# AFRICA
## and Change

# Colin M. Turnbull

Hofstra University

**Alfred · A · Knopf**     **New York**

# AFRICA and Change

First Edition

987654321

Copyright © 1973 by Alfred A. Knopf, Inc.

Library of Congress Cataloging in Publication Data

Turnbull, Colin M. comp.
Africa and Change.

CONTENTS: Economy, morality, and anthropology: Hughes, A. J. B. Some Swazi views on land tenure. Cohen, A. The social organization of credit in a West African cattle market. Ottenberg, S. Improvement association among the Ibo. [etc.]
1. Africa—Social conditions—Addresses, essays, lectures. 2. Africa—Politics—1960–    —Addresses, essays, lectures. 3. Ethnology—Africa—Addresses, essays, lectures. I. Title.
HN773.5.T87   309.1′6′03   70–39817
ISBN 0–394–31520–0

Manufactured in the United States of America. Composed by Cherry Hill Composition, Pennsauken, N.J. Printed and bound by The Kingsport Press, Kingsport, Tenn.

Design by James McGuire

PHOTO CREDITS
P. 231: Bruno Barbey from Magnum Photos, Inc.; pp. 17, 129, 229, 361: Marc & Evelyne Bernheim from Rapho Guillumette Pictures; p. 358: Bruce Davidson from Magnum Photos, Inc.; p. 128: Elliott Erwitt from Magnum Photos, Inc.; pp. 20, 130, 360, 362: Susan Gilbert; p. 18: Bettye Lane; p. 230: Danny Lyon; p. 357: Marc Riboud from Magnum Photos, Inc.; pp. 19, 127: George Rodger from Magnum Photos, Inc.; p. 359: Colin M. Turnbull; p. 232: Burt Uzzle from Magnum Photos, Inc.

The following articles are reprinted from *Africa* by permission of the International African Institute.

A. J. B. Hughes, "Some Swazi Views on Land Tenure," 32, 3 (1962), 253–277.

Abner Cohen, "The Social Organization of Credit in a West African Cattle Market," 35, 1 (1965), 8–19.

S. Ottenberg, "Improvement Associations among the Afikpo Ibo," 25, 1 (1955), 1–27.

Gustav Jahoda, "Love, Marriage, and Social Change: Letters to the Advice Column of a West African Newspaper," 29, 2 (1959), 177–189.

J. H. Chaplin, "Wiving and Thriving in Northern Rhodesia," 32, 2 (1962), 111–122.

Kenneth Little and Anne Price, "Some Trends in Modern Marriage among West Africans," 37, 4 (1967), 407–424.

David J. Parkin, "Types of Urban African Marriage in Kampala," 36, 3 (1966), 269–284.

Kenneth Little, "The Political Function of the Poro," Part 1, 35, 4 (1965), 349–365; Part II, 36, 1 (1966), 62–73.

P. C. Lloyd, "Sacred Kingship and Government among the Yoruba," 30, 3 (1960), 221–237.

I. M. Lewis, "Modern Political Movements in Somaliland," Part I, 28, 3 (1958), 244–260; Part II, 28, 4 (1958), 344–362.

T. O. Beidelman, "Swazi Royal Ritual," 36, 4 (1966), 373–405.

Rodney Needham, "The Left Hand of the Mugwe: An Analytical Note on the Structure of Meru Symbolism," 30, 1 (1960), 20–33.

William A. Shack, "The *Mäsqal*-Pole: Religious Conflict and Social Change in Gurageland," 38, 4 (1968), 457–468.

Robin Horton, "African Traditional Thought and Western Science," Part I, 37, 1 (1967), 50–71; Part II, 37, 2 (1967), 155–187.

For Joseph Allen Towles, anthropologist and friend.
If anthropology had served mankind better, my people
might have served his less ill.
With gratitude.

# Acknowledgments

First and foremost, acknowledgments must be made to the International African Institute, from whose journal *Africa* all the articles reprinted in this volume are drawn. This exclusiveness, which in no way reflects on the Institute itself, is deliberate. By selecting articles from this one source, I have been able to capitalize, for the reader's benefit as well as my own, on the uniform excellence of the Institute's publications and on the consistency of style and content that is the mark of their journal.

My editorial comments and introductory essays, although largely descriptive, are based on a wide field experience that has covered almost all the major areas of the African continent, with the exception of South Africa, from which I have gladly segregated myself. My comments are also based on a rigorous training received from the Institute of Social Anthropology at Oxford University (which at the time was almost exclusively Africanist), under the leadership of Professor E. E. Evans-Pritchard, as well as on the personal stimulation received from Dr. Rodney Needham and Dr. John Peristiany.

I would also like to thank Hofstra University and its Department of Anthropology for giving me the opportunity and encouragement to strike out in a new direction and actively join the ranks of those who feel that it is time that anthropology showed some sense of relevance in a world desperately in need of all the guidance it can get. The methodological weaknesses of this volume are too manifold and obvious to be enumerated; any virtue it may have is due either to the authors of the articles and to the editorial board of *Africa* or (the only claim I can make for myself) to the sincerity of the attempt to suggest one direction in which anthropology may find a more vital role to play. In a world in which social change has taken the initiative and in which man blindly follows in the comforting but possibly mistaken belief that this is progress, it may be the function of anthropology to show man where his progress is leading him with such alarming rapidity and seeming inevitability and to suggest that "retrogression" might more accurately describe the direction in which he is moving.

My own generalizations and personal opinions in this volume are, I hope, sufficiently tempered by experience and training to qualify as acceptable working hypotheses, which is what they are intended to be. To those mentioned above and to the authors of the articles, I extend my apologies if they would have preferred not to be associated with such an endeavor.

To Dr. Peter Rigby, of Makerere University, I am indebted for both criticism and encouragement, and for the patient reading of the manuscript. Finally, I owe thanks to the many friends and colleagues whose ideas have influenced the formation of my own and to the various institutions and people who have enabled me to spend so much time in the field. The first of these are my parents, who financed my education and my first venture (in India) into that incomparably exciting world of alien culture. I am also grateful to the Emslie Horniman Trust, the American Museum of Natural History, the National Science Foundation, and last, but by no means least, the Wenner Gren Foundation for Anthropological Research.

Hempstead, New York                                    C.M.T.
December 1972

# Contents

x    Contents

# AFRICA
## and Change

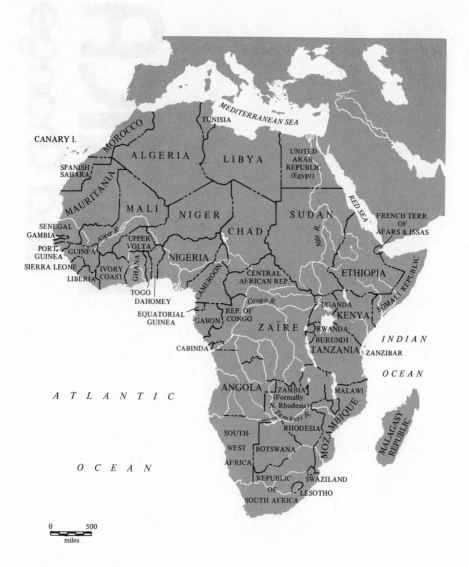

# Introduction

As its title suggests, this volume is primarily concerned with a central focus of interest, social change, and with the use of the comparative method in examining our own society (whatever that society might be) and, in this case, African society.

There are several ways in which comparison can be made to serve the cause of academic inquiry, although not all of them are valid and acceptable methods. The facile juxtaposition of similarities or dissimilarities is frequently passed off as the comparative method, but it does not deserve the name. Juxtaposition can, however, be a useful stimulant when it is employed with discretion (as I have frequently tried to use it) and when certain essential common characteristics provide a basis for the comparison. A comparison that produces the conclusions it was designed to produce (as has been done by the more ethnocentric evolutionists) is not a method, at least not a very honorable one.

There are various legitimate aims and various legitimate methods, and social anthropology in Britain and France owes much of its acute insight to the proper formulation of both. If a method is truly comparative, something new should arise as a result of that comparison, such as the proof or disproof of a hypothesis. What I am suggesting and attempting in a limited way in this volume is that although the refinement of man's understanding of social structure and the discovery of increasingly significant generalities (which some might term "laws") certainly continue to be legitimate aims of the comparative method, there is another equally legitimate aim that seeks to relate anthropology directly to contemporary social problems that are to be found in almost all human societies. The aim of this study is to use comparison, occasionally in a methodical manner, to provide new insights into the process of social change and to suggest more perceptive ways of inducing and controlling change than have been achieved up to the present. To this end, I suggest that each reader take his own society as one reference point (as I do in my personal comments) and Africa as the other reference point. The objective should be the better understanding of the reader's own society.

This volume is certainly not offered as a casebook of social change in Africa. My aim is steadfastly subjective because I believe it is high time that social anthropology returned to its starting point and continued the task it originally set out to accomplish, and for which it has, for three centuries, been forging and sharpening its tools.

The foundations of social anthropology are to be found in the writings of the moral philosophers of the seventeenth and eighteenth centuries, who were concerned with their own societies and with the processes of change that were then beginning to take control of events, the direction of which, although unforeseen, gave rise to serious misgivings on the part of these exceptional humanitarians. No matter how scientific it tries to be (and should be) in the rigor of its methods and techniques, social anthropology is still very much one of the humanities; it is an art, at times almost creative. The dichotomy between the sciences and the humanities is artificial and misleading; it belongs to anthropology's largely unglorious nineteenth-century past.

The shift of interest from "primitive" societies to "civilized" societies is something new in modern anthropology, although it is where the journey began. In recent years, anthropologists have focused their attention on exotic societies, mostly small in scale, for diverse theoretical objectives. The techniques and methods of study were fashioned for other purposes, but, with some modification, they are nonetheless suited to the present investigation.

One of the major changes, perhaps *the* major change, that is called for is a relinquishing of the obsession with objectivity that has become almost a religion with social anthropologists who, it seems, are more concerned with their scientific respectability than with academic viability and the advancement of knowledge. To pose the issue as a dichotomy is to introduce an artificial barrier that has successfully blinded so many to the potential role of social anthropology in contemporary affairs. Objectivity is not only desirable but indispensable at certain levels of inquiry. But anyone who denies the value of subjectivity denies his own existence. Each anthropologist brings to the field and to the worktable his entire social personality, from which he can never entirely divorce himself. The most he can do is be as objective as possible when objectivity is called for. If he carries the striving for objectivity further than that, then he ceases to be a human being and becomes a thinking machine instead (which is a fair description of some anthropologists today). On the other hand, it is dangerous to identify too closely with the object, by becoming what we are studying; the very basis of objectivity is then lost.

In arguing for a combination of the two approaches I am not simply suggesting a compromise on a terminological quibble. I am suggesting that anthropologists actively make use of their own identities, both as individuals and as members of social groups, in the tasks of field research and subsequent analysis. There is room for intuitive speculation, and the reader will find plenty of it in the following pages. I believe that it is a neglected technique, just as subjective inquiry is a neglected method. In the Western world, intuition is commonly regarded as a female substitute for reason. This ascription is doubly fallacious: the female sex does not hold a monopoly on intuition nor is intuition a substitute for reason. The process is not rational, but when it is properly used, it can provide just those illuminating insights that ultimately are "proven" by reason, which then claims all the credit. It is well known that science would get nowhere without shrewd guesswork. The posing of a hypothesis is a prerequisite for its testing. And some of the shrewdest guesswork is achieved by that direct, nonrational form of perception that is ridiculed as intuition. There is nothing particularly mystical about it, although, as a process, it has been relegated to the realm of mystery. It is a neat by-passing of the meticulous, complex, and painstaking logical process that reasoning should be, but too frequently is not. It derives from the wealth of subconscious experience that lies dormant and inutile until it is allowed expression in this way. But given a chance, it can produce the answer to a question that perhaps has not even been asked, suggesting, at the same time, the question itself or the most significant way of formulating it. In short, intuition is the superintelligent guess that makes use of both the subconscious and the conscious; and like all guesses, once it has been made, it has done its work, leaving open the task of rational formulation and verification.

The anthropologist, particularly the field worker, has a special potential in this direction because the very nature of his work involves him intimately in the lives and thoughts of others, with complex results on his own personality that can never be more than partially recognized. In an unguarded moment, when the pretentious façade of objectivity is lowered, his complex, rich, subjective experience may provide him with a brilliant insight; and he will wonder why he had never thought of it before. Such insights are simply not accessible to thought.

I am not suggesting that the anthropologist should assume the lotus posture and wait for divine revelation (which is how some regard intuition), but I am suggesting that he allow his wealth of "forgotten" experience more credit than it is generally given and deliberately make more use of that personal experience which is available at the conscious level.

A moral issue is involved here, too, and it will emerge in Part 1 of this book. It hinges on the issue of subjectivity because it is only when the anthropologist claims total objectivity that he can excuse himself from making a commitment of an essentially moral nature. By allowing, indeed by encouraging, a partially subjective approach, he will not only be inviting himself to commit the cardinal sin of social anthropology, the making of value judgments, but he will also be *requiring* it of himself. It is part of the purpose of this book to examine the position of the anthropologist in human society and to see what, if any, moral obligation he has and how it can be fulfilled. By combining the comparative method and the technique of subjective inquiry, the anthropologist may achieve what he set out so long ago to do, and what in moments of nostalgia he still says he hopes ultimately to achieve: the better understanding of himself and his own society. But I confess that even in moments of the most divine of revelations, it has not been given to me to perceive how the goal of self-comprehension can be achieved while pursuing the phantom of total objectivity.

Social change lends itself to this form of inquiry. It is necessarily different in time depth and perception as studied by the anthropologist than as studied by the historian or any other social scientist more accustomed, for one thing, to dealing with literate societies that have many hundreds of years of recorded history. The tools of the anthropologist were forged on nonliterate, small-scale societies. That is what differentiates the anthropologist from the sociologist. Rather than attempt to duplicate the work of the sociologist by imitating his methods, the anthropologist should try to approach the problem of change in his own way. If the attempt is not productive, it can be abandoned. But in light of current events not to make the attempt would be highly irresponsible, to say the least, regardless of whether the refusal derived from genuine doubt of ability, from stage fright, or from sheer indifference.

The anthropologist brings to the inquiry not only his own methods and techniques but several important concepts. Those that first (intuitively) come to mind are the interrelationship and integration in human society and the relativity of culture. If carried to excess, the concept of cultural relativism would obviously put social anthropology out of business. It would invite a reversion to old-time ethnographic description in lieu of structural-functional analysis through the use of the comparative method. But the concept provides an effective antidote to excessive ethnocentrism (among other things). It enables the anthropologist to attain, briefly, a condition of detachment during which the fullest measure of objectivity is possible. Then, surprisingly perhaps, it allows the anthropologist to make value judgments as he develops the facility for hopping from one culture and set of values to another while temporarily leaving himself behind. But it leaves open the question, which is ultimately a personal one, of whether the anthropologist actually chooses to make judgments about his own society in terms of his own values.

In his *Persian Letters*,* Montesquieu used the subtle critical technique of looking at his own society in terms of the values of another culture; the attempt has been repeated since. For example, Horace Miner has examined American society as if he were describing some exotic, "primitive" culture.†

---

* Baron de Montesquieu, *The Persian Letters* (New York: World, 1960).
† H. Miner, "Body Ritual Among the Nacirema," *American Anthropologist*, 58 (1956), 503–507.

This technique is frequently enlightening, and the anthropologist who has identified himself to any extent with the people he has studied almost inevitably uses it when he looks at his own society. But in the greatly advanced state of their field today, social anthropologists can surely be more direct and, after rigorously examining themselves as they examine others, pass judgments on their own society by taking a stand as members of that society. They are, by virtue of their training and experience, in the position of Montesquieu's Persians (to a greater or lesser extent, depending on their techniques of inquiry). The more subjective they have been in their field work and the more they have identified with the people they have studied, the more objective they can be in looking at their own society. Conversely, the self-study proposed in this volume will not be wholly subjective, and perhaps only anthropologists can bring a reasonable degree of objectivity to bear on such a study.

Insofar as social anthropology has until now largely dealt with nonliterate societies, historical data have been minimal, highly conjectural, and entirely lacking in the kind of detail that is available to the student of change occurring in literate societies. The base that anthropologists have for comparison of the present with anything but the very immediate past is such that through archaeological evidence, it is possible to hazard guesses at the nature of change but guesses only of the grossest order, such as are indulged in by many of the evolutionists whose theories are built on such flimsy and selective evidence that their technique verges on the unscrupulous. The results of such endeavors must remain at least as conjectural as the data, and in this case the data are politely termed "reconstructed" history, which is rather unfair to history. Thus anthropologists can justifiably examine change only over a much more recent time span and from the perspective that their methods and techniques provide, primarily of integrated societies with systems of interrelated institutions. The full meaning of "integrated societies" should emerge in the course of this book, here it refers to the kind of solidarity that is found in small-scale societies in which there is a great deal more consistency between, and a great deal more acceptance of, uniform ways of life and thought than exist in a nation such as the United States, to which the term "integrated" can hardly be applied in any respect.

I have selected Africa as one reference point not only because it gives me the greatest opportunity for the expression of personal opinion drawn from personal experience but also because Africa is a clearly defined area, a continental land mass with a remarkable degree of cultural homogeneity and an unremarkable degree of diversity. I have chosen Africa also because it has been singularly well studied by social anthropologists over the past half-century, when the pressures of change were at their maximum. There are well-documented examples of change having been fully accepted with the minimum of apparent distaste by the most "traditional" of peoples, and there are other cases of change being resisted with the utmost vigor by the most "progressive" sectors of a population. But change does not have to be imposed from without; it is nothing new in Africa, and indigenous institutions are sometimes perfectly capable not only of coping with change, even in its present form, but of actively initiating it. Examples of all these aspects of change have been included in this volume. Here it is only necessary to stress that the old picture of Africa as a primeval, unchanging continent may be laughable, but the persistent implication that change has always been moderate and slow is inexcusable. Ancient Egyptian texts and the admirable records of the early Arab historians, as well as the findings of archaeology, indicate that in the past, Africa has known change every bit as dramatic and rapid as the change taking place today. Although, I repeat, this volume is not intended to be a casebook of social change in Africa, the selected articles should provide some idea of the possibilities that exist for a comparative study of change within that continent. Such a study would be greatly enriched by the use of the sources mentioned above because the Arab texts provide historic documentation for the past thousand years (for West and North Africa, but for a shorter time span for East Africa) and the Egyptian texts, for up to 5,000 years. There is also valuable information that dates from the beginning of the colonial era in the form of acutely perceptive, if largely descriptive, accounts by district commissioners, administrators, missionaries, and others who had prolonged contact with the peoples of Africa before the new pressures of change began to take effect. There have also been studies, undertaken by various anthropologists, of the same people or institutions over a rather smaller time interval; and although these studies were made by people with different approaches, techniques, and interests (the subjective element is relevant again) and are therefore not strictly comparable, the data that they provide often *are* comparable. Thus even in areas untouched by the Arabic historians, anthropologists sometimes have an opportunity to study a time depth of a hundred years or even more. It is possible to study change in still greater time depth if further attention is paid to the oral tradition that in many cases is a much more vital way of recording history than is freezing it in print, and that can achieve just as great a degree of factual accuracy.

Another way in which change can be studied, but necessarily over an even shorter time span, is for an anthropologist to undertake a restudy of an earlier work. However, most of the articles in this book are synchronic studies of change, if such a thing is possible. They are studies of the process of change, either "natural" or induced, as observed during one period of field work. Most of the change described has come about through the process of modernization that has resulted from the introduction by the colonial powers of new systems of government, new systems and technologies of economics (including the introduction of a cash economy), new systems of thought and belief, and new attitudes toward family life and responsibility. In some of the articles, the authors (none of whom, incidentally, are Africans) describe the techniques they used to gather the data or to increase the time span. Such studies are generally descriptive rather than analytical because of the limitations imposed by the data. But sometimes the anthropologist has been able to enhance the analytical value of his study by the use of his own experience, sensitivity, and proximity to the problem and by his willingness to step beyond the safe confines of conventional anthropology to hazard intelligent guesses, knowing them to be no more than guesses. Many of these articles are by people who are so concerned with the moral and social implications of change that they attempted an examination of the process, knowing that it could not be as rigorous as the kind of examination for which anthropological methods were originally devised. Thus a number of the essays do not claim to be more than forays into a new but vital field.

That many of the articles are out of date is of no special importance because, in a sense, all descriptions of social change are out of date before they are written. I have not tried to bring the articles up to date because the attempt would have failed before it was begun. The reader, in his own time-space niche, will be in a better position to do this if he feels so inclined. The articles are of historical importance in helping the reader to achieve a better understanding of Africa's recent past and, therefore, its present. They are important stepping stones toward the use of the comparative method in a study of social change. Finally, I believe they are important because they represent a trend that anthropology may do well to take up, a new interest for which new techniques and methods will ultimately have to be fashioned.

Although all the articles are about Africa, they are in no way representative of all the major areas of study, geographical or theoretical. They were chosen because they highlight different possibilities and problems in the general anthropological study of social change. In my introductory essays, I have attempted to provide an adequate, although highly generalized, background for the reader who has little or no knowledge of African societies. But this account is more discursive than descriptive, and for those who wish fuller information, I recommend four compilations edited, respectively, by Gibbs, Middleton, the Ottenbergs, and Southall* and, beyond these, the host of excellent monographs that are available for really specialized study. For those readers who are totally unfamiliar with problems of social change, I suggest two volumes by Arensberg and Niehoff† as a good introduction both to social change and (in the Arensberg-Niehoff volume particularly) to judicious ethnocentricism.

My introductory essays may seem to indicate a greater homogeneity in African society than there actually is, but I believe the suggestion to be valid at this level of generalization. The introductions attempt to provide an idea of at least some major types of social organization and structure that existed before the recent, often violent, changes began to affect African society. They also indicate a more limited focus of interest, reflected in the articles themselves, on the specific interconnection between tradition and change. Tradition itself is as subject to change as is anything else, although it is often mistakenly thought to be irrevocably opposed to change. Too often tradition is mistaken for a condition, a state of being, whereas in fact it is an attitude, a state of mind. A traditional institution, as I see it, is one that has the sanction of the past; whether that past is relatively recent or distant is, in this respect, immaterial because although traditions tend to grow stronger with time, they do not always do so. Tradition is a dynamic force, and traditional societies are far from static. The colonial era brought such rapid changes that traditions did not usually have time to change soon enough to provide continuity or sanction. Thus "nontraditional" institutions or societies are, as I use the term, simply those that have not yet been sanctioned by reference to the past, whether it be real or mythical, recent or distant. They may well be traditional tomorrow.

The introductory essays also attempt to suggest various topics the reader might wish to pursue on his own and to indicate the possible significance of the articles for a comparative study of our own societies, their significance, in fact, for a new, contemporary, vital, and more truly social anthropology. The four divisions of the book correspond to the general fourfold division of social life into its economic, domestic, political, and religious sectors, and the articles are grouped accordingly; but the

---

* J. R. Gibbs (ed.), *The Peoples of Africa* (New York: Holt, Rinehart and Winston, 1965); J. Middleton (ed.), *Black Africa* (New York: Macmillan, 1970); S. Ottenberg and P. Ottenberg (eds.), *Cultures and Societies of Africa* (New York: Random House, 1960); and A. Southall (ed.), *Social Change in Modern Africa* (London: Oxford University Press, 1961).

† A. H. Niehoff, *A Casebook of Social Change* (Chicago: Aldine, 1966); C. M. Arensberg and A. H. Niehoff, *Introducing Social Change* (Chicago: Aldine, 1964).

introductions also follow a fourfold division of their own, considering, in turn, morality and anthropology, cultural relativism and self-criticism, comparative evaluation, and finally, the making of value judgments as a new goal (or an old one reintroduced) for social anthropology. The correlation between these two fourfold divisions is obviously not one to one; it is one to four or four to one, as will be seen, which makes tidy classification difficult. It is strictly a question of emphasis (as it is with the articles) that determines where in the format anything is placed; there are no exclusive categories.

By themselves, the articles could have been, and in many cases will have been, read in *Africa*. The only valid reason for a compilation is either to increase the accessibility of articles or to link them in a new and significant manner. The latter is what I have attempted in this book, suggesting a specific use to which they could be put, and indicating some of the ways the resulting data could be applied. I have tried to raise general questions rather than to answer them in the hope of initiating experimentation with new goals and techniques and methods. The reader must do the rest and, according to his own interests or concerns, pursue the matter further and find the answers to his own specific questions. I propose to do the same.

# 1

# Economy, Morality, and Anthropology

A. The wealth of the Deji (king) is based on the size of his family, not on the elaborateness of his court or the number of his material possessions. The Deji of Akure, shown here seated at a ritual function, is surrounded by his family, advisors, officials, and ritual specialists, who all work to help achieve an equable distribution of his wealth as well as of his authority.

B. In the Brownsville section of Brooklyn, these children play amid the garbage and debris of their slum neighborhood.

C. The Nilotic peoples of East Africa lead a seminomadic pastoral life which makes the accumulation of material wealth impossible. They do, however, possess a different type of wealth: a mutual cooperation and sharing that bind them in a voluntary group cooperative and give them a security that can never diminish in value.

D. The three-car family in this suburban Long Island community illustrates the belief, in America, that wealth can be measured by material accumulation.

Nothing strikes "civilized" man so close to home as economic crisis. It is not without significance that we sanctify our currency with portraits of sacred emblems or deified personages and pass laws forbidding defacement of the coin of the realm as though that were the supreme sacrilege. Even war raises the specter of economic ruin or impoverishment more than the fear of death, since we always assume (and hope) death will claim others rather than ourselves. Apart from this personal, and therefore debatable, point of view, I think it is clear that the very problem of survival is undoubtedly central and that it has prime economic implications for most of us.

How does economic crisis strike "primitive" man? In a rather similar fashion, to judge by the Ik of northern Uganda, among whom I had the misfortune to live for eighteen months. During that time, I witnessed the effects of endemic starvation on social organization and on interpersonal, as well as intergroup, relations. I also observed the effects of hunger on myself and on my own relationships, for however much I believe in subjectivity, I was unprepared to starve.

A superficial glance at the Ik might seem to justify the opposition between "civilized" and "primitive". The Ik react to economic crisis by leaving their children to fend for themselves at the age of three and by helping their parents to die more rapidly by stealing what little food the old people (anyone over twenty-five is old) have managed to scavenge for themselves; certainly nobody is going to give them any. And when one of the Ik gets an unexpected windfall, such as famine relief, which some misguided official has entrusted to one person for the use of his whole family, he makes himself ill by consuming it all, secretly and in haste, so that no member of his hungry family can suggest that the food should have been shared.

Actually, what has happened is that the Ik (whose plight, incidentally, is a result of social change induced by the colonial obsession with drawing neat boundary lines) have learned at last to act like so-called civilized people. Although we behave in a more decorous manner—sending our children away to school and to holiday camps, if possible, or otherwise farming them out, and disposing of tiresome parents by placing them (for their own good, of course) in nice "old-folks" homes where they join the pathetic line of those waiting to die—we have, in fact, developed a "civilization" that is the very negation of sociality, if not of society. Thus we honor individualism and initiative, and, consequently, cutthroat economics. Survival for us means survival first for oneself, then for anyone who might be of use. By comparison, the Ik make a rather good showing in terms of consideration for others. At least they do not kill each other, even if their behavior does suggest the bomb-shelter tactics of survival, whereby survival of the fittest becomes survival of the most unscrupulous and cold-blooded. The African border police who had to cope with the Ik gave a telling appraisal when they referred to them as "Europeans" because they spoke an incomprehensible language, referring not so much to the fact that the language itself was indeed difficult, as to the fact that the Ik seemed to speak only in lies, and because they behaved in such an incomprehensible and inhuman (which is to say, un-African) way.

The Ik are an extreme case, but they illustrate the aim of this book: that it is time to remember that anthropology's original objective was to help man to achieve a better understanding of himself. Looking at the Ik is similar to looking in a mirror; the hasty judgments that leap to the viewer's lips rebound and strike him squarely. But what of less extreme cases, such as those presented in the following articles? How do other Africans react to economic crisis? Again, comparison is likely to strike home, this time by reminding us of how many, and even which, specific qualities we preach so glibly but fail with such facility to practice.

I am particularly concerned in this part of the book with the issue of morality; but the term has to be defined in a way that renders it equally applicable to our own and African society. That is not likely to be entirely possible, but the exercise is revealing. The concept of morality involves a difficult mixture of relativity and absolutism. If we were to judge each other by what we exhort our fellows to do in terms of prescriptive and proscriptive behavior, we would find each other as different as can be. But if we were to judge each other in terms of what we sought to achieve by a diversity of behavior, we would find little difference at all. Forms of behavior vary widely, but social goals and institutional functions are remarkably similar. Thus a comparison of practice may reveal nothing of significance; whereas a comparison of actual achievement or of function may reveal everything. A definition of morality that centers on behavioral forms is going to beg the question from the start.

Morality certainly implies a felt obligation to behave in a certain way, even in the absence of physical or other formal means of coercion; but it is the sentiment rather than the form of behavior that is important. Morality is a recognition of obligation to others without any necessary conscious expectation of reward or reciprocation. The obligation is most frequently expressed in familial or religious terms that bind the individual to a moral community defined and delimited by common kinship (fictional or otherwise), common belief, or both. The essence of morality, then, is that the obligation should be felt rather than rationalized or compelled.

There are striking correlations between morality and economic crisis. Economic crisis strikes home in all societies because of its obvious and immediate threat to our most basic urge: the urge to survive. Perhaps life may best be considered as an essay in survival; and society, as a mechanism that assists our attempt to survive. Indeed, society is indispensable for human survival. Thus the antisocial Western trend toward ever-increasing individualism points in the direction of extinction.

If we are honest, we come to realize that under economic stress, morality is a luxury to be afforded—like other virtues such as generosity, consideration, and compassion—only in times of affluence. Respectable aristocratic ladies of impeccable pedigree could be seen in wartime England stealing sugar from restaurants. Meanwhile, their equally respectable husbands were using their wealth and prestige to acquire illicit food and clothing coupons so that their wives would not be forced into such demeaning behavior. If the aristocracy represents the pinnacle of English culture and civilization, it is significant that while the aristocrats were purchasing coupons so that they could preserve the illusion of honesty, the lower classes were being less devious by simply buying food and clothes directly, when they could afford them, on the same black market that sold the coupons. That particular economic crisis was one of goods rather than of cash. But judging by the scale of black-market activities and the obvious way the black market enabled those with means to gain at the expense of those without means, it successfully dissolved all professed sense of obligation to kin and country.

In a cash crisis, too, the normal civilized reaction varies according to social class. At the upper-class level, swindling and exploitation abound, while at the lower-class level, theft is a more usual reaction to economic deprivation. Theft, although technically less honest in legal terms, is also less immoral than exploitation, however legal the latter might be. In moralistic, as opposed to legalistic, societies the same act may be judged right or wrong, moral or immoral, according to contextual differences. In such societies integrity of motive is a key factor.

The example of social class may mislead us in trying to determine just what essential ingredient in our own society makes for a moral scale that slides in the direction of corruption and immorality in times of crisis. Plainly it is not just pedigree, the white- versus blue-collar occupational difference, or wealth. Many sets of social opposites frequently parallel one another: upper class and lower class parallel rich and poor; rich and poor parallel white collar and blue collar; and, in supercivilizations like the United States and the United Kingdom, white skin and black skin fit the same pattern of parallels. But one set of opposites cuts across them all: rural and urban. The opposition between the rural and urban ends of the crisis scale parallel the moral and immoral ends of the same scale. Among the many ramifications is the possibility that the migration of rural workers to towns is a factor contributing to the greater morality (as morality has been defined here) in the poor areas of those towns. It is not possible here to examine this rural-urban opposition except to mention one or two factors that might be critically important in determining a relative level of morality. These are suggested by the African data, and they bear close comparison.

One such factor is the relative lack, in rural (and African) areas, of emphasis on cash as a means to the acquisition of goods, power, or prestige. Cash is not seen as direct and necessary to security. Barter is still frequently employed in many rural areas in England and the United States, if only to a small extent. But that small extent survives because it maintains the vital tradition of interpersonal and intergroup relationships that is lost in a full cash economy. This tradition retains such vitality that people may go for miles to exchange goods that they could have purchased much more easily and quickly at the local supermarket.

Another factor is the importance placed in rural communities on land and lineage and on the relationship between the two. When groups of people, familial or otherwise, have been associated with specific territories over long periods of time, they often have greater access to power and prestige than other groups, regardless of wealth. The longer the time span, the greater the tradition and the force it carries and the greater the felt obligations. Often a rural family's land continues to be regarded by the community as "theirs" long after it has been sold, while the new, legal owners are treated as usurpers and ostracized.

Because these rural societies are closer to African societies in their lack of cash emphasis and their positive stress on land and lineage, this comparison between the traditional African and the rural American or English scenes can be of real analytical value. Other factors that suggest themselves for comparison are egalitarianism (often conjoined, in an apparently paradoxical manner, with social stratification), democratic government (often paradoxically conjoined with an apparent centralization of power), and religiosity (by which I refer to the presence of a vital, functional religious belief and practice). Community of belief and kinship are, as I have suggested, prime means for defining the area of moral obligation. The rural African scene has an ample measure of both; the urban setting tends to have neither.

Another relevant factor is population size. Obviously, the larger the population, the less the likelihood of community of belief or kinship. The fact that modern cities are constantly broken down into areas, quarters, districts, and ghettos indicates a felt need for a greater sense of community than would otherwise be possible. Thus there appears to be a correlation between community and security at one end of the economic scale and between wealth and security at the other. This correlation emphasizes the different uses to which cash is put at the two extremes of society—differences not accounted for by variations in spending power. The comparison helps us to be rather more perceptive than those who point to the poor black with his white Cadillac and enough money for one month's payment, using him as proof that poor blacks have no sense of responsibility, no comprehension of money. The phenomenon is due rather to the fact that, perhaps because they are poor and black, or perhaps due to the not-impossible persistence of a strictly functional African tradition, they have a high sense of responsibility, but to the wider community rather than for their personal profit; and to the fact that they have a particularly acute awareness of what cash means. It is entirely likely that in many cases the "abuse" of cash is deliberate, a form of ridicule, a desecration of a value system that keeps them in economic subjection. The tightly packed, closely knit slum areas in Western cities differ in appearance from the diffuse, detached, isolationist areas of the wealthy just as vividly as they differ in their sense of communal responsibility and in their perception of security.

The larger societies cannot, by previous definition, be called moral; indeed, it is doubtful that the term "society" can even be meaningfully applied since it implies the kind of obligations already described as moral. In fact, moral obligations are, or should be, coterminous with social obligations; and a society, if it is to be more than a legal and political convenience, must surely be a moral community, which few modern nations are.

These generalizations need to be tested and either proved or discarded. First, however, must come the task of gathering adequate data, which cannot be attempted here. But the data at hand give good evidence that civilization has much to learn from small-scale societies and that it had better learn quickly if it is to survive. Likewise, the small-scale societies had better learn not to imitate the ways of civilization too readily and not to fall for the lure of technological progress and material benefit that will, in the end, place them in the same dilemma that Western society is now facing.

In view of the limitations of available data and the scope of this volume, I can do no more than present an opinion and suggest that the selected articles be used, along with others of the reader's own choice, as partial evidence in support of that opinion and for comparison with the reader's own store of experience. The articles have the advantage of being unbiased in their present context because the authors are up to this moment still unaware of my views, with which they may well disagree.

The following broad outlines of the nature of traditional economy in

Africa places the articles in a wider perspective. It may be of some help to the reader who has no time for deeper study and who is not already informed in this area.

Any attempt to describe what economic systems were like in prehistoric or even protohistoric times is an exercise in courageous but excessive imagination. Archaeological discoveries indicate a great deal about technology, but they are usually too divorced from significant social context or data to allow for any talk of systems. A great deal can be inferred about the more immediate precolonial past from eyewitness accounts of that time and from oral tradition. Certainly the level of technology reveals much about what economic systems were *not*. Archaeological research indicates quite clearly that the period following Africa's equivalent of the Industrial Revolution (which came with the discovery of iron some 2,000 years ago) was characterized by rapid and far-reaching change that was largely attributable to the greatly improved agricultural technology. It was a period of significant increase not only in the size of the total population but also in the size of the local population units. That is to say, people gathered in increasingly large communities that were increasingly sedentary and increasingly complex in structure. But from the moment the agricultural revolution was accomplished (which, if judged by the rapidity of its spread, must have been in a remarkably short time), there was in all probability little dramatic change until the colonial era. The most frequent and dramatic feature of this long period was warfare, which probably resulted from the ever-growing demand for land and the attendant migrations and hostilities. Warfare was not, however, a major and constant part of Africa's past as it is sometimes thought to have been. There were certainly a series of brief engagements between those people being forced on from behind and those whom they were forcing out ahead. But this kind of conflict excludes institutionalized warfare and slavery as the West knows them, which came to Africa with the Islamic and European invasions.

During this long, relatively quiet period, there must have been continuous changes of a smaller order, affecting not just the economic sector but the entire social organization of each population. Although the agricultural revolution affected the bulk of the population, there were significant groups that resisted it or were unable to take advantage of it, because of unfavorable ecological circumstances for instance, and that remain to this day relatively or totally aloof from agricultural activity. They might be described as the arch conservatives of Africa. I am referring to the hunters and gatherers and the pastoralists. In fact, most pastoralists do engage in a limited form of agriculture, and despite the popular notion to the contrary, they may always have done so. It is even possible that the number of pastoralists who were originally cultivators but who were forced into cattle herding by the loss of their arable land was larger than is commonly believed. Even hunters and gatherers may not be, or may not ever have been, as "pure" as the evolutionists would like to think.

Many hunters and gatherers certainly know and practice the principles of vegeculture (the nomadic version of agriculture), and there is absolutely no reason why, even with the most limited techniques, they should not always have done so. The Ik, who in recent times were forced to abandon hunting and take up farming, have demonstrated remarkably detailed knowledge of agricultural techniques without guidance, even of specialized forms such as terracing. But raising the issue of purity is misleading because it plays with guesses as though they were facts and thus requires supporting these guesses with still more guesses. Definitions of purity seem designed to support specific arguments for which there is a lack of adequate evidence; thus, deviations from the arbitrarily defined norm can promptly be dismissed as "impure."

A more reasonable consideration than the issue of purity is that of emphasis. Even such people as the Nuer and Dinka,* who practice agriculture extensively, are still true (if not pure) pastoralists insofar as their value system revolves around their cattle-herding activities. Similarly, hunters and gatherers are often properly referred to simply as hunters, because although gathering is to them a far more important economic activity as far as subsistence is concerned, their dominant value is placed on hunting. The term "hunters" is technically less accurate than "gatherers," but it conveys more of the truth about them, just as "pastoralist" conveys more than "pastoral cultivator," except for the purposes of technical or technological classification. (Indeed, in the case of the Pygmies of Zaïre, I would be tempted to classify hunting as a political or religious, rather than an economic, activity.)

The question of which type of economy came first is not relevant to this discussion. On technological grounds, anthropologists can be sure that hunting preceded agriculture or pastoralism (although it may always have been associated with vegeculture), but beyond that they really have no definite knowledge; there are plenty of ideas but too few facts. What *can* be said is that for the past 2,000 years, most of the peoples of Africa have tended to be predominantly agricultural but that there have been large

---

* See E. E. Evans-Pritchard, *Witchcraft, Oracles and Magic among the Azande* (Oxford, Eng.: Clarendon Press, 1937), *The Nuer* (Oxford, Eng.: Clarendon Press, 1940), *Kinship and Marriage among the Nuer* (Oxford, Eng.: Clarendon Press, 1951), *Nuer Religion* (Oxford, Eng.: Clarendon Press, 1956); and R. G. Lienhardt, *Divinity and Experience: Religion among the Dinka* (Oxford, Eng.: Clarendon Press, 1961).

groups of pastoralists and smaller groups of hunters. There are also still smaller economic groups: fishers (riverein, lacustrine, or littoral, each involving a significantly different form of organization) and traders.

Obviously, each of these major economic groupings has a distinct social character because each necessarily demands different forms of association and organization and finds support for its own form of social organization in its system of values and religious belief. Not only the economies but also the family structures, the systems of government and social control, and the world views of each group differ. So, frequently, does the environment, a factor not to be ignored by those who wish to explore further the differences between these economies.

At this point, it is more beneficial to consider the similarities of economies rather than the differences, which are quite obvious (traders will be excluded because they introduce a foreign element). The most important similarity is that all these groupings operated without cash. Much that is often referred to as trade was, in fact, barter, in which goods are exchanged for goods rather than for cash. This distinction is of special significance because barter introduces into transactions a relative scale of values; whereas the use of cash involves an absolute scale of values. The barter of a goat for a pot does not determine that one goat is worth one pot on an absolute scale, or that, if one pot fetches on egg in another market, one goat is worth one egg. Rather, it determines that one particular goat and one particular pot, at a particular moment and place, are of equivalent worth insofar as each matches a need. Barter should be regarded more as a mutual assistance program than as a primitive form of trade.

Even today, it is common to find cash trade in Africa taking on the form of barter. (I am not referring here to the Oriental passion for haggling often so wrongly termed "bartering.") For example, if a man has a hoe he knows is worth two dollars, and if he does not need it but does need a box of fishhooks worth twenty-five cents, and particularly if he can sell and buy on the same market or in the same vicinity, he may well sell the hoe for exactly twenty-five cents. I have observed this type of transaction in forest villages, in urban markets, and even in city stores. This practice reveals two important things: that the traditional African prefers to complete a transaction without the intervention of money, which so effectively depersonalizes human beings, and that he defines his needs rather more clearly than we are apt to define ours. We are usually willing to expand our needs beyond any probability of satisfaction. It is a rare man in our world who is content with what he has. Such a man is likely to be characterized by his fellows as backward, lacking in initiative, not likely to get anywhere, a failure. He may also be happy. Whereas we define our own individual needs, to a large extent, the African has his needs defined for him (in traditional society) by the limitations of his technology, the existence of a widely accepted system of values, and the essentially social, as opposed to individual, nature of his personality. Thus a transaction is not a deal in which he expects to make a profit; it is a mutual fulfillment of needs, another thread in the web of human relationships, binding together more effectively people who know and rely on each other. The African society is a *true* society, where economic relationships are human (and moral) rather than commercial (and legal).

The issue of technology is important in this respect. It has often been said that Africa's limited technology has made progress impossible. While this is a good ethnocentric point of view, and as such, it has some validity, its validity depends on what is meant by "progress." Africa's limited technology did prevent the *illusion* of progress that is brought about by constantly invented "aids to better living." Such aids are usually invitations to indulge in yet another luxury that will relegate a previous luxury to the status of a necessity. The endless, mindless inventiveness that produces them leads to progress in only one sense: technological. It is technology that progresses, not humanity. With an unlimited technology, the gap between what men have and what they want widens, leading to a deterioration in personal and group relations. With a limited technology, the gap remains constant, and it is a necessary, socially functional constant, for the filling of the gap by other people who can supply the needs of those in want is as much a political mechanism as it is an economic one.

Similarly, division of labor and development of specializations also respond to political as well as to economic needs. The economic factor becomes more important as the society becomes more complex, and particularly as cash is introduced—in other words, as social relationships become more depersonalized. This does not mean that the society has to be so small that everyone knows everyone else. On the contrary, the very strength and vitality of the African system is shown by the fact that people may be strangers, in the sense of never having seen or heard of each other before, but still feel bound to each other by a system of mutual obligations and therefore honor those obligations. All that is required is that they be part of the society, whether the society defines itself as nation, tribe, clan, lineage, or family. At different levels of segmentation there are different sets of obligations; which of them is brought into play depends on the context.

In the same way that these major traditional African economies share a lack of cash, they share a communal nature since transactions are conducted in terms of interpersonal relations. This is another vital similarity between them. While the nature of a community may differ vastly at any level, all levels have their roots in the most basic community of all: the family. It really does not matter, for our purposes, whether the family is matrilineal or patrilineal, monogynous or polygynous, nuclear or extended. What matters is that, whatever form it takes, the family serves as the model for all social relationships, including economic ones. There is frequently a strong correlation between the precise nature of the family and the precise nature of the economy, but the family is always the basic unit.

The family may also be the major economic unit. If it is not, the major unit is nevertheless frequently familial. Other important bases of economic association are age and residence. Often all three factors overlap. In any case, all are significant and are structurally important in each of the major economies.

Age is frequently used as a device for cutting across kinship lines which, if followed too strictly, are as divisive at the wider extent as they are cohesive at the narrower. Territorial considerations are nearly always linked to kinship, although sometimes they are linked more directly to age, as in the case of the Nyakyusa with their "age villages."* (Age will be discussed in Part 2.) The factors to concentrate on here are the absence of a cash economy; the communal, social nature of economic transactions; and the importance of family and land. All these are supplied by just that element that is missing in traditional African society: cash. They add up to security, which is much the same as survivability.

A brief look at what is often called "traditional money" will help to make this point clear. According to a popular misconception, a cash economy not only existed in traditional Africa but was quite widespread. Paul Bohannan puts it nicely:

It is an astounding fact that economists have, for decades, been assigning three or four qualities to money when they discuss it with reference to our own society or to those of the mediaeval and modern world, yet the moment they have gone to ancient history or to the societies and economies studied by anthropologists they have sought out the "real" nature of money by allowing only one of these defining characteristics to dominate their definitions.†

---

* See Godfrey Wilson, "An African Morality," in S. Ottenberg and P. Ottenberg (eds.), *Cultures and Societies of Africa* (New York: Random House, 1960), pp. 345–364; and M. Wilson, *Rituals of Kinship among the Nyakyusa* (London: Oxford University Press, 1957).

† Paul J. Bohannan, "The Impact of Money on an African Subsistence Economy," in J. Middleton (ed.), *Black Africa* (New York: Macmillan, 1970), p. 14.

Each economist, according to his persuasion, emphasizes the form of money that he champions as the "earlier" form. Bohannan supports Karl Polanyi (1957), who designates as "general purpose money" what I have simply called cash; namely, money that can fulfill any of the three major monetary functions: payment, exchange, or evaluation. Polanyi contrasts this with a form he calls "special purpose money" which serves only one or, at the most, two of these functions. As Bohannan points out, special purpose money was the most common form found in traditional Africa. The fact that in recent years special purpose money has on various occasions been used as cash does not mean that it was used in that way in the past; the evidence is to the contrary.

Special purpose money was largely symbolic of certain important human activities and relationships, and was used to convey the obligations associated with those relationships. A Mangbetu did not "buy" his wife with his "money," which was in the form of a curved bush knife; he assumed certain obligations toward the girl's family, just as the family assumed certain obligations toward him and his family. He no more bought the girl with the knife than they bought the knife with the girl; if one wishes to argue that the knife was used as money to affect a purchase, the same argument converts the girl into cash. The example is perhaps not a good one because marriage in Africa is better regarded as a political, rather than as an economic, transaction; but I use it because of the lasting popularity of the term "bride price."

This is not to say that there was no concept of wealth; far from it. But wealth had nothing to do with cash or money, as such, in any form. For the traditional African, as for us, wealth implies security. But whereas we see security in terms of a bank balance or investment portfolio, the African sees it in terms of land and lineage. What we regard as economic activity is closely related to wealth and, consequently, to security in terms of money. Position is also considered a form of security; this, too, implies cash income because in our society position is mainly defined in occupational terms. In Africa, what is usually conceived of as economic activity has little to do with security; it is ordinarily aimed at filling stomachs (bananas and manioc cannot be conveniently put into savings accounts). Security is sought through other, diverse activities such as marriage, childbearing, proper child rearing, the fulfillment of one's obligations in the total network of social relations, drinking palm wine (an essentially male occupation on the whole), and gossiping (a correspondingly, but not exclusively, female occupation). Security, then, is understood in terms of social relationships rather than economic success. And insofar as security involves land as well as lineage, land also should be discussed elsewhere, for its economic importance is incidental. Land only serves as a vehicle, so to speak, for the transmission of food; it is the produce of the land, rather than the land itself, that is the economic factor. Land has economic implications, just as it has familial and political implications, but its greatest importance, perhaps its most fundamental importance, is spiritual. This underlies the connection between land and lineage because, in a sense, lineage is also spiritual in concept. If the reader wishes to continue to classify land and land tenure under "economy," well and good; classification can be made for many different purposes, and the categories by no means always coincide. But what I am suggesting here is that in dealing with African institutions, it is helpful to use African categories of thought rather than to impose our own categories and then wonder, in a superior way, why "those Africans" so abuse the land. (The article by A. J. B. Hughes, "Some Swazi Views on Land Tenure," discusses in greater detail both approaches.)

Perhaps one more economic factor should be mentioned: the essentially egalitarian nature of most traditional African societies. I think I have already suggested an adequate rebuttal to the counterexample of the many African societies where social stratification is accompanied by stratification in terms of wealth. The fact that one man has twice as many cattle or twice as much land as another does not mean that he is twice as rich, but rather that he has twice as many obligations. Chiefs are singled out by would-be detractors of the primitive and described as despots and exploiters. Judged by superficial appearances, they may well be. Chiefly courts are often lavish. According to the early Arabic historians, such courts were lavish well over 1,000 years ago and aroused the admiration and envy of the civilized world, which did not then include Europe. Going back some 5,000 years, Egypt, which was essentially African, can also be characterized as despotic, with its enormous contrasts of wealth and poverty, license and servitude. Much the same can be said of many of the more recent African states and nations. Certainly there was and still is an enormous concentration of wealth and power in many traditional societies. But in Africa this phenomenon in no way contradicts the principles of democracy and egalitarianism. A chief, in common parlance in many parts of Africa, is there "to be eaten"; and the wealthier he is, the better the "meal." It is a suitable metaphor. Many field workers know from professional experience what it must be like to be a chief, in terms of being eaten, because in Africa the field worker is also considered a storehouse of power and wealth to be consumed. A chief is often the apex of the lineage system and thus has the control of the land in his hands. But the power and the wealth are not his; they are merely held by him in trust for the benefit of the people. Control is always exerted over him, even when he is expected to be apparently arbitrary and extravagant in his behavior. The often-considerable tribute that is paid to a chief is not his to do with as he likes; a whole host of considerations force him to use it in the socially approved manner. There are numerous mechanisms for getting rid of chiefs who abuse their position of trust. Like chiefs, lesser individuals do not own their wealth. It is, in effect, security for others, for those who have a right to "eat" it in times of need.

Inheritance rules exemplify this essentially egalitarian nature of the African economy, assuring that wealth in any form does not accumulate in the hands of a few, except when held in trust. This assurance may be achieved in a diversity of ways, one of which is to maintain the same principles of division even before death, by complicated rules of sharing that in some cases seem to make all property communal. The rules, if followed to the letter, would be utterly impractical in many cases; but like other African rules they are intended to convey the spirit of the concept and to be tempered, in practice, with reason and good social sense. They are invoked when, and to the extent that, the occasion demands. Like the chief's storehouse, they are potential security for times of emergency.

The picture of the traditional African presented here is too often dismissed as idealistic and romantic. It is neither; it is factual and anything but romantic. No suggestion is being made that there is anything particularly noble or self-sacrificing about the African's behavior, or that the African is more virtuous than others. Indeed, what to us would be a highly virtuous act would to the African be merely good sense, if he thought about it, and good manners if he did not. This does not imply that Africans are only considerate toward each other because they expect a just return. Rather, the acts that Western society considers virtuous are simply part of the African system, which is accepted and followed because it has long proven itself by fulfilling the needs of its members. Nearly all forms of behavior that we consider virtuous, such as generosity, kindness, and consideration, are regarded by the African as normal, reasonable adult behavior.

How much has all this changed under the impact of such a different form of economy as was imposed on Africa by the colonial powers? Obviously, the question is too vast to be answered fully here because the situation varies from area to area and village to village, from virtually no significant change to almost total acceptance of the new system. Instead, I would like to examine briefly those aspects of economic life that I have been discussing.

The three articles that follow make clear the validity of the social anthropological tenet that social institutions are interrelated. There is no such thing as economic change in the exclusive sense because any change in the economic sector will have repercussions in all other sectors; sometimes these will be even more profound than the economic change that was originally contemplated.

"Some Swazi Views on Land Tenure," by A. J. B. Hughes, gives a splendid example of simple-minded thinking on the part of the authorities trying to introduce land reform among the Swazi. It is also an example of ethnocentric thinking. The authorities assumed that the Swazi would share the exclusively economic values that they placed on land. Thinking only in economic terms and only within the British conceptual framework, they could see so clearly and indisputably what needed to be done that their only concern was with how to do it. The notion that different cultural and organizational complexities existed and could be of significance apparently did not occur to them. Although they made use of the Swazi to implement their plan, they made use of the wrong Swazi. Probably they shared the common view that traditional authorities would resist change, so they by-passed those authorities and trained "progressive" young Swazi for the job. The trainees evidently recognized the nature of the land-shortage crisis and agreed that something had to be done. Yet they rejected the plan for introducing individual land ownership, which would theoretically have taken land out of the control of the despotic chiefs and distributed it fairly among the subjects, because they saw that it struck at the very roots of their being and identity. From their point of view, they were being asked to change their nationality and their religion, as well as to abandon their families, as they understood the terms. Not unreasonably, this seemed a high price to pay. The article describes a classic study of failure; it shows that nearly all the cardinal rules for successful social change were violated.* Yet even under such conditions, with understanding, changes as far-reaching as those attempted with the Swazi can be achieved if the necessity for change is accepted as a felt need and is given the approval of the traditional leaders of society.

Attitudes toward land, however, offer the maximum resistance to change. The assumption here is that land meets such resistance because it is a spiritual rather than an economic entity. I think Hughes' article supports this assumption.

One might well ask, then, how it is that the introduction of cash, which

---

* Niehoff establishes six conditions as generally necessary for successful change: two-way communication, participation on the part of the people affected, utilization (which implies comprehension) of existing culture, utilization of a *felt* need as distinct from the *defined* need as seen by the agents of change, establishment of a sound motivation, and utilization of local leadership, religious, secular, or both. A. H. Niehoff, *A Casebook of Social Change* (Chicago: Aldine, 1966).

according to the arguments presented also strikes at the social personality of the individual, an essentially spiritual entity, appears to have been completely successful. First, the introduction of cash, both in coin and paper forms, has not always met with precisely the expected results. Early coinage was frequently perforated. This was the most popular form of currency because it lent itself so readily to use as personal adornment. Such coins could be strung from the neck, wrists, waist, and ankles; hung from the ears; and even braided into the hair. They were highly desired for these purposes and consequently had a greater value than the nominally and intrinsically more valuable silver coins, which were not perforated. Coins had other decorative uses. They could be inlaid in wood, strung from musical instruments (where they were also often used for their acoustical properties), and embedded in the clay walls of houses or in pottery. Paper money could also be used as adornment. It could be tightly rolled and inserted through holes in the ears, lips, or nose; occasionally I have seen it rolled into the hair. These uses often kept money both safe and handy, but their prime purpose was decorative. The utilitarian value of money was not ignored; for instance, pierced coins made admirable sinkers for fishing nets, and paper money made reasonable though expensive wrapping paper for commodities such as snuff and hemp seeds.

Moreover, when the variety of conceptual attitudes toward cash is taken into account, the claim that cash has been fully accepted requires serious modification. In preindependent Zaïre (Congo, Kinshasa), the market prices were often kept under rigorous control by the Belgian authorities; prices were fixed. In postindependence Zaïre, the Congolese administrators in rural areas have a hard time trying to maintain even a semblance of stability: they are not prepared to be as ruthless as their predecessors were in imposing official policy and the notion of fixed cash value still meets with enthusiastic opposition. For the foreigner, it is disconcerting to find that a budget based on today's market prices is likely to be useless tomorrow. Plantains that cost five *makuta* today may well cost twenty tomorrow, depending on a host of considerations, few of which are economic. For instance, raising and lowering prices is a good way to control political relationships either at the group or at the personal level. Tribal hostilities are frequently demonstrated this way, as are personal animosities. The same mechanism can be used to settle both kinds of disputes. Overcharging and being overcharged are ways of recouping a loss and paying a debt without losing face and without bringing the case to court or to public attention. Such a mechanism is particularly useful under the present circumstances in the eastern province, where there has been a sudden influx of Congolese officials, government workers, public works laborers, and others from tribes hitherto entirely unknown in the area and toward whom there is considerable mistrust. A powerful national sentiment encourages people to find an amicable settlement for the many disputes that arise out of the situation, but in this highly traditional area, no traditional mechanism exists that could encompass people as far from home as the BaKongo or BaLuba. Thus manipulation of market prices provides an effective alternative. It is a technique not unknown in our own society, where the institution of awarding gratuities, for example, might be said to be political at both group and personal levels.

When cash is substituted for special purpose money, as it now is in marriage, it fulfills the same function as the traditional bush knife, raffia mat, iron ingot, or hoe and establishes the same sets of obligations both by being given and by being received. It does not, except in certain circumstances, bring with it the commercial concept of purchase. However, the original symbolism is lacking. In African society, the symbolism was not a romantic nicety; it was a functional necessity. Thus, the use of cash is a step in the direction of less-effective human relationships.

There are also practical difficulties involved whenever cash is introduced as a compulsory means for paying taxes or other national dues in an area where little or no wage labor is offered (as is the case in the more remote rural areas) and where there is no viable cash economy. In such an area, the few government workers and other wage earners become the sole source of cash and the center of the local cash circulation system. The farmers or herders may have remarkably few opportunities for finding even the minimum amount required for annual taxes; they may be forced to sell what they can ill afford to sell or to accept part-time labor, if available, that will take them away from full-time subsistence activities. In some cases, the problem is unexpectedly compounded by nationalistic fervor. For example, people with no cash resources nonetheless feel obliged to dress in a certain manner, such as in clothing displaying portraits of national leaders. Fervid nationalism is part of the process of traditionalizing a new nation and granting it the sanction of the past, but for a wage earner in a remote area, one party shirt might cost a month's wages. Furthermore, wage earners inevitably acquire other expensive tastes for trade goods. In situations like this, nomadic hunters are the least adversely affected. Their need and desire for trade goods are almost nonexistent. They are entirely self-sufficient with regard to life's necessities and, in their view, its comforts. This is particularly true of forest hunters who live in an abundant environment. Because meat is a highly prized commodity at any market and in any village, and because their trade needs are so minimal, the hunters have no difficulty in fulfilling their cash obligations when they wish to do so. But on the whole, the introduction of a cash economy has drastically increased the traditional African's felt needs and has opened the gap between desire and achievement. Greed is now possible.

The most significant change that has accompanied the introduction of a cash economy in Africa is the depersonalization of economic relationships. Abner Cohen's article, "The Social Organization of Credit in a West African Cattle Market," explores the ways in which interpersonal relationships may be retained as the basis for transactions despite the use of a cash economy. In the credit system he describes, following the initial transaction, the actual handling of cash is indirect and involves different participants. Delayed reciprocation of this sort is a common feature of gift exchange in small-scale societies. Moreover, some economic transactions in the traditional system might be said to have existed primarily for the purpose of invoking and thereby reaffirming (with the possibility of denial) specific interpersonal and intergroup relationships. The Pygmy village relationship was long misunderstood by outsiders because it was taken at face value, as an economic relationship, whereas it was and is first and foremost a political relationship, using exchange as a means of maintaining a delicate balance between two potentially hostile groups.* Where cash has been introduced, such a balance has been destroyed, and hostilities have erupted.

S. Ottenberg's article, "Improvement Associations among the Afikpo Ibo," is more general in scope but still has a strong economic bias. He shows how change that threatens established sets of relationships is handled in order to retain those relationships, even if in modified form, perhaps by creating an additional set of relationships. A traditional system can be remarkably adaptive, providing the whole system is allowed to adapt. The case of the Afikpo Ibo is a fascinating example of change being not only adopted and adapted but also actively initiated within the framework of a semitraditional pattern. It is another strong argument against the simplistic opinion that tradition is opposed to change and antagonistic to national interests. (Cohen makes this same point in describing the positive use of tribalism in the cattle market.)

Like the cash economy, technological change has come to stay, receiving wide acceptance and striking deep at the essence of traditional African society. But, like cash, tools are often used for purposes other than those intended. This is not done out of ignorance, as may be asserted by frus-

---

* See C. M. Turnbull, *Wayward Servants* (Garden City, N.Y.: Natural History Press, 1965).

trated overseers. Rather, it stems from the African's deeper understanding of the consequences of accepting proposed changes and his unwillingness to reap the "benefits." This has been true particularly in the case of the introduction of technological devices designed to save labor in situations where labor did not have to be saved, except from the Western orientation toward ever-increased production for the sake of increase. Of course, it is possible to ignore a specific local situation and maintain that in the wider national (or international) context, increased production is needed everywhere to cope with the ever-expanding population. But this is not likely to be recognized as a felt need by the people at the local level. Although the problems of population growth are not ignored in Africa, even in the most rural areas, increased production is recognized as a futile attempt to catch up with an ever-receding goal, serving only to push the goal still farther away. At this level, something more basic is needed to deal with population increase. A highly significant factor in traditional African economy is demographic: many societies developed subtle, indigenous birth control mechanisms that maintained a proper ecological balance even under conditions of change. Any alteration in the traditional labor pattern threatens the whole network of human relations, including the lines of kinship with which economic relations and labor patterns so often coincided. Thus, the introduction of a plough becomes a potential threat to a community.

On the wider scale, the drastic changes brought by industrialization to the entire social and demographic situation, such as urbanization and systematic migration, merit special study. Despite the apparently total disruption of traditional life that industrialization has caused, tradition frequently remains, not merely as an obstinate holdover but as a dynamic force in a new situation where new forms of cohesion are called for. It remains not because other logical reasons for cohesion are lacking, but rather because other reasons would not have the same force. The presence of some traditional element, however modified or divorced from its original context, provides a sense of continuity with a past that offered, above all else, precisely the condition that is lacking in the present: security.

What does all this tell us about ourselves? Again I refer to the three articles that follow. They provide abundant evidence that, in the economic realm, the African has retained a high degree of concern for the maintenance of what he considers proper human relationships. The kinds of economic transactions that are preferred occur between members of a community, people who know each other and who therefore are subject to moral pressure. Legal coercion, even in such a modern setting as the Ibadan cattle market, is avoided, and the security offered against credit rests on the concept of community. In the Ibadan market the community is not familial; elsewhere it often is. Ottenberg's article describes two levels of community-advancement organization. It is particularly worth noting that only at the local level, where people know each other, does the organization make cash loans. It is the sense of community that is vital, rather than the desire for economic gain. Economic needs must be satisfied, but not at the expense of the community.

We seem to take the opposite approach. In general transactions we prefer cash and fixed prices, and even value the impersonality of a transaction often to the point of reaffirming, when it is between friends, that "this is business," that the friendship is irrelevant. There is something satisfying about the cut-and-dried nature of the business deal, about its finality and inflexibility. Yet, unlike the African, if it is possible we avoid cash deals, particularly loans, with family and close friends. It is worth asking why. Do we show this reluctance because, as is often stated, lending cash to friends is a good way to lose friends? Or because it is a good way to lose cash? The latter possibility would at least indicate that we implicitly recognize certain human obligations, however much it would also show our devotion to the dollar.

The common denominator between the African and our own situations is frequently the stated values; the difference lies in the way these values are implemented. We say we believe in community, society, and nation. But our loyalties become rather diffuse when put to the test. Our ultimate loyalty, like that of the Ik, is to ourself. Nowhere is this more true than in the economic realm. Where economic associations exist in Africa, even in the form of guilds of craftsmen or other specialists (somewhat comparable, at first glance, to our trade unions), they function for the benefit of the total community and not merely for self-advancement—a direct contrast to the situation in the United States and elsewhere in the Western world, where unions often seem to exist for their own benefit without regard for the rest of the community. To any member of a trade guild in traditional West Africa, the vicious hostility to students displayed by that remarkable segment of American society which takes as its symbol the hard hat would be incomprehensible and its often vicious opposition to the ideas of students would be taken as a glorification of ignorance and stupidity. It is not only the division of one segment of a so-called society against another that would be incomprehensible to the traditional African; so would the fact that different occupational groups should be so hierarchically arranged in a powerful and effective value system contradicting the nominal value system. For in Western society, these systems seem to work in opposition. "All men are equal" could hardly be less true.

The question of whether Western society can be called a society is not just a quibble over a term; it is a challenge to define that term. To me "society" implies more than a mere conglomeration of individuals accepting a common government and (relatively) common law while frequently finding excuses to further their own interests at the expense of others in the same conglomeration. It means, or should mean, more than a group of people who behave in an ordered manner because they are compelled to by such civilized incentives as night sticks, fire hoses, cattle prods, dogs, guns, and tanks. A certain element of cohesion seems to be lacking when such drastic measures have to be taken to hold the fabric of a society together. The traditional society in Africa requires a minimum of physical coercion. In the past there were no police forces comparable to those of the West, although in some of the more complex societies institutions did exist to discourage and punish offenders. This does not mean there was a general lack of coercion; in all societies there must be forces of social control. But whereas in Western society, social control is achieved by threats and the use of physical violence, including incarceration, physical and psychological torture (I refer the reader to any good account of the prison system), and execution, in the so-called primitive society, exactly the same goal is achieved by powerful but nonviolent forces that create an equally powerful and positive urge to act in the approved manner. The sanctions are positive rather than negative, and the result is a moral community, a society, rather than a legal, political technicality.

Negative sanctions do exist in Africa, and in some of the larger societies, such as the nation-states, they sometimes include quite appalling methods of physical punishment, such as the *atopere* death dance of the Ashanti. But I suggest that these should not be interpreted as arguments to contradict what I have said about positive sanctions, merely because of their apparent horror, least of all by anyone who has failed to examine with some attention his own society's penal system. It is unrealistic to compare only the outer forms of the punishment; who is to judge being sliced to death within a few days, at most, of being sentenced, as opposed to months and years of waiting in a sanitary death cell, knowing that at the end comes the last month, the last week, the last day and night, and finally the last hour, all of which must make those last minutes infinitely more horrifying than any amount of physical pain.

There is also something singularly dishonest about the way we do our dirty work, and the way we get others to do it for us, in private. An execution is an unpleasant event, but it is a shade less so if it can be said, with some conviction, to serve a useful purpose and to be the genuine will of the people. A private execution in an antiseptic green gas chamber in front of a few chosen observers does not seem to achieve anything except revenge for some, the tying up of a loose end for others, and the removal of a nuisance for still others. It must seem singularly pointless to the person having his life taken from him when he looks for the last time at humanity and sees a few strange, unknown, uncomprehending faces.

I have seen a public execution in Africa, and, although it was not exactly a happy event, it made sense. For one thing, a goodly proportion of the populace of Kisangani was present, at the exhortation of the governor. They were not there, as members of the foreign press so often like to claim, for the fun of it, but because to be there was, in the traditional African sense, a social duty. They knew that *they* were hanging the two men, not the hooded figures who did the job (very inefficiently) on the gallows. In our world, we read a short paragraph in the daily paper stating that so-and-so was executed at such-and-such prison yesterday, then pass on to something more meaningful to us, like the weatherman's report that it is going to rain. That stupid, wasteful death has achieved nothing. But this execution at Kisangani, in the rain, was what execution is claimed to be in the West (and what statistics say it is not): a deterrent. Even the inefficiency of the hangmen was functional in this respect, as was (for the spectators) the horrifying moment when one of the condemned men fainted while sitting beneath the noose and was hung in his unconscious state. He did not have a chance to say much. The other spoke loudly and clearly, and at considerable length, through a bull horn. Evidently the whole thing made perfect sense to him. He said that his desire had not been to kill, but that nevertheless he *had* killed (there had been a succession of killings; these men were two ex-Simba bandits), and that the killing had been wrong because it had been for his own safety. He said he was glad to have an opportunity to make amends, and he ended, much to my surprise but probably nobody else's, by thanking everyone present, with obvious and touching sincerity, for coming to see him die and helping him, as he put it, to undo the wrong. What he was trying to do in his last moments was be himself—a murderer, but still a human being with a human and social conscience. The people who were part of the system that condemned him to die recognized their part, and they came to hang him; yet they cried with sympathy when the other condemned man fainted. It was a positive effort by everyone, including the condemned, not merely to right a wrong but to remove it. The few thousand faces the condemned men had to look at belonged to the people they had wronged and who had asked for amends. The execution was a sort of mutual compact between the condemned and the wronged, an intensely intimate meeting of the two; and of everyone involved, I think the human being who spoke was probably the most satisfied with the outcome.

The preceding account does not stray as far as it may seem to from the general economic theme of this discussion. Human life deserves consideration as an economic factor; and the traditional African seems to make better use of it, in many ways, than we do, and to be infinitely less wasteful with it. With our civilized technology we can now easily kill millions; whereas it is hard work for an African to kill even a single person with a *panga* (a home-forged bush knife). Concern for life is the core of traditional African behavior, and the power it gives to the positive sanctions is so enormous that the people in traditional society seem to behave in a moral manner, without any coercion, when in fact they are merely behaving in a sensible manner.

It must be said at this point that in Africa the traditional view of life is not confined to the notion of a single existence, although it does not usually include the notion of rebirth. To the African there are, in a sense, three coexisting planes of existence: the past, the present, and the future. The unborn, the living, and the dead all exist. This is one reason why land frequently cannot be alienated from its owner by sale; it belongs to all three planes. A piece of land may belong to only one man now, as it belonged to his father before him; but it also belongs to the countless unborn who will follow. It was the failure of the British colonials to grasp this point that led, among other things, to Mau Mau.

Thus, the coercive element contributing to moral behavior is the expectation of afterlife, which amounts to certainty for the African in these societies. But the coercion is not couched in negative terms, as in the threat of hellfire, even though an equivalent to hellfire is implicit. It lies, rather, in the African's positive desire to follow his ancestors, who are, after all, his family; who are demonstrably the source of all well being; and without whom there can be no existence. Much of his religious belief and practice seems designed to support this positive attitude.

The promise of afterlife is the main focus of African social interest and behavior, although it is not common subject matter for casual conversation, any more than God is a popular drawing-room topic in our society. It is not, therefore, generally given enough credit. Yet, because of it, many factors that seem to us to be incontrovertibly economic are removed to other sectors of social life, leaving as the objective of economics the filling of stomachs, and familial rather than individual stomachs at that.

Hughes examined a situation that had been treated by the authorities in exclusively economic terms. The factors that arose as a result of his more perceptive inquiry had little to do with land tenure as such but much to do with community. The answers to the questions Hughes raises show concern for the inevitable loss of the respect that every Swazi must traditionally show his ruler, his parents and friends, and the aged; good-neighborliness is said to be in jeopardy if the reforms are carried through. Land pressure is the problem, and it is recognized as such by the Swazi. However, their most fundamental sense of security lies in the land, not as an independent entity, but as the common property of the nation, which includes the unborn. They represent the community at its widest extension. The reform proposed for them suggested individual land ownership with right of alienation. Yet the individual in such traditional societies (as has already been seen and as will be seen in greater detail in Part 2) is not entirely what we understand by that term in the West, and traditional African societies are not plagued to the same extent that Western societies are by a conflict between the individual and society. The African individual sees himself only as a social entity, as part of a whole system of inter-personal relationships without which he would be nothing. One of the Swazi essayists put it bluntly when he stated that the introduction of individual land ownership would "poison us with envy." Hughes thinks that prediction to be rather extreme and unlikely to happen. I disagree; in the West it has already come to pass.

Many of these points will be further clarified and justified in the remaining sections of the book. In order to close this part on a more strictly economic note and relate it more directly to the theme of morality, let me suggest that traditional African morality, humanity, or concern for and with others is not a virtue but a necessity; and yet it is this direct function of the African's limited technology that we deplore as evidence of backwardness. When defined in economic terms, virtue is no more than a corollary of greed; the one implies and even necessitates the other. And since a limited technology makes greed almost impossible, it also, in a sense, makes virtue impossible. The result is Max Gluckman's "reasonable man,"* which is one of the best definitions of a traditional African (although, of course, Gluckman was applying the term specifically to the Lozi ideal).

The question that arises is: Just what has technological progress achieved for us in human terms, other than an obvious worsening of human relationships? With their backs to the wall, some defenders of the technological faith reply that medical technology, at least, has prolonged human life and alleviated human suffering. But the truth of that reply is not much comfort if life is less worth living or if other technological advances make it less likely to be livable.

---

* Max Gluckman, *The Judicial Process among the Barotse of Northern Rhodesia* (Manchester, Eng.: Manchester University Press, 1955).

# Some Swazi Views on Land Tenure[1]

# A. J. B. Hughes[*]

Virtually all sub-Saharan Africa is in the throes of rapid social and economic change. The recent fashion for meteorological allegories has merely served to stress the fact that these changes are also causing very considerable problems. The dilemma facing most administrations throughout the continent is that while much of the old way of life must inevitably disappear if the tribal groups involved are to hope to survive as viable populations in the modern world, this same process can, if it occurs too fast, threaten the whole social order and the systems of social control and social organization, which have hitherto bound them together as groups and governed the day-to-day lives of their members.

[*] A personal communication from Mr. A. J. B. Hughes comments on "the advance in thinking about traditional African land tenure since my article appeared in 1962. Much of this has appeared in rather obscure publications not obviously connected with anthropology. For example there is some pertinent material at page 71 of the published *Proceedings of the Ninth Ordinary Meeting of the Southern African Regional Commission for the Conservation and Utilization of the Soil* (1964); and in the very recently published *Proceedings* of the special symposium on traditional systems of land tenure arranged by that same body in May (1968). I myself have gone rather further than my 1962 thinking in a paper delivered (1967) at a symposium with the title of "Drought and Development."

Doubtless all the contributors to this volume would have similar qualifications concerning their earlier thinking and would wish their work to be considered especially in light of the time at which it was written. [Ed.]

[1] The material on which this paper is based was collected while carrying out a social-anthropological study in Swaziland, as a research worker of the Institute for Social Research of the University of Natal. My thanks are due to the Swaziland Government, who initiated this project, and arranged for C. D. and W. funds to finance it; to all the many government officials who provided invaluable assistance; to the Ngwenyama and the Swazi Nation who permitted the research to be conducted; to J. D. Hunter-Smith, Principal Agricultural Officer, who enabled me to obtain this particular material; and to the writers of the essays themselves. I owe a special debt of gratitude to Professor Holleman, Director of the Institute for Social Research, whose comments on and criticisms of earlier drafts of this paper were of the greatest help; a debt I also owe to J. D. Hunter-Smith, A. Dicks, J. B. Purcell, and other Swaziland Government officials, who likewise read and commented on these earlier drafts. As far as the views expressed are concerned, however, the responsibility is mine alone.

Nor has the process of change always been an even one. Some traditional institutions have adjusted readily to the new conditions, others have shown remarkable powers of resistance, the last class including many which from the point of view of western economic thinking would seem to be those where radical alterations were most essential.

A case in point is the widespread survival of traditional systems of land tenure throughout the area. By and large, these are agriculturally most inefficient and are becoming more so every year. Something must change, and soon, if the land of Africa is to make an adequate contribution to the feeding of its inhabitants. Yet the close connexion in the traditional systems between control over land, political authority, and the whole system of sanctions, removes this question from the purely economic sphere. This is the essence of the dilemma. Economic planners and agriculturists can argue with considerable force that change must come if economic chaos is to be averted. Students of African land tenure, and many of the Africans involved, argue that purely economically oriented legislation to this end would inevitably bring social chaos in its wake.

Owing to a fortunate chain of circumstances, I was able to obtain the views of a group which could reasonably be classed as 'progressive' Swazi on the situation in Swaziland. With the co-operation of the Swaziland Government's Department of Land Utilization, a question on this subject was set in the passing-out examination for trainee Land Utilization Officers at the Mdutshane Agricultural School. A discussion of the short essays produced by these Swazi in answer to this question provides the main subject-matter for this paper.

This type of research technique has certain obvious limitations. It lacks the controls and scientific selectivity of a properly planned attitude survey. It is also unfortunate, in some respects, that the Swazi students had to write in English rather than in their mother tongue. This was inevitable, in view of the circumstances under which the answers were produced, but it did force the writers to translate into a foreign language concepts that are well known to be singularly unamenable to this process. Nevertheless, these essays would still seem to provide valuable information about a contentious and still little-studied issue.

## The Background to the Question

In Swaziland the question of whether or not some change is needed in the traditional system of land tenure in the Swazi areas is a very live issue.

Change is in the air. This territory of some 6,705 square miles has seen remarkable economic advances during the last decade, and seems poised for even more spectacular advance in the near future. There is general acceptance of the fact that these economic changes must inevitably mean great social changes. All are agreed on the need to associate the Swazi as closely as possible with the development of the Territory, and it is generally appreciated that this involvement must have considerable effect on their traditional way of life.

The fundamental question is, What adjustments will the Swazi have to make in their social and political organization so as to fit in most satisfactorily with the changed economic conditions?

The local situation is in many ways atypical as far as the general Southern African scene is concerned. The territory has an African and a European population,[2] a remarkably strong Paramount Chieftaincy and social organization among the Swazi, and what amounts almost to a federal system of government within the country. While overall political control is vested in the agents of the United Kingdom Government, headed locally by the Resident Commissioner, the Swazi National authorities have considerable powers of government over Swazi living inside the territorial frontiers.[3] This is a formalized division of authority, enshrined in statutory pronouncements and statements of policy. Though it is based technically on population groups rather than territorial areas, there is some territorial basis to this division owing to the fact that the Territory is divided approximately equally between areas where land is held on freehold tenure and the Swazi Area,[4] where the traditional system of land tenure operates. It is in the latter that the majority of Swazi live, and it is here that the powers of the Swazi National Administration are most exercised and most evident.

The issue is further complicated by the peculiar history of early contacts between Swazi and Europeans. In the latter part of the nineteenth century the then Swazi king, Mbandzeni, issued a vast number of concessions to Europeans who flocked to his court armed with liquor, money, peacocks, greyhounds, and other inducements designed to win favours from an African monarch.[5] There followed a turbulent and confused period until after the end of the Anglo-Boer War in 1902, when the incoming British Administration was faced with the problem of the concessions, and had to reach some decision regarding the rights of Swazi and concessionaires respectively.

The position was that the entire territory had been signed away to various concessionaires, often several times over, while mining and other

---

[2] 5,919 Europeans; 229,744 Africans; 1,378 Eurafricans (1956 Census).

[3] For details see B. A. Marwick, *The Swazi*, Cambridge, 1940, pp. 288 ff.; H. Kuper, *An African Aristocracy*, London, O.U.P., 1947, pp. 54–71; H. Kuper, *The Swazi*, Ethnographic Survey of Africa (S.A. Part I), International African Institute, London, 1952, pp. 39 ff.

[4] In this paper the term 'Swazi Area' is used to include three technically distinct categories of land: Native Areas, Lifa Land, and Native Land Settlement areas. In all these (with one or two small exceptions in the Native Land Settlements) land is held according to Swazi customary rules of tenure.

[5] For details see Kuper, *An African Aristocracy,* pp. 20 ff.; H. J. R. Way, *Mineral ownership as affecting mineral development in Swaziland.* Special report No. 2 of the Swaziland Geological Survey Department, 1949.

concessions often overlapped the land concessions. Under the Concessions Partitions Proclamation of 1907 one-third of the land was allocated to the Swazi to be held under traditional systems of land tenure, while the remaining two-thirds was allocated to the concessionaires. It was also ruled that all expired concessions should revert to the Crown, not to the Swazi nation.

Since then more land has been acquired by the Swazi authorities, either purchased by the Lifa Fund (a fund set up by the Swazi with the specific aim of buying back land lost through the granting of concessions) or through grants of Crown land, bringing the total Swazi Area to just over half the total area of Swaziland.

The Swazi have always argued that Mbandzeni did not sell the land, in the European sense of the term 'to sell', and was, in fact, not entitled to do so according to Swazi customary law. The view taken by the Territorial Administration and the paramount power is that these concessions did transfer ownership, and it was this decision that resulted in the settlement of 1907.[6]

Thus, the differences between European and traditional Bantu systems of land tenure have come to have great emotive significance for the Swazi. Any discussion about land-tenure problems invariably comes back to the history of the concessions. Swazi will constantly stress that the selling of land (*kudayisa umhlaba*) is not a Swazi custom, but a European one; the implication usually being that the speaker considers it a thoroughly deplorable custom at that.

Nor has the issue been allowed to acquire the respectable patina of an ancient injustice which must now simply be accepted as an historical fact. The Swazi authorities have never ceased their fight against the Partition decision. A delegation was sent to the United Kingdom in 1907, to plead for its reversal; the present Ngwenyama (Paramount Chief) went over in person in 1922, shortly after reaching his majority, for the same purpose; and the latest Petition to the Secretary of State on this subject was sent as late as 1956. Legal actions, the raising of funds to finance these and other official efforts to challenge the Partition, and the attempts to regain the 'Swazi heritage' by purchase through the Lifa Fund,[7] have all served to keep the 'land question' alive in Swazi minds.

## The Traditional System of Tenure

Without going deeply into this system, it can be said that it is very similar to the general traditional pattern found among other Southern Bantu. The

---

[6] Kuper, op. cit., pp. 30 ff.

[7] *Lifa* could be directly translated in this context as 'Inheritance, Heritage'.

term 'communal', by which it has often been described, is partially justified
in that an individual's rights to land are derived from his membership of a
community, from his position in the political organization. Rights to
allocate land to others are similarly based on the allocator's political position. The Swazi ruler, the Ngwenyama, is technically the ultimate authority
as far as land distribution goes, but in practice this power is effectively
vested in the subordinate territorial authorities, the local chiefs who rule
160 chiefdoms into which the Swazi Area of Swaziland is divided.

A married man derives the right to arable land and a site on which to
erect a dwelling from being a member of a local community and a subject
of the chief ruling over it. He can acquire this membership either through
birth, or by offering allegiance (*kukhonta*) to the chief and being accepted.
His individualized right to any given piece of arable land is normally
established either through his own legitimate use of it (with the knowledge
and approval of the chief and community), or by inheritance.

Grazing land is not allocated to individuals; only arable land and homestead sites are so distributed.[8] A man can lose his rights to land in any specific chiefdom by voluntarily relinquishing them, by formally handing them
over to others, or by being banished from the chiefdom by the chief and
his council (*libandla*).

In this context it is the last, banishment, which is of greatest importance,
as many Swazi argue that this inhibits agricultural development because of
the general insecurity of tenure. The argument runs that a man who is too
successful economically is liable to become unpopular with the political
authorities in the chiefdom and runs the risk of banishment.

Technically, every man who is so banished has the right of appeal to the
Ngwenyama, and no sentence of banishment will be confirmed unless the
local political authorities can show good cause why the person in question
should be driven out of the area. The fact remains that many men are
banished and forced to make new lives in other chiefdoms. In this connexion, it is interesting to note that numbers of Swazi have left the Swazi
Area and are living on land that they have acquired on freehold title in
other parts of Swaziland. This process is continuing, though slowly, which
would suggest that there is some substance in the suggestion that many
people find the lack of security of tenure in the Swazi Area a sufficiently
real problem for them to make considerable economic sacrifices in search
of something more satisfactory.

In their essays the students make frequent mention of the national
*Incwala* ritual, and of other national and local rituals in which the mystic
connexion between rulers, people, and land is symbolically expressed.
While the symbolism of many of these ceremonies, particularly of the

---

[8] It is now becoming increasingly common for special allocations to be made to
individuals for timber plantations.

*Incwala,* is often obscure or disputed, the central theme of all is clearly the need for the cohesion of the community, and the dependence of the welfare of all its members on the continuation of that cohesion. In the case of the *Incwala,* the so-called 'First Fruits Ceremony', which Kuper styles 'a drama of kingship', the community involved is the whole Swazi nation and the central part is played by the Swazi ruler, the Ngwenyama.[9]

The *Incwala* ritual complex is undoubtedly the most important of all public national ceremonies among the Swazi, but there are others that also serve to stress and reinforce the traditional relationship between ruler and subject, both at the national level and in the local chiefdoms. There are the *luselwa* ceremonies of certain chiefs, performed after the *Incwala* in those chiefdoms which 'have their own kingship' (*bukosi*), as Swazi put it. There is the ceremonial attached to the now largely formal tribute-labour gatherings such as the national Reed Dance (*umhlanga*). There is the *umcwasho* ritual whereby the young girls of a chiefdom (more rarely a selected group from the whole nation) form an association for a fixed period under the leadership of a girl of the ruling house.[10] An adequate discussion of the full significance of these and other rites would not be practicable here, but it is of interest that our students did see a clear connexion between these ceremonies, stressing the unity of the community as they do, and the land question.

### The Essayists

Apart from this general background, which they share with all Swazi, the writers of these essays had been subjected to special influences as the result of their course as Land Utilization Officers.

They had been shown that increased agricultural production was a real possibility, by the use of techniques within the reach of all Swazi. They had been trained in the advantages of building up soil fertility, rotational grazing, the proper cultivation of cash crops and long-term crops (such as timber). Their whole course had been oriented so as to demonstrate that increased agricultural productivity, with consequent economic advantages to the farmer, was dependent on long-term planning, rational integration of agricultural and pastoral activities, and increased capital investment. They had also received lectures stressing the virtual impossibility of the small farmer raising this capital except on the security of the land itself; something quite impracticable with the existing system of tenure.

---

[9] Kuper, op cit., pp. 197 ff.; Marwick, op. cit., pp. 182 ff; S.T.M. Sukati, *The Incwala* (Swaziland Government duplicated publication).

[10] Kuper, op. cit., pp. 130–2.

Their answers show that they had accepted these premises, and the majority also accepted the desirability of an improved standard of living for the Swazi farmer—better housing, more assured food-supply, an increasing cash income to pay for other needs. In this they were not unique in any way, as the desirability of increased production and an improved standard of living is today widely accepted among the Swazi people.

They had been selected from those answering an advertisement put out by the Territorial Administration. At least a Standard VII education was essential,[11] and the final choice of students was made by technical officers of the Territorial Administration. Thus, there is no reason to believe that those selected represented a group that particularly supported conservative views. On the contrary, it is reasonable to suppose a certain amount of personal selection by the applicants themselves in favour of those who had a predilection for European ideas and values.

To sum up, one can say of this group that they had reached a reasonably high educational standard, had deliberately chosen a career that would label them as *emakhulungwane* (westernized Swazi), and had been through an intensive course based on European ideas regarding the most rational use of land and labour, the overriding importance of getting the best economic returns possible from agricultural holdings, and that farming should be conducted as a business. Not only had they learned these things themselves; the whole purpose of the course was that they should spread these ideas among the rest of the Swazi. It is in the light of these considerations that one should consider the subject-matter of their essays on land tenure.

### The Question and the Answers

The question read, 'What in your opinion are the main differences between land rights held in Native Area according to the traditional Swazi system and land rights held by the few individual Swazis who have purchased their land?'

It would not be practicable, nor is it necessary, to publish the full text of all the essays. Owing to a certain uniformity in the contents, some generalizations are possible without reference to all the texts. However, in order to give an idea of the type of answer given in this question, two complete versions are given below. They were originally written in English, and no attempt has been made to alter or 'correct' this, except in minor points such as punctuation and the use of capital letters, or where the sense would have been obscure otherwise.

Thus, one student writes:

---

[11] The majority had passed the Junior Certificate examination.

When one considers land held on a commonage[12] against that held on individual tenure one finds striking difference between the two in so far as land rights and privileges are concerned.

Both the individual land owner and the man on land held in accordance with Swazi tradition and custom have the right to use and plough the land, and make use of the produce therefrom. But the individual land owner has the advantage of selling the land, which his neighbour cannot do.

Under individual tenure land can be loaned and some interest reaped. But under commonage you can only 'beka'[13] somebody.

Under individual tenure there are far-reaching benefits, and bright prospects of unlimited and unrestricted progress agriculturally or otherwise. For instance, you can farm and develop your lands, as well as modernise your homestead, without any external interference and disturbances, such as being ordered to vacate the area because the chief does not like you, or your financial standpoint renders his powers ineffective over you.

Under commonage land cannot be granted as security if any financial aid is sought from either bank or society. Therefore, enterprise of any form is considerably hampered; and here it may be legitimate to point out that this form of land tenure has considerably crippled our Swazi colleagues in business.

The individual land owner, on the other hand, has unrestricted commercial progress and freedom in as far as security[14] is concerned.

Legal defence can be procured with ease under the single land tenure system because lawyers readily uphold immovable property as security, e.g. building or land; which is virtually a practical impossibility by law and tradition under commonage.

Traditionally, individual land ownership inevitably destroys and degenerates Swazi social life, and ultimately undermines and invalidates the honour, power, and significance of Royalty and chieftainship, with respect to Swazi rule.

Custom orders and commands that every Swazi subject will pay homage and respect to Royalty, by being called upon to render some service and perform duties of any form; for example, 'kumemeza'.[15]

Kumemeta, emahlahla, umhlanga, kuhlepula Incwala[16] are customs that not only require service by Swazi subjects as [a] whole; but also teach good morals and courtesy to Royalty—Swazi rule.

Further, one fears that land held under a system of individual tenure may end by being sold and owned by foreigners who will have no regard for Swazi tradition and custom, as evidenced by conditions found over Swaziland to-day, as a result of non-Swazi who have ownership of vast tracts of land. One also dreams that Swaziland will be Swaziland no more, but a mine of individual wealth and treasure.

---

[12] i.e. The traditional Swazi system.

[13] Kubeka, to put or place. When used in this sense it refers to the customary legal process whereby Bantu ownership in a piece of arable or building land is transferred to an individual as the representative of the group of which he is the recognized head, normally the polygynous or elementary family.

[14] i.e. security for a loan.

[15] Kumemeza is the Zulu or Zunda form of the Swazi term kumemeta, which is used to designate the official (traditionally 'shouted') summons to subjects to perform tribute labour.

[16] The last three refer to occasions when Swazi are expected to come to the National capitals to render homage and tribute to the Ngwenyama, the Paramount Chief.

Under such circumstances it is not surprising therefore that a rise of slavery and coming into being of politically independent landlords will inevitably shape out.

A dimming of all progress and civilization that has paced such gigantic strides within our boundaries can undoubtedly be the resultant booming phenomenon in our modern history in Swaziland.

Let alone the modern system of land settlement; it can be the only foundation on which the future of a happy, contented Swaziland can be built. Here chief and Royalty still retain their power over Swazi people; hence order and peace —the demands of modern civilization.

Another student, expressing himself at slightly greater length, makes many of the same points. He writes:

In my opinion, the main differences between a public and individual land tenure are to start with the advantages of individual land tenure.

1. *Advantages.* If the owner of the land wants to be come a progressive and conspicuous farmer, but he finds it impossible to furnish himself well with all the implements he needs, he can go to any man well equipped financially to make a petition for assistance. If the rich man agrees to help the land owner with the money he wants, a bond can be signed, so the land can in this case be used as security. If the landowner does not come to such rich men, he can go to any bank and do as above. The bank, of course, will as a matter of fact assist him, and it will obviously require of him an immovable property, such as [the] house or the very land.

2. Say the farmer has got all his requirements, he can now then put the whole land under good soil conservation measures; that is, protecting all eroded areas or parts in the land, divide the land into many required blocks, integrate arable with grazing lands. He can use the land economically, by ploughing any kind of cash crops, annuals, bi-annuals, or even peren[n]ials. He can procure pecunia from what is enclosed in the land.

He can enable himself to manage all the properties in his land. Commercially all that belongs to the land is his; not even his *lusendvo* [family], but his own; with it he can do what thing he wants to do, to get money. People kraaling in the land can be taxed unjustly or justly. Nobody else, not a single soul, can say a word concerning the land; except, of course, the prominent authorities such [as] *Hulumende*,[17] the only person or people [who] can interfere with him about his land or any property of his.

3. *The disadvantages of individual tenure in Swaziland.* Unless Swaziland was born white in colour good order of authorities would she maintain. It is our Swazi custom that we people born and bred in Swaziland, we must uplift her, by paying and rendering due respect to our authorities; people like the Government of Swaziland, The *Ngwenyama*,[18] chiefs, indunas and parents, including all old people.

We render to the chiefs our due respect by responding to chiefs' calls for *amahlahla esibaya*,[19] ploughing of the *indlunkulu*'s fields,[20] as well as harvesting.

---

[17] The Government.

[18] The Paramount Chief.

[19] One of the traditional tribute-labour gatherings.

[20] Fields of the 'great house', i.e. fields of the Nation or the chiefdom.

To the Ngwenyama we Swazi people pay due respects by leaving our kraals for years to go and *butheka*,[21] for nothing but honour. There is an annual *Incwala*[22] ceremony, which requires unmarried men and young boys to go and fetch the *usekwane* tree for the Ngwenyama. If the use of the tree is carefully examined, there is absolutely nothing; but we go there because of honourship, and perhaps the Lion[23] wants to see his people.

There is an *umhlanga*[24] dance [reed dance]. This is also held annually. It requires unmarried girls to go and cut the reeds. Examining its use, too, it has no other value besides honourship and respect to the Lion. After all, the Ngwenyama has many wives (*makosikati*) and princesses; they can easily do the job themselves, as would be the case if an individual person would be allowed to hold a piece of land for his own, not for the nation. We are told and educated formally that we must respect those people of nobility, medium, base and lastly ourselves. I would not like to be interfered with if I were to be allowed to hold my own land tenure. I would not respond to any call, any chief, *induna*,[25] and the Lion himself. I would not even like any white man to interfere with my grounds, as the case might be.

So I think individual land tenure would into many a man's mind plant too many undesirable seed[s] of self confidence and self relying.

There would, in fact, be no need of chiefs and *indunas*. There would perhaps be an Ngwenyama by name, but working for himself. Each and every owner of land would be the King, chief, induna of everything himself.

I personally would not allow or favour people having their own lands. I would have a fear that rate of death would rise rapidly; people would poison themselves on their own. This would happen in this way; envy would be one of the main factors, as well as poverty. We would very soon have a Swazi revolution as it happened in France, the French revolution. I personally enjoy and like the system practised in Swaziland; that is, one man must be in charge of a piece of land not for his own need, but for the benefit of the nation.

Each man given a piece of land to utilize, he must try his best to introduce into the authorities his ability of utilizing the land. Even when time for removal comes the authorities are going to make great meditations over the man with citrus, about 2–3 acres, planted next to his kraal, a very beautiful house, gorgeously furnished, and many valuable things next to his house. I am practically sure they cannot just simply remove him away; something of beneficial to him can be done, or [he] cannot be moved at all.

Even if the man is removed, it [is] quite good; for during the time when [he] was still young his education was that whatever thing he does, it [is] not his, but for the *usendo*,[26] and [the] Nation. So, if he has been improving the land given to him, he has been doing it for the nation.

I repeat, there is absolutely no need for individual land tenure in Swaziland,

---

[21] To go and join the regiments.

[22] See pp. 49–50 above.

[23] The Paramount Chief.

[24] See p. 50 above.

[25] A subordinate political official; a deputy of either the Paramount Chief or of a local chief.

[26] Normally written *lusendvo* in Swazi. The family group, or group of agnates who should be consulted in all matters which Swazi consider to be family business, as distinct from purely personal affairs.

not unless it was in Europe. If a man wants a security for something else, he must work hard to gain prosperity. At least build a nice looking house, fill it with gorgeous furniture, and make the security.

If our motto is to work for the nation, why then should we be worried about individual tenure? If some of our Swazi men have realized the value of money they should go to work for it under Europeans. I, as an individual, realize the value of cattle. My grandfather did work for money, but he died having not got enough to buy a bicycle. On the contrary, he had 250 head of cattle here in Swaziland. Apart from that, he had 24 wives, all *lotsholwa'*d.[27] So it stands to reason that there was no need for money by the family except himself alone.

Although in places the writers' meanings may be obscure, the general tenor of their arguments is clear enough. Both appreciate that there are certain advantages in a system of land tenure offering more individual security than the traditional Swazi system; both are most definitely opposed to any change of this traditional Swazi system in a direction of more individualized tenure.

In this they agree with the rest of the students. Out of a total of fourteen, twelve made clear statements expressing strong disapproval of any change to individual tenure, or any change at all in the traditional system. Many even expressed disapproval of Swazi being allowed to hold land on individual tenure outside the Swazi area. Of the two remaining, one contented himself with listing the advantages and disadvantages, as he saw them, of both systems; the impression is given that the weight of the evidence, as stated by this student, is strongly in favour of the traditional system. Finally, one expressed disapproval of any extension of individual tenure to areas where the traditional system operates, but suggested that individual holdings should be made available (presumably outside the Swazi Area) for those Swazi requiring them, 'provided he will use the land as a farmer properly'.

Thus, all the students appear to have been in favour of the traditional system. The majority appreciated that there were certain disadvantages in this system, and certain definite advantages in a system of individual tenure. However, they argued that the disastrous social consequences of any change would far outweigh any economic advantages which might result.

Some idea of the arguments advanced, and the contents of various answers, may be obtained from the table given below. A threefold breakdown into 'Disadvantages of the traditional system', 'Specific advantages of individual tenure', and 'Specific disadvantages of individual tenure' has

---

[27] i.e. for whom bridewealth cattle had been passed. At the present time this would involve, in a similar case, the man or his agnatic group producing at least 12 beasts for each marriage, making a total of 288 beasts for 24 wives. The bridewealth might be higher in cases where the women were of high rank.

been attempted. It will be appreciated that the first two virtually amount to different ways of stating the same thing. No attempt has been made to isolate a class of statements dealing with the 'Advantages of traditional tenure', since the students themselves mostly indicated these by implication when dealing with the disadvantages that they considered would be the result of the introduction of individual tenure.

In this table the figures in brackets after each item represent the number of students specifically making each particular point.

## A. Disadvantages of the Traditional System

1. Progressive farmers are unable to obtain loans on security of land or buildings (7).
2. The danger of eviction by the political authorities (6).
3. Good farming practices are hindered, and the cultivation of long-term crops is not encouraged (3).

Other disadvantages listed by individual students were the impracticability of improving one's standard of living by building better and more permanent housing; the danger of arousing the jealousy of one's political superiors if one's farming is too successful; no compensation is obtainable for improvements when one departs; no compensation is obtainable if a neighbour's stock damages one's standing crops. Only one student complained about the burden of tribute labour; 'the chief may send you very far and you get no provision, yet sometimes you were busy ploughing your land'.

It is worthy of note that three of the students listed no disadvantages in the traditional Swazi system of land tenure.

## B. Specific Advantages of Individual Tenure

1. Loans can be obtained on the security of land or building (11).
2. Security of tenure (7).
3. Good farming and conservation practices are possible, and also the cultivation of long-term crops (6).
4. One can fence, and thus obtain security from one's neighbour's stock (4).
5. The land can be sold or rented (3).
6. Holders of land on individual tenure have greater opportunities of economic advancement (3).

Other advantages listed were the possibility of raising one's standard of living by building better housing; the possibility of settling friends and relations on one's land; and the possibility of evicting people from one's land. It is not clear whether the last was listed as an advantage or as one of the deplorable results of this type of tenure.

## C. Specific Disadvantages of Individual Tenure

1. The danger of the emergence of a landless group and economic classes; some of the students speak in terms of 'slavery' (10).
2. The great national ceremonies[28] would come to an end (10).
3. The traditional Swazi political authorities, the Ngwenyama, and the local chiefs, would lose their power over the people (9).
4. People holding land on individual tenure would impound the animals of other Swazi which strayed on to their land (4).
5. 'Foreigners' (presumably Europeans) may buy up all the land, leaving the Swazi landless once again (3).
6. Owners of land held on individual tenure may be unable to pay back the loans that they have raised, and so lose their land (2).
7. Owners of land held on individual tenure may close paths which Swazi have been accustomed to use (1).

## The Implications of these Arguments

Owing to the relatively small number of individuals involved in this study, and the necessarily crude categories of thought that have had to be employed in the table, the numerical analysis can do no more than indicate the general trends of the opinions expressed. None the less, the nature of these trends does emerge reasonably clearly. While the students appreciated that an individualized system of land holding offered certain practical advantages not available under the traditional system now in operation, they were far more preoccupied, by and large, with the social dangers attendant upon any change in the latter, than with the obvious economic dangers of leaving things as they are.

From our point of view, therefore, the greatest interest would seem to lie in section C of the table, listing the disadvantages of individual tenure. These fall into three main classes, namely:

(a) The effects on the national and local political organization.
(b) The economic effects.
(c) The effects on good neighbourliness at the local level.

Points 2 and 3 (in section C) are definitely political effects; 1, 5, and 6 refer largely to economic effects; while 4 and 7 are primarily effects on the tradition of good neighbourliness in the rural community.

---

[28] See pp. 49–50 above.

It is the qualitative aspects of the arguments that are of greatest interest, and these can probably be analysed most conveniently in terms of these three major classes.

## Political Effects

The close connexion between certain Swazi national and local rituals and the traditional political organization has already been mentioned earlier in this paper.[29] The importance of a 'ceremonial charter' as a support for political authority is well attested in other African societies, and in the case of the Swazi themselves Kuper's detailed analysis has clearly demonstrated the political content of one of the ceremonies most frequently mentioned in these essays, the annual *Incwala*.[30]

The probability of these rituals coming to an end were land tenure to be individualized is mentioned specifically in ten out of the fourteen essays, and hinted at in one other. In many cases the threat to them is given pride of place over the threat to the traditional authority system, being mentioned first and dealt with at greater length; yet the link between the two was made quite clear. 'I have said that persons who have purchased their lands, they act like kings in their lands' runs one comment, 'therefore they cannot attend these national meetings or dances.' In the first text given above we have the remark that 'Individual land ownership inevitably destroys and degenerates Swazi social life and ultimately undermines and invalidates the honour, power, and significance of royalty and chieftainship,' this being followed almost immediately by the statement that certain named ceremonies and occasions of customary tribute labour 'are customs that not only require service by Swazi subjects as a whole, but also teach good morals and courtesy to royalty'.

In the second of our quoted texts there is a relatively sophisticated analysis of the function of certain national rituals, which the author concludes have 'no other value besides honour and respect to the Lion'. He continues to argue that this would cease 'if an individual person would be allowed to hold an individual piece of land for his own, not for the nation'.

The fear of banishment is sometimes specifically cited as a sanction enforcing obedience to political superiors, and the dictates of tribal custom. Thus, one has the comment, with reference to the *Incwala* and other customary gatherings, that 'everybody fears that he might be deprived of his land if he does not maintain [obey?] orders, whereas if one owns land nobody can be forced, thus the national power is lost'. In other cases the existence and operation of this sanction is implied by the argument that

---

[29] See pp. 49–50 above.

[30] Cf. Kuper, *An African Aristocracy*, pp. 197 ff.

the introduction of individualized tenure must inevitably result in a refusal to render these customary services or to attend these politically significant ceremonies.

There is the surprising remark in our second text that the writer would 'not respond to any call, any *induna,* and the Lion himself' if he had land on individual tenure. This reads oddly in the midst of an essay devoted largely to deploring the possibility of this type of behaviour by others; but it would also seem to suggest that the writer believes firmly that the existing system of social control is primarily dependent on sanctions operating through the present system of land holding and allocation of rights over land.

It is possibly significant that no mention was made of the possibility of other sanctions being introduced to maintain the overall authority pattern and existing system of social control; and this despite the fact that such sanctions already exist and operate. Thus, the present penalty for 'unreasonable failure' to attend the *Incwala,* or to respond to a national tribute-labour call, is a fine (a beast or an acceptable monetary equivalent), not automatic deprivation of land rights. Local chiefs also impose fines for failure to render customary services. This omission may have been due, in part, to the students' unfamiliarity with the operation of such alternative sanctions. It may also have been due to an appreciation of the lack of machinery available to the traditional political authorities for their effective enforcement. At the present time there is virtually no other way whereby the community, or its leaders, can enforce conformity to the communal will and rulings other than by withdrawing the advantages of community membership from the recalcitrant, and this in effect means banishment.

In general the authors of these essays seem to subscribe to the view, often advanced by anthropologists and others who have concerned themselves with non-Western land tenure, that control over land is very often the only real power left in the hands of traditional leaders of tribal groups that have been incorporated into larger states. That such a situation should exist among the Swazi of today is not unexpected; what is possibly of more moment is that this should have been appreciated, and so clearly formulated, by this particular group of young students.

## Economic Effects

It is clear from the essays that the economic implications of any change in the system of land tenure evoke a strong emotive reaction. Running through nearly all of them is the fear that a new landless class would be created, and that this would be accompanied by increasing differentiation between rich and poor.

Western technical and economic thinking about rural problems is usually based on the assumption that the endless subdivision of agricultural holdings to accommodate an increasing population is economic suicide; that the result could only be over-ploughing, over-grazing, increased erosion, and the holdings ultimately becoming too small to make any significant contribution to either national or personal incomes. This leads to the conclusion that, in the near future, there must come a division between a class of farmers, with holdings of a reasonable size and adequate security of tenure, and another comprising Swazi who will have to seek other means of livelihood.

Our group of students are obviously not willing to concede the inevitability of this process. They apparently consider that such a division could only arise as the result of a change to individualized tenure; and since they consider this differentiation to be deplorable, they resist anything which might (in their view) contribute towards it.

The emotional significance of this whole aspect of the problem is emphasized by the repeated references to 'slavery' in the essays. In one of those quoted above, there is the explicit statement, 'under such circumstances it is not surprising that a rise of slavery . . . will inevitably shape out'. In a similar vein one has the fear expressed that 'people who are [too] poor to buy lands or provide security for a loan can be the slaves of those with lands', and 'the unfortunate [landless] ones would become their [the landowners'] servants, working for the land which once belonged to everybody, and they that are workers will never recover; they could remain workers for life, as they are not paid. As a result, classification could take place'.

While ten of the students expressed fears that a landless class might come into being, only three specifically mentioned the danger of landed Swazi being bought out by 'foreigners'—a surprisingly small proportion in view of the constant complaints by the National authorities against the 1907 Partition. Possibly the last-mentioned body's preoccupation with this issue is not reflected in the thinking of the majority of the Swazi people. For our essayists, the spectre of any repetition of the concessions era was seemingly overshadowed by the horror engendered at the thought of landless Swazi, and by the possible rise of an economic class structure.

Traditionally, the Swazi are anything but an egalitarian community. Kuper's analysis has brought out the great importance of rank in Swazi life; and complex social, economic, and psychological issues are raised by the possible connexion between this emphasis on traditionally recognized rank and the objections expressed in the essays to any economic 'classification'.

No great psychological insight is needed, however, to see how these objections might well derive from an unexpressed, and largely unformulated, fear that any economic differentiation would inevitably cut across the existing rank divisions, and could ultimately make the latter almost meaningless.

When discussing the principles underlying the traditional system of tenure Swazi often advance the argument that arable lands should be allocated according to needs. Field studies suggest that this theory bears little relation to the reality, and when one turns from general principles to a discussion of particular instances Swazi informants almost invariably come back to the relative position of individuals in the traditional hierarchy of rank. So-and-so should have rights over a large arable area since his wife is the sister of the chief, or because his father was chief deputy to the previous chief; while the relatively small arable holding of another family is easily explained in terms of their being new arrivals in the area, with no close connexions with any of the mighty.

There is also considerable variation in the sizes of cattle holdings (which nowadays can provide both prestige and income), and in cash earnings from other sources. These differences exist, and are an accepted part of the present Swazi way of life; which might suggest that there is little point in the students' arguments that they would only arise if tenure were individualized. However, one can only presume that underlying these arguments there is not so much a lack of appreciation of present economic differentiation, but rather the fear that individual tenure would entrench the economic criteria of status at the expense of all the other criteria at present recognized in Swazi society.

Thus, while a Western agricultural economist might regard the individualization of tenure as a means of creating a prosperous land-owning peasantry, the students appear to see the economic implications primarily as a threat to existing Swazi values, and as an open invitation for the creation of an elite of parvenus.

The loss of economic security for the financially unfortunate was another aspect of the matter which received considerable attention in the essays. This fear is easy enough to understand, and the problem is certainly not confined to Africa. European history can supply many instances of the painful transition from a system where the cultivators had a considerable measure of economic security as members of a peasant community to other, more 'rational', systems of agriculture.

Excessive agrarian indebtedness is a lamentably widespread phenomenon in societies where individual tenure is the accepted norm. The breaking up of various forms of latifundia has characterized land-reform movements in all ages; as has their reappearance whenever periods of financial strain encourage small proprietors to raise too large loans on the security of their land.

For Swazi, most of whom still find the deeper implications of our money economy most confusing, and who have had little opportunity to study the workings of any comprehensive social security scheme, the prospect must seem very alarming indeed. 'Let us think of the poor widow', we are admonished in one of the essays. 'Will our coming sons and daughters find any farms left for them?' asks another. A third, listing the advantages of the traditional system, points out that 'the owner of the kraal[31] may have many lands to lend to the widows, to [the] family who have no father, and to mothers'.

Several essays specifically mention the landlessness that may befall those who fail to pay back loans raised on the security of land. One sums the position up thus: 'The advantages of the Swazi system [are] that the land is not sold to you, so even if you are careless, or you have no idea of farming, you do not trouble yourself so much'; whereas, on bought land, 'you are forced to improve the land to bring back the money. If you have borrowed money and do not bring it back at a fixed time, the land may be taken from you and given to somebody who will improve the land.' Shocking as this way of putting things might seem to an agronomist anxious to improve productivity, it does suggest that for the author of this statement the role of land as a provider of security (in the sense of security for the individual and his family, rather than for the bank manager) far outweighs its importance as a productive asset. Arguments in favour of radical changes in the traditional systems of land tenure in Bantu societies are normally based on the economic assumption that only by such changes can the cultivators be given the incentive to undertake permanent improvements and long-term planning, and thus raise their own standards of living. It is interesting to see, therefore, that in these essays economic arguments are used to support the opposing point of view—that the traditional system of tenure should not be changed for fear of the economic results of such a change.

One thing which does emerge in this connexion, however, is the general lack of appreciation by the students of the simple economic arithmetic underlying the whole issue. There is the frequently recurring assumption, only to be expected in modern Africa, that all economic problems would be solved if only more land were available for occupation on traditional tenure. While there is some force in this contention (since the main economic problem of today is the Malthusian one of increasing human and stock populations pressing ever harder on a fixed supply of land) there is little evidence of any realization of exactly how much new land would be needed, or how temporary such a solution would be. Nor does there appear to be any real knowledge of the amount of land already available for settlement in the Swazi Area. One student firmly states that it is less than a quarter of Swaziland, others imply that it is only a small proportion of the whole country; in fact, it is over half the country.

---

[31] i.e. the head of a homestead group.

Of greater interest is the argument advanced by several of them that an increasing population could be satisfactorily settled even on the present land available if traditional tenure were retained, but that this would be impossible if tenure were individualized. 'If Swaziland had been big enough to satisfy everybody who could afford to buy his own land the European system would be preferable', as one essay puts it. Another poses the following question, with regard to individual tenure farms: 'Say this Swazi farmer gets thirty sons and daughters, and these get their sons and daughters, how on earth are they going to fit themselves there once the farmer father dies?' The contention here, also found in other essays, is apparently that while under individual tenure land would tend to be locked up, as it were, in the hands of a specific number of owners, under the traditional system a man can always find a place to live and plough somewhere. The students undoubtedly knew of the situation in Basutoland and elsewhere, where, even though the traditional system still operates, the proportion of completely landless individuals is high; but they seem to think that the present situation could persist indefinitely in Swaziland.

If one takes the short-term view this argument is not completely unjustified. It takes account both of the flexibility of the traditional system, and of the fact that an appreciable proportion of the real income of many Swazi homesteads now comes from sources other than agriculture; from wage labour elsewhere. This flexibility allows for a redistribution of holdings to fit the situation of the moment. The lands of migrant labourers need not lie idle. The grazing area provides a convenient pool from which more arable land can be drawn when required, and the dangers of overgrazing are not so widely appreciated by Swazi for this last process to worry them as much as it does the Administration's conservation and veterinary officers.

Not all the comments were purely destructive criticism of the alleged advantages of individualized tenure. Attempts were made to suggest alternative ways of overcoming the disadvantages of the present system; rather more so than in the case of the comments dealing with the political effects of any change. As far as the productivity of the land was concerned, the general feeling expressed in most of the essays was that this could be increased to a satisfactory level simply by example and encouragement, both to be provided by the Administration. There seemed to be little appreciation of how very low Swazi agricultural productivity is by world standards, of the relative lack of success of the very strenuous efforts made by the Government during the past two decades to improve it, nor of the seriousness of the soil-erosion menace.

Most of our subjects seemed to realize the need for capital by the cultivators wishing to adopt improved techniques, and the virtual impossibility of raising this on loan under present conditions. Suggestions were made that a Swazi National Bank should be established for this purpose; that loans could be made on security of cattle, or to the farmers' associations that have grown up throughout the country. The latter would accept collective responsibility for repayment and re-lend the money to their members.

Although there are technical difficulties in all these suggestions, none is completely impracticable.

One suggestion, not mentioned in any essay, but made during a discussion after a lecture given to this same group of students earlier, was that loans should be made on the security of daughters. Strange as this might sound to Western ears, it was made in all seriousness, and is quite in accordance with Swazi conceptual thinking. A debt (*umbhalo*) may arise from bridewealth arrangements as well as from other transactions, 'and a debt never dies', as the Swazi proverb runs. If not settled in this generation, it can be settled in the next. The advocates of this solution argued, rightly, that Swazi were not traditionally accustomed to reckoning their wealth in terms of money, but rather in terms of cattle and dependents. 'A man's wealth was in his family and his daughters', as one of them put it.

Accepting this, and also that unpaid bridewealth was 'secured', as it were, by the right of the wife's agnates to claim the bridewealth of her female children, it seemed a logical extension of the idea to use daughters as security for agricultural loans.

In West Africa the 'pawning' of individuals was formerly developed into a workable and locally acceptable system, so the plan was not completely original. However, the general feeling of the meeting was that this particular scheme, sound as it seemed in terms of Swazi customary law, was unlikely to find favour in the eyes of orthodox financiers in Southern Africa. In this they were, unfortunately, probably right. Tragic as heavily encumbered farms might seem to an agricultural economist, the vision of a land bank heavily encumbered with the daughters of insolvent farmers would probably appear infinitely worse.

### Effects on Good Neighbourliness

Apart from the economic and political changes envisaged by the students as a result of any change in the system of land tenure, they also mention certain probable developments in the field of personal relations, and appear to regard these last as being of as great importance as the other effects, if not greater. Thus, the impounding of straying cattle by private landowners is listed as one of the disadvantages of individual tenure. This and the closing of footpaths crossing farms are points which Swazi very frequently bring up in any conversations dealing with land-holding. 'He may treat people going . . . through his farm cruelly', runs a statement from one of our sources; 'or sometimes close their shorter ways of travelling. . . . Fourthly, he troubles his neighbours by [im]pounding their cattle or stock when they happen to come into his land. . . . People round him are never happy with their stay because he may act so cruelly to them and their stock.' Some of the examples given are obviously based on the stereotype of behaviour expected from European landholders. These do tend to claim damages for crops damaged by straying Swazi cattle, and to impound the beasts in question to ensure payment; they also fence farms and so cut off recognized footpaths. On the Swazi area an individual will seldom claim damages for crops damaged by someone else's cattle; the accepted thing is for the injured party to beat the erring herd-boy. Informants have argued that, although nowadays compensation could be claimed in the Swazi National Courts if the damage caused were severe, few would be willing to go to these lengths, since their own cattle could easily be involved in a similar incident at some future date.

An even more calamitous state of affairs is anticipated in the second text, quoted above, where the author fears that people would 'poison themselves' and that 'the rate of death would rise rapidly', all this resulting from 'envy'.

While non-Swazi familiar with the working of individualized tenure elsewhere might consider it unlikely that things would ever come to such a pass, we cannot dismiss as completely unjustified the fear expressed by so many of the students that inter-personal relationships would deteriorate catastrophically if the traditional sanctions at present operating in the local rural group were removed. Great emphasis is laid by the Swazi on the vital importance of good neighbourliness, as is the case in most other Bantu communities. Wilson has made a penetrating analysis of this aspect of the social organization of another Bantu people, the Nyakyusa of Tanganyika.[32] Among them it appears that good neighbourliness is conceptually closely linked with witchcraft beliefs, and it is possible that similar linkages could be traced among the Nguni-speaking peoples, including the Swazi. One might, possibly, go so far as to argue that witchcraft beliefs are, in a sense, essential for the cohesion, internal peace, and survival of the rural African community. The fear of being accused of 'hatred' (*kutonsa*), which is virtually synonymous with a wish to bewitch, is ever present. The use of the term 'to smell one another out as witches' (*kunukana*) to describe a situation where mutual recriminations and accusations (of witchcraft) are flying between persons or groups would appear to provide further linguistic support for this view, as does the linkage frequently made by informants between the presence of 'people who hate' (*abantfu abatondzako*) in a particular place and the fear of being bewitched if one goes there. Since it is essential not to be thought a witch, it follows that one should make earnest efforts to avoid any suspicion that one is showing signs of 'hatred'; and the result of these efforts is usually to lessen tensions that a more

---

[32] Monica Wilson, *Good Company*, O.U.P., London, 1951.

stiff-necked insistence on one's rights might only serve to increase. In Swaziland witchcraft accusations are usually a prelude to banishment, with the consequent loss of all rights, including those over specific parcels of land derived from being accepted as a member of this particular community. What our students seem to fear is that were this obvious material sanction to be removed, it would also decrease the incentive for individuals to strive to reduce tensions at all costs, even if this involves personal sacrifice. Whether or not any of these students actually believe in witchcraft is immaterial. That many Swazi do so is a fact, as is the existence of interpersonal and inter-group tensions, and the material incentive offered by the present system of land tenure for everyone involved to try and reduce these as much as possible. If this incentive were removed, and nothing else put in its place, it is only logical to suppose that these tensions might become greater and more obvious.[33]

The loss of economic security if the tenure system were changed has been discussed above. The authors of the essays were, apparently, also worried about the more intangible, but none the less real, danger of losing the security of 'good neighbourliness', a loss which could have just as disruptive effects on the social order as any more direct threat to the material well-being of individuals.

## General Considerations

'In the extensive colonial areas in which the system of land-holding is based on the conception of a collective right in the land,' runs a comment of Lord Hailey, 'the most conspicuous effect of economic development will . . . appear in the progressive individualization of holdings. That process will have the economic advantage of giving to the holders a greater sense of security and a greater incentive to a more intensive type of cultivation; on the other hand, its undue acceleration may hasten the disintegration of the present social structure, and thus weaken the basis on which the institutions of local self-government are now being built up.'[34] Elsewhere, this same authority has shown a full awareness of the last-mentioned dangers, and of the different connotations that the concept of 'security' may have in different contexts. Speaking of the 'fundamental difference in the conception of the place of land in the life of the community', in African and Western thought, he points out that while the case for individualization of tenure is based largely on the premise that it will offer greater security

---

[33] Cf. L. P. Mair, 'The Contribution of Social Anthropology to the Study of Changes in African Land Rights', in *Applied Anthropology*, Athlone Press, London, 1957, p. 55.

[34] Lord Hailey—Introduction to C. K. Meek, *Land Law and Custom in the Colonies*, London, 1956, p. xix.

to the cultivator, 'African customary procedure already secures to him a right of occupation in which he is protected not merely by the custom of the tribe or group, but by the action of the Native Courts.' If, the argument continues, 'there is any feeling of insecurity in his right of occupation it arises not so much in fear of interference by members of his own community, but from the apprehension that the Government may, for its own purposes (such as the needs of land for public use or for alienation to colonists), disturb him in the possession of his holding'.[35]

The first of these quotations sums up succinctly the conclusion of much administrative and technical thinking about this issue. The second touches on one of the main fears expressed by the authors of these essays; that increased security of tenure for some by the granting of individual titles to land could only be obtained at the cost of very greatly increased economic and social insecurity for everyone else. The students clearly do not accept the inevitability of 'progressive individualization of tenure', nor that this would provide greater incentives for improved farming, or 'a greater sense of security for the holders'. They do not, admittedly, seem to have been unduly concerned about the possible alienation of land for use by non-Swazi. This was mentioned but not stressed. More fear seemed to be felt that legislative action designed to help Swazi economically might actually take away more than it offered.

Not only do the students disagree with some of the conclusions in the first quotation above and lend modified support to those of the second; they also say specifically why they disagree, and indicate what they consider security. In this lies the main value of their statements, offering as they do both the point of view of members of a society directly faced with this problem, and also something more tangible than the vague concept of 'African conservatism' so often invoked to explain any resistance to change.

It is now reasonably widely appreciated that the simple dichotomy between 'communal' and 'individualized' tenure leaves the greater part of the story untold; that even in the most economically individualized societies the rights of landowners are subject to limitations, while in the so-called 'communal' system these rights are still, in the last resort, actually exercised by individuals. 'There is a common saying', states Meek, 'that property is a bundle of rights, and to no form of property is this more applicable than to land.'[36] If we analyse the present situation in Swaziland in terms of rights held over land under different systems of tenure, rather than in terms of opposed systems as wholes, it is easier to understand how our Swazi students could argue that a man has greater security under the traditional system than under the Western system, despite the fact that they admitted there was also some lack of security inherent in the former.

---

[35] Hailey, *An African Survey* (1957 edition), London, pp. 685, 807.
[36] Meek, op. cit., p. 1.

Here again they have indicated what they consider to be the most important of these rights, and which of these they feel would be threatened, or bound to disappear, under a system of individualized tenure.

Even if we reject the contention that there is no real need for any alteration in the present system of traditional tenure (which we well might, in view of the known economic results of that system), there still remains the question of how likely any specific changes are to produce the results desired. The latter might be summed up as a greater return from the same amount of land, a greater investment of both capital and energy by the cultivator to produce this return, and a radical change in agricultural techniques to halt the present process of rapidly falling soil fertility and increasing erosion. We should examine the arguments in the essays to the effect that individualized tenure, and the 'magic of property' presumed to result, would not automatically provide sufficiently strong incentives for the landholders to strive for these goals.

The essays themselves give little indication as to why their authors think these incentives would be lacking, and mostly contain little more than simple assertions that this would be the case. However, they cannot be considered completely in isolation, and in this connexion some of the evidence from other parts of sub-Saharan Africa where experiments in individualizing African tenure have been tried is revealing.

Thus, in Buganda, the chaos which followed Sir Harry Johnston's introduction of freehold tenure on the English pattern has long served as a warning to those inclined to rush into such changes before acquiring an adequate knowledge of the full social role of land in the society it is wished to 'reform'. Many decades earlier, individual tenure had been introduced in the Ciskei (in the Cape Province of South Africa) and evidence can also be produced from Swaziland itself, where an appreciable number of Swazi have acquired freehold land outside the Swazi area by various means.[37] In Buganda, it is true, increased agricultural prosperity followed ultimately, but it is still an open question whether this was due to Johnston's changes or despite them. An equally important factor may have been the increased world demand for a single crop, for the cultivation of which Buganda's soil and climate were particularly well suited. In any case, the recurrent riots and agitations following this settlement have demonstrated in no uncertain fashion that these changes in land tenure did have a disruptive effect on the traditional system of social and political organization, and that these results were felt and resented by an appreciable proportion of the Ganda people.[38]

In the Ciskei some Africans have held land on individual tenure for over

---

[37] For a fuller analysis of the Buganda and Ciskei situations see Mair, op. cit., pp. 56 ff.

[38] Hailey, op. cit., p. 811; A. B. Mukwaya, *Land Tenure in Buganda*, Nairobi, 1953.

a century. Mills and Wilson make the point in their Keiskammahoek study that this individually held land is no better or more intensively farmed than that held on 'communal' tenure near by. Many of the freeholdings are now held in undivided shares by a large number of individuals, thus reproducing something very like the traditional pattern within the boundaries of each farm. Here it appears that in many instances the security offered by individual tenure actually militates against intensive and sustained cultivation. The freeholders, with nothing to fear from community pressure if they leave their land lying idle, are more prone to long-term migration away from the rural area than men living where tenure is 'communal', and where the effective and continued use of arable land is essential if one wishes to ensure the continued right to use it.

The authors of this study give some clues as to how this situation has arisen. Writing on inheritance, they point out that 'it is felt that to "eat the inheritance alone" is not just, no matter what the circumstances, and anyone who insists on his rights is scorned by members of the village. . . . Thus, though the right of disposal of land by will, and the right of primogeniture, are established by law, they are limited by public opinion.'[39] As a result, farms that were individually owned in one generation become group-owned in the next, and the joint property of a yet wider group in the third. Instead of being farmed as single, integrated wholes, they have become split up into a number of separate arable holdings, each managed according to the wishes of the particular holder, while grazing is shared as in the traditional system.

Elsewhere Mills and Wilson show how the distribution of land within these theoretically individualized holdings follows the traditional pattern; how people are 'placed' on the holdings by the head of the owning lineage exactly as they would be by a chief in the traditional area. Witnesses are summoned and food is provided 'both to attract the people to witness the subdivision and to impress the occasion on their memories'.[40] Thus, despite the title-deeds, it appears that everything is done to ensure that the person 'placed' and the head of the farm-owning lineage have rights similar to those of subject and chief respectively in the 'communal' areas.

In Swaziland, the latest information available is that there are 67 Swazi-owned freeholdings, totalling 8160 morgen.[41] Slightly over half of these are of less than 20 morgen each, and in many cases they are used primarily as residential plots, the owners holding arable lands on traditional tenure in the Swazi Area, where they also graze their cattle. The remainder are

---

[39] M. E. Elton Mills and M. Wilson, *Land Tenure*, Keiskammahoek Rural Survey, vol. iv, 1952, p. 57.

[40] Ibid., p. 51.

[41] One morgen is approximately 2⅑ acres. The figures given here refer to the situation in 1960.

larger, with the largest of all covering 1,926 morgen. The owner of this last-mentioned farm is at present striving for government recognition as a chief. Though he has not yet succeeded in gaining this, he 'places' people on his land exactly as a chief would in his own area, and is recognized by the neighbouring chiefs as the leader of the community residing on his farm. On another Swazi-owned freehold farm of 647 morgen, which I investigated, there were, in 1959, a total of 143 inhabitants distributed among 16 separate homesteads. The majority of these homestead heads belong to the agnatic group owning the farm,[42] and of the remainder all but one are closely related, either cognatically or affinally, to this group. They are all regarded for most purposes as subjects of the chief of the chiefdom in the Swazi Area adjoining the farm. They are registered under him for tax purposes; take their cases to his court, and provide tribute labour when called upon to do so by him. They do not, it seems, officially attend the *Incwala* or other National ceremonies, or National tribute-labour gatherings,[43] and do not appear to be fined for staying away; a significant fact in view of our students' expressed fears on this score.

Members of the farm-owning group are insistent that their land does not form part of the neighbouring chiefdom, though they themselves do. This attitude is apparently not of recent origin, since the grandfather of the present chief was evicted by them from land he was ploughing on the farm after a quarrel, although those who evicted him seem to have continued to regard him as their political superior in all other matters. Both this farm and the larger one mentioned earlier are agriculturally indistinguishable from Swazi Area. Each homestead has its own lands, cultivated independently by each holder, and the grazing is used indiscriminately by cattle coming both from homesteads on the farms and from outside.

These few instances, selected as they are, cannot be held to 'prove' (in any sense of that term) that individualized tenure can never be an economic success in an African community. Evidence suggesting the contrary could be adduced from areas such as the West African coast, where individualized tenure appears to have become widely accepted without much specific encouragement by the State, or from Kenya, where African demands for freehold tenure became a major political issue. Government inspired schemes in Tanganyika, the former Belgian Congo, Southern Rhodesia, Mozambique, and, more recently, in Kenya have all been reported as showing varying degrees of success. However, it is most certainly not my aim here to attempt to reach any conclusions about the value of individual tenure as such; nor would it be possible to examine all the

---

[42] I was unable to discover the exact position regarding ownership of this farm in terms of Western law. It is recorded in official records as belonging to 'the so-and-so family'.

[43] See pp. 49–50 and 57 above.

relevant evidence, and all the arguments for and against it, within the limits of this paper. My purpose in citing these examples was far more modest. It was merely to put the Swaziland situation, and the points made in the essays, into some sort of perspective by considering some instances of what had actually happened when individual tenure had been introduced to Bantu-speaking groups where it was previously unknown. One fact which does emerge, particularly from the Keiskammahoek and Swaziland evidence, is that the simple legislative recognition of individual tenure does not by itself *automatically* ensure the agricultural 'great leap forward' that agrarian reformers in Bantu Africa so earnestly desire. As Mair sums up her own excellent analysis, 'These facts abundantly demonstrate that proprietary rights in themselves have but little magical effect.'[44]

Great stress was laid in the essays on the dangers to the existing traditional social system if land-holding were to be effectively individualized, and the land itself thus commercialized. The operative word here is surely 'effectively'. What none of the students envisaged was the possibility that the inertia of traditional patterns of organization might prove too strong; that the close interrelationships between land-holding and other aspects of the social organization might, as at Keiskammahoek, result in a survival of the general traditional pattern of land holding and land utilization, regardless of any legislative changes.

One of the advantages that individual tenure is held to have is that it provides 'a greater incentive to a more intensive type of cultivation', to borrow Hailey's phrase. The assumption is that this incentive stems from the cultivator's desire to reap a richer financial reward from his holding and the labour he puts into it, and that more intensive cultivation will be achieved once one adds to this desire a greater certainty that he will actually obtain this reward. Yet the results of this incentive are certainly not very obvious on the African-held freehold farms of the Ciskei or Swaziland, and we should examine the implicit assumption of our students that it would also be negligible in any other schemes based on individualized tenure that might be introduced here.

Some support for their point of view is given by data gathered in the 1960 sample survey of Swaziland.[45] This suggests that the possibility of greater rewards from agriculture may not, in fact, provide as great an incentive as one might think for an individual to change his agricultural techniques, and possibly his whole way of life, and devote his entire time to farming; for the simple reason that equal or greater financial rewards may be obtained, more surely, and perhaps more easily, from other sources, such as migrant labour. For instance, it has been estimated that an 'enter-

---

[44] L. P. Mair, op. cit., pp. 60–61.

[45] Conducted by the Institute for Social Research of the University of Natal, for the Swaziland Government.

prising peasant farmer', cultivating a developed holding (individually held), using the best techniques[46] and with assured markets, could reasonably expect an annual cash income of the order of R180 a year for himself and his family. This, needless to say, is far in excess of the cash income obtained *from agriculture* by more than a minute proportion of Swazi homesteads at present. However, if one takes cash income *from all sources*, the picture is very different. In a selected sample of forty-five homesteads (selected on the basis of their having poor agricultural records during the previous year), nearly a quarter had cash incomes of R480 a year, or more, while the median figure for this group was R122. In a random sample of homesteads from the best agricultural region in the territory the median was R54 and the upper quartile fell at R134. The bulk of these cash incomes was derived from wage labour, only a very small proportion coming from sales of agricultural produce or other rural sources. Apart from suggesting that the economic incentive would have to be considerably greater to provide any real drive for radical changes in agricultural practices, these figures also suggest what may be a very significant difference in the approach of the Western agronomist and the rural Swazi to this issue; a difference that may result from totally different conceptions of the economic role that land *should* fill.

Throughout the essays great emphasis was laid on the function of land as a provider of security for the individual. This concept of land as a provider of security is fundamentally different from that of security of tenure *of* land. The agriculturalist tends to regard land primarily as an economic asset, the more successful exploitation of which could be encouraged, once it could be demonstrated how this could be achieved. Our students mostly ignore this function of land, and tend to stress its role as a resource of which every member of the community is entitled, simply by virtue of his or her membership of that community, to make reasonable use. This point of view becomes more intelligible if one also accepts the decreasing importance of land as an income provider suggested by the figures given above.

This is only one aspect of the 'fundamental difference in conception' of the role of land that Hailey mentions, but it is obviously one that would-be agrarian reformers must bear in mind. So much stress has been laid on the non-economic functions of land in traditional African societies that one may tend to overlook the possibility that, even where its economic importance is recognized, ideas may differ considerably as to what its 'obvious' economic function is.

That these comments were made at all in this context, in answer to an examination question, is also remarkable. One would have assumed that

---

[46] i.e. the best agricultural techniques one could reasonably assume the majority could employ with their limited means, and with the possibility of raising a small amount of capital on the security of the holding itself.

here the main aim of the examinees would have been to please their examiners by demonstrating how well they had absorbed all that they had been taught. Lectures had been given about land tenure, and the need for 'reform', and the students were well aware that their instructors regarded the traditional system as one of the main obstacles in the way of improving agricultural techniques. The whole purpose of the course was to train the students to encourage wholesale changes in these techniques. Yet, in answering this particular question, they expressed views that disagreed fundamentally with those their instructors had advanced.

Discussions among the students must have followed the lectures on land tenure, and the possibility that the similarity of the views advanced by them all is largely the reflection of a predetermined 'party line' cannot be overlooked. At all levels of organization the Swazi lay great emphasis on the importance of reaching unanimous decisions before any action is taken or statement of principle made.[47] The land-tenure issue has been a subject of discussion between Swazi for many decades, owing to the concessions. Coming from this cultural background it would have been perfectly natural for our students to have consulted together and arrived at a 'proper position' for themselves, as Swazi.

Thus, while the uniformities listed in sections A and B of the numerical analysis might be an indication of how well they had learned the lessons forming part of their formal course of training, those in section C could equally be an index of how well they had learned other lessons; the teachers in the last case being their elders and the Swazi National authorities. Nevertheless, regardless of how they had reached their conclusions, the students obviously felt strongly enough about this matter to advance these views in an examination answer, in spite of the certainty that they differed from those of their instructors. It also seems very probable that they are not alone among their compatriots in having these feelings about this particular issue.

## Conclusion

In the essays we can discern a clear conflict between two loyalties. On the one hand there is loyalty to the traditional Swazi system of land tenure, standing as a symbol of Swazi culture and national unity, with all the

---

[47] Thus the Ngwenyama stated publicly, in connexion with the proposed formation of a new political party in Swaziland, that 'the Swazi custom was for all matters to be brought to the Libandla (Council) for discussion, and for the proper position to be arrived at by all men putting their heads together. . . . If they [the organizers of the new party] had something good in their organization they should have brought it to the Council and discussed it with the other men, and perhaps convinced them of its benefits, when all could have gone forward together as Socialists.' *Times of Swaziland*, 16 May 1959.

emotional overtones that such an identification involves. On the other hand, there is the loyalty to the progressive urge of this generation; the acceptance of the social desirability of accumulating a wide range of material possessions as a sign of success, the duty to show one's adherence to this modern school of thought by 'acquiring a beautiful house and filling it with gorgeous furniture', as it is put in one of our sources.

Most of the students solve the conflict between these two loyalties simply by ignoring it; by arguing that acceptance of individual tenure can only lead to universal poverty, while retention of the old ways will enable every Swazi to attain the goals of Western-style success. The use of the term *modern* Swazi system of land settlement' to describe the traditional system (in the first of the essays quoted earlier) exemplifies to some extent this urge to combine these two sets of aims. As I pointed out, none of the students seems to have appreciated the simple arithmetic of the economic and agricultural problem. Nor have any of them suggested why, if the economic potential of the traditional system is what they claim it to be, greater improvements in techniques and productivity have not resulted from the Administration's very considerable educative efforts during the last decade or so. What one has in most of the essays is not so much a series of sober, detailed assessments of the economic situation as it is, but rather a number of inevitably emotionally charged comparisons of features identified with the Swazi and Western ways of life, respectively. Never-. theless, the fears expressed about the probable course of events, were tenure to be individualized, cannot be ignored, and these seem to be based on a real appreciation of what the essential elements in the present Swazi social system are.

At the beginning of this paper I mentioned the general acceptance of the fact that most of Bantu Africa is in the throes of rapid social and economic change. Coupled with the acceptance of this is the widespread belief that 'progress' and 'traditionalism' must always be opposed to one another. The popularly accepted picture is only too often one of the traditionalists making a last-ditch stand, more successfully in some areas than in others, against the inevitable onward march of progress towards a society based almost entirely on the Western pattern. Anthropologists who have worked in rural African communities are often loath to accept this simple bipolar model. They have lived with Bantu tradition, and experienced its vitality at first hand. They have known and talked with members of these communities who show all the outward signs of being 'progressives', but who often prove to be the staunchest and most deliberate supporters of certain aspects of traditionalism. We appear to have such a group in the writers of these essays. They are of the generation and educational standard that is usually associated with the rejection of all that is traditional, of the authority of all traditional leaders, and with advocating wholesale adoption of Western patterns of life by the African. Yet, faced with this particular question, they have shown a most determined opposition to any change in the traditional ways. They have stated clearly why they consider that such a change is unnecessary, and would do harm. Above all, they have brought out the differences between their views and those of the agronomists regarding what is the most important 'security' for the modern African cultivator. 'In African customary law', states a recent report dealing with the situation in Southern Rhodesia, 'the permanence and inviolability of the land rights of individuals are not conceived (as is ownership in our law) as a relationship to a specific holding in perpetuity, but as a perpetual relationship with any such unencumbered portion of the land of the community as may be available for individualized occupation, whenever required as such, from time to time. Herein lies the individual's security, that is, in his vested right to claim a share.[48] This, as I point out above, is a theme running through all these essays, phrased in other words, perhaps, but all making essentially the same point.

The problem is now thrown back to the administrator and the research worker. For the former it is primarily a question of communication; of how those most closely concerned can be shown why certain changes are necessary, and what the realities of the overall economic situation are. Where fears have been expressed that changes, which the policy-makers consider essential, would bring social chaos in their wake, more thought is obviously needed to decide if such chaos is inevitable, or whether (which is more probable) it could be avoided, if only it is anticipated and some deliberate adjustments made, when any particular aspect of the existing social order is threatened.

For the research worker the problem is, mainly, one of more detailed research; of a deliberate and directed investigation of the extent to which the interrelations between various aspects of the Swazi social organization, suggested by these students, do correspond to the modern reality; of adjustments that have been made in the past to meet changed economic and social conditions; and of the changes that are occurring now. The most that research as such can offer, however, is a clarification of the issue—a clearer picture of the social mechanisms involved, and of what is at stake. My aim in this paper is certainly not that of making any specific recommendations. Policy will be decided in any case, and based on such evidence as is available to the policy-makers at that time. My purpose here has been simply to offer further relevant evidence, collected, in this case, from representatives of the Swazi people, whose co-operation and trust in the aims of any particular policy are essential, if this policy is to have any hope of success.

---

[48] *Report of the Commission of Enquiry into Discontent in the Mangwende Reserve*, Southern Rhodesia Government, Salisbury, 1961, p. 35.

# The Social Organization of Credit in a West African Cattle Market[1]

## Abner Cohen

Credit is a vital economic institution without which trade becomes very limited. In the industrial Western societies, where it is highly developed, it operates through formal, standardized arrangements and procedures by which the solvency of the debtor is closely assessed, securities against possible default are provided, and the conditions of the agreement are documented and endorsed by the parties concerned. Ultimately, these arrangements and procedures are upheld by legislated rules and sanctions administered by central, bureaucratized, fairly impartial, efficient, and effective courts and police. In West Africa, on the other hand, where long-distance trade has been fostered by varying ecological circumstances, such organization has not yet evolved, particularly for long-distance trade. Nevertheless extensive systems of credit have been developed.

I discuss in this paper the organization and operation of credit in one Nigerian market which I studied intensively. After a preliminary description of the formal organization of the market and of the credit by which it functions, I discuss some non-economic social relations which, while formally exterior to the market situation, are in practice built into the structure of the credit system in such a way that they make its functioning as a going concern possible.

Nearly 75,000[2] head of cattle are sold every year in the cattle market of Ibadan, capital of the Western Region of the Federation of Nigeria. The forest belt of West Africa, of which Ibadan is part, is infested with the

[1] The material on which this paper is based was collected in the course of field study among Hausa migrants in the Western Region of Nigeria between September 1962 and November 1963. I am grateful to the School of Oriental and African Studies, University of London, for financing the project and to the Nigerian Institute of Social and Economic Research and the University of Ibadan for their invaluable help in carrying it out.

[2] This is an approximate figure which is higher by about 12 per cent. than that obtained from the records of the veterinary service offices.

disease-carrying tse-tse fly which is fatal to cattle. The inhabitants depend for their beef supplies on herds of cattle brought from the savannah country, hundreds of miles to the north. These herds are collected mainly from the semi-nomadic Fulani by Hausa dealers from Northern Nigeria and are then brought south to be sold with the help of local Hausa middlemen. In the Ibadan market, which is locally known as 'Zango',[3] the buyers are Yoruba butchers and are total strangers to the Hausa dealers. Nevertheless, all sales are on credit and there is always an outstanding total amount of about a hundred thousand pounds current debt.[4] No documents are signed and no resort is made to the services of banks or to the official civil courts, and the whole organization, which has developed over the past sixty years, is entirely indigenous.

The cattle are brought to Ibadan either on foot or by train. In the market there is a sharp distinction between the two categories of cattle, not only in price but also in the organization and the scale of the business. After about five weeks of continuous travel, the foot cattle[5] arrive at the market thin, weak, and already having been exposed, for many days, to the disease[6] as they penetrated the forest area. The manoeuvrability in selling them is therefore limited in both time and place and dealers are always eager to sell. This eagerness is further enhanced by the need of the dealers to release, as soon as possible, the capital invested in the herd in order to have a quicker business turn-over. In recent years, cattle have increasingly been brought south by train, but between 30 and 40 per cent. still come on foot, either because they are brought from districts which are remote from a railway line, or because no train wagons happen to be available at the time. The principal advantage of bringing cattle on foot is that part of the herd can be sold on the way to small towns and villages which are not served by the railways or which are not large enough to have cattle markets.[7]

---

[3] Throughout the Western Region of Nigeria the cattle markets are locally known by the Hausa word *Zango* (literally meaning a camping place of caravan or lodging place of travellers), while the local Hausa quarter is known as *Sābo*, short for *Sābon Gari*. In Ghana, on the other hand, the word *Zango*, which is usually pronounced as *Zongo*, is used for the native strangers' quarter which is often predominantly Hausa.

[4] This, again, is an approximate figure derived from the number of cattle sold in the market, the average price per head, and the average length of the period of credit.

[5] *Shānun kasa.*

[6] Trypanosomiasis.

[7] According to figures from the veterinary service offices, for the years 1959 to 1962, 20 per cent. of all the cattle which started the journey from the North towards Ibadan as the final destination did not actually reach Ibadan, which means that they were sold on the way. As nearly all the cattle brought by train eventually arrive at Ibadan, this percentage represents the foot cattle which are sold on the way. This means that about 50 per cent. of the foot cattle originally destined for Ibadan are sold on the way.

Foot cattle are brought by smaller-scale Hausa dealers, each dealer making an average of four journeys to Ibadan in a year, bringing to the market each journey an average of seventy head of cattle.[8] The herd is driven by hired Fulani drovers, an average of one drover[9] for every twenty-five head. The herd owner walks with his cattle as far as Ilorin, where he usually parts with the caravan and starts a reconnaissance trip, by lorries and mammy wagons, along the ninety-five-mile route to Ibadan, stopping at the cattle markets in Ogbomosho and Oyo, and also at other, smaller towns, choosing the most advantageous place to sell. The more southerly the place, the higher the price, but the greater the hazards to the health of the cattle and the longer the period in which the capital is engaged.

The train cattle[10] are either brought by smaller-scale dealers, who travel with the herd, or are sent by relatively larger-scale dealers to their permanent agents in Ibadan. The cattle are transported in special wagons, each wagon accommodating between twenty and thirty head.[11] The herd in each wagon is looked after by an attendant[12] whose main task is to guard the beasts against theft. The journey to Ibadan takes two to three days and the few cattle who show signs of sickness in the meantime are slaughtered and sold in the several intervening stations, where local butchers are always waiting for such opportunities.

According to men in the business, the life expectancy of cattle after arriving in Ibadan is about two weeks for those brought on foot and about two and a half months for those brought by train. Train cattle therefore fetch a higher price than foot cattle of the same size and quality, particularly because they are demanded by butchers, not only from Ibadan, but also from neighbouring towns and villages. Also, when prices in Ibadan are unfavourable train cattle can be taken south as far as Lagos.

Despite the sharp distinction in the market between the two categories of cattle, the organization of credit is essentially similar in both cases.

When the cattle dealer,[13] whether he is the owner of the herd or only an agent of the owner, is in Ibadan he lodges with his usual 'landlord' in the Hausa Quarter. The word 'landlord' is a literal translation of the Hausa term *mai gida*, but the *mai gida* plays several kinds of roles in the cattle business which are not denoted by the English translation and need to be analytically separated. In the first place, the *mai gida* is a house-owner,

---

[8] These figures are from a survey covering 118 dealers in foot cattle.

[9] *Dan kōre.*

[10] *Shānun Jirgi.*

[11] Depending on the size of the animals. Usually the horns of the cattle are cut short before the journey so that more cattle can be accommodated in a wagon, and in the market, train cattle can usually be identified by their shorter horns.

[12] *Dan taragu*, literally 'son of the wagon'.

[13] *Mai shānu.*

having, besides that in which he and his family live, at least one more house for the accommodation of his dealers from the north. Of the twelve cattle landlords who operated in Zango in 1963, one had six such houses, a second had four, two others had two houses each, and the rest had one each. The landlords usually own additional houses in which their assistants, clerks, servants, malams, and other men of their entourage are accommodated, free of charge. The landlord also provides three meals a day for his dealers and entertains them in the evenings, but this function as inn-keeper is by no means the most fundamental of his roles.

The landlord is also a middleman[14] who mediates between his dealers and the local butchers in the market. Each landlord has for this purpose a number of middlemen[15] working under him, but responsibility for their business conduct remains always with him. Thus, when the herd of the dealer arrives at the market, the landlord entrusts its sale to one of his middlemen. The dealer then accompanies the middleman in the market and remains with him until the whole herd is sold. But no transaction can be finally concluded without the approval of the landlord.

Here we come to the role of the landlord as insurer or risk-taker, which is the most crucial factor in the operation of the whole market. As sale is on credit, the landlord is the guarantor that the money will eventually be paid, and that if the buyer should default, he would pay the full amount to the dealer himself. This obligation means that he must be very well acquainted with the buyers, and it is only through long experience in the business that he comes to acquire the necessary knowledge. He has to know not only where a buyer slaughters the cattle, or where he has his shop or market stall, but also where he lives, who are his relatives and associates, what is the size of his business, and how honest and trustworthy he has proved himself to be in his dealings so far. In this way, every butcher in the market is informally graded by the landlords and their middlemen on a scale of credit-worthiness from nil up to about £1,000 of credit, for a period of up to four weeks. No sane landlord would give a butcher credit in excess of the latter's 'quota'. Misjudgement in this respect can ruin the business house of the landlord. This actually happened early in 1963 to one of the landlords, when a number of butchers who had bought cattle

---

[14] *Dillāli*.

[15] Between them, the twelve cattle landlords operating in Ibadan in 1963, had fifty-two middlemen working for them. The senior among these middlemen had assistants under them, as they were usually given more cattle to sell than were the junior middlemen. Some of these senior middlemen provided food, cooked by their own wives, to the dealers who were 'allotted' to them, and they therefore received a greater proportion of the commission. There were a few middlemen in the market who were not attached to any particular landlord but who worked on a temporary basis for landlords who had more business on their hands than could be dealt with by their permanent middlemen.

through him defaulted, and he eventually failed to pay the money himself to the dealers. These stopped lodging with him and complained to the Chief of the Cattle Market. He finally sold his only house of strangers to meet his obligations and became an ordinary middleman.

Thus landlords need to have not only a precise assessment of the buyer's social background and of his business conduct in the past, but must also be continuously vigilant as to his day-to-day purchases in the market. For while a dealer is attached to one landlord at a time, the butcher is free to buy through any landlord, and he usually makes his purchases through many landlords. It is conceivable, therefore, that he may succeed in buying, within a short period of time, from several unsuspecting landlords in excess of the limits of his credit-worthiness. The only way in which the landlords can meet this potential danger is by the continuous exchange of business information. No formally institutionalized channels for such an exchange exist in the market, but the objective is nevertheless achieved through informal relations.

Landlords interact very intensively among themselves, since it is in the nature of their business both to compete and to co-operate. They compete fiercely over business, and countless disputes arise among them over what they describe as 'stealing of dealers'. Generally speaking, a dealer has one landlord to whom he is accustomed to entrust the sale of his cattle whenever he comes to Ibadan. This attachment of a dealer to one landlord usually holds for years and sometimes continues to hold between their sons when they die. Landlords do much to keep their dealers attached to them, offering them various services, some of which have little to do with the cattle business. When a dealer finally goes back to the North, after selling his cattle, his landlord gives him a present, the minimum standard being a bottle of French perfume costing (as in 1963) 18 shillings.[16] But some dealers, particularly those of foot cattle who come to Ibadan only occasionally, *do* change their landlords, for one reason or another, and sometimes landlords send emissaries as far as Ilorin to meet such dealers, offer them presents, and direct them to lodge with their masters.

Disputes between landlords over dealers have often led to political crises within the Hausa Quarter. The basic principle of political grouping among the 5,000 Hausa of the Quarter is that of the client–patron relationship, which is essentially diadic, holding between the patron and each client separately, without leading to the formation of corporate groups. A man's clients are his employees, attendants, and tenants. The patrons of the Quarter are the thirty landlords, in the various economic fields, who control much of the employment and of the housing of the rest of the population. Each one of them is the head of what may be described as a 'house of power'. Clients often 'change house', i.e. change their allegiance from

---

[16] It is customary for Hausa *men* to wear perfume.

one landlord to another, which often means literally moving from one house to another. Generally speaking, landlords are old residents in Ibadan while most of their clients are new migrants.[17]

The landlords and their clients pay allegiance to the Hausa Chief of the Quarter,[18] who mediates between them and the authorities, adjudicates—with the help of his advisers—in cases of disputes within the Quarter, and appoints men to titled positions who regulate communal affairs. One of these positions is that of the 'Chief of the Cattle Market',[19] who is responsible for keeping order in the market and who arbitrates in cases of disputes within it.

Of all the patrons, the cattle landlords are the most powerful as they have dominated the Quarter politically ever since its foundation in 1916. The Chief of the Quarter has always been a cattle landlord and, since 1930, he has also been the Chief of the Cattle Market.[20]

The cattle business is thus directly involved in the politics of the Quarter. The same men who meet in the cattle market as landlords confront each other in the Quarter as political leaders, and their behaviour in the one role affects their behaviour in the other. For example, one of the duties of the Chief of the Quarter is to give accommodation to any Hausa stranger who comes to him, and the Chief runs many houses for this specific purpose. When a new cattle dealer comes for the first time to Ibadan and lodges in one of these houses, as a stranger, it is only natural that he should eventually sell his cattle through the Chief, in the latter's role as cattle landlord.

Within the context of the Quarter, one major source of dispute between the landlords has been the struggle for the control over houses, since from the early 1930's these have become relatively scarce because of overcrowding. A man needs housing in the Quarter to secure membership of the community, to establish himself in business, to gather clients around him, to enlarge his family by marrying more wives, to foster the sons and daughters of his kin, and to accommodate malams whose services in the mystical world are indispensable to his success and well-being. Thus, command over housing is in no small measure command over economic and political power. When the Quarter was first established, the land, which had been allotted for the purpose by the city's native authority, was distributed in equal plots among the first settlers. But since then many changes have taken place in the ownership and distribution of houses and land. In 1963 only five of the many hundreds of houses of the Quarter

---

[17] According to census material which I collected in 1963, only 12 per cent. of the Hausa migrants in the Quarter had been in Ibadan for twenty years or more.

[18] Known as *Sarkin Hausāwa* and sometimes as *Sarkin Sābo*.

[19] *Sarkin Zango.*

[20] These two positions, the *Sarkin Sābo* and the *Sarkin Zango*, have become so involved in each other that in some situations it is difficult to separate them, even analytically.

were registered as deeds. There were no documents of any kind to establish ownership over the rest of the houses. Most of the original houses and plots have changed hands many times through sale or the death of their owners. The houses of persons who died without leaving heirs have been 'inherited' by the Chief of the Quarter, who is presumed to use them for the general welfare of the community. In this way the Chief has come to control scores of houses in which he accommodates, rent free, several hundreds of people who have in this way automatically become his clients. Landlords thus struggle over the ownership of houses in the Quarter because these are the means to political and economic power.

In the cattle market the landlords also compete over the buyers and each landlord has a number of young men who act as 'advertisers', trying to draw the attention of the butchers to the herds marketed through their employers. But landlords are at the same time forced to co-operate in the market in several respects, the most important being to present a united front *vis-à-vis* the butchers. These are very powerfully organized through an association which has played an important role within the Ibadan polity and only a strong landlords' front can keep the necessary balance in the market.

The market is held twice a day, once in the morning, between 9 and 10, and again in the afternoon, between 5 and 7. These official hours are enforced by the Chief of the Market.[21] But landlords come to the market about an hour before each session to sit informally together and 'joke', often very clumsily, and it is in the course of this joking that much of the vital information on the buyers is exchanged.

Another informal channel through which business information is exchanged is the interaction between the clerks. Every landlord has a clerk[22] whose main duty is the registration of sales and the collection of money from the debtors. As soon as a transaction is concluded, the middleman involved calls the clerk of his landlord to note down the details. These include the date of the transaction, name of dealer, name of middleman, name and address of buyer, the number of cattle sold, the price and total amount as well as the exact time and place of payment.[23] The clerk occupies a central position within the structure of the 'business house' because, while the middlemen and the other assistants are individually related to the landlord and are not formally related to each other, the clerk is formally related to everyone within the house, and thus knows about all the transactions concluded through the house. Being also the collector of substantial

---

[21] The beginning and the ending of a session are announced by a whistle blown by one of the 'boys' of the Chief of the Market.

[22] Known as *mālam*, in the sense of 'literate', not of 'religious functionary'.

[23] The register in which these details are written down serves as a reminder, not a document. The details are neither checked nor ratified by the buyers.

amounts of money, he is always a man who is fully trusted by the landlord. Of the twelve landlords in the Ibadan market, three have their own sons as clerks, two their "fostered"[24] sons, and three perform the task themselves. The clerks are young, educated 'in Arabic',[25] and are Ibadan-born. They speak Yoruba as well as Hausa and belong to the same age-group. Sharing the same background, they belong to the same group whose members pray, eat, learn, and seek entertainment together.[26] They thus meet in various social situations every day and in the course of their interaction they exchange information about the solvency of the butchers, which they eventually pass on to their respective masters.

These exchanges of information, however, relate only to the behaviour of the butchers in the past and it is conceivable that a butcher may in one hour buy from several landlords who, in the pressure of business, may not realize that he is exceeding his limits. A protection against such a possibility is obtained through the informal activities of, and interaction among, the 'boys',[27] who perform various jobs in helping their landlord and his middlemen in the market. These 'boys' can be seen everywhere in the market, and indeed the literal meaning of the Hausa word *kankamba* is 'going hither and thither'. Their tasks take them to many parts of the market and they mingle with the 'boys' of other landlords. When, in the course of their activities, they notice a butcher who, having already bought cattle in other corners of the market, comes to buy also from their landlord, then they alert the middlemen to the impending danger.[28]

Thus, joking and gossiping between the landlords, informal meetings among the clerks, and the activities of the 'boys' serve as means of disseminating business information and help to guard against the hazards of credit.

But the conflicting interests of the landlords are implicit even in this very fundamental issue of exchanging information about the butchers' purchases, and it sometimes happens, though not often, that a landlord tries to suppress information. I witnessed in 1963 a case of a butcher who failed to pay, on time, a debt of a few hundred pounds to a landlord, but promised to do so as soon as his business improved. The landlord withheld this news from the other landlords, since otherwise these would have refrained

---

[24] Child fostering is very widespread among the Hausa.

[25] All education in the Hausa Quarter is 'Arabic' education which consists mainly in learning to read the Kor'an and to write in Arabic.

[26] The overwhelming majority of the Hausa in Sabo adhere to the Tijaniyya order which enjoins intensive collective ritualism and ties initiates to a ritual leader known as *mukaddam*. Groupings emerging in the course of ritual performance tend to become fraternities whose members co-operate in many social fields.

[27] *Kankamba.*

[28] The butchers are always under constant observation by the landlords and their subordinates. The absence of a butcher for three or four days in succession is always marked with suspicion in the market.

from selling cattle to the butcher, who would thus have been without business and would have failed to settle his original debt. An unsuspecting landlord eventually sold cattle to the butcher in question, who duly settled his debt to the first landlord but defaulted in payment to the second. When the first landlord was later blamed for his unethical conduct he replied that no one had asked him to give the information which he had withheld. The landlord who suffered in this case had himself acted as his own clerk and had therefore no means of knowing of the default of the butcher except from the first landlord. Landlords are thus sometimes in an invidious position about revealing information concerning their sales.

The credit is given for a period of two to four weeks.[29] Dealers in foot cattle usually remain during this period accommodated and fed by the landlord, and when the money is finally collected it is kept by the landlord until the dealer arranges transport for himself to go back to the North.[30] Dealers in train cattle often go back to the North as soon as their cattle are sold and collect the proceeds when they come back with the next herd.

The landlord receives no direct reward whatsoever from the dealer for accommodation, food, mediation, banking, or risk-taking. On the contrary he gives the dealer not only presents but also part of his own earning from the sale of the cattle. The landlord's remuneration is a fixed commission, known by the Hausa term *kudin lada* or simply *lada*, which he collects from the buyer, in cash, on the conclusion of the sale. During 1963 the commission in Ibadan was 13 shillings on each head of cattle, irrespective of the price. From this amount the landlord pays 3 shillings to the middleman who arranged the transaction, about a shilling to the clerk and the 'boys', 2 shillings to the dealer himself, and retains the rest to cover his expenses and to remunerate himself for the financial risks he has taken in assuring the credit.[31]

This credit arrangement is not fool-proof and cases of default occur, but, barring political or economic upheavals, the risks are greatly reduced by a variety of factors.

In the first place a loss is always distributed among several individuals because a butcher is usually indebted not to one landlord but to many, and a dealer's herd is sold not to one butcher but to many butchers. Thus, if a butcher defaulted the loss would be shared by the several landlords who

---

[29] As the Hausa are Muslims, the dealers do not in principle charge interest for the credit they give to the butchers. But cash price is always lower than credit price by £1 to £3 for a head of cattle which is usually sold at sold at £20 to £40.

[30] Landlords often keep in their houses several thousands of pounds, in cash, for their dealers. The money is kept in simple wooden chests which are protected from thieves by amulets prepared by the malams and are also watched night and day by trusted attendants.

[31] There are slight variations in the distribution of the commission between foot cattle and train cattle.

gave him credit. The incidence of the loss is spread still wider when the case is eventually arbitrated, and in nearly all the cases I have recorded the dealer was made to share in the loss even though the formal principle is that the whole loss should be borne by the landlord.[32] I am talking here of loss, but it nearly always happens that an arrangement is reached, as a result of arbitration, by which the butcher undertakes to pay his debt by instalments over several months. During these months he is allowed to buy from the market but must pay in cash.

Unless a butcher is prepared to go out of the business altogether he is forced to abide by such an arrangement, since according to municipal rules he would forfeit his licence as a butcher if he did not slaughter at least one beast every week. This is a very important source of pressure on him because a licence is very difficult to obtain and is also very expensive. He cannot evade payment by buying cattle elsewhere. The Hausa throughout the region, indeed throughout southern Nigeria, monopolize the sale of cattle and control all cattle markets. These markets, together with the Hausa Quarters to which they are attached, constitute a widespread network of highly interrelated communities. In each of the three large cattle markets which are within a radius of sixty miles of Ibadan (Ogbomosho, Oyo, and Abeokuta) the Chief of the Cattle Market is himself the Chief of the Hausa Quarter, as well as being a cattle landlord. Thus, when the landlords in the Ibadan market decide not to sell to a defaulting butcher, they usually send a word to the neighbouring cattle markets about him and if he ever appeared there no one would sell to him even if he paid cash.

An equally important form of pressure on individual defaulters comes from the butchers themselves, who are organized in eight slaughter-houses, as well as within the overall occupational association. When one butcher defaults, the landlords are often forced to retaliate by declaring a temporary boycott of all the butchers within his slaughter-house. I witnessed one such case in 1963 when a butcher failed to pay a debt of about £700 which he owed to many landlords. In their gossiping time one day the landlords decided to refuse selling any cattle to the whole slaughter-house of the defaulting butcher in order to mobilize the pressure of his colleagues on him. This action was so effective that the butchers involved, together with the chief of the whole Association,[33] as well as the defaulting butcher, came to the Chief of the Hausa Quarter, in his capacity as Chief of the Cattle Market, on the same evening and an arrangement was made there and then to settle the matter. Indeed it happens sometimes that when a butcher shows signs of financial difficulties, some of his colleagues within the same

---

[32] A landlord would run the risk of losing all his dealers if he did not meet his obligations. The payment of compensation to the dealers is always by monthly instalments, in accordance with the ruling of the Chief of the Market in the case.

[33] The *Sarkin Pāwa*. The incumbent of the office is of course a Yoruba man.

slaughter-house will caution some of their trustworthy middlemen not to sell to him. Thus, the butchers on their part watch each other's conduct in business and can exert a great deal of pressure on potential defaulters.

The market is therefore not seriously disturbed by the occasional default of individual butchers. Indeed, from the study of cases seen against the background of the history of the market organization, it appears that occasional default (as crime in Durkheim's analysis[34]) has led to continual re-examination and retightening of the control mechanisms in the market and thus made the continuity of the credit system possible. The cattle landlords' main worry is not the individual defaulter but the sudden collapse of the market as a result of a concerted hostile action on the part of the butchers.[35] The position of the landlords is particularly vulnerable, since the pressure which they can exert on the butchers is limited in degree and is not without its dangers. This is because the cleavage in the market between buyer and seller, debtor and creditor, is also a cleavage between Yoruba and Hausa and, indeed, both sides describe their mutual relationships in tribalistic terms. The landlords often talk of the 'machinations' and the 'treachery' of the Yoruba and the butchers of the 'exploitation' and 'greed' of the Hausa. When the Ibadan cattle landlords appeal for support and solidarity from the cattle landlords in other markets in the region they actually do so not in the name of the profession but in the name of Hausa-ism, and the communication between the markets is effected through the respective Hausa chiefs, acting *as* Hausa chiefs, and not as chiefs of the cattle markets.

In the same way, the butchers confront the landlords as a tribal group and rely on the support of various other Yoruba groupings in this confrontation. The butchers resent the fact that it is they, and not the Hausa sellers, who are made to pay the commission to the landlords, and for years they have been agitating against it. In this agitation they have often succeeded in mobilizing support from the press and from the city's traditional chiefs, who on several occasions in the past reminded the Hausa that they were strangers, that the Quarter stood on the Olubadan's land, that if they did not behave they would be made to leave, and so on. The landlords are always afraid that the city council or the regional government may impose on them new taxes or new restrictions on the movement and sale of cattle,

---

[34] See E. Durkheim, *The Rules of Sociological Method*, pp. 64–75, translated by S. A. Solovay and J. H. Mueller, and edited by G. E. G. Catlin, The Free Press, Glencoe, Illinois (1950).

[35] Such an action is not unlikely to happen. It happened in 1963 in the Abeokuta cattle market, when the butchers stopped paying their debts to the dealers and completely paralysed the market for about five weeks, until the two sides accepted arbitration by the Ibadan Hausa Chief. The dispute arose when some of the Hausa cattle landlords attempted to enter the butchering business by slaughtering a number of cattle and selling the meat to local retailers. The arbitrator eventually ruled that no slaughtering should be done by the landlords.

or that they will decide to remove the Hausa Quarter or to 'scrap' it altogether.

The cattle landlords have not been passive in the face of such threats. When during the 1950's the butchers affiliated themselves within the predominantly Yoruba Action Group Party, which was until 1962 in power in the Western Region, the Hausa landlords reacted not only by joining the same party themselves, but also by dragging almost the whole Hausa Quarter with them in joining it, and in successive elections the Ibadan Hausa gave their votes to it.[36] In the 1961 election for the Ibadan local council, 93 per cent. of the votes in the Quarter went to the Action Group candidate. Within the party, the Hausa eventually formed a strong pressure group. According to the 1952 Census of Nigeria there were in the Western Region nearly 41,000 Hausa residents and even then it was realized that there were many more Hausa who for a variety of reasons had not registered themselves. In 1953 the chiefs of all Hausa communities in the Region formed a joint Hausa association[37] and unanimously elected the Ibadan Hausa Chief as their chairman. This occurred on the eve of the 1954 Federal Election and there is little doubt that the association played an important role in mobilizing Hausa support for the party chosen by their chiefs. At that time the Action Group was struggling to establish itself, not as a regional, but as a national, party which was to gain the support of the masses from the other tribes of the Federation of Nigeria. For that purpose the party fought particularly hard to gain a foothold in Hausaland in the North, as that region contained more than half the population of the Federation. A party with such objectives could not allow the persecution of a Hausa minority in its own capital. Thus, the party not only prevented hostile action being taken against the cattle landlords, but even tried to prevent individual butchers from defaulting, by exerting pressure on these to honour their obligations, and sometimes by granting loans to those among them who did not have the cash to pay.

The risks of the credit system have thus made it necessary for the cattle landlords to act politically within the Hausa network of communities, as well as within the Ibadan, the regional, and the national polities. To do so, they have had to act not on occupational but on tribal lines, and it has therefore been essential for them to control the Chieftaincy of the Hausa Quarter. Under the prevailing conditions it is only through the Chieftaincy that political interaction with other Hausa communities, on the one hand, and with the Yoruba, on the other, can be effected.

The cattle landlords are few in number and, together with all their middlemen, clerks, and assistants, constitute only 6 per cent. of the working

---

[36] Men in the Quarter do not conceal the fact that in their political behaviour they follow the instructions of their patrons unquestionably.

[37] The association was formally called 'The Federal Union of the Western Sarkis Hausawa'.

Hausa male population of the Quarter.[38] And yet they have always been so dominant that the history of the Quarter is to a great extent the history of the cattle trade in Ibadan. From the very beginning of Hausa settlement in Ibadan, at the beginning of the present century, until today, the Chief of the Quarter has always been a cattle landlord. And this is the case not only in Ibadan but also in the other Hausa communities in those Yoruba towns where a cattle market exists. Indeed it was initially this sociological problem, i.e. 'How is it that a handful of cattle landlords have come to dominate the whole Quarter politically?', which led me to study the organization of the cattle market.

There are various factors involved in this phenomenon, but it is beyond the limits of this paper to discuss them in detail. It is sufficient to point out that the landlords not only 'need' the Chieftaincy because of its role in the organization of credit, but also have the power and the organization to dominate the Quarter. They interact among themselves most intensively, as they meet in a relatively small place (the market) twice a day, seven days a week. In contrast, the kola landlords, for example, who run business on similar lines and who, as an occupational group, constitute nearly 18 per cent.[39] of the working Hausa males in the Quarter, and certainly command greater wealth, do not have opportunities to interact so frequently and so intensively, since they have to leave the Quarter every morning and disperse in all directions within a radius of about forty miles in quest of supplies. They also operate mainly with cash and, since they are dealing in a local product for export from the area, whenever credit is involved, they are the debtors, not the creditors, and hence are not impelled to political action to the same degree as are the cattle landlords, who seem to be always beset by great anxieties over the thousands of pounds of credit which continuously weigh on their conscience. Another factor which should be taken into account is that of continuities from the past. The cattle landlords and middlemen were among the very first of the Hausa migrants to Ibadan. In a census taken in the Quarter in 1916, a few months after its establishment, 56 out of 261 (20 per cent.) Hausa males were described as cattle traders, which means that men working in the cattle trade constituted a much higher proportion of the working population in the past than today. On the other hand, the kola men came to the Quarter mainly during the past generation, since kola has been grown in the Western Region of Nigeria only in recent decades. For the cattle landlords, seniority in the Quarter has meant greater opportunities for acquiring houses, for rallying clients, and for establishing connexions with local sources of power and authority. These are advantages which help the cattle landlords, within the contemporary situation, to control the Quarter.

---

[38] Ninety-seven out of a total of 1,570. The figures are from a general census which I took in Sabo with the help of local assistants.

[39] 285 out of a total of 1,570.

I am not arguing here that the majority of the Quarter blindly align themselves for political action behind the cattle landlords, to the latter's private interests. I am only suggesting that, because of their role in the cattle market, the cattle landlords are more politically active and better organized for political action than any other group within the Quarter. They are also the group most sensitive to any changes in Hausa-Yoruba relations. When the 1962 emergency situation in the Western Region of Nigeria came to an end, in January 1963, and the former Prime Minister, Chief Akintola, returned to his previous position in Ibadan, the cattle landlords and middlemen, who had been ardent Action Groupers until the emergency, went *en masse,* taking with them any Hausa they could mobilize, to greet the returning Premier and to express allegiance to him and to his party (at the time the UPP), which had emerged in opposition to the Action Group. They did this not as cattle men but as Hausa, representing the whole Hausa Quarter. It is significant, incidentally, that at the doors of the Premier they came face to face with another delegation who had also come to express their allegiance—it was the delegation of the Yoruba butchers.

The cattle landlords have very serious reservations about submitting their disputes with the butchers to the civil courts. There are many reasons for this attitude. When a butcher defaults he is usually indebted to many dealers from whom he has bought cattle. As these dealers are the legal creditors, it is they, not the landlords, who should apply to the courts for adjudication, which means that a number of dealers should act jointly in order to pursue their case against the defaulting butcher. But this is highly impracticable. The amount due to each dealer from the defaulting butcher is relatively small, while the expenses of adjudication are high. Furthermore, court procedure is long and the dealers, whose residence is usually far in the North, cannot wait in Ibadan indefinitely. There is also the problem of language and cultural differences. Furthermore, the landlords believe that court rulings in cases of this nature are not effective, since a butcher who pleads that he has no money can be asked to pay only a few pounds a month to his creditors until an amount of hundreds of pounds could be finally settled.[40]

Arbitration by the Chief of the Market, on the other hand, is prompt, convenient, and effective. It is performed by a Hausa, but in nearly all cases of dispute, the Chief of the Butchers, a Yoruba, participates in the arbitratory process. The ruling of the Chief of the Market is final and is nearly always honoured.[41]

---

[40] The landlords often skip over most of these factors and dismiss the case for submitting disputes to the courts by saying: 'After all these are *Yoruba* courts'.

[41] One of the most striking phenomena I witnessed in this respect was the obedience which the Yoruba butchers showed towards the Hausa Chief, whose authority was so strong that he could send his messenger and summon any butcher to his office.

Thus the organization of credit in the market is ultimately upheld, not by the civil courts, but by what may be labelled as 'tribal politics'. In the market, debtors and creditors face each other as tribesmen as well as business men. This double cleavage is basic to the operation of the credit system. It is the product of a number of processes which have driven the Hausa out of the butchering business, on the one hand, and prevented the Yoruba from performing the functions of the cattle landlords, on the other. Until the early 1930's many of the butchers of Ibadan were Hausa, and the Quarter's Hausa 'Chief of the Butchers' was a very powerful man. But today there is only one Hausa butcher[42] in the city, and the title 'Chief of the Butchers' within the Quarter has sunk into insignificance.[43] On the other hand, all the attempts that have been made every now and then by some ambitious Yoruba to act as cattle landlords or even as cattle dealers have completely failed.

I have attempted to show that in order to understand the operation of credit in the cattle market in Ibadan we need to consider such phenomena as informal gossiping and joking, age-grouping, and inter-tribal politics. These are essentially non-economic factors which seem to be exterior to the market situation. In considering credit in Western society, it is equally essential to take into account some non-economic factors, but because of the highly developed centralization, communication, and bureaucratization, these factors are fundamentally the same throughout the society and there is therefore one unitary system of credit. In his analysis, the economist can thus regard these factors as constant, take them for granted, and never mention them. In a pre-industrial society, on the other hand, there are many systems of credit, each having its own structure which consists of both formal and informal relations. This is why, in order to explain such a system, the economist has to rely much on anthropologists or become one himself.

---

[42] Besides this licensed butcher there are a few Hausa men who work as 'meat cutters', buying wholesale from Yoruba butchers and selling within the Quarter or in the neighbouring Mokola Quarter.

[43] The case of dispute between the local Yoruba butchers and the Hausa cattle landlords mentioned in footnote 35, p. 86, points in the same direction.

# Improvement Associations among the Afikpo Ibo[1]

## S. Ottenberg

In recent years a new type of association, the improvement union or 'meeting', has become common in Southern Nigeria. Associations of this kind may be formed on a lineage, clan, village, village-group, divisional, or tribal basis, and may carry out various economic, educational, political, social, and general improvement activities directly related to changing cultural conditions.[2] The present report is concerned with the development of this kind of association in the Afikpo village-group of the Ibo-speaking people. Its growth in this section of Ibo country has been more recent than in the more central Ibo areas, where European contact has been of longer duration, a circumstance that has made it possible to study its initial development in detail.

The Afikpo are Eastern Ibo,[3] who live between the headquarters of Afikpo Division, Ogoja Province, South-eastern Nigeria, and the Cross River, a few miles to the east. Though sometimes referred to as Afikpo Clan, the twenty-three villages, with a population of 26,305,[4] do not form

[1] This paper is based on research carried out in the Afikpo area between December 1951 and February 1953, with the aid of grants from the Social Science Research Council, New York City, and from the Program of African Studies, Northwestern University, Evanston, Illinois. The portion of the paper dealing with the village 'meetings' is a revised version of a paper originally submitted to the Second Annual Conference of the West African Institute of Social and Economic Research, Ibadan, in March 1953. I wish to thank Professor M. J. Herskovits of Northwestern University, Mr. G. I. Jones of Cambridge University, and Mr. Nnachi Enwo of Afikpo for suggestions in the preparation of the final draft of this paper. The publication of this paper in *Africa* has been made possible by a grant from the Program of African Studies, Northwestern University, to defray additional publication costs involved.

[2] For general discussions of these unions in Nigeria see Coleman, 1952; Lord Hailey, 1951, pp. 18–20; Offodile, 1947.

[3] See Forde and Jones, 1950, pp. 51–56.

[4] Nigeria, Census Superintendent, 1953, p. 25.

a clan in the anthropological sense, being composed of numerous lineages, only some of which are related. Many of the people came originally from the Aro Chuku area, and the Afikpo people as a group consider themselves socially and politically distinct from the people living around them. While they possess many characteristics common to other Ibo peoples, including the lack of political groupings more extensive than the village-group, they also have cultural features which are not typical of the Ibo. These include a system of double descent, a highly organized age-grade and age-set system, limited economic independence of women, and the grouping of compounds (*ɛzi*) into geographically compact villages (*ogo*). There is also a somewhat sharper division of social and political groupings on the basis of sex than in other Ibo areas.[5] Since the Afikpo women, unlike those of other Ibo regions, at present hold no 'meetings', this report, unless otherwise indicated, concerns men only.

The Afikpo people are predominantly agriculturists, though fishing and trading activities are also an important part of their economy. The basic subsistence crops are yam, coco-yam, and cassava, and these are also the major cash crops, though the sale of fish and of pottery is also a source of income. Little money comes from palm products, Afikpo being peripheral to the main Ibo palm-belt to the west. Afikpo traders are active on the Cross River, moving foodstuffs (particularly yams) and pottery southward and European goods and dried fish to the north-east. The presence of the Divisional Headquarters at Afikpo has made it possible for many local people to obtain salaried jobs, an important source of cash. In the past 30 years British West African currency has largely replaced barter and the use of brass rods as a medium of exchange, and it is increasingly being used as a substitute for ceremonial foodstuffs and goods. The form and functions of the Afikpo village 'meetings' will be seen to be related to the expanding cash economy.

## Village Organization

The Afikpo village usually consists of a number of compact compounds grouped around a village square, or, in larger villages, around two or three village squares, each serving a group of contiguous compounds. A compound—in some cases a group of compounds, and in a few cases the whole village—is composed of a patrilineage. Exogamous matriclans also exist in Afikpo as corporate groups without a common residential basis,

---

[5] For discussions of women's 'meetings' in other Ibo areas see Ardener, 1953; Green, 1947, pp. 44–48 and 217–31; Leith-Ross, 1939, pp. 106–10, 163–5, and 214–15; Leith-Ross, 1944, pp. 98, 110.

the members of each matriclan being widely spread throughout the village-group.

Age is a major factor among the men in determining social and political authority in the village. This is reflected in the well-organized village age-set system. An age set is composed of almost all the men of a village within an age span of approximately three years and, by the time the members are about 20 years old, is informally organized with recognized leaders, a name chosen by the members, and a definite meeting-place. It becomes an official village organization when its members are about 30 years of age. Throughout the life of its members, it keeps its organization, name, and meeting-place. Each village has about 20 official sets ranked by age.

In every village two or three age sets, next to each other in age, of men of roughly 35 to 45 years of age, are formed as an age grade usually called *ukɛkpe*. This is an executive grade which has well-defined village duties, largely of a supervisory nature, in which it receives orders for communal village work from the village elders and calls on the two or three age sets below it in age to perform the duties under its supervision. Such work includes the repair of village and farm paths, the building of log bridges, and the clearing of debris and bush from the village area. In addition, most villages own a palm-grove, and it is the responsibility of this grade to determine the days on which palm-fruit may be collected, to collect annual fees from those who use the grove, and to levy and collect fines from violators of rules regulating palm-fruit collection. Most of the money collected is turned over to the village elders, who share it among themselves. *Ukɛkpe* can be called upon by the elders to lead the search for people who become lost or are missing in the farm areas, to direct operations when there are farm or village fires, and they are responsible for providing animals and goods used in certain village ceremonies, though the ceremonies are largely performed and attended by priests and elders. The age-grade members are also responsible for keeping peace in the compounds in which they live, especially in the case of disputes between spouses and between the women of a compound. They have the power to fine persons in the compound who refuse to stop quarrelling, and when this occurs the matter must be discussed and tried before the compound elders (and in some instances the village elders), who will decide whether the fines should stand as collected, be returned or be increased. *Ukɛkpe* will take only an explanatory part in such a trial, as they are considered too young to take a major part in the actual judgement.

With this grade authority is usually in the hands of the active and interested members of the señior age set, though younger men who show skill and interest are sometimes found in positions of leadership. It is rare for the grade to take a major part in initiating new activities, and when it does it is usually only after consultation with the village elders. It plays only a minor role in making decisions concerning the village, which are the province of the elders. These last two factors are important to the understanding of why the village 'meeting' developed.

The village elders (*Ndicie*) consist of the men of the oldest nine to twelve age sets, the exact number varying from village to village. The youngest members of this group are rarely less than 55 years old. These senior sets are organized into three age grades on the village-group basis, where they play a major role in the social and political leadership of Afikpo, and where, in the past, they also performed important judicial activities. These village-group grade members act, within their own villages, as a loosely organized aggregate of elders who are the leaders and the judiciary in many village matters. Qualifications for leadership are here based on age—the older the man the greater his authority—on speaking ability and knowledge of Afikpo affairs and history, and, to a lesser degree, on wealth and relationship ties, and on the number and kind of titles a man has taken. Village shrine priests are rarely active politically, restricting themselves to matters directly concerning their shrine, for it is a common Afikpo belief that if a priest becomes too much involved in social and political affairs the shrine he administers will lose some of its power. With regard to age it occasionally occurs that one of the younger elders who has taken many titles and is a good speaker will take a leading part in village activities, while an older man who is a poor speaker and who has taken few titles will play a minor role. However, the main factor in determining political and social leadership in the village is age and, for those within the proper age range, speaking ability and general knowledge.

The village elders come together each year after the yam harvest to decide which sections of the village farm-land will be used in the coming year, to review farming regulations, to see that the *ukɛkpe* age grade recognizes its responsibility for carrying out certain farm rules and to collect palm-grove rents from this executive grade. Throughout the year they meet whenever there is a matter of concern to the village to discuss, such as the clearing of paths or the settling of disputes between sections of the village. As a rule women do not attend these meetings, but the younger men may come to all but the first meeting mentioned above and are free to speak their minds, though it is the elders mainly who make the decisions. The three or four village age sets that are between the executive age grade and the elders in age are free to attend village meetings and learn how they themselves will some day conduct village matters, but apart from taking their turn at guarding the village during the early part of the farming season, these sets have no regular village duties to perform. However, they may be liable for village labour at the request of the elders.

The activities of the village elders are not usually dominated, except in the case of some of the smallest villages, by any one patrilineage.[6] While matrilineal relationships are important in some village matters the village is not dominated by single matriclans.

The village men's secret society[7] takes part in various village religious and social activities, though it is less concerned with political matters. However, within the society there exists a judicial group of members who have taken certain of the society's titles. When any male social, religious, political, or relationship group within the village makes a ruling affecting its members, if its leaders feel that the ruling is sufficiently important, or if it is likely to be disobeyed, they place a palm-frond on the roof of a village square rest-house while announcing the ruling; anyone who, in these circumstances, violates the rule, is said to have broken the secret society's regulations and is tried at the annual meeting of the society by this judicial group; title members from other Afikpo villages will usually be called in to help judge. This title group is considered by Afikpo people to be the highest court in Afikpo. The palm-frond is not always used, but the threat of its possible use is a strong factor in making people conform to rulings.

## Village 'Meetings'

Although British administrators began to control the Afikpo area in 1902, it was not until about 1920 that frequent contacts between them and the Afikpo people began. As a result of these contacts there has arisen a group of men, of about 45 years of age and younger, who have developed certain interests and activities which differ from those of men of a similar age who are more completely oriented in terms of the traditional culture,[8] and from those of young men of the pre-British period. This new grouping includes a few who are educated, who work as clerks for the local British Administration, who teach in local schools, who work for traders, or who are traders themselves. The majority of this group are unschooled traders, farmers, and fishermen, some of whom speak a little English. In

---

[6] A system formerly existed whereby patrilineal owners of a religious shrine called ɔtɔsi possessed strong political and social authority in the villages and the village-group. It became non-functional under British pressure and through the efforts of certain non-holders of the shrine during the 1930's. It had existed side by side with the authority of the Ndicie. While this shrine forms a part of the traditional Afikpo culture it seems to be in no way related to the more recent development of 'meetings' in Afikpo.

[7] Commonly called ogo, but known by various other names as well.

[8] When the term 'traditional' is used in this paper in connexion with culture, activities, attitudes, and so on, it refers to the culture existing about 1910, and to those elements of that culture which persist today in much the same manner.

none of the Afikpo villages does this group appear to form the majority of the young men of the village, though no accurate statistics are available. The leaders of this group are usually men between the ages of 35 and 45, though not necessarily educated or English-speaking men. A few older men, even several members of the village elders, also belong, at least partially, in this grouping. These are people interested in guiding the younger men and interested in some of their activities and points of view. They do not dominate the activities of this new group. Certain of the interests of this group are reflected in the development of village 'meetings', and an examination of one of the first organized and best developed of these will help to show exactly what some of these activities and interests are.[9]

Our analysis will be concerned with Mgbom, one of the larger Afikpo villages, which consists of 2,058 persons[10] settled in three groups of compounds and three nearby sub-villages. The village contains a number of unrelated patrilineages, but no single dominating lineage or compound is found. In 1944 a group of about fifteen Mgbom villagers, most of whom traded up and down the Cross River, organized the Mgbom Traders' Union. They met once a month at the house of an interested member, collecting 3d. dues per person at each meeting. The accumulated money was let out on loan to members at low interest-rates. While the need for loans was a major impetus to the formation of the group, the desire for mutual assistance in trading was also a factor, and agreements were made to help one another in cases of trouble or disputes while trading, and to prevent competitive buying and selling among themselves.

In 1947 the Union was reorganized on a broader basis, with many non-traders as members. The traders became assimilated to the larger groups, while informally maintaining their trading regulations among themselves. The change was led by a middle-aged educated son of a prominent deceased Warrant Chief of Mgbom who had recently returned from work in various Nigerian cities. This man and his friends and relatives who aided him were interested in furthering the schooling of village boys, and in forming an effective political organization to influence the elders in village matters to the point of view and interests of these young men. However, the majority of the members of the new Union were primarily interested in a loan system. The members were mostly between 20 and 45 years of age, men who were not yet village leaders, their number including only a few who had had schooling. No age-limit on membership existed,

---

[9] The terms 'new interests' and 'new activities' are used in this paper to mean interests and activities which at the level of observation differ from traditional ones. This does not imply that at a more analytical level they are new, or that they are unrelated to traditional interests and activities. In fact, many of them are old and deep-seated interests and activities which are expressed in ways that appear to differ at the level of observation.

[10] Nigeria, Census Superintendent, 1953, p. 26.

and though a few interested elders did join, the elders, as a whole, were not interested in the Union, although they did not oppose its organization. In several years the membership increased to seventy-five.

During the reorganization the group changed its name to the Mgbom Family Union,[11] establishing the offices of President, Secretary, and Assistant Secretary.[12] The first men selected for these offices, by majority assent, were the leaders in the reorganization. Though the Union has remained active since the first election there has been no further election except when the President died.[13] The members decided on procedures for future meetings and accepted a brief written constitution in English.[14] In practice, the bulk of the organizational work and the responsibility for the financial records belongs to the Secretary, the President acting as general guide of the Union's affairs, while the Assistant Secretary takes over the Secretary's duties whenever necessary. The Union also selected one man to represent each compound in the village, and these men, together with the officers, form a council which the educated members of the Union frequently refer to as the Executive. Between meetings the Executive collects unpaid dues and fines and, if sufficient money is raised by this method, let it out on loan. These activities are reported at the next regular meeting. Since the money is constantly circulating, opportunities for the misappropriation of large sums are minimal. Although women are not specifically excluded from the Union none has attempted to join. A strong feeling against bisexual organizations exists in Afikpo except for those which are primarily based on relationship. Some members attempted to form sub-unions in Calabar and in Victoria, British Cameroons, where small groups of Mgbom people live, but these groups never became active. The impetus for the formation of the Mgbom Union came from within the village, not from Mgbom people living elsewhere.

---

[11] Though the members were frequently unrelated the term 'Family' stresses the unity of the village, especially in terms of the outside world. The term 'meeting' (frequently pronounced *mitini*) and the Ibo term *ozuzu* are used for the Union as a whole, and for any of its meetings. *Ozuzu* is also used in Afikpo for almost any Afikpo gathering or work group. The Afikpo Ibo term *nciko* is used when referring to any improvement union.

[12] Respectively: *onye isi oche* (person-head-chair), *ode ɛkwuwke* (write-leaf or book), and *iyaka ode ɛkwuwke* (help or lend hand write-leaf or book).

[13] This is in keeping with the traditional practice of permitting those elected to a position to keep it until they die, become totally incompetent, or in certain cases move into a different age category.

[14] The constitution prescribes aid for any member in trouble, the donation of a coffin for the burial of any member, the general improvement of social conditions, the making of loans, and the payment of fines for failure to attend meetings. It lays down fines for failure to aid another member in trouble and for bribing another member, and stipulates that disputes between members should be tried within the Union before being taken elsewhere. These last three rules, common in age-set regulations as well, help to maintain the internal solidarity of the Union.

Meetings are held every three months, when 9*d.* per member is collected. This money is let out at 5*s.* interest per year for each £1 loaned, with lower interest-rates for shorter periods. Loans, which are usually limited to £1 per person, must be repaid with interest at the annual meeting in December, when most of the Union's funds are redistributed in new loans, conveniently before the principal fishing season is fully under way and before the new farming season and the new school term begin. Fines of 3*d.* for failure to attend a meeting, and of 3*d.* a day for failure to repay a loan on time are levied, while an entrance fee of 2*s.* is collected. No special ceremony is performed for or by a new member.

Meetings usually take place in the spacious house of the President, though the members can meet in any village house they choose, in accordance with a traditional Afikpo pattern. The meeting, usually held on a Sunday evening, is conducted in Ibo. The older members, as they enter, take the most comfortable seats; if none is available, a younger person will give an elder his in keeping with the traditional respect for age in Afikpo. The fifty or so persons who usually attend sit on chairs or benches along the walls, while the three main officers sit at a table in the centre of the room. No formal opening prayer usually occurs, in contrast to traditional Afikpo meetings. The Secretary reads the names of the members, who then pay their dues and fines. He counts the money, announces the total amount, and makes loans to members; at these quarterly meetings, however, only a few loans are made as little money has come in, most of it having been returned at the annual meeting. Should anyone object to loaning money to a specific person the meeting will discuss the matter and decide on the advisability of making the loan. The best means of dealing with the few who, during the past year, have not repaid their loans is then considered, frequently in terms of attempts to induce friends and relatives of the defaulters to put pressure on them to pay. This is followed by a consideration of any problems that the members bring up, such as loan regulations or plans for some project, and is accompanied or followed by the serving of refreshments, which always include palm-wine, and which are considered by many to be the most interesting part of the meeting. The refreshments were at one time served without regard to age, but owing to the objections of some of the older members, it is now done according to the traditional system of age-set seniority. The meeting is concluded by the oldest man present giving the traditional Afikpo blessing.

The annual meeting, which is held during the Christmas season, is similar in form, though the attendance is larger, members wear good cloths or European clothes, and there is more feasting. Loans are the major topic of interest. At the 1952 annual meeting seventy-three loans of £1 each were made, the sum representing almost the total working capital of the Union; nearly every member received a loan. Sometimes a few members pool their loans and lend the total to one member for the year to help him get started in business or to bring some other major project into operation. At the annual meeting scholarships for Mgbom boys are sometimes discussed, but matters not directly concerned with finance are rarely brought forward.

The activities and interests of the Union since its inception are as follows:

LOANS. A loan system has been developed to make money accessible for trade, farming, title-taking, and other activities. This augments the traditional system of informal loans between friends and relatives, and avoids one disadvantage of the latter, which may involve obligatory deferential behaviour on the part of the borrower towards his creditor. Village elders have not shown much interest in the loan system. There seem to be other reasons for this than merely a reluctance of the older people to change. They are usually members of more title-societies than the young men, and receive a moderate, though irregular, income from this source. In addition they may have set money aside through the years and, while they may obtain only a small income from farming operations, they receive rather more from judging disputes. For these and other reasons they seem less likely to need loans than the younger men.

CONSTRUCTION. There is a strong interest in non-traditional construction activities which are often in accord with British interests in Afikpo and are likely to receive government approval. The Mgbom Union engaged in two such projects. The first was a bicycle path from Mgbom to the Afikpo market, and to build this the village elders gave the Union Executive the power to call labourers from any village age set necessary to perform the work, the project proceeding on occasional Sunday mornings under the direction of the senior working set and the Executive until it was completed. The second project was a plan, developed by the Union, to dam the stream used for village washing, bathing, and drinking-water, and to separate the drinking-water from the water for washing and bathing. When the village elders agreed to the plan they gave the Union authority to handle the matter, and arrangements were promptly made with the senior women's village age sets for women to carry rocks and sand to the site. This work was done and the Union officers are now attempting to procure cement from the Afikpo Native Authority to complete the task.

EDUCATION. In 1948 a scholarship was given to any Mgbom boy who took first, second, or third place in his class in any of the seven primary schools in Afikpo, whether his father was a Union member or not. In that year several scholarships were given, but the students did not do well, so the scholarships were discontinued, though in 1952 the Union rather reluctantly set aside £10 for a secondary school boy.[15] Except for these the

---

[15] This sum was never used, since the student obtained a larger scholarship from the village-group union.

only money put aside for educational purposes has been a donation of £3.3s. to a newly opened secondary school at Afikpo. The subject of a village school has been brought up at several meetings, but it has met opposition from those who are primarily interested in loans and who do not want the capital of the Union diverted to other uses. There is an active desire in the Union to foster education for village boys, however, and there is considerable competition among Afikpo villages to increase the schooling of their own boys in comparison with those of other villages. The villages possessing primary schools are much envied by the young men of those which do not. The Mgbom elders have shown no interest in building a local school, and in fact some of them strongly oppose it. Nevertheless, at the 1952 annual meeting the Union decided that it should attempt to raise £300 by 1957 to demonstrate to the elders that they were ready to build a school. No funds, however, have as yet been set aside.[16]

FUNERALS AND INHERITANCE. When the President died the Union paid for his coffin and most of the members attended the funeral ceremonies.[17] No other members have died, but they will probably receive similar respect. The President's death precipitated a dispute between his matriclan and his patrilineage over the inheritance of his money, and the Union came in actively on the side of the patrilineage, thereby affirming the close friendship and patrilineal ties of some of the Union members with the President and his patrilineage, as well as the fact that the patrilineage of the dead man is a local residential group while the matriclan is not. This dispute reflects a growing tendency for some of the young men to favour father–son inheritance over the traditional matrilineal pattern, a tendency which all the Union members do not agree to, and of which the village elders do not approve. The Union leaders, it may be noted, do not feel that they are committed to entering into every dispute over the property of a deceased member which might occur in the future.[18]

TRADE. One of the members of the Union lost his trade goods and his personal belongings in a storm on the Cross River, and the Union helped him by buying him a wrapping cloth worth about 30s. The influence of the traders in the Union has continued after the period when they were in control.

---

[16] The attitude towards female education is a mixed one, with some Union members favouring it, and others feeling that it is not of much value or of much use to the girls.

[17] The coffin is a new burial element of considerable prestige among some of the young men of the Union. The funeral ceremonies in Afikpo seem as a rule to be still carried out pretty much in the traditional manner.

[18] The pattern of burial assistance and of a loan organization in Afipko would seem to be akin to the widespread insurance and burial societies among the New World negroes. See Herskovits, 1941, pp. 161–7.

THEFT. Many cases of stealing of articles left at the Mgbom village washing-stream were occurring, and the Union had discussed the matter and had asked the village elders to erect a shrine at the stream to prevent further thefts of clothing, machets, and other items. The elders, however, put off the matter, and had taken no action by the time this research was terminated.[19]

RECREATION. Most members look forward to the opportunity of taking refreshments together at meetings and consider this of major importance. The abruptness with which discussions at the meetings are sometimes ended in order that refreshments may be served indicates this and some-times slows down action on the projects of the Union.

POLITICAL AMBITIONS. Certain of the more active Union members are politically ambitious and are attempting to use the association to help them gain experience and increase their social and political prestige. They feel that they have a right to a much more important place in Afikpo political life than would be traditionally open to them at their age, and that their interests today differ more from those of the elders than in traditional times. This matter will be more fully discussed below.

RELATIONS WITH OTHER ASSOCIATIONS. Informal contacts exist between the Mgbom Youth Association, an organization of all Mgbom students of both sexes, the purpose of which is helping its members do well in school, and the Mgbom Family Union officers, who give guidance to the students' group and like to consider it as a junior adjunct of their own organization. No formal ties exist between these two groups, and no combined activities occur.

A village-group union exists in Afikpo which until recently had no con-nexion with the village 'meetings', though many of the members of the latter groups take part in the village-group union. This union, called the Afikpo Town Welfare Association, decided in 1952 that it did not have an effective working organization and that a larger membership would increase its financial resources and its ability to carry out its projects. In 1953 it came to an agreement with the senior village-group elders whereby the elders of each Afikpo village that posseessed a 'meeting' should determine that all members of certain village age sets, to be designated by the village elders, should join the village 'meeting' under threat of action and fine from the village elders themselves, and that in villages where no union

---

[19] It is to be noted that the Union was willing to use a traditional religious technique, the efficacy of which some of the members did not strongly believe in, in order to prevent stealing.

existed the elders should see that the youths formed one. Such unions were to become branches of the village-group union.[20] This association of 'meetings' had not been advanced at the time of writing. In Mgbom, however, as a result of this action, the membership in the Family Union increased from about 75 to over 250 members in the first part of 1953, without causing any change in the basic organization or the interests of Union members. The Executive backed this action because they are interested in developing the local Union, and some of them and some of the general members feel that an enlarged group will help their own political ambitions. The officers are aware that this increase in size may mean shifts in policies and changes in its officers in the future.

While the Union in Mgbom is the major village focus for new activities of the young men, it does not cover all the new activities and interests that are arising. There are other new village associations, including the Mgbom Youth Association, and informal drinking clubs that are much less inclusive in organization and activities than the Union. Certain new interests are related to traditional social groupings: thus the changing attitudes of some of the young men with regard to the duties and the place of their wives in the family are directed towards attempts to modify kinship and family behaviour. Other new interests, as in new forms of dress, do not seem to be specifically related to any one organization or social group, while others, such as those in church and sports, are cared for by new groups on the village-group or other levels broader than the village. Certain interests and activities of the Mgbom Family Union are also the concern of the village-group union, which will be discussed below.

CHARACTER AND PROCEDURE OF THE MGBOM FAMILY UNION. It is apparent that a conflict exists within the Mgbom Family Union as to its primary purpose, which, together with the increase in new members, gives the Union a certain instability at the present time. Most members favour the loan system, but a minority, including some of the Executive, feels that in addition the political cause of the young men of Mgbom should be advanced and that the Union should strongly stress educational and construction activities and back them with financial contributions. Those favouring loans have acted as a check on Union actions requiring an outlay of capital, but have co-operated in village projects needing little or no money, such as the construction of the market path. The Union's few educated men appear to favour the broader programme, but the new members, most of whom are without schooling, are more concerned with loans than with these other activities and are likely to swing the interests more towards loans than before.

---

[20] The Afikpo elders seems to feel that a widespread organization of unions will help them to maintain their position of authority in the village-group.

The Union shows an interesting fusion of traditional and new procedures. The latter include the holding of meetings on Sundays, offices patterned after European models, the existence of a constitution, and the keeping of record books. Traditional procedures include the use of Ibo in meetings, the use of a closing blessing, and respect for age in seating. Certain others show a blend of new and traditional practices, such as the method of reaching decisions.[21] The only conflict between the traditional and the new procedures occurred in the matter of the order of serving refreshments at meetings, and this was quickly settled. Space does not permit a detailed examination of the reasons why certain new procedures have been accepted and others rejected, but it may be stated that the new procedures, such as the holding of meetings on Sundays instead of on the more traditional major market day (every fourth day), do not strongly conflict with traditional methods. For, in the traditional manner, there is no restriction on holding meetings on other days, the day chosen being one convenient to those concerned. Hence, since some of the members hold jobs on a European work schedule and can best gather on a Sunday, the Union has adopted this day for its meetings and work activities. Some of the new procedures have come to be held in high esteem by the young men. For example, the keeping of written financial records has proved so popular that today even traditional village organizations will enlist the aid of a literate village boy to help keep their financial accounts. It is difficult to show precisely where the new procedural techniques, activities, and interests originated. Some came through individuals who had traded or lived in other parts of West Africa, some from strangers living in Mgbom or in other areas of Afikpo, some from the activities of the village-group union, and some from the schools. The origins are varied and do not derive from any single source.

While the Mgbom Union has initiated non-traditional projects, the village executive age grade, *ukɛkpe*, has not. The Union must consider the authority of the village elders, and any major project started without their approval would probably fail, since they control the allocation of village age-set work groups and since dissension with them would be likely to lead to interference by the elders in other Union activities. Thus the cycle path, the dam, and the school all required this consent; in the case of the first two it was given and the projects are under way, but the school has not been approved, and the Union will probably have difficulty in constructing

---

[21] The traditional method is informal discussion until a consensus is reached, with the discussion led and dominated by the older men who are taking part. In the Union age does not have so much weight. Informal discussion until consensus is reached also occurs, the discussion being guided by the Executive, even though a few older men are usually present. The Executive's views, as previously noted, are frequently not agreed to by the rest of the members and thus the checks exercised on the Executive are stronger than those exercised by young men on older ones at more traditional gatherings.

it by itself, even if the members are unanimous in their desire to do so. They have, however, at no time seriously opposed the elders, but rather prefer to seek their co-operation by persuasion, even though the elders are sometimes slow in deciding matters brought before them, as in the case of erecting a shrine to prevent theft at the village stream. It is, however, quite traditional for the elders not to make an immediate decision on a project, so that delay in approval does not necessarily imply disapproval. While the elders may oppose some of the projects of the Union, they do not appear to be antagonistic towards the Union itself; their position has been rather one of indifference. It might be surmised that the leaders would be concerned with the financial affairs of the Union, but this has not been the case, probably because their traditional rights to shares are not involved, as they are, for example, in the control of the village palm-grove by the executive age grade.

Other Afikpo village 'meetings' are, in general, not as well organized as the Mgbom Union, though they exhibit similar characteristics. In Amamgballa village there is an active 'meeting' concerned almost exclusively with loans. Ugwuagu has a 'meeting' concerned with both loans and scholarships. In another village a 'meeting' formerly existed, but the treasurer obtained a job away from home and left, taking £10 in 'meeting' funds with him, and the members have refused to pay any more dues until the money has been repaid. Ukpa has no village 'meeting', but its largest compound, larger in numbers than some of the smaller Afikpo villages, has an active one which is the only example of an Afikpo compound 'meeting'. All compound men not elders belong to it and it has regular officers. It makes loans to its members up to £2 annually, and has given several scholarships to boys from the compound. It performs two functions that the Mgbom Union does not: it makes loans of more than £2 for marriage purposes and collects funds for compound projects from the compound members as a whole.

Slightly more than half of the Afikpo villages have no 'meetings'. As might be expected, the villages having them are those which had early contacts with the British, as well as those which are today close to the Afikpo Government Station. None of the 'meetings' is more than seven years old. There is no record of different village 'meetings' having attempted to work together for any purpose. None possesses a shrine, commonly found in traditional Afikpo social groupings, or has a religious ritual other than giving blessings at meetings, which is commonly done in most traditional meetings in Afikpo. No costumes and dances are associated with the 'meetings' and they do not carry out judicial activities.

REASONS FOR THE DEVELOPMENT OF VILLAGE 'MEETINGS'. One might ask why the 'meetings' in Afikpo villages developed at all. Why were the new interests of the young men not dealt with through traditional organizations or by altering traditional groupings? It is clear, first of all, that in some villages the young men interested in change and in the loan system formed such a small minority that they could not hope to dominate *ukɛkpe*, the village executive organization. Again, assuming that in some villages they could influence this age grade, the grade represents only certain sets in the village, and to broaden its membership to include other ages might cause confusion as to who should be responsible within the grouping for carrying out its traditional functions.[22] A third factor is that some of the young men fear that if they attempted to work through *ukɛkpe*, the elders would apply to them their traditional controls, and attempt to dominate the loan system, expecting rewards from it. The various Afikpo title societies do not seem interested in forming themselves into loan societies as some of them have done among the Mba-Ise Ibo to the west.[23] The reasons why this has not occurred in Afikpo are not quite clear, though the predominance within many of these societies of elders who are not particularly interested in a loan system is a factor; the small size of some Afikpo title societies and the widespread distribution of members of some societies throughout Afikpo are probably also factors. The village men's secret society, *ogo*, is a most unlikely organization for these young men interested in loans to use because of its concern with some of the most conservative (and secret) aspects of Afikpo culture.

Another factor in the development of these associations is related to the attitude of the older and younger men towards one another. The introduction of 'meetings' is an attempt, whether consciously made or not, on the part of many of the men interested in change to increase their authority and prestige in the village, authority and prestige that they claim belong to them because they believe that they understand and can handle changing conditions, which they feel that the elders do not understand and therefore cannot adequately deal with. The elders consider these young men to be 'small boys' lacking the necessary experience and maturity to handle such matters. They are sure that they can very well take care of whatever new problems arise in their own way. Nevertheless, the elders today admit a kind of dependence on some of the younger men *as individuals* in dealing with conditions that did not exist before, which probably

---

[22] In certain villages lacking unions non-traditional construction activities are sometimes advocated by the young men as an informal group who convince the elders of the desirability of the project. The elders then appoint certain younger age sets, or *ukɛkpe*, to direct the project. This alternative solution for new projects has the disadvantage that the groupings of young men are only temporary and must be reformed for every new project to be advocated, and that such groupings are too informal to act as a loan society. Nevertheless, it is out of such informal groupings that many of the village 'meetings' undoubtedly arose. There is no record of an *ukɛkpe* grade ever forming a loan system.

[23] Cf. Ardener, 1953, p. 133.

reflects a change in the former status of such younger men.[24] This is well illustrated by the manner in which educated young men, especially those who have contacts in the British Administration at Afikpo, are constantly being consulted by the elders on the best means of dealing with matters that the elders want presented to or kept secret from the Administration, as well as on various Native Authority Court procedures.

None the less, though the prestige position of specific individuals is changing, the village elders still firmly guide and control the activities of the executive age grade, so that for young men interested in change to attempt to work through *ukɛkpe* is to risk challenging the authority of the elders. The Afikpo men of the 20 to 45 year-old age group who have developed new interests still have a strong pattern of respect for the elders and do not desire to become involved in conflict with them. What these younger men wish is to increase their prestige and their freedom of action without antagonizing the elders. It is thus more satisfactory for these young men to form separate organizations which quietly concern themselves with financial matters such as loans or scholarships and which work with the elders on certain construction projects, while at the same time propagandizing, largely along traditional lines, for other projects towards which the elders are less favourably inclined, such as the building of schools in certain villages. In this way they hope over a period of time to persuade the elders to endorse projects which they oppose at present. To this end the 'meeting' serves as a method not only of promoting new activities but also of institutionalizing and giving recognition to these young men as a group—a recognition that until the formation of the 'meetings' the village elders were only willing to grant on an individual basis.

The economic aspects of the 'meeting' are very important because the collection of money and the system of loans form a focal activity which stimulates the local economy, makes possible improvement projects of the 'meetings' and, in addition, attracts and holds people to these associations. The system of loans serves as a means by which individual wealth, and the prestige associated with it, may be acquired through the skilful use of borrowed money. This loan system has not as yet become such an integral part of the local economy as it has in the Mba-Ise area to the west.[25] This is probably because at Afikpo, unlike Mba-Ise, farm-land is still relatively easy to obtain, and the population is less dependent upon non-farming economic activities, particularly trading, for meeting their subsistence needs.

---

[24] Before the arrival of the British the elders, like everyone else, were dependent on the young men for physical protection and for conducting warfare. This activity gradually ceased after the British settled in Afikpo, apparently causing a decrease in the importance of the young men in village activities involving matters of authority.

[25] Ardener, 1953, contains an interesting description of the place of unions, primarily of an economic kind, in the total economy of the Mba-Ise Ibo people south-west of Okigwi.

In the Afikpo 'meetings' the amount of money loaned to any one individual is smaller, the interest-rates on loans are lower, and there seem to be fewer people desiring loans than among the Mba-Ise 'Contribution Clubs'. In view of the steadily increasing cost of living at Afikpo, the increase in non-agricultural population due to the development of the area as an administrative and educational centre, and the migration of young Afikpo people to other areas which makes necessary the hiring of foreign farm labourers in increasing numbers at increasing wage-rates, it is possible that the loan system will assume greater importance in the economy in the future, though it will probably have its economic base in a combination of farming, fishing, trading, and salaried positions, rather than primarily in the trading of palm products, as it seems to do at Mba-Ise.

## Village-Group Organization

In order to understand the rise of the village-group union certain facts concerning this group of villages should be understood. While traditionally the ɔtɔsi shrine-holders played an important part in Afikpo,[26] today lineage authority in matters of the village-group as a whole is minor. The major authority on the village-group level in recent times has been the village-group age grades, secondarily the Afikpo Native Authority Court, while in the last few years the Afikpo Native Authority Council has also begun to play a significant role.

There are three men's village-group age grades composed of twelve village-group age sets. A village-group set is made up of a grouping of single sets from each village of men of roughly equivalent age. The junior village-group grade consists of men in their fifties and early sixties, is called ɛkpuke ɛto (age set three), and is composed of three village-group sets. The middle grade, consisting of six village-group sets, is named ɛkpuke ɛsa.[27] Above this three further village-group age sets combine into a grade called ɔni ɛkara, in which there were only ten surviving members in 1952. There is also a residual classification of men older than ɔni ɛkara called hɔri, which in 1952 contained only one very old man. Since hɔri has little functional importance it will not be further considered.

These three village-group age grades, which include almost all the Afikpo elders, are the source of much of the social and political authority on the village-group level. Each grade has its own shelter in the Afikpo market-place where its members can come and sit and where it meets on market day, every fourth day, and each has its place to sit at ɔkpo·ta, the traditional Afikpo meeting-place, where the age grades meet to discuss Afikpo affairs whenever the need arises. Each grade has specific duties

---

[26] See page 94, footnote 6.

[27] Although ɛsa means 'seven' the grade consists of only six sets.

and activities, though ɔni ɛkara, the senior grade, takes part in village-group activities only occasionally, as its few members are frequently too old or too ill to be active. When men of this grade are present, however, they are given every opportunity to speak their minds and to take part in judgements, and their advice and knowledge are highly respected. The major responsibility for making village-group decisions, such as regulations concerning marriage procedure and market rulings, falls on ɛkpuke ɛsa, the middle grade. This grade formerly acted as a judicial body for the village-group, deciding matters which the villages, lineages, or individuals were unable to settle. However, the Afikpo Native Authority Court has taken over most of these judicial functions, and the grade therefore acts mainly as a pre-judicial advisory body. The junior grade, ɛkpuke ɛtɔ, enforces the decisions made by the three grades together, as well as those made by the middle grade alone. It sees that peace is kept in the Afikpo market and it intervenes in the initial stages of disputes and difficulties in which the village-group as a whole is likely to be involved. At joint meetings of all three grades its opinions do not usually carry as much weight as those of the two older grades, but its dissent from a decision passed by the older grades must be carefully considered. It may be recalled that these three grades, in their own particular villages, usually constitute the ruling elders—the Ndiciɛ.

The Native Authority Court consisted, at the time of this field research, of eighteen men, sitting in panels of nine each month, one judge being chosen by each village (certain of the smaller villages being grouped for this purpose). Most of the Court members belong to the village-group grades, and in their decisions strongly favour traditional views, though these are sometimes reversed in the Administration's courts of review. The Court, in general, acts as the judicial arm of the village-group age grades.

Several large Afikpo Native Authority councils existed until 1948, when a smaller council, consisting of one member elected from each Afikpo village, was organized under the British Administration. This group functioned until 1952, when new elections produced a council of almost completely new members. The council is a major channel through which working contacts between the District Office and the Afikpo people are maintained. The 1948–52 council was dominated by educated and 'progressive' men, its successor by men of more traditional orientation. Since 1948 these councils have taken some legislative action, have stimulated road building and other construction projects, and have passed a number of health regulations. They have also attempted to resolve a number of disputes in Afikpo: one concerning the social position of slaves, and another concerning the killing of children whose births are considered 'unnatural'. In certain of these disputes the council dominated by 'progressive' members showed considerable differences of viewpoint from the opinions of the village-group elders, the council often favouring non-traditional points of view. Up to the present, the councils have held an insecure position in Afikpo, though they are a potentially strong authority. They have had only limited legislative powers and they have not been regarded with real respect by the village-group elders.

While there are several village-group shrines, Afikpo religious authority is mainly based on smaller units, particularly village and lineage groups. A yam priest for all of Afikpo exists but he does not take an active part in social and political affairs other than those concerned with the ritual regulation of the farming seasons.

## The Village-Group Unions

With this background we now turn to the development of the village-group union, called the Afikpo Town Welfare Association. During the five years prior to 1950 several attempts were made to form an active village-group union in Afikpo, but owing to lack of interest none of these attempts was successful, though since the 1930's Afikpo communities in various Nigerian cities had formed local unions varying from informal organizations to highly structured groups. For some years prior to 1950 a union, called the Federal Afikpo District Union, which claimed to be an association of all village-groups in Afikpo Division, was in existence. This union had a definite organization, and had at one time collected over £100 in dues and donations. It was dominated by Afikpo and Unwana village-groups, the two most advanced in European contacts and education in Afikpo Division at that time, and this, coupled with the lack of interest on the part of certain other village-groups, led to its gradual dissolution. No divisional union exists today.

The establishment of the Afikpo Town Welfare Association (hereafter abbreviated to ATWA) resulted from the mass arrest of a group of Afikpo fishermen at Umon on the Cross River, as a result of a dispute with the local Umon people over fishing rights. An educated Afikpo man working at a trade-union post in Aba, who had travelled widely in the course of his work and was in contact with many Afikpo communities outside Afikpo, realized the need for a protective union to aid Afikpo people living and working abroad. At his own expense he had 400 membership cards printed to organize Afikpo people at Umon and other Afikpo traders and fishermen, naming the organization the Afikpo Fishermen and Traders Association. In March 1950, at the first general meeting, the name was changed to the present Afikpo Town Welfare Association, since it was felt by most of those present that it would be better to have one union representing all Afikpo people at home and abroad.[28]

---

[28] The Afikpo village-group is frequently called 'Afikpo town' by strangers and educated Afikpo people. The Union dispute was not finally settled by ATWA, but by Government agencies.

At this meeting an Executive, consisting of a President, Vice-President, Financial Secretary, Treasurer, Honourable Under-Secretary, General Secretary, and two Auditors, was selected; the rate for dues was decided upon; a plan was made for the first annual meeting in December 1950; and the general aims and possible activities of the union were discussed. The Executive and most of the initial membership were young educated and uneducated English-speaking men, though a considerable number of uneducated and non-English-speaking traders, farmers, and fishermen, as well as a number of older uneducated Afikpo politicians and leaders who belonged to the village-group age grades, and who were interested in 'progressive' activities, also participated. The man selected as President belonged to *ekpuke etɔ*, the youngest village-group age grade, and had done considerable travelling in Nigeria, though he lived at Afikpo. He, in general, approved of the traditional point of view of the village-group grades, and his selection helped to make possible good working contacts of ATWA with the village-group grades. The bulk of the administrative work fell to the General Secretary, to which post the founder had been elected. Contacts were soon made with groups and unions in other parts of Nigeria that had not already taken part in the initial meeting, and most of the Afikpo communities away from home rapidly joined as branch unions. The development of ATWA was stimulated by a tour of these branches in April, May, and June of 1950 by the General Secretary and other Executive members.[29]

The first annual meeting, held at the Afikpo Native Authority Court Hall in December 1950, gave the organization a solid basis on which to function. At this meeting, attended by about fifty people, the office of Honourable Under-Secretary was changed to that of Permanent Under-Secretary, who became the only paid officer at a salary of £36 per annum. He cared for correspondence, checked all records, co-ordinated all ATWA functions, and kept contact with the branch unions. His duties were not precisely agreed upon or written down, nor were the duties of the other officers. The President presided over all ATWA meetings and saw to it that the work of the union was properly done, the Vice-President assisted and acted for the President when necessary, the Financial Secretary collected and distributed funds, the Treasurer banked and cared for the funds collected, the money being kept in an African bank in Aba, and the Auditors kept a check on the financial records. The General Secretary was responsible for organizing activities, keeping good working relations with all members, initiating new policies, and guiding the Executive. At their first meeting, the Executive appointed six Members-at-Large, whose title at the 1952 annual meeting was changed to Publicity Members, having the duty of increasing membership as much as possible. A local trader, a

---

[29] Afikpo Town Welfare Association, 1951, pp. 11–13.

member of the Executive, donated a room in his store as an office, and plans for a permanent office building were made, though because of lack of funds this had not been built at the time of writing.

At the first annual meeting it was decided that the initial membership fee should be 5s. 6d., with an annual fee of 2s., and that special rates should be established for branches, depending upon the size of their membership. It was also suggested that every Afikpo village should pay £1 as annual membership fee, but this proposal was never carried out. Elections were to be held every year, except for the post of Permanent Under-Secretary, and the Executive formed itself into a committee to prepare a constitution.[30] By the time of the first annual meeting over £280 had been collected in dues and donations. From the beginning a heavy emphasis was placed on the collection of voluntary contributions, and these were received from most of the branches, reflecting their relative wealth as compared to the home branch.[31]

During 1950 a principal source of income, which in 1951 and part of 1952 was to form almost half the total, was money derived from the tax rebate. In Afikpo each tax collector was permitted by the British Administration to keep 5 per cent. of the tax collected in lieu of a salary. It had become the Afikpo custom for the money to be 'shared among the Tax Payers or in some areas among the Village Elders'.[32] However, in 1950 the Afikpo Native Authority Council, many of whose members were also active in ATWA, decided that this money should be set aside for development, education, and general welfare purposes, and delegated its expenditure to ATWA. The village-group elders did not care for this arrangement, involving about £100 a year, but they were undecided at the time as to what action to take about it. In 1952, however, the new council, which, as has been stated, represented a more traditional point of view, agreed to the elders' demands that the tax-rebate system should revert to its earlier form. At this time, however, the British Administration took a firm stand, ruling that the money belonged to the tax collectors for the work that they had done, and since then it has gone to them, though in some villages the collectors have been forced to turn their money over to the village elders. Early in 1953, in order to offset this loss of almost half its annual income, the Association decided to initiate a village-to-village campaign within Afikpo to

---

[30] They failed to prepare it, and at the 1951 annual meeting a committee of four was appointed to write one. Their version has been printed, though it has not yet been accepted by the membership as a whole. See Afikpo Town Welfare Association, 1952a.

[31] Receipts for 1950 show collections of £16.11s. for the home branch and over £180 for 19 other branches, e.g. Abakaliki, Aba, Enugu, Onitsha, Port Harcourt, Obubra, Obudu, Oron, Aro Chuku, Calabar, Adiabo, Calabar/Mamfe Road Camp, Ikot Okoro (Abak), Makurdi, Jos, Zaria, Ife, Ibadan, and Lagos, Afikpo Town Welfare Association, 1951, p. 22.

[32] Ibid., p. 13.

obtain new members, and an agreement was reached with the village-group elders to make all young men of certain age sets in each village join their village unions or create such unions, and for these unions to become local branches of ATWA, as has been indicated.[33] The success of this plan is as yet uncertain; however, some means of increasing the Association's income is necessary if it is to carry out an active programme.

The annual meetings are held during the Christmas season, when the farming and fishing activities are not extensive and many men are home on leave from salaried positions. The meeting, which is conducted in Ibo and lasts two days, is called to order by the President, after which a roll-call of the branches is taken by the General Secretary or the Permanent Under-Secretary. The oldest man present rises and recites the traditional Afikpo opening prayer. The General Secretary then reads long, flowery, enthusiastic, and hortatory goodwill messages from various individuals and branches. The minutes of the previous annual meeting, which are printed and distributed previous to the meeting, are next discussed and accepted. This is followed by the report of the year's activities by the General Secretary, and the Financial Secretary's report, to which the Auditors usually add comments.[34] There is then a discussion of activities and plans, after which elections take place according to parliamentary procedure with voting by show of hands, and the meeting closes. If guest speakers are invited, they speak early in the programme. The meeting is held at the Afikpo Native Authority Court, a central place, though the members gather and the opening prayer is pronounced at the traditional meeting-place of the village-group grades a short distance away. Entertainment and feasting take place in the evening, frequently at the Executive members' houses. Careful attention is paid to the proper hospitality towards branch members, for which purpose union funds are set aside by the Executive.

The Executive meets as often as it feels it necessary, usually at the President's house, and these gatherings are more informal than the annual meetings. This body takes considerable initiative, often preferring not to wait for the sometimes cumbersome annual meeting to make decisions.[35] At times the Executive calls an emergency general meeting to discuss an issue it prefers not to decide itself, such as the question of whether to send

---

[33] See pp. 101–102 above.

[34] There is suspicion among some members as to the accuracy of financial reports. In the more traditional manner of handling money large sums controlled by a group are not usually handled by one or a few representatives, but are divided among the members for safe keeping.

[35] In the more traditional way, the village-group age grades or the village elders, when involved in a matter, frequently discuss it at several meetings over a period of weeks or even months before a decision is reached. With ATWA the items on the agenda must be presented, discussed, and decided upon in one general meeting, or put off until next year's annual meeting, discussed at a special general meeting, or left for the Executive to decide by itself.

delegates to the Conference on the New Igbo Orthography at Aba in 1952. It also arranges meetings of its group with the village-group grades at ɔkpoˑta, the traditional age-grade meeting-place, to discuss matters of common concern. For example, a meeting was held there with the elders to discuss the tax-rebate system. In addition it appoints committees for special purposes, as it did with regard to certain branch disputes (see below).

The Executive decides when to hold receptions and send-offs for prominent local people, for delegates from other organizations, and for distinguished visitors, and establishes programme committees and authorizes expenditure for entertainment. It can appoint touring committees for special purposes, as it did in 1950. However, the heavy expenditures of this committee and the subsequent decline in available funds have prevented further tours.[36]

The original members of the Executive remained in office by re-election until the third annual convention (1952), when only four officers were returned. At the time of this meeting the total membership was estimated to be over 200, but this included many who were in arrears in their dues, and it is more likely that the active effective membership was not over seventy-five. Almost all of the educated and English-speaking men living in Afikpo are members, as well as many educated Afikpo people living elsewhere. Membership cards are used. Women are permitted to join, and some of the small number of educated women have done so. Membership is open to strangers who have resided in Afikpo for a long while, though there are only a few such members and they are not in a position to dominate policy.

The union has no well-formed cliques representing special interests, though there is a division of membership into a small minority group, some of whom are educated, interested in 'improvement' but desirous of continuing to recognize the authority of the village-group grades, and a majority group, greatly interested in 'improvement', who do not particularly desire this age-grade leadership. Though this division has caused some friction and political manœuvring it has never caused a serious split within the union. Village or sub-village-group cliques, so common in traditional politics, have not found a place in ATWA, possibly because matters affecting single villages or groups of villages within the village-group rarely come to the union for action.

ATWA has not attempted to dictate the organizational structure and functions of its branches, which vary from occasional informal gatherings to well-formed groups who sponsor loans, engage in welfare activities, and aid in funerals. Members of branch unions who come to the annual meeting hold full voting rights as individuals, though such persons do not

---

[36] Afikpo Town Welfare Association, 1951, p. 7; 1952b, p. 4.

formally represent their branches unless they have been specifically instructed by them to do so. Members living in Afikpo come as individuals and do not represent their villages. There are no important groups of Afikpo people living away from home who have failed to join the union, though some of them have defaulted in payment of their dues.

The activities of ATWA since its inception clearly indicate the kind and diversity of interests with which this association is concerned.

CASES INVOLVING BRANCH UNIONS. In 1950 a dispute arose among Afikpo people at Adiabo, near Calabar, over the question of whether the local union should pay the funeral expenses of two deceased Mgbom village men or whether the Mgbom people should pay the required amount. At the same time a series of disputes over house rentals, over the use of the local union's funds, and over sexual violations, developed among the Afikpo people living at a Calabar–Mamfe Road work camp. In both cases the local groups were unable to reach satisfactory settlements and called on the newly formed ATWA to adjudicate the matter. In May 1950 the Executive sent three of its members and an unschooled but literate political leader of the village-group age grade ɛkpuke ɛtɔ, and temporary settlements were effected. In 1951 the Permanent Under-Secretary helped to initiate activities to secure a debt settlement in the Aba branch. Since 1951 several branch unions have asked for aid in resolving local or internal differences. However, the Executive has turned down all these requests, since the cost of sending out committees is heavy and the local branches concerned have refused to help defray the costs.

WORK PROJECTS. The union stimulated interest in rebuilding the main Afikpo market, a project later taken over by the Afikpo Divisional Authority Council. They were active in interesting people in work on a road to a nearby Cross River factory and proposed the construction of several cycle tracks within the village-group area. Their position with regard to work projects has been to stimulate projects rather than to execute them themselves.

MORAL ISSUES. The union, by resolution at its first annual meeting, condemned the pecuniary activities of the agents of an Ibo 'oracle' from the Owerri area. Some of the members took part as individuals in attempting to end the agents' practices by legal means, but most of the controversy over the 'oracle' had ended by the time the Association was firmly founded, and it took no further action in the matter. The members of ATWA, on the whole, seem to be suspicious of any activities of a religious or ritual kind which involve large outlays of money to any one priest or religious representative, and the controversy over the Owerri 'oracle' helped to draw people of this mind into the union during its formative period. The major moral issue involving the union grew out of a decision by the Executive that it was immoral for physically mature unmarried girls to wear only strings of beads around the hips in public. (Nudity or wearing only beads is equated with chastity and the unmarried state, cloths being reserved for married women in the more traditional Afikpo culture.) The Executive, however, felt that they possessed no authority to give a ruling for the whole village group. They could not turn to the village-group elders, since the elders follow the belief that girls who wear cloths are pregnant and are trying to hide their condition. The Executive therefore turned to the Afikpo Native Authority Council, many of whose members were also members of ATWA. The Council, however, felt that it had authority only to present the matter in the form of an appeal, which it did. This was supplemented by the Councillors and Executive circulating rumours that girls who went unclothed in the Government Station area would be arrested by the police, while the members of the Council and of ATWA made it a point publicly to ridicule girls who did not respond to their appeals. The campaign, really directed at the parents and future husbands of the girls, was on the whole successful. This incident illustrates the active interest of certain ATWA members in what seems to them to be one of the main points of European morality. In this particular case the ATWA members acted as an informal group representing a particular point of view when they could not reach their objective by working through their union.

TRADE. In 1952 a small group of Afikpo traders, most of whom traded on the Cross River, formed a union without a definite set of officers, regulations, or a constitution, but with a recognized leader. They proposed a set of trading rules, centring around non-competition and mutual aid, which they hoped to apply to all Afikpo traders. This group in 1952, and again in 1953, asked the ATWA Executive to help them enforce their regulations. Though the Afikpo elders had approved these rules the traders' union included only a small minority of Afikpo traders, and it was questionable whether the elders or ATWA could exert authority over the rest, especially those away from home. The Executive suggested that all traders should organize, or that they should all join ATWA, but that until one or other of these things was done there was little that could be done to enforce their regulations.

EDUCATIONAL ACTIVITIES. At its first annual meeting ATWA unanimously agreed to award in 1952 a scholarship to study law overseas, but this was not done because of insufficient funds. At the 1952 annual meeting it was agreed that three scholarships, renewable each year, should be given to three Afikpo boys who had passed the entrance requirements to the new Government Secondary School at Afikpo. The cost to ATWA will be about £90 a year, almost equal to its present income. Because of this heavy commitment it must either expand its income or limit its activities in the coming years. The desire for education in Afikpo is strong and some ATWA members feel that scholarships should be the primary purpose of the union.

DISPUTE BETWEEN THE AFIKPO COUNCIL AND ELDERS. During 1950–2, the Afikpo Native Authority Council became involved in a series of disputes with the village-group age grades, notably *ɛkpuke ɛtɔ*, the executive grouping. The age grades felt that the Council was usurping their authority and that it did not represent the real attitudes of the Afikpo people. The Councillors, in turn, believed that changing conditions favoured new kinds of action. The dispute crystallized around the proper punitive action to be taken following the shooting, in 1951, of a Native Authority messenger by a bandit in the presence of the Council while it was in session, something that resulted in a series of fines being imposed on the Councillors by the age grades. Some Councillors objected to any sort of fine, and some claimed that a group fine, rather than individual fines, was proper, and many Councillors refused to pay. The dispute seriously interfered with the usual activities of the Council and of the village-group grades during 1951 and part of 1952. At the 1951 annual meeting of ATWA the membership appointed a committee of thirteen to reconcile the two groups, including five members representing Afikpo interests away from home, a person to act as spokesman, and another to record the proceedings. After two preliminary meetings with some of the Afikpo elders a general meeting was arranged by the committee of all those interested or involved, and at this gathering, held at the traditional Afikpo age-grade meeting-ground, both sides presented their case. Somewhat later the committee formulated a complex decision, which in the main favoured the age grades.[37] The decision was not backed by powers of enforcement, and left both sides dissatisfied. The dispute passed into obscurity in 1953, by which time most of the Councillors had paid their fines and a new Council had been elected. ATWA's action brought it publicity, indicated its interest in village-group affairs, its willingness to arbitrate between factions for the sake of maintaining harmony within the community, and helped to establish it, as well as the Native Authority Court, the age grades, and the Council, as a group concerned with village-group matters.

RECEPTIONS AND SEND-OFFS. ATWA gave send-offs to two Executive members who went to England to study, and held receptions for them upon their return. It also made loans to them to help them purchase equip-

---

[37] Since both the Council and ATWA at that time represented persons holding predominantly 'progressive' viewpoints, one might have expected that ATWA's committee would favour the Council. However, personality factors, strong social pressures, as well as other considerations entered into the judgement. Afikpo Town Welfare Association, 1952b, pp. 30–38.

ment for their travels. In 1950 it gave receptions to delegates of the Ibo State Union, the large association claiming to embrace all Ibo-speaking peoples, and the Executive authorized ATWA's enrolment in the Union. It does not appear, however, that close working relations between ATWA and this Union developed.

The members of ATWA feel strongly that they should honour important people by special ceremonies, and that failure to do so would be a sign of backwardness and lack of interest in the outside world. The ceremonies are usually elaborate and lengthy evening affairs, frequently including a Master of Ceremonies, a Chairman, Sub-Chairman, Supporters, and Invitees, and the presentation of toasts and testimonials, often with gifts, as well as eating, drinking, and rejoicing.

DELEGATES TO CONFERENCES. At an emergency general meeting to which all local school teachers of both sexes were invited and to which four women teachers came, two delegates were selected to go, at ATWA's expense, to the Conference on the New Igbo Orthography held at Aba on 23 August 1952. It was decided at this emergency meeting that the new orthography was preferable to the old one for the Afikpo dialect, and the delegates, who were both Afikpo teachers, one of them a woman, were instructed to keep this in mind when they went to Aba.

OTHER ACTIVITIES. No funeral activities are associated with the union. No regular system of loans exists, such as is found in the village unions, and the only loans made were to the two scholars who went to England. Judicial activities are absent, and the union has not organized dances or traditional Afikpo plays. The group has no religious shrines.

The union's activities are thus not concentrated in any one field. It has no broad plan of future action, but meets each situation as it arises. It seems to lack a central goal and a major focus of activity, and no one specific activity exemplifies its existence. It is really the nature of the activity which serves as a focus—activity of a non-traditional kind, often associated with certain European attitudes, which possess high value for its members. ATWA does not exhibit an orientation of complete rejection of traditional behaviour and does not claim that all things traditional are 'bad' *per se*.

The union is beset with certain basic organizational difficulties at the present time, which are, perhaps, partly due to its recent origin and to the fact that some of its members are not familiar with the European organizational procedures it is attempting to adopt. There is a lack of confidence in the union due to the suspicion of some of the members as to the accuracy of the financial reports, a lack of adequate finances, at the moment, for extensive improvement activities, and there is the failure of annual meetings to cover all the points placed on the agenda by the Executive. In addition, the relationship of the branches to the whole organization is still being worked out. While the branches have played a vital role in the union's development, and their numerical superiority and their financial and social backing have helped to maintain it, they do not dominate it, since the Executive, the group most active in initiating policy, is mainly composed of people living in Afikpo. This active interest and financial support of the branches which characterized the period of the formation of the union seem to have slackened and some branches appear to be losing interest and contact with the home branch. In addition the union has yet to work out a satisfactory system of financing the settling of disputes within its branches.

While the union has had little contact so far with large-scale tribal or divisional unions or with Nigerian political parties, it is likely that, as more educated and 'improvement-minded' people arise in Afikpo, and as these large unions and parties reach farther out from the more highly acculturated areas, such contacts will become frequent.[38]

ATWA has adopted the role, limited by financial considerations, of arbitrator for Afikpo people living in other parts of Nigeria. Groups of labourers, traders, and fishermen are frequently suspicious of the existing tribal or colonial authorities where they live, since these are controlled by strangers, who often speak a different language or dialect, so that some of the normal social, political, and religious sanctions of Afikpo are difficult to maintain. The frequent absence of elders, who at home effect settlements, tends to make disputes linger on. Under these circumstances it is not surprising that these groups appeal to ATWA to arbitrate for them. Since these groups usually contain people from various Afikpo villages they are not likely to appeal to any one village union or organization to settle disputes. It does not appear to be customary to call village-group elders to settle disputes in these distant communities. Such communities were apparently non-existent in pre-British times, so that no such precedent developed. In addition some members of these groups away from home feel that the elders would not fully understand the conditions and problems of living in a strange environment and therefore would not judge them well.

ATWA is finding a place for itself within the village-group. At present, because of the gradual change of Afikpo governmental forms from those that were traditional in orientation to others more in accord with British local government systems, considerable confusion exists in the minds of both the educated and uneducated, whether traditionally or 'progressively' oriented, as to the exact functions and sphere of influence of the local British Administration, of the Native Authority Council and Court, and of the village-group age grades. There is no longer certainty as to who has legitimate authority to pass certain rules, whose authority should be

---

[38] Although no detailed analyses of larger Ibo unions have been published the following are of value: Coleman, 1952; Comhaire-Sylvain, 1950; Lord Hailey, 1951, pp. 18–20; Ibo State Union, 1951; Leith-Ross, 1939, pp. 248–9; Offodile, 1947; and Offonry, 1951.

respected in specific cases, and whose can be neglected. Persons with different concerns naturally tend to interpret the value of various authorities in terms of their own interests. In consequence of this change in the system of authority ATWA has had the opportunity to step in as an arbitrator and a potential authority in its own right, and its attempts in this direction, as well as the kinds of problems it raises in terms of specific actions, are clearly indicated in the case of the dispute between the Native Authority Council and the village-group elders, in the case of the traders' union, and in the issue of the unclothed girls.

## Other Modern Associations

In addition to the associations that have been considered, there are other non-traditional Afikpo associations which merit brief description. Between 1947 and 1951 a women's union, called *ovu ɛjo*,[39] existed in the area, drawing its members from various villages. It had no officers, though its one literate member kept its financial records. These women wore Yoruba cloths as well as the Yoruba head-tie. They considered themselves more 'civilized' than other Afikpo women. They met monthly and collected dues to help members with their own title-taking ceremonies or to support their husbands when they took titles. Improvement activities were also carried out by this group, which at one time numbered about fifty members. Internal disputes, partly over finance, caused its disintegration in 1951. This was the only women's non-traditional association in Afikpo that was in any way comparable to the men's unions. The absence of such groups among the Afikpo women, compared to Ibo women in other areas,[40] is associated with the relative lack of social and economic independence and the relatively limited trading activities of the Afikpo women as compared with the women of other Ibo groups, as well as their limited acculturative contacts. Furthermore, the facts that after marriage women join a women's age-set in their husband's village which renders mutual aid (of a non-financial kind) and that they frequently receive assistance of various kinds from matrilineal relatives in this village, seem to remove some of the need for a women's union for mutual-aid purposes.[41]

Another 'modern' Afikpo association, the African Recreation Club, is a group with no political interests, whose members play tennis together and occasionally sponsor social evenings and receptions. There are several Church of Scotland and Catholic Church groups and a branch of Jehovah's

---

[39] *ovu*: one who carries; *ɛjo*: head pad for carrying loads. In this case referring to the Yoruba style of women's head-tie, worn by Afikpo women who have been in other areas of Nigeria, or have experienced considerable culture contact at Afikpo.

[40] See references, p. 92, footnote 5.

[41] I am indebted to my wife, Phoebe Ottenberg, for information concerning *ovu ɛjo*.

Witnesses, as well as an organization of teachers working in the Afikpo area, a small branch of the Nigerian Ex-Servicemen's Welfare Association, and an inactive branch of the National Council of Nigeria and the Cameroons. All of these, while including Afikpo residents, have a membership consisting of many persons who are not Afikpo-born, though they live and work there. Many of these 'strangers' are educated, and live in the Government Station area or near the schools. While these organizations form a contact point between Afikpo people and outsiders living in the area, none of them is primarily concerned with Afikpo village-group affairs, ATWA being the major village-group association through which Afikpo people at home who are interested in non-traditional activities can express their interests.

### Comparison of Village and Village-Group Associations

The organization and procedures of ATWA show a greater change from the traditional culture than do those of the village unions, and this is related to the larger number of educated and enthusiastic 'progressive' members within its ranks. Nevertheless, both ATWA and the village unions show compatible blends of European and Afikpo cultural elements. The structural organization as well as the interests of both groups are, of course, likely to change, since these unions are still in the formative stages. The village unions show a primary concentration of interest around one activity, loans, while ATWA is characterized by a diffuseness of goals. Both express quite clearly certain of the new interests of the young men most affected by culture contact, including a striving for increased social prestige despite their youth. Both show similar interests in trading rules and regulations, and have similar points of view regarding education. Both lack religious shrines. This, however, is not really a radical departure from tradition, since traditional Afikpo associations, especially village and village-group age sets and grades and Afikpo title-societies, either possess shrines of little ritual importance or have none at all. (Almost all other Afikpo groupings, especially those based on relationship and residence, have shrines with which important rituals are associated.) The members of ATWA and of the village unions frequently appear sceptical of some of their traditional religious beliefs and practices, but few would consider themselves Christians. Both ATWA and the village unions give an opportunity for political experience of a kind and intensity not so readily available to men of the same age in the traditional culture, and both comprise groups to which these younger politicians can look for support. Both show considerable interest in 'improvement' work projects, though, despite the higher percentage of educated and 'progressive' members in ATWA than in the village unions, most of this activity is carried out on the village level by the 'meetings', probably because the traditional work unit is the village and its age-set system, and it has always been difficult, even in pre-British times, to organize co-operative work on the village-group level. The village-group union offers no burial assistance, but burials in Afikpo have always been primarily family and lineage affairs. It is likely, however, that ATWA would participate in the burial of a prominent member.

There are a number of reasons for the absence of a loaning system in the village-group union. In the first place such a system requires either a group with considerable authority over its members, or, in the absence of direct controls, strong external sanctions which can be applied if financial irregularities occur. This is apparent in the case of the village unions which give loans, for here defaulters on loans are likely to be subjected to traditional village sanctions of a very effective kind if the union itself cannot settle the matter. In addition the high degree of familiarity of the village-union members—their frequent face-to-face contacts in daily activities—is related to a considerable degree of knowledge of, and faith in, each other's financial honesty. ATWA, the village-group union, does not possess strong control over its members, and the conflict in authority of the Native Authority Court and Council, and of the village-group age grades, makes external sanctions weak.[42] In addition the membership of ATWA is drawn from a more widespread population than any single village, and the familiarity of the members with each other is not as strong as in the village unions. A loan system in ATWA would probably be associated with considerable suspicion and hostility among the members.

The development of ATWA expresses the increased consciousness of the outer world by a growing number of Afikpo people, which is perhaps an inevitable consequence of acculturative forces acting upon a small and hitherto relatively isolated group of people, and is related to the rapid increase in physical mobility and contact following the arrival of the British. In this context one senses that the individual's village-group identification is increasing. The consciousness that Afikpo people have that they should deal with this outside world is apparent in the receptions given for visiting dignitaries, and in their emphasis on scholarships so that Afikpo boys may 'get ahead' in competition with boys from other parts of Nigeria.

At the same time the village 'meetings' help to perpetuate village unity and inter-village rivalry under changing cultural conditions *within* the village-group. These 'meetings' promote face-to-face contact for the young village men. The members carry out village projects as a group and accomplish certain work activities in a manner similar to that in which *ukɛkpɛ*, the village executive grade, carries out traditional activities. Again, while inter-village land rivalries continue to the present day, traditional inter-

---

[42] Nevertheless, ATWA collects dues and donations and maintains a financial account. Though the financial system is safeguarded by keeping the money in an Aba bank, and by a public announcement of expenditures and receipts at the annual meeting, suspicion concerning the accuracy of the accounts exists.

village warfare has disappeared, and inter-village educational and economic prestige rivalries seem to be taking its place. The village 'meetings' thus help to maintain the identification of individuals as members of a village, and the position of the village in the village-group.

While lineage and kinship considerations influence the actions of ATWA and the village unions, as well as the interests and attitudes of individual members, these Afikpo associations do not generally show themselves to be a projection of the relationship system, but rather are expressions of residential affiliations in which kinship and lineage factors play a part. In the case of the previously discussed compound 'meeting' in Ukpa village the union members are from a single large patrilineage, but this seems to be an exceptional case.[43] The idea of village and village-group associations on a non-lineage basis is, of course, not new in Afikpo, since the age sets and grades are organized in this manner.

Coleman has suggested that tribal associations in Nigeria accelerate the acculturative process, but also that the expatriate branch unions tend to perpetuate certain aspects of the traditional culture, such as dances, the use of the vernacular language, and 'adherence to customary ideas of social morality and discipline'.[44] The situation is much the same with regard to ATWA. The home branch is primarily concerned not with perpetuating the traditional but with culture change. This may possibly be because the traditional culture is still relatively unchanged as compared with some other areas of Nigeria, and there remains little need consciously to preserve what is still very much in existence. While some ATWA members at Afikpo have expressed a desire to record their culture and history, and many traditional cultural elements mark the Afikpo association, such as the use of Ibo in speaking, the primary conscious orientation of this group is toward satisfying relatively new interests. However, as Afikpo culture continues to change, this union may become more concerned with the preservation of traditional values. Although apparently employing a greater number of traditional cultural elements in their organization, much the same can be said of the village 'meetings', which are, of course, not strictly 'tribal' associations.

Coleman's suggestion, however, has considerable applicability to ATWA's expatriate branch unions. These, in a foreign environment, help to sustain the identification of their members as Afikpo, acting as channels through which contacts with home are maintained and perpetuating the Afikpo dialect, the family, kinship, and lineage structure, and other aspects of this culture. The orientation of these branches is to preserve among

---

[43] There are a number of small Afikpo villages which are either composed entirely of one major patrilineage or seem to be dominated by one such group, but none of these seems to have developed a union at the present time. In these cases, such unions, if they existed, could be said to be organized on a relationship basis.

[44] Coleman, 1952, p. 2.

themselves certain traditional modes of behaviour, and to maintain the identification of the members with home, as well as to raise the educational and economic standards of the home community to the level which many of the branches find they possess and to organize their own local mutual aid and loan activities. Hence, while both branch and home unions show many traditional elements in their behaviour, the branch unions in a foreign environment verbalize and are conscious of a need for the preservation of some aspects of the indigenous culture, as well as for certain changes, while the home unions, existing in the more traditional environment, put their greatest emphasis on 'improvement' and change.

## Bibliography

AFIKPO TOWN WELFARE ASSOCIATION, 1951, *Minutes of the 1st Annual Convention of the Afikpo Town Welfare Association, holden at Amaizu Native Court Hall on December 23 and 24, 1950,* Aba.

———— 1952a, *Afikpo Town Welfare Association, Constitution,* Afikpo.

———— 1952b, *Minutes of the Second Annual Convention of the Afikpo Town Welfare Association, held at Afikpo Native Court (Amaizu) on 22nd and 23rd December 1951,* Afikpo.

ARDENER, SHIRLEY G., 1953, 'The Social and Economic Significance of the Contribution Club among a Section of the Southern Ibo', *Annual Conference, West African Institute of Social and Economic Research, Sociology Section,* March 1953, Ibadan, pp. 128–42.

COLEMAN, JAMES, 1952, 'The Role of Tribal Associations in Nigeria' (summary), *West African Institute of Social and Economic Research Annual Conference,* 1952, Ibadan, 4 pages.

COMHAIRE-SYLVAIN, SUZANNE, 1950, 'Associations on the Basis of Origin in Lagos, Nigeria', *Amer. Cath. Soc. Rev.* (Chicago), vol. xi, pp. 234–6.

FORDE, DARYLL, and JONES, G. I., 1950, *The Ibo and Ibibio-Speaking Peoples of South-Eastern Nigeria,* London.

GREEN, M. M., 1947, *Ibo Village Affairs,* London.

HAILEY, LORD, 1951, *Native Administration in the British African Territories, Part III, West Africa,* London.

HERSKOVITS, M. J., 1941, *The Myth of the Negro Past,* New York.

IBO STATE UNION, 1951, *Ibo State Union, Constitution,* Aba.

LEITH-ROSS, SYLVIA, 1939, *African Women,* London.

———— 1944, *African Conversation Piece,* London.

NIGERIA, Census Superintendent, *Population Census of the Eastern Region of Nigeria, 1953, Bulletin No. 4. Ogoja Province,* Port Harcourt, 1953.

OFFODILE, E. P. OYEAKA, 1947, 'Growth and Influence of Tribal Unions', *West African Review,* vol. xviii, no. 239, pp. 937, 939, 941.

OFFONRY, H. KANU, 1951, 'The Strength of Ibo Clan Feeling', *West Africa,* No. 1787, p. 467, and No. 1788, pp. 489–90.

OTTENBERG, SIMON, 1953, 'The Development of Village Meetings among the Afikpo People', *Annual Conference, West African Institute of Social and Economic Research, Sociology Section,* March, 1953, Ibadan, pp. 186–205.

# 2

# Family,
# Cultural Relativism,
# and Self-Criticism

A. This Ugandan family exemplifies the traditional African family: a functional unit serving to educate future responsible adult members of society. The family represents above all a cooperative effort; here—where the husband has three wives—young and old, male and female, work, learn, and play together.

B. This view of Detroit typifies overpopulated conditions in American cities which tend to reduce, rather than widen, individual horizons and social responsibility. In each house the family is an independent entity, isolated both economically and emotionally from surrounding families.

C. Special efforts were made to design a functional community such as this modern middle-class apartment dwelling on the Ivory Coast. The well-planned location of facilities encourages mutual cooperation between families and the continuity of tradition into modern life.

D. Where African families unite, American families seem to separate. Old-age and nursing homes, such as this one, are sad but necessary institutions in a country that finds its elder citizens of little use to society.

If, as can hardly be denied, the family, the most fundamental of social units, is the cornerstone of social life, then it can be said that the concept of cultural relativism is equally essential to the construction of a sound moral life. However one defines society, it can be broken down into smaller and smaller units until finally one reaches the family (at its most basic a family may be only a woman and her dependent children). At each level of society, from this fundamental unit up to the society as a whole, there is a specific set of values. Only some of these values are applicable at other levels of society, but, in general, each unit must be judged according to the values of its own level. Any attempt to judge one unit by the values of another is plainly unworkable.

This is not a new concept in small-scale societies, where the different units are clearly recognized and often formalized and where the appropriate values are defined. Such societies recognize that an individual is many things, bound by as many sets of values that sometimes conflict. A man may be a father, but he is also a son, a brother, an uncle, a nephew, an affine, and a friend or an enemy. He may be a member of a nuclear family, a lineage, a clan, a tribe, and a nation. He may also be a member of an age-set, a guild or union, a cooperative, a church, and so forth. In each role, he has different social horizons and different rights and obligations governed by different values. It is the genius of small-scale societies that they recognize the complexity of the individual's social life and avert what would seem to be the inevitable conflicts arising from such a multiplicity of roles. Where conflict exists or emerges, it may even be turned to advantage. It is the idiocy of Western civilization that it ignores this complexity of man's social obligations and attempts to impose a single, universal, inflexible standard of behavior by which he can be judged at all times and in all contexts. The result is an ever-increasing conflict between the individual and society, a conflict largely avoided in small-scale societies because there the individual *is* society.

Once it is admitted that a man's obligations as a brother are not necessarily directly applicable to his role as an uncle, that his values as a member of a construction worker's union are hardly pertinent to his role as a countertenor in the church choir (although he might adopt certain techniques learned in the one role to further his efficacy in the other), then it should also be considered illogical to judge his actions as a union member or as a father in terms of his proficiency as a countertenor or as an uncle. Why, then, judge Roman Catholics as though they were Protestants, Chinese as though they were Americans, city dwellers as though they were villagers, and so forth, as if the sets of relationships and values involved in being a member of the one unit are identical with those involved in being a member of the other? Few people manage to avoid making such illogical, egocentric criticisms.

In saying this, I am becoming involved in the issue of value judgments, which will be discussed in Part 4, but I mention it here because unicentricism *can* be a valuable tool, and one that will be examined here (although in its more usual form it is disastrous). It can lead all too easily to the sometimes unconscious narrowness of vision that is the mainstay of all the insidious forms of conscious racism that plague man today. Here I use the term "racism" in a wide sense to refer to bigotry however and wherever it exists, rather than to refer exclusively to race, in which context it is meaningless. In this wider sense, racism is all-pervasive. Differences between economic class, political party, and religious conviction tend to be permeated by self-interest and self-superior attitudes that are only more obvious, not more prevalent, when they are applied to race. My concern is with the racist attitude and its flagrant opposition to truly social and moral life. The concept of cultural relativism offers an excellent means for demonstrating the illogicality and danger of such exclusive attitudes; it leads us to exercise great caution before making judgments of other peoples and other groups. In fact, it turns our natural tendency to judge inward, in the form of critical self-appraisal.

It is sometimes said that cultural relativism limits anthropologists to a study of the particular and eliminates the possibility of generalization afforded by the comparative method. That would be true if cultural relativism were carried to an extreme as unintelligent as the position of such detractors. Much defamation and criticism is made to sound convincing by the simple expedient of defining a term or concept in such a way as to open it to defamation. I will frankly ignore such methodological and theoretical criticisms here and try rather to understand concepts such as that of cultural relativism in a general way in order to extract from them their maximum value, without supposing them to be perfect.

Cultural relativism has the practical and humanitarian value of broadening our outlook on other ways of life and thought while at the same time making us more critical of our own; it also has considerable academic value. Although I have suggested that total objectivity in anthropology is not only undesirable as a goal but also impossible to achieve, a certain measure of detachment is essential. Cultural relativism does not assert that there are no general truths; it merely suggests that the particular aspects of any society should be understood with reference to the totality of that society. Once understood in this way, it is possible to consider the applicability of cultural relativism to an examination of other societies.

On entering a strange society it is hard for most people, including anthropologists, not to form hasty judgments by making superficial comparisons with our own society: for example, how dirty a people are in their personal habits, how poor their architecture, how noble their egalitarianism, how spiritual their religion. Such comparisons are inevitable, and they are not without merit so long as we recognize that they primarily inform us about ourselves, not about others. The eating of food with fingers rather than with utensils may strike those who see it for the first time as a dirty custom, yet given the climatic and social conditions that exist where such customs prevail, this way of eating generally involves far less danger of spreading germs than would be involved with the use of utensils. Utensils would very likely be washed in unclean water and contaminated by disease-bearing flies. It is a simple matter to wash and dry your hands before a meal; it is not so simple to make sure that the knives and forks and plates and cups you use are as clean . . . observe the more fastidious clients in a cheap diner, surreptitiously wiping their forks on their napkins. Similarly, architecture can only be understood as a response to the total environment; there are no absolute terms by which it can be judged. Many a lofty European has lived an uncomfortable and difficult domestic life in a foreign land because he has insisted on transporting his preconceived notions on how a house should be built, furnished, wired, plumbed, and staffed. And a wistful, envious remark, on how egalitarian primitive man is, is really a comment on how inegalitarian civilized man is. In any case, further inquiry might well reveal that primitive man is not quite so noble as he was thought to be, but rather that he shares because he expects to consume that of others. (This would probably inspire an equally hasty judgment in the opposite direction.) A close examination might also reveal that his religion is not quite so spiritual, but rather that it is practical.

These first reactions are almost inevitable, even for the most *blasé* of field workers; they are not without value insofar as they make the anthropologist question his own ways of life and thought. Too often, however, once having made this superficial comparison he stops there, convinced of his superiority or inferiority.

But cultural relativism makes it possible for us to go further than that, to examine each aspect of a foreign culture in relation to the whole, to understand not only what a people do and how but also why they do it. This may be possible to explain in the culture's own terms, or it may require intensive analysis, the given reason being a conscious or unconscious red herring. Thus, when an African turns his back on his mother-in-law and walks away without a word of greeting, we learn not to say "how rude" (or even, as many might say with greater perspicacity, "how sensible") but rather to note the fact and set out to discover the reason for it. Nor should we believe we have discovered the reason when the son-in-law says that he did not see his mother-in-law, that he merely went out to the toilet, or that if he had greeted her, his child would have fallen sick. The same custom may prove to have different functions in different societies, in which case it is not the same custom, but merely a similar act. Such consideration of this custom might make us reflect that if in our society men were obliged by law never to speak to their mothers-in-law, many divorces might have been avoided. Of all interpersonal relationships this one is fraught with the most obvious dangers of conflict. It is with this functional aspect that we should be concerned, not with whether a man turns his back or his side to his mother-in-law, refuses to talk with her, or openly abuses her, as is sometimes required of him. There are many modes of behavior designed to deal with the same situation; therefore, if any judgment is to be made, it should be made with reference to the one common factor, the situation itself (in this case the mother-in-law–son-in-law relationship), and of how effectively the institutionalized form of behavior deals with it. Here I suppose it is necessary to ask "effective from whose point of view?" Mothers-in-law have different points of view from sons-in-law. The answer is as simple as it is significant: the only reasonable and universal way to judge a custom's efficacy is from the point of view of the particular society as a whole, in terms of its well-being and its survival.

This provides a more valid base from which to make comparisons, not of how other sons-in-law behave, but of how effectively other societies resolve the same basic problem of inherent, latent conflict. If a given society does not solve the problem so well, it is necessary to examine the possibility that there is a valid reason even for that. This applies particularly where there is change in family structure as brought on by the process of urbanization, Westernization, or conversion from one religious belief to another. It is even conceivable that we might be led, through the double process of understanding others while critically appraising ourselves, to discover a way of improving our own chances of survival in either role.

Mother-in-law avoidance is not an insignificant example, but there are others that could be examined with equal profit. It might be possible to make similar discoveries in the economic or political realm. And if a nation were fortunate enough to have a government that was either intelligent or had any respect for intelligence, there might be some chance of consequent reform being initiated, as it should be, at a governmental level.

The crucial factor is the definition of what is meant by "society." It can be defined at almost any level, from elementary family to nation, alliance, or bloc; it can even be defined in global terms. It is a provoking question and one that I shall attempt to tackle shortly, but here I wish to point out that the very existence (its utility aside) of an organization such as the

United Nations indicates how vastly our concept of society has expanded since those not-so-distant days when half the world did not even know that the other half existed. The trouble is that now we know we either do not care, refusing to acknowledge the other half as part of "our" society, or we *do* care and consciously dismiss the other half by the illogical act of denying it as part of our society while judging it by our standards and from our point of view. England provides a prime example of a modern nation's facility for such two-facedness. In that country, diplomacy is frequently indistinguishable from deceit except for its polish, and even the allegation of hypocrisy does not always ring true because the English are often genuinely unaware of the blatant contradictions between their pontifications and their inability to practice what they preach. One might say they are liberal-minded racist extremists. There is no room in their world for anyone to be *non*-English, others can only be *un*-English. And many a black Commonwealth citizen has found out just what it means to be considered un-English.

These occasional sallies at nations and governments are not gratuitous expressions of personal disenchantment or rancor; they are intended to suggest topics for anthropological inquiry. Anthropologists should be interested in whatever happens, regardless of personal opinion; and there are few who, having experience with other societies, can maintain an uncritical attitude toward their own society. Everyone who has been raised in the Western tradition can probably feel something of the conflict that is inherent in his way of life; this manifests itself in embarrassingly pertinent ways to remind him of his lack of perfection. I like to think of myself, for instance, as not being a racist; yet it has been pointed out that in *The Forest People*,* I took what might be construed as a racist attitude toward the villagers (an attitude that I still found hard to shake off when I was again living with those villagers some twelve years later) and that my own ethnocentricism showed nicely when I described the Pygmies as beautiful and in the same breath remarked on their lightness of color and on the "Greek-like" features of some of them.

Perhaps the answer is not to try so hard to love the whole of humanity but, instead, to be content to belong to one's chosen part of it, to follow one's chosen way, and to allow others the courtesy of the same freedom of choice. It is necessary, then, to be a member of a part before it is possible in any sense to be a true member of the whole. But we cannot honorably ignore the rest of mankind any longer nor merely consider them

---

* C. M. Turnbull, *The Forest People* (New York: Simon and Schuster, 1961).

inferior versions of the ideal, as represented by ourselves. The world has reached a point where even the old concept of nationalism is indeed immoral; now all men belong to a much wider, more universal society.

The apparent contradiction is not a contradiction at all; rather, it is a matter of the multiplicity of roles we are called upon to play. It is necessary for us to feel that we are a part of a smaller-than-global society; we can do this because of the happy diversity of cultures that is one of our greatest riches. As members of that society, we should act in accord with its precepts, but morally such smaller units (whether state or even national) can no longer be as exclusive as they once were, nor as self-interested and concerned. We cannot dismiss or ignore others just because they are not like us, nor can we judge them as though they *are* or *should be* like us. If we wish freedom to follow our chosen way, we are compelled to allow others that same freedom, thus the diverse ways, if viable, cannot be mutually antagonistic.

Morality itself is relative, and the same apparent contradiction applies. Although a man binds himself to a moral code specific to his own smaller society, he must develop a more universal sense of morality if he is to consider himself a part of humanity as a whole. At the moment there is an enormous diversity of self-contained systems that were perfectly adequate when their relevant social groups were more isolated than they are now. But today, in terms of the global society of which we are all a part, these systems must be integrated; and integration is going to necessitate modification. I suggest that cultural relativism is one appropriate way to approach the problem.

Before attempting to define "society," it is necessary to define "family"; and before that can be done it is necessary to look at the phenomenon that is anathema to so many social anthropologists: the individual. Many anthropologists, with more veracity than they may realize, claim that the individual is of no concern to them in their studies of society. But the truth of this assertion does not rest in the methodological reasons they usually put forward; rather, it rests, in a very real sense, in the fact that in many small-scale societies, the individual simply does not exist: that is to say, personality in such societies is defined not in individual terms but in strictly social terms. Thus an individual, if he is anything more than a biological specimen, is essentially a social phenomenon. This may be one of the most significant differences between small-scale societies and the larger Western civilizations, and it holds true no matter what form the family or society takes.

In Africa there are traditionally many types of families. A family may consist of parents and children only, or it may include grandparents and/or uncles and aunts. In the case of the Ashanti, the family (*abusua*) consists of a mother, her children, and her brother; the father is almost an outsider who belongs to another abusua. It can, of course, be said that in America and Europe there are also many variations of who is included or excluded as a member of a family. But the nature of the genealogical relationship is not the main point at all. One major difference between the Western family, whatever form it takes, and the traditional African family is that the latter formalizes the interpersonal relationships between its members into a tight, miniature social system in which the so-called kinship terminology defines *not* so much kinship as social relationships. Thus "mother" does not mean, as it usually does in the West, the woman who gave birth to the child; rather a mother is a person, not necessarily even a female to whom the child behaves, and who behaves toward the child, in the manner appropriate to that term. Although the pattern of behavior is most often established with respect to the biological mother, the pattern itself is more important than the individual. If the individual biological mother dies there are many others to take her place and fill the same roles in relation to the child. A child may call all his mother's sisters "mother," with or without qualification (big, little, and so forth). He may even call his mother's brother "mother," as the Nyoro do, because the essence of that man is that he too is ready to act toward the child as anyone on its mother's side of the family would act, fulfilling the same obligations, expecting the same rights.*

Thus when a child says "mother" he is not addressing an individual, but a class of individuals. This is the essential point we have to grasp for our present purpose, for we have to compare not the form of the family, but its function. The reader has available to him a wealth of excellent documentation on the wide variety of family forms in Africa, particularly *African Systems of Kinship and Marriage.*† Rather than attempt here what would have to be an inadequate summary, I want to concentrate on this one point, for it seems central, and directly related to the equally central conflict between the individual and society in our Western world.

African society is modeled on the family. Although the form of the family varies, in most cases the generalizations that follow are still valid. All forms point to the concern of society that its members should be social beings,

---

* In LuNyoro, the word for "mother" is *nyina,* and the word for "male" is *rumi.* "Mother's brother" is *nyinarumi,* that is, "male on the mother's side."

† A. R. Radcliffe-Brown and D. Forde (eds.), *African Systems of Kinship and Marriage* (London: Oxford University Press for the International African Institute, 1950).

not individual beings. Thus African society has the characteristic of being a network of multiple personalities, interrelating in an almost infinite number of ways; it is not a mere assortment of individuals bound together by certain discrete economic, political, or religious ties. In African terms, a society is more than a legal technicality; it is a vital organism.

It is important to consider the diversity of family forms found in Africa because it makes the element all the more apparent. But it is also necessary to realize that the differences in forms are not quite as rigid or as clear-cut as terminology may suggest. There is a much greater overlap in descent systems than is indicated by such terms as "patrilineal," "matrilineal," "dual," and "bilateral." The terminology has more to do with intellectual constructs, with analytical tools, than with actual societies. Some societies are more rigid than others in the application of their rules of descent, and in some societies the rules are more exclusive than in others. But these differences are more interesting to theoreticians than to the families involved, and they can too easily obscure an essential unity.

One clue to that unity appears when we ask why there is such diversity. Again, the urge to classify frequently leads us to make generalizations such as that hunters (contrary to the Steward-Service allegation*) are generally bilateral; herders, patrilineal; and cultivators, mostly matrilineal. This at least is better than trying to explain the descent system in terms of the geographical area, as though, for example, there is something inherent in occidentality that makes West Africans matrilineal. The first generalization indicates a correlation between economy and descent, but only when individual cases are examined in greater detail does it become apparent how close the correlation often is. Thus, a society that changes its economy may, with remarkable readiness, change its descent system. Within any system, matrilocality and patrilocality also vary with the least apparently significant ecological differences, such as the type of palm favored or the type of animal hunted. Once again this demonstrates the concept of social organization as an essay in survival, although survival may not be the first conscious concern of a society. Sometimes the environment virtually dictates the nature of the subsistence economy; at other times, it is a matter of choice, history, or accident. It may even be that a family system that was established under other conditions may affect the choice, but economy and descent must be closely interrelated.

In a broad sense, then, the family is an economic unit, and familial rela-

---

* See Elman R. Service, *Primitive Social Organization* (New York: Random House, 1962); and Julian H. Steward, *Theory of Culture Change* (Urbana: University of Illinois Press, 1955).

tionships may be categorized in the same way at the most basic level. The family may *become* a political unit, a religious unit, and a legal unit; but its most immediate, inescapable, and fundamental relationship is economic. The economic relationships that are necessary for the survival of any particular society in traditional Africa are exemplified in its familial relationships: between husband and wife, father and son, mother and daughter, and so forth. These relationships are much better understood in economic terms rather than in the cozy terms of warmth and love with which we beguile ourselves so habitually. The African family is essentially effective rather than affective. This does not deny the existence of warmth and love in the African family; quite the contrary, when a family begins to lose effectiveness, as the Western family is now doing, it also begins to lack in affection. The converse is just as likely to be true.

It is immediately apparent that the African concept of family is necessarily much wider than the Western concept. A pair of adults and three or four children do not usually have much chance of survival as an independent economic group, although under certain ecological conditions, the effective family can indeed be remarkably small. But even when a tiny band of hunters manages with ease to fill its subsistence needs, it must still expand its social horizons for other economic purposes, such as procreation. Thus, although a Pygmy or Bushman band may be considered a family, it is not a society; and although the wider society may not be considered a family, the family model provides the necessary pattern for all its relationships.

For those who think the affective basis of family relationships is being underestimated as a fundamental and necessary part of the family, and for anyone who sees love as a romantic, isolated emotion detached from anything as mundane as economic need, I recommend a look at the Ik.* The Ik represent humanity at its most basic. At first sight, in good ethnocentric fashion, I refused to accept them as an example of anything but the degree of inhumanity to which people can be reduced by external forces. But after living with them for eighteen months, I came to a better understanding of myself and therefore of the Ik. The Ik live in seemingly neurotic villages that have no center. Every compound backs onto another, each with its own private entrance from its own private outside world, each facing a different direction. Inside these compounds live "families" (that is, biological parents and unmarried children). Only the parents have a house; the children have to sleep outside. There is no family life even within the

---

* Colin M. Turnbull: *The Mountain People* (New York, Simon and Schuster, 1972).

compound; it is merely a place to sleep, protected by its fences and stockades against marauders from both outside and inside the village. At dawn or shortly afterward, each compound releases its members, who go their individual ways in search of their own food and water for the day. When they find it, they consume it alone and in haste, lest they be discovered and have it taken from them. The country is extremely arid and excessively mountainous, gouged with precipitous rocky ravines. The old, infirm, or unlucky die rapidly because under such conditions they cannot travel far enough to find sufficient nourishment, and no one will bring anything to them. Even the young and healthy can find themselves trapped without water if their search for food has carried them too far from that other vital commodity. Mothers bear children with boredom and distaste, reluctantly feed them until they are three years old, then leave them to fend for themselves. Parents are equally unloved, and not surprisingly, they are ignored by their offspring when they become old and feeble, which is usually in their early thirties. And if, by any mischance, an old person should find some food and be foolish enough to try and eat it in public, the Ik consider it great sport for a child to grab the food out of the old person's mouth. The curious thing is that even the old person, who is thus brought a step closer to death, joins in the merriment; he has been caught in an act as ridiculous as an octogenarian lady dressing in a miniskirt. The Ik consider eating an act proper to youth; old people are expected to die gracefully and not to make spectacles of themselves. I used to see them coming to say goodby and then hobbling off to find a comfortable place to die, where they would not be a bother to anyone. The old ritual priest was roundly scolded for asking to be allowed to die inside his daughter's or son's house. He was reminded that this would involve his offspring in a burial feast, and surely the old man did not want them to waste food like that? Whether he did or not, he went off like the others; three days later he was found dead on a rocky spur.

During those eighteen months, I saw no sign of love and little affection in any form. The Ik simply could not afford such luxuries. But neither did I see any hatred, bitterness, or resentment.

It was not always this way with the Ik. When I first arrived, there were still some old ones alive who remembered days when children used to help their parents, not because they were any more loving, but because they could afford to help. But under the present conditions of utter deprivation and periodic starvation, love is uneconomic because it implies mutual economic and political obligations that simply cannot be fulfilled. Survival is an individual affair for the Ik. Thus, ironically, although only the strongest individuals survive, the Ik as a people continue to exist, even though they are drastically reduced in number.

At the opposite extreme, the Mbuti hunters of the Congo, who live in a superabundant environment, display a corresponding abundance of love, affection, and mutual help. But they also display the same curious indifference to the biological family. The biological family is recognized, and generally the members live together; but any Mbuti will call all the people of his parents' generation by the same terms of address that he uses for his biological parents, without qualification. The same is true of the way he addresses his grandparents and children, for the entire hunting band of perhaps a hundred people is his true family, both effective and affective. A band is the totality of people who cooperate in hunting and gathering within a given area; it can be defined in no other way. Kinship is almost irrelevant.

Whereas the childhood education of an Mbuti emphasizes that his very existence depends on the multiplicity of different cooperative roles that he gradually learns to play, the childhood education of an Ik consists of systematic neglect, which teaches him the first thing he needs to know— that he must look to his own survival. At the age of three, he is hardly equipped to survive on his own. Therefore, he is forced into a measure of cooperation with his age-mates in a gang of children aged three to seven. Within the gang each child must get his or her own food (mainly remnants of figs partly eaten by baboons), but having found it, they are allowed to eat it in peace; no one will take it from them. If a member of one gang is attacked by another gang, his own group will usually protect him. At age seven, the child finds his gang turning on him. He is driven out into the next age-level gang, where he will stay until he is about thirteen years old. Once again his "friends" throw him out, just as he, as a younger member of the group, helped throw out many older members. Then he enters the world truly on his own. Nonetheless, he has learned the necessary patterns of cooperation. In times of relative plenty, when by some freak chance his fields might yield fruit and need tending, or when he wants to build a house, he knows he can get help from his age-mates if he is willing to reciprocate. Much as the band is the family for the Mbuti, so to a lesser extent the age-group is the family for the Ik. It is the only kind of group that may be said to be both effective and, at least to a minimal extent, affective.

This is not as dismal as it sounds, and it does not deny the enormous value of love and affection under certain, probably under most, circumstances. But for those like the Ik who live in utter deprivation, love is an economic and psychological burden too great to be borne. It is nonfunctional. By way of comparison, the cynic might well say that love is rapidly becoming the same in our own society, that we are becoming more Ik-like daily. A quick trip through the many orphanages, old people's homes, and mental hospitals will tell us much about our sense of family devotion. Although "primitive" man seems to have a less-romantic notion of love, given the bare economic means, he displays an enormous capacity for an affection the warmth and sincerity of which would put most Western lovers to shame, both by its depth and by its durability. With all our talk of love, it is too often either a brief moment of passion (or a series of them, interspersed with periods of increasing frigidity) or a possessiveness that is equally self-oriented and extreme. The African family may provide a means for distinguishing more clearly between love and affection, the one perhaps usefully considered a response to psychological needs, the other a response to economic needs. Both are functional.

As a functional unit, the biological family is frequently adequate from the child's point of view, and in most societies other than that of the Ik the child is therefore carefully taught that his "real" family is much wider in extent. The terminology he has to use teaches him this, as do the related modes of speech and behavior; but he is still likely to feel more bound by the affective ties than by the effective, the reality of which may not be apparent to him in his early years. Thus in such small societies, the kinship terminology functions in the educational process as one means of expanding the child's social horizons beyond the basic nuclear family model, and one finds the related modes of behavior operating to teach the child the difference between affective and effective relationships. In a matrilineal society, for instance, a boy may have a singularly free-and-easy relationship with his father, from whom he will inherit little or nothing in the way of material wealth, but a constrained and disciplined relationship with his mother's brother, from whom he will acquire land, status, and wealth. It might be just the opposite in a patrilineal society. One often finds adjacent generational relationships as effective (and constrained) as alternate generational relationships are affective (and free).

The double process of expanding the child's social horizons and teaching him the essential difference between these two types of relationship is sometimes brought to a head during the formal initiation rites by which a child is transformed into an adult. This often involves a symbolic break with biological parents, followed by a period during which the child is further encouraged to reject the biological link by acts of ridicule and by scornful or offensive speech. At the same time he is taught to respect the wider clan or tribal society in the way he has already been taught to respect his parents, and thus the patterns already learned in crucial formative years are transferred to the larger social context. In a very real way, becoming an adult means assuming adult (which is to say, social) horizons and responsibilities. The respect that is shown for the parental level (adjacent generation) is transferred to the same level throughout the wider society, as is the affection felt for the grandparental (alternate) generation. And perhaps even more significantly, the child, in becoming an adult, learns that at his own generational level the effective and affective elements may be most satisfactorily combined. The age-set (or the less formal age-group) becomes another form of family and again helps to break down the insularity of the biological family model though continuing the pattern of sibling relationships established by it.

The very process of naming a child bears out this emphasis on the social character of the African individual. For instance, an infant is usually not named until it has shown that it has "come to stay" (a matter of days, weeks, or sometimes months). He is then given his first name, and thereafter more names are added at different intervals. The least important of these names will designate him as an individual; the others will identify various lines of rights and obligations, familial and otherwise. The Ashanti give one name according to the day of the week on which the child was born, theoretically ensuring that one out of every seven Ashanti will be the child's namesake (the number seven has important ritual connotations for the Ashanti). Throughout Africa, a shared name implies shared obligations. In societies with formal age-set systems, members of a set or subset often share a common name that is exclusively theirs. In this way, a child is born with a fixed set of relationships determined by his biological kinship, and as soon as he shows signs of surviving the critical periods of infancy and early childhood and is therefore going to be of social significance, he is endowed with further rights and obligations, his sociological kinship, implicit in the names he bears.

From then on, the process of widening his horizons continues until initiation, after which he is expected to marry and actively create still further relationships, both by the act of marriage and by the act of procreation. The political aspect of marriage cannot be overemphasized, for in such societies, marriage is above all a relationship between two groups of people rather than between two individuals. This does not mean that the individuals have no say, which is how Westerners usually interpret the institution of arranged marriages. Because the individuals are already endowed with such a strong sense of social identity, their wishes frequently correlate with those of the groups concerned. They recognize their futures as inextricably bound together. There may be differences of opinion at the outset; but the limits prescribed are often so broad that the individual has a wide range of choice ensuring personal as well as political compatibility. Increasingly, however, the individual is now going against the wishes of the group, thus voluntarily exiling himself. In renouncing his obligations to his family, in asserting his "individual" rights, he also renounces his familial rights, which may represent as much security as most modern social security systems.

The articles that follow examine some of this conflict between the individual and society as seen by young Africans who are caught in the dilemma. They display an almost intuitive recognition of the validity of the old way, which spelled less individual freedom but far greater security, and show some recognition that the new commercial world, although encouraging and making individual freedom possible, imposes shackles as rigid as, and often less comfortable than, those imposed by the traditional family. The freedom to marry according to individual taste and desire (hardly the most enduring of criteria) is synonymous with the freedom to divorce oneself from kith and kin effectively and sometimes affectively.

Gustav Jahoda's article, "Love, Marriage, and Social Change: Letters to the Advice Column of a West African Newspaper," raises an important point. It is not necessarily change itself that brings about so many problems in family life; rather, it is the uneven way in which change affects society. It affects the young more strongly and in a different way than the old. In Africa this creates a particularly traumatic form of generation gap because the young are often still attached to the old way emotionally and economically while at the same time their education leads them to model their values on the new ways. Jahoda's article deals both explicitly and implicitly with the basic conflict between the individual and society as that conflict is heightened, if not induced, by changes in education, economy, and religion. The younger people, aware of their different and, in new-world terms, superior education, regard those not so educated as backward or unprogressive. Because at the time the article was written, the education of girls lagged behind that of boys, this view often applied to prospective wives. It nearly always applied to parents. The result was a lack of respect for the views and wishes of others, rationalized in terms of their educational inferiority. Young men feel free to make their own decisions, and the new world often makes it economically possible for them to do so. Salaried employment makes them far less dependent upon their parents and families. The cash economy has also introduced a new measure of status and power that further complicates the scene. A man of wealth is viewed with mixed respect—"carful and fridgful," as one letter writer put it. A man may thus be regarded as superior to his elders in education and wealth and, consequently, as more powerful. Why, then, should he listen to them? Yet there is the nagging recognition that the security offered by the new way of life, with its emphasis on cash wealth, is more ephemeral than that offered by family.

Conversion to Christianity has undoubtedly added to the basic problem by undermining various beliefs and practices that emphasize the individual's social personality and, hence, his social responsibility. This is particularly true of Christianity's aggressive fight against initiation rites, arranged marriages, and traditional forms of marriage (especially polygyny), without the least understanding of them; automatically judging them to be evil because they were non-Christian. But according to Jahoda, Christianity has also compounded its errors by introducing a new and bewildering concept of love. (This is also discussed in J. H. Chaplin's article, "Wiving and Thriving in Northern Rhodesia.") It suggests that the only requisites for a stable marriage are "love and understanding," as though no other considerations pertained; for true love is seen as coming "from Heaven," and many a new convert (like many an old convert) is not quite sure how to recognize the true from the false. Undoubtedly the somewhat-austere notion of love as it is most often depicted in the Bible is the source of much difficulty for people who take their new values from that source but who traditionally have other notions of love and consequently confuse respect and a selfless sense of obligation with sexual attraction, mutual need, and mere liking. This new doctrine of love, which evolved under totally different circumstances, and the Christian notion that marriage is a sacred union between two individuals (although the church ritual—separating the bride's family from groom's family, the "giving away" of the bride, and so forth—shows that it once thought otherwise) help to make marriage for the new convert an exercise in self-indulgence, strengthening still further the case of the individual against society.

At the time the data for the article were gathered (1955), despite a long association with Europeans, the education of Africans had been limited and had not made too many drastic inroads into traditional life and thought because there was, in most colonies, the feeling that "an educated native is dangerous." Many of the letters dealt with in the Jahoda article show a real sense of conflicting loyalties (some also show a nice sense of conflicting economics and politics). Today the situation may no longer exist, for there is now a generation of educated parents. There is and always will be a gap, but not so wide a gap as that between literate and nonliterate. Similarly, the economic and political gaps have tended to close. But many parts of rural Africa are only beginning to face the problem, and the new generation of leaders, less influenced by a strictly colonial education than their predecessors were, is beginning to question the dangers to society involved in the loss of the old family system and the consequent loss of a firm foundation for moral and responsible citizenship.

"Wiving and Thriving in Northern Rhodesia," by J. H. Chaplin, uses the same approach (the analysis of letters to an advice column in a newspaper) but deals with a different geographical area, where there is a smaller percentage of literates. The article explores much the same kind of general problem and reveals the same concerns and conflicts and many of the same causes. There is the same confusion, for instance, over the Western notion of love. One writer uses the biblical "Love without works is dead" as an argument that his girl friend is acting dishonorably by not jumping into bed with him. There is the same insidious triumph of the individual over society, even when some respect for the family still remains. Thus the man who says "I have a terrible hunger of family" is merely concerned with getting one of his own. Chaplin refers to incidental dangers brought about by the new educational system (as opposed to the education itself), which necessitates long periods of implied celibacy, frequently resolved by extramarital sexual activity. Again it is a case of an institution that was functional in one time and place being imposed on a totally different context.

"Some Trends in Modern Marriage among West Africans," by Kenneth Little and Anne Price, and "Types of Urban African Marriage in Kampala," by David J. Parkin, examine the personal problems discussed by Jahoda and Chaplin as such problems have developed in an urban context. Among the problems brought by migration are the rapid spread of venereal disease and the near impossibility of its eradication. The results are diminished fertility and an increasing incidence of complete sterility. Women thus affected are no longer desirable in the rural setting, where traditionally one of the main purposes of marriage is to perpetuate lineage, clan, or tribe. Consequently, such women move to towns, where they find a ready welcome and answer the needs of men who are compelled by economic, religious, or social considerations to be unmarried, celibate, monogamous, or restrained in their sexual lives. The article by Little and Price deals with a predominately polygynous area. It indicates that prostitution may become an institutionalized alternative to polygyny, allowing a man to preserve his status as established by his adopted European and Christian values and at the same time preserve his traditional right of access to a plurality of women.

Whereas the Little and Price article is broad in its approach, the Parkin article, "Types of Urban African Marriage in Kampala," is a more detailed study of a specific community in a single town. It deals more fully with the role of tribalism. Although restricted to one community, this study is valuable because it suggests the structure that can lie behind the social organization of an urban setting and indicates that such organization is by no means as haphazard as it may seem. Dealing as it does with different tribal elements within the same community, the article shows that the problem of individualism is much greater among people from centralized tribes than among those from segmentary societies.

Insofar as every viable society is constantly undergoing social change, these articles have much to contribute to an understanding of the European or American family and the changes taking place there. The fact that the role of the family *is* changing is perhaps the best thing that can be said about it, since this indicates greater vitality than might be suspected from a study of the divorce rate, the increasingly open practice of adultery, the increasing number of institutionalized means (such as summer camps) for keeping the child out of the home, and the open rejection by much of today's youth of the old, nominal, family ideal. The state is increasingly taking over functions that until very recently were considered the prerogatives of the parents: health care, sex (and general) education, nourishment, even clothing and shelter, and, ultimately, responsibility for launching the child into gainful employment and for his maintenance if he fails to find such employment. Marriage, birth, naming, coming of age, death, and burial have all become legal formalities.

The greatly heightened pace of change in Africa, while superficially making the two situations less comparable, nonetheless serves to indicate certain basic factors. It helps us, for instance, to better understand the growing lack of respect for authority in the United States and Europe, for there is a correlation with the increasing lack of respect for the nuclear family, undermined, as it is, by state control. In the African situation the relationship is made very obvious to us, and, in reading some of the letters in the Jahoda and Chaplin articles, we may well wonder what kinds of citizens these romantically (and selfishly) inclined individuals are likely to make. Many a foreigner traveling through the new nations has made a similar observation upon noting the graft and corruption. Really, he should be surprised that graft and corruption are not more widespread; they are the inevitable consequences of the change that was introduced starting with the destruction of the traditional sense of family. In the West, where change has taken place over a longer period of time, the all-important lesson of sociability that was once learned in the personal intimacy of the family, where daily life was a constant example of its efficacy, now has become an impersonal and remote intellectual exercise learned in the classroom. We may not perceive the results immediately in the same terms of graft and corruption with which we criticize many a new nation, but there is little difference. Graft and corruption are the subjugation of moral, social interests to individual interests, or, in modern terms, of the larger society to the smaller part of that society. It is difficult in the huge, impersonal nations of the West for the individual to feel a direct sense of responsibility to the nation as a whole. It is an intellectual feat, if he achieves it, rather than a sentiment, and is correspondingly fragile. Similarly, it seems difficult for a nation to feel itself part of the international, global society. Nationality and nationhood are legal political conveniences, and merely conceal the same basic lack of responsibility with which we attack others by the use of terms such as "diplomacy," "expediency," "legal responsibility," "political necessity," "realism," and so forth.

One of the strengths of tribality (to avoid the loaded term "tribalism") lies in its emphasis on familial obligations and on the family as the foundation and model of society as a whole. A leader like Kwame Nkrumah who had a genuine sense of devotion to the new nation turned this to advantage and used tribal sentiment as the model for national sentiment by expanding the family concept from tribe to nation. Another leader, Obote of Uganda, who was less scrupulous and less devoted to the nation, used the tribal sentiment by restricting it and converting it into the most vicious form of tribalism (in the sense of intertribal hostility) in order to secure his own ascendancy. In comparing the two leaders and their methods, it is notable that Nkrumah, who during the first critical years of his rule enjoyed the affection of the entire nation, left behind a truly united people, even after his personal collapse. This unity was achieved by the temporary use he made of his image as a common founding ancestor, an image by no means destroyed by his evident fallibility. Obote, on the other hand, could hardly be said to have enjoyed anyone's affection, except that of some of his own Lango tribe. Obote came to power through bloodshed, was welcomed with fear, and ruled through oppression. He left behind a nation divided by bitterness and hatred, ruined by corruption, and reunited only by the act of his overthrow, which was greeted with almost universal joy. His successor, General Amin, was welcomed to power with widespread demonstrations of affection. Obote never managed (and never tried) to win the affection of the nation and establish himself (or anyone else) as a symbol evoking the common sentiment of nationality or nationhood. The family model, at every level of society, shows how essential such a symbol is and how the affective and effective elements may (or may not) be combined.

It is difficult to love a flag, a national anthem, or a passport as much as a human being, even when the ideals for which they stand are intellectualized, and it is more difficult to love a president who occupies office for a short time than a constitutional monarch one comes to know over a lifetime. When the president is expected to take an active part in political life, as he is in the United States, this is especially true; he inevitably alienates even his supporters at some time or another. Consequently, the nation is left without an affective leader and has instead one whose efficacy is constantly in question—a precariously balanced idol to which the people cling, all the time suspecting its emptiness.

With a monarchy, there is more of a perceived affective relationship between the monarch and the people, but European monarchies have still lacked the enormous symbolic and unifying power of African monarchies. In Africa the monarch is considered the apex of the family pyramid, repeating at the tribal or national level what is already established and familiar to all at the basic family level. In looking at the general social malaise to be found today in our own Western world, especially as manifest in the open disregard for law and order, perhaps it would be better to examine the system and what it does to the family, rather than blame specific governments or policies. Perhaps we are more like the African than we think in transferring habits of cooperation and social responsibility, learned in infancy and childhood through family example, to the wider national level. There is often little or nothing to transfer.

The Western family, instead of being the foundation of social life, reinforces the ideal of rugged individualism The idealized family is further associated with the notion of a pure, selfless, and undemanding love, a notion that is as untenable as the concept of the pure gift.* These notions of love and individualism lead us to expect, even to demand, something for nothing; but unfortunately the system fails to teach us how not to be infuriated and genuinely outraged when the same demand is made of us. The African family, on the other hand, rests and acts, survives and thrives on a well-ordered and frank system of reciprocal relationships, rights, and obligations under which the individual can see his survival only in terms of

---

* See Marcel Mauss, *The Gift* (New York: Norton, 1967), for a deeply perceptive examination of the gift as a functional institution.

the survival of the whole. This is not as brutal as it may sound, for it is often institutionalized that reciprocation is either delayed or diverted or both. Thus, a man is not expected to return equivalent value for what he receives at the moment, within any given period, or even necessarily to the same individuals, which he may be asked to fulfill at a mutually convenient time. In fact, gifts (including offers of friendship) are often made or demanded as political rather than economic gestures, in order to establish or reconfirm a system of interrelationships.

At the same time, the concept of cultural relativity makes it clear that we cannot simply adopt the African family model. It is as proper to its society as the Western family is to Western society. But an understanding of the traditional African notion of society as defined by his notion of family reveals that there is a similar correlation in Western society. Using the family model, the African defines society in both effective and affective terms, whereas Western society is generally defined exclusively in effective terms, perhaps with intellect running a poor substitute for sentiment. Further still, whereas African society works from the smallest unit outward in a series of coherent expansions that differ only in extent, not in form, in our society there is little coherence, merely a number of discrete units to which we belong for different purposes, with no common theme, familial or otherwise, structuring our diverse relationships. Far from judging ourselves by African standards, it is more profitable to eschew judgment at this stage and merely use African (or other) societies as a means of illuminating our own, adding to the depth of our self-awareness, which in this case means merely noting that rather chilling correlation between our family relationships (as practiced, not preached) and our wider social relationships.

Whereas traditional African relationships are based on mutual exploitation, ours, thanks to our misguided concepts of love and individualism, tend to be founded more on unidirectional, nonreciprocal exploitation. And if the African is not virtuously affectionate to the point of a possessiveness that connotes emotional instability, neither is he cold and without human affection, even when he calculates. The African sees human relations as a necessary, vital network to be created, maintained, repaired, expanded, and contracted according to need, relevant to his entire social life. He sees and uses the family as his model. In traditional African life, it is on this solid foundation of mutual need that affection is built and love is found. The African's human relations are based on a realistic appraisal of their social worth, but as well as being realistic they are also essentially human.

If on further inquiry we find that, in our own world, the destruction of the family and of moral human relationships is an inevitable corollary of the expansion of the state and the dominance of purely legal relationships, then we merely have to ask ourselves which do we value the more highly. Do we want to behave toward each other in an approved manner because we *want* to, because it is natural to us, or simply because we *have* to under threat of physical coercion? Society, it seems, can be defined as either essentially moralistic or essentially legalistic. In the former, equitable human relations are maintained by the reiteration of basic patterns of behavior learned during childhood; in the latter, they are maintained, if at all, through the imposition of contrived laws enforced by constraint, often violent.

Having asked the question and knowing at least some of the implications, we may then be in a position to do something about it. To assert that nothing can be done, that the direction on which we are embarked is irreversible, or to argue against going "back," is nonsensical. Society changes all the time; there is no reason why that change should not be guided. It is not a question of a reversal of direction, but merely one of a change in course. The engineering of social change is a highly disputable issue, fraught with dangers; but considering the ever-diminishing chances of survival with which contemporary society is faced, it is surely time to make some attempt to do more than merely add to the growing list of this year's comforts that are going to be next year's necessities, and call that "progress."

# Love, Marriage, and Social Change: Letters to the Advice Column of a West African Newspaper

## • Gustav Jahoda

The effects of major changes in the social system on the mental state of individuals have been the subject of a recent controversy. Miss Ward (1956), in a paper discussing the significance of an alleged increase in the number of witch-finding cults in Ashanti, argued that this can be taken as evidence of a widespread rise in the general level of anxiety resulting from rapid structural changes. In a subsequent rejoinder Goody (1957) challenged not only the view that such cults have in fact become more numerous, but also the underlying assumption, shared by many social scientists, that rapid social change produces an emotional malaise in the people caught up in it.

Without entering into the details of this dispute, a few comments may be justified as serving to introduce the present topic. Goody was clearly right in pointing out that we have no means of assessing comparative happiness or misery, so that statements about an *overall* increase in malaise are necessarily always speculative. One can also sympathize with his attack on the idea that rapid social change leads to anomie (normlessness), although it is doubtful whether many sociologists would really believe this; the problem here is probably at least partly of a semantic nature. Even if one rejects the notion of a drift towards anomie, it does not affect the likelihood that *conflicting norms* will exist side by side during the transition phase, so that individuals may lack a firm guide for their conduct in various situations. Or again, as a consequence of social changes people will tend to adopt new goals, which may be difficult to achieve, and this is liable to generate anxiety and discontent. There are certainly many ways in which social change can make life more difficult for some people, and these are worthy of study in their own right: one does not have to be able to balance them against the unquestioned gains in terms of personal security or material welfare with which social change can often be credited. The present study, carried out in Ghana, was part of a wider attempt to gain information both about the transformations of attitudes and norms, and the accompanying stresses.

In his discussion of the use of personal documents in anthropology, Kluckhohn (1945, p. 105) refers to letters to the press as one of the 'yet unexploited research resources' on acculturation. In the present study an effort was made to secure all letters addressed to the advice column of a newspaper with a national circulation in Ghana (then still the Gold Coast) during a period of about three months at the beginning of 1955. Owing to the haphazard method of storage, and the fact that many of the letters were not dated, there is a certain overlap with earlier and later months. This means that the number of letters cannot be related to specified units of time, but there is no reason to suppose that it introduces any systematic distortion as regards content.

At the outset it may be well to evaluate this kind of material, and in particular to indicate its limitations. There is first the question of the motives for writing a letter; generally one may expect two main ones, namely the need to get outside help with a personal problem, and the wish to appear in print. In practice these cannot be easily disentangled, though it is possible to eliminate those letters which contain merely statements of fact or opinion. The bulk of the letters unmistakably relates to definite personal problems, freely and spontaneously described in the writers' own words.

It is clear, however, that for a variety of reasons the range of problems included in the letters cannot be considered as typical, both in character and frequency, for people in the society as a whole. Obviously only literates are likely to write letters to the press, and even if one makes a very generous estimate these can hardly have constituted much more than about one-quarter of the population aged 16 and over. Furthermore, there are a number of other institutions and agencies, modern and traditional, which people can and do approach with their troubles; among these would be doctors, social welfare agencies, ministers of religion, native doctors and herbalists, and finally some persons and organizations intermediate between the traditional and the modern.[1]

Lastly, while editorial screening does not enter directly, the policy guiding the selection of letters for publication will influence the kind that are being sent in. The emphasis in the present case, undoubtedly patterned on British women's magazines, is on love, courtship, and marriage, and this is the salient theme of the letters.

Before presenting the actual problems, something has to be said about the social characteristics of the letter-writers. It is one of the drawbacks of this sort of research that one has to be content with such information as

---

[1] The intermediate type is a characteristic product of social change, embodying a blend of western religious and occult notions with traditional indigenous beliefs.

the writers choose to give about themselves. The temptation to put forward plausible inferences will not always be resisted, but in Table 1 below only information directly contained in the documents is listed.

In spite of this limitation a few trends emerge quite clearly from the table. First, the bulk of the letters came from unmarried young men; from internal evidence it is very likely that most of the 40 men whose marital status is not definitely known also belong to this category; if one adds them to the previous total this accounts for nearly 90 per cent. of all letters. It may be noted that this is almost exactly the reverse of the position in Britain as set out by Greenland (1957). One important cause of this is probably the higher literacy rate among men; in 1952, for instance, nearly three times as many boys as girls were enrolled in all types of educational institutions, and in earlier years the discrepancy was far greater.

Almost two-thirds specified their age, hence one may feel confident that the typical seeker for advice is in his or her late 'teens or early twenties. This is confirmed by the high proportion (among those who mention what they are doing) still undergoing full-time education.

The other reliable piece of information concerns the places from which the letters were sent. Over half of them originated from the four largest towns (Accra, Kumasi, Sekondi-Takoradi, and Cape Coast), whose combined population in 1948 represented only 7 per cent. of the country's total. Owing to the concentration of literates in the large towns this is, of course, not unexpected.

With education and jobs one is on far more precarious ground. Only some 16 and 24 per cent. respectively provide any details, and one cannot be sure how representative they are. An impressionistic judgement, based on style of writing as well as other indirect clues, suggests that rather more than half the writers had received an education beyond the elementary level. As far as jobs are concerned, clerical and teaching ones clearly predominate; in addition there seems to be a fair sprinkling of men in minor technical government posts. In view of the subsequent discussion of the nature of their problems it is important to stress that nearly all people in such occupations are, by virtue of their conditions of employment, liable to be transferred from one part of the country to another.

The analysis will concentrate on the largest single category, i.e. unmarried young men; problems of married men will be outlined in so far as they help to throw additional light on those of unmarried ones.

## Unmarried Young Men

Their letters were subdivided according to the predominant causal factors, as viewed from a sociological standpoint. The most important of these were the persistence of traditional mores, and the influence of new patterns of living.

TABLE 1 SOCIAL BACKGROUND OF WRITERS

| | | No. | Numbers Given | Ages | | Education | | | Occupations | | | | | Place of origin | |
|---|---|---|---|---|---|---|---|---|---|---|---|---|---|---|---|
| | | | | Median | Range | Elementary only | Secondary or Teacher training | Other post-elementary | Clerical or teaching | Trading | Artisan | Unem.ployed | Full-time education | Large town | Other |
| Men | Unmarried | 251 | 185 | 22 | 16–31 | 13 | 27 | 6 | 20 | 9 | 6 | 3 | 22 | 123 | 100 |
| Men | Married | 35 | 19 | 28 | 21–35 | ? | ? | ? | 1 | ? | ? | ? | ? | 15 | 15 |
| Men | Not known | 40 | 17 | 20 | 18–25 | 5 | 2 | ? | 6 | 1 | 1 | 1 | 7 | 14 | 16 |
| Women | Unmarried | 33 | 24 | 18½ | 16–24 | 3 | 1 | 1 | 7 | ? | ? | ? | 2 | 15 | 12 |
| Women | Married | 4 | 3 | 21 | 21–45 | ? | ? | ? | ? | ? | ? | ? | ? | 1 | 3 |
| Totals | | 363 | 248 | 21 | 16–45 | 21 | 30 | 7 | 34 | 10 | 7 | 4 | 31 | 168 | 146 |

Persistence of Traditional Mores

1. MARRIAGES ARRANGED BY PARENTS OR RELATIVES. There were 20 cases of this kind. In 15 a young man's parents or relatives wanted to force him to marry a girl of their choice, to whom he objected. Four of these girls were explicitly stated to be illiterate, but the actual proportion was probably a good deal higher. The remaining 5 letters describe a situation in which the young man wanted to marry a girl, whose parents were exerting pressure for her to enter another marriage they had already arranged regardless of her wishes. Here is a summary of a letter illustrating the former problem:

A young man aged 22, from internal evidence an Ashanti, has an uncle who took the responsibility of helping him with his education and assisted him whenever he was in any financial embarrassment. After he had held a job for a year, the uncle considered that he was almost ready for marriage and offered him one of his daughters, an illiterate than aged 10. The young man already has a girl friend who is educated, but does not hail from his town. The uncle, on the other hand, is anxious that he should not marry a 'stranger'. He does not wish to marry an illiterate girl, yet at the same time is afraid to reject the offer of his uncle, who helped him in the past and on whom he might perhaps have to depend in the future.

This letter shows the nature of the dilemma very clearly. In a matrilineal society like Ashanti, the mother's brother stands in a very special relationship to his sister's son, who inherits his property. The good uncle creates an obligation on the part of his nephew by his generosity; moreover, cross-cousin marriage is traditionally favoured, and the rejection of his uncle's offer would constitute a grave hurt and insult. Similar situations do of course arise *vis-à-vis* parents and other relatives.

2. FAMILY OPPOSITION TO PROJECTED MARRIAGES. There were 52 letters focused on this theme: in 27 the opposition came from the man's side, in 21 from the girl's and in the remaining 4 from both sides. The distribution of such grounds for opposition as were given is to be found in Table 2.

The traditional reasons, which clearly predominate, require some explanation. The term 'stranger' may refer to someone from outside the home town[2] (3 cases), someone belonging to a different tribe (6 cases), or a national of another West African country (2 cases). An example of the first kind is outlined below:

---

[2] The word 'village' does not form part of the ordinary vocabulary and all places, irrespective of size, are called 'towns'; this usage will also be adopted here.

TABLE 2 REASONS FOR OPPOSITION

|                        | No. |
|------------------------|-----|
| Traditional reasons    |     |
| 'Stranger'             | 11  |
| Prohibited kin         | 6   |
| Total                  | 17  |
| New kinds of reasons   |     |
| Disturbs studies       | 1   |
| 'Scholarship'          | 1   |
| Political feud         | 1   |
| Girl illiterate        | 1   |
| Total                  | 4   |
| Not applicable         |     |
| Boy too young          | 1   |
| Woman a widow          | 2   |
| Family quarrel         | 1   |
| Total                  | 4   |

This young man's mother objected to his marrying a girl who, though from within the district, was not from his town. He commented that the Creator could not have intended any such restrictions, and emphasis ought to be only on 'love and understanding'.

After elaborating somewhat upon this theme, the writer ended with two revealing questions:

1. 'Would it be better if I marry such a girl?'
2. 'If so, then what can I tell my mother just to [make her] understand the word "love and understanding in marriage"?'

Although he uses a universalist argument derived from Christian teaching, he is in fact plagued by grave doubts as to whether he ought to marry the 'stranger' of his choice in the face of his mother's objection. And if the advice is to marry her, he appeals for help in conveying to his mother a conception obviously quite foreign to her, namely that what matters most in marriage is the harmonious personal relationship of the partners.

The next example concerns tribal differences.

The writer, who comes from a poor Ga family, met a Fante girl from a well-to-do background at secondary school. The girl agreed to marry him, but his father said he would 'never allow any of his sons to marry anyone who is not a Ga born'.

Owing to variations in customs, marriages across tribal boundaries may involve complications, so that parental opposition in such instances cannot always be put down just to deep-rooted conservatism. This applies especially where one tribe is patrilineal and the other matrilineal, with the associated son-versus-nephew inheritance, which was referred to several times. Nevertheless, there is evidence that inter-tribal marriages are becoming increasingly prevalent in the larger urban centres.[3]

The other traditional reason for families withholding their consent was that the marriage would contravene rules about prohibited degrees of kinship. None of those mentioned related to direct blood relationships, and would thus not constitute reasonable objections in European eyes; and to the extent that the 'young men have adopted a western outlook, they are equally unacceptable to them.

The 'new' kinds of reasons can be dealt with more summarily. The first, disturbance of studies, is self-explanatory as a ground for postponing marriage. 'Scholarship' has nothing to do with learning, but is an expression coined to characterize the relationship between a man and a woman by analogy with that of a student to the government: it refers to a relationship in which the woman has a higher position and/or greater wealth than the man, and does in fact keep him. In the present instance the girl's parents opposed the union because her status in the teaching profession was senior to his, so that her salary was also higher.

The political feud divided, on the one hand, a family enthusiastic in their support for the CPP, and on the other a family devoted with equal fervour to the opposition party.

The last case is that of a man wanting to marry an illiterate girl, who found that his educated family were greatly disappointed by his choice. Their disapproval has made him rather uneasy, so that he is evidently seeking for outside support. Here we have what amounts to a complete reversal of the earlier problems, and one closely akin to that of the son of a western bourgeois family who wishes to marry an unskilled factory girl. It seems likely that, as social differentiation along western lines proceeds, this type of problem will become more common, while the incidence of the ones described earlier will decline.

### Influence of New Patterns of Living

1. THREATENED OR BROKEN RELATIONSHIPS. Two kinds of difficulty are included under this heading: first, the man states that his girl has ceased to care for him, and asks how he can win her back (24 letters); second, a rival has appeared with whom the girl has started 'playing', the question being what can be done about it (35 letters). In over half the cases of both

---

[3] Busia (1950, p. 29) reported that in Sekondi-Takoradi nearly one-third of the marriages in his sample were inter-tribal.

types it was specifically stated that a more or less prolonged separation had occurred, of which details are given below.

Gone to work elsewhere, transferred: 11 men and 2 girls.
Went to school or college: 3 men and 5 girls.
Met at school or college and separated after leaving: 8.
Unspecified separations: 3 men and 1 girl.

These problems are to a large extent a consequence of the high degree of geographical mobility among the literate section of the population, brought about by social changes. Such enforced absences are liable to make the heart grow less fond, in spite of the exchange of letters that was frequently mentioned. In such circumstances one or other of the couple may look elsewhere for consolation—the present letters can, of course, tell only one side of the story.

Some additional features emerge from the cases where another man came into the picture. Seven of the writers stated that their girl had intercourse with the other man, and in 4 more pregnancy had resulted. It is of interest to note that 1 in 5 of the rivals was actually a friend of the writer. This is no coincidence, for a friend often acts as a go-between in love affairs; he cannot always be relied upon to remain detached, especially when friction has already arisen. Here is a summary of a typical instance:

A young man of 23 had a quarrel with his girl. He called in a friend 'to settle the case between them'. The outcome was that the friend stayed with the girl, and as the writer somewhat naïvely elaborated 'I hope you know what happens when a man and a woman sleep in the same room till the next day'. On the following morning the friend came to say that the girl still did not want to resume their former relationship. The writer, who heard what had happened, did not know what to do next.

Finally, in several cases not involving separation there were direct or indirect indications that the man who had stolen the girl's affections was of higher socioeconomic status; e.g. 'he is holding a European post'[4] or he was said to be 'a man of wealth—carful and fridgful'.

2. MULTIPLE ENTANGLEMENTS. The issue here may be regarded as complementary to the one just discussed, with similar causal factors. A schematic presentation would run something like this: a man travels around, entering into liaisons with girls at two or more stations, in addition sometimes to a girl at his home town; or again, his girl may go away for further education or to another work place. Pregnancies frequently occur (5 single,

---

[4] i.e. one of the higher administrative posts formerly reserved for Europeans.

3 double, 1 multiple). The man is then faced with a conflict situation: sometimes he wants to know which one he ought to marry, or keep up relations with (which one out of two in 8 cases, out of three in 2 cases); alternatively, if he has a definite preference, the question becomes one of finding means of getting rid of the others (4 cases). The remaining 6 do not fit clearly into the scheme; none referred to any transfers or separations, but in 3 of them the writer lived in a large city, whose size and anonymity permit the same basic pattern. The others were variations on the theme in which the different girls knew each other, or were about to collide.

An example of the problem first outlined will be given.

A 23-year-old clerk writes about his wife-to-be, who is being trained as a telephone operator: 'I love this girl to the bottom of my heart'. However, as she lives far away, he unfortunately made two other girls pregnant and consequently is 'perplexed mentally'. He asks: 'What can I do to repel . . . these two girls . . . and get hold of my own darling as my ever and one wife?'

One means whereby dilemmas of this sort might be resolved would be polygyny, which was in fact referred to in the present context. In 5 cases this was only to reject it with varying degrees of vehemence, largely on the ground of what one called 'my natural distastes'. Two more objected mainly because of the expense and only one man, in a very special situation, was seriously toying with the idea: both his girl friends came together and announced their intention to marry him.

3. APPROACH TO GIRLS AND ROMANTIC LOVE. In presenting the problems grouped under this heading the main types will be listed with brief examples.

(a) How can I get a girl friend? How does one approach a girl? (15 letters)
   'I am a boy of 19 years of age. As I don't have any girls as my friend, which step should I take to get one?'
   'I often meet a girl near the bus stop. This girl I love very much, but the first steps I should take to approach her is now my difficulty.'
(b) Complaints of feeling shy and nervous about girls (5 letters)
   '. . . several times I have been attracted by nice girls, but always I have been beaten by nervousness. When in the 'teens I masturbated. Do you think this shyness of mine could be [the result of this]?'

It should be explained that this reference to masturbation was the only one of its kind, otherwise the letter was typical.

(c) How does one choose a good wife? (5 letters)
   '. . . I cannot make my choice at all because [I] cannot distinguish between a good and a bad girl, and aged woman and a young woman . . . the old women

. . . are all racing or scrambling for young men by "pan-cacking", "lip-sticking" and painting of nails.'

(d) Does she really love me? (10 letters)

'I wonder if she is really in love with me. Please, how can I know that she has fallen for me?'

'Is she a true lover?'

'How can I be sure she will love me more than ever?'

'Is this love really from Heaven?'

What is noteworthy about many of these problems is their resemblance to those experienced by young people in western societies. Types (a), (b), and (c) stem largely from comparative social isolation, either due to the impersonal atmosphere of life in a city as contrasted with a village, or to being a stranger in a small town. In such circumstances the establishment of relations with the opposite sex requires the exercise of individual initiative, which some people find harder than others. In the small village community, where nearly everybody has some sort of contact with everybody else, and where relatives have a hand in the choice of a marriage partner, such difficulties will be almost entirely absent.

The boy who worries about the effects of masturbation probably derived this idea from imported popular magazines and books. The same source[5] no doubt also contributes to foster the notion of romantic love, but they are perhaps outweighed by the long-term influence of certain facets of Christian teaching and, more recently, the cinema.

In connexion with the concept of romantic love a certain caution is advisable. From the fact that the phrasing employed is familiar, one is apt to jump to the conclusion that the referent, i.e. the emotional bond, is identical with that in western societies. While it is not possible to make any dogmatic pronouncements in such an elusive sphere, there are indications that matters may not be so simple. In the first place the frequent request for reassurance, for some sign that the love is really 'true', suggests that many young people are in fact groping for the full meaning of what is symbolized by the word 'love', for some criterion by which they could judge that it is really there. Secondly, in the West the concept of romantic love carries the connotation of exclusiveness; the usage frequently exemplified in the letters shows that this is not necessarily true of the writers. Thus it appears that although western influences have given a wide currency to the language of romantic love, its actual content of meaning remains circumscribed by the existing matrix of social values, which can alter only gradually.

---

[5] In a reading survey carried out under the direction of the author it was found that popular books and magazines on psychology and etiquette are widely read; women's journals and such publications as 'True Romances' enjoy a considerable circulation. Cf. Kimble (1956).

## Other Problems of Love and Marriage

This is a residual category of 65 letters that do not fit into any of the preceding ones. The largest single subdivision consists of questions as to how a marriage the writer had originally envisaged could be avoided or postponed. The main reasons given were that they felt too young or poor (5), that the girl was illiterate (2), or that she did not come up to expectations in some other way (6).

Next is a large and very mixed bag of problems, whose variety will be illustrated by outlining the essential elements of a few chosen at random:

His girl brings two others for breakfast every day, which ruins him financially. His girl is too jealous. His girl refuses to come and see him in his room. He would like to get love letters from girls abroad. His girl gets too many 'offers' from other men. His school-girl friend washed his clothes and the head teacher confiscated them.

There are, in addition, some letters whose theme is more directly relevant in the present context, and these will be treated in more detail.

A young man of 21 fell in love with a girl while they both attended secondary school. The relationship lasted for three years, when the girl's parents sent her to Britain for further education. Although she writes regularly, he is anxious about the future and wonders if she will still care for him after her return, 'I being just a junior clerk in one of the local firms. And if she does, am I worthy of her hand in marriage if she comes back a "been-to"?'

The increasing importance of status differences is also brought out in another letter where a young man expresses himself bitterly about the attitude of his girl who is better educated than himself. Forthcoming in private, she hates to be seen in his company. As he somewhat ambiguously put it 'In the night she is a "devil", during the day she is an "angel"'.

In another letter a young unestablished government servant, who plans to marry a teacher, is worried because his work is not stationary and he is required to have a Christian wedding, which is far more expensive than the customary rite.[6] Again, a man would like to marry a divorced woman, yet fears that this may be contrary to the teaching of the Bible.

Finally three letters are worthy of special note, each being the only one of its kind. The first is phrased in terms strongly suggesting that the writer is a homosexual; he asks how one can get men friends, and complains that girls gossip about him and call him names. Nothing seems to be known about the incidence of such deviants in West Africa, but it is generally

---

[6] Cf. Busia (1950), p. 41. This is a very common and widely debated problem.

held to be very low. It is therefore of interest that a case should occur in such a small sample.

The second letter is from a man about to be married, who is afraid that he might be what he calls 'impotent', though it is evident from the context that he really means 'infertile'. This is contrary to the widely held assumption, at least until the opposite is established in any particular case, that infertility is the fault of the woman.

The last letter is from a young man who says that he cannot bring himself to kiss his girl, because her breath is so bad. The interest here lies not so much in the topic of halitosis with its usual accompaniment ('I can't tell her about her breath'), but in the reference to kissing. For this is not an indigenous practice, being in fact strongly disapproved of by older people as immoral. There was one other mention of kissing among the letters, which similarly implied that it was common. In this respect, therefore, western sexual mores seem to have been adopted, and one may suspect that films are largely responsible.

### Other Observations and Summary of Problem Types

A great deal of incidental information may be gleaned from the content of the letters, and some of this is valuable in providing further pointers to the general picture.

The ages of 89 of the girls or women concerned were mentioned; these range from 12 to 45, with a mode of 18. In 79 cases it was possible to compute the age-differences: at one extreme the woman was 15 years older, at the other the girl 10 years younger; the general tendency was for the man to be 2 or 3 years older (respective mode and median).

In 42 letters the place where boy met girl was stated: in 23 cases it was their home town, for the rest elsewhere; and 22 of the meetings occurred in schools or colleges.

There were 14 young men who mentioned gifts and/or remittances to their girl, and 10 more referred to reciprocal gifts; in three cases the man assumed financial responsibility for the schooling of the girl to whom he was engaged.

Although physical relations were explicitly said to have taken place in only 18 letters, the numerous oblique references to intercourse indicate that it is the norm rather than the exception. One has, of course, to add the 27 cases where the girl's pregnancy was reported. In this connexion it should be explained that the quotation under the heading of 'multiple entanglements', where pregnancy was apt to produce special difficulties, may have been somewhat misleading as regards the usual attitudes to such an event. It appears to have been greeted mostly with pleasure and pride, a fact reflecting the persistence of procreation as a predominant value even among educated Africans. A more representative extract would be the following:

'Very fortunately enough my Darling conceived . . . My Darling was fed, clothed and cared by me until she delivered and the daughter and the mother are under my care.'

Like many other descriptions of this kind, it showed not only the acceptance of an obligation to look after the mother with her child, but also to marry her according to custom. In cases where attempts are made to evade this obligation, one will mostly find that special circumstances are operating; e.g. paternity may be in doubt, or more than one girl has become pregnant.

In concluding this section on unmarried young men, the frequency of the different types of problems for which they sought advice and help is listed below (percentages rounded to the nearest whole number):

|  | per cent. |
| --- | --- |
| Threatened or broken relationships | 24 |
| Family opposition to marriage | 21 |
| Approach to girls and romantic love | 14 |
| Marriages arranged by parents or relatives | 8 |
| Multiple entanglements | 8 |
| Miscellaneous other | 26 |

## Married Men

The purpose of the majority of their letters was to ask what could be done about some defect of character in the wife. It was sometimes possible to infer that differences in education and social background may have had something to do with the lack of marital harmony. In several cases the circumstances were quite explicitly set out, and these will be briefly considered.

First, there were those marriages which had taken place in opposition to the wishes of the family, usually because the girl was a 'stranger'. In one case there was no offspring from such a union, in another the child was born with a hare-lip. Anything of this kind was seized upon as showing that the marriage was an ill-fated one—the men clearly had not succeeded in overcoming the conflict experienced as a result of marrying in the face of parental disapproval.

Second, there was the more common problem of those who had been pushed or driven into marrying illiterate girls. In view of the importance of this topic one of the most articulate of these letters, which brings out most of the difficulties of such a situation, is reproduced in full.

'I am 28 years old. I am married to an illiterate girl for the past three years. The marriage was arranged by my parents without my consent. My parents and the girls' parents are close friends. The girl was sent to me but I had not the courage to refuse her, fearing that the refusal would anger my father and also cast a blur on his friendship with the girl's parent. Again, I learnt that my father had spent much money on the girl on my behalf, so I decided to give her a trial. Fortunately for her our first mating resulted in pregnancy and we have now got a nice baby girl of whom I am very proud. But the girl is not the ideal wife I dreamt of in my college days. I have tried hard to bring her to the standard required of her, but she is still unprogressive. I feel shy to bring my friends to my house because no one likes to wash his dirty linen in public. The nature of my work is such that I spend most of the days of each month outside my home and I am entertaining the fear that my children will be ill-bred because the girl herself lacks training. However, she is honest and economical, but I feel she is not the right type of girl I ought to have married.

Recently I have fallen in love with an educated girl who I am sure is the girl I have been looking for. But polygamy is the first thing I detest. I am afraid of losing the confidence of my parents by putting away my wife and marrying the girl of my own choice. This is a hard nut for me to break. I don't in the least feel happy in my wife's company at all. I am a public-spirited fellow, but when I ask my wife to accompany me to a social gathering or church she always puts up a lame excuse and refuses to go.

The picture emerging from this and the other letters is a pathetic one: two people thrown together who soon realize their incompatibility, without an easy way out. Some marriages with illiterate girls undoubtedly turn out more successful than this; nevertheless, the unwillingness to marry illiterates voiced by many of the young men appears amply justified.[7]

Lastly it may be mentioned that only 4 of the letters were written by polygynous husbands, one of these being an attempt to defend and justify his having three wives in view of what 'gossipers' say. This fits in with the tenor of the material as a whole, which suggests that opinion is moving against polygyny as an institution.

## Conclusions

An attempt will now be made to offer a broader perspective on the various aspects of social change, in so far as they are liable to give rise to the prob-

---

[7] The previous attitude of the men is probably the crucial variable. By no means all young men who have had some schooling prefer literate wives. It is reckoned by some that a wife with education is too great a financial liability, and they would rather have an illiterate who earns money by trading. For a more detailed discussion of this issue, cf. Jahoda (1958).

lems considered. The grouping of causal factors is inevitably to some extent arbitrary, as most of them are closely interrelated.

GEOGRAPHICAL MOBILITY AND URBAN LIFE. Both of these widen the potential range of contact with members of the opposite sex. At the same time this means that a person is more often thrown back on his own resources in establishing relations, which creates difficulties for shy and diffident people. Attachments are also liable to spring up between men and women of different tribal as well as social and educational backgrounds, and a proposed marriage across such barriers may lead to friction in the respective families.

Frequent movement for reasons of education or work tends to make for instability of relationships, occasioning distress to those who have been abandoned. Simultaneous friendships and/or engagements often land people in a net of incompatible obligations from which they are incapable of disentangling themselves.

ADOPTION OF WESTERN NORMS, VALUES AND CRITERIA OF STATUS. The main element in the present context is the taking over of the notion of romantic love, and of marriage as a partnership of like-minded individuals. A corollary to this is the rejection of traditional restrictions on the selection of a marriage partner, i.e. from outside a prescribed range of classificatory kinship and within the tribe. A relatively minor problem here is the difficulty experienced by some young people in recognizing the presence, especially in their partner, of the intense emotional bond which is regarded as the essential prerequisite of a satisfactory relationship. The consequences are much more far-reaching when the dictates of love clash with the wishes of the family of origin; this often results in the most acute anxiety. Even where the idea of romantic love is not in the foreground, and the family leaves a man free to choose his wife, this new freedom may itself produce a state of uncertainty and doubt if he is not sure what he is looking for.

In this connexion reference should be made to the effect of the emergence of a status system of the western type, for this erects new kinds of barriers. As social differences become more pronounced, there are increasing hazards for matches in which there is a great disparity in terms of education and/or material wealth. The trouble is that many young people, brought together by their families, are of comparable status within the traditional system; and their incompatibility is revealed only when they live together in sections of society that no longer form an integral part of that system. The typical case is of course that of the educated young man who marries an illiterate wife, but other variants have been described in this paper. It is likely that assortative mating along western lines will in the long run operate cumulatively in building up a new class structure.

DIFFERENTIAL RATES OF CHANGE OF NORMS AND VALUES. It is implicit in much of what has been said that the underlying cause of many of the problems is not just social change as such, but rather the fact that the reorientation it brings about is not uniform; it affects the older generation far less than the younger people. This greatly exacerbates the divergence in outlook between successive generations which is found in varying degrees in all societies. Moreover, the ties of kinship, which are rooted in the old cosmology, have always been extremely close and powerful in West Africa; and the feelings of respect and dependence towards the family of origin have not weakened in proportion to the acceptance of new norms in other spheres. Youth or girls may have their own ideas about the kind of marriage partner they want, yet at the same time they are frequently not able or willing to ignore the pressures or objections of their elders who remain attached to traditional standards. Severing of the ties which bind them to the kin group is not only difficult because it runs counter to deeply entrenched sentiments, but would also be risky in practice in a society where as yet no safety net is provided by the welfare state. Even educated Africans derive comfort and security from the knowledge that they can confidently look forward to help from their kin if they should happen to fall upon evil days; it requires a very independent cast of mind to be able to cut oneself loose under such circumstances. Therefore it becomes necessary to tread an uneasy middle path between following the time-honoured customs as expected by one's elders and pursuing one's own goals and aspirations.

A large proportion of the letters consists of cases where there has been failure to reconcile the conflicting demands, and they are of three main types: first, family pressure has been disregarded, with consequent doubt, remorse or anxiety; second, having given way to family pressure, the result is unhappiness and chafing against the yoke; the most common outcome (and this above all leads to the writing of a letter) was a paralysing feeling of indecision, an inability to act.

There is, of course, no intention of suggesting that the whole of the younger generation is necessarily thus afflicted. The responses to such problems are always a matter of degree, depending on individual differences. No doubt many young people are either sufficiently tough-minded to do what they want irrespective of their family's wishes, or pliant enough to adjust themselves to these wishes without undue mental anguish. Furthermore, many families will tend to show an increasing readiness to compromise, and with the spread of literacy the more rigid of the older norms are likely to lose ground at an ever-increasing rate. Thus in time the conditions giving rise to the particular kinds of problem described will probably cease to exist. The material analysed indicates, however, that during the present period of transition the incidence of conflict and anxiety associated with social change is by no means negligible.

## References

BUSIA, K. A. 1950. *Report on a Social Survey of Sekondi-Takoradi.* London: Crown Agents.

GOODY, J. 1957. 'Anomie in Ashanti?' *Africa,* xxvii. 356–63.

GREENLAND, C. 1957. 'A study of the correspondence addressed to an "Advice Column" in 1953'. *Case Conference,* iii. 255–62.

JAHODA, G. 1958. 'Boys' images of marriage partners and girls' self-images in Ghana.' *Sociologus,* viii. 155–69.

KIMBLE, H. 1956. 'A reading survey in Accra.' *Universitas,* ii. 77–81.

KLUCKHOHN, C. 1945. *The Persona Document in Anthropological Science.* Social Science Research Council. Bulletin No. 53, New York.

WARD, B. E. 1956. 'Some observations on religious cults in Ashanti.' *Africa,* xxvi. 47–60.

# Wiving and Thriving in Northern Rhodesia

## J. H. Chaplin

'In wiving and thriving a man should take counsel. . . .'
(Sixteenth-century proverb)

With the publication of Jahoda's (1959)[1] study of letters addressed to the advice column of a Ghanaian newspaper, my plans for a similar study in Northern Rhodesia crystallized into action. Fortunately at about the same time the country's sole independent newspaper aimed at the indigenous population began publication. The paper, which is weekly and is written in English throughout, has a circulation of some 20,000 copies, and with shared readers may be expected to reach a public of about 70,000 all told. (The total African population is somewhat over 2½ million.) Through the kindness of the editor, I have been allowed access to the complete incoming correspondence dealt with in a feature offering advice to inquirers; letters addressed to the editor have been excluded from this survey.[2]

While wishing to avoid plagiarism, for convenience of comparison I have tried generally to follow Jahoda's pattern but adapting it to local circumstances. There is also no point in duplicating here the work he has already so adequately done in discussing the use of such material, to which the reader is referred.

Jahoda's sample was collected over three months; the present group, though of similar size, is an accumulation of approximately one year's letters, but this is hardly surprising in a country with a smaller population and fewer literates[3] than Ghana. Only 20 per cent. of writers mention their

---

[1] G. Jahoda, 1959, 'Love, Marriage and Social Change . . .', *Africa*, xxix, pp. 177–90.

[2] I am most grateful to Mrs. B. Hall for allowing me access to the original letters on which this paper is based, and for her interest in the whole matter. To Dr. R. J. Apthorpe I must also acknowledge my debt for reading the manuscript while in draft and making several helpful suggestions.

[3] In round figures, during 1959, only 60 per cent. of children between 8–15 years of age had any opportunity of going to school. There were 34,000 boys and 29,500 girls in their first year; 13,000 boys, 4,600 girls in the fifth; 5,400 boys and 1,300 girls in the eighth year; 136 boys and 19 girls in the twelfth year (quoted in *African Digest*, London, vol. viii, no. 2, p. 49).

educational attainments; of these 17 per cent. are Standard V and below; 83 per cent. Standard VI and above.[4] Tribal affiliation is hardly ever mentioned except in cases of inter-tribal marriage difficulties.

An analysis of the places of origin (where known) of the letters gives: Copper Belt, 41 per cent.; Lusaka, 20 per cent.; balance of line of rail towns, 15 per cent.; rural areas, 17 per cent.; extra-territorial, 7 per cent. As could be expected, the commercial and administrative centres provide the bulk of correspondents, since these will attract the more educated men, who, in turn, will have the money to buy the paper, the ability to read its English, and the need to seek advice where traditional sources are either lacking or rejected.

Only 41 per cent. of the letter-writers give their occupations. Of those who did, almost half (49 per cent.) are still at school or under training; junior Government workers and clerks form 29 per cent. of the total; miners 10 per cent., and the remainder domestic servants, shop assistants, and so on. It is important to remember that, although the school age is dropping rapidly, many of the young men who are still at school are in their early twenties, with vocational courses as teachers, orderlies, or the like, of two or more years' duration beyond their schooling. Throughout this time they are expected to remain single, a state unnatural to their physical age, and contrary to traditional thinking. As far as marital status is concerned 74 per cent. are single, 15 per cent. married; the remainder make no statement on this point.

The background is now filled except for the age composition of the inquirers. In an attempt to do two things at once Table 1 is presented. Here, an analysis is made of the age of the male inquirers, together with that of the girl who generally forms the subject of the query. In addition, the ages of other, 'non-romantic', letter-writers are given. The total of this table exceeds that of the sample because of multiple entanglements where the age of each partner is included. The average age of the correspondent is 21.1 years (median 20.4), while the girls with whom they are involved average 17.2 years (median 16.4).

There will be seen to be close similarities between the writers of letters in both West and Central Africa. The majority of correspondents in both places are young unmarried men, with little more than basic education, living in an urban setting.

---

[4] African education begins with two years of pre-primary schooling (Standards Sub-A and Sub-B), then follow six years of Primary education (Standards I to VI). In Secondary school a further six years lead to University Entrance level (Forms 1 to 6).

TABLE 1  AGES OF CORRESPONDENTS AND THEIR PARTNERS

| Man's age | No partner mentioned | Age of Partner (Female) | | | | | | | | | | | | | | | | | Partner's age not given | Total |
|---|---|---|---|---|---|---|---|---|---|---|---|---|---|---|---|---|---|---|---|---|
| | | 10 | 11 | 12 | 13 | 14 | 15 | 16 | 17 | 18 | 19 | 20 | 21 | 22 | 23 | 24 | 25 | 26+ | | |
| 12 | | 1 | | | | | | | | | | | | | | | | | | 1 |
| 13 | 1 | | | | | | | | | | | | | | | | | | | 1 |
| 14 | 3 | | | 1 | 1 | | | | | | | | | | | | | | 2 | 7 |
| 15 | | 1 | | | 1 | | | | | | | | | | | | | | 6 | 8 |
| 16 | 1 | | | 1 | | 4 | 3 | | | | | | | | | | | | 6 | 15 |
| 17 | 3 | | | | | 2 | 3 | 1 | 1 | | | | | | | | | | 1 | 11 |
| 18 | 3 | | | 1 | | 6 | 5 | 1 | 1 | 2 | | | | | | | | | 8 | 27 |
| 19 | 1 | | | | | | 4 | 2 | 1 | 1 | | | | | | | | | 2 | 11 |
| 20 | 2 | | | | | 1 | 2 | 4 | 3 | 3 | 1 | 1 | | | | | | | 4 | 21 |
| 21 | 2 | | | | | 1 | 1 | 4 | 4 | 6 | 2 | 2 | | | | | | | 5 | 27 |
| 22 | 3 | | | | | | 1 | 2 | 2 | 3 | 2 | 1 | 1 | | 1 | | | | 8 | 24 |
| 23 | | | | | | 1 | | 2 | 2 | 2 | 1 | 1 | 1 | 3 | | | | | 8 | 21 |
| 24 | 1 | | | | | | 1 | 1 | 1 | 1 | 1 | | | 1 | | | | 1 | 6 | 14 |
| 25 | 1 | | | | | | | 1 | 1 | 2 | 1 | 3 | 2 | | | | | | 3 | 14 |
| 26+ | 8 | | | | | | 1 | 1 | | 2 | 3 | 2 | | | | | 2 | 2 | 6 | 27 |
| Age not given | 46 | | | | | 1 | 2 | 1 | 2 | 3 | 3 | | 1 | | | | | | 65 | 124 |
| Total | 75 | 2 | 0 | 3 | 2 | 16 | 23 | 20 | 18 | 25 | 14 | 10 | 5 | 4 | 1 | 0 | 2 | 3 | 130 | 353 |

## Categories of Correspondence

No clear-cut divisions are possible, there are always the borderline cases (this is particularly true of the first two categories); even so, broad divisions can be made and I have kept to those given by Jahoda, whose figures are shown for comparison. It should be noted that the Ghanaian figures are for single men only, those from Northern Rhodesia for the whole male sample.

|  | N. Rhodesia per cent. | Ghana per cent. |
|---|---|---|
| Threatened or broken relationship | 28 | 24 |
| Approach to girls and romantic love | 27 | 14 |
| Multiple entanglements | 9 | 8 |
| Family interference in marriage | 16 | 29* |
| Miscellaneous | 20 | 26 |

* This combines 'Family opposition to marriage' and 'Marriages arranged by parents'.

As will be shown later, the type of problem facing the correspondents is very much the same; the difference between the two areas is one of emphasis depending on the social circumstances of each country. It is apparent that the waning of family control is much greater in the more industrialized economy of Northern Rhodesia, bringing with it a greater number of personal socio-romantic troubles. In some rural areas the absentee rate for taxable males (ages 16–60) is as high as 70 per cent., while on the other side of the picture, third-generation town-dwellers are beginning to reach nubility. Men writing in towns have few opportunities for receiving advice from older relatives, either by way of definite instruction or in answer to queries. It is true that men from the same tribal area will tend to live as close to each other as possible, and form drinking-clubs at beer-halls. These are associations of contemporaries, however, and are important to their adherents because of ease of communication in the home language, rather than as definite attempts to maintain customs. It is equally true that such men are outside the immediate interference of relatives in their personal affairs.

## 1. *Threatened or Broken Relationships*

It is perhaps hardly surprising that the largest total of letters under this heading is concerned with the writer's girl being too friendly with other boys (16 letters). There is, however, only one instance where the man is honest enough to admit that his girl is jealous of his attentions to others, and even then he is on the defensive. Linked with this question are three instances where rivals (always called friends, however) are interfering between the couple.

Almost as common a complaint is that the girl does not reply to letters (15). The length of silence varies from 'a monthfule' to 9 sold [*sic*] months have elapsed'. The common complaint is of writing 'so many letters' without reply. Mention was made above of continuation at school while well into marriageable age, and this gives rise to difficulties on all sides. While thirteen students are worried because their girl friends want them to leave school and marry them, only one is concerned that his future wife insists he stay there until he has finished. Three girl friends want to remain at school; two wish to leave at once against their partners' wishes, and one man is annoyed because his fiancée will not give up her job to marry. A rather atypical case of the majority in this group is of a boy both younger and less well educated than his friend. A more ordinary situation is the problem in which a young man is in love with his cousin who has been asking him to marry her: '. . . I refused because I was at school. But I was playing her in private till she got wombed. . . . When she gave birth to a baby boy that month, I decided to complete my secondary Education.' On the other hand we have the example of the young man who says: 'I wish to stop her now [from being at school] because I seem to be at the age of keeping a family near by otherwise I lose my time for nothing. . . . I have a terrible hunger of family.'

The Form II friend of a younger Standard IV man insists he go back to school before she will marry him, but he is already working and does not want to go back. The opposite problem is seen in the youth who wants his girl to stay at school, though there is another factor here as well, since, at the age of nineteen, he is wondering: 'Is my years fit for the marriage and am I able to produce a baby at this age?'

A group of six letters reflects a serious social problem; five of these letters are from married men and each is troubled by the excessive drinking of his wife, though there is, as often as not, a clear double standard being used in this matter. The monopoly of the sale of African beer in towns belongs to the municipal authorities and is a factor peculiar to the Central African situation, and one that produces a host of unnecessary problems. The police find it difficult to control the large unruly crowds that fill the barn-like premises, especially at the month's end when men are paid. Religious and political leaders are united with social workers in their concern at this problem, but apathy at town council level is hard to shift. Beer-hall profits are large and subsidize the provision of amenities such as street lighting and welfare work.

Clearly linked with the foregoing is disobedience, and here three out of four letters are from married men. Obedience is a virtue highly praised by a husband; a girl with a reputation for pride is unlikely to marry easily. A domestic quarrel almost bristles off the page in such a letter as this: 'When I try to tell her something she replied in abusive word so I come also angry and start quarrel . . . when I leave the house she also leave the house she come at 4 Oclock and flie [fry] this fish called Kapenta[5] so how do you advise.'

In this case the man is wondering whether to divorce his wife. There are four letters from men whose wives are seeking a divorce. Yet another side of the divorce question comes in three letters from single men, whose attachment to their friends is threatened because the girls will not leave their present husbands and seem to be making the best of two worlds.

The remaining letters in this category consist of single instances; some of these might seem better considered under the next section, but are included here because in each there is a threat to break the relationship rather than a plain statement of fact or query for advice: 'Dear me the madly loved girl belongs to the other church and I also to the other.'

A reference to tokens comes from a man who has been jilted. He writes: 'I feel I should not refund her tokens as she has been so unfaithful to me.' The exchange of gifts is an important preliminary to marriage. It exists traditionally and, in slightly different form but with equal significance, survives in towns. There is a recognized but undefinable difference between these token gifts and those that might pass in the usual way of love and friendship.[6] Another town problem is well emphasized when a Nyasaland man wishes to marry a Bemba girl; between themselves they speak English but her parents do not know his language, or he theirs, and this is likely to cause a breach.

A letter which appears to record a homosexual relationship may not in fact do so; 'She says she will not mary me if I shall not stop to play with my best friend who is her brother.' The word 'play' has almost always a sexual meaning, the doubt arises because a mixture of personal pronouns he/she, his/hers, is not uncommon, neither is the use of 'brother' for 'sister'; on the other hand this correspondent has got all his other genders correct, so the deviation may be there after all, especially as he is a nineteen-year-old schoolboy.

---

[5] This is *Engraulicypris,* a species of fish also known as *nshembe* caught in Lake Tanganyika, which, when dried, is exported in large quantities. The same word is also the common 'two-Bantu' for a prostitute. It it not clear whether the fish is named after the woman or the woman after the fish. Whether it got this name because it is quickly cooked, and so is a useful stand-by for a woman with little sense of house-keeping, or because it is a 'quick-time' foodstuff as she is a 'quick-time' woman, it is difficult to say.

[6] See the account of the betrothal present, *nsalamu,* in A. I. Richards, 'Bemba Marriage and Present Economic Conditions', Rhodes-Livingstone Paper No. 4, 1940, pp. 52 et seq.

## 2. *Approach to Girls and Romantic Love*

Rather than treat the letters in this section in the strict numerical pattern of subjects, it would seem more reasonable to deal with the correspondence in the natural way of the development of a young man's fancy.

There is a single instance of genuine concern about the why and wherefore: '. . . where ever you get Boys and Girls sex is a Piriminary topic. I have often heard boys of my own age telling me "Boy! There is no life without girls or damsels", what do they meant?'

In contrast to this naïve attitude there are three letters, clearly written to get into print, conveying opinions rather than queries. One of these is headed, 'A page for town girls as they call themselves' and deals at length with the mercenary attitude of girls, and the fights over them.

A group of seventeen letters is from men anxious in one way or another to have a girl friend. Some have no specific reason keeping them back. There are others who have so far conducted their love affairs by correspondence and wish to bring about a meeting but do not know how to do so. This is particularly common among students, where a boy can exchange an introduction to his sister, cousin, or girl-friend's friend, for such a moderate consideration as a visit to the nearest tea-room. But some of the most poignant letters in the whole sample are to be found in the seven that seek guidance on how to overcome shyness: 'I have failed to meet the right girl. I am growing old. I am now 27. I see years going faster than they used to go during my teenages.'

Finally a letter written in despair by a man of 21 who is 'ashamed to propose girls': 'I even think to go and hang myself up the tree or to contact the electric wires and die. As I am useless under this world. I think I am alone under this world who is like that. My friends they tell me that you don't want to propose girls, you don't want to drink beer. Why don't you want to enjoy yourself before your days? You are a fool. I only be silent as I have nothing to do.'

The most numerous letters in this section deal in one way or another with the difficulty the writer is having in persuading his girl to have intercourse with him. There are thirteen letters in this part, each written with a frankness that seldom escapes the editorial blue pencil; the man who refers to 'night-time business' never sees the light of print, but a more romantic phrasing was happily passed: 'I want her to be my lovely attractive flower of winter during night time. What should I do to win this lovely flower?'

Two men write in very aggrieved tones, one of whom seems to have a rather literal way of thinking: 'When ever I went to play with her she refuses. While she says she loves Greatly. When I read in the Bible the

Bible says love without works is dead, is this the love spoken in the Bible?' Two other men are both restrained by fear of financial responsibilities; and 'can not afford the outbreak of pregnance'. Perhaps of relevance here is the single letter from a man of twenty-eight who is impotent and feels this may derive from masturbation.

Having got a girl friend, there are eleven correspondents asking how they can tell if she is really in love with them, or how to keep her. And there are the same number of letters that ask how to be rid of either a girl friend of whom the writer is now tired, or a persistent admirer he is not really interested in. The balance of letters in this section are for the most part problems of conduct with regard to girls, or indecision as to whether certain characteristics are a bar to marriage. Five letters complain that the girl is after money and three that she uses insulting behaviour (there is no threat of break-up here, only a request for advice to correct these faults). One man gave a promise not to have another girl friend while his own was away and wishes to know if this is binding. Two men are preparing things for marriage but are not yet ready; however, they have to endure their friends' scorn—is this fair?

Contrasts between the two partners are a source of concern. An uneducated man fears to marry an educated girl. Three educated men love uneducated girls, an increasingly serious problem: 'My all relatives like the girl and I like and love her, she loves me too, that I be married to her, but she is an uneducated.'

As Table 1 showed, the preference of men is for partners younger than themselves. In some areas the betrothal of a girl well below the age of puberty to an older man is traditional. She will live with him and be introduced gradually to domestic and marital duties. This was considered the gentlest way of introducing a girl to her wifely estate, but has been condemned by authority as repugnant.[7] An extreme case is the sixteen-year-old, whose friend is only ten; less wide is the gap of ten years between twenty-five and fifteen. The reverse, and unusual, side of the situation is given in two letters. While a somewhat older woman may introduce a youth to intercourse, too big a gap in age between them might well be the basis for an accusation of witchcraft.[8]

Tribal differences account for three people's problems. Interdenominational differences occur in two instances, while a pending tragedy lies in the letter from a man whose parents chose his bride for him: 'As I am new in the world of married people, I did not observe that my girl was pregnant, she gave birth to our first child, when she was completing her sixth month's stay with me. Do you sincerely believe that I am the father of this child?'

---

[7] A. I. Richards, 1940, loc. cit.

[8] J. A. Barnes, 1951, 'Marriage in a changing society'. Rhodes-Livingstone Paper No. 20, p. 33.

### 3. *Family Interference in Marriage*

Whereas in Jahoda's sample the boy's family was responsible for greater interference than the girl's (42 cases against 26), in our own the roles are reversed: 33 of the objections were the girl's parents and only 19 were the boy's. (One case cannot be allocated to either but will be discussed later.) With a matrilineal society this is perhaps not surprising; the group into which the young man is marrying is likely to be more careful. But against this the objection to inter-tribal marriage is higher in the case of the boy's parents (7 cases) than the girl's (3 cases), though the sample is of course very small. Other instances will be found when discussing multiple entanglements.

By far the greatest number of letters telling of the girl's parents interfering deal with their insistence that the boy marry her at once. There is only one letter actually ordering a 'shotgun' wedding: 'I am a boy of 17 and wombed a schoolgirl of 15. . . . I am forced to marry her by her father [who] again says I spoored [spoiled] his daughter.'

There are two letters with the problem that the girl's parents think education unnecessary for a girl. One case can be mentioned for both. The couple were betrothed before the girl matured, the parents agreed that the boy should pay her school fees as she was only at Standard II level, but when she matured her parents changed their mind, saying 'It was of no need why she should continue and said Standard III was enough to a girl'. The young man asks: 'What can I do to amend this trouble among these premitive homeside people having fixed ideas?'

The question of maturity arises in another letter in which the girl's stepfather refuses to let her marry until she is 'inciated' and wishes her to be so, but the mother says she can be married without it. The boy's uncle, sent as mediator, cannot reconcile these opinions. In four cases the girl has been married off to someone but the correspondent still loves her, and in every case she loves him.

The payment of *lobola* (to use the term that avoids controversial translation) raises problems, as might be expected. For a seventeen-year-old girl £15 was asked and £9 paid, and, because the remainder was not following, the girl's mother took her away. For a girl of Standard VI education £55 was asked but the boy's family could only find £15.5s. Another young man writes: 'I was eloped with a girl of 18 years in 1959. . . . I was charged three cattle and £18 for the lobola. As a result I was just able to give her parents three cattle and £11, but they didn't accept, [but] I had given them according to Native Authority'. This reference to authority is interesting, as there is no uniformity at all as to these payments. Areas differ widely and in many of them definite figures have not been laid down.

Two young men are faced with the same difficulty: the girls' parents demand cattle and they have only money to offer which is unacceptable. One is asked for £5 plus '2 herds of cattle' [surely 'head']. The other writes 'I love this girl to Kingdom come. She is a M'cewa by tribe while am Tumbuka. The Cewa people use cattle for paying lobola and yet in our tribe we do not own cattle for paying lobola. Should I deliver buffaloes from the forest and pay for lobola?'

A rather different question of lobola is given by a Tonga correspondent: having had a second child by his wife a man is asked by her parents to pay 5 cattle and £45. On this his own parents are adamant in saying: ' "We have not to pay for so much for one person. You must leave her and get another." But I love my wife very much and she loves me so much. . . . What can I do for my wife and the two opposite parents?' Conversely, and rather unexpectedly, there is one man whose parents refused to let him marry in his own district although he wishes to do so.

Tribal custom arises in another way in the case of a boy wanting to marry, but being told the girl's elder sister should be married first. This difficulty hardly arises in another case where the girl's elder sister wants him to marry her instead. The most frequent objection by the boy's parents is that he should not marry a girl from another tribe. A solid prejudiced answer comes from one man's father who told him: 'I must not marry a Muzezulu because she may be a vagabond, because Mazezulu are wanderers. I can't believe it, is that true?'

A further letter comes from a man who married a girl of another tribe against his parents' wishes. They were glad when they saw his two children, but are now urging him to divorce. Tribal difficulties also occur in the case of the man working away from home who falls in love there but whose parents write: 'We have found a girl for you to marry, just send your picture and money for lobola.' He goes on: 'I was born in town, educated in town and knows nothing about my hom. Should I get this girl [here] without the consent of my parents or should I just send my picture and money and get my home girl "cash with order"?' Three almost exactly similar letters are from boys who consider they are not ready for marriage but whose parents insist that they are. 'I am not prepared to marry and I feel it is too early for me, but God hears parents much more than their sons.'

Other opposition is raised, though of no great interest here, apart from the boy whose elder brother says his fiancée is too fat, an unusual comment, since plump girls are usually very much admired and desired as partners. The remaining letter concerning family interference is an unusual one as much for the query it contains as for the circumstance. A man sends his wife to his home, and whilst there she becomes pregnant by his father. The writer is not concerned at this, he only wants to know what relation the child bears to him: is it his brother?

## 4. *Muliple Entanglements*

Indiscriminate affairs are clearly more easily conducted in towns than in rural areas, and almost every letter in this section has an urban origin. The fact that there were comparatively few letters is that the activity is so generally recognized and accepted that it is unlikely to cause a great deal of difficulty. The most frequent cases are those where a man already married has fallen in love with another woman (8 letters). The claims of the rivals are seldom straightforward, there may be more than one attribute to be considered: uneducated home-girl/educated town girl (2); brown girl/black girl (2); betrothed home girl/wombed town girl-friend (2). More than once they are exactly the same: 'Same Standard, both brown, clean and charming, modern and know little things about romance' or, 'Same Standard, all brown, clean and same height'. The question of a colour preference is of interest and has been noticed in other contexts. The word 'brown' has acquired a high value in the scale of social approval. Girls from Southern Rhodesia, who are considered lighter-skinned, are very popular partners for this reason.

A situation with no jealousy between the two girls concerned occurs in the following case: '. . . her young sister came from her home and found that I have already made the elder sister pregnant. The older sister told me that I cann't just stay without any action so instead I should take an action with the young sister, of course I did and without wasting any time she reported to me that she is also pregnant. So they are all pregnant. What can I do to both of them? I feed them alright.' The obvious traditional answer would be to marry both of them, both in this particular case and in the others. Such advice had already been given to one man, and several others think of it. Finally there are two men with more than a pair of possibilities, one with three girls and another who writes: '. . . All these four girls love me greatly and they shall have their holidays very soon and I don't think I will manage to occupy these girls, for everyone will be in need of me visiting her daily.'

## 5. *Miscellaneous*

Highest in this section, and, indeed, the third highest in the entire collection, stand the fourteen letters asking about educational opportunities. That universal educational opportunity is far from being attained has already been mentioned, but the bottleneck is particularly severe after Standard VI, when secondary education begins, school places are few, and annual payments run to more than £20—two or more months' salary of the brother, or another relative who has to find the money: 'My parents are both too old but I want to higher my education.'

There are five people wanting to ask for work, and two complain of their present conditions. Considering that according to one set of criteria, about 80 per cent. of the urban population (in one town for which data are available) live below the Poverty Datum Line,[9] it is surprising that only three correspondents ask for advice concerning their financial difficulties, but although these are endemic throughout the population, or perhaps because they are so, they do not appear to affect emotional life in any deep respect.[10] More serious, as there is clearly a feeling of breach of duty, are the five letters of complaint at family maltreatment. In four cases a family responsibility of care is not fulfilled. To whom else can the writer turn when, the proper channels have failed, other than the newspaper's columnist?

The usual correspondence columns are open to writers wishing to ventilate their political views, so there are only seven in the present sample. Even the four which deal with the colour bar could perhaps be called 'social'.

There are seven specifically medical queries at least two of which are so outspokenly frank on sexual matters that at first glance they would appear exhibitionistic, though on reflection they seem to be genuine and without shame. The topic is one so frequently spoken of that it can therefore be written about in all normality.

Six letters ask for publication of the writer's name in an attempt to find lost relatives. In rural areas the postal service, albeit slow, is fairly sure, as everybody knows everybody, but in towns, unless a man is working or has a friend who is working, it is almost impossible for him to receive letters. Postal deliveries to houses are confined to the European housing areas, and, in any case, post-boxes are the rule. Many people get badly out of touch and at times of family or personal stress seek any means to contact their relatives. One letter in this section is unusual, since the writer is seeking his sister, who left school while young at her parents' insistence, 'School is a thing which is useless especially to girls.' Her father's white employer wanted to marry her, offering £50 and a bicycle, but despite the father's wishes the girl refused and ran away with a cook.

---

[9] Of Lusaka it has been written, 'The average wage of just over £7 per month is in itself inadequate to supply the minimum needs at Poverty Datum Level standards of a couple and one child. . . . Some 80% of households with children do not currently receive a wage sufficient to supply their minimum needs excluding any rent payments.' D. G. Bettison, 1959, 'Numerical Data on African Dwellers in Lusaka', Rhodes-Livingstone Communication No. 16, at p. xxiii. However, Bettison's criteria have been challenged by Kay (Rhodes-Livingstone Communication No. 21, 1961) and Thomson and Kay (Human Problems No. 30, 1961).

[10] In a study on suicide in Northern Rhodesia, economic causes lay behind only about 3 per cent. of the sample. See J. H. Chaplin, 1961, *Africa Studies,* vol. xx, No. 3.

Three letters are of religious inquiry: '. . . please tell me the Language which God will judge me because I am Lungu by tribe?'

As the column-head shows a very attractive young lady, it is perhaps not surprising that there are two offers of marriage in the sample, in fact others were earlier destroyed. The remaining dozen letters are all very varied.

## Letters from Women

As there are only thirteen letters from women the problems of each may be considered. Five do not give their ages, but the remainder are between fifteen and twenty-two. Five writers are in main towns, four in rural areas, and the remainder do not say where they are writing from. None mentions educational standard, but one asks, 'you can forgive me for bad written English and wrong spellings for I am not very much educated?'

Only two pairs of letters share the same topic. Two girls are teachers and are worried by gossip because they are not married and are accused of being 'loose'. Two others are pregnant by a boy already married and want to know whether they should become his second wife. One woman's husband is unfaithful and they are still working to pay off the £18 damages of an adultery case—should she divorce him or remain because, although often drunk, he provides for her and the children? A similar, newly wed, wife hears her husband has a girl-friend as well—how can she keep him for herself alone? Another girl was married young against her wishes and was not allowed to continue with her education. She still loves another man—what can she do about it?

Difficulties of engagement are common: one girl thinks she is not pretty enough; another wants to know how to tell if her boy really loves her; the friend of another is of a different religion, can she marry him? Two years ago a girl jilted a boy, she has now changed her mind, can she write to him again? A lovers' quarrel lies behind the query that ends 'What shall I do to make him forget about the big NO!?' Finally there is the girl troubled by her friend's repeated requests for intercourse which she has so far refused—should she continue to do so, otherwise she'll lose him?

All in all these letters are complementary to those from men. The problem of single women is an acute one: they are usually girls of advanced education and training, yet such are so few that they are in great demand as wives by men of similar or higher educational standards, the disproportion of educational achievement being very marked. The other letters call for no comment.

## Social Function of the Column

When we come to consider the value of this type of newspaper column it is clearly considerable. As already mentioned, traditional sources of comfort, advice, even of firmly laid down rules of conduct, are either missing or are considered old-fashioned. The smart and modern thing, which also carries the added glory of getting your name in print, is to write to the newspaper.

It is not without relevance that the most popular radio programmes are those in which a man's name is read out together with his greetings to a string of friends and a piece of music played which he has chosen for their entertainment.

Most of the letters received are answered in print, the exceptions being the educational queries and one or two of the more intimate medical difficulties, which are dealt with privately. The style of the printed replies is that which seems to be standard to correspondence columns throughout the world. A brisk, no-nonsense approach with an occasional change into humour. This has the disadvantage of ignoring the accepted behaviour of the correspondents. A man will be told to talk things over with his father, who in the circumstances would be the last person he would consider. Philanderers are always told to marry the girl they have impregnated; on the other hand, where there is a choice between a 'chosen' and a 'loved' girl, the romantic view is taken and the inquirer advised to follow his choice. The difficulties of inter-church, inter-tribal, and discrepant-age marriages are usually minimized. As can be seen, the advice given is that of the imported social pattern—middle-class western norms with the virtues and conventions of such an attitude.[11]

Some of the replies will clearly be acted upon, others, especially those advising western sexual *mores,* will almost certainly be ignored, since the free pattern of 'town marriage' has already a firm hold. It is probably true to say that a looser adherence to Western tenets now obtains among African Christians than, say, twenty years ago. In village areas, where once the missionary was administrator and as powerful as the chief, if not more so, there are now schools, dispensaries, and other social amenities outside his control. The shock of dismay at the colour bar in towns maintained by White Christians has been well recorded in African writing, so need not be elaborated here. These factors have combined to lessen the power of the school-learnt Western sexual ethic. Economic difficulties prevent many men from marrying at a suitable age, and apart from drinking, recreations are limited, with the result that there is a tendency to observe the Italian proverb, 'Bed is the poor man's opera.' Very few young men do not have liaisons of some sort while in town, and only a minority are not involved

---

[11] Of particular relevance here is the statement by a leading Nyasa politician: '. . . Lastly it should be made clear to social leaders that their job is not to throw overboard everything African nor merely to process foreign ways but to uphold African ways of life where necessary, to adopt foreign ways where possible and to strike practicable compromises where need be.' D. K. Chisiza, 1961, *Realities of African Independence*, Africa Bureau, London.

in a paternity case at one time or another in their lives even if this does not come to court but is settled privately. An instance comes to mind of one young man who was transferred to a town for one month but had to return to face six such cases resulting from his activities during that time. Fights over women are common in beer-halls, but there is almost no social stigma attached to such a liaison, rather the reverse, in fact, as several of the letters have shown.

Advice concerning defiance of parents is rather differently treated. Respect for elders is placed amost at the top of any list of traditional virtues, and even though the natural man rebels, the power of public opinion will be strongly against the man who deviates. Several of the letters under this head are worded as if the query is not so much 'What shall I do?' but 'I want to break, please bolster up my courage to do so'. Once or twice correspondents have written to give thanks for the advice received, which has been acted on with satisfactory results.

The whole value of the column may be summed up in the following extract from a correspondent, who answers a man who had complained of the letters on love affairs: 'In your village where you are come from don't little children play games during the moonshine for the pleasure? Do the big people chase them away? No, of course you as father of them when you go there and join them you can't be interested in clapping hands, running here and there. Those who write such are interested by themselves, they have great pleasure with it, in fact they are between the ages of 10 and 21. It is only Josephine who is interested in them she knows young ideas and thoughts and she is even giving them best advices and knowledge which they want. . . .' Such a spontaneous tribute would appear to reflect the general opinion of readers. By those with whom the feature has been discussed verbally the same opinion of its value has been expressed.

# Some Trends in Modern Marriage among West Africans

## Kenneth Little and Anne Price

This article describes and attempts to analyse the nature and content of marital relationships in the 'modern' West African family.[1] To an increasing extent educated young people[2] apparently want a companionate marriage on Western lines (Marris, 1961). Evidence comes from interviewing and from studies made of the attitudes of students and of secondary school boys and girls in a number of countries, including Ghana, Nigeria, and Sierra Leone. Omari, for example, collected data from 293 students in a sample of eight Secondary and Teacher Training Institutions throughout Ghana. About three-quarters of these subjects said they would like to be married either in church or before a magistrate (1960, pp. 197–210). A statutory marriage of this kind, unlike traditional marriage, makes bigamy a crime, and so we may assume that the young people concerned had monogamy in mind. A group of Nigerian secondary school girls also declared, with a single exception, that monogamy was the ideal form of marriage; they insisted that they wanted to choose their own husbands (Baker, 1957).

### Courtship and Romantic Love

No doubt these attitudes are in part the product of Christian evangelization. In propagating the Christian ideal of marriage, missionaries have insisted not only on monogamy but on the responsibilities that spouses have towards each other. The contractual nature of the union has been made clear but according to the authoritative *Survey of African Marriage and Family Life* (ed. Phillips, 1953) much of the teaching on the Christian

---

[1] The authors wish to thank Professor Daryll Forde for some very helpful comments on the original draft of this article.

[2] Throughout this article the expression 'educated person' refers to one who has completed a course of study at a secondary school, or its equivalent.

marriage ideal has been negative. It has concentrated on prohibitions resulting in the common belief that sin is 'the wrong use of sex'. 'By an unconscious transition, the sex impulse and the sex act came to be associated with and to become sin' (Harries, 1953, pp. 379–80). In contrast, the young people cited above attached positive value to the emotional side of the conjugal relationship. It is possible, therefore, that they have gained their idea of love through a different medium from the missionary;[3] through, for instance, the Hollywood type of film, by travel abroad, etc.

Young people in traditional society frequently form romantic attachments. Among the Mende of Sierra Leone, for example, the marriage of a man to his first or to a subsequent wife may sometimes be the result of mutual physical attraction and she will be known specifically as his 'love wife' (*Ndoma nyaha*) (Little, 1951). Quite frequently, too, although her motives may be commercial as well as amorous a member of the polygamous household will elope or enter into an illicit relationship with a man much younger than her husband. Another West African people, the Gonja of Northern Ghana, have a species of trial marriage (*jipo*) (Esther Goody, 1962, p. 20), and among the Tallensi it is a point of honour for a boy to find a girl for himself (Fortes, 1949). Courtship, though often formalized, is also a common institution. The many peoples among whom it is part of the preliminaries of marriage include the Yakö and the Hausa (Forde, 1941; Mary Smith, 1955).

What is different about the contemporary situation is the extent to which romantic values are socially emphasized. According to Omari, Ghanaians nowadays want 'to fall in love' with a girl before they marry her. This implies that, in contrast to most traditional patterns, 'love' is becoming nowadays an initial requirement for mate selection (1962, pp. 14, 43). Omari says:

While in grandfather's time he was lucky if he was permitted to edge in a word as to whom he would rather marry; today a young man wants to do everything for himself. Grandmother had even less to do or say about these things: she only found herself with a husband. She did not know anything about 'love' and never expected her husband 'to say sweet things' to her. She knew she had to get along with the man—for her own happiness, and for the happiness of her family which had taken 'head money'.                    (Ibid., p. 15.)

This preoccupation of educated youths with their feelings towards the opposite sex is illustrated in Jahoda's study of letters addressed to the advice column of a Ghanaian newspaper in 1955. One problem often

---

[3] In support of this suggestion is the fact that none of twelve well-known African writers who discuss African reaction to missionary teaching make any reference whatever to this matter. Cf. *Christianity in Africa as seen by the Africans*, Ram Desai (ed.), 1962, Denver.

mentioned was how to recognize true love and be sure of one's partner's feelings. Letters written by unmarried young men referred mainly to two kinds of difficulty. First, the man states that his girl has ceased to care for him and asks how he can win her back; a rival has appeared and the girl has started 'playing'; the question being what can be done about it. A twenty-year-old clerk wrote about his telephonist wife-to-be: 'I love this girl to the bottom of my heart.' However, as she lives far away, he unfortunately made two other girls pregnant and consequently is, to quote his own words, 'perplexed mentally'. He asks: 'What can I do to repel these two girls . . . and get hold of my own darling as my ever and one wife?' (Jahoda, 1959).

Among educated Yoruba, too, the ideal for two partners is to get married because they are in love (Baker and Bird, 1959). In Freetown, Jellicoe found five men out of a sample of twenty-six Creoles who got married between eighteen and twenty-three because of 'a modern Western type of romantic attachment' (1955); even in small towns of Sierra Leone, the choice of a spouse among skilled workers, clerks, and civil servants is based on Western patterns of love (Gamble, 1963).

In Freetown and in Western Nigeria, educated young people meet at work, or at literary or social circles, dancing places being looked down upon as immoral by members of the élite.[4] The method of courtship is for the man to write to the girl's parents, asking whether he may visit her at her home. When accepted he pays the girl frequent visits, escorts her to public functions, but in fact there is little privacy for the couple (Jellicoe, op. cit.; Bird, 1958). In Ghana, very often the parents of the girl do not want their daughter to associate with a man until she is engaged. To have a 'date' is a very recent pattern and it is only when the man has given the girl a ring and a bible that he is allowed to take her out and court her. Therefore, the engagement often precedes dating and courtship except when these have been carried out secretly (Omari, 1962, pp. 37, 41, 44, 45, 53).

Once engaged, fiancés often have regular sexual relations; this is partly because the high cost of marriage prolongs the engagement period and also because 'marriage is only the final stage in a relationship which is regarded as established at an earlier stage' (Izzett, 1961, p. 313). Often, too, a man will not marry his fiancée before she conceives a child (Omari, 1962, p. 57). As the Ordinance marriage is monogamous and it is difficult and expensive to divorce, men want to be sure that their future wives are not barren, sterility being regarded as the worst thing that can happen to a married couple. Although public opinion on premarital sexual relationships

---

[4] The term 'élite' refers here and hereafter to highly educated, well-to-do members of African society, such as persons in the senior ranks of the Administration, including Ministers and top civil servants, the professional class in general, university teachers, and holders of important traditional titles. This categorization corresponds broadly with the Smythes' definition of the 'top-level' élite in Nigeria (1960, p. 92).

varies according to traditional culture, sexual experience is quite wide-spread among educated adolescents and, even if virginity at marriage is the ideal state, it is not expected in Ghana where few boys and few girls are chaste when they reach twenty-one (Omari, 1962, p. 55; Crabtree, 1950). Chastity is not an essential condition of marriage and provided girls have had no sexual relations with Europeans or Lebanese, they have the same chance of getting married (Little, 1959). Nevertheless, girls are worried nowadays about this problem, mainly because they fear to have a baby, which would be a burden in view of their hope for independence and a career (Omari, 1962, p. 118). In Cotonou there are 'trial marriages' among young evolués; afraid of the cost of marriage payment and the fact that Christian marriages are indissoluble, young men prefer to have a trial with their possible wife-to-be for one year or more (Lombard, 1954, p. 162).

### Choice of Partner

Marriage is still, in the eyes of the parents at least, a union between two groups (Jellicoe). As, however, the following examples show, personal choice is nowadays more important than in the past. Thus, in Cotonou, after a secret engagement, young people tell their families officially; their parents then start the traditional presentations to conclude the marriage; all the fiancés interviewed there by Lombard had chosen their partners themselves (Lombard, 1954, p. 356). Few of the Nigerian élite in Ibadan had their marriage arranged by their family and most met their spouses during their students days (Lloyd, P. C., n.d.), while in Porto-Novo, 96 per cent. of a sample of women had chosen their husbands (Tardits, 1958, p. 60). In Lagos, four-fifths of a sample of men had chosen their wives themselves; even in first marriage, only a quarter had left the initiative to their parents (Marris, p. 44). Again, in Ghana, 86 per cent. of 275 students said they had gained their girl or boy friend by their own efforts. Twenty-four per cent. declared that they would not accept their parents' choice of spouse; 31 per cent. were uncertain; but as many as 41 per cent. would accept their choice. The last figure, however, consisted mainly of girls and it seems that although 'modern' girls want to make their own choice of a partner, they are more influenced by their family and often married to men they would rather not have married (Omari, 1960, p. 204; 1962, p. 125).

The conclusion, therefore, is that the influence of parents (other relatives' comments are no longer taken into account) often consists only in the formal agreement to a choice already made. Nevertheless, there are still educated men who say that they accept their parents' choice either because they can then obtain financial assistance to get married or because of their sense of loyaly to their parents is still very strong[5] (Crabtree). This is the case because it is often more difficult in practice than in theory to disregard parental wishes; contemporary African novels, which show characters traditionally engaged by their family and who happen to fall in love with another partner, illustrate this point.

Choice of a spouse is widened by the fact that one may not have to marry any longer in the same tribal group. Admittedly, Crabtree found that in 1947 among 150 marriages of educated men and women in Accra, 127 were married with persons of the same tribe. Also, in Lagos, two-thirds of the marriages studied by Marris had taken place between people of the same birth-place. He also discovered that marriages between men and women of different places were commonest when one or other had been born in Lagos (1961, p. 44). Marris does not specify the educational status of his subjects but there are indications that the percentage of inter-tribal unions increases at the higher levels of the social ladder. In Dakar, for example, Mercier found that professional men, skilled workers, and senior civil servants marry more often with women of other tribes than do farmers, fishermen, and unskilled workers (1954, p. 29). That tribal influence has less significance than education or religion is also suggested by inquiries made among 184 educated young Sierra Leoneans most of whom were Christians (Little, 1966). On the other hand, any tendency on the part of men with post-secondary education to marry outside their own tribe may be due to the relative scarcity of educated women. A tribe like the Ijebu of Western Nigeria, who have many educated women, tends to marry endogamously (Lloyd, op. cit.). Possibly therefore a lot of educated young people still prefer to marry in their own tribe though it is more by their own choice than to obey their parents (Lombard, 1954, p. 367; Omari, 1962, pp. 48, 50, 51).

## Social Implications of Monogamy and Education

The fact that personal selection of the spouse is now much more widespread is in tune with the emphasis that Western marriage places on the conjugal relationship. However, a different attitude is taken towards such matters in the traditional homes in which many of the young people concerned have grown up. There they belonged to an extended kinship grouping whose members formed a community, often living and working on lineage lands and inhabiting the same compound. Domestic life was largely communal and each individual was expected to follow fixed patterns of behaviour in order not to disturb the unity and balance of the group.

---

[5] According to Jahoda, an uncle would be gravely offended if the offer of his daughter was refused by his literate nephew, to whose education he had contributed (1958, p. 156; 1959, p. 180).

Therefore, selection for marriage was mainly a family matter and the domestic life of husband and wife was adapted to the general organization of the compound, any marital dispute being settled by the lineage itself. This made the spouses more responsible to relatives round them than to each other for their action. In contrast to Western marriage, it meant that husband and wife were called upon to make relatively few personal adjustments to each other's individual personality (Little, 1959; Lombard, 1954; Omari, 1962).

The 'old' families of the Coast[6] are accustomed to homes organized on Western lines, but the bulk of the educated class does not have this kind of background. Even among students at the new universities it seems to be rare for a person to have more than one parent who is literate, and in an appreciable number of cases both parents are illiterate (Johada, 1955, II, pp. 71–72). How successful then are individuals brought up in the traditional environment in adopting new patterns of marital behaviour?

In the English-speaking countries, acceptance of monogamy is reflected in an insistence on being married according to statute.[7] We can start, therefore, by examining expectations of this kind of marriage. So far as the men are concerned, an important motive appears to be prestige, because to marry in this way is a sign of superior status. It implies that the person concerned is 'progressive' and has sufficient means to live in a modern up-to-date style. Members of well-to-do and highly Westernized families marry in church as a matter of course. However, for men lower down on the social scale it represents a definite achievement and such a person may be married according to native law and custom for a number of years

---

[6] This term refers to certain families of Sierra Leonean and Brazilian extraction and to the earlier *evolués* in Senegal who possessed wealth and position long before Independence.

[7] In the Anglophone countries, Ordinance marriage can take place in a Registry Office or be celebrated in church. The civil ceremony seems quite common in Lagos, and particularly among the young people who prefer to use their money for some more useful purpose than on an expensive wedding (Izzett, 1961, pp. 308 and 310). A religious wedding which should include 'all the elements which characterize it in a European culture' (Mair, 1953, p. 153) is very expensive, but it carries much more prestige than a simple civil ceremony. In Freetown, only a church wedding is socially recognized by Christians and marriages under the civil Ordinance are still rare (Jellicoe, 1955). It seems that in Ghana, too, religious marriages are much more in favour than a civil ceremony. Sixty-five per cent. of students in Omari's sample cited above want to marry in church, as against only 7 per cent. who would prefer a civil ceremony (Omari, 1960, p. 201). This is not only an ideal: Crabtree found as many as 69 out of 113 educated men and 29 out of 37 educated women who had married in church, while only 10 men and 3 women had married in front of the magistrate (Crabtree, 1950). When customary unions have been previously contracted, Ordinance marriage cannot take place at church; what is called a 'parlour wedding' is celebrated at the home of one of the spouses and the minister gives his blessing (Bird, 1958). However, it should be remembered that, even in the case of highly educated people, the statutory marriage still operates within the common law and custom system. For instance, if a young couple met and married in England while studying they must, on their return to Nigeria, perform all the customary rituals if they want their marriage to be recognized by their families (Bird, 1958).

before feeling sufficiently advanced in his career to afford the expense of a church wedding, amounting to several hundreds of pounds.[8] Nor, for that matter, will a man have much hope of an educated bride unless he agrees to be married in this fashion. Although the number of educated girls is growing, the proportion of women who have been to college or even to a secondary school is generally small. Consequently, to have such a wife brings social distinction, and the higher her education the greater the husband's prestige[9] (Little, 1951; Marris, 1961).

In principle, educated men want to marry educated girls. In the Sierra Leone sample cited above, some 72 per cent. of the men considered that an educated partner was an advantage (Little, 1966). Indeed, one of the common complaints made by young men is that their tribally oriented parents want them to marry illiterate girls (Jahoda, 1959, p. 178), when they in fact are looking for a woman of roughly similar educational standard and also similar financial and social position.[10] Consequently, in Western Nigeria it often happens that to make sure that they will get an educated wife, men get engaged to school-girls and pay for their further education: but the girl, once trained, often marries a younger man (Bird, 1963). Educated girls are still so rare that in Ghana men sometimes travel abroad to find an educated Ghanaian woman (Omari, 1962, p. 52).

In addition to bringing him prestige, an educated wife is also able to support her husband's social position. In Little's Sierra Leone sample some 21 per cent. of the Creole girls mentioned that education for a woman is an advantage as she is then able to converse in society and her husband is not ashamed of her. Some educated husbands, particularly if they have been to England, divorce their illiterate wife to marry an educated one (Omari, 1962, p. 51), it being claimed that illiterate wives are shy in public, feel ill at ease, and are more interested in local gossip than literary or political activities (Crabtree). A letter written by a twenty-eight-year-old husband married by his parents to an illiterate girl makes this point very clearly: 'I have tried hard to bring her to the standard required of her, but she is still unprogressive. . . . I feel shy to bring my friends to my house. . . . I spend most of the days outside my home and I am entertaining the fear that my children will be ill-bred because the girl herself lacks training. . . . Recently I have fallen in love with an educated girl. . . . But polygamy is the first thing I detest. I am afraid of losing the confidence of my parents by putting away my wife and marrying the girl of my own choice. . . . When I ask my wife to accompany me to a social

---

[8] See p. 200, n. 27 for further information about this point.

[9] The larger also the amount of bride-wealth expected in cases when this traditional payment is made (Marris, et al.).

[10] Lloyd (op. cit.) found that in Ibadan half of the men with university education married women with secondary education. Only one-tenth took women with no more than primary education.

gathering or church she always puts up a lame excuse and refuses to go' (Jahoda, 1959, p. 187).

In other words, any educated man is embarrassed if his wife does not know the appropriate etiquette, when she has to act as a hostess or accompany him to social parties. This is so much the case that in some of the French-speaking countries where there are hardly any educated wives, a special class of sophisticated prostitute is sometimes called in to deputize at official balls and other formal functions for a diplomat's wife. When doubt is felt about her deportment, these *femmes libres* help the official party to feel at ease (*New Society*, 1963, pp. 4–5). Such a husband also wants a wife who knows enough about modern tastes to furnish and decorate his home in up-to-date style. Moreover, most men being ambitious for their children wish them to be suitably reared and this is facilitated if their mother understands modern practices of child welfare. She should also be capable of checking their homework. Members of the élite are no longer disposed to send their children away to kinsmen. Instead, a child attends school either as a day pupil or as a boarder and may then be sent, on reaching puberty, to Britain to complete its education.

Nor, in view of the significance of education,[11] is it surprising that a large proportion of the young women as well as of the men insist on having a well-educated partner. Thus, in Omari's Ghanaian sample, 35 per cent. of secondary-school seniors, the main part of whom were girls, wanted college or university graduates for spouses; 35 per cent. wanted secondary-school graduates, and 23 per cent. would be content with primary-school graduates; the 7 per cent. left did not think that educational achievements would influence their choice (1962, p. 52).[12] Similarly, in Little's Sierra Leone sample, the Creole girls said that education was the main quality which would influence their choice of a spouse: girls of tribal origin, too, stressed education, but they put religion on the same level and also mentioned that the physical appearance of their future husband would play a large part in their choice (Little, 1966). Men who have studied abroad, particularly if they are of the professional class and wealthy, are much sought after (Ekwensi, p. 31; Bird, 1958). Some girls even prefer to have an irregular relationship with an educated man if the only alternative is to marry a man of lower class and education (Bird, 1958).

---

[11] Education today tends to divide African society into two major classes; the educated and the non-educated. In addition to being the means of attaining a well-paid job, education also implies a relatively luxurious way of life. As a character in one of Achebe's novels says: 'A University degree is a philosopher's stone. It transmutes a third-class clerk on one hundred and fifty a year into a senior civil servant on five hundred and seventy with a car and luxuriously furnished quarter' (p. 92).

[12] Omari comments: 'Since only a small proportion of both men and women in Ghana have even the School Certificate, it is quite clear that a large proportion (70%) of the youngsters with higher than Form 4 (Standard 7) education in this country are going to be dissatisfied with their choice of a marital partner' (1962, p. 52).

On the other hand, although educated young men want sophisticated wives to grace their households, they do not necessarily share the idea of education being intrinsically valuable. Men wish their wives to be good looking and smartly dressed, but, at the same time, they have a stereotype of educated women as troublesome, critical, demanding, insubordinate, neglectful of husband and children. They admire a woman who has the same academic and cultural interests as they have; they are attracted by the smart Westernized girl who is at ease in society and can discuss any topic, but they still praise the qualities of the traditional wife. 'At one extreme', writes Jahoda about Ghana (1958, p. 198), 'there is the traditional illiterate African woman where the emphasis is on child-rearing, housework and trading . . . at the other extreme an educated lady whose work, if any, is done in an office, who dresses in European clothes and is not tied to the house as she will have other people to work for her'. And Jahoda's study shows that two-thirds of a sample of educated boys expressed preference for both the traditional and the 'modern' type of woman.[13] In short, men want to keep their personal and sexual superiority and are jealous of the independence of educated girls and of their work, especially when they are in a profession such as teaching; Jellicoe found cases in Freetown when the husband tried to get his wife dismissed from her job. The ideal seems to be a well-mannered wife who looks after the house and children, cooks, earns money, if required, obeys and respects her husband, and puts his interests before those of her own kin (Crabtree, 1950; Jahoda, 1958; Jellicoe, 1955; Little, 1966; Omari, 1962).

Educated girls agree that the man should be the dominant character; they do not always expect, therefore, to be treated as an equal, although they want to be their husbands' first interest. They want their husbands to be young, but of the professional class[14] and wealthy enough to provide modern luxuries and a high standard of material comfort. In other respects, their attitude is as ambiguous as that of the men. Although they wish to be accepted as partners, they also want a good deal of independence—to have a career of their own if they work, to have their own friends, and so on (Baker, 1957; Banton, 1957; Izzett; Jellicoe; Marris).

It is largely on the latter account—the desire to feel themselves 'emancipated'—that women are anxious to contract a statutory marriage. A girl is just as aware as the men of the social implications—for one thing it entitles her to style herself 'Mrs.' or 'Madame', and to command respect. A very important reason, however, is that such a marriage makes her legally

---

[13] Needless to say, in Ghana, as elsewhere, some highly educated men do have non-educated wives (Crabtree, Omari, 1962, p. 22). Naturally, it would be interesting to have precise figures showing how many educated men marry educated women and how many prefer to hold to the illiterate type.

[14] A character in one of Ekwensi's novels wants a 'gentleman'. 'A man can have money and still be crude'. Op. cit., p. 165.

free of her husband's lineage, including the right to sue him on the grounds, *inter alia*, of adultery; the right to inherit property from him, etc. (Baker and Bird, 1959). A highly educated woman may be in a position to cope successfully with economic difficulties; but a less literate girl may need the above kind of security if, at her husband's death, his kinsmen claim the entire estate and she is left homeless. Even if her marriage was made without her own family's consent, they will probably receive her back, but only if she submits herself completely to their control—perhaps the very thing she wants to avoid (ibid.).

The men, on the other hand, favour monogamy partly because for most of the educated class it is the socially approved form of marriage.[15] Indeed, it is virtually incumbent on professional people as well as upon church men. Thus, out of Omari's sample of 292 Ghanaian students, 73 per cent. believed that 'polygamy is definitely a backward practice which must be discouraged' (Omari, 1960, p. 202). Needless to say, economic pressures strongly support this attitude. Formerly, several wives were married to have as many children as possible but nowadays young educated people want only a small number of children to whom they can give a good education. Formerly the wives made their contribution by helping the man to improve his economic position; but today, except in certain occupations such as trading, they are expensive to maintain. And, whereas to be linked by marriage ties to several families used to be regarded as important the stress now is on the individual and not on the kin. There are also social as well as religious reasons for the decline of polygamy. In Dakar, Mercier found that monogamy is the ideal of both upper civil servants and members of professional occupations. Christians represent only 11 per cent. of the sample studies, but they represent 20 per cent. of the upper civil servants for whom monogamy is not yet widespread in actual practice. Since only 15 per cent. of the teachers and professional men, who practise monogamy, are Christian, this last figure shows that members of the teaching and professional occupations are starting to value monogamy for its own sake and not as a corollary of Christianity (1954, p. 202). In other words, monogamy is correlated with education as well and increases as educational standards improve (Bird, 1963). It means that to have a plurality of wives is no longer the way to increase influence and status and that, in short, the reasons which made polygamy an asset no longer obtain.

However, in this regard, there are significant differences in attitude between the sexes. In the Sierra Leone sample, for instance, one-third of a sample of male students wanted more than one wife, whereas only five girls out of 119 preferred polygamy (Little, 1966). Again, in Ghana, 86 per cent. of the girls rejected polygamy as a backward practice, as against

---

[15] Mercier differentiates between a 'monogamy of fact' and a 'monogamy of choice'; if unskilled workers are monogamous it is because they cannot afford polygamy, but professional men choose to be monogamous (Mercier, 1960, pp. 40–41).

61 per cent. of boys (Omari, 1960, p. 203). The same difference in outlook has been observed in Nigeria (Baker, 1957). Women do not want to
share their husband or to share his love and they would be jealous of
another wife (Banton, 1957, p. 198; Little, 1966); neither, presumably,
do they want to share their husband's income with co-wives.

 To sum up, then, for the man monogamy is basically a method of achieving or of consolidating superior status in the new Western context. The
woman's attitude is more complex because in breaking away from her
husband's lineage she jeopardizes the social position she would traditionally enjoy by having children. She knows that if she wants independence,
to use her education, and to have a career, she may have to fight for a
different status in the new form of society she will enter. Consequently,
her expectations of her husband are not the same as in the past. Requiring
his co-operation and support she wants him to be a companion and a
partner.

## The Clash of Modern Marriage and the Traditional System

If the above account is correct, it follows that the notion of romantic love
may be seen partly as a rationalization of changes going on in the social
structure. It justifies certain social tendencies. This does not mean that the
individual feelings professed are insincere; but political independence and
the expanding economy have opened up a large number of new and
important posts for younger people. Educated men, in particular, have the
prospect of rapidly advancing their status and for educated women, too,
there are new opportunities in the civil service, business, and the professions, as well as in nursing and teaching. But these occupations are specialized ones and require specific training; trained individuals and not
members with a predetermined status in a group have to fill these posts
and be able to move geographically, if necessary.

Upward mobility, therefore, requires an individualistic attitude and this
may be difficult to implement without seriously offending relatives and
kinsfolk who, for example, if they have partly paid for a man's education
will expect a return with each substantial increase in his income. Their
demands may take the form of the partial support of a yet younger relative
while at school, or of monetary assistance when they themselves are in
need.[16] They will expect to be generously entertained and to stay as long

---

[16] There are many illustrations of this point in the writings of West African novelists.
In *Wand of Noble Wood*, one of the principal characters remarks: 'The rate at which
demands were being made on my income was terrific. I did not know a good many
people who claimed to be my paternal or maternal relatives. Uncle knew them all
and always said their claims were true. They came at all hours and after explaining
what close ties bound us together begged financial help' (Onuoro Nzekwu, 1961, p.
85).

as they wish at the home of their more successful relative.[17] They will also look for a monetary contribution at every christening, wedding, and funeral.[18] These and other demands are difficult to refuse because socialization in the traditional system has ingrained in each of its members a very deep sense of obligation and loyalty to kinsfolk in general. They have been brought up to give these attachments priority over all other interests.[19] In the urban economy, by contrast, friendships develop on a different basis, including education, common interests, work, and residence; and a person's achievement of any social position is likely to depend on factors and relationships outside the kinship circle. Nevertheless, since deeply felt emotions persist,[20] it is only by replacing familial feelings with an alternative and equally strong moral sentiment that many individuals who have been so reared can avoid an acute feeling of personal guilt.[21]

This suggestion may explain why many of the younger men as well as the women find in the notion of love for a single partner a solution for their emotional dilemma. Psychologically, it would mean that by fixing their attention upon the conjugal relationship they can substitute for the wide circle of kinsfolk a much smaller group. The latter being limited in size to the parental family would imply that the scale of personal obligations was reduced, thereby providing some justification for concentrating economic and other resources upon a person's own interests and ambitions.[22] In other words, people find ways of satisfying their need for

---

[17] Of 190 households studied by Banton in Freetown, 92 reported visits received within the past 12 months; 23 of these visits lasted less than a week; 47 from a week to a month; and 15 over a month (op. cit.).

[18] For example, in Cotonou 37 out of 50 persons regularly sent money to their parents of other kinsmen for family ceremonies (Lombard, 1954, p. 370).

[19] In Chinua Achebe's novel, *No Longer At Ease,* one of the characters sent 'all he could find for his mother's funeral, but it was already said to his eternal shame that a woman who had borne so many children, one of whom was in a European post, deserved a better funeral than she got. . . . That is what Lagos can do to a young man. He runs after sweet things, dances breast to breast with women and forgets his name and his people' (pp. 18–9).

[20] Even residence overseas appears not greatly to alter this sentiment. West African students in the United States were interviewed by Zalinger (1960), and no less than 45 per cent. of the sample said that the fulfilment of one's family obligations was still 'the proper thing'; only 3 per cent. claimed that they would have absolutely nothing to do with such obligations.

[21] An example of the way in which this emotional conflict may extend to quite minor matters occurred when one of my informants came in some distress to see me (K. L.). There had been a quarrel between him and his illiterate mother—to whom he was very much attached—because he had criticized the lack of sanitation in her home. He had considered it his duty to point this out, and was upset because she had described his attitude as unfilial.

[22] Possible support for the hypothesis that educated young people have a conflict of emotional interest which they attempt to resolve in the manner suggested above is provided by the response of the Sierra Leone group. The questionnaire they answered

reciprocated love which can be more easily reconciled with society's new structure.

A more obvious reason why traditional influences are difficult to resist is structural. It is that the economic needs of the domestic group of man, wife, and children are different from those of a household in Europe. As yet, West Africa offers few of the safeguards of a modern welfare state: there are no schemes for social insurance to cover sickness or disability, and no pension for widows, orphans, and old people; nor is there any public assistance to provide for the destitute or the unemployed. Civil servants have their pensions, but only a very few men are wealthy enough, in every such crisis, to shoulder the financial handicap of sickness and unemployment on their own. Many people prepare for the rainy day by joining friendly societies which organize mutual aid, including benefit in the case of illness and bereavement (Little, 1965, ch. 3). On the whole, however, these associations are patronized by, and cater for, the less literate and well-to-do sections of society, and so in general an élite person's kinsfolk are still the main standby. He or she knows that so long as their goodwill is retained assistance and sympathy will always be forthcoming.

In these circumstances, few married couples of the first generation find it possible to make the break from their extra-familial ties sufficiently complete. They tend, for reasons which have just been described, to compromise. In other words, although the husband's main concern may be the education of his own children he may also feel it necessary for the sake of satisfactory lineage relations to see that his nephews and nieces receive a good schooling as well. A fifth of a man's income may be spent in this way (Lloyd, P., n.d.), in addition to remittances made to his mother and other maternal relatives.[23] The wife, too, will spend money on presents for her brothers and sisters and for her mother (Crabtree, 1950) when the available cash could have been used to provide her own children with clothes or to decorate the home. Again, rather than offend his lineage's sense of propriety, the husband may insist on his wife making customary obeisances

---

offered a number of alternative replies to the question of what their attitude would be in the event of a serious quarrel between their relatives and their spouse. Some 25 per cent. of the men and some 15 per cent. of the girls said that they would be impartial while only some 7 per cent. of the men and 4.5 per cent. of the girls said they would be on their spouse's side. On the other hand, in answer to a further question about residence, slightly more than 90 per cent. of the entire sample said that, after marriage, they would prefer to live in a house or compound of their own rather than with relatives.

[23] In Lagos, for example, 70 per cent. of the heads of households gave some regular help to at least one member of their natal family; 55 per cent. of them gave an average of over £1 (out of a monthly average earning of £20); 25 per cent. spent regularly £4 on relatives, and 12 per cent. £6. These sums did not include gifts and expenses of family ceremonies (Marris, pp. 36–38).

to female relatives, younger and much less educated than herself (Bird, 1963).

Furthermore, since the traditional family system is more concerned with procreation than with the husband–wife relationship, the husband's lineage is more likely for purposes of procreation to encourage than to condemn his relations with other women. This may happen when conservative senior kinsfolk, particularly the man's mother, resent the wife as an interloper who is seducing the boy from them. If she proves unsatisfactory in any way they seize on this with avidity in order to try to prejudice the husband against her. If her fault lies in her infertility they may 'marry' a young girl for him by customary law, paying the bridewealth and installing her in another house. It is recognized that there is some kind of statutory bar to this further union, but this recognition tends to be vague and inaccurate (Bird, 1963; Izzett). Traditional attitudes are also on the husband's side if, despite his statutory marriage, he has not put away former wives married according to customary law. This may make him guilty of the crime of bigamy in the eyes of the law, but he is not regarded as culpable by popular opinion.

Nor may there be any public objection to a husband having an irregular union with a single woman.[24] In western Nigeria, popular parlance calls these women 'outside wives', not mistresses or concubines. If these unions persist for some time they receive social acceptance and may form the basis of an elementary family. Man and woman regard themselves as husband and wife, and the woman is expected to remain faithful to the man. Any children born are usually recognized as their father's children by all concerned—the father, his kinsfolk, and society generally—and he often spends as much money on these women and their children as he does on his legal wife and her children (Baker and Bird, 1959; Crabtree; Izzett, p. 310).

In addition, in the cities, sexual contacts are facilitated by the presence of numbers of pleasure-loving women-about-town as well as ordinary prostitutes. One kind of union, which is not usually lasting, is the type contracted with *femmes libres* who, as indicated above, are a species of courtesan. These women are living by themselves with or without children. They like luxuries and have liaisons with wealthy civil servants who, fearing the reactions of their educated wives and also gossip, prefer a clandestine union (Lombard, p. 30). Another category are the 'Jaguars' or 'Hotel girls' who are found in towns like Accra, Lagos, and Ibadan. Dressed in

---

[24] In Yoruba (as in French) the same words used for legal wife and husband also denote the man and his 'outside' wife. The union may or may not be secret; if the parents of the girl take notice of it, the man may 'feed' them with small presents. The outside wife often appears at kinship functions but when European etiquette prevails she leaves the place to the legal wife (Bird, 1958).

a European way, they frequent dance halls, bars, and hotels.[25] Also, some mothers of illiterate girls prefer their daughters to have temporary unions with educated and well-to-do men rather than marry men of poorer class (Izzett; Little, 1959; Rouch and Bernus, 1957). The result, as Omari has pointed out, is that monogamy tends to be functually associated with concubinage and mistress relations.

## Organization of Modern Marriage

Circumstances of this kind, therefore, may determine the way in which a marriage becomes organized. A girl may start with the ideal of marital partnership, but come to feel that the competition of her husband's other women is too much for her. Legally, she may be in a position to take him to court but she also realizes that public opinion is not yet sufficiently on her side for it to be worth while. In addition, she may come to resent, but be unable to stop, the continuous draining away of money from her home to her husband's relatives, as well as to some other woman (Busia, 1950; Crabtree, 1950; Jellicoe, 1955).

In the event, since it may be economically impracticable for her to leave her husband, a wife may consider that the only way of dealing with her unsatisfactory marriage, of offsetting insecurity, and of safeguarding her children, is to become financially independent. One important opportunity open to women in general is in trading and so she may endeavour to build up a profitable business of her own (Marris, 1961). Alternatively, if she has enough education, she may take a full-time job in one of the professions open to women.[26] If such work is to be successful, it will necessitate her spending most of the day, and sometimes months, away from home (ibid.) and forming connexions with customers or colleagues outside the domestic circle. There are numerous voluntary associations to which women in trade can belong and an educated woman can join women's institutes, ladies' dining clubs, and other groups. Such activities provide scope for leadership and initiative among the latter class of women. A neglected wife, therefore, may compensate for her loneliness by founding such societies and actively helping to run them (Izzett; Little, 1965; Lombard). It means, however,

---

[25] In Accra and Abidjan, prostitutes include the *'tutu'* who usually live in reserved districts of the town. They take up a position on the doorsteps of their house, allowing the client to make his choice. Another group in Accra are the 'Karuas' who cater mostly for migrants from the north. Their practice is to rent a small house in the *zongo* where they lodge and feed passing strangers (Rouch, 1954).

[26] It must be pointed out, however, that many educated women work for other reasons; sometimes to repay parents for their training, or to provide extra money for the household. A good many girls have the intention of working after their marriage; otherwise, they say, their 'studies' would be a 'waste' (Baker, 1957; Little, 1966).

that in these various ways she becomes involved in a network of social relations which has no personal connexion with her husband.

The husband, too, may begin with some desire for a companionate relationship, but his position tends to be different from the start. For one thing, his statutory marriage is likely to be costly,[27] and so, as already explained, many men delay so marrying.[28] The Sierra Leonean respondents said that the best age for marriage is twenty-four (Little, 1966) but the actual evidence is that statutory marriage is not contracted by most men until they are twenty-five or much older. In Ghana, more men marry between thirty and forty than between twenty and thirty (Crabtree; Rado, 1956). In the meantime, some of them have had children by illiterate women with whom they cohabit or marry by customary law. This means, since such unions may have lasted for ten years or more, that on their statutory marriage, the men concerned have already strong ties and obligations which they cannot ignore. Relationships with their former customary wives or concubines may have ceased, but the bond with children is invariably continued. In addition, there are the husband's relatives with whom he keeps closely in touch, including attendance at family councils at least once every month, as well as birth, marriage, and other ceremonies. It is also in keeping with the traditional pattern for him to spend his leisure time with men friends as well as with other women. He and his male associates spend the evening together in each other's homes or meet in social clubs modelled on European lines which are formed for dining and drinking (Bird, 1958; Crabtree; Smythe, 1960).

The results of this situation is that familial activities tend to be organized on the basis of the husband's and the wife's respective social networks. Some of these activities complement each other, but in the main man and wife have a considerable number of separate interests. This kind of rela-

---

[27] Bridewealth still plays an important part and, although some educated parents refuse any money, or give it to their daughters, the amount is usually higher for an educated girl. In addition to the bridal gown, the bridegroom may have to pay for the clothes of the bridesmaids, and pages, provide food and drink and musical entertainment for a large number of invited and uninvited guests, and distribute money among the girl's relatives. There are also many traditional expenses prior to the wedding itself, including maintenance of the girl during the engagement period. The total cost of the wedding, therefore, may be as much as £500. In his study of Sekondi-Takoradi, Busia estimated that men marrying under the Ordinance spent £154 on the average. That was in 1950. Sometimes the cost can reach a sum representing a year's salary. A member of a well-to-do family in Lagos told Marris that he would try to get married in England to save money (p. 47). See also Crabtree; Tardits, 1958, p. 61; Mercier, 1954, p. 28; Izzett, p. 309.

[28] Young men sometimes borrow money and pay it back during the first months of their marriage; it even happens that the father gives his future son-in-law a loan so that he can marry his daughter. Out of a sample of 91 educated men, 18 got into debt in order to get married; out of 34 individuals interviewed, 17 had borrowed money to marry; 12 paid it back in 2 years; but 7 cases ended by imprisonment or separation of the spouses (Crabtree).

tionship in which complementary and independent types of organization predominate involves a segregation of roles between the spouses. Elizabeth Bott used this phrase in describing variations in the ways that the husbands and wives she studied in London performed their conjugal roles. She found that those families that had a high degree of segregation in the role-relationships of husband and wife had a close-knit network; that is to say, many of their neighbours, friends, and relatives knew one another. Families, on the other hand, that had a relatively joint role-relationship between husband and wife had a loose-knit network; few of their relatives, neighbours, and friends knew one another. Bott's suggestion is that the degree of segregation in the role-relationship of husband and wife varies directly with the connectedness of the family's social network. In other words, the more connected the respective networks of man and wife, the greater the degree of segregation between their roles.[29] At the other extreme, however, was a family in which husband and wife spent as much time together as possible. They stressed that husband and wife should be equals; all major decisions were made together, and even in minor household matters they helped one another as much as possible. To the latter kind of family in which joint organization is predominant Bott applied the term joint conjugal role-relationship (ibid., pp. 52–61).

Since they indicate polar types of family organization the latter term and the term segregated conjugal role-relationship are employed by the analyst merely as models of marital behaviour. These formulations are mentioned, however, because they may help to clarify the conflicting tendencies in West African marriage. On the one hand, according to several observers, successful and durable marriages are the exception rather than the rule among the educated class[30] (Bird, 1958; Busia; Crabtree). A large number of marriages do not necessarily end in the courts and, so far as Christian and civil marriages are concerned, the divorce rate

---

[29] Bott explains that the social relationship of other people with one another may affect the relationship of husband and wife in the following way: 'When many of the people a person knows interact with one another, that is when the person's network is close-knit, the members of his network tend to reach consensus on norms and they exert consistent informal pressure on one another to conform to the norms, to keep in touch with one another, and, if need be, to help one another. If both husband and wife come to marriage with such close-knit networks, and if conditions are such that the previous pattern of relationships is continued, the marriage will be superimposed on these pre-existing relationships, and both spouses will continue to be drawn into activities with people outside their own elementary family (family of procreation). Each will get some emotional satisfaction from these external relationships and will be likely to demand correspondingly less of the spouse. Rigid segregation of conjugal roles will be possible because each spouse can get help from people outside' (p. 60).

[30] Writing of the African urban family in general, Gutkind says that on the whole there is no evidence that the Christian form of marriage may, perhaps, have a better chance of survival than common law unions (1962, p. 193).

appears to be low by Western standards[31] (Banton, 1957; Bird, 1958, Crabtree, 1950). But, needless to say, the available figures do not cover all marriages that have failed. Some marriage partners have separated (Jellicoe) and some are living in an unhappy state.[32] On the other hand, as we have seen, many young Africans obviously desire a companionate form of union in which there will be a degree of partnership between husband and wife.

### Marriages of the Companionate Type

As yet, for reasons already mentioned, marriages of the latter kind are not achieved very frequently. Nevertheless, there does exist a trend in the companionate direction and it has developed in two different ways. Firstly, in the earlier days, what has been called the 'Victorian' family was introduced largely by missionary education among a number of peoples on the coast, especially Liberated Africans in Sierra Leone. In this type of family as it existed among the Yoruba, domestic roles remained segregated and the husband tended to be an authoritarian figure, quite often having more than one wife. The fact, however, that a much greater stress was placed on the individual rather than on the corporate group enabled the nuclear family to emerge at that stage as a unit on its own. The members of these early families were among the first Christians of their towns and ranked as an educated élite (Lloyd, P. C., n.d.). There are many staunch Christians among educated Africans today who have this 'Victorian' type of family as a background.

However, in organizing conjugal relationships the modern élite also show a more secular pattern which is derived from different experiences. This is the case because these high civil servants, professional men and women, university lecturers, and so on have received almost invariably part of their training overseas. They have met and mixed with European or American university students and have frequently stayed as guests or as lodgers in middle-class homes. They have observed for themselves a contemporary Western way of life and élite men and women prefer the con-

---

[31] Even in the same country, however, the situation varies. In Cotonou, according to Lombard, divorces seem to be quite frequent. In Porto-Novo, on the other hand, Tardits (1958) found a lower incidence among educated people than illiterate.

[32] One of the reasons for marital instability is that nowadays man and wife are under less social control. Formerly, it was the responsibility of the relatives to see that they observed their marital obligations. Any such disputes were settled 'in the house', both family groups having an interest in keeping the marriage intact. Today, marriage being an individual affair, it is not rare that the kinsfolk of the one party are strangers to the kinsfolk of the other party. It may no longer be a union of two lineages or families and so today there is less pressure on the couple to maintain the marriage (Little, 1965). For example, in the Sierra Leone Colony 1941–52 there were only 53 divorces compared with 3,700 Christian marriages, 39 civil marriages, and 701 Muslim marriages (Banton, op. cit., p. 209).

temporary style rather than the image given by the missions to their parents. They seek, in particular, to apply these Western standards to their social activities and this includes emulating many of the domestic practices seen abroad. The result is that among younger married couples at least, egalitarianism is considered 'good form', and a husband cannot, with impunity, publicly treat his wife as an inferior (Jellicoe). He would run the risk of being stigmatized as 'bush' and losing prestige. In any case, having the same kind of advanced education, husbands and wives have more interests in common, including intellectual ones, than is the case among married couples lower down on the educational scale. Sharing domestic tasks is not often called for because most of the manual work is done by servants or housemaids. Also, since the existence of servants who act as baby-sitters removes any obstacle to spouses going out together, some amount of visiting of mutual friends takes place,[33] facilitated by the family car (Lloyd, B. B., 1966).

Another important bond is created through the children in whose upbringing husband and wife frequently co-operate with zeal. The élite father plays ball with his children, reads to them, and actively seeks a warm, friendly relationship. Parents take care to see that in their absence the servants never use physical punishment[34] but instead report the children's misdeeds when the parents come home. A child's subsequent career brings prestige to its parents, and so, since husband and wife want the same élite status for their sons and daughters, they both take pains with their education, very often with the university in mind. Almost universally, one parent, usually the mother, checks each child's homework daily (Gamble, p. 220; Lloyd, B. B., 1966).

In many such families, then, the husband and wife take equal responsibility in domestic matters, and the emphasis is on shared roles in the life of the home and in leisure-time activities (Baker, 1947; Lloyd, P. C. and Lloyd, B. B., op. cit.). In this way, new patterns of marital conduct are being set because many of the uneducated inhabitants of the larger towns are Western-oriented and ready to follow the lead of the élite (Little,

---

[33] If the spouses work in the same place they inevitably share more friends. In Ibadan, P. C. Lloyd found that half of the best friends of élite men and women are well known to one another: a clergyman's wife cited as two of her best friends the wives of her husband's closest friends. Either spouse may gain new friends through the other; a third of the men Lloyd interviewed claimed between one and three friends gained through their wife and one half of the women had between them one and four friends gained through their husband. However, the degree to which husbands and wives share their leisure time is still fairly low; they may watch television together or go to cocktail parties to friends of either of them, but they spend much of their spare time in monosexual gatherings, and among one half of the Ibadan élite no shared friendship was found. (Lloyd, n.d.)

[34] Gamble (op. cit., pp. 214–22) points out that in up country towns in Sierra Leone one of the practices which distinguishes educated families from families of men in unskilled work is the punishment of children. In the latter families it is often very severe.

1965, pp. 154–6). However, these new norms are mainly adopted when the spouses have been reared in families in which both boys and girls have been given some sort of preparation for a joint conjugal role-relationship. If they have been brought up traditionally there is already a barrier to their companionship and understanding in the husband's reluctance to behave differently from his non-literate kinsfolk's expectations. He may wish to raise his wife's standing to an equal position but fears criticism if he does so (Omari, 1962).

Also to be considered is the general effect of cultural and economic change. The sale of novels and popular magazines, and the cinema as well as schools and colleges themselves, all propagate directly or indirectly a Western view of marriage (Jahoda). And, since it stimulates migration, industrialization is particularly significant. Development schemes, the expansion of the civil service, new mining and commercial enterprises, new towns themselves—all these things make families as well as individual men and women more mobile. Thus, to quote only two examples, Kumasi, in Ghana, has grown from about 24,000 inhabitants in 1921 to about 190,000 in 1960, and Enugu, the administrative capital of Eastern Nigeria, founded on an empty site, had a population of 82,000 by 1962. The people who move into these and other rapidly growing towns come from different parts of the country and a large proportion of them are transient (Little, 1965, pp. 87–88). Precise data are lacking, but the impression is that members of the educated class change their residence as often as other migrants, especially as it helps promotion. Civil servants, for example, are frequently transferred from one post to another part of the country. The result is that the married couples concerned find themselves in a different environment from their home town and its associations. They are obliged to rely more on their own resources.

These young people who move away do not lack new neighbours and friends; nor do they lose contact with or forget the lineage at home. As already indicated, family sentiment invariably remains strong and through periodical visiting and in various indirect ways the network of kinship is preserved. Nevertheless, since there is less face-to-face interaction, kinship norms are correspondingly less compulsive and man and wife have a greater incentive to adjust to each other's personality. They may for this reason look towards one another for co-operation in the joint enterprise of making a home (Bird, 1958; Crabtree, 1950; Marris, 1961).

## Conclusion

In this paper the connexion between notions of romantic love and the social aspirations of educated young West Africans has been examined. The suggestion is that this connexion largely explains the contemporary popularity of monogamous marriage. Although romantic attachments between young people are by no means unknown in traditional culture 'falling in love' was not regarded hitherto as a necessary prelude to marriage. Moreover, the idea of love for a single partner is in conflict with the traditional family system in which more emphasis is placed upon the procreative and economic functions of marriage than upon the personal feelings of the spouses for each other. Consequently, since traditional norms continue to influence and regulate the extra-familial relationships of man and wife, the organization of modern marriage generally involves a segregation of roles between the spouses. In this regard, there is apparently a close similarity between West African marital behaviour and one of the polar types of British family organization that Elizabeth Bott has described in East London.

On the other hand, trends in African marriage are also affected by the growth of an industrial economy in which the domestic group has significance as a socioeconomic unit on its own. Urbanization, involving increased physical mobility, also lessens the pressure of kinship. The result is to be seen in the appearance, mainly among the highly educated, well-to-do classes, of marriages of the companionate type. Possibly the organization of these élite families also accords with Bott's model. Further data, however, are required in order to show whether it is characterized by the same kind of joint conjugal role-relationship as that postulated by Bott.

## References Cited

ACHEBE, CHINUA. 1960. *No Longer At Ease.* London.

BAKER, TANYA. 1957. 'Women's Élites in Western Nigeria.' Unpublished MS. Department of Social Anthropology, Edinburgh University.

BAKER, TANYA, and BIRD, MARY. 1959. 'Urbanization and the Position of Women' in Special Number on 'Urbanism in West Africa', ed. Little, Kenneth. *Sociological Review,* vol. 7, no. 1, new series.

BANTON, MICHAEL. 1957. *West African City: A Study of Tribal Life in Freetown.* London.

BIRD, MARY. 1958. 'Social Change in Kinship and Marriage among the Yoruba of Western Nigeria." Unpublished Ph.D. Thesis, Edinburgh University.

————— 1963. 'Urbanization, Family and Marriage in Western Nigeria', in *Urbanization in African Social Change.* Centre of African Studies, Edinburgh University.

BOTT, ELIZABETH. 1957. *Family and Social Network.* London.

BUSIA, K. A. 1950. *Report on a Social Survey of Sekondi-Takoradi.* London.

CRABTREE, A. I. 1950. 'Marriage and Family Life among Educated Africans in the Urban Areas of the Gold Coast.' Unpublished M.Sc. Thesis, London University.

DESAI, RAM (ed.). 1962. *Christianity in Africa as Seen by the Africans.* Denver.

EKWENSI, CYPRIAN. 1961. *Jagua Nana.* London.

FORDE, DARYLL. 1941. *Marriage and Family among the Yakö in South Eastern Nigeria.* Monographs on Social Anthropology, No. 5. London School of Economics.

FORTES, MEYER. 1959. *The Web of Kinship among the Tallensi.* London.

GAMBLE, DAVID. 1963. 'The Temne Family in a Modern Town (Lunsar) in Sierra Leone', *Africa,* vol. xxxiii, no. 3.

GOODY, ESTHER N. 1962. 'Conjugal Separation and Divorce among the Gonja of Northern Ghana', in *Marriage in Tribal Society,* ed. Fortes, Meyer. Cambridge.

GUTKIND, PETER C. W. 1962. 'African Urban Family Life', *Cahiers d'Études africaines,* vol. iii, no. 2.

HARRIES, LYNDON. 1953. 'Christian Marriage in African Society', in *Survey of African Marriage and Family Life,* ed. Phillips, A. London. (For International African Institute.)

IZZETT, A. 1961. 'Family Life among the Yoruba in Lagos, Nigeria', in *Social Change in Modern Africa,* ed. Southall, A. W. London. (For International African Institute.)

JAHODA, GUSTAV. 1955. 'The Social Background of a West African Student Population, II', *British Journal of Sociology,* vol. 6, no. 1.

———— 1958. 'Boys' Images of Marriage Partners and Girls' Self-Images in Ghana', *Sociologus,* viii.

———— 1959. 'Love, Marriage and Social Change: Letters to the Advice Column of a West African Newspaper', *Africa,* vol. xxix, no. 2.

JELLICOE, MARGUERITE. 1955. Unpublished London University Diploma in Social Anthropology Thesis.

LITTLE, KENNETH. 1951. *The Mende of Sierra Leone.* London.

———— 1959. 'Some Patterns of West African Marriage and Domesticity', in 'Urbanism in West Africa', ed. Little, Kenneth. *Sociological Review,* vol. 7, no. 1, new series.

———— 1965. *West African Urbanization: A Study of Voluntary Associations in Social Change.* Cambridge.

———— 1966. 'Attitudes Towards Marriage and the Family Among Educated Young Sierra Leoneans', in *New Élites of Tropical Africa,* ed. Lloyd, P. C. London. (For International African Institute.)

LLOYD, B. B. 1966. 'Education and Family Life in the Development of Class Identification Among the Yoruba', in *New Élites of Tropical Africa,* ed. Lloyd, P. C. London. (For International African Institute.)

LLOYD, P. C. n.d. 'The Élite of Ibadan.' In Mabogunje, A. *et al.* (eds.). *City of Ibadan* (forthcoming).

LOMBARD, J. 1954. 'Cotonou: ville africaine', *Bulletin de l'Institut français d'Afrique noire,* vol. xvi, nos. 3 and 4.

MAIR, L. P. 1953. 'African Marriage and Social Change', in *Survey of African Marriage and Family Life,* ed. Phillips, A. London. (For International African Institute.)

MARRIS, PETER. 1961. *Family and Social Change in an African City.* London.

MERCIER, P. 1954. 'Aspects de la société africaine dans l'agglomeration dakaroise: groupes familiaux et unités de voisinage', *Études Sénégalaises,* no. 5.

———— 1960. 'Étude du mariage et enquête urbaines', *Cahiers d'Études africaines,* i. 1.

NZEKWU, ONUORA. 1961. *Wand of Noble Wood.* London.

OMARI, T. PETER. 1960. 'Changing Attitudes of Students in West African Society Towards Marriage and Family Relationships', *British Journal of Sociology,* vol. xi, no. 3.

———— 1962. *Marriage Guidance for Young Ghanaians.* Edinburgh.

PHILLIPS, A. (ed.). 1953. *Survey of African Marriage and Family Life.* London. (For International African Institute.)

ROUCH, JEAN, and BERNUS, EDMOND. 1957. 'Note sur les prostituées "toutou" de Treichville et d'Adjamé', *Études Éburnéennes,* 6 (Institut français d'Afrique noire).

———— 1954. *Migration in the Gold Coast* (English translation). Accra.

SMITH, MARY F. 1955. *Baba of Karo, a woman of the Muslim Hausa.* New York.

SMYTHE, HUGH H., and MABEL M. 1960. *The New Nigerian Élite.* Stanford.

SOFER, C., and SOFER, R. 1955. 'Jinja Transformed.' *East African Studies,* no. 4. Kampala.

TARDITS, C. 1958. *Porto Novo.* Paris.

ZALINGER, ALVIN D. 1960. 'A Study of African Students in the United States', Working Paper in *Tropical Africa,* ed. Kimble, George H. T. New York.

# Types of Urban African Marriage in Kampala

## David J. Parkin

This paper analyses factors affecting the variable character of urban marriage patterns in the predominantly African city ward of Kampala East, Uganda.[1] Kampala city comprises two other wards, both of which accommodate considerable proportions of Asians and Europeans. Skirting the west and south of the city is the Kibuga, meaning capital in the local vernacular, Luganda.[2] The Kibuga, like Kampala East, is also predominantly African. The city and Kibuga are administratively and culturally highly distinct. The city has its own council and is the nation's capital. The Kibuga is the capital of the quasi-autonomous kingdom of Buganda. The latter is alternatively a province of Uganda.

Though they are both predominantly African urban residential areas, Kampala East and the Kibuga differ in many other respects. The Kibuga is a relatively self-sufficient community commercially. Only a small proportion of its population, which includes a mostly Ganda professional *élite*, work in the city. Ganda are the dominant tribe. Migrants from other tribes are much less numerous and many are transitory, short-term, unskilled, and unmarried. Kampala East comprises six housing estates and development areas. These have come to provide accommodation for the more skilled worker who is of longer than average urban residence,[3] of higher than average income, and who has married monogamously and has his wife living with him in town for much of the time. Moreover, Ganda are not in all areas numerically dominant. Indeed migrants, such as the Kenya Luo

---

[1] Between July 1962 and March 1964 I studied intensively two city council housing estates in this ward. I am grateful to the Commonwealth Scholarship Scheme for making the study possible. I acknowledge the invaluable assistance of the East African Institute of Social Research. I especially thank Professor A. W. Southall for commenting on a draft of this paper.

[2] In accordance with the 1961 Buganda agreement the Kibuga is now administered by a new Mengo municipal council. Before 1962 Mengo was a township of the Kibuga.

[3] I estimate the average length of urban residence by migrants in this area at about seven years, against only approximately two or three years for Greater Kampala.

and Luhya, are the most numerous and, before disfranchisement, were the most active politically.

The people of Kampala East thus consitute a wide cross-section of migrants from different tribes who appear to have assumed many characteristics of urban commitment, including the creation of and subscription to urban norms. My figures and other data were obtained from two city council housing estates. The number of household heads, mostly male, on these estates is 1,468. Seventy-nine per cent. of them are married. Eighty-seven per cent. of these have children.

Immediately impressive in Kampala as a whole is the distinction into two super-tribal categories of migrants from traditionally politically centralized and uncentralized tribes. People from the Ganda, Toro, Nyoro, and Soga kingdoms are included among the former.[4] The Luo, Acholi, Lango, Alur, Luhya, Lugbara, Teso, and Kiga are uncentralized tribes-peoples. A third somewhat residual category is that of the so-called Nubi, who are Muslims.

Bridewealth among the centralized tribespeoples is generally low and/or irrecoverable. Marriage has increasingly come to be regarded as a contract between bride and groom rather than between the two respective sets of kin. Regardless of whether or not bridewealth has been paid for a woman, a genitor has the right to claim his children. This right is upheld in the courts of these kingdoms. A special feature of these centralized societies is a marked emphasis on highly individual rights in land, which in parts approaches de facto freehold land tenure, especially among Ganda. Political office at any points in the hierarchy is largely based on the possession or control of land. Many decades of social and physical mobility have brought about the dispersion of patrilineages and clans. The contemporary highly developed cotton and coffee cash crop economy has continued the process by encouraging the spatial separation of fathers and sons and of brothers from each other, who attempt to move to bigger and more productive plots of land. Their rather special land tenure systems and highly developed cash crop economies immediately distinguish these societies from most other centralized tribes in Africa.

Property is transmitted patrilineally in most cases, a chosen heir of any wife and of any seniority receiving by far the greater portion of the legacy. Daughters occasionally inherit. Women may own valuable property, includ-

---

[4] The Bantu Rwanda and Ankole societies are also politically centralized. But they are structured into 'castes' rather than 'classes'. Most Rwanda and Ankole in Kampala are of the lower 'caste'. Ankole lower 'caste' or Iru marriages have much in common with those of the uncentralized peoples with their stress on high bridewealth payments for genetricial rights. Whether through assimilation or cultural factors of longer standing the few Rwanda lower 'caste' or Hutu marriages known to me seemed to be governed by regulations similar to those of the other centralized societies. Neither is particularly significant in my sample.

ing land and money, and may choose their heirs. There is thus really only a relatively weak emphasis on patriliny.

Among the uncentralized tribespeoples bridewealth continues to be of high value and is generally recoverable. It guarantees a man's rights to claim his wife's children as his own, regardless of their genitor.[5] The bride and groom's respective agnates maintain an economic and ideological interest in the marriage. For many of these peoples patrilineages of all levels are frequently localized and are land-holding units. The smaller lineages possess a relatively high degree of economic, jural, and political autonomy, so that close agnates especially are united in a number of ways. More distant actual and putative agnates subscribe to a fairly common ideology regarding marriage. Inheritance is strictly patrilineal, all sons receiving approximately equal shares of their father's property. Daughters do not inherit and women do not own or control property except for certain gardens and cattle or livestock which co-wives hold in trust for their own sons.[6]

The Nubi stem from the Sudan, but in many cases were born in Uganda. They derive from a number of Sudanese tribes, though nowadays their original tribal affiliations are irrelevant to or superseded by their Muslim status, which underlies their cohesion and sense of community. I do not have the data to discuss the Nubi in detail, nor do I know how numerous they are, though they probably do not exceed a few thousand, the majority of whom are clustered in or near towns.

The very approximate sizes of the centralized tribes are Ganda a million, Soga half a million, Ankole half a million, and Toro and Nyoro nearly a quarter of a million each. For the uncentralized tribespeoples the approximate sizes are Luo and Luhya both a million, Teso half a million, Kiga just under half a million, Lango 364,000, Acholi 285,000, Lugbara 236,000, and Alur 123,000.

According to the 1959 census the African population of Greater Kampala was 76,729, though the actual figure may be over 100,000. According to the same census the populations of these peoples in Kampala expressed as percentages were: Ganda 48.8, Toro 7.6, Rwanda 3.7, Ankole 3.2, Nyoro 2.5, and Soga 1.3; Luo 7.2, Luhya about 3.5, Acholi 2.7, Kiga 2.6, Teso 1.7, Lugbara 1.2, Lango under 1, and Alur even fewer; and Nubi 1.9.

I have defined the three super-tribal categories according to broad social and cultural criteria. Linguistic affinities may cut across these categories.

---

[5] See Southall, 1960. Southall's distinction between 'Nilotic' and 'Interlacustrine Bantu' marriage types corresponds with my distinction between the marriage systems of uncentralized and centralized societies.

[6] I do not propose these features as universal correlates of centralized and uncentralized societies respectively. The Zulu, for instance, are centralized but place a strong emphasis on agnation and are similar in very many institutions, including marriage, to an uncentralized tribe like the Luo.

Thus, the Kiga are linguistically Interlacustrine Bantu but are not centralized as are others in this category. The Luhya are also Bantu. Politically and culturally, however, they are close to their fellow Kenyans, the Luo. The latter are Nilotes. Their dialect and those of the Uganda Nilotes, the Acholi, Lango, and Alur, are more or less mutually intelligible. The Lugbara are Sudanic speakers and, in this respect, are somewhat isolated from migrants of other tribes. The Teso are the only Nilo-Hamites but are not so isolated because so many of their migrant population speak Swahili and English. English, Swahili, and Luganda severally serve as a limited *lingua franca* to blur somewhat the lines separating the wider ethnic and other groupings. These cultural and linguistic affinities and differences constitute one major set of factors limiting the incidence and type of intra- and inter-tribal conjugal union among residents.

Other related factors are embodied in statements made very generally by neighbours themselves about given marriages. These statements begin with a distinction which residents themselves make between 'permanent' (or 'real') and 'temporary' wives. It is important to note that, like some other English expressions, these are used by persons who otherwise know no English.

A 'permanent' wife is one who has married according to tribal custom in the rural district, one who has undergone a Christian or Muslim ritual, or one who is partner to a civil or District Registrar marriage. These three forms of marriage may be accompanied by a transaction of bridewealth. Christian and civil marriages are alternatively referred to as 'ring' marriages. By far the greater proportion of 'permanent' marriages in my sample are those established according to tribal custom in the rural home area.

But there is a further fourth category of 'permanent' wives. These are women who are partners to some intra- and inter-tribal unions, which were established in town, and in which bridewealth may have been paid and/or children previously or subsequently born. Neighbours select one or both these criteria, in conjunction with the length of the union and degree of harmony between the partners, in ascribing 'permanent' status to the wife. Such wives were once 'temporary'.

A 'temporary' wife is usually one who has been secured in town by a man to satisfy his domestic and sexual needs. No bridewealth will have been paid for her. Normally she will be childless, but occasionally a man may impregnate his 'temporary' wife, and both partners, and eventually also neighbours, may begin to regard the union as permanent, with at least the stated expectation that the union will be continued at one spouse's rural home when the period of urban employment ceases. There is a parallel here with the concept of 'outside wives' described by Fraenkel in Monrovia. A man's lover who bears him children may become his 'outside wife'. The 'outside marriage' is not legally defined as a marriage but is a long-term extra-marital union of 'civilized' men who are also partners to a Christian marriage. But, like 'permanent' wives in Kampala who were initially 'temporary', 'outside wives' in Monrovia achieve recognized social status.[7]

I am using the concept of marriage or conjugal union broadly. I am less concerned with legal and administrative definitions[8] than with public recognition, both by kin and neighbours, of such unions. Hence the importance of pursuing analytically the local distinction into 'temporary' and 'permanent' wives.

In 1957 Southall and Gutkind, for two areas in the Kibuga, distinguished 'different types of marital union and sexual activity, although no hard and fast lines can be drawn between them, and one type is constantly turning into another'. They first distinguished the three administratively recognized forms of marriage I outlined above. They termed all other unions 'based on continuous cohabitation and common domestic economy for a longer or shorter period' as concubinage. They further distinguished prostitution, as 'an *ad hoc* commercial transaction between strangers, and love affairs, in which the parties do not establish a common *ménage* but simply visit one another, the woman receiving gifts and even some sort of maintenance allowance from her lover'.[9]

I do not describe prostitution or love affairs, but only those unions in which people do 'establish a common *ménage*'.

On the basis of the categories and criteria outlined, common *ménage* unions may be divided into:

1. Unions arranged in the rural districts;
2. Unions arranged in the town:
   (*a*) Intra-tribal unions in which wives are regarded as 'temporary'.
   (*b*) Inter-tribal unions in which wives are regarded as 'temporary'.
   (*c*) Intra-tribal unions in which wives are regarded as 'permanent'.
   (*d*) Inter-tribal unions in which wives are regarded as 'permanent'.

The data relating to the 166 common *ménage* unions dealt with were not collected by systematic sampling, and the number is too small for analysis of all variables. But they indicate the general differences between the populations of the two housing estates in Kampala East and of Greater Kampala.

In the housing estates of Kampala East the tribal proportions of household heads, mostly male, expressed as approximate percentages of the total household head population of 1,468, excluding tribespeoples who are not

---

[7] Fraenkel, 1964, pp. 113–14.

[8] See Mitchell, 1957, in which the social significance of marriage certificates is explored. I do, however, follow up ideas suggested in Mitchell's analysis, such as the implications for a union of the choice of spouse in an area accommodating migrants of different tribes.

[9] Southall and Gutkind, 1957, p. 71.

significant in my sample, are: Ganda 12, Toro, Nyoro, and Soga together 6, Rwanda 2.5, Ankole 1; Luo 22, Luhya (including Samia) 12.5, Acholi 9, Lugbara 5.5, Kiga 4.5, Lango 3, Teso 2.5, Alur under 1; and Nubi 5.5.

Thus, though, as already seen, the Ganda preponderate in Greater Kampala, they are less numerous than the Luo and Luhya in the housing estates. There the Kiga, Lugbara, Lango, Teso, and Nubi all exceed their proportions in Greater Kampala, the proportion of Toro being reduced, while those of Nyoro and Soga are about the same.

There is, of course, no direct relationship between size of tribe and the proportion of its members in town. Nor is distance always the dominant factor. Rural economic conditions are also important. Of those from the Western Province of Uganda, the Kiga come nearly 250 miles, and the Ankole, Toro, and Nyoro between 150 and 200 miles by road to Kampala. The Teso from the Eastern Province, like the Soga, are some 150 miles from Kampala. The Lango, some 150 miles, and the Alcholi, Alur, and Lugbara, between 250 and 300 miles from Kampala, are in the Northern Province. The Luo and Luhya in Kampala have come 200 to 250 miles from the Kenya side of Lake Victoria. Although the Ganda are the local tribespeople, their area is extensive, and many Ganda in the estates appear to stem from fairly distant parts of the province.

The Soga, Lango, and Teso living in the estates, who come from rural areas of higher economic development, claim that only people with enough education to find a lucrative job will find it profitable to migrate to Kampala. Others can be profitably employed at home growing cash crops. Certainly, most people of these tribes in the estates hold above average clerical and skilled posts, as also do the Ganda. The Toro and Nyoro are also mostly clerks and skilled workers.

The Kiga and Lugbara suffer land shortage at home, more severe in some areas than others. Most of the Kiga in the estates are short-term migrants who rarely stay for more than a year and hold such unskilled jobs as sweepers and cleaners; but a small number are clerical or skilled workers. The Lugbara have been in the estates the longest and are mostly in the lower artisan class. They claim that they have lost effective rights to their land at home, unlike other Lugbara in Kampala who are mostly short-term migrants.

The Luo and Luhya are scattered fairly evenly over a range of clerical, skilled, and unskilled occupations. The Acholi include many skilled and unskilled workers, but with a small minority of clerks.

The tribal membership of male 'spouses' in the sample of 166 common *ménage* unions is 17 Ganda, 10 Soga, 8 Toro, 7 Nyoro, 4 Rwanda, and 1 Ankole; 40 Luo, 16 Acholi, 14 Luhya, 12 Lango, 11 Kiga, 8 Lugbara, 5 Alur, and 3 Teso; and 10 Nubi. Thus, males from centralized tribes account for 28.3 per cent., uncentralized for 65.7 per cent., and Nubi for 6 per cent. The corresponding proportions of household heads in the estates as a whole are: centralized tribes 21.3 per cent.; uncentralized

71.7 per cent.; and Nubi 5.5 per cent. Females from centralized tribes account for 39.7 per cent. of the 166 unions, uncentralized for 57.8 per cent., and Nubi for 2.4 per cent., so that there are more females than males from centralized tribes, while the converse applies for the uncentralized and Nubi.

All men in the sample are between twenty and thirty-five years of age. With the exception of a few Luo, Acholi, Luhya, and Lugbara unskilled workers, most are of the artisan and clerical classes and have been in Kampala in most cases over four years, in some cases well over this period. Broadly they may be said to represent a stable element in the Kampala labour force.

## 1. Unions Arranged in the Rural Districts

Of the ninety common *ménage* unions established in the rural districts under customary law, all except two Luo/Luhya[10] marriages are intra-tribal, as might be expected. Direction and restriction of choice of spouse is most marked among the uncentralized tribes, where local groups of agnates are concerned in the proceedings and course of the marriage and regard the economically valuable bridewealth as guaranteeing genetricial rights. Cohabitation without marriage is rare among these peoples. Of the eighty-eight customary intra-tribal unions 30 were Luo, 14 Acholi, 13 Luhya, 8 Lango, 6 Kiga, 4 Alur, 4 Lugbara, 1 Teso, that is, altogether eighty from uncentralized tribes. The rest were 4 Soga, 3 Ganda, and 1 Toro. Thus, in the sample much greater proportions of men from uncentralized tribes have been married in the rural, customary manner than have men from centralized tribes who are mostly partners to urban-established conjugal unions. Among the latter there is a relatively high frequency of cohabitation without marriage in rural districts as well as in town.

When couples from uncentralized tribes move from rural district to town their marriages continue to be subject to the surveillance and control of urban-dwelling agnates, clansmen, and wider-scale formal urban tribal associations. Adulterous wives and errant unmarried girls are forcibly dispatched to their husbands' or fathers' rural homes. There are remarkably few prostitutes of these tribes in Kampala, or, apparently, in any East African town. This control exerted over urban-dwelling couples from uncentralized tribes contrasts most strongly with the situation for couples from the centralized tribes.

Table 1 supports the impression that much larger proportions of men

---

[10] Luo/Luhya marriages occur not infrequently at the territorial boundary of these two peoples.

TABLE 1* COMMON *MÉNAGE* UNIONS ESTABLISHED IN TOWN AND REGARDED AS INCLUDING A 'TEMPORARY' WIFE

| Husband \ Wife | Luo | Acholi | Lango | Alur | Luhya | Kiga | Lugbara | Teso | Ganda | Toro | Nyoro | Soga | Rwanda | Ankole | Nubi |
|---|---|---|---|---|---|---|---|---|---|---|---|---|---|---|---|
| Luo |  |  |  |  |  |  |  |  | 1 | 1 |  |  |  |  |  |
| Acholi |  |  |  |  |  |  |  |  | 1 | 1 |  |  |  |  |  |
| Lango |  |  | 1 |  |  |  |  |  | 1 |  |  |  |  |  |  |
| Alur |  |  |  |  |  |  |  |  |  |  | 1 |  |  |  |  |
| Luhya |  |  |  |  |  |  |  |  |  |  |  |  |  |  |  |
| Kiga |  |  |  |  |  |  |  |  | 1 | 1 |  |  |  |  |  |
| Lugbara |  |  |  |  |  |  | 2 |  |  |  |  |  |  |  |  |
| Teso |  |  |  |  |  |  |  | 1 |  |  |  |  |  |  |  |
| Ganda |  |  |  |  |  |  |  |  | 7 |  |  |  | 1 |  |  |
| Toro |  |  |  |  |  |  |  |  |  | 1 |  |  |  |  |  |
| Nyoro |  |  |  |  | 1 |  |  |  | 1 |  |  |  |  |  |  |
| Soga |  |  |  |  |  |  |  |  | 2 |  |  |  |  |  |  |
| Rwanda |  |  |  |  |  | 1 |  |  |  |  | 1 |  |  |  |  |
| Ankole |  |  |  |  |  |  |  |  |  |  |  |  |  |  |  |
| Nubi |  |  |  |  |  |  |  |  |  |  |  |  |  |  |  |

Only two women in this table have children. One of them, a Teso living with a fellow tribesman, had her two children through previous relationships. A Kiga and a Ganda woman are household heads, i.e. their houses are rented in their names.

* This and Table 2 are based on that recorded by J. C. Mitchell, op. cit.

and women of centralized tribes are partners to 'temporary' common *ménage* unions, and that these are complemented by much larger proportions of men and women of uncentralized tribes living in town as partners to rural-established and controlled marriages.

Unmarried male migrants of uncentralized tribes do, of course, have access to the town's prostitutes, who are practically all women of centralized tribes.[11] They may even have regular acquaintanceships with 'lovers', though they rarely establish a common *ménage*. Informal groups of agnates, clansmen, and fellow tribesmen, or formal associations made up of these, actively discourage inter-tribal common *ménage* unions, particularly when the 'wife' or 'lover' is of a centralized tribe. A man is condemned for entering into a mixed union on the grounds that 'she (the wife) will never understand our customs nor the home people. Her own people will have different customs and may refuse to pay back cattle' (i.e. if the girl is barren or leaves her husband, though neither cattle nor high bridewealth may necessarily have been requested in the first place). The reference here is to the fear of uncentralized tribesmen that genetricial rights cannot be guaranteed.

It is recognized that urban 'temporary' unions may become 'permanent' and migrants are criticized for contracting even 'temporary' inter-tribal unions. Permanent status even for 'temporary' intra-tribal unions is urged in suggestions that initial payment of bridewealth be paid to secure genetricial rights.

By contrast, in the absence of economic interests such as recoverable bridewealth, and owing to the other differences in values and social organization already mentioned, kinsmen of migrants of centralized tribes do not condemn tribally mixed unions, 'temporary' or 'permanent'. A genitor has the right to claim his children if he wants them, whether or not bridewealth has been paid for the woman who has borne the children. Men and women of such tribes may thus move relatively freely from one union to another. This explains the higher incidence of 'temporary' unions, many of them inter-tribal, involving one or more partners of a centralized tribe (Table 1).

The relative freedom of choice of spouse enjoyed by men and women of centralized tribes also explains why they constitute a higher proportion of partners in urban-established marriages, in which a wife, usually initially 'temporary', has come to be regarded as 'permanent' (Table 2).

The Nubi, on whom little general information is available, are only significant in marriages established in town on account of their urban residence, their major preoccupation with retail trading, the unifying influence of Islam, and their lack of association with any particular tribal lands. When they marry non-Nubi, they tend to marry Ganda Muslims, or, as in

---

[11] Many prostitutes are Haya, a Tanzania centralized tribe, who are not significant in my sample nor in the estates, though they are fairly numerous in Kampala generally.

TABLE 2 COMMON *MÉNAGE* UNIONS ESTABLISHED IN TOWN AND REGARDED AS INCLUDING A 'PERMANENT' WIFE

| Husband \ Wife | Luo | Acholi | Lango | Alur | Luhya | Kiga | Lugbara | Teso | Ganda | Toro | Nyoro | Soga | Rwanda | Ankole | Nubi |
|---|---|---|---|---|---|---|---|---|---|---|---|---|---|---|---|
| Luo | 3 | | | | | | | | 3 | | | | | | |
| Acholi | | | 1 | | | | | | | | | | | | |
| Lango | | | 1* | | | | | | | | | | | | |
| Alur | | | | | | | | | | | 1 | | | | |
| Luhya | | | | | | | | | | 1 | | | | | |
| Kiga | | | | | | 2 | | | | 1 | | | | | |
| Lugbara | | | | | 1 | | | | | | | | 1 | | |
| Teso | | | | | | | | | | | | 1 | | | |
| Ganda | | | | | | | | | 5 | 1 | | | | | |
| Toro | | | | | | | | | 1 | 3 | 1 | | 1 | | |
| Nyoro | | | | | | | | | 1 | | 4 | | | | |
| Soga | | | | | | | | | 2 | 1 | | 2 | 1 | | |
| Rwanda | | | | | | | | | | | | | | | |
| Ankole | | | | | | | | | 1 | | | | | | |
| Nubi | | | | | | | | | 5 | | | | 1 | | 4 |

All women have borne children in these relationships.
* The wife is in fact a Padhola who agreed to 'become' Lango.

one case in my sample, Ganda who become Muslims. The four intra-tribal Nubi unions recorded in Table 2 did not pass through an initial temporary phase. They were urban-established but arranged and contracted according to Muslim law.

## 2. *Unions Arranged in the Town*

(A) INTRA-TRIBAL UNIONS IN WHICH WIVES ARE REGARDED AS TEMPORARY. For migrants of uncentralized tribes the obligation to provide money for bridewealth cattle has in many cases shifted from the father to the son. It is not so easy to accumulate money in town as some fathers imagine, and many men, unable to save sufficient money for bridewealth, stay unmarried for longer than might traditionally be expected.

A 'woman of the town' is commonly accorded less status than her rural counterpart, and younger men frequently state that they would expect to pay less bridewealth for her.[12] Rather than incur the disapproval of kin in striking up a liaison with one of the many available Uganda Bantu women, they may contact men of their own tribe whose sisters, but rarely daughters, may be living with them in Kampala, usually undergoing a course of study or training. For the few unmarried girls of uncentralized tribes in Kampala are mostly accompanied by a brother or father. The latter are reluctant to allow a fellow tribesman the opportunity of a trial period of urban cohabitation unless they are quite sure he sincerely intends a permanent marriage and will make the customary payment of bridewealth.

Relatively few migrants of uncentralized tribes desire to enter into urban-based trial and error agreements of this kind with fellow tribesmen, most preferring to wait until they can afford a rurally arranged marriage. In Table 1 only the Lango and two Lugbara unions had been established in this way. The Teso intra-tribal union recorded in Table 1 was unusual in that both partners acted independently of kinsmen in establishing it. Both were fairly highly educated: the husband was a senior clerk and the wife a high-grade secretary. Both, however, declared a commitment to their respective careers and confirmed the temporary sexual and domestic convenience of the union.

There are eight intra-tribal unions of centralized tribespeople recorded in Table 1. Seven are Ganda, reflecting the preponderance of unattached women and balanced sex ratio of this tribe in Kampala. One is Toro. Most men and women in these unions are of skilled and clerical status. But this is not the relevant point, since there are many temporary intra-tribal unions

---

[12] As an example a traditional Luo payment of bridewealth may be 14–15 head of cattle with sometimes an additional cash payment of from Sh 100 to 1,000. Urban migrants claim that at least the extra cash payment should be dispensed with for a 'town woman'.

of centralized tribespeople of much lower status in Kampala generally. The relevant factors are that such people are largely unworried by bridewealth obligations and uncontrolled by kin. A genitor is entitled to claim any children born regardless of bridewealth payments. Such intra-tribal common *ménage* unions need not therefore be regarded as final and binding. They are typically fluid and unplanned relationships.

(B) INTER-TRIBAL UNIONS IN WHICH WIVES ARE REGARDED AS TEMPORARY. A very few uncentralized tribesmen do ignore the prospects of incurring the disapproval of kin and establish temporary common *ménage* unions with unattached centralized tribeswomen. There are seven of these unions in Table 1. Both unmarried and married uncentralized tribesmen, whose wives may not be in Kampala, tend to regard such unions as relationships of convenience. The 'wife' receives gifts of money and clothes, as well as the security of a shelter, in return for the performance of her domestic and sexual duties. The unmarried man will be subject to attempts by urban and rural kin and fellow tribesmen to dissuade him from continuing in the union. The married man has to contend with the additional disfavour of one or more customary wives, who may travel from home to town to admonish their husband.

An Acholi clerk, who has two customary wives and five children at his tribal home, 'fell in love' in Kampala with a Ganda woman who became his temporary wife. This Ganda woman, however, bore him a child. This appeared to strengthen the affective bond between them. But the two permanent Acholi wives, who 'love each other as sisters', travelled the 250 miles to Kampala, beat the man and his temporary wife, and demanded her dismissal. The man, because of his affection for the woman, was reluctant to eject her. Eventually, agnates and fellow tribesmen exhorted him to do so. The Ganda woman took custody of the child, even though she knew it would be a liability and possible impediment to any future marriage, because the Acholi's two permanent wives had refused to accept it.

The married uncentralized tribesman who has his customary wife with him in town is faced with similar difficulties.

Joseph, a Luo, has his customary wife with him in Kampala. He is a driver and his job for a woodworking firm takes him to and from Toro district once or twice a week. He had a Toro lover in Toro district whom he brought back with him to live in Kampala, establishing a separate household for her there. His Luo wife does not get on well with this Toro woman, (1) because she is of a different tribe and linguistic group, and (2) because she is only a temporary wife. Joseph's emotional and sexual attachment to his Toro temporary wife is strong and he has tended to frequent the household of his permanent wife and children less often. Inevitably the relationships between him and his two wives are strained. Joseph would like his Luo wife to accept his concubine as a permanent co-wife. But neither of the women relishes integration of this kind.

In these two cases, affective ties were paramount and conflicted with existing ties and obligations. Both the Luo and Acholi tribes practise polygyny. Clearly, however, their wives do not accept multi-tribal polygyny. Yet both these phenomena—relationships based affectively according to chance or situational acquaintanceships, and multi-tribalism—are features of urban life. Some married uncentralized tribesmen have attempted to solve this problem of conflicting expectations by clandestine arrangements. They maintain a concubine of a centralized tribe in a quarter of the town separate from that in which their customary wife is living. There are only seven cases in Table 1 of uncentralized tribesmen living with women from centralized tribes, which, considering the larger proportion of uncentralized tribesmen in the sample, indicates a very low incidence of this type of union.

As well as having similar customs regarding the function of bridewealth and the legitimacy of offspring, and being uncontrolled in their choice of spouses, men and women from centralized tribes are linguistically and culturally very close. In Table 1 there are five temporary inter-tribal unions of these peoples. There are only eight temporary intra-tribal unions among them, including seven Ganda, so that they appear to have no marked preference for temporary spouses of their own tribe, though such factors as a tribe's adult sex ratio and its proportion of unattached women in Kampala are relevant also. A feature of these unions is that the partners to them often communicate in Luganda, though neither may in fact be Ganda, except where, as with Nyoro and Toro, the dialects are mutually intelligible.

The temporary spouses of both centralized and uncentralized tribesmen tend to be centralized tribeswomen, that is, Interlacustrine Bantu women, with the exception of Kiga, who, though Interlacustrine Bantu, are uncentralized and generally subject to the same practical and ideological controls as women from other uncentralized tribes.

The widespread association of 'promiscuity' with infertility reflects itself in the *a priori* assumption that the unattached centralized tribeswomen in Kampala are only fit for temporary unions of domestic and sexual convenience. Not surprisingly, temporary wives labelled in this way have to look to their own future and security and tend to expect inordinate economic benefits from the unions. In circumstances of this kind, mutual trust is difficult to achieve, unions may break up, and women move from one temporary common *ménage* to another. These urban Bantu women do in fact tend to be infertile. The situation is thus circular, and is only arrested with the birth of a child, which then confers permanency on the union, providing linguistic and cultural differences and pre-existing obligations do not deter this graduation of a temporary to a permanent union.

(C) INTRA-TRIBAL UNIONS IN WHICH WIVES ARE REGARDED AS PERMANENT. The passage from a temporary to a permanent common *ménage* union is obviously more easily realizable when both partners are of the same tribe. The migrant of an uncentralized tribe tends to regard the temporary union as a preliminary to a full customary marriage in the rural area. His and his temporary wife's respective agnates living in the town assume more or less the same roles as in the rural districts.

There is relatively little preference for intra-tribal temporary unions by migrants of centralized tribes. Those that are established are not generally regarded as preliminary periods of cohabitation before marriage.

(D) INTER-TRIBAL UNIONS IN WHICH WIVES ARE REGARDED AS PERMA-NENT. Incorporating the two major ethnic/cultural groupings, and including also the Nubi, six broad categories of inter-tribal marriage may be distinguished. It is within these categories that temporary inter-tribal unions are sometimes accorded permanent status by each spouse's respective kin, fellow tribespeople, and by neighbours.

Illustrated diagrammatically these broad inter-tribal categories are:

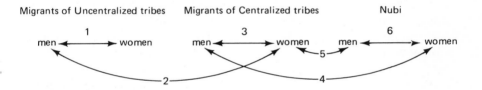

CATEGORY 1. Migrants of uncentralized tribes regard marriage as an interlineage affair involving recoverable bridewealth of high value, which guarantees rights of genetrix in a woman. Marriage may therefore occasionally be permitted between persons whose respective tribes share these features of social organizations. Thus, an Acholi married a Lango woman (Table 2) after an initial temporary union in Kampala, agreed by the Acholi, his agnates, and the Lango woman's brother and agnates; a Lango man married a Padhola woman after a similar period of cohabitation. For both cases the birth of a child led the woman's urban-dwelling agnates to demand an initial bridewealth payment by the husband. These agnates provided a vehicle for the extension of rural expectations to urban conditions.

The single case in Table 2 of a Lugbara marrying a Luhya girl is unusual in that the Lugbara had been born and brought up on a sugar plantation in eastern Buganda and was familiar with the tongues and customs of many Bantu tribespeople. This, and a relatively high level of education, distinguished him from other Lugbara in Kampala who are generally isolated in various ways from other tribespeople in the town, and facilitated his marrying a woman of a Bantu tribe, though it is interesting to note that she is a Luhya, a member of an uncentralized tribe similar in many respects to the Luo, and to a lesser extent the Lugbara. As in the previous two cases, the birth of a child effectively endorsed the expectations of recoverable bridewealth guaranteeing genetricial rights and agnatic control.

CATEGORY 2. This category includes marriages which have successfully overcome the widest cultural, organizational, and linguistic obstacles. But while men of uncentralized tribes do marry women of the centralized Bantu tribes, the strong control exerted over their sisters and daughters by the former inhibits the reverse inter-tribal unions: that is, males of centralized tribes do not marry, or even establish temporary common *ménage* unions with women of uncentralized tribes.

There are eight marriages in this category (Table 2). The fact that they are more numerous than those of category 1 is explained by the much greater availability of Uganda Bantu women in Kampala. That they are not more numerous reflects the disfavour in which such marriages are held by migrants of uncentralized tribes.

All eight marriages began with an initial period of temporary common *ménage* subjected to open condemnation by the man's close kin and neighbours and friends of the same tribe. The normal annual or biannual visits to the rural home were rarely made. One Luo who had been living with a Ganda woman for six years and had four children by her, had not been to his rural home during the whole of this period.

While kin and fellow tribesmen neighbours may continue to condemn, other neighbours and associates begin to confer more established status on the union by calling it 'permanent', after the birth of one or usually more children.

In all cases children born of these unions speak their mother's language, or, in the case of the Lugbara/Rwanda and Lango/Nyoro unions, Luganda, more frequently than their father's language.

The Kiga/Toro union has become rurally uxorilocal in so far as the Kiga has already built a house of permanent materials in his wife's tribal district, having more or less severed contacts with his own rural home and kinsfolk. Like a Lugbara discussed earlier, the Lugbara married to a Rwanda woman was born and lived outside Lugbara district. He and his wife speak fluent Luganda and each has relatives living in Buganda where they intend to settle eventually. The Teso and his Soga wife, who are both in good clerical jobs and are above the educational average of the sample, intend remaining indefinitely in Kampala and can avoid returning to settle in either of their rural homes.

The men in the other five unions claim that they desire to settle in their own rural tribal districts eventually, though not for a long time. Their wives are mostly reluctant to accompany their husbands if this should happen. One Ganda woman, however, had been to her Luo husband's rural home about five times in their seven years together. She had borne five children,[13] had herself acquired a fair knowledge of DhoLuo and now wanted her children to regard DhoLuo as their first language. Of these five unions, this seemed the most likely to persist in the husband's rural home area after his period of urban employment ceased.

In nearly all cases, the exceptions being the Teso/Soga and Lugbara/ Rwanda unions, some bridewealth payments were made after the birth of one or more children. The payments, in keeping with the wives' parents' expectations, were small, and regarded as neither recoverable nor guaranteeing genetricial rights.

The problem of the ultimate tribal attachment of the children in those unions in which this is undecided may never be faced. Most couples have more than two children. Going to Kampala or nearby schools and having their most effective relationships centred in the town, they will presumably take up employment in this or another town. Since most couples envisage remaining in urban employment certainly until their younger children are adult or adolescent, the children may not be confronted with the choice of a single, permanent affiliation with either their mother's or father's rural tribal homes. They will be urban-based, while, in the last resort, their parents will separately return to their respective tribal homes.

CATEGORY 3. The problems of language and custom, and of post-urban residence do not loom so large for unions in which partners, although of different tribes, are both within the centralized Bantu super-tribal category.

These unions also commence on the basis of a temporary common *ménage,* and the birth of one or more children does not automatically put the union on a permanent footing. There are, for instance, many unmarried Uganda Bantu women with children by different fathers. Some, especially retired successful prostitutes, establish their own households which develop as matri-focal units. But the birth of children may strengthen the existing bond of affection, and within the context of their urban local relations, neighbours and friends may regard a couple as 'permanent' man and wife.

These unions are not only established in town but also by the man and woman themselves, largely without reference to kin, who are unlikely to discourage or condemn the union and do not act out of common economic and ideological interests to exert sanctions. In all except one of the nine unions of this category recorded in Table 2, two or more children have been born. Except in the case of the Toro/Nyoro union in which the husband's and wife's dialects are very close, the language used between

---

[13] Traditional Luo expectations stress the high child-bearing qualities of a wife. This fact may have eased the integration into rural Luo society of this relatively prolific Ganda woman. Ganda women, it may be noted, have a popular reputation for low fecundity. Cf. Richards and Reining, 1954.

husband and wife and by children is Luganda. All except the Ankole/
Ganda and one of the Soga/Ganda couples, who already had plots of land
and houses in Buganda, intend to settle in the husband's tribal district.
Spouses visit each other's kin, though not frequently. There is no indication, however, of any more than slight apprehension for the future of their
conjugal relationships. They, too, intend to remain in urban employment
for many more years, so that their children are also likely to constitute part
of the slowly growing urban-born generation of Kampala.

The greater freedom of choice existing for partners in these unions,
during both the 'temporary' and 'permanent' phases in town, and thereafter, suggests that, of the urban-established inter-tribal marriage categories, they are likely to increase the most. Reducing somewhat their rate
of increase, however, is the fact that this same freedom of choice and
action for both men and women contributes to the general instability and
unenduring nature of unions into which they enter.

CATEGORIES 4, 5, AND 6. In these marriages, where one or both partners
are Nubi, features of Nubi social life are dominant.

Nubi men and women appear reluctant to enter into casual, temporary
liaisons. But they are not opposed to inter-tribal or inter-ethnic group marriage, provided both spouses are Muslim. Four of the five Ganda women
married to Nubi men (Table 2) were already Muslim. The other adopted
Islam during the initial relationship with her husband. Couples usually
meet in the context of one or other of the Muslim religious gatherings or
festivals, or through involvement in the fairly close-knit network of retail
selling and trading carried on by Nubi. Such unions are thus urban-
established and, by virtue of the general urban location of Nubi, are likely
to continue so. The Nubi Islamic community provides the norms and
sanctions determining the general course of the union.

No marriages between Nubi and members of uncentralized tribes are
recorded. Few of the latter are Muslim, and the Nubi do not share their
features of social organization and so are regarded as unsuitable for mixed
marriages. An uncentralized tribesman will not throw off his own tribal expectations regarding his marriage by becoming Muslim. A Nubi will not dis-
card his own concept of Islamic marriage any more than he will leave the
Nubi Islamic community, which is, of course, economic as well as ideological. The two ethnic groups are thus mutually exclusive with regard
to marriage.

## Summary

In a complex field like urban marriage, there are many other factors which
are relevant. Spouse's occupation, education, precise length of urban resi-

dence, age, and number and type of previous unions are the most important. Further analysis would relate these factors to the connexion of the conjugal role-relationship with the spouses' respective social networks.[14]

In this account I have confined myself to choice of spouse in the context of a tribally heterogeneous urban community and a continuum along which temporary common *ménage* unions may receive permanent public assent.

Features of tribal social organization are seen to be significant either because they narrowly define the range of choice of spouse, or because, even more than in the rural area, they allow a wide range of individual choice and action. The former characterizes the situation for migrants of uncentralized tribes, and the latter the situation for migrants of centralized tribes.

Uncentralized tribes are commonly referred to as egalitarian in that they lack established hierarchies of authority and established and specialized political and economic roles. Local descent groups are the agents through which marriages are contracted, and contracts are only entered into with like groups. Thus, these tribes constitute a set of closed societies when it comes to most forms of inter-tribal marriage under urban conditions.

The greater political and economic individualism of centralized tribes expresses itself in a reduced influence of descent group or other kin expectations and sanctions. They are quite open to all prevailing forms of inter-tribal marriage.

The Nubi are similar in their exclusiveness to the uncentralized tribes. They accept in mixed marriage only those who are Muslim, or who are prepared to become Muslim, and will shift a large proportion of their relationships to the Nubi economic and ideological community.

For most urban migrants, the Nubi excepted, inter-tribal marriage is a passage from a temporary common *ménage* to recognized permanent union. Though differences of language and custom inhibit the development of many forms of permanent inter-tribal union or marriage, it is the availability and independence in Kampala of many unattached women of the centralized tribes which make possible most of those few which are achieved. A long period of cohabitation, the birth of one or more children, and evidence to neighbours and kin that the couple enjoy harmony, may enable the widest cultural barriers to be overcome. Permanence usually necessitates one of the partners 'becoming' a member of the other spouse's tribe. The greater the cultural and linguistic differences, and these do not always coincide, between the two partners, the more difficult it is to achieve. That at least a few of the widest barriers have been overcome reflects special features of the area studied; a city ward, accommodating migrants generally above the Greater Kampala average in socio-economic status

---

[14] Bott, 1957.

and length of urban residence. In most cases monogamy is preferred by both men and women, with the special exception of the Nubi. Residents are far from being Kampala's top *élite*, but they are also quite distinct from the many unskilled and transitory migrants living at the city's periphery. It is within this category of mostly clerical, skilled, and semi-skilled workers of some stability that we may expect some of the most immediate developments in patterns of urban marriage.

## References

BOTT, E. 1957. *The Family and Social Network,* Tavistock, London.

FRAENKEL, M. 1964. *Tribe and Class in Monrovia,* Oxford University Press for International African Institute.

MITCHELL, J. C. 1957. 'Aspects of African Marriage on the Copperbelt of Northern Rhodesia', *Rhodes-Livingstone Journal,* no. 22.

RICHARDS, A. I., and REINING, P. 1954. 'Report on Fertility Surveys in Buganda and Buhaya', in *Culture and Human Fertility* (ed.), Frank Lorimer, Paris, Unesco.

SOUTHALL, A. W. 1960. 'On Chastity in Africa', *Uganda Journal,* vol. xxiv.

———— and GUTKIND, P. C. W. 1957. *Townsmen in the Making,* East African Studies no. 9, E.A.I.S.R., Kampala, Uganda.

# 3

# Politics, Values, and Comparison

A. In many traditional African societies, actual power is entrusted to the young. The elders, who serve as advisors, are often thought of as symbols of a superior, divine authority. This Masai elder is giving counsel to the young tribesmen, and rarely is any important action taken without some such form of group discussion.

B. The pressures of our modern society combine to make it nearly impossible to settle disputes or to govern by mutual discussion. Physical coercion has become the main, if not the only, way of maintaining order in a society lacking uniform values and beliefs.

C. In modern Africa, conformity is growing, together with individual action and individual decision making. The influence of modern technology seems to be encouraging this substitution of communication between individuals for that among groups.

D. In a society of conformity, we find our world increasingly impersonal and devoid of close human relationships.

Again, rather than try to be all-encompassing and definitive, in this part I propose one or two broad generalizations that may reasonably be said to characterize traditional political systems in Africa, examine the impact of accelerated change upon their validity, and suggest implicitly and explicitly profitable comparisons with our own political life and values.

The two major generalizations are of the utmost significance in any consideration of our own Western societies because they concern cherished values, the practice of which we frequently regard as being our monopoly; whereas in fact, the practice of these values is probably most distinguished by its absence. First, in Africa the concern is for justice rather than for law. This can be related to the second generalization: that African political systems, whether segmentary or centralized, are traditionally highly democratic. I can at once foresee that there will be cries of protest that these are precisely the characteristics of Western civilization, but at this point it is important to refrain from making judgments and instead simply observe the facts, consider the values involved, and make comparisons.

Part 1 discussed morality. Part 2 suggested an arbitrary classification of societies into two major types: moralistic and legalistic. This classification, which corresponds to small-scale versus large-scale or primitive versus civilized, was made with the purpose of helping us to understand the nature of society and to clarify the meaning of that term. It may seem rather odd that we should use the term "social change" so glibly when it is so difficult to find a satisfactory definition of society, but an examination of the concepts of justice and democracy may prove to be helpful in achieving a better understanding of the meanings of both change and society.

I have already made some remarks about American and European notions of justice, but these have been more personal opinion than critical evaluation. When the matter is considered with less emotion and, therefore, with less humanity, it is apparent that the general lack of concern for justice in Western nations is largely a function of the grotesque size and incoherence of what is generally referred to as modern society. In such large societies, with a diversity of peoples and beliefs, and even with significant linguistic and cultural variations, justice has become equated with the fulfillment of law, which, as Shakespeare said, "is a fool." Some concern for justice remains and is indicated by such devices as extenuating circumstances, which enable a responsible judge to twist the law in order to effect justice. Sometimes, perhaps quite often, a legal decision is a just one; but that seems both accidental and almost incidental. The focus is undeniably on law, and many a judge sighs as he dons the black cap and sentences someone to death—as if to say "this is going to hurt me more than it hurts you"—because he has no alternative and knows the penalty is unjust. He has not been allowed to take into consideration immaterial and irrelevant facts that may, in fact, have contributed, if indirectly, to the crime: a broken marriage, a starving family, a fatal sickness, and so forth. Such petty considerations are deemed unworthy of note in the eyes of the law. Furthermore, the judge is bound by the decision of a jury of twelve possibly ignorant (or worse) jurors with no special qualifications. It is not for nothing that Justice, in our world, is portrayed by a blindfolded woman, with her scales tipped unevenly and a sword in readiness. This more accurately represents law, for justice has its eyes wide open, and the result of a just decision is harmony between the disputants, not the decapitation of one for the individual satisfaction of the other.

We think of ourselves as progressive if we talk of rehabilitation of criminals or if we aim at corrective measures. In small-scale societies, there is no single criminal; rather, the whole society is to blame. There is also no rehabilitation or correction, let alone punishment (as we understand it), but rather a restoration of the norm of harmony. In the segmentary societies, this is achieved informally by what is misleadingly called "self-help." This really means the absence of a court, judge, or jury; society as a whole steps in, usually activated by an initial retaliatory move made by the offended party. It certainly does not mean that the offended party can settle the dispute by himself, without the concurrence of the total society.

In the larger and more complex African societies, there may be a more formal hearing, with a court or tribunal presided over by a council or judge. In such a hearing, however, each person is generally allowed to state his case fully and as he pleases, citing all the facts that he considers relevant. This provides not only an adequate background for an equitable resolution of the case but also a mechanism for raising many related disputes and tensions, which are also discussed with care. In this way, the entire local society is, in a sense, purged by this one act of self-examination. Judgment in smaller societies is seldom penal; rather, it is restitutive. Inequalities are equalized; disharmonies are resolved. Fines may be imposed, but often on both sides, since no one side is likely to be without fault. Frequently, such fines are in the form of food and beer, at least a portion of which must be shared by the disputants in the symbolic (and pleasurable) act of eating and drinking together.

It is often required at both formal and informal hearings that all those concerned or connected, perhaps an entire band or village, be present and take part. Thus, the final decision is the decision of all. Whereas our jury is expected to be impartial (an impossibility if one is a sentient being), here all participants are expected to be partial and not to disguise their personal feelings under the false cloak of detachment. Only the judge (if there is one) is expected to be remote from the case and is often an outsider, chosen for that very reason. When the judgment involves a penalty, as it does in some of the complex societies, and particularly when the penalty is severe, the judge frequently wears a mask, and sometimes a costume covering the entire body, in order to conceal his personal identity. Even when his identity is, in fact, known, the ritual of masking serves to emphasize the social nature of the judgment; it also emphasizes the spiritual nature, since the judge's authority is usually derived from ancestors or other spiritual beings. The mask removes the judge as a human member of the society with specific social ties, so that he and his kith and kin are not themselves penalized or victimized by an adversely judged party; once he removes the mask, he resumes his human personality. In some cases judgment is left to specialized groups formed into sacred or secret societies, again emphasizing the social nature of the judgment and the sacred origin of its authority. Whereas secular judgment is as questionable as the omniscience and infallibility of the judge, divine judgment, resting on an act of faith, is beyond question.

The cause of justice is pursued in many elaborate and, to us, strange but effective ways. The strangeness is often due to the African's recognition of the power of belief, his constant use of symbolism, and the concept of the supernatural and suprarational. Thus, witchcraft (or the belief in it) may serve as the mainstay of justice, enabling a culprit caught in the act to deny not the act but any intent to harm, which would be the real crime. He may do this on the grounds of either having been bewitched or actually being a witch without knowing it. He thus absolves himself of blame while admitting the act, and he is not ostracized from society. He is treated as a sick person, to be cured by ritual purification, which may or may not involve payment to the offended party. It is, however, a claim he can usually make only once, since from then onward he will be eyed with caution in case his sickness should recur. Any further culpable act will be regarded as doubly sinister, and he will then be blamed either for not having maintained his ritual purity (an act of social irresponsibility) or, even worse, for having deliberately used his supernatural powers as a witch for antisocial purposes (which would brand him as a sorcerer).

Implicit in all this is the belief that man is essentially social but not perfect. Great care is taken from birth to ensure his sociality; this is his nature, and any unsocial or antisocial act is thus unnatural. Such an act is seen more as a sin than as a crime, and what is called for is expiation rather than punishment, understanding rather than vengeance or retribution. In any society, the former attitudes are obviously less divisive than the latter, but it does not take much firsthand experience of traditional jural procedures to know the sometimes-exasperating lengths to which the people go to secure a thorough understanding of a case. Yet every point raised, however irrelevant it may seem to us, is listened to with attention, examined, and usually brought into play. The thought of vengeance is by no means necessarily absent; human emotions run the same gamut in Africa as elsewhere, but the system of controls is different and creates different forms of expression. Vengeance is remarkably rare. Even in feuding societies, where we frequently use the word "vengeance," there are other, more important considerations in pursuing the feud. In African thought, vengeance, although a human emotion, is properly left to the ancestors or to God. Thus, even the vengeance that may be spoken of in the feuding societies has strong religious connotations, and the feud may appear more to resemble a holy war.

Undoubtedly, the smallness and corporateness of the society is, once again, a major factor, for fission of any kind threatens its viability. It is in everyone's interests that a dispute be settled as soon as possible, preferably by a restoration of the harmonious human relationships essential to cooperative life. This is not so with the larger societies and in the traditional African states penal systems have developed, although the earlier sentiment of natural sociability is largely maintained and antisocial acts are still regarded as sins rather than as crimes. So-called crimes against the state are also correctly regarded as sins because the state, represented in the person of the king, is sacred. It is highly questionable whether a truly secular state existed in Africa until comparatively recent times, and even those states arising in response to Muslim invasions and the introduction of trade in slaves as a profitable alternative to a dwindling trade in gold were usually not without a strong religious element. In such states, physical coercion emerged as a means of social control, whereas in the earlier and more traditional kingdoms (which are more pertinent to this discussion), control was achieved through moral coercion.

In our more haughty moments, we should stop to reflect on what would happen in our civilized societies if we were to entrust individual security to everyone's moral conscience. The thought that we could ever advance far enough as human beings to be able to disband the police force or even to unarm it is almost laughable, although it is debatable whether the mental anarchy that already reigns could be any greater than it is. To suggest that religious sanctions such as the threat of hellfire and everlasting damnation would effect much social control is equally nonsensical. Yet when we grudgingly admit that the small-scale societies do in fact achieve at least as much, and often more, control than we do, but without either physical coercion or even the threat of it, we turn and snap at their religious beliefs and say such people are ruled by superstition and fear of the supernatural. Undoubtedly, the threat of hellfire would affect a few impressionable Africans just as it does a few impressionable non-Africans, but it could only attain a significant hold under the most puritanical, isolated conditions. It is wishful and malicious to say that if we behave "morally" because we are forced to by a policeman with a gun (that is, not morally at all, only legally), the African also behaves in a given way because he is afraid of being cursed with leprosy or transformed into a water animal. That implies, among other things, that the African is as negative in his sociality as we are, quite apart from relegating his religion to the realm of superstition. Certainly, in most African societies, there are supernatural sanctions against particular forms of behavior, but fear of these sanctions, although real, is not dominant. It is certainly not an everyday part of life, whereas, alas, policemen with guns are very much a daily part of life in our Western societies.

On the contrary, the African acts in a given manner because he has been educated so to act with positive rather than negative sanctions. And again, it is a mistake to liken these positive religious sanctions to the promise of a halo and a pair of wings in heaven if we behave well on earth, particularly on Sundays. Although the right to join the ancestors after death is highly cherished and a goal to be desired, the *need* to follow the way of the ancestors is equally strong. This need effectively constitutes what might be called a moral code. It not only brings favor with the ancestors, it rejoices those who are loved and, above all, manifestly enables the living to survive. It is the latter consideration that is more immediately important to most people, especially if they are truly social in nature. Ever practical, the traditional African may be said to act in a given way because it proves to be the most sensible and effective way, not only for him but also for society. Sociality itself is sensible and effective. Thus, even the act of being selfish and concerned with his own survival may be a social act, although it is hardly likely to be moral.

Conversely, with us it would be impractical to expect morality to provide a Western nation with an adequate incentive toward social behavior, for in the small-scale societies, individuals are taught to be social beings; but more important, they can actually see the efficacy of their sociality in their everyday relationships. Their effective social horizons are small enough for them to feel an obligation toward the total network of which they are each a part. Their education has, indeed, been so effective that they may often think they are making a free and moral choice when they have in fact been conditioned to make that choice because it is social. Thus, the illusion of individual freedom is maintained at the same time that social control is enforced.

In the West, with our much-idealized notion of individual freedom, the concept has become a farce, synonymous with anarchy at the individual level and despotism at the governmental level. The size and complexity of the modern nation is such that, except in relatively isolated rural areas that have not yet been polluted (morally as well as physically) by industrialization, many people do not even know the names of their neighbors. An inegalitarian economic structure ensures a certain economic homogeneity in restricted areas, but despite our Western genius for the most refined forms of racism, the cultural purity of such sanctuaries is seldom untainted. Thus, even if a man knows his neighbors, he may not share the same values. And once outside his sanctuary—be it a private estate, a block, or an apartment floor—he is alone. If someone is run over on the street in front of him, it is not a person; it is a stranger, and therefore merely spoils his lunch if he does not like the sight of blood. He may, however, get a slight satisfaction at the thought that it was not he. A body in the gutter is passed by with the assumption that it is a drunk and therefore needs and wants no attention, with seldom a thought that it might be a human being in need of help, perhaps even a neighbor who has suffered a heart attack. In self-defense, in this monstrous, teeming, inhuman world of mutual strangers, we surround ourselves with an effective, functional shield of solitary individualism. It is not immoral; it is a sheer necessity.

The problem is also one of values. In the small-scale society, all individuals are educated into a single system of values and belief, even in a nation as large as that of the Yoruba. In our perhaps mistaken pursuit of freedom, we pride ourselves in allowing exactly that particular freedom—religious— that immediately establishes a diversity of values and conflicting moralities. Although there is a certain, often large, overlap of values held in common among many religions, the differences are sometimes crucial; and the sentiments engendered by the diversity of interpretations of even these common values may be in direct opposition. Since morality, as defined, rests on sentiment, no common morality is then possible. Unhappily, this is as much in perfect accord with the unwieldy size of the modern nations as it is with the diversity of their linguistic and cultural subdivisions. In place of a common sentiment, a common morality, there can only be a common law; and since man tends, with wisdom, to follow his own sentiment rather than that of the lawmakers, the law is accepted sometimes unwillingly, sometimes not at all. There can be no question that the degree of unity achieved through a common belief is infinitely higher and more powerful than that achieved by a common law, and the increasing amount of force with which the law has to be backed is sufficient evidence of its intrinsic weakness.

The question of a common sentiment also affects the nature of democracy. It is notable that few political leaders style themselves as despots and that few countries admit to being anything other than democratic. In saying that traditional African forms of government are essentially democratic, then, I am suggesting that there is a difference between concepts of democracy as well as between methods of implementation, and that in African political systems exists the essence, not the superficial form. Sentiment is one measure of democracy, for to be truly democratic, a society must be bound by ties that are affective as well as effective. The amount of power the people confer upon their leaders and the degree of concentration of this power are secondary. A nation with a popularly elected government may prove to be less democratic than a feudal monarchy if the degree of affection between rulers and ruled is less. If there is less national sentiment, there will be less coincidence between the political views of the two, less coincidence between desire and fulfillment. Even in some of the most apparently despotic African monarchies, the ultimate power seems to belong to the people; and if it does not do so, this is most often a result of the introduction of modern firearms and the consequent introduction of physical force as a means of effecting control.

Democracy supposes a connection between politics and people, between rulers and ruled. This connection may be formal or informal, nominal or real, distant or intimate, weak or strong. The larger the society (to continue using the term with abandon, for the moment, to cover any kind of social grouping from a nuclear family to an empire) the more formal, more nominal, more distant and weaker is the connection; the smaller the society, the more informal, real, intimate and strong the connection. It can also be said that the connection is either rational or sentimental, without implying that the one excludes the other. As with other categories, it is more a question of degree than of alternatives.

A look at the mechanisms that exist in any society to distribute the power, to effect adequate checks on its abuse, and to ensure the proper representation of the people reveals the nature of the difference between the Western type of formal democracy and the small-scale type of informal democracy. The mechanisms of the one are artificial; those of the other are human.

How many voters in a modern nation ever see their representative to the central government, let alone speak to him, really know him, or have ready access to him except through occasional correspondence? In the larger societies, this same question may well be asked at the level of local government. The connection between the representative and the ruling elite (the cabinet or supreme council) may be equally distant and indirect. The system of checks on the abuse of power is so mechanical and inflexible that by the time it is brought into operation and completes its gyrations, the damage has most likely been done. Thus, power and authority are effectively concentrated in a handful of individuals elected by a dubiously democratic process that involves more guesswork than intelligence but that seems to be the best system such a society can come up with. This ruling elite has virtually no contact with the people, as demonstrated by the pantomime of presidential electioneering, with all its toothpaste smiles, clammy handshakes, and theatrical changes of costume, speech, and eating habits. Yet, given the mechanical system of checks, the power of the elite is almost absolute during the term for which it is elected. The elite has control of the power of physical coercion, access to vast wealth, and daily coverage by the mass media over which it can exert considerable control. It can coerce by violence, bribery, and sheer dishonesty, since it is not bound by a common morality. As everyone knows, telling the public one thing while doing another is a not-infrequent act and is lightly passed off as being "in the public's best interest." Thus, the people frequently, indeed usually, do not even know what their leaders are really doing, let alone intending to do, with the result that they begin not to care, voluntarily resigning what little power they have.

Let us look at some of the institutions that in Africa manage to achieve, without the electoral system we deem so necessary to democracy, a democratic government that is also popular. For the sake of brevity and in order to offer a reasonably wide sample, I shall take the three major economic categories (hunters, herders, and cultivators) in the order of their increasingly complex social organization.

At the simplest level, the hunting band presents the unusual picture of direct rule by the people without any delegation of power or authority. Such a hunting band may number as many as thirty nuclear families or as few as two or three. Even in the larger bands, it is not difficult for all adults to sit down together and discuss any problem that needs to be resolved. Although some individuals have more influence than others, it is likely to vary as their circumstances vary. Thus, a man who does well at hunting this month may be listened to with respect this month, but not next month if he does badly or is sick and cannot go hunting. Such bands are strictly egalitarian. They have no chiefs or even formal councils of elders; decisions are made by common assent at informal gatherings or by discussions shouted from hut to hut throughout the camp. If someone disagrees with a decision to go hunting in a certain direction, he may simply stay behind that day; no attempt is made to coerce him. If he finds himself continually in disagreement, or if he disagrees over a matter that is likely to cause strong feelings, he simply leaves that band and joins another. Disputes are settled in the same informal but effective way. The two disputants argue it out if they can, and if they fail, then the whole band joins in. If it still cannot be settled, the dispute is dropped by one of the parties, who leaves to go elsewhere, either temporarily or permanently. The goal is the restoration of harmony within the band, and a disputant's removal obviates the necessity for any judgment and any penalty.

The settlement of disputes by removal indicates how little a people can be concerned with a crime per se, how unwilling to judge or to condemn. They are concerned with the solidarity of the band as a whole. The individual who leaves one band because of a dispute, possibly one in which he was the main instigator (for example, an adulterer), is made perfectly welcome in another band. He is judged, if at all, by his present and immediate effectiveness as a member of his new society. The process is aided by the fact that hunters are continually on the move, and at each move it is normal (except perhaps in times of economic stress) for some members to break off and join other bands and for new members to come in, according to the availability of game and vegetable resources or to the need or desire to visit relatives, as well as in response to actual or latent disputes. The adulterer simply says he is going to visit his relatives elsewhere, and this is accepted. Thus, there is no loss of face involved in leaving a band.

In such a fluid society, it is plain that there can be no permanent body of leaders. Political relations between bands are maintained through the myriad kinship relationships that can be evoked as and when necessary but that are usually left dormant. The band is considered the family and is the only real political unit; except, for example, insofar as Pygmies or Bushmen may be opposed as a whole to their Bantu neighbors, and may be unified by a common sentiment despite the lack of formal political interconnections over large areas, leading them to react to outsiders with remarkable unanimity.

Within the band, authority is not centralized, then, nor is it confined to one segment divided along lines of kinship, age, or sex. It is distributed throughout the entire band; among the Mbuti Pygmies,* for instance, age is the prime institutional, regulatory device. Thus, children have control over the hunting fire, without which a successful hunt cannot take place; youths have control over the *molimo madé* which, as the "voice of the forest," can express the forest's displeasure at disputatious or troublesome members of the band. Adults have control over the hunt and other daily

---

* See C. M. Turnbull, *Wayward Servants* (Garden City, N.Y.: Natural History Press, 1965).

subsistence activities. Elders act as arbitrators, control the education of the young, and may even be said to control death, since they have authority over the *molimo mangbo*, the means by which the Mbuti communicate with their forest deity in times of major crisis. There is some division of labor according to sex, but it is insignificant in terms of economics. Of greater importance is the way the latent hostility between the sexes is resolved by ritual reversal (especially the *ekokoméa* dance) and ritual conflict in the form of a tug of war (*amabongio*), which also involves role reversal. In societies with more complex kinship structures, latent hostilities between various classes of kin are also forestalled by similar role reversal and other devices, such as joking relationship and avoidance. The latent conflict between ruler and ruled may also be expressed and expelled in these ways. The lack of such devices among the Mbuti and Bushman hunters is evidence of the degree of harmony inherent in their social structure.

It is particularly significant that at the band level kinship should occupy such a subordinate role in determining lines of association. Residence and age are much more significant; loyalty is to the hunting territory in which one resides at a given moment and to those also residing there at the same moment. Within that complex of loyalties, the prime divisions are age and sex, with kinship lagging far behind as a structural force.

Among herders, age and residence are also powerful factors, but kinship acquires a major structural role, providing the basis for the segmentary system that is characteristic of these societies. Age is formalized into the age-set system (also a pastoral characteristic), and there may be strong loyalties to given pasture lands or water holes. Authority is still not vested in any one individual or small class of individuals; it is widely distributed. Kinship, age, and residence all play roles in this distribution. The lineal elder (at any level of segmentation) is the nominal leader of his segment, but his authority is not backed by power, except such as he can command ritually. His influence, however, is powerful, and the lineal unit sees its solidarity in the person of the elder. Disputes that cannot be settled between individuals may be adjusted between the elders of their respective lineal segments, which may involve minimal or maximal lineages, family heads, or heads of clans. The largest political unit is sometimes defined as that widest extension of a segmentary society within which the most serious disputes can be settled without recourse to war.* It is a group of people who share a common sentiment as well as a common system, and

---

* For the most detailed account of a pastoral people (in this case, the Nuer), see E. E. Evans-Pritchard, *The Nuer* (Oxford, Eng.: Clarendon Press, 1940), *Kinship and Marriage Among the Nuer* (Oxford, Eng.: Clarendon Press, 1951), and *Nuer Religion* (Oxford, Eng.: Clarendon Press, 1956).

that sentiment is symbolized by the lineal leader at all levels, with a possibly hypothetical common ancestor at the apex.

There are many variations, particularly with regard to the point at which the process of segmentation reaches its apex. In some societies, it is the maximum point to which genealogical connection can be traced; in others, hypothetical ancestry is allowed, even invented, to maintain or create a wider unity. But in all cases, although kinship is a highly integrative device creating strong loyalties, it is also divisive.

One of the main checks against both this divisiveness and the abuse of such authority and influence as reside in the lineal elders is the institutionalization of age. Age-sets unify people of similar age regardless of kinship or residence, establishing a crosscutting complex of loyalties. Moreover, they provide for the further dispersal of authority, with different sets or grades holding different areas of authority. Insofar as age-set loyalties cut across those of kinship, the age-set system also operates in the just settlement of disputes by providing an alternative point of view, an alternative set of rights and obligations by which a person may be judged. Default toward one's kin might be excused, at least partially, if that default were occasioned by an obligation toward an age-mate. But when a dispute among herders reaches major proportions, removal is not the easy resolution mechanism it is for hunters. Whereas hunters have few personal possessions to encumber them, herders have many more material belongings, quite apart from their cattle, and many more fixed loyalties that cannot be left behind lightly. Removal means virtual exile.

Among many herders, a ritual figure (or a number of them)—diviner, priest, or prophet—plays a prominent role in the settlement of major disputes as well as in the regularization of political rifts. This ritual figure is often an outsider, perhaps himself an exile from another segment or even another tribe. In this way he is not an integral part of the local kinship network and is less subject to pressure or prejudice. He is, in a real sense, outside the system because he is outside the kinship structure, and, as such, he provides a check over lineal elders. Even if they are part of the kinship structure, such figures often place themselves outside the system by peculiarities of speech, dress, or behavior and may cultivate these differences to such a degree that they are almost the antithesis of the norm. (This occurs at the band level, though as may be expected in a much less formal way, in the figure of the fool or clown.)

In such societies, the lineal elder may be regarded as the representative of all members of that segment of the population and can be relied on for help or support and for the furtherance of the interests of their segment as a whole, although not to the detriment of other segments. But as with the hunters, most decisions are made by all those immediately involved, in concert. The lineal elder and the ritual specialist are figures to be appealed to only in times of particular need. The interests of the segment as a whole are the main concern of its members, just as those of the band are the main concern of the hunters. The major difference is that whereas the individual hunter can change his loyalties by moving from one geographical area to another (as well as by moving from one set of relationships to another), the herder makes an ideological shift from one level of segmentation to another, using alternative sets of relationships as needed. And like the Mbuti who see themselves as a single people, although they never act in unison, taking the forest as their supreme symbol and distinguishing themselves from nonforest people, the herders also distinguish themselves from others at the wider tribal or national level, taking cattle as their symbol. It is also significant that just as the Mbuti place the education of youth in the hands of the elders, who are in closest touch with the forest deity, the herders also place education largely in the hands of their religious or ritual figures. "The Master of the Fulani Way" is one of the clearest examples.*

It is less easy to generalize about cultivators because their economy is both more permissive and more variable. The obvious differences are the shift to a sedentary occupation and the consequent trend to centralization, specialization, and technological development. Centralization uses the same principle of segmentation that is dominant among the herders, who in turn use the same principle of mobility that is dominant among the hunters. With the cultivators, however, the terms "justice" and "democracy" take on special meaning and appear in more recognizable forms, with the advent of courts and governments. But the principles have already been established—concern for the society (at any level) as a whole, concern with intent rather than with behavior, and the renunciation of individual or centralized authority, especially when associated with power that is absolute in any area.

Among cultivators, there is a whole range of tribal structure from that in which each village is virtually a small autonomous unit under the ritual authority of the lineal elder, which is similar to some of the forest cultivators, to confederations of tribes into nations and empires under apparently despotic monarchs. There is an equally wide range of jural systems. However, the basic generalizations remain valid, and the same kinds of

---

* See the articles by D. J. Stenning, "Transhumance, Migratory Drift, Migration: Patterns of Pastoral Fulani Nomadism," in S. Ottenberg and P. Ottenberg (eds.), *Cultures and Societies of Africa* (New York: Random House, 1960), pp. 139–159; and "The Pastoral Fulani of Northern Nigeria," in J. R. Gibbs (ed.), *The Peoples of Africa* (New York: Holt, Rinehart and Winston, 1965), pp. 361–401.

mechanisms are at work in the interests of justice and democracy. In addition to kinship, age, and residence another factor that is always implicit among hunters and herders but that now becomes explicit is of major importance: belief, and its manifestation in ritual. Hunters have remarkably little concern with ritual, and their beliefs are informal; God and the ancestors are rarely referred to, and belief in spirits and supernatural powers is minimal. Life is a practical matter of man's relationship to his environment, which includes neighboring human beings, to be dealt with in a practical manner. Herders share this characteristic, but their problems are more complex and less easily and definitively resolved by practical effort, and ritual and belief take on a correspondingly more important role. Among cultivators, ritual comes into full play and is the mainstay of justice and democracy, but this does not mean that the cultivators are any less pragmatic than the others.

The institution of Divine Kingship is an excellent illustration. It may be found among certain pastoral cultivators, and some anthropologists see its origin in the ritual priests and prophets of the herders. It may also be found in the great African states and nations and is almost certainly present in some form wherever the institution of kingship is found, at any level from petty chief to emperor. It is only with the coming of foreign powers, with their more truly secular forms of government and their notions of physical coercion, that divinity begins to lose ground.

The Divine King was one who primarily was a symbol not only of the unity of the people but also of their prosperity and success. We grossly misjudge when, as evidence of African despotism and injustice, we point to a corpulent king, with many wives, innumerable children, and enormous wealth, living in a luxurious palace surrounded by the huts in which his less-fortunate subjects live. To start with, those subjects would usually not consider themselves less fortunate at all. Kingship, for all its material splendor, was not something many would desire. Furthermore, many kings were expected to give such visible evidence of their nation's prosperity and happiness and would be sharply criticized for reducing themselves to the level of the common man. The king's wealth, gained through what often seem unjust demands of tribute, was in reality the nation's wealth; and the king's storehouse was a storehouse against any national emergency. Long before Louis XIV ever made his famous pronouncement, the Africans knew that King and State were one. And since the king was divine, he was expected to be perfect. Thus, any demonstration of imperfection—such as the abuse of his (the nation's) wealth or power, an act of injustice, or failure to support his people in time of need or to lead them to victory in time of war—may be taken as an indication that he was not divine at all, but an imposter or a body that the divine had seen fit to vacate; in either case, he was disposable. It is said that the Shilluk king was supposed to be so divine that if he sneezed, he was put to death. The veracity of this has not been established, but the sentiment is right.

In effect, then, the Divine King had no power. His safest course was to do nothing himself but to appoint or confirm a council of ministers who could then be blamed for any default or imperfection. Even they were sometimes thought to be touched by his divinity, expected to be perfect, and considered removable. The mechanisms for removal were many and varied. Ashanti kings and chiefs sat on royal stools in which the ancestral soul resided. The authority lay in the stool itself and thus in the king only as long as he occupied it. Destoolment was all that was necessary to depose a king and was often accomplished by no more than the physical task of separating the two. A Yoruba king might be sent a gift of pigeon's eggs, a sign that he should commit suicide or expect worse. An Anuak chief could be stripped of authority by being deprived of the royal beads, which, until they were confiscated by the British authorities, were evidently constantly in demand. And of the Shilluk, it is said (again with some lack of evidence that it had ever actually happened) that the king was killed at the expiration of a given period (accounts vary concerning the number of years, the minimum being one), a fate the king-elect readily accepted because of the honor accorded to him both in this life and the next as the chosen vehicle for the divine spirit of Nyikang.

All these devices obviously militate against any abuse of the people, who are the sacred trust of the king. At the same time, his word was absolute when given, so in times of crisis and division, he could at once unify the country into concerted action or persuade it to accept a controversial edict; and his future might depend on the outcome of any such intervention. The king was also the ultimate court of appeal, and his decision, being divine, was unquestionable. When a kingship became more secular, as with the Ganda, a higher appeal was sometimes provided. For the Ganda, the ultimate appeal was to the Royal Drums, which served much the same purpose as the Ashanti Stool, symbolizing the ultimacy of ritual and belief over physical power.

Customs separated the Divine Kings from their people, except on ritual occasions. This not only helped conceal the king's possibly obvious imperfections but also increased the aura of divinity with which he was surrounded. For example, when Yoruba kings appeared in public, their faces were heavily veiled with beads. Accession rituals, more than anything, emphasized the divine nature of the king's authority, making it quite plain that his body was a mere receptacle, sacred only while inhabited by the divine.

Succession in itself involved a wide diversity of means to ensure the nonabuse of the kingship. The choice was seldom inevitable, although primogeniture or some other system might be preferred. Sometimes the means was election. Councils of ministers, hereditary and otherwise, existed to decide which of many royal sons was the most suitable for the role, a flexible system that allowed for the choice to be made according to the needs of the moment. The Ganda moved the kingship around from clan to clan so that there was no one royal clan. The Shilluk, with a more linear population distribution, alternated the kingship between the northern and southern halves of the kingdom. In thus distributing the kingship, both kinship and residence factors were utilized to secure an equitable distribution. Although once the king was enthroned, all authority was enshrined in him, the same factors, working through a hierarchy of ministers, chiefs, subchiefs, and headmen, not only dispersed this authority throughout the nation but also provided channels by which the people had access to their king.

In many such states and in others that were less centralized, what are sometimes called secret societies came into play. Perhaps "sacred" would be a more appropriate word because although some of their activities and occasionally even membership were secret, some societies held power that, like the authority of the king, derived from a sacred source. The function of such societies was manifold. Sometimes it was educational; sometimes it was corrective or even penal; sometimes it was administrative or executive. These societies existed and operated quite independently of the king and in some cases were able to advise and even to reprimand him or to demand his removal. Membership was made up of ordinary people on either a voluntary or a compulsory basis. The strength of the societies lay in their sacred nature, in the oaths taken by members to uphold the tribal ideals, and in the belief, shared by all, in the efficacy of those oaths.

Thus, even under a highly centralized government, there were some institutions that ensured that ultimately the power remained in the hands of the people, others that gave the people more immediate access to and control over the power, and some that placed the power directly in the people's hands for specific purposes, including the deposition of a king.

Such a system was as open to abuse as any other system is, but this was largely avoided by two factors: the absence of physical coercion and the presence of religious belief. This belief was, above all, common within any given society and formed the core of the traditional education that generally accompanied the ritual of initiation into adulthood. The education stressed an adult's responsibility to society as a whole, as opposed to a child's responsibility to his nuclear family; and this responsibility was given the full sanction of both ritual and belief. Belief is not something that can be acquired in a brief period of schooling; it has already been acquired in the child's family experience, through teaching and example, including ritual. The formal education of the initiation school reinforces the childhood experience and in a number of ingenious ways demonstrates the validity of the belief and of its associated values. The belief becomes associated directly with practice and provides a moral coercion more effective than any physical coercion could be. Further, this deep-seated belief, which is intensified during the formative years, forms the basis for community of action. Even in dispersed societies such as those of the forest cultivators or the cattle herders, the teachings of the initiation schools serve to provide what might be called a national sentiment, unifying even the most widely separated segments and providing a basis for cooperative action should such action ever be called for.

I have been discussing the ideal rather than the actual situation. Undoubtedly, abuse did occur, but it was less likely to occur in this system because the strength and social nature of the values and beliefs meant that there was less need for it to occur. If a father sees his future as necessarily bound to that of his children, he is likely to take good care of them; and this is just what the family model teaches him to do. So, too, with the lineage elder, chief, or king; his future is inextricably bound up with that of his people, just as the future of the people is bound up with that of their leader. It is a natural tendency, not a legal requirement, for the one to reinforce and support the other in working for their mutual interests. The disparities in wealth, status, and power are only disparities from our point of view and are indications of the weakness of our own form of democracy. Whereas we emphasize community of action (and a purely theoretical communality of wealth, status, and power), the African system emphasizes community of belief. And although community of belief does not stem from community of action, community of action does stem from community of belief.

The same community of belief is responsible for the African focus on justice rather than law because it allows for a diversity of action. An action is not judged for what it is but for what it achieves and, still more important, what is intended. Thus, a man is not judged a thief because he undeniably stole a chicken; rather, he is judged according to his reasons for stealing the chicken.*

A nation based on community of action through the establishment of a common law and backed by physical force cannot boast a community of

---

* For a profound study of this kind of approach to justice, see M. Gluckman, *The Judicial Process Among the Barotse of Northern Rhodesia* (Manchester, Eng.: Manchester University Press, 1955).

belief. It cannot properly be called a society because its members do not share a common sociality; rather, they merely behave, under constraint, as though they did. A nation based on community of belief (and some of the smaller European nations approach this model), that incidentally demonstrates community of action, *is* a society because its members possess a common sentiment, a common sociality. Yet the mere existence of common belief is not enough either, as Franco's Roman Catholic Spain clearly shows. Belief has to be the very foundation of social order (although, of course, not in the sense that one starts with a specific belief and proceeds to build a specific social order).

The three articles that follow illustrate some of these points and raise others, although they do not deal directly with either justice or democracy as such.

Kenneth Little's article, "The Political Function of the Poro," deals with a typical "secret society." Little shows how such a society, which frequently crosses even tribal boundaries, can create a common sentiment that extends far beyond the bounds of the individual's experience or comprehension and provides the basis for a national sentiment. He clearly shows the powerful role of belief. The Poro held so much ritual power that they were able to intervene in almost any realm of life, to effect justice where there was injustice, and to avert the abuse of the secular power by kings and chiefs.

P. C. Lloyd's discussion of "Sacred Kingship and Government Among the Yoruba" illustrates the many ways in which centralization of authority can be counterbalanced. Through a controlled interplay between king and chiefs, both are prevented from abusing their positions. Here, also, belief and ritual play vital roles, and there is an absence of physical coercion.

In "Modern Political Movements in Somaliland," I. M. Lewis deals with three political movements and discusses what I have not discussed here: the relationship of traditional tribal structures to modern national politics. Lewis's article raises issues that, although specific to Somaliland, have much wider significance. Kinship and residence are the bases for the formation of clan and regional parties; and the national party (the third movement) attempts to override the fissive tendencies of the other two parties by the establishment of a national sentiment. Lewis also indicates the importance of the smaller groupings, as a member of which a person more often acts, and with which his identity and sentiments are most closely bound.

These articles illustrate not only the workings of democracy, the ways in which the power is vested in the people (a point of view that will be strengthened in Part 4), but also the importance of belief as a political force and of a community of belief in establishing the boundaries of a society. The latter is perhaps debatable, but it is useful in that it indicates a possible contributing factor to the nonsocial nature of most modern nations, to which, if the same criteria are applied, the term "society" cannot be given.

The concept of society can be defined in many ways—geographic, economic, political, functional, and so forth. But all these relegate to secondary status the primary consideration: that society is comprised of people. A definition of society that took people as its focus of interest would be at least as valid as any of the others and possibly of more general significance. Society would thus not be seen as a group of people contained within given geographic boundaries or influenced by a given environment nor as a group of people within a given political system. It would certainly not be regarded as a system of interrelated social institutions, although this concept, like the others, has its own worth. Instead, it would be regarded primarily as a web of human relationships integrated by a system of mutual rights and obligations. The essence of such a concept of society is the interrelatedness of its members. After having examined economic, familial, and political relationships, I am suggesting that a fourth kind—religious (based on belief and sentiment)—may be the most important of all.

In African societies, the moral society (people who share common values) is most often coincidental with the political, economic, and familial society. Such a conjunction evidently is possible only when the society is small. When it becomes large we have to content ourselves with fewer or only one criterion, and the choice is ultimately between politics and values, between the legalistic and the moralistic society. The former, which is the fruit of centuries of civilized progress, has become increasingly inadequate to the point where the modern nation is threatened with disintegration. To some, such disintegration is already a fact; to others, it is merely imminent. The most gloomy see the future in terms of global disaster. which is by no means impossible if disintegration is inherent in the system and if it continues to be dismissed as a mere temporary malfunction. The alternative suggested by a consideration of the traditional African society at its smallest band level or its largest national level is that we switch our emphasis from behavior to belief, from politics to values. This is in fact what may well be happening in countries like the United States, where youth (the age principle at work), dissatisfied with the current system of nonhuman relationships, are trying new systems such as living in communes (the residence principle), where the most basic demand is community of belief (the religious principle), the distinct values of which are manifested in speech and behavior. It is not too strange that this revolt against the established order should spring from the inadequacy of the modern American family, but it is wrong to interpret it as a denial of family values or as a purely divisive factor. It is nothing of the sort; it is rather a reemphasis on the family as a truly vital, functional unit that is not limited by biological kinship but is bound by common belief and is thus on all grounds the basis of a wider society.

Perhaps it is not necessary to go quite so far in breaking down the old society in order to build a new one; perhaps it is. Significant realignments are taking place at a higher level of segmentation as well, and it seems that even racism may prove to be functional in this respect. The separatist ideals of some Black Americans are by no means the fantasy some people suppose them to be, and if a New Africa were indeed to be founded on American soil, it might be the most significant contribution yet made to the world by the United States. This segment of the American population is probably the most united of all in terms of community of action and, thanks to the new surge of pride in black identity, also in terms of community of belief. Physical separation, which may or may not prove to be a necessity, is not the main factor at all. What is of central importance is the moral separation, the establishment of what is almost certainly the largest single moral community in the not-so-United States.

None of this would necessarily mean that the United States would cease to exist as a nation, particularly if these and other separatist movements were regarded not so much as a breaking away from the nation as a breaking down of the nation into moral rather than political parts. Such a process may well be necessary if the nation is to survive in any form other than a police state. What is being suggested is that a new basis for unity is necessary if we are to find a moral basis for living and that a political federation of states formed primarily on a moral basis might lead to a much greater unity than the present nominal unity. The power of the principle of segmentation is that it uses a single model—the nuclear family—to provide the structure for unity at any level, including the national level. The family is the most intimate of all units, where human relationships are the closest, the most effective, the most affective, and the most moral. All these qualities are transferred, by use of the family model, from one level to the next. They enable the individual to see himself in relation to the state in much the same way that he sees himself in relation to the family. The process of segmentation is continuous and gradual. But in our society there is no such model, no such intimacy that can be transferred. Between the individual and the state there are merely a series of political institutions, party organizations, and the like, to which he may or may not belong, as he likes. His individual membership is unessential; he is unessential. He may feel a loyalty to his family, but this is not transferred to a larger context. Between family and nation there is a perfect hiatus. The establishment of smaller, intermediate groupings, to which the individual could *feel* a loyalty, rather than owe one, seems vital. The alternative is a nation of solitary, isolated individuals, in which case morality ceases to have any meaning.

It is not a question of what we do, how we behave, that ultimately unites or divides us, but in what we believe. Tiny Northern Ireland is a current example of a modern "society" wrecked by a division of belief subjected to the full pressure of an artificial political unity. It is not the beliefs that have done the damage but political behavior and the refusal of the politicians to acknowledge the power of belief. If the United States, with all its diversity, lacks division along these lines, perhaps it is only because religious beliefs are not so profoundly held there; other, more material considerations are more important to the American. I would say, in that case, that there is more hope for Ireland.

Some may openly prefer to maintain the materialistic, technological notion of progress, mistakenly thinking of religion, values, and morality as otherworldly. One thing that is clear about African society in its political as well as its other aspects is the essential practicality and this-worldliness of religious belief, without which the society, as it is structured, would collapse. But even so, the opponents of so radical a change as one leading to a moral way of life might say that our society, being differently structured, has no need for primitive superstition and ritual. This is perhaps the point that should be examined most carefully. It might well be that despite the enormous outward differences between our form of society and traditional Africa there is a great deal of structural similarity. It is precisely because we have, in the name of expediency, thrust aside such vital elements as religious belief, thinking them to be mere embellishments, that we are now faced with an increasingly unstable structure. So, still eschewing judgment, I suggest as a useful exercise the functional comparison of African and American political systems and institutions and of their interrelationships within the total social system. There is hardly room for that here, and in any case it is perhaps better made by each individual who is so motivated, since each will bring his own American (or other) experience and his own beliefs to bear. If anything is to be done, it may be a matter for state legislation; but first and foremost, it is also a matter of individual belief and its communality.

We have our share of secret societies, such as the Ku Klux Klan, the Mafia, and the CIA. By comparison, however, they can hardly be considered sacred, nor do they operate in the interests of the nation as a whole, although they are a functional part of it. The religious element is by no means absent and, with the first two, it is a powerful factor. But the interests represented are sectional: racist, criminal, and governmental. It is therefore more pertinent to ask the question differently. What do we have in our society that functions as the Poro and similar societies function in Africa? We might be tempted to say that our schools fulfill the educational function, but they do not. Formal schooling is concerned with the material aspects of life; whereas Poro schooling is concerned with the source of life, with belief and values. Increasingly, our schools are forbidden to give instruction in religious matters; therefore, such values as they can impart are strictly secular and are better termed conveniences than values. The fact that religious education is both voluntary and highly diverse is directly responsible for the moral fragmentation of the nation and the dissipation of what should be a major source of unity and strength.

Similarly, we should ask what do we have that fulfills the function of the mask, when used in passing judgment, depersonalizing the judge and giving the judgment of the society rather than that of the individual. The robes and other court paraphernalia have a similar function, but whereas the mask symbolizes sacred judgment, the robes now merely symbolize the state's secular law. And the judgment is that of twelve men who may very well be neither just nor true.

We laugh at witchcraft, but what device do we have that enables us to maintain a code of socially approved behavior but allows for human frailty, and, therefore, does not condemn a man when he is caught doing what many of us are merely not caught doing? The judge is permitted a measure of discretion in our society, but too often that merely allows him room for the exercise of his personal beliefs and prejudices, as any study of court decisions can show. If we compare courts, which in both cases allegedly aim at achieving justice, the difference is equally revealing. An African court is filled with all those concerned (family, friends, and members of the same community), and all are expected to participate. Our court is filled with strangers, sightseers and sensationmongers, ushers and guards, none of whom have a word to say. Only witnesses who are called may speak, and then only to answer specific questions. Many recognize the inadequacy of the procedure and the danger of vital evidence remaining ungiven but deem it necessary in the interests of saving time in our busy, expensive world. Yet no one has come up with an equation relating the value of a court's time to the value of a man's life or future.

In the realm of democracy, what do we have that functions as a ritual of accession, investing a fallible human being with divine authority? We have a secular ceremony that effectively gives authority and power to what we know to be a fallible human being, already making allowances for the errors we expect him to commit. By not expecting our leaders to be perfect, we give them full rein to be imperfect and excuse them in advance for their future faults. Since they are human beings, like everyone else, and since in our democratic way we often compel them to be even more banal than they may already be, they are brought down to the level of the ordinary citizen. They do not project an image that all can respect, let alone worship. One of the great virtues of the beaded veil of the Yoruba kings was that it made it possible for the Yoruba to accept their kings as divine. With due respect for the physiognomy of American presidents, they seldom present a divine image; a veil or two would do much to lessen the anxiety caused by the appearance of some. It is said that if man looks on the face of God, he will die. If the institution of the veil is removed, man is compelled to look upon God; and as God is thus sometimes revealed, the reaction may be one of mirth rather than terror. It is the notion of God (and godliness) that dies. We are left with nothing to respect or trust, except ourselves.

What do we have that functions as religious belief functions in an African society, providing the basis of a truly unified society? It is a curious tenet of Western democracy that half the nation should ideally be opposed to the other half and that leaders should occasionally have rotten eggs thrown at them to prove that they are democratic. The African notion of democracy holds that the power resides in the people and that through the existence of a community of belief the people should be united in the exercise of that power. We agree that power should reside in the people, but we take care to see that they do not exercise it as they see fit if we can term them a minority. The interests of the "whole," even if representation were more equable than it is, might thus deny the interests of 49 percent of the population. In the absence of communality of belief, we are increasingly driven to the use of repressive measures. Preventive detention is the up-and-coming thing of the new, enlightened democracy, Western style. Yet rather than consider a common belief and a united nation, we quaintly favor a diversity of belief and a disunited nation, even encouraging with fanfare the bitter opposition of political parties. Thus, opposition to government is liberally invited, yet acceptance of its laws is demanded.

These are tentative suggestions of lines along which comparisons might usefully be made. Indications are that what will be revealed is a difference of values rather than of structure. Through this kind of comparison we are not misled by the difference of outward form, and a fundamental rather than a superficial difference may be discerned. If any judgment is to be made, it can most usefully be made in terms of the issue of morality versus legality. Efficacy being a supreme criterion, we can claim that there is no judgment to be made, since the size of the modern nation determines its legalistic form. Or we can openly continue to choose technological, as opposed to human, progress, which will come to the same thing. Or we can opt for human values and then see what steps have to be taken to protect our chosen path. The basic values we are faced with here are those of justice as against law, belief against compulsory obedience, morality against conformity, sociality against individuality, humanity against formality, unanimity against disunity, and identity with the government as against mere acceptance of it.

# The Political Function of the Poro

## Kenneth Little

### Part I

*Traditional Background*

One of the most interesting problems of pre-colonial history is the relation of so-called secret societies to indigenous government.[1] In West Africa they are concerned mainly with the ownership and use of supposedly super-natural medicines and the propagation of certain cults.

These are the functions also of other associations, but what principally distinguishes secret societies from the ordinary medicine society or cult is the esoteric basis of their activities. Not only do the secret societies employ particular rituals, signs, symbols, and forms of knowledge which are with-held from non-initiates, but these things are regarded as a special source of power through being kept private. Associations of this kind are prevalent in southern Nigeria, and are particularly numerous in the coastal area of rain-forest in general, including the Ivory Coast, Liberia, Sierra Leone, and parts of Ghana and Portuguese Guinea. They are not secret in any other respect. On the contrary, not only is the existence and general pur-pose of these societies known to every grown-up person, but in many places the wide range of their activities makes them the dominant social force. They are frequently responsible for tribal education, regulate sexual conduct, supervise political and economic affairs, and operate various social services, including entertainment and recreation as well as medical treatment.

Sierra Leone, where secret societies are as numerous and influential as anywhere else, is a case in point. It contains a host of societies like the Humui and the Njayei of the Mende, and the Tuntu, the Thoma, and the Yasi of the Sherbro, practising medicine; but the best known and most

---

[1] I have to thank Professor Daryll Forde for a number of very helpful comments on my original draft of this article.

widely spread association of all is undoubtedly the Poro. The Poro is important not only because it is the men's association *par excellence*—into which the boys are initiated on reaching puberty—but because of the part that it has played in community affairs from time immemorial. Valentim Fernandes, whose description of the West Coast is dated 1506–10, mentions that in Sierra Leone '. . . there are certain houses or churches of idols where women do not enter called *baa*. Another of these idols they call *piçaa* and another *cõ tuberia*. And these houses are only for men' (1951, ed. Monod, da Mota, Mauny). Another sixteenth-century author, André Alvares d'Almada, has also referred to *Contuberia*, an evil spirit, whom the common people regard as God: 'and before he appears it is shouted through the village, because the evil spirit is coming to visit them. Therefore they must stay at home and shut their doors and not appear in the street because the evil spirit is coming to visit them.'

D'Almada suggests that this 'spirit' and his followers are none other than the king and his nobles who go naked through the streets, blowing on a hollowed reed as if it were a trumpet. They kill anyone in their path unless the king comes to his aid and enrols him in the *Contuberia*, which is a cult.[2]

Fragmentary as these accounts are, they both imply that the Poro society existed 400 years ago, and that it was regarded with much the same kind of awe as today. The earliest European visitors to Sierra Leone itself were all impressed by Poro, and most of them speak of it as the principal means by which the country was governed. The *Report of the Chalmers Commission*, which is our main source of information about indigenous methods of government during pre-colonial times, bears particular witness to the large number of activities that were under Poro control. Both the harvesting of palm fruit and fishing were regulated by Poro, since the placing of the society's sign prohibited the use of the plantations or fishing grounds concerned until it was removed (1899, pt. i, pp. 51–52). The Poro also decided trading practices and fixed prices at which various commodities should be sold and at which certain services—for instance, a day's load carrying—should be performed (Vivian, 1896, pp. 29–31). It had its own tribunal which took precedence over other authorities in the settlement of certain disputes, and to which cases involving murder or witchcraft had to be taken. It arbitrated in local wars, and no fighting was permitted while Poro was in session. At the same time, the fact that its symbols were understood and obeyed all over the country meant that they could also be used as a general call to war (*Chalmers Report*, pt. i, p. 52).

The latter point is illustrated historically by the part played by the Poro in the Mende Rising of 1898. This rebellion, as is well known, was

---

[2] These excerpts from Fernandes and d'Almada are both taken from Christopher Fyfe's *Sierra Leone Inheritance*, 1964, pp. 27, 32.

prompted ostensibly by the collection of a hut tax in the recently established Protectorate. Following an initial outbreak in Temne country, fighting spread to Mendeland where an almost simultaneous attack was made
on all government posts. Within less than a week the male British subjects
in Bandajuma, Kwallu, and Sulima Districts, with few exceptions, were
murdered, and all property belonging to British subjects up-country was
plundered. According to evidence supplied to the Chalmers Commission,
plans for the rising were laid in specially convened meetings of the Poro
society. Common action was effected on this very wide scale by placing
the whole country under Poro oath, before its actual object was known.
After this, everyone was bound to adhere to whatever plans had been
decided upon in the Poro inner council, hence the expression used in this
connexion—*ngo yela,* 'one word', or 'unity' (ibid., pp. 51–52). Evidence
given to the Chalmers Commission also suggests that the almost simultaneous nature of the outbreak was accounted for by the sending round of the
Poro symbol for war—a burned palm leaf. This is said to have been carried by Poro messengers who, starting from Bumpe as the centre, bore it
rapidly to the different places where the rising was to begin and delivered
their message that the time had come. Sir David Chalmers, in summing
up these operations, cautiously states that there was no trace of any secret
society having been instrumental in the Rising. However, he does suggest
that it was facilitated through the organization of Poro (p. 52).

Another important incident in which Poro is supposed to have played
some part was the more recent disturbance in the northern and southwestern provinces of the then Protectorate. These took place between
November 1955 and March 1956 and involved the destruction and looting
of a large amount of property as well as loss of life. The immediate cause
was resentment of the way in which certain chiefs and big men had
allegedly been misruling the country. In many cases, the houses and compounds of the chiefs in question were attacked, and they were obliged to
fly for their lives. The rioters were generally armed with sticks and slings
for hurling stones, and on a number of occasions they were stopped only
by rifle fire. In fact, so well drilled and organized were the young men
who made these attacks that the police had frequently to fight a pitched
battle in order to restrain them. This fact, coupled with evidence of the
chanting of Poro songs and the consistent pattern of complaint at the subsequent Commission inquiry, led the Commissioners to suggest that the
disturbances had been partly facilitated by Poro and that the society had
also been responsible for the extreme secrecy which shrouded the prevailing discontent. The extent of the latter had been underestimated, and the
whole outbreak took the Government entirely by surprise (*Report of Commission of Inquiry,* 1956, pp. 11–12).

The question which naturally arises from both the Mende Rising and the
Protectorate Disturbances is how a purely traditional institution operating

beneath the formal surface of African and colonial society could exert so much influence upon events. This question is the more relevant because very little attention seems to have been paid officially to Poro until recent times. The Government's original arrangements for administering the Protectorate employed chiefs and headmen, but no serious attempt was made to understand the political function of the secret societies (Hargreaves, 1956, pp. 62–63). Only in a negative sense was their influence recognized as when, in 1897, the Poro was declared illegal by Ordinance. It was made a criminal offence to employ, or to connive at the employment of, Poro laws as a means of interfering with trade.[3] This occurred after the society had placed a ban on palm trees in the Sherbro. Possibly the Poro's action in holding up trade on that occasion was attributed by Governor Cardew more to the local influence of particular chiefs than to any other factor. However, the fact that he made absolutely no comment upon the secret societies in replying to the findings of the Commission seems to suggest either ignorance or apathy on his part. He replied in detail to the other twenty-three sections of the Report (*Chalmers Report,* pt. i, *passim*).

### Eighteenth- and Nineteenth-Century Impressions of Poro

That Cardew's own officials were informed about Poro and knew something of its activities is indicated by the evidence which Mr. Parkes, the Secretary for Native Affairs, and various District Commissioners offered to the Commission (ibid., pt. ii, *passim*). As indicated above, much earlier European visitors to the Coast had also recorded their impressions of the society. The most important of these accounts dates back to 1668. It was compiled by the Dutchman, O. Dapper, and translated into English by J. Ogilby in 1696, as part of a description of the inhabitants of the Guinea Coast. In the course of relating tribal manners and customs in the region of Cape Mount, Dapper mentions the initiation of youths into a society called Belli. That this association was very probably a Vai version of the Poro school is indicated both by the geographical context and by the practices and ceremonies described in the passage concerned which, as translated by Ogilby, reads as follows:

There is by the King's order a place in the Wood appointed of about two or three miles compass, whither are brought the Youths that have not been Marked, by main force and against their wills, because they believe they shall be kill'd or chang'd; and therefore they take a sorrowful farewell of their Friends and Parents, as if they went indeed to their death.

When now they are lodged in the Wood, continually some Ancient persons which have had the Tokens of *Belli-Paaro* very long, attend to teach and in-

---

[3] Ordinance no. 14 of 1897. To protect and safeguard the trade of the Colony of Sierra Leone and its Protectorate and those engaged and interested in the same.

struct them what behaviour they shall use; leading them a strange and *uncouth* dance, and causing them to learn some *Verses* which they call *Belli-Dong,* being Songs and Encomiums of *Belli,* stuffed with obscene and scurrilous language. . . .

Hither the women bring rice, *Bonano's,* and all sort of Fruit, prepared for an offering, and give it to the *Soggonoe,* that is the *Ancientest Marked,* whom the women hold for Saints. . . .

This living in the Wood continues four or five years, during which time there are new comers daily brought thither.

None unmark'd may come near this place, only women in manner before mention'd, and they too must go singing with a loud noise for if it fall out that any pass by silently, they are taken by the Spirits, without ever being heard of more. . . .

At their first coming abroad, they behave themselves as if they then came newly into the world, not knowing (or at least wise so pretending) where their Parents dwell, and so totally changed, that they have forgot their Names; nor indeed do they the meanest or most common act of Childhood, without being first tutor'd therein by the *Soggonoe.* . . .

Lastly, every one of them must swear by *Belli-Paaro,* that is, *by Divine Justice, that he will do the Command impressed on him: that he will not withdraw out of this or that Town; nor reproach any persons or places, or carry anything away, or hinder the passing of the canoo's, or keep Oyl, Nuts, and Houses.* . . . (Ogilby, vol. i, 1696, pp. 403–4.)

Further reference to this early account of the Belli society will be made in later paragraphs. It describes the judicial functions of this association and indicates that it existed during the seventeenth century in the coastal territories of Sierra Leone as well as in the north-western corner of what is now Liberia.

Nicholas Owen, who was a slave trader on the island of Sherbro during the 1750's, and the Reverend John Newton, formerly captain of a slave ship, came into close contact with the Poro society there. Both of them describe it as a method of maintaining law and order (ed. Martin, 1930, pp. 48–49; 1788, pp. 25–26). A similar point was made by Lieutenant John Matthews who lived in Sierra Leone between 1785 and 1787. He wrote in one of his letters to a friend in England that:

This wise, political institution is desseminated through the country for the purpose of putting an end to disputes and wars, as the jealousy, pride, and irritability of the natives are such as will not suffer them even when conscious of being the aggressors, to make concessions. . . . This law is never used but in the dernier resort; and when it is in force, the crimes of witchcraft and murder are punishable by it. (1788, pp. 82–83.)

Matthews's letter goes on to describe the very summary and violent way in which the Poro dealt with further resistance, once its ruling had been declared. It sent down a party of forty or fifty men, all armed and disguised. They put to death anyone who was out of doors, and removed as much livestock and provisions as they pleased (pp. 84–85). The legal and political functions of Poro have also been referred to by Thomas Winterbottom, who was a doctor with the Sierra Leone Company. His book, too, stresses the judicial functions of the society and gives a certain amount of information about its organization, including methods of initiation and the role of initiates (vol. i, 1803, pp. 135–7).

Most of this earlier experience of Poro seems to have been gained among the Bullom of Sherbro, but it was not long before European travellers were also coming into personal contact with the society in the course of expeditions into the interior of the country. One of these journeys was made by Major Gordon Laing, an officer of the West India Regiment, who claims that his party was attacked by a Poro gang when passing through Temneland *en route* to Falaba. Laing's account suggests that there were large stretches of territory over which Poro had complete control, completely superseding the authority of local headmen. He also compares the society to the Inquisition in Europe (1825, pp. 91–99). Some ten years later, another European traveller, F. Harrison Rankin, also made a trip into Temne country, working his way up the River Rokell as far as Magbele. Rankin had evidently been warned in advance that he was likely to be stopped on reaching a certain boundary beyond which white men were prohibited by Poro from moving further up-country. This duly happened, but from Rankin's light-hearted description, he does not appear to have been particularly awed by the encounter. Nevertheless, his account seems to suggest that the Poro ban was being used at that time as a means of controlling trade with the Colony (1837, pp. 299–303). There are several recorded instances, in earlier as well as later trading contacts, of produce being held up in this way, it being a native method of driving a better bargain with the Colony merchants.

Finally, so far as the nineteenth century is concerned, there is Augustus Cole's *Secret Orders of Western Africa,* as well as the *Chalmers Report.* Cole was an African teacher in a Mission school in the Sherbro, and his short account of Poro is interesting mainly because of its author's claim to have been initiated as a junior member of the society. That Cole did not penetrate very deeply into Poro secrets is evident from his somewhat garbled version of its activities and organization. He does confirm, however, Major Laing's impression of Poro constituting a law unto itself, and he also implies that the society's ritual powers were sufficient, irrespective of physical force, to put an abrupt end to local hostilities (1866, pp. 49–53 and pp. 63–64).

## The Supernatural Basis of Poro

As already mentioned, the *Chalmers Report* placed special emphasis upon the Poro's political function. Among the witnesses from whom Sir David Chalmers derived his information were a number of missionaries and Creole traders (pt. ii, *passim*). The latter, in particular, were people who might be expected to have a close familiarity with native life. Most of them had lived and carried on their business either in Sherbro or further up-country, and it is likely that some of them had native wives or consorts, that being a fairly common custom among Creoles trading in the interior. These witnesses are nearly unanimous in testifying to the widespread influence of the society, and some of them distinguish between what are referred to as the 'religious Poro' and the 'civil or political Poro', though without explaining their relationship. What is even more important, but is left equally obscure, is the precise meaning which Poro had for its own members and for the community at large. 'The whole system', wrote one witness, 'is wrapt up in a mass of superstition, trickery and fetish, which appears to be merely intended to impress the native mind and so give importance to the craft' (*Chalmers Report,* pt. ii, app. L (1), p. 146(1)).

This, no doubt, was how Poro activity appeared when judged by late Victorian standards of morality and rationality,[4] but it obviously omits the question of motivation. Nor does it explain what nearly every witness was concerned to stress, namely, the strict adherence of every person joined in Poro to his oath, irrespective of knowing its purpose. In our own society the latter attitude of mind would imply either intense religious faith or fear of the strongest kind. Both conditions, indeed, are largely involved in Poro, and since psychological factors are also fundamental to Poro's organiza-tion, it will be convenient to discuss these first.

The principal consideration in this respect is the central position that belief in the supernatural attributes of Poro occupies in indigenous cos-mology. 'The (Poro) spirit was made by God and not by man' was the reply of a native informant to a comment on the apparently very material nature of this particular spirit (Little, 1951, p. 226). Similarly, the native assumption is that 'God' handed down the rites of initiation, practised in the bush, to human beings. 'This is what *Leve* (an old name for God) brought down long ago', chants the *Mabole* (see later paragraph) officiat-ing over the final ceremony of initiation into Poro (ibid., p. 124).

The Mende word for 'Poro' is *Poe*, meaning literally 'no end', 'far behind' (ibid., p. 241 f.n.). It is called *Polo* by most Liberian tribesmen, and in Gbunde its full name is *Polo gi zu,* i.e. 'in the Poro society'. In Mano it is called the *Bo*: the term is said here to mean 'to cut', or a 'cut-ting', and refers, according to Schwab, to the circumcision and excision done in the bush (1947, pp. 266–78). An educated informant told the latter author that Poro means 'earth'—of the earth, pertaining to or having to do with the earth or ground. Schwab's conclusion in this respect is that Poro is an elaborate modification of earth-mother worship (ibid.).

There are also myths to explain the origin of Poro. These mainly empha-

---

[4] Mary Kingsley, one hastens to add, is an exception to the rule. Not only did she regard the tribal secret societies as 'admirable engines of government' but she strenucusly rebutted the notion of there being anything very repulsive about their rites and ceremonies (1901, pp. 448–9).

size the atmosphere of secrecy which surrounds the society (Little, op. cit., pp. 242–3). From the point of view of its adherents, however, the supernatural nature of Poro is manifested in a number of ways. There are, first of all, the 'spirits' of the society. Among the Mende these spirits are impersonated by Poro officials disguised by carved wooden masks, raffia capes, and other accoutrements. They are believed to have power to cause sickness and death. The most potent of them is the *Gbeni,* who may be seen only by society members, and even they are in danger if they approach too near to him. For this reason, when the *Gbeni* is 'pulled out' of the Poro bush, his followers turn about according to the way the spirit faces in order to avoid coming in front of him. Word has also to be sent on in advance of the arrival of the *Gbeni,* so that people can hide themselves out of his sight (ibid., pp. 246–7). Doubtless the terrifying effect of these 'spirits' derived largely from the violent way in which the individuals impersonating them were licensed to behave. Several earlier writers, as well as Matthews, have described how such a Poro party of masked officials descended with irresistible force upon any community rash enough to ignore the society's dictates.

These special spirits of the Poro supposedly reside in the secret bush of the society and, as described below, they are instrumental in the psychological conversion of novices into Poro men. This part of the forest is also sacred to the spirits of former Poro members. The latter supposedly watch over the society's activities in much the same kind of way as ancestral spirits are believed to interest themselves in the living members of the family. Since, therefore, these Poro spirits are particularly concerned with the welfare of young initiates, their blessing is specially invoked on behalf of new members.

The result is that the Poro enclosure may be regarded as a veritable power house of supernatural force. This is largely because of the enormous influence which spirits, particularly of the dead, are thought to exert upon human affairs. Not only do they canalize supernatural powers, but they are the principal means that human beings have for communicating with its ultimate source, which is God. There is, in fact, a good deal of evidence to suggest that it is mainly upon this ancestral conception, rather than upon any other mystical factor, that the Poro is fundamentally based. Among the Mano of Liberia, for example, spirits are impersonated by masks, and a boy belonging to the hereditary class of priests would be told that his mask represented the 'old people' who lived as spirits in 'God's town'; that it also represented himself, because he would one day go as a spirit to live in God's town with other spirits (Harley, 1950, p. 4).[5] In short, 'the Poro

---

[5] According to Schwab (op. cit.) masks served as Poro medicine among the Mano. A certain mask was always left outside the camp in which the boys were being initiated. See also p. 269, footnote 13.

may be thought of as an attempt to reduce the all pervading spirit world to an organization in which man might contact the spirit world and interpret it to the people, where men became spirits, and took on godhead' (Harley, 1941, p. 7).

In addition to spirits, the Poro supposedly possesses a number of medicines of great strength. These medicines are used for promoting society business, including the initiation of new members, and they are also available for various purposes affecting the wider community. The notion of medicine in indigenous thought is as pervasive as that of spirit. It is conceived of as an efficient, though impersonal, force. In theory, most grown persons are capable of using medicine, but the fact that medicine is potentially dangerous as well as potentially helpful confines its production and employment to people who are specialists. Mishandling of it may bring down harm upon its manipulator and on those associated with him. Indeed, the more powerful medicines might be compared to electric batteries of high voltage. They are charged with energy, and so it is risky for an inept or unauthorized person to tamper with them, even to go anywhere near them. A medicine has to be tended and nurtured as carefully as a child, and part of the technique consists in talking to it in a certain way every day. The more powerful the medicine, the more harm it is likely to cause, but it is also capable of greater benefits to all concerned, hence the need for properly qualified and responsible people to look after it (Little, 1951, pp. 227–30; 1953, pp. 128–9).

Of all such specialists Poro men are regarded as the most skilful and highly trained. The society's spiritual endowment has already been stressed. These two facts combine to make the Poro the main arbiter in the indigenous culture, and, in effect, they enable it to perform a role analogous to that of the medieval church in Europe. Like the latter institution, Poro was also in a position to indoctrinate the 'laity' with its own particular beliefs and practices, and could use its professed knowledge of supernatural matters to control most of the general life of the community (Little, 1951, p. 240). Incidentally, like the medieval church, Poro also has power to excommunicate. According to Schlenker (1861), the placing of the society's sign in a person's compound signified that he had incurred the society's displeasure, and was a warning that he must not move outside his farm or have anything to do with his neighbours until the ban was removed.

More will be said later about the society's organization. It is difficult to be specific because arrangements probably varied with political and other conditions. In general, however, there appears to have been a large number of local chapters or 'lodges' which were based upon important towns and villages. These local 'lodges' usually organized their own activities, but when the time came for the chief's son to be initiated the youth of neighbouring towns and villages might be convened for a chiefdom 'poro'[6] (Harley, 1941). On other occasions the activities of the society transcended not only chiefdom but tribal boundaries.

## The Implications of Initiation

In fact, initiation of boys into Poro, and of girls into Sande, the parallel women's society, was virtually compulsory, if only because of its implications for adult membership of the tribe. Marriage, for example, was impossible without it, and no non-initiate, irrespective of biological age, was treated as a grown-up person, much less allowed to hold a position of importance. This largely explains Poro's control, as well as its political power, in the respects just noted, because initiation was the principal medium of tribal education. As is well known, the Poro ran its own school for boys, and according to Harley (1941, p. 27) it was also customary for the head woman of Sande to confer with the leader of Poro. The latter was overlord of Sande and so the men's society had indirect supervision of the girls' training as well as charge of the boys. Mary Kingsley, who also mentions the Sande head woman's practice of attending Poro meetings,[7] goes even further in this respect, claiming that the boys' and girls' initiation schools represent two sides of the same institution (1899, p. 452).[8] According to Westermann and Sibthorpe the two societies must never be in session at the same time in one chief's jurisdiction (1928, p. 231). Poro also overlaps a number of other societies, such as Yasi, the Sherbro medicine society, whose woman head is *ex officio* a leading figure in Poro (Hall, 1939) and, according to Cole (1886), is entitled to Poro burial. Ordinary members of Yasi include initiates of both Poro and Sande.

Initiation into Poro has been described in detail in a number of places (see *inter alia* Harley, 1941, *passim*, and Little, 1951, pp. 117–26), and it will suffice for present purposes to indicate its political implication. The procedure is partly ceremonial and symbolical and partly instructional, and it is designed, first and foremost, to turn the initiate into a good Poro man. In addition to various practical techniques tribal history is taught, and training for the position that a person will hold in tribal life is also given; but all this is secondary to the main function of initiation which is to impress upon the new member the sacredness of his duty to Poro. This is

---

[6] For a distinction between Poro as a general institution and a 'poro' see pp. 275–276.

[7] Mary Kingsley adds that this Sande representative was not allowed to speak at these meetings, and was supposed to be invisible to all except the head of Poro. I am unable to vouch for this. It may just possibly be a misreading of the fact that women members of Poro (see later paragraphs) are regarded ritually as men.

[8] This is a matter about which there is very much more material for the Liberian side of the Poro than exists for Sierra Leone. (See Harley, 1941, *passim*, and Schwab, 1947, pp. 266–78.) Details of Sande and its organization have been omitted for the sake of brevity, but a description may be found *inter alia* in Little, 1951, pp. 126–30.

done psychologically by subjecting the youths to a number of terrifying experiences during which they are symbolically 'eaten' by the Poro spirit and are ultimately shown that their 're-birth' is due to the same spiritual force. They also take part in a series of ceremonies, involving the killing of fowl by brutal methods. The object is to demonstrate how the initiates, too, would be treated should they ever divulge any Poro secrets. This ritual takes place in the special camp in which the boys have been segregated, but it is not until the final ceremony that they are allowed into the most sacred part of the Poro bush. The climax comes when, bound symbolically by thread and moss to his fellow initiates, the new member takes his final vows of loyalty to the society in the presence of its spirits. As a sign of his incorporation, he carries out with him into the world, not only the marks on his body of the 'spirit's teeth', but the new name that Poro has bestowed upon him in the bush (Little, loc. cit.).

A good deal of the practical training, too, is calculated to produce among the initiates a sense of *esprit de corps* and solidarity as members sharing the same institution. For example, they are taught the meaning of various signs and symbols and to use certain pass words which are secret to Poro; most allusions to society business are so cloaked in proverbial language as to be obscure to an outsider. Initiates must also be familiar with Poro prohibitions and taboos, referred to as *kassi*[9] by some writers. They recognize each other by the use of certain phrases and inflections of the voice, and by more elaborate tests, which consist of set questions and answers. These, too, are of a proverbial kind and they are a part of the Poro ritual (Migeod, 1916 (*a*) and (*b*); and Little, 1948, pp. 7 and 8).[10]

Again, not only are the boys sorted out for purposes of residence and instruction into groups of approximately the same age and size, but they undergo common experiences of hardship and tests of endurance. Pain is inflicted deliberately upon them to instil habits of self-discipline, and they are taught to obey the elders of the society without question. In the old days training lasted for two or three years, and sometimes longer; and throughout the whole of this time the Poro had complete control over

---

[9] The term *kassi* implies a ritual sanction, and, according to Augustus Cole, it should only be used in connexion with Poro. Tying grass upon plants or fruit-trees, 'with the notification that Poro is on it, makes the tree from that moment sacred, and picking fruit from it is to be guilty of the Purrah laws, or to buy Kasey' (1866, pp. 49–53).

[10] Augustus Cole says that there are three kinds of salutation. The first is given by scratching the palm of the hand of the stranger with the middle finger of the grip, the second, by kneeling, laying the right hand on the ground, and in this position moving round and nodding the head gracefully to all the members; the third is used by a person who, though not a member of Poro, belongs to a kindred society. Such a person coming in contact with Poro, quickly picks the leaves of a certain common herb. With these leaves in his right hand, which he places flat on the ground, he kneels, uttering words to the effect that Poro secrets will remain as sealed up in his heart as the leaves in his hand (ibid.).

virtually every youth in the country. Should a boy die during the session, he was simply buried in the bush and no particular attention was paid to the matter. Notice was not sent to the parents until the sesssion was over. Then one of the elders would go round to the mother's house and break a pot in front of her saying: 'Of the pots you asked us to build, we are sorry that yours was broken.' His explanation was accepted without question, and there would be no 'crying' for the lad—the usual mourning custom— because, to quote the native rationalization of the matter the mourners 'might breathe in the same kind of disease' (Little, 1951, p. 126).

It only remains to point out that this Poro initiation was undergone at puberty. This is generally regarded by psychologists as the most impressionable stage of a person's life, and every technique was used to imbue the young initiate's mind with awe of the society and ensure his conformity with its aims. Not only was he snatched, sometimes without warning,[11] from the security of family and kinsfolk and exposed to terrifying experiences; but he was systematically deprived of sleep to make him still further open to suggestion. He was also subjected to a constant round of admonition, backed up by gruesome examples of the fate in store for him should he default.

## The Organization of Poro

(A) THE JUNIOR MEMBERS. The significance of this Poro indoctrination for the society's political role becomes even more apparent if it is appreciated that the great majority of initiates never advanced beyond the most junior grade. Individuals who did not belong to Poro were regarded as ceremonially unclean (Schlenker, 1861). In Liberia they were called, according to tribe, by terms meaning 'outsiders', 'sinners', 'shadow' or 'image' (Schwab, 1947, pp. 266–78). By joining the society they established their status as men. They became so hinga, to use the Mende term, i.e. 'those entitled to procreate', and enjoyed, henceforward, the society's protection. This meant, according to contemporary writers, that a Poro man could ride roughshod over ordinary people to the extent of evading responsibility for debt and insulting non-members with impunity (Cole, op. cit., pp. 63–64, and Vivian, op. cit., pp. 29–31).

But junior Poro men had no rights within the society itself. They were completely without voice in its affairs although bound to carry out Poro commands (Little, 1951, p. 245). 'Poro' in the political sense consisted solely of the higher grades of the society. These comprised men who in some cases had risen to a position of seniority by further and more exten-

---

[11] However, the extent to which the initiate's abrupt removal terrified him probably depended upon whether he appreciated that this experience, like his subsequent ordeal, was all part of the Poro ritual.

sive periods of instruction,[12] and men who through membership of certain descent groups had an hereditary right to high position in the society. In addition to the taking of an oath of greater and greater solemnity, each upward step involved payment of fees, and so only a very wealthy man of advanced years could hope to pass initiation into these higher degrees. Among the northern tribes of Liberia, according to Harley, there are said to be ninety-nine degrees in all, in which members of two or three 'families' (descent groups) were eligible for initiation into the final secrets (1941, pp. 5 and 6).

(B) THE 'INNER CIRCLE'. It was this top group of Poro elders, including certain hereditary officials, who constituted what has been described as the 'inner circle' of the Poro. This 'inner circle' was the executive council and tribunal of the society. It decided policy and was the court of final appeal when Poro was not in sesssion.[13] According to Matthews and Laing—the earlier writers already cited—there were certain offences which could not be tried even by the chief. These had to be taken before the Poro elders assembled secretly, preferably in the bush (*Chalmers Report, pt. ii, passim*). Among the Mano of Liberia, these senior grades wore masks and were regarded and treated as spirits. When these masked spirits came to town, the chief 'stood in a corner'. He had no jurisdiction over them, and they could be tried only by their peers. They could not be insulted or made the object of physical violence (Harley, 1941, p. 7).

(C) GRADES AND DIVISIONS WITHIN THE SOCIETY. Although there is insufficient evidence for close comparison with Liberia, the Poro inner circle among the Mende in Sierra Leone seems to have possessed somewhat similar powers. It was this body which decided on intervention in wars, which placed embargoes on trade and on farm work, and which decided when the society as a whole should be called into session. It was possible for the 'inner circle' to meet and plan Poro action without the ordinary members knowing anything about the matter. According to some writers, its executive role was facilitated by the organization of the society into three divisions, consisting respectively of men of chiefly rank, priests, and ordinary members (Harley, 1950, vii; Migeod, 1926; and Wallis, 1905). Each division had its own function in the activities of the society. For

---

[12] Vernon R. Dorjahn has provided a contemporary account of the initiation of Temne Poro officials (1961, pp. 1–5).

[13] There are a number of references to the Poro 'inner circle' in the literature, but Harley is the only author to attempt a detailed treatment of this complex but still obscure matter (1941 and 1950). Harley came to doubt if the pinnacle of power, represented by the inner circle, was *within* the Poro. He suggests that it was within the cult of the masks of which the Poro was the most highly developed form for manifesting the power of the ancestors toward the people (1950, vii).

example, chiefs served as judges; priests were in charge of the ceremonial affairs of the society and operated its medicines; and commoners acted mainly as messengers. Allocation to a particular division depended upon the person's position in the wider community or his membership of certain hereditary descent groups. He generally remained within the same division all his life, but could advance his status within it by taking further degrees. The marks on his body increased with the grading. Membership of a higher grade entitled him to be an office-bearer, and to take charge of the society's paraphernalia, including such things as drums, masks, initiation knives, etc. Among the Mano of Liberia, the scarifying operations were conducted by hereditary members of the priestly class (Harley, 1941, p. 8), and, as already mentioned, masks represented the spirits of former Poro members.

In the Poro of the Mende the less important spirits of the society, such as the *Ngafagoti,* the *Gobai,* and the *Yawei,* were impersonated by minor officials who also assisted with initiation. Other officials acted as the 'spirit's' interpreter, or served as his attendants. For example, the *Gbeni's* followers include a broomholder who sweeps the road in front of the spirit, drummers, a bugler, and a number of individuals beating sticks. Nowadays, they wear head ties, head-dresses of animal skin, and a head tie wrapped round the body in the form of a tunic; short trousers of country cloth are also worn. The *Gbeni's* own costume consists of cloth and leather. He wears a leopard skin, and carries medicines and glass accoutrement in addition to his wooden mask (Little, 1951, pp. 7 and 8). According to Cole, the Sherbro Poro had seven grades or degrees. The first was the *Bangan,* or the Entered Apprentice; the second the *Pornor,* or the Fellowcraft; the third, the *Lakka,* or the Herald; the fourth, the *Ba Kasey,* or Lawyer; the fifth, the *Famanja,* or Moderator; the sixth, the *Ngaygbana,* or Revenger; the seventh, the *Soekoe* (*Sopwaywee*), or Master-Mason. The Herald summoned the society; the duty of the Lawyer was to watch the movements of every member, particularly misdemeanours amounting to *kassi.* Members found guilty of the latter offence had their punishment mitigated by the Moderator. The Revenger stood in defence of the society, and it was the duty of the Master-Mason to establish new lodges as well as to judge cases and preside over the affairs of his own lodge (pp. 49–53).

(D) THE HEAD OF PORO. Among the Mano, a priest, or *zo,* belonging to a senior grade, though not the most senior grade, was head of each Poro chapter (Harley, 1941, p. 8). Westermann refers to this official as the Grand Master, and says that when appearing in public he wears a state dress consisting of wide-knee breeches, a narrow jacket with short sleeves, and a head-dress in the form of a cylindrical hat of metal plates, ornamented with the skull of a hornbill and trimmed with cowrie shells and white otter or monkey skin. On his forehead is a white bandage, round his neck a collar or skin ornamented with cowries, and hanging from the throat a medicine bag and other charms. In his hand he generally carries a horsetail or cowtail, sometimes hung with bells (op. cit., pp. 219–20). The head of Poro among the Mende is *Gbeima* (most senior), the Sherbro name being the *Taso*. The *Taso*'s head-dress consists of the plumes of feathers supported by a framework consisting of the thigh bones of his predecessors in office. His attendants carry turtle shells which they beat with a short stick to announce his coming, and to make the time for his dancing. The *Laka*, according to Hall, comes next in rank in the Poro of the Sherbro, and he carries a sword and shield (1938). The *Sowa*, who is second in rank in the Mende Poro, has charge of the bush school and officiates at most of the initiates' rites. According to one of Schwab's informants, a Poro man's standing is indicated by the marks on his breast. Seeing him, one knows at once how to shake his hand. Certain gestures also reveal a person's status in the society; perhaps the way he walks out of the house; always the way he sits down, crosses his legs, and folds his hands, or waves the cow's tail that he holds (Schwab, op. cit., pp. 266–78).

(E) WOMEN AS MEMBERS. Another important official is the *Mabole*, who, as already mentioned, is a woman. This office, according to tradition, derives from the first Poro spirit, the old man who was the legendary founder of the society. Before he was put to death he decreed that a woman should be co-opted in memory of his wife, who had his name. The *Mabole*'s principal duty is to act as matron to the young initiates during their course of training. She also takes the leading part in the final ceremonies, invoking the ancestral spirits on behalf of the initiates and pronouncing the society's blessing on them as they depart from the bush. She is held in the highest respect and, when the session is over, she takes charge of the spirit's pipe, and the razor used for marking the boys. The *Mabole* is the only woman to hold office in the Poro of the Mende, although women who suffer from barrenness may be initiated as a means of obtaining a cure. Any woman who becomes a paramount chief must also be initiated, but she remains a junior member (Little, 1951, pp. 245–6). There are also certain individuals known as *Sami*, who have a hereditary connexion with the society and who, irrespective of sex, must be initiated. The Poro of the Sherbro includes a somewhat similar custom whereby one woman of a certain 'family' (descent group) in which the right is hereditary, is initiated as a *deboi*, becoming technically a man. She goes into the bush with the initiates and performs a role similar to that of the *Mabole* among the Mende. It is also customary, in some parts of Sherbro, to initiate women who have seen a Poro candidate or learned a Poro secret. Such women are called by the Mende term *mamboi*. This means that, if married, their husbands have no case for 'woman damage' in the event of adultery (Hall, 1938).

(F) HAD THE PORO A SUPREME COUNCIL? Whether Poro possessed a centralized form of administration is a moot point. The earliest information about it is supplied by Winterbottom whose book, as already mentioned, was published in 1803. He speaks about the Bulloms of Sherbro having a head 'purra' man, who was assisted by a grand council. Its commands were received with the most profound reverence and absolute submission by the subordinate councils and by individuals. According to Butt-Thompson (1929, p. 71), the Bullom Poro council was headed by the Grand *Tasso*. It had twenty-five members consisting of the chief officers of the branches, or District *Tassos*. Fifteen of these members acted as the inner council, or court of appeal, and five as the executive. Butt-Thompson's reference is presumably to the Sherbro, but he does not indicate the source of his information. A number of other modern authors have apparently gained the same idea of the Poro's organization. For example, Migeod (1926), who visited Sierra Leone during the 1920's, speaks of Poro acting as the grand national council of the Mende, controlling the otherwise independent chiefdoms.

More convincing in this respect is the fact that Harley's comprehensive description of the inner workings of Poro leads to the same conclusion. He thinks that there was undoubtedly a wide network binding all the priests together under a supreme council. 'This was presided over by high officials selected by a kind of divine right from two or three families of supreme hereditary standing in the whole of Liberia.' Harley was given a definite clue to this effect from a member of one of these families, though he provides no detailed or supporting documentation (1950, vii).

Harley's reference is to an area where the Poro was probably more highly developed than anywhere else in West Africa. However, whilst not discounting the complexity of the Poro's administration, the present writer is doubtful if it generally involved the hierarchically ordered system of government thus pictured. When a European outsider is confronted by such widespread and co-ordinated activity as the Poro was undoubtedly able to organize, it is tempting to explain it in terms of a culturally familiar model. Having regard, however, to the virtual absence of first-hand information about what actually went on behind the scenes, such an explanation is bound to be somewhat conjectural. That the society as a whole was made up of a number of localized chapters or lodges is clear. It is also probable that there was inter-tribal communication, but to regard these local lodges as branches of a single unified organization is probably to exaggerate the extent to which the association as a whole was integrated.

There is, in fact, a much simpler and more plausible explanation of the Poro's capacity for action on a territorial scale, which will be readily understood if the function of initiation and of the bush school is recalled. The latter, as has been explained, had the effect of imbuing virtually the entire youth in the country with a sense of loyalty and duty towards the Poro order, and of teaching on a universal scale a similar set of habits and practices. As a result of his initiation, every new member learned not only to think and feel, but to act completely in concert with his fellow initiates, both near and far. When, therefore, the moment arrived for what might appropriately be termed general mobilization of Poro, there was no need for special administrative machinery, or for the issue of detailed instructions. Everything expected of the junior members, constituting the body of the movement, had already been rehearsed in the bush. This assumes, of course, that the particular purpose of Poro action was something that could be carried out along traditional lines, such as a piece of farm work, an ambush, or a raid. That Poro 'troops' were not trained to deal with novel or unaccustomed situations was demonstrated by the Mende Rising. This began as a grand and almost simultaneous assault, which took the British by surprise. Subsequent African operations, however, degenerated rapidly into mere plundering, and little attempt was made to follow up the initial advantage or to consolidate what had been gained. The latter pattern of behaviour was entirely consistent with indigenous methods of warfare, but it showed a complete lack of adaptation to the fresh situation created by the European organization of warfare as a sustained campaign.

(G) RELATIONSHIP BETWEEN PORO 'LODGES'. Examination of the method whereby the Mende Rising was set in motion does, in fact, throw a good deal of light on the wider organization of Poro, as well as on the point just made about its spontaneous mobilization. In this regard one of Sir David Chalmers's best informed witnesses was a Mr. Harris—a Creole merchant —who had carried on business for several years in the Sherbo and Sulima districts. Harris had been on intimate terms with the native people there, and had joined a 'porro' on one occasion. Though not professing to know anything about what he and other witnesses call the 'religious porro', i.e. initiation, Harris said that the 'civil porro'

is formed for any special purpose. For instance, if going to war they would form a porro in which the chiefs would compel all their people to join, and under oath would organise their raids. . . . I have seen several porros brought down from the interior. These have always been the forerunner of some new law they wished to promulgate in the district. They would have a visible symbol. (*Chalmers Report,* pt. ii, p. 488.)

After explaining Poro's practice of placing the whole country under oath through *ngo-yela,* Harris went on:

The head Chief is always at the head. . . . As a rule the porro is brought down to the head Chief of the country who forms a porro bush in his town, and he will then initiate the Chiefs of various districts under him, and they, as they call it, buy the porro bed from him and take it to their own town where they initiate the people. . . . Several Head Chiefs may combine in a porro—indeed very rarely is anything attempted by one man. There is always a tribe of several. . . . When several Head Chiefs resolved on a war they would meet and form their porro, then communicate with the Sub-Chiefs and spread it through the country. A one word porro would mean a one opinion. (ibid., p. 489.)

Our reading of Harris's statement is that the initiative was invariably taken by a high chief. After convening his own meeting of the 'inner circle' he would place the chiefs subordinate to him under Poro oath and they, in turn, would see that their people swore in similar fashion to carry out whatever objective had been decided on.

Augustus Cole, whose personal association with Poro has already been referred to, supplies further information about how instructions were passed on. In a letter to the Commission he explained that *ngo-yela,* which he terms, 'Go-yella', was something established by the chiefs. The place where it originates is called its birth-place. The name of that place is sacred, and is used as a password and as evidence that the person knowing that name is a member of the society. For example, 'Bompeh' was the pass-word used in the raid on Sherbro, Bumpe being the place where, presumably, the Rising originated. Every member of the 'inner circle' which originally determined the purpose of the oath swears in a similar group in his own home town, and the members of the latter group, in turn, pass word on to every place where they have a friend or a relative, and so on 'until the fire takes the whole country'. Cole also says that the society had its emissaries who travel about the country, keeping members mindful of their oath, and watching for the most favourable opportunity for implementing the plan. The reason for their sudden appearance in a town is known only to the initiated (*Chalmers Report,* pt. i, app. H, pp. 141–2). In his book Cole says that the signal for war, or rebellion, is made by the Lakka (herald) running desperately through the country, in his official dress; or, 'in moderate cases, he walks quietly around the country with his sword unsheathed' (p. 63).

Though neither Harris nor Cole described the general organization of the society, they both implied that all over the country there were local cells constituted of Poro's most senior local members, each in a position to mobilize its own lodge at quite short notice. The signal for such a meeting is the small branch of a tree, held by a messenger and carried around to the members, without saying a word. The number of small dry sticks tied to the branch signifies the number of nights before meeting. Pepper tied on it shows that the members are to appear with weapons and in readiness to defend or protect a member in difficulty, or to fight with somebody who is an enemy of the order (Cole, p. 62).[14]

---

[14] Many lodges use a tortoise-shell for calling Poro together. Any Poro man, hearing the sound of the tortoise-shell being beaten, has to go at once and attend the meeting (Warren, 1926).

Doubtless, it was quite a simple matter for these local 'inner circles' to maintain continuous contact with each other through messengers, and thus to keep themselves constantly informed of what was going on in other parts of the country. When matters of special importance arose requiring the determination of a common policy personal contact would be facilitated through the fact that Poro higher degrees hold good wherever a man might travel. A man of standing in the society could enter the Poro school and be immediately received according to his rank. The one in charge would put him through his paces, degree after degree, until one of the two dropped out (Harley, 1941, p. 7). (It is perhaps unnecessary to add that it is this aspect of Poro which most resembles the Freemasonry of Western society to which the Poro has frequently been likened.)

Gatherings of the top ranks of Poro, though of an *ad hoc* nature, might be likened, perhaps, to a 'supreme council' as referred to by Harley. As already implied, the oath taken by these senior officials would be even more binding than the one which they would administer, in turn, to their local lodges. The question of who took the initiative in convening such a meeting is, however, another matter. Possibly it largely depended on what was in view. So far as Poro organization for war is concerned, both Harris and Cole make it clear that it was the head of the chiefdom, more specifically the head chief, who took control of the entire situation. Harris also implies that a chief could use Poro to promulgate legislation, mentioning that (in Gallinas country) there was no longer a chief powerful enough 'to raise a porro' (*Chalmers Report,* pt. ii, pp. 488–9). Another of Chalmers's witnesses, a missionary from Tikonko,[15] reported that the Poro had largely been done away with in his neighbourhood, except for purposes of initiation. In answer to a question as to what class of persons are leaders of Poro, he said that the 'King' usually takes the chair, but he had latterly refused to enter the bush (ibid., pp. 66–67). All this seems to suggest that the Poro's political role and its capacity for widespread activity were largely a function of purely secular forms of government. However, as the question of the chief's relationship to Poro involves a much wider problem, it will be more convenient to deal with it later.

(H) THE 'PORO' AS A FUNCTION OF PORO. What does seem to be fairly clear about the society's organization is that there was no permanently existing Poro in the sense of a continuous round of activities involving every member or even officials and elders. Butt-Thompson states that meetings of the Poro council were never terminated in the formal sense, and he quotes a saying that 'society business never ends' (1929). This was probably true, as far as the Poro elders were concerned. Speaking col-

---

[15] A town in middle Mende country well known as a warlike centre in pre-colonial times.

loquially, they had a finger in every pie, and in addition to performing judicial functions they were doubtless consulted about every important happening in the local community. However, ordinary members were only called together as an assembly at indefinite times and for specific objectives. When these objectives had been gained the 'poro' broke up or dissolved (Warren, 1926). The initiation school for new members was no exception to this rule or principle. Nowadays, there is a tendency for the Poro to initiate almost as an annual event; but in former times its session appears to have been much less regular, probably because it lasted very much longer. In other words, there is a fairly clear, but subtle distinction to be made between the Poro as a society or general institution, and a 'poro' which is a gathering of Poro members called together for a specific purpose, hence the use of the small letter in the latter case.

This point needs to be emphasized because the habit of previous writers in referring to the 'religious' and the 'civil' Poro might seem to imply that two more or less separate institutions are involved. The so-called 'religious Poro', and the 'civil Poro' are, in fact, simply functions of the same organization which, as already indicated, was under the control of the senior men. According to the evidence of Mr. J. C. E. Parkes, Secretary for Native Affairs, at the time the Sierra Leone Protectorate was established, these functions included, in addition to the (religious) poro of initiation, the following 'political' and 'civil' poros: (a) the poro of prohibition by which a general rule was imposed, for instance that no palm fruits be cut for a certain time, or certain land occupied; (b) the peace poro, or poro of alliance, by which certain parties bind themselves to make peace; (c) the one-word poro, by which everyone who participates takes a secret oath for some particular object which may not be told to any outsider (*Chalmers Report*, pt. ii, p. 34).

## Part II

### The Relation of the Chief to the Poro

#### (a) Evidence of Poro Supremacy

In the concluding paragraphs of Part I of this article it was pointed out that in addition to its judicial functions the Poro society possessed some important powers of administration. On the other hand, there was also evidence to suggest that the society carried on this wide range of activities, amounting almost to government of the country, as an instrument of the chiefs.

Clearly, this raises a difficult problem, because far from describing the Poro as subordinate, most earlier writers seem to have regarded it as a law unto itself. According to them, it overrode all other forms of authority as well as being the principal means of arbitration. Nicholas Owen, for example, had a poor opinion of native methods of justice because a rich man could buy his way out of any crime. He added, however, that this was impossible when Poro was concerned with the case (p. 48). Matthews' account also illustrates the limited nature of the Sherbro chieftaincy. Although the executive power and final decision in all cases were vested in the 'king', yet every head, or principal man of a village, considered himself sole authority in his own 'town'. The 'king' had no power to issue orders without the council's consent; he could only entreat people to carry out his wishes. His family ranked no differently from any one else who had wealth, and there was very little competition for the royal office (pp. 77–79). As already noted, both Matthews (p. 83) and Winterbottom mentioned that witchcraft and murder were punishable by Poro; and according to the latter author, it also composed family feuds (p. 136). Laing's impression of the political power of Poro was similar. He adds that 'palavers of great weight', such as disputes between rival towns and capital offences are always settled by the society—'the headmen of towns not having, at the present . . . the lives of their subjects or dependents in keeping' (pp. 98–99).

Laing also points out that at stated periods Poro held conventions or assemblies, 'placing the country in the greatest state of confusion and alarm'. No public proclamation was made, but a communication from the head of the society by signs hung up announced the meeting. Chiefs, apparently, were completely without say in the matter. In fact, according to Laing, no chief or headman would dare to bring a palaver against a Poro man for fear of retribution, and his conclusion is that 'the purrah may be therefore said to possess the general government of the country' (pp. 98–99). In addition, there is also supporting evidence in the *Chalmers Report*. For example, Captain Carr, who was a District Commissioner at Bandajuma for two years before the Rising, gave it as his opinion that a chief's authority depended much on his character, and on the position he held in Poro (pt. ii, p. 13).

The limited amount of ethnographic information available about this particular matter also seems to support the historical data. Hall says that in former times Poro was practically supreme in the government of a chiefdom. Decisions affecting both its internal affairs and relations with other chiefdoms were made in the Poro council. The chief was a member of that council, but its authority could override him, and the Poro's ascendancy over the chief was also asserted at his installation through the institution known as *kungh* (1938). Harley's more detailed remarks are to a similar effect. He stresses that although the chief was the nominal centre of civil life, the real power lay in the hands of the Poro 'inner circle', who could act through the council of elders or even depose a chief. A chief could not declare war without their consent and that of the 'old women's cult' (1941, p. 7 and p. 31). Harley's own explanation of this paradox, developed in his later paper (1950, viii), is that indigenous government functioned at two levels, not mutually exclusive, but overlapping. The first, which might be termed the civil phase, was concerned with the management of the town and its citizens, common laws governing conduct, etc. It included what Harley terms the external organization of chiefs and minor officials. This was perfectly evident to casual observers, being known and understood by all members of the group, including women and children. On the second level, which may be thought of as religious, were the mechanisms for handling the crises and emergencies of life. 'It was in this second level of government, calculated to deal with the powerful, hidden, spiritual forces, that the (Poro) masks found their special place' (ibid.).

## (b)  Chiefs and High Chiefs in Traditional Society

Harley's suggestion explains, no doubt, the general division of authority between Poro and secular administration. However, it should also be noted that according to his own description of the Mano there was usually one chief in the community who was a peer of the Poro elders. 'He was something of a king and had power of life and death over his subjects provided he worked through the Poro, never against it' (1941, p. 7). Taken in conjunction with the references of Chalmers's witnesses to the 'high chief', as cited above, the latter observation seems significant. It raises a question that has not so far been considered—that of relative status and of the meaning attached to the term 'chief' in the political context of indigenous society as distinct from the form that it subsequently took in colonial times. Let us, therefore, examine this matter in the light of pre-colonial Sierra Leone.

When the Protectorate was originally organized little was known about the extent of local authority. The Government simply consolidated what they believed to be the existing political boundaries between the various rulers with whom treaties had already been signed or other forms of contract made. In a number of cases, persons were recognized as chiefs whose position and standing in the chiefdom concerned was of a very minor and subordinate character. The status of other native rulers was misrepresented or misunderstood through mistakes, deliberate or otherwise, on the part of interpreters; and, in some instances, too, the chiefly staff of office was awarded to individuals whose only claim to the territory concerned lay in the fact that they had managed to bring in House Tax for it. Again, in the early days, the Frontier Police virtually created chiefs out of persons, including women, who won their favour or were useful to them. Finally, in adopting what was believed to represent the native hierarchy, for administrative purposes, the Government limited itself to individual chiefdoms, putting all the native rulers whom they recognized as 'paramount chiefs' on the same footing (Little, 1951, pp. 176–7).

Needless to say, quite apart from the question of Poro, the indigenous system was much more complex than this. True, a number of individual chiefdoms existed, each relatively independent and under the control of its own chief, sub-chiefs, and headmen. But, according both to tradition and the earliest written accounts of conditions in the Guinea Coast, the underlying situation involved an intricate network of political ties and affiliations corresponding, in some ways, to quite large hegemonies or confederacies. The impression gained is that these arose out of the exigencies of tribal warfare, which seems to have been almost continuous in certain areas, prompting a constant need for military alliance and for protection on the part of weaker chiefdoms. For this reason, but also as a result of conquest, there was often a single chief, or 'high chief', whose general leadership over a group of chiefdoms was recognized by his neighbours. Each of the latter kept his own administration, but the arbitration of the high chief was accepted in important cases, including disputes between fellow members of the 'confederacy'. Fealty was displayed, sometimes, in the shape of periodical payments of tribute, and it might also involve the provision of military assistance, if the high chief were attacked. He, in return, would go to the aid of chiefs whose towns lay within his sphere of influence when war threatened them. The alliance was also symbolized by the periodical exchange of customary presents (Little, op. cit.; Kup, 1961, ch. iv).

In this connexion, Astley's eighteenth-century *Collection of Voyages and Travels* contains a passage from Barbot's description of Guinea, which, if the latter is to be trusted, points to another important prerogative of the high chief, namely, that of crowning each new chief who succeeded to office in the tributary state. This right probably derived from the original conquest of the chiefdom concerned, it being the custom of the victor to leave one of his warriors in charge. It was then the duty of this viceroy to 'look after the country' on his own chief's behalf. Alternatively, a weaker chiefdom might invite a well-known warrior from outside to serve as its leader. The fact that this political affiliation was continuously confirmed by the high chief's ceremonial right of coronation probably explains the following further complication in the system. It was quite possible for a tributary state situated geographically on the borders of the confederacy to undertake military conquests of its own. This would give rise to an additional pattern of overlordship, but without altering the original relationship of the chiefdom concerned to its own high chief. Finally, a tributary member of the second hegemony might, in its turn, carve out yet a further 'empire', while continuing fealty to its own overlord. It was also possible for a given people to pay homage to more than one high chief at the same time (vol. ii, 1745–7, pp. 529–42).

Evidence of the kind of hegemony described above was given to the Chalmers Commission. It was claimed, for example, that Chief Bai Forki had under him all the Temne, Loko, and Limba peoples living in the Port Loko District. In addition to seven sub-chiefs of his own, he had jurisdiction over the Alikarli of Port Loko to whom about a hundred villages belonged, all of them under headmen (*Chalmers Report*, pt. ii, p. 555). It is said that the same kind of paramount role was played by the chiefs of such towns as Panguma, Bumpe, Mongeri, and Tikonko. Conditions, however, were unstable and it is difficult, in any case, to describe the Sierra Leone situation in its indigenous form because political relations up-country were affected by Colony intervention long before the Government arrived to take actual control. For a clearer illustration of the traditional system we must return to the coast where, during the seventeenth century, tribal warfare, although stimulated by the Slave Trade, was carried on without interference by Europeans, except occasionally as participants.

## (c) The Kingdom of Quoja

In this regard Barbot says that all the local rulers between what is now the north bank of the Sierra Leone river and the western corner of Liberia were subject to the King of Quoja (Astley, op. cit., pp. 529–30). Quoja was situated about two days journey into the interior from Cape Mount, presumably in country belonging to the Vai people. This meant, in other words, that Quoja controlled the coastal part of the Sierra Leone peninsula, both banks of the Sierra Leone river, Sherbro, Krim, and Gallinas country. Towns in most of these places had viceroys appointed by the king of Quoja, although the office of king was hereditary in Burré before its subjugation. Burré (or Bureh) was a town on the south bank of the Sierra Leone river, about twenty miles from its mouth, which had some 600 adult male inhabitants (ibid., pp. 322–33). What is now Sherbro was known as Massaquoi, this being the name of its viceroy. The king of Quoja was a descendant of a Carow (Kru?) general, who had conquered that country in former times on behalf of a neighbouring people, the Folgians. For this reason Quoja itself paid homage to the Folgians who, in turn, were subject to the king of Manu, the head of a further hegemony.[16] The latter's tributaries paid homage to him in the shape of slaves, iron-bars, bugles, cloth, etc. In acknowledgement of their fealty he presented them with a gift of Qua-Qua[17] cloths. The same procedure was followed in relations between Folgia and Quoja, and between Quoja and her tributaries. The

---

[16] Johnston (1906) suggests that Quoja may have been the name of the dominant caste of the Vai at the time; that the Folgians may be people belonging to Gora stock; and that the king of Manu is possibly a Mandingo chieftain.

[17] Qua-Qua is an old name for the Ivory Coast.

people of Folgia called the subjects of the king of Manow by a term signifying 'lord', although the king of Folgia had complete jurisdiction over his
own towns and was entitled to make war or peace without the consent of
his overlord. Kings of Quoja were crowned by the king of Folgia and those
of Bulme Berre (Sierra Leone) by the king of Quoja. In the ceremony the
person to be crowned prostrated himself on the ground, earth was scattered
over his back, and he was asked what name he desired to take. The title
of 'king' and the name of his country were then added to it and proclaimed aloud. The new king was then told to rise, and a bow and quiver
of arrows were presented to him, signifying his duty as defender of the
country. He then did homage, giving his overlord a present of linen,
sheets, brass kettles, basins, etc. Another way in which the tributary king
showed respect was by allowing an envoy from his overlord certain privileges not permitted to other visitors (ibid., pp. 529–35 and pp. 538–40).

It is hardly necessary to repeat that under the warlike conditions obtaining, the system of political relationships just described was largely the
result of military factors. Fighting being on a limited scale, personal qualities of leadership, including audacity and skill in ambush, were more
important than the number of a man's followers or the ethnic and kin
relations between groups. It was quite possible, therefore, for a warrior
chief of resource, backed by a competent band of mercenaries, to win one
or two quick victories and thus to overawe a whole chiefdom within a
short space of time. To keep it permanently under control by military
methods alone was another matter. Should war break out afresh, his communications with the area affected were likely to be impeded not only by
forests and rivers, but by the presence of fortified towns on the route. He
had also to reckon on the possibility of treachery at home should he move
his personal bodyguard of trained warriors too far from the capital town.
Additional means, therefore, had to be found. They consisted partly in the
diplomatic and other measures described above. However, the extent to
which a puppet ruler could be used was obviously limited, and there was
the constant danger of a viceroy's authority being locally usurped, or of his
loyalty being weakened through intermarriage or his association with the
people under his charge. In other words, some sanction was necessary
which could operate more widely and more effectively than mere physical
force or even traditionally ingrained attitudes of allegiance.

*(d)  The Poro as an Instrument of Government*

It is possible that this sanction was supplied by the Poro. A belief in the
supernatural power of spirits and of medicine was common to all the
peoples of the region, and according to Dapper, the relationship of Belli—
the Vai version of the Poro society—to government was very close indeed.
We have already cited Quoja as an example of 'high chieftainship'. In that

country the king was head of the society and boys were collected by his orders for initiation. As already mentioned, the session of the Belli lasted from four to five years. The king himself stayed a few days in the camp, but he appointed elders to look after the training. Membership of Belli, according to the account in Astley (p. 541), was a qualification for various offices and appointments in the king's service, and it also conferred certain privileges denied to non-members who were known as Quolga—'Idiots'. The society investigated cases of murder, theft, and perjury, and had its own magical methods of trying such cases. It also dealt with infidelity in women. A woman accused of adultery had to swear to tell the truth on Belli medicine, and was threatened with the direst consequences if she did did not mend her ways. If she repeated the offence she was carried away by the officials of the society, disguised as spirits, to the sacred grove of Belli, and (presumably) put to death.

A further basis of the society's power over the people was a certain dough-like substance manufactured by its chief priest at the order of the king. It was supposedly capable of inflicting frightful punishment, but only with his consent (ibid., pp. 539, 542).

As explained earlier, it was also the king who gave the command for initiation. Given, therefore, as much control over Belli as the king of Quoja seemingly possessed, he would have a powerful instrument of government at his disposal.[18] There was the bait of preferment and special privileges to attract people in the tributary countries into the society and, once initiated, these groups would be under oath to do whatever the Belli, in effect, the king, commanded. In this way he would be able to organize a body of secret agents, already trained through Belli, to police the particular territory to which they belonged. These agents would keep the king continuously informed, in his role as head of the society, about what was going on and he would be able to use them, if the need arose, to stamp out disaffection or civil unrest.

Admittedly, these suggestions are somewhat conjectural so far as Quoja is concerned. Nevertheless, the employment of the Poro as a striking force under chiefly control seems to be fully vouched for and it could be employed to regulate economic affairs in the same way as it was used to mobilize the country for purposes of military aggression or defence. The method of bringing down a 'porro bed' in the latter connexion has also been described above and we are told that the Poro's 'police' was 'by no means contemptible' (Newton, p. 26). In other words, the suggestion is —following Hutton Webster—that with growing political centralization,

---

[18] According to Butt-Thompson (1929) Belli or Belli-Paaro, was founded by an old-time king of Gbandi, whose trained and disciplined bodyguard became its first members. The supreme grades of Belli were in close affiliation with the civil governments of their district, and its council formed a recognized court of justice. Unfortunately, Butt-Thompson does not particularize the source of his information.

the judicial and executive function of a secret society may be retained and its members as the personal agents of the ruling chief may constitute the effective police of the state (1908).

The latter kind of political adaptation involving the use of men's secret associations is known in other parts of West Africa. For example, in southern and western Yoruba kingdoms there were the Oro and Egungun cults whose members wore masks. As well as punishing witches and sorcerers in the name of supernatural powers, these cults were also used to threaten or even to make away with those who, while lacking a titled office, were by wealth or following in a position to challenge the instituted authorities (Morton-Williams, 1964, p. 256). It may also be noted that several important functions similar to those of Poro were performed by another Yoruba secret association, the Ogboni. Thus, since Ogboni members worship and control the sanctions of the Earth as a Spirit,[19] this cult was called in to judge the dispute and to perform rites of purification whenever human blood was shed upon the ground in a fight. In addition to this judicial and ritual function Ogboni is thought of by the Yoruba generally as supporting the power of the ruler[20] (Morton-Williams, 1960, pp. 362–74).

The comparative evidence does not permit us to say that in Sierra Leone the more powerful chiefs had the Poro directly under control. It may, however, help us to explain the unification of different districts which seemed to be, in many respects, independent of each other, and how it was possible for peace to be forced upon warring tribes by a third party. Matthews, writing in 1788 when indigenous methods of government were still in full swing, says:

When two tribes, or nations, are at war, and begin to be tired, or wish to put an end to it, but are too haughty and proud to make overtures to each other, they apply to the ruler of a neighbouring state for his interference as a mediator: if the offer be accepted, he immediately sends to the contending parties, to inform them he will act as umpire if they choose to refer their disputes to him: and that if they do not agree to terminate their differences amicably, he will no longer look on with indifference, and see those who ought to be friends destroy each other and depopulate their country (pp. 83–84).

It is therefore particularly pertinent to note, as we know historically, that the pacification of the Gallinas was completed by a a 'peace poro' inaugurated by Mendegra, an influential Mende chief. This was just a century later than the year in which Matthews wrote. The report of T. J.

---

[19] Note in this connexion Schwab's conclusion mentioned in Part I, page 263, that Poro is an elaborate modification of earth-mother worship.

[20] In Oyo, one of the leading officials of the cult there once said to Morton-Williams: 'Every Obo must have Ogboni so that the people may fear him' (op. cit., p. 364).

Alldridge, a Government Travelling Commissioner, shows clearly that Mendegra was in a position to use the Poro:

. . . I will here digress for a moment to offer an explanation as to how Chief Mendingrah could, while ruling the Goura country, situated as it is with the Barri and Toncha countries to the south, the Koya and Damah countries to the south-west, Jowveh-Mano and other places to the north, undertake such obligations as he did when he signed the treaty, until he had satisfied himself that he was certain of the co-operation of the rulers of those and of other countries which were in proximity to his own. After my first notifying Mendingrah on the 27th of last January that I would be glad to meet him at Bandasumah on the 15th of the following month, February, he had recourse to what is known in the country as a 'Porroh'. This being an ignorant, illiterate and superstitious country, and the Chiefs being unable to impart their wishes to one another in a written document, when anything of importance is undertaken in the country, and it becomes necessary, as in the present instance that the distant Chiefs should be notified of what is taking place, the Chief desiring to make such communication makes known his secrets to two or three of his most trusted headmen, who 'carry' them down to such places as may be necessary, and the 'Porroh men' selecting some very secluded spot in the bush near to a town there, in the utmost privacy, and under terrible fetich oaths, they administer the 'Porroh', i.e., they divulge the secrets to such persons as may be qualified to receive the 'Porroh'. Nothing of very great importance ever takes place in the country until a 'Porroh' has been sent down.

Chief Mendingrah did not arrive, as I have had the honour of stating, until the 11th of March. In this interval his Porroh was going about, and upon my reaching Bandasumah all of the Chiefs whom I met there had already accepted the 'Porroh' which, so far as I could learn, had reference to a permanent peace being maintained in the country. When passing through Juring on my returning from the interior, I met several Chiefs still engaged in this same Porroh. Now the town of Juring is over 90 miles distance from Chief Mendingrah's town of Juru, which will, I venture to think, show how an important Chieftain like Mendingrah is able to make known his laws, whether for good or for bad, over a very considerable area of country.[21] . . . (C.O. 806/325, p. 112).

The observations of Chalmers's witness, Mr. Harris, in a similar connexion have already been quoted (see Part I, pp. 273–274). We may therefore summarize the hypothesis that the more powerful chiefs had control of Poro, explaining at the same time the paradox created by the statements of earlier writers. The latter noted an apparent subordination of the civil ruler, but they may not have realized that a particular chief's pusillanimity was a function of his relationship with political authority higher than his own rather than of his relationship with Poro. In other words, the alleged supremacy of Poro—its ability to regulate the actions of a lesser chief, or headman—may have been a purely local phenomenon, constituting merely a segment of a wider system of government.

There is, of course, the alternative possibility that Poro domination did, in fact, exist, but was the result of social change in the shape of a general diminution of the chief's office. This kind of change actually occurred when

---

[21] Quoted by Christopher Fyfe, op. cit., pp. 247–8.

the Sierra Leone Government declared a Protectorate, because one of its first actions was to ban slave-dealing and to encourage 'legitimate' trade in its place. This, in removing one of the chief's main sources of wealth, made his followers less dependent upon him. His personal position and authority were additionally reduced by restrictions on the power of native courts which limited their jurisdiction to cases of minor importance as well as providing a right of appeal (Little, 1951, pp. 202–3). Also, as pointed out above, the Government completely ignored differences in status between individual chiefs and recognized other individuals who had no indigenous claim to the office. One of the consequences of this levelling down of authority and prestige was that chiefs were no longer able to control Poro. As Mr. Harris remarked, 'The power of the chiefs is entirely gone. . . . The war boys when once they get on foot, no one can stop them. . . . Now there are no chiefs who have power to stop them . . .' (*Chalmers Report*, pt. ii, p. 489).

*(e)  The Chieftainship and Poro as Complementary Institutions*

The implication of the latter remark is that political power was normally balanced between the Poro and the chieftainship. This is perhaps the best way of summing up the situation. In ordinary circumstances it was the prerogative of the society in any given political unit as main custodian of tribal tradition to watch the chief; to ensure that his actions as ruler conformed with customary practice. Among the Sherbro, as already mentioned, the Poro supervised his installation. When the new chief was chosen he was put into *kungh*, i.e. remained in seclusion, for some weeks, or longer in a building erected on the outskirts of the Poro bush. During this time he was under instruction and practically under the control of the elders, who were necessarily Poro men and included those who direct Poro affairs (Hall, 1938). In some Temne chiefdoms a chief who is not already a member of Poro must receive initiation and enter the bush, if only for a day. This is so that he may be taught the traditional lore underlying the country's way of life (Ture, 1939). In fact, in those Temne chiefdoms which have the Poro, a clear relationship exists between the chieftainship and the society. The Poro corresponds in this respect to the Ragbenle or Manyeke society of other areas, whose function is, among other things, to maintain the chief's authority. So close is this connexion that chiefs may be spoken of as Poro or as Ragbenle chiefs[22] (Thomas, 1916, pp. 143–4).

---

[22] In fact, in Temne country, the ceremonies connected with the installation of a paramount chief are conducted by one of four agencies: the *Ragbenle* society in the east, the Poro society in the south, the *Ramɛna* society in the central region, and by Moslem ceremonies in the north and west. Traditionally, Ragbenle installed chiefs in the southern chiefdom, but Poro took over these functions during the tribal wars of the eighteenth and nineteenth centuries. Vernon R. Dorjahn, 'The Organization and Functions of the Ragbenle society of the Temne', *Africa*, vol. xxix, no. 2, 1959.

Among the Mende, not only had questions of succession to the chief's office to be decided in Poro, but all important cases affecting the chiefdom at large had also, in theory, to be taken there.

The chief, on his part, was expected to hold the Poro in check, and to see that its officials did not take undue advantage of their special privileges by exploiting the people. He could, for example, withhold his permission when the society wished to initiate new members. A session which lasted for three years or more was a serious drain on the public wealth. Among the Mano, the Poro usually waited until the chief's son was old enough so that he could be the leader of his age-group (Harley, 1941, p. 8). The chief and other 'big men' were entitled to the labour of Poro initiates on their farms.

In general, therefore, the two institutions of chieftaincy and Poro complemented, rather than opposed, each other in the general management of the state. Harley's remarks about Liberia have already been quoted in this connexion (page 278) and it will suffice to offer one or two final examples from Sierra Leone. Thus, where mystical elements are lacking from the business of administration, as in the purely secular figure of the Mende chief, the Poro remedies this by appearing publicly at his coronation and funeral. The *Gbeni*, its principal and most sacred spirit, proceeds to the grave of the dead chief and bows over it. The same ritual is performed for all political figures, including sub-chiefs. Also, the chief, when dying, is taken to the Poro bush, where his body must be buried unless he is a stranger to the chiefdom. His death is subsequently announced from the roof of his house by an official (Little, 1951, pp. 184–5). Both Newland (1916) and Migeod (1926) suggest that any important Sherbro chief was accompanied on ceremonial occasions by the Taso, the head of the local Poro.[23]

Political control, then, was divided between the two institutions. Also, it was vested in the hands of relatively few individuals. Principally, there were the officials of the Poro, and there was the chief, who, as well as directing the civil affairs of the chiefdom, might also occupy a senior grade in the society. In these terms, positions of leadership were hereditary or could be achieved by ritual means. In addition, individual chiefs obtained

---

[23] Again, the functional parallel with Yoruba cult organization is very marked. Like the Poro, the priests of Ogboni play a part in the ceremonies following the death of a ruler and during the installation of his successor. In Oyo they are summoned to the palace as soon as the Alafin has died and they carry out a ritual dissection of the corpse. Also, as part of his installation the succeeding Alafin is taken to the Ogboni shrine were a rite is performed to enable his ears to discriminate between the true and the false and to give compelling power to his words. Nor can he be properly installed at all without the acceptance and collaboration of the Ogboni. Particularly in the case of Temne chiefs the ceremonies performed by both the Poro and its counterpart, Ragbenle, were very similar to these, and, as has already been mentioned, questions of succession had to be decided in the Poro Bush.

extra power through military success which they were able to retain because an interlocking organization of local Poro lodges cut across kinship lines and the local group. The latter organization kept the scale of political interaction potentially wider than that encompassed by a single chiefdom. It offered, despite continuous warfare and inter-chiefdom rivalry, a framework of relationships upon which political integration could proceed.

By these arrangements—to paraphrase Morton-Williams's analysis of the Yoruba state—there was produced a system of social control capable of working in a small community, or in one of several thousands, and adapted to a confederation of petty chiefdoms.[24]

## References Cited

ADDISON, W. 1937. 'The Wunde Society', *Man*, xxxvii. 3.

ASTLEY, THOMAS. 1745–7. *New General Collection of Voyages and Travels*, vol. ii. London.

BUTT-THOMPSON, F. W. 1929. *Secret Societies of West Africa*. London.

CHALMERS REPORT. 1899. Parts I and II (Parliamentary Papers).

C.O. 806/325. Report by T. J. Alldridge, of 12 May 1890, enclosed in Governor Hay's dispatch no. 248, of 6 June 1800. (From extract quoted in Fyfe, Christopher, 1964, *Sierra Leone Inheritance*.)

COLE, AUGUSTUS. 1866. *Secret Orders of West Africa*. London.

D'ALMADA, ANDRÉ ALVARES, 1841. *Tratado breve dos rios de Guiné do Cabo Verde*.

FERNANDES, VALENTIM. 1951. *Description de la Côte occidentale d'Afrique*, ed. Th. Monod, A. Teixeira da Mota, R. Mauny. Bissao.

GORVIE, MAX. 1945. *Our People of the Sierra Leone Protectorate*. London.

HALL, H. U. 1938. *The Sherbro*. London.

HARGREAVES, J. D. 1956. 'The Establishment of the Sierra Leone Protectorate', *Cambridge Historical Journal*, no. 1, vol. 2.

---

[24] Morton-Williams says: '. . . I will remind you of Hutton Webster's theory that the scale of a society limits the possibility of using the secret association as an effective agent of social control. It seems that the Yoruba have extended the use of this kind of social system so that it has at times been effective over a society of some millions of people. They limited the categories of social relationship under the control of one organization and, restricting the size of the membership in each, made the functions of each society overlap those of the others in any one town; by fictions of kinship they linked the leaders in every town with the leaders of the society in Oyo. In general, not all the men of one lineage were recruited into any one cult association, with the result that lineage solidarity was broken into, in the political sphere. The balance between the different associations could be arranged so that none became over-strong. The leaders of the different associations were combined into a central council, meeting often together and necessarily reaching (on the surface at least) unanimous agreement before their decisions appeared as "the will of the town" expressed by the single voice of the sacred king' ('The Egungun society in southwestern Yoruba kingdoms'. *W.A.I.S.E.R. Proceedings of Third Annual Conference*, March 1954, publ. 1956, pp. 102–3).

HARLEY, G. W. 1941. 'Notes on the Poro in Liberia', *Peabody Museum Papers*, no. 2, vol. 19.

———1950. 'Masks as Agents of Social Control', *Peabody Museum Papers*, no. 2.

HORNELL, J. 1928. 'The Tuntu Society of the Dema Chiefdom', *Sierra Leone Studies*, no. xiii.

JOHNSTON, SIR HARRY. 1906. *Liberia*, vol. i. London.

KINGSLEY, MARY. 1899. *West African Studies*. London.

KUP, A. P. 1961. *A History of Sierra Leone, 1400–1787*. Cambridge.

LAING, A. G. 1825. *Travels in the Timmanee, Kooranko, and Soolima Countries in Western Africa*. London.

LITTLE, K. L. 1948. 'The Poro as an Arbiter of Culture', *African Studies*, vii, 1, 1–15.

——— 1951. *The Mende of Sierra Leone*. London.

——— 1953. 'The Mende in Sierra Leone' in *African Worlds*, ed. Daryll Forde. London.

MATTHEWS, JOHN. 1788. *A Voyage to the River Sierra Leone*. London.

MIGEOD, F. W. H. 1916a. 'The Building of the Poro House', *Man*, 61.

——— 1916b. 'Mende Songs', *Man*, 112.

——— 1926. *A View of Sierra Leone*. London.

MORTON-WILLIAMS, PETER. 1960. 'The Yoruba Ogboni Cult in Oyo', *Africa*, vol. xxx, no. 4.

——— 1964. 'An outline of the Cosmology and Cult Organization of the Oyo Yoruba', *Africa*, vol. xxxiv, no. 3.

NEWLAND, H. O. 1916. *Sierra Leone: its Peoples, Products and Secret Societies*. London.

NEWTON, J. 1788. *Thoughts upon the African Slave Trade*. London.

OGILBY, J. 1696. *Africa, the Regions of Egypt, Barbary, Lybia and Billedulgerid*. London.

OWEN, NICHOLAS. 1935. *Journal of a Slave Dealer*, ed. Martin, E. C. London.

RANKIN, F. HARRISON. 1836. *The White Man's Grave*, vol. i. London.

SCHLENKER, C. F. 1861. *Temne Translations and Vocabulary*. London.

SCHWAB, GEORGE. 1947. 'Tribes of the Liberian Hinterland', *Peabody Museum Papers*, vol. xxxi.

SIBLEY, J. L., and WESTERMANN, D. 1928. *Liberia—Old and New*. London.

SIERRA LEONE. 1956. Report of Commission of Inquiry into the Disturbances in the Provinces, November 1955 to March 1956.

THOMAS, N. W. 1916. *Anthropological Report on Sierra Leone*, vols. ii and iii. London.

TURE, A. B. 1939. 'Customs and Ceremonies attending the Selection and Crowning of a Bombali Temne Chief', *Sierra Leone Studies*, no. xxii.

VIVIAN, WILLIAM. 1896. 'A Visit to Mendeland', *Journal of the Manchester Geographical Society*.

WARREN, H. C. 1926. 'Secret Societies', *Sierra Leone Studies*, vol. v, no. 2.

WEBSTER, HUTTON. 1932. *Primitive Secret Societies*. New York.

WESTERMANN, D. 1921. *Die Kpelle*. Göttingen and Leipzig.

WINTERBOTTOM, THOMAS. 1804. *Account of the Native Africans of Sierra Leone*, 2 vols. London.

# Sacred Kingship and Government among the Yoruba

# P. C. Lloyd

Interest in African sacred kingship has for long been centred upon its ritual aspects; descriptions of highly colourful ceremonies have provided a convenient introduction to the study of a people's religious beliefs, yielding also examples of the ritual sanctions by which the ruler enforces obedience. As a result the constitutional aspects of kingship have been largely ignored.

Among the best-known West African examples of sacred kings are the oba (ɔba) of the Yoruba kingdoms of Western Nigeria. Though little has so far been published about the rituals of the kingship itself, much material exists on Yoruba religion with its pantheon of deities and cults which rivals that of ancient Greece.[1] But the constitutional relationship between the oba and his chiefs has not been discussed. This is probably because, in a century of such rapid change, the traditional relationship is thought to exist no longer. As a result of continuous tribal wars and the spread of Islam in the nineteenth century and the colonial administration of the twentieth century, the obas are no longer hidden within their palaces, appearing to their people only on a few ceremonial occasions; they have become popular figures and often highly autocratic rulers. The roles of the chiefs too have changed; many of them, whose functions were in the past ritual or of specialized executive importance, have tended to rank themselves with those chiefs whose role is primarily legislative, the incentive usually being a seat on the Native Authority or Local Government council.

It is thus often difficult to elucidate, from the day-to-day meetings of obas and their chiefs, the traditional principles of constitutional law which have governed their behaviour. But these laws do still become apparent today

---

[1] R. E. Dennett, *Nigerian Studies*, 1910; J. O. Lucas, *Religion of the Yorubas*, 1948; G. Parrinder has outlined the sacred attributes of Yoruba kingship in *West African Religion*, 1949, pp. 211 ff., *African Traditional Religion*, 1954, ch. vi, and in 'Divine Kingship in West Africa', *Numen*, vol. iii, 1956, pp. 111–21.

in the conflicts which occur over the installation of a new ruler or in the attempts to depose an unpopular one, the traditional role of the oba being contrasted here with the modern autocratic roles which he has tended to assume. By 'traditional role' I mean, in this context, the role which he is held by his chiefs and people to have performed traditionally, and which he ought therefore to perform today. I do not wish to suggest that there ever existed, in Yoruba history, an idyllic period when obas performed exactly the roles expected of them, though in periods of less violent change the deviations from the ideal role would tend to be less striking. I do consider, however, that the ideal traditional roles described today are probably little different from those operative a century ago. Contemporary documentary evidence on this point is scarce, but it does not contradict this assumption.

The constitutional aspects of the oba in one kingdom—that of Ado Ekiti—will be described here. Between the many Yoruba kingdoms there are striking differences in social and political structure; among the northern Yoruba the patrilineage is the dominant social group, among the southern Yoruba (Ijebu and Ondo) it is the cognatic descent group.[2] In some areas chiefs are selected by and from among lineage members; in others appointment to a grade rests, basically, with the existing members of the grade.[3] Yet throughout Yoruba country the rituals of kingship and the constitutional roles of the obas tend to form a common pattern. In analysing Ado Ekiti I have consciously stressed those points which I know to be applicable to the numerous other kingdoms in which I have worked. There are, of course, some kingdoms to which these generalizations do not apply in their entirety—e.g. Ibadan, technically not a kingdom at all, has no royal lineage, the Olubadan, the most senior chief, having been promoted from the lowest hierarchies of chieftaincy on the deaths of those ranked above him; Abeokuta, also founded in the 1830's, where the people of the numerous Egba townships (140 is the number often cited) struggle with the problems of federal government; and Iwo, where the rapid influx of refugees from the nineteenth-century wars (Iwo's population is now 100,000), the consequent territorial expansion of the kingdom, and the fifty-year reign of a single oba have somehow resulted in the assumption of considerable political power by the descendants of this one ruler.

---

[2] For a more detailed description of the variations in Yoruba social structure see my article 'Some Notes on Yoruba Rules of Succession and on Family Property', *Journal of African Law*, vol. iii, 1959, pp. 7–32.

[3] These differences are elaborated in my article 'The Traditional Political System of the Yoruba', *Southwestern Journal of Anthropology*, vol. x, 1954, pp. 366–84.

## The Origin of Sacred Kingship

Sacred kingship is, among the Yoruba, an ancient institution. We do not know how or when it was introduced to this part of Nigeria, though we suspect that it was more than a thousand years ago. We presume that the Yoruba peoples are descended from several waves of migrants moving from the savanna into the forest. Yet the Yoruba today see themselves as a homogeneous people; each town, as we shall see below, has its own royal and non-royal descent groups but there is among the Yoruba no ruling clan or aristocratic group, such as the Fulani of the emirates of Northern Nigeria.[4] It is not difficult to accept that, with polygyny on the scale prac- tised by Yoruba rulers and chiefs and with a considerable internal move- ment of population consequent upon struggles for titled office in the numerous kingdoms, any ethnical differences between the indigenous people and a more powerful incoming group—whether this power be the result of superior numbers or techniques—would be occluded within a relatively short period.

In the nineteenth century the Yoruba kingdoms were independent of one another and the people remember no period, besides that subsumed in the origin myths, when all Yoruba formed a single political unit. The term Yoruba was applied originally not, as it is widely used today, to the whole people, but only to the Oyo;[5] in some areas the word *anago* was used by the Yoruba to describe the common language, and this term has been adopted in Dahomey as a name for the people. But it seems that the Yoruba of the early nineteenth century and before knew themselves as Ifes, Ijeshas, Oyos, &c., after the designations of their kingdoms and had no word to describe themselves collectively.

Yet the origin myths, known to all Yoruba, do provide the concept of unity; into these tribal myths the people of each kingdom fit their own important ancestors. The myths fall basically into two groups—those telling of the creation of the world and those describing conquest. Typical of the former is one which tells how Olorun (lit. owner of the sky), the high god to whom sacrifices are not made, let from the sky a chain down which climbed Oduduwa carrying a cock, a handful of earth, and a palm nut: Oduduwa threw the earth on to the waters, the cock scratched it and it became land, and the nut, when planted, grew to a palm tree with sixteen branches, symbolizing the sixteen original crowned rulers. The conquest

---

[4] The Fulani political system is described by M. G. Smith, 'The Hausa System of Social Status', *Africa*, xxix, 1959, pp. 239–52.

[5] Ekiti, for instance, still on occasion use the term Yoruba to designate the Oyo people. In this paper I shall use the term to embrace all Yoruba-speaking peoples.

myth tells of Oduduwa coming from the east and settling at (a presumably uninhabited) Ile Ife—the centre of the world according to the creation myth—where he had seven grandchildren, the youngest of whom was Oranyan who founded the present ruling dynasties of Oyo and Benin.[6]

Oduduwa is conceived in these myths as the father of the original crowned rulers. Ile Ife is pictured as a city which became so burdened with royal princes that on a certain day Oduduwa dispatched them all into the forests and savanna to found their own kingdoms. Yet all Yoruba today think of themselves as the descendants of Oduduwa.[7] The present Alafin is the fiftieth in succession to Oranyan, and the Oba of Benin the thirty-eighth in succession to Eweka, the son of Oranyan by a local woman. There seem, however, to be no myths telling of the character of Oduduwa or of the nature of his reign, to provide a model of the ideal roles of the oba.

A detailed analysis of these myths and their variants would perhaps contribute towards a clearer understanding of Yoruba pre-history. With our present knowledge only the vaguest hypotheses are possible. My own is that immigrants travelling from the Benue valley first brought sacred kingship to Ife, together with such arts as yam cultivation and perhaps iron working. Then, perhaps in the thirteenth century, Ile Ife and its dependent kingdoms were conquered by a small ruling group, with which is associated the cult hero Oranyan, which came from the area of the Middle Niger, perhaps near Bussa, and established the kingdoms of Oyo and Benin.[8]

In the succeeding centuries Oyo and Benin grew to become large empires which, at the heights of their power, were contiguous in northern Ekiti; but at other periods of weak central authority the small kingdoms on their peripheries were practically independent. Between Oyo and Benin lay a zone of such small kingdoms, some of ancient foundation and others of more recent creation by rebel princes and chiefs from the great empires. There would seem to have been no marked immigration into Yoruba-Benin country since the thirteenth century.

### The Origins of Ado Ekiti

The origin myth of Ado tells how the Ewi (the title of the oba of Ado) was a junior brother of the Oba of Benin (and thus a son of Oduduwa) who followed that oba to Benin when the princes of Oduduwa dispersed from

---

[6] A fuller account of the conquest myth is given by S. Johnson, *History of the Yorubas*, 1921, pp. 3 ff., 15.

[7] The Yoruba cultural association is known as *Egbe Ɔmɔ Oduduwa*—the society of the children of Oduduwa.

[8] Similar outlines of the early history of Western Nigeria are given by S. O. Biobaku, *The Lugard Lectures, 1955*, Federal Information Service, Lagos.

Ile Ife; here the brothers quarrelled and the Ewi retraced his steps, halting at Idoani before reaching Ado, where a small indigenous group accepted him as their oba on account of his royal birth.[9] The myth tells in detail of the Ewi's route to Ado, details which are today commemorated at rituals performed at shrines along the route.[10] Subsequent to the arrival of the Ewi other groups of migrants settled in the town, founding their own lineages; each of these has its own myths of origin described below.

Myths current in Ado, but not forming part of the 'official history', suggest the previous existence in the Ado area of a number of small settlements. Those no longer exist, the villages having been destroyed (or abandoned) and their people absorbed into the lineages of Ado town. One occasionally meets a sole survivor who insists that a certain name represents not merely the name of a geographical feature but of a lineage and its village.

## The Structure of Ado

Ado is a compact town of 25,000 people, almost the largest settlement in Ekiti Division. It is anomalous, however, in that it consists of three distinct but adjacent settlements—Oke Ewi (population approx. 16,000), Odo Ado (approx. 7,000), and Oke Ila (approx. 1,500). Each of these has its own chieftaincy system but the Ewi, whose palace lies in Oke Ewi, is oba of all three settlements; Odo Ado and Oke Ila, unlike the subordinate towns of the kingdom, have no ruler of their own; their chiefs, however, have no right to appoint or depose the Ewi.[11] In the following paragraphs I therefore refer to Oke Ewi alone.

The palace, a walled area covering some 15 acres, lies in the centre of Oke Ewi. Around a large courtyard live the royal servants and migrant Hausa. In a series of small courtyards at one corner the Ewi used to meet his chiefs, and in the innermost one he lived. The present Ewi, an educated ruler, has built an imposing modern house behind the traditional structure.

---

[9] The Idoani myths state that their own founder-oba, the Alaini, was a Benin prince sent to rule a border town of the empire, and that the first Ewi was an Idoani prince who fought for the throne, and, losing, emigrated. Other myths told in Ado suggest that the first Ewi gained secular power in the town by intervening in the title disputes of the indigenous people, so overcoming first one faction and then another.

[10] In most Yoruba towns the first ruler of the dynasty is said to have 'founded' the town—a small group of indigenes accepting his rule. In other cases, Ijebu Ode for instance, the ruler arrived in a sizeable town, and here the myths ascribe the acceptance of his rule primarily to his royal birth and descent from Oduduwa.

[11] The most senior ranking *Ihare* chiefs—the Odofin of Odo Ado and the Alarierin of Oke Ila—are rather more important than their opposite number—the Odogun of Oke Ewi; meetings of the chiefs of their respective settlements are regularly held in their houses.

In front of the palace lies the town's principal market, and beyond this is a quarter in which lived the royal slaves. Close to the palace are the compounds of descendants of the past Ewis; beyond these, in a circle around the palace, are the large compounds of the other lineages of the town.

SOCIAL STRUCTURE. The royal lineage (*idile ɔba*) comprises all those persons who trace their descent in the male line from the first Ewi, who is held to be the founder of Ado. Structurally the royal lineage differs from others in the town; its peculiarities are described in more detail in a later section.

In Ado, as in every Yoruba town, the king-lists give the name of every oba believed to have ascended the throne; at ceremonies the drummers describe the characteristics of the reigns of each oba. The present Ewi is the twenty-first in succession to the founder of the town. There seems to be no evidence that Yoruba obas were ever killed, or 'asked to die', at the end of a reign of seven or fourteen years. It is difficult to calculate the average length of a reign, but we might ascribe the foundation of Ado to the seventeenth century. Most persons claiming membership of the royal lineage and thus describing themselves as *ɔmɔ ɔba* (children of the oba), and using the appellations of the royal lineage—*ɔba* (m), *ɔja* (f.)—seem to trace descent from recent rulers. In Oke Ewi and Odo Ado are compounds whose male members claim descent from an early Ewi, but these people do not describe themselves as *ɔmɔ ɔba* and these segments, as we may term them, function to a large degree as if they were independent lineages.

There is no term used in Ado (or in most other Yoruba towns) which collectively describes the non-royal lineages; each is merely an *ɛbi* or *idile*.[12] In Oke Ewi are twenty-four lineages, each with its own compound. Each has its myths of origin: in some cases it is said that the lineage founder 'came with the Ewi', for such an origin confers prestige on lineage members as it establishes the antiquity of the group; in other cases the lineage founder is said to have fought for an oba's title in a far kingdom and, losing the contest to a junior brother, to have emigrated to Ado. The myths describe how the lineage came to worship its own particular deity and relate the origin of the lineage's members' distinctive appellations. They describe too how the reigning Ewi gave the immigrant land in the town for his compound and beyond it for his farms, and bestowed on him an hereditary chieftaincy title to recompense him for the one he failed to win in his home town. Thus the lineage is a corporate group, its male members living together and having common rights to land and chieftaincy titles. Elderly men conceive their town as composed of lineages little

---

[12] I have described the structure of the patrilineage at greater length in 'The Yoruba Lineage', *Africa*, 3, xxv, 1955, pp. 235–51.

dependent one on the other, but each dependent individually on the oba. Though tracing their origin from the home town of their founder, they make no attempt to trace genealogically their ultimate descent from Oduduwa.

Most Ado lineages seem to have been founded by men coming from kingdoms east of Ado and particularly those in the Akoko District of Owo Division. Oke Ewi provides no example of a lineage founded by a son of a ruler, such as the Oni of Ife or Alafin of Oyo, through whom ascent can, of course, be traced to Oduduwa. Such an origin does confer prestige on lineage members, though it is but one of many factors, such as lineage size or titles held. Where it does occur, a royal origin of this nature gives the lineage no special political rights.

In the non-royal lineages no attempt is made to remember the names of all those men who have held the lineage's hereditary chieftaincy title; only holders in the past century can be named, together with one or two earlier heroes. The genealogy as presented is foreshortened, so that the founder is placed four or five generations above the living elders. The two, three, four, or five sons of the founder are themselves founders of the constituent segments of the lineage. These segments function as corporate groups; sometimes they hold usufructory rights to homogeneous blocks of farm land; the hereditary chieftaincy title should be held by a member of each segment in turn. There is evidence that small segments tend over the years to unite while larger ones split into two, for one of the main purposes of segmentation seems to be to enable every member of the lineage to be eligible for the chieftaincy title at some period of his life; as the segments are more nearly equal in size, so is every member of the lineage given an equal chance of achieving the title.

POLITICAL STRUCTURE. The Ewi is king of Ado, a sacred king. He is the direct descendant of the first ruler of the dynasty, said to be the founder of Ado. It is this descent from the founder of the town which validates the rule of the Yoruba oba; it is not sufficient to trace descent from Oduduwa, for every Yoruba claims such an origin. But while it is not relevant that members of non-royal lineages should so trace their ancestry, it is obligatory that an oba should be able to show how he is descended directly from Oduduwa; only when such descent is shown may the oba validly assume the beaded crown and other symbols of royalty.[13]

There are three grades of chiefs *(oloye)* in Oke Ewi. Most senior are the *Ihare* chiefs; the *Olori Marun* (lit. five heads) rank highest in this group—

---

[13] In some recent instances, where an oba has granted the ruler of a subordinate town the right to wear a beaded crown, local historians have disagreed on the 'official' myth—some holding that the founder of the subordinate town came direct from Ile Ife while others argue that he was a son of a past oba of the metropolitan town.

these five titles are hereditary within the five largest lineages (large, perhaps, because they hold such a title). Below these are the junior *Iharɛ*, grouped as the *Elesi* (five chiefs) and the *Ijɛgbɛ* (ten chiefs). Some of these titles are hereditary within the smaller lineages while others are filled by appointment by the oba and senior *Iharɛ* chiefs. The second grade is of *Ijoye*, a group of at least twenty-two chiefs (though most titles are today vacant); only the most senior title in the group is hereditary within a lineage. The third grade is the *Elɛgbɛ*; again most titles are now vacant, though in the past it would seem that each lineage had two or more *Elɛgbɛ*. The most senior title is hereditary and some other titles are reserved for members of the royal lineage. In Oke Ewi, as in other Ekiti towns, the chieftaincy titles seem to be as equitably distributed among the non-royal lineages as their number will allow.

Titles which are hereditary within a lineage are the corporate property of all lineage members. On the death of a chief the lineage meets to elect a successor. The title should pass in rotation to each segment, though this is rarely followed strictly; a title can never pass directly from a man to his own son. The lineage is guided in its choice by the pronouncements of the *ifa* oracle. The oba and other chiefs may not interfere in such an election, save only to ensure that it is fairly conducted. The oba should accept the selection of the lineage and perform the ceremonies installing the new chief. Lineage meetings are presided over by the oldest man (*olori ɛbi*) and in these meetings the chief is ranked according to his age. His office as chief gives him such prestige in the lineage that he is often regarded as the head of the lineage.

In selecting men to hold those chieftaincy titles which are not hereditary, the *Iharɛ* chiefs have a determining if not final voice. Since no *Iharɛ or ijoye* titles may be held by members of the royal lineage, it will be appreciated that the chiefs are the elected representatives of the non-royal lineages in the Yoruba town.

The functions of these grades of chiefs are described in later sections.

## The Appointment and Installation of the Oba

The right to the throne is held by the members of the royal lineage—that is by those persons who can trace patrilineal descent from the first Ewi. The mode of succession of the early Ewis is not clear. Today the royal lineage is divided into two segments, named after rulers of the mid-nineteenth century, and the oba is selected alternately from these segments. Not all male members of a segment are eligible as candidates for the throne. Firstly, only a son born to an oba while on the throne—excepting the first such son —is eligible. (In Ado the eldest son born on the throne is allowed considerable licence in his behaviour.) Secondly, the son must have been born to a free woman and not to a slave. Thirdly, he must be free from physical blemish; in a recent instance one man was rejected as being too tall—he would have looked down on his people!

After the death and burial of an oba the elder members of the royal lineage present the *Ihare* chiefs with a list of those candidates whom they consider eligible and suitable—they do not necessarily put forward *every* eligible candidate. The chiefs consider the merits of each candidate and were, in the past, guided to a considerable degree by the pronouncements of the *ifa* oracle upon the length and prosperity of the reign of each candidate should he be chosen. Public discussion was limited (though today it is not so), for the mass of the people felt that the duty of selecting the oba lay with the chiefs alone; nevertheless, the chiefs would of course be guided by any strong popular feelings about a candidate. The senior *Ihare* chiefs, the *Olori Marun,* make the final choice of the new oba and put in train the installation ceremonies. These are long and complex but they tend to follow a similar pattern throughout the Yoruba kingdoms.

It is presumed that the Ewi elect will be most reluctant to assume office; he is therefore 'captured' by the *ɛfa* (town police) while hiding in his house. These men take him into the bush and tell him how he should rule the town. The new oba then traces much of the route traditionally taken by the first Ewi, performing ceremonies at shrines along the route and eventually reaching Ado where, in the compound of the lineage of the indigenous inhabitants, he renews his ancestor's promise to govern well. Here too he is clad in rags and beaten; he then assumes a white cloth and announces his new name in a rite which symbolizes his rebirth as oba.

Most Yoruba are today reluctant to admit that the custom of eating the excised heart of the late oba was practised in their own town; it was, however, probably universal throughout Yoruba country. It constituted the most important of the rituals by which the new oba became a consecrated ruler. All the sacred powers of preceding obas (and ultimately those of Oduduwa) thus pass to the new ruler. İt is believed by the Yoruba that a man who performed these rites, if not eligible by descent for the throne, would die. Conversely, an eligible ruler who omitted the rites would not be able to withstand the magic potency of the charms incorporated within the royal regalia and he too would die. Consecration gives to the oba the wisdom to rule well; his rule is good because he is consecrated.[14]

For three months after these ceremonies the oba lives in the compound of one of the chiefs—in Ado that of the Arowa, an *Ijɛgbɛ* chief, whose compound is opposite the palace entrance. Here he is visited daily by his

---

[14] It was widely believed that the late Awujale of Ijebu was not duly consecrated at his installation because the last consecrated oba was still alive in exile; in addition his eligibility for the throne was dubious. His reign was marked by a succession of political crises disturbing the peace of the town and his people were apt to murmur 'But what can we expect when we do not have a proper oba?'

chiefs, who instruct him in the arts of government and in the history of the town. Then he enters his palace, a point at which he used in the past to lose all informal personal contact with his chiefs and people, save only those whose titles conferred the right to enter his personal apartments.

The ceremonies of installation and burial of the oba provide duties for each chief and non-royal lineage of Oke Ewi and for the members of each subordinate town in the kingdom. These duties are jealously preserved by their holders; they symbolize the participation of each lineage in the government of the town.

The sacred character of the oba is expressed in numerous customs. He does not 'die' but 'goes away'. He may not be seen eating and his food was, at least until the nineteen twenties in Ado, prepared by royal wives working naked. His bare foot should not touch the ground. He may take any woman as wife and a royal wife (olori) may not be seduced by any other man: the penalty was death for both parties. All royal wives passed to the successor to the throne and not to the kin of a deceased oba. But the health of an oba is not held to affect the prosperity of the town—the failing ruler was not put to death. Nor does he perform ritual sexual intercourse to promote crop fertility.

The oba formerly appeared to his people on very few occasions and on these he was barely visible as a person. Surrounded by trumpeters, umbrella carriers and the like, he sat clad in voluminous gowns (in Ado sometimes made of coral) and veiled by a conical beaded crown. But he is not a priest, though he is the ritual head of the town. As elsewhere, the town ceremonies of Ado seem to fulfil two purposes—the blessing of the oba, as representative of the town, by its deities and the oba's conveyance of these blessings to his people in return for their homage. In Ado the cycle of ceremonies begins with *Etado,* when the priests of the spirits living in the hill overlooking the town dance before the Ewi; this is followed by three ceremonies at which the three grades of chiefs—the *Elεgbε* first and finally the *Iharε*—dance before him and prostrate to him to receive his blessing.

## The Wealth of the Oba

As the oba is the personification of his town, his wealth—reflected in the magnificence of his palace and his regalia—establishes the prosperity and rank of the town among its neighbours. The Yoruba despise as backward those neighbouring peoples without institutions of kingship.

Under traditional law the oba brought little to the throne with him; his house and farms were taken over by his immediate kin. But everything which came to him while on the throne belonged to the throne. The maintenance of the palace demanded a considerable income. The palace was built by the people and compulsory labour was due on the royal farms; on these farms the palace slaves also worked. Annual tithes, usually in the form of crops, were paid through the chiefs at festivals; special levies might be ordered in addition. Tolls were levied on all produce entering the town. One-third of all war booty was handed over to the oba, and a further third to the chief under whose jurisdiction the captor lived. Death duties were exacted on the estates of wealthy men. Part of the fines levied by the oba and chiefs, sitting as the highest judicial court, passed to him, as did part of the fees paid by a new chief before his installation. The greater part of the income of the oba was collected by the chiefs, who kept a share as their own perquisite; in general, however, the share of the oba tended to equal that of all the chiefs together. The wealth accumulated by an oba passed, at this death, entirely to his successor in office. But the wealth of a powerful chief passed to his sons and near kin, following the normal rules of succession to property; since each chief would have many sons, his estate was divided into small lots and the power which such wealth represented was broken; it was thus almost impossible for the oba to be rivalled in wealth by one of his senior chiefs.

### The Sacred Ruler, Democratically Elected

The ceremonies of installation and burial of the sacred Yoruba oba, together with the sanctity of his person, are attributes similar to those described for the so-termed divine kings of other parts of Africa. But as the previous section demonstrates, an oba is chosen by the chiefs who are the representatives of the non-royal lineages of the town. We thus have the apparent dichotomy of a sacred ruler who is democratically elected. The Yoruba themselves see nothing untoward in this, for while they hold their rulers in great reverence they are quite ready to add that he 'belongs to the people' and can be removed if he becomes unpopular.

It has been suggested that sacred kingship of this type is associated with a lineage structure in which the lineages, or the small territorial units which their villages form, are virtually politically independent; the king unites these groups in rituals but does not constitute a centralized form of government.[15] The lineage structure of Ado would seem to support the first part of this hypothesis; but in other Yoruba kingdoms the chiefs are not elected by the descent groups (though the members of a group may co-operate in seeking that a non-hereditary title be bestowed on one of their members, and having won such an honour seek to retain it thereafter). It is also difficult to conceive the oba merely as the overall ritual head of a number

---

[15] Cf. E. E. Evans-Pritchard in *The Divine Kingship of the Shilluk of the Nilotic Sudan*, 1948.

of independent lineages, for the government of the Yoruba town is highly complex and centralized, and the oba is at its apex.


## The Government of the Town

The oba is the personification of his town. 'Without the oba the town would cease to exist', say the Yoruba; the implication is that without the kingship peace could not be maintained between the descent groups composing the town. 'When we . . . try . . . to dispense with the position of king we immediately find the town with people concerned thrown into confusion; we find lawlessness and general disorder.'[16]

The Yoruba say that the new ruler jɛ ɔba (becomes, or eats the oba), the term ijɔba connotes government—the Yoruba used to refer to ijɔba gɛsi—the British or Colonial government—but it also connotes a reign. The phrase 'the king governs' can only be rendered ɔba j'ɔba or ɔba ʃe ijɔba (the oba does the work of the oba). Distinctions between 'govern' and 'reign' are not possible in Yoruba except, of course, through long explanation. The oba is said to 'take care of the town' (ʃe tɔju ilu), 'to exercise restraint upon the town' (sakoso ilu). Under a good oba the town is said to be 'improved' (tunʃe—connoting to renew, improve); under a bad oba the town is 'spoilt' (bajɛ—to spoil, corrupt, defile, or destroy).

The government, of which the oba is the head, is sovereign; it is concerned with the public affairs of the townspeople. Nothing is theoretically outside its competence, though it is little concerned with those actions of individuals or small groups which do not affect other groups. There is in Ado, as elsewhere, the distinction between the rights of the government or oba and those of the individual which it is the duty of the government to protect. But an analogy of federal government—with some political powers held by the obas and chiefs and others by the lineages—is misleading and wrong.

The government of the Yoruba kingdom was, in the last century, much concerned with relationships with neighbouring kingdoms, in the conduct of wars, and in controlling the admission of refugees into the kingdom. Lineages possessed what might loosely be termed rights of ownership over lineage land, but the oba and chiefs had unlimited power to control the use of the land, as for instance by regulating bush firing or the export of certain crops. On behalf of the people the oba and chiefs safeguarded the common rights of the people to hunt on any land within the kingdom, and to collect firewood or stone. Through the collection of tolls and in the organization of long-distance caravans they could control much of the trading activity of the town.

---

[16] The Odemo of Ishara, oba of a town of Ijebu Remo, speaking in the Western Region House of Chiefs on the occasion of the death of King George VI.

The political views of the mass of the people were expressed in their lineage meetings; these views were carried by the chiefs, sitting in these meetings as ordinary members, to their own assemblies. In common with most elected representatives, the Ado chief not only has a duty to his lineage but also to the town; at his installation he promises to obey the Ewi. Each grade of chiefs meets separately and its conclusions are reported to the next higher grade. The *Olori Marun*—the most senior *Ihare* chiefs—used to sit daily on the veranda of one of the palace courtyards, discussing the town's affairs. Their decisions were then communicated to the oba by one of these chiefs or by a palace slave. The oba then announced this decision as his own. The decision of his chiefs thus became the decision of the oba. The royal 'ban' gave such decisions the highest authority and attached to them, in the event of their violation, the most extreme sanction.

The meetings of the chiefs were not only legislative but also judicial. The two functions were not in fact sharply separated but were dealt with in one and the same meeting. Disputes within a lineage were, in the first instance, dealt with by lineage elders; these were taken on appeal to the chiefs, who also heard cases involving members of different lineages. Cases of homicide, treason, and offences against deities were heard in the first instance by the oba and chiefs. They might fine the guilty party, imprison him, expel him from the town, or sentence him to death. (In the last instance the oba had the prerogative of mercy.) The oba rarely, in the past, sat with his chiefs in council. If he did so he spoke little during the debate but his final conclusion reflected an opinion which the chiefs could accept unanimously.

Political power is segmentary and in Ado the segments are the lineages each struggling against its neighbour for its own aggrandisement—rights to more land or to new titles. Administration is however hierarchical.[17] In Ado three channels of administration are recognized. The decisions of the oba and chiefs were announced through the town by one of the oba's palace slaves. Other slaves acted as general messengers and would be sent, with the oba's staff, to other towns of the kingdom; they would also summon persons to the palace. The *ɛfa* association whose members were recruited from all the lineages of the town acted as a police force, seizing rougher criminals and breaking up minor riots. The age-grade system has now disappeared in Ado, being without a modern function, but it seems that the work of the *Elɛgbɛ* chiefs was, in the past, concerned with the organization of these grades in war and public works. (The senior *Elɛgbɛ*, the Barafon, was the war-leader in Ado.) The functions of the *Ihare* and *Ijoye* chiefs were primarily deliberative but they usually had some executive functions in respect of their own lineages and quarters.

---

[17] For the concept of segmentary power–hierarchical administration I am indebted to M. G. Smith, 'Segmentary Lineage Systems', *Journal of the Royal Anthropological Institute*, vol. lxxxvi, part ii, 1956, pp. 39–80.

THE KINGDOM. We have referred so far only to the government of the town of Ado (or more strictly of Oke Ewi). The Ewi is, however, the ruler of a larger kingdom, the seventeen subordinate towns of which have a total population of 35,000. The largest of these towns, Igede, has today a population of 6,100 inhabitants.

Each of the subordinate towns is organized in a manner similar to the metropolitan town. Some of these towns claim an origin earlier than the foundation of Ado, having acknowledged the Ewi as ruler on his arrival; in others the first rulers are said to have been exiled Ado princes. These towns, in common with the Ado lineages, usually have specific duties at the installation and burial of the Ewi. Their rulers usually take their title from their town—Onijan of Ijan, Oluyin of Iyin, the prefix *oni* or *olu* denoting possession. They hold the same constitutional position *vis-à-vis* their chiefs as the Ewi has towards his chiefs in Oke Ewi. The appointment of the subordinate ruler must be ratified by the Ewi, though he is installed in his own town by his own chiefs with the Ewi's messengers as witnesses. The subordinate towns have a large measure of internal independence but they could have in the past no separate foreign policy. Disputes between towns and all cases of homicide were referred to the Ewi and his chiefs. Tribute was paid annually to the Ewi. Each of the five senior chiefs of Oke Ewi was responsible for the subordinate towns along the road which passed out of the capital through his own quarter. All matters affecting the subordinate town were brought to the responsible chief, who presented them before the chiefs in council. The same chiefs collected the tribute from the subordinate towns. The subordinate towns had no part in the selection of the chief responsible for them or of the Ewi.

This pattern of government for the kingdom seems to have been fairly general among Yoruba kingdoms. Here, perhaps, it may be appropriate to use the analogy of a federal constitution with specific powers, those of internal government, being reserved for the subordinate towns; these towns would claim that the powers are not delegated by the oba but are inherent in the foundation of their own settlements, and represent the powers which remain to them after ceding their sovereignty to the oba, whom they acknowledged by virtue of his royal birth or by conquest.

## The Balance of Power

The chiefs sitting in council make decisions; the oba, wealthy and sacred, ordains them. This is the ideal pattern—a delicate balance of power. Sometimes a senile and effete oba leaves his chiefs to govern the town, taking little interest himself in its affairs. At other times the new oba is a man of strong personality anxious to govern, and thus almost bound to clash with his chiefs who find themselves overruled or ignored. The balance is maintained by a variety of sanctions.

If oba and chiefs disagreed there was little by which the former could coerce the latter. The army of the kingdom was controlled by the chiefs. In Ado Ekiti it was the senior age grade, organized by the *Elegbe*, which provided the warriors. The oba could not call upon the army to quell a mass insurrection against his rule; but through the chiefs he could mobilize it to put down a minor rebellion within the metropolitan town or to bring to heel a recalcitrant subordinate town. During the period of tribal wars the palace slaves were often increased in number so that they formed a bodyguard around the oba, protecting him against any sudden attack by his people. Intrigue was the oba's prime weapon. The chieftaincy titles were, according to the myths, granted by the oba and could accordingly be withdrawn by him. He might convert a title to one hereditary within a lineage. He might make changes within the ranking of chiefs. In most Yoruba towns myths tell of such alterations in the pattern of chieftaincy.

Although the possession of a senior chieftaincy title, a famous origin, a long history in the town, and even of mere numbers, can confer prestige on a lineage, there is no formal ranking of the non-royal lineages: all are, in theory, equal. Yet each lineage competes for its own aggrandisement and royal recognition. Concerted action against an unpopular ruler was often foiled by tale-bearing chiefs who believed that the oba's rewards might benefit them more than a successful rebellion. The oba's messengers were largely instrumental in gathering rumours of threatened sedition and in spreading gossip to divide the chiefs against one another. The oba might also curse an opponent, a most terrible sanction. The Ewi still on occasion addresses formal meetings through his spokesman, an *Elegbe* chief of the royal lineage: on one occasion, at the installation of a chief, his reprimands to the lineage concerned for creating an acrimonious dispute were couched in the mildest terms—the spokesman embellished these considerably.

The oba might forbid one of the chiefs to enter the palace, thus preventing him from participating in the government of the town, and bringing disgrace upon his lineage. The oba could not depose a chief unless he could be proved guilty of crimes against the town as a whole; thus he could not easily rid himself of a chief who merely displeased him. Similarly, a chief could not be deposed by his own lineage, though if he died mysteriously it would often be believed that the lineage members had poisoned him.

The chiefs have had far greater power to coerce their oba, though it was often difficult to get unanimous action. Initially they might boycott the palace and govern without the oba, relying on their popularity in the town to ensure obedience to their orders. However, such a boycott would involve the chiefs in a refusal to participate in rituals carried out by the oba on behalf of the town, and would thus endanger its prosperity. Ultimately the chiefs might ask their oba to die; (such precautions were taken in preparing the royal food that it was difficult to poison the oba). Deposition could only be effected by death and never by exile or abdication, for only by the death of one oba could his successor perform the consecration rituals necessary to validate his own rule. The demands of the chiefs were usually conveyed symbolically; in Oyo the Alafin was sent a gift of parrot eggs. The oba was then expected to take poison and thus commit suicide. Should the chiefs be slow to take action or should their demands go unheeded the people might themselves demand that their oba should go—either symbolically, as in Ado in 1940, when the Ewi's subjects clapped stones together in the market-place, or, practically, by stoning or firing the palace.

The deposition of a Yoruba oba is a constitutional procedure. The rights of the royal lineage are not questioned. The opposition of the chiefs is solely to the individual whom they selected and who has not fulfilled their hopes. When deposition has been decided upon, the chiefs probably have an alternative candidate for the throne in whom they feel confidence, and the opposition to an unpopular ruler may be formulated partly by listing the virtues existing in his rival; particularly is this so where the former failed to perform the due consecration ceremonies, and thus has no legitimate claim to rule. The procedure was simple. Yet it seems to have been rarely used. There is, for example, no record of such an occurrence in the Ado king-list. The oba's protection was his sacred right to rule. He did not stand above the customary law of his people; the law, ancient and supreme, stood unquestioned. His commands were valid, in the sight of his people, so long as they were within the law. He did not make new laws; he ordained the law to suit particular current needs, making the necessary rules. By his consecration the oba received wisdom to interpret the law— wisdom not possessed by his chiefs who had performed no such ceremonies. Thus, mere disagreement with his chiefs was not sufficient cause for the people to turn against their oba.[18]

## The Royal Lineage

In a society where the ruler is so powerful, is the wealthiest person, and has far more wives than anybody else, it would perhaps seem inevitable

---

[18] In Shaki, a town in the north of Oyo Province, ten out of the eighteen rulers of the nineteenth century were deposed. The oba of this town, the Okere, traces his descent from an influential warrior from Bussa, who settled in Shaki. So good, say the myths, was he at settling disputes that the Onishaki (at that time oba) suggested that he, the Okere, should deal with such secular matters, leaving the Onishaki to look after the ritual. Thus the Okere became oba and the Onishaki is now a priest. A similar myth is related in Ikere, ten miles south of Ado, where the Ogoga (descended from an elephant hunter from Benin) similarly displaced the Onikere. The Ogogas have suffered from much unpopularity.

that the royal lineage should be large and powerful and able to support its oba against the chiefs and the non-royal lineages. But in Yoruba towns several mechanisms exist for curbing the size and the political power of the royal lineage.

In Ado the royal lineage would seem to be small, considering that the present dynasty has probably ruled for three centuries; it numbers less perhaps than 2,000 persons. Those descended from recent Ewis live in Ogbon Ado, immediately west of the palace, while the compounds of six or more segments tracing descent from earlier rulers are scattered through the town.

In Ado a royal wife may not bear a child in the palace; she returns home to the compound of her own patrilineage, remaining there until the child is weaned when she again sleeps with the oba. Her status is recognized in the town by her peculiar hair style and by the palace messenger, who, in the past, invariably accompanied her. Her children often remain in her compound, growing up with the children of their mother's brother. In Ado little land, either in the town or outside on the farms, is held corporately by the royal lineage as distinct from the land attached to the oba's title—the palace and the royal farms. A member of the royal lineage must usually obtain land from his mother's lineage.[19] A prince who is able and wealthy will build his compound at one edge of this lineage land and his children will later extend it. A modern example is provided by Ogirigbo, son of the eighteenth Ewi, who unsuccessfully contested the throne; he is now 100 years old and his compound, in the quarter of his mother's lineage, is surrounded by the houses of numerous and prosperous sons and grandsons. Less prosperous men become absorbed into their mothers' lineages, losing after three or four generations their status as ɔmɔ ɔba, the genealogies usually featuring them as the direct issue of their mothers' fathers. There is no formal adoption ceremony; thus, once absorption has occurred it cannot be proved ever to have taken place. That it does occur can only be demonstrated by the absence of members of the royal lineage tracing descent from many of the earlier obas.

Yoruba often say that the post of oba was, in the past, so little to be envied that no disputes over accession to the throne ever occurred. Yet many of the immigrant lineages in Oke Ewi claim that their foundation arose from a title dispute in another town, the losing candidate emigrating because he was unwilling to acknowledge the rule of the successful man. Such recalcitrant emigrants would almost certainly travel beyond the confines of their own kingdoms and there is thus no reason why the home town should remember them in their myths.

A more loyal but still powerful prince could be sent to rule an outlying

---

[19] By the same process a large non-royal lineage may absorb members of smaller ones. Royal wives who are not members of Ado lineages are often lodged with chiefs.

part of the kingdom; within the Ado kingdom the rulers of three subordinate towns—Aisegba, Igbimo, and Iluomoba—trace their descent from Ado princes. Once appointed to such a post, the prince becomes the founder of the ruling lineage of this subordinate town; although he may not describe himself as an oba or assume the regalia of royalty, his constitutional role towards his chiefs is similar to that of the oba towards the chiefs of the metropolitan town. The subordinate ruler may not live in the metropolitan town; he is buried in his own town; he cannot be promoted to any other office. Such an appointment of a prince has not been made in Ado within living memory; its occurrence in the past is evinced by the myths of the subordinate towns.

There are, however, on the outer limits of Ado farm land, where the town bounds the lands of larger subordinate towns, a number of very small farm villages, each of which is headed by a royal prince taking his title from his village. Today nearly thirty such villages are listed. Many of the title-holders at present live in Ado town, but it is believed that in the past they were confined to their villages and did not participate in the government of Ado. It would seem that the villages were founded by important princes with a small personal following, and that these princes and their issue became hereditary rulers; if the village attracted other settlers a chieftaincy system developed and the village gradually achieved the status of a subordinate town within the kingdom. Odo, headed by the Akitipa, situated nine miles from Ado and only two from its erstwhile subordinate, Ilawe, is the largest village today (population c. 300); it has its own chiefs, but the Akitipa now lives in Ado (where he has achieved posts such as native court and local government council membership to which his title does not traditionally entitle him). Odo still ranks as a village.

Thus, the size of the royal lineage is reduced by the slow absorption of the weaker members into the non-royal lineages and by the expulsion of the more powerful ones.

The non-royal lineages of Ado extend the limits of their farm land to the boundaries of those of the subordinate towns or to the frontiers of the kingdom. The oba has little land on which to settle his own children. His entire income should be used for the benefit of the town and not for the advancement of his own family. At his death all his wealth should pass to his successor—his children should receive nothing. In the past the close kin of the Ewi were not allowed to enter his private apartments in the palace. The oba is ministered to by his wives, palace servants, and those chiefs with rights of access to him—in Oke Ewi one chief from each grade. (Today the degree to which an oba may use his income from his salary and gifts to build private houses, and educate his children in the manner of other wealthy men of the town has become a problem.)

Members of the royal lineage are not eligible for any of the *Ihare* titles.

They are thus debarred from full participation in the government of the town. They cannot, of course, be omitted from its administration and certain *Elɛgbɛ* titles are reserved for them.[20] Poor and without political rights, the status of the royal lineage is debased. Often it is difficult to discover the eligible heirs to the throne, so humble are they. Some princes are, of course, prominent men, but they might have become even more influential had they belonged to a non-royal lineage and thus been eligible for a chieftaincy title. Absorption into the maternally related lineages is thus encouraged. Yet a vacant throne is often bitterly contested, not only by the candidates themselves but by their own close kin and members of their own segment of the royal lineage. One might well ask why members of the royal lineage who are not eligible for the throne struggle so tenaciously to support a candidate who could (in the past) bring them so little material reward. Why do they not allow their membership of the royal lineage to fall into oblivion?

It takes at least three generations, and probably longer, for a man and his descendants to become completely absorbed into his mother's lineage. And although a lineage, lacking a suitable member, may sometimes elect to its hereditary chieftaincy a son of one of its own female members, it would never choose an acknowledged member of the royal lineage. Thus, members of the royal lineage see participation in a contest for the throne as a rare but legitimate method of exercising *some* political influence even at the expense of delaying still further absorption into a non-royal lineage. Furthermore members of each segment which may put up eligible candidates have some pride in their own group and are anxious to ensure that the rotation of the kingship between the segments is followed. In Ado, with only two such segments, the rotation has been observed during the past century. But in other towns, with three or more segments, there is always a danger that the rotation may be upset in order to install a popular candidate. If a segment misses a turn there is a possibility that its own eligible candidates—those born to a reigning oba—will be dead before the next succession, in which event the segment will have lost its rights as a ruling house and will lose its prestige in the town.

The chiefs too are not necessarily unanimous—at least initially so—in their selection of a new oba. We should be mistaken in regarding a contest for the vacant throne as a struggle for political power between the segments of the royal lineage, in which rival candidates seek the support of the chiefs to improve their chances. The members of the royal lineage have no political power and strive merely to enhance their own prestige. In all the instances I have encountered, in which deposition of an unpopu-

---

[20] In some Yoruba towns titles, usually termed chieftaincy titles, are conferred by the oba on leading members of the royal lineage; such titles confer on their holders no rights to sit with the chiefs governing the town.

lar oba has been mooted, the opposition to the oba has invariably been led by the senior chiefs or by an educated man (representing the literate group); members of the ruling lines who, as eligible candidates for the throne, were alternative rulers, played no active part in the campaigns against the oba. In most cases it has seemed likely that those leading the opposition to the oba have not had in mind any particular successor to the throne.

## Conclusion

In this paper I have described only the constitutional aspects of Yoruba kingship, but I do not wish to infer that I consider the ritual roles of the sacred ruler to be unimportant, though today the decline in traditional religious beliefs and the development of modern local government institutions is leading many Yoruba to conceive the roles of their oba not as those of the sacred king, but as the secular roles of the constitutional monarch. As the oba becomes less sacred, so is he less free from criticism should he overstep his constitutional rights.

To recapitulate: we have seen that in the Yoruba town the kingship is hereditary in the lineage of the ruler who founded the town (or who was accepted as ruler by the indigenous inhabitants on account of his royal descent). In many towns only those princes born to a reigning oba are eligible for the throne. There is thus a clear distinction between the royal lineage and the non-royal descent groups of the town. But while the candidates for the throne are proposed by the elders of the royal lineage it is the chiefs, representing the non-royal lineages, who make the final selection. Although the oba is at the head of the government of his town and kingdom he may act only on the advice of his chiefs. The balance of power between oba and chiefs depends ultimately on personalities. The position of the royal lineage is the key to the system. No member of the royal lineage may hold any chieftaincy title giving political power, though they may hold titles conferring administrative duties. Princes have no economic power from the control of land; they may not share in the wealth of the throne. The size of the royal lineage has been reduced by the expulsion of the more prominent princes and the absorption of others into their maternal lineages. Membership of the royal lineage confers less prestige than of the non-royal lineages.

This political system is markedly different from, for example, that of the emirates of Northern Nigeria, where the Fulani are a ruling aristocracy clearly established by conquest. There the contents for power lie between the segments of the royal lineage; the commoners have no direct representation in the government of the emirate (though individual commoners may be selected by the emir for high posts). The senior princes rule over subordinate towns and villages, but these offices are but stepping-stones to the highest posts in the metropolitan town. Emphasis on the sacred aspects of kingship and on the complexity and centralization of government has tended to obscure the constitutional variations which occur among tribal kingdoms. The points raised here may provide useful criteria for a more detailed classification of such kingdoms.

# Modern Political Movements in Somaliland[1]

## I. M. Lewis

. . .

**I**

As is well known, the Somali (*Soomaali*) are a proud, even haughty, Muslim people with a highly democratic political organization. In their semi-arid environment they are predominantly camel-nomads. Latest estimates suggest that the total Somali population numbers some 3 million souls. A little sorghum is cultivated in the north-west—in Harar Province of Ethiopia and in the British Protectorate—where some 5 per cent. of the Protectorate population are thought to practise plough cultivation. Agriculture, mainly hoe-cultivation, is most extensively practised in southern Somalia by an estimated 40 to 50 per cent. of the population.

Physically, and to a certain extent culturally, the Somali are 'Hamitic'. But looking to their agnatic Arabian eponyms, whom they venerate as Sufi saints, they claim Arabian descent. Their ultimate ancestors, according to Somali tradition, are of Quraysh, the lineage of the Prophet Maḥammad,[2] and of the progeny of His Companions. Historically these traditions reflect the contact, over centuries, with Arabia, and the settlement at various periods in Somali history of small groups of Arabian immigrants. Sociologically they represent further the application of Somali lineage principles to Islam, in which the founders of Somali patrilineal descent groups are canonized and venerated as Sufi saints.[3] Sufism is highly developed.[4] But

---

[1] 'Somaliland': the French *Côte des Somalis* (Somali pop. *c.* 30,000); The British Somaliland Protectorate (pop. 640,000); Harar Province of Ethiopia (Somali pop. probably *c.* 500,000); the Italian administered United Nations Trusteeship Territory of Somalia (pop. *c.* 2,000,000); and the Northern Province of Kenya (Somali pop. 80,000).

[2] In the orthography adopted in this paper, long vowels are indicated by doubling, as, e.g., *aa, oo,* &c. The Arabic and Cushitic aspirate h is indicated by *ḥ,* and the Cushitic post alveolar plosive by *ḍ.*

[3] I am not suggesting that such traditions are necessarily mythological. The research through historical documents in southern Arabia which is required to examine the

for a small minority in the towns and government service who have been influenced mainly by western values, all Somali belong nominally to the local Somali Dervish Orders. But the number of adherents of the Orders who are formal initiates is comparatively small.

The entire Somali population can be comprised within one vast genealogy recording all the relationships of the numerous patrilineal descent groups into which Somali society is divided. At every level descent is reckoned agnatically through named ancestors to the descent group eponym. At the highest level there are seven great descent groups which I propose to call 'clan-families'. The relationships of these in the total genealogy are shown in the chart.

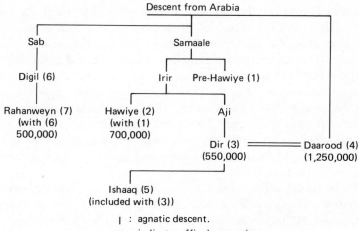

It will be seen that the primary and genealogical bifurcation of the Somali people is between those who descend from Samaale and those who descend from Sab. The Daarood, who claim and trace affinal relationship only, are classed with those clan-families descended from Samaale who, in their order of generation, are the 'Pre-Hawiye',[5] Dir, Daarood, and Ishaaq. The Ishaaq are classified by other Somali as Dir, but themselves

authenticity of these traditions has still to be undertaken. For a summary account of known Somali history see Lewis, 1955, pp. 45–48, and Lewis, 1957 (2).

[4] Sufism: the mystical interpretation of Islam which emphasizes the powers of mediation between God and man of saints with special revelations from, and direct experience of, God and the Prophet. The adherents of Sufism (known in a religious sense as 'brothers') belong to the congregations or communities (*jamaa'as*) of the various Orders (*tariiqa*, 'The Way') into which the movement is divided according to the doctrines and services (*dhikr*) ordained by the saintly founders of the Orders. See Lewis, 1956.

[5] This term was usefully coined by Colucci, 1924, to represent clans genealogically anterior to the Hawiye clan-family. Those so designated are now of little importance and have no collective unity.

deny this grouping, claiming that they are a clan-family of Arabian descent in their own right and without the intermediacy of other Somali ancestors.[6] Those descended from Samaale whom I refer to as the 'Samaale', in opposition to those descended from Sab, are almost entirely nomadic stock-herders, although, as noted, a little cultivation is practised by the Isḥaaq and Dir in the north-west of Somaliland and by some of the Hawiye of Somalia. The Digil and Raḥanweyn clan-families descended from Sab are, in contrast, mainly cultivators. Possessed of the relatively fertile region (to the nomad almost a paradise) between the Shebelle and Juba Rivers of southern Somalia, cultivation of millets, durra, and Indian corn, with other subsidiary crops and fruits, has largely replaced camel-nomadism. The Sab own also extensive herds of cattle and, as a whole, are culturally distinguished from the five Samaale clan-families. The northern Samaale dialects differ from the speech of the southern Sab by about as much as French does from Italian. Other differences cannot be gone into here.[7] As far as habitat is concerned the Samaale—to make a broad generalization— inhabit northern and central Somaliland while the Sab occupy the southern regions approximately up to the Juba River where they come into contact with a wedge of nomadic Daarood and Hawiye Samaale extending into the Northern Province of Kenya.[8] The former are primarily nomads and the latter principally cultivators. When, therefore, we speak of 'northern nomads' we refer to the typical Samaale, and when we speak of 'southern cultivators' to the typical Sab.

Below the clan-family, subsidiary descent groups are indicated according to their order of segmentation and special properties, as clans, sub-clans, lineages, and segments of lineages. Genealogically, however, all these descent groups, from clan-family to smallest lineage-group, have the same properties. All are lineages, to the eponymous ancestor of which a person traces exactly his agnatic relationship through named ancestors. The number of generations counted, and the number of ancestors named, vary with the size and strength of the group concerned.

Somali society is thus an agnatic lineage society in which the primary bifurcation is between those who descend from Samaale and those who descend from Sab, and each division comprises a vast system of balanced segments. Segmentation and lineage-group affiliation is at every level relative; the various orders of segmentation do not constitute permanent cleavages. Those who at a given time and in a certain situation act as one

---

[6] These contradictory genealogical traditions are discussed in their social contexts in Lewis, 1957 (1), pp. 81–94, and will form the subject of a later publication.

[7] In general the physical characters of the Sab are more Negroid than the Samaale and this, with cultural differences, reflects the mixed origin of the Sab from south-driving Somali conquerors and pre-Somali Negroid and Galla populations of southern Somalia.

[8] Clan distribution is shown fairly accurately in the map at the end of Lewis, 1955.

unit are on another occasion and in a different situation divided by hostility into opposed units. This relativism is characteristic of the whole structure and all political groups are relative units although some, it is true, have greater permanence than others.

The Samaale nomads are a warlike people and their society is highly militaristic. Ranging over wide distances in the search for pasture and water, the nomadic social units are hamlets of a few closely related nuclear families, with their sheep and goats, and burden camels for their transport. The grazing camels, mostly female, constitute a separate unit. They are herded in camel-camps containing the camels of a few siblings, or other close relatives (mainly agnatic), in the charge of youths and unmarried men. The camel-camps are usually out in the far grazing, often hundreds of miles from the nomadic hamlets to which the herds belong. This primary division reflects the greater mobility and less demanding water requirements of camels which, when the grass is dry, are watered every two weeks or so and marched over long distances, frequently above a hundred miles between the pastures and the wells. The weaker sheep and goats need to be watered almost every four or five days when the grass is dry, and cattle more frequently. Thus the nuclear families grouped in threes and fours[9] in nomadic hamlets cannot move far from water in the dry seasons. Women and children, with from time to time the male head of the nuclear family, move with the flocks which, because of their slight powers of endurance as compared with camels, limit their range of movement.

When in an area with pasture and water, hamlets and camel-camps congregate in temporary settlements. In these people who are close agnates tend to pitch camp side by side. But the grazing settlement has no residential solidarity of any importance. As the grazing and water are exhausted after a few weeks or days, according to their abundance, the settlement disintegrates and individual hamlets, nuclear families, or small parties of kinsmen set off in search of new pasture. New settlements are formed with a new configuration of individual nuclear families and hamlets, but again, one in which people of the same small lineage-group tend to camp close to each other. The same is true of the settlements of camel-camps. Just as the settlements of nomadic hamlets with the flocks of sheep and goats, these form and dissociate in time of peace at random and without engendering any sentiments of residential solidarity.

Lack of any clearly defined territorial units is indeed characteristic of Samaale society and is in keeping with pastoral nomadism in a semi-arid country. The distribution of rain is very scattered and it is—in peace-time —mainly in relation to the availability of grazing and water that move-

---

[9] The nomadic hamlet commonly contains up to four nuclear families in peace-time. It is not, however, unusual, and especially common in time of war, to find hamlets which contain more than four nuclear families grouped together within the same thorn fence enclosure.

ments correspond. People, often of different clans and even clan-families, congregate and interpenetrate in an area of reasonable pasture and in their movements follow the distribution of good grazing. It is thus inappropriate to speak of a 'tribal' structure among the nomads, for the social units are not tribes but lineage-groups.[10] While lack of territorial solidarity is characteristic, lineage-groups sometimes do assume transient territorial formations for the purposes of self-defence. This is a matter of tactical convenience and policy, and reflects the political unity of agnates and not the association of territorial divisions with political interests. At the level of the clan, however, and sometimes at the level of the sub-clan, a certain degree of localization and of attachment to territory occurs. But even so, prescriptive rights to grazing, even between potentially hostile clans of different clan-families, are not usually asserted in the absence of hostilities. Another property of the clan which distinguishes it from other orders of lineage-group is that it is with clans that the only clearly defined political office—that of Sultan—is associated.[11] Most clans, although not all, have titular leaders dignified beyond their actual power and authority by the Arabian title Sultan. The office, which is sometimes hereditary, is, on the whole, an empty one and is little more than of a representative and symbolic kind. There are no formal courts attached to Sultans. Although they usually own considerable herds of camels, flocks of sheep, and other property, their riches are often surpassed by the wealth of merchants and other private persons. A Sultan is always spoken of with great respect but he is often in practice shown little consideration. Only leaders of exceptional personality and character succeed in investing their titles with authority beyond that of *primus inter pares* in their clans.

At every level of segmentation it is the elders of the nomadic hamlets who control political relations. All adult free-born males[12] may speak at the councils (*shir*) which are summoned as need arises to debate the policy of a lineage-group. There are no permanent councils. In settlement of disputes resort may be had to a panel of arbitrators (*guddi*) also appointed on an *ad hoc* basis. Unbiased assessors are chosen who are also expert authorities on Somali custom. They have, however, no direct sanctions with which to implement their findings. Ultimately a settlement

---

[10] This contention, which contradicts the terminology employed in previous publications (Lewis, 1955; 1956), is substantiated in Lewis, 1957 (1), where a fuller description of the nomadic social organization is given than is possible here.

[11] In Somali, *Suldaan, Boqor, Ugaas, Garaad*, and *Islaam* are all used in the North with much the same sense. Formerly some of these titles seem to have distinguished different ranks. See Lewis, 1957 (1), pp. 25–27.

[12] The so-called 'outcast', but more correctly bondsmen, Midgaans, Tumaals, and Yibirs, now few in numbers and partly emancipated, but formerly bound to almost every large Samaale lineage-group, traditionally have not the right to speak in council. This stigma is now to some extent removed, at least in the case of wealthy and influential members of the class. See Lewis, op. cit., pp. 8–9.

depends upon the willingness of the parties to settle, and upon political expediency in terms of the relations between the lineage-groups to which they belong. In negotiation and arbitration religious men (sheikhs and *wadaads*)[13] play an important, though not exclusive, role. But they cannot enforce a ritual settlement of a dispute. Only the Administrations have established courts with effective juridical powers. Outside these self-help remains the basic mechanism for redressing wrongs. This is explicitly recognized by the nomad, whose code is that might is right and that the weak must yield to the strong. The notion of the paramount importance of force is expressed in the proverb: 'Either be a mountain, or attach yourself to one.'

The Somali expression *heer,* usually translated 'custom', means basically treaty or contract and the reciprocal code of duties and privileges founded upon it. Two or more lineage-groups at any level may enter into a *heer* agreement binding themselves together by a specific treaty and for specific purposes, usually for defence or agression.[14] Policy is determined by treaty mainly in relation to hostility, to forward or combat which as occasion demands, different lineage-groups ally together. A particular treaty, when no longer appropriate to a new set of conditions, is rescinded. By treaty, explicit obligations and rights are laid down and superimposed upon the implicit bonds of agnation. In a narrower sense, the word *heer* describes the agreement to pay blood-wealth (at a statutory rate of 100 camels for a man)[15] in common, by a few small, mainly directly related, lineage-groups. This is further an alliance for mutual defence in opposition to other stronger groups which the parties to the agreement could not combat individually. These small political units are generally known in the British Protectorate by the expression 'Dia-paying group' from the Arabic *d-y-t,* blood-wealth (Somali, *mag*). Although this name suggests a greater rigidity and stability than in fact exists we retain it here for convenience. The strength of a single Dia-paying group varies between a few hundred and a few thousand men. It rarely exceeds a thousand. In the British Protectorate in 1957 there were over 300 Dia-paying groups of relative stability. In a system of shifting agnatic attachment and loyalty Dia-paying groups are the most stable and effective political units. While outside them, disputes are settled basically in terms of self-help and administrative intervention, within them there may be said to be a rule of law, for their

---

[13] See below.

[14] It is the practice in the British Protectorate to register and maintain a file in District Offices of such agreements, which thus become a source of law.

[15] A woman's life is valued at 50 camels. These are the statutory Shariah values which in practice are not always rigidly adhered to, and which are sometimes used as bases of negotiation rather than absolute assessments. In an article on 'Diapaying groups' I discuss the subject of compensation more fully than is necessary here.

members have some powers of punishment with which to impose the terms of the treaty which unites them. They have no constitutionally defined leaders and their affairs are regulated by the component elders in *ad hoc* councils.

The practice, introduced during the Egyptian administration of the Somali coast, of appointing salaried representatives ('*aaqils*) for Dia-paying groups has been retained in all the Somali territories. In many cases, too, co-operative Sultans have been recognized by the Governments of the Somalilands and receive salaries as clan representatives. Both the '*aaqils* and Sultans are in this context often called 'Chiefs' and it is implied that they have authority over the lineage-groups which they are chosen to represent. This may be true of a handful of exceptional Sultans, but generally, and particularly in the case of '*aaqils* (now in the British Protectorate styled 'Local Authorities'), these are representative offices only. The holders of the offices are usually little more than mediators or go-betweens between Government and lineage-group. Although usually they have little or no power over their kinsmen they are useful in maintaining liaison with the Administrations.

In contrast to those who hold political authority (elders and Sultans), men of religion—*wadaads* and shiekhs[16]—are not normally invested with secular authority.[17] Their sphere, as is indicated in the division between warrior (*waranleh*, lit. spearbearer) and *wadaad*, man of religion, is usually restricted to religious matters. This does not of course mean that sheikhs are not expected to be partisan, for in lineage-group disputes, sheikhs always, except in very exceptional cases, support their own agnates and are expected to intercede with God on their behalf. But at the same time, they are to a certain extent, by definition, and more in theory than practice, divorced from worldly affairs and dedicated to the promotion of Muslim solidarity. Through the Sufi Dervish Orders (*tariiqas*) in which they hold office, and through which they are bound by the doctrine of the brotherhood of the faithful, they achieve some independence from clan and lineage squabbles. They are the champions of the Religious Law as opposed to clan custom (*heer*), and where the two conflict, as, for example, in the payment of blood-wealth by lineage affiliation, they should stand on the side of the Shariah. Their greatest freedom from clan obligations is achieved in the *tariiqa* cultivating communities, of which there are but few

---

[16] *Wadaad* is the Somali equivalent of the Arabic sheikh. In practice both words are used more or less synonymously; although the appellation 'sheikh' is generally reserved for a man of religion whose knowledge and learning are the greater.

[17] Except of course where they have been appointed by the Administrations as Government *Qaadis* with jurisdiction in matters of personal status, inheritance (mainly in the towns), and marriage and divorce, &c. Occasionally, too, through figuring as leaders of the *jihaad* against Christian administration or Ethiopia, they have, as in the case of Sayyid Maḥammad ʿAbdille Ḥassan (the celebrated 'Mad Mullah'), assumed civil powers.

in northern Somaliland, though considerable numbers in southern Somalia. Some of the latter have developed into small theocratic polities engaged in strife with surrounding Somali clans.[18] But at least in theory, whether or not the members of a ṭariiqa are established as an independent cultivating settlement, membership of the Dervish Orders provides a new principle of aggregation and one that is nominally opposed to clanship.

So far we have considered the Samaale nomads, now we turn to examine the social organization of the mainly sedentary Raḥanweyn and Digil. While the political structure of the northern nomads is acephalous, highly anarchic, and extremely fluid, and at all times relative, the political structure of the Sab appears to be more formalized and hierarchical. There are, broadly, two types of agricultural settlement. In one, the land-holding political units are lineages composed of a usually small nucleus of those descended agnatically from the original settlers. They include a majority of later arrivals, of various clan and lineage-group origin, who, through adoption as clients with fictional agnation, have become identified with the genealogy of their hosts. In the second type, purely residential units have emerged in which rights to land are not tied to agnation, and in which lineages serve little or no political function. Here it seems legitimate to speak of a tribal organization with a hierarchy of territorial subdivisions. Any fully satisfactory study of Sab political structure is lacking, but on the basis of information which I have reviewed elsewhere[19] it seems possible to describe their administrative organization as hierarchical. There is a much wider range of ranked offices, of specialized functionaries, and tribal Sultans, at any rate before the arrival of the Colonial Powers, seem to have wielded greater power than among the northern nomads. Similarly, the investiture of a new Sultan is a much more elaborate affair than in northern Somaliland. Such a hierarchical state-like organization is, on the one hand, founded in the adoption of agriculture and a sedentary life. On the other, it is historically the consequence of the conquest of southern Somalia by Somali of nomadic origin and northern provenance, who wrested control of the arable land from pre-Somali Negroid and Galla populations. Remnants of the latter still survive in the riverine regions of Somalia,[20] and have left behind them indelible traces in the present physical and cultural characteristics of the Sab. Compared to the northern Samaale nomads, the Sab are less warlike, less individualistic, more co-operative, and more biddable. The nomad recognizes these qualities and despises them. For him they are well named 'Sab', since this word has for him the derogatory

---

[18] See Lewis, 1956, p. 597; 1957 (3), pp. 36–37.

[19] Lewis, 1955. The description given here is a summary of the argument in Lewis, 1957 (1), pp. 37–41. The best work so far is Colucci, 1924.

[20] For these groups and other minorities see Lewis, 1955, pp. 41–43; 1957 (1), pp. 9–14.

connotation of Midgaan, Tumaal, or Yibir bondsmen. To the nomad, the Sab are *masaakiin*, poor not so much in material wealth as in spirit.

## II

The preceding brief account will, it is hoped, suffice for an understanding of the modern political movements which we now consider. Among the nomads, with their segmentary lineage political organization, the main barriers to the formation of national unity are the disuniting forces of clanship (*tol*) and blood-compensation rules (*ẖeer*). Among the Sab, where clanship has to some extent lost its traditional political force in favour of 'local contiguity',[21] the impediment to national patriotism is a diminished clanship supplemented by tribalism. In the following pages I suggest that the organization of the new political parties reflects these different forces.[22] On the whole, however, in describing pan-Somali nationalism, it is with the retarding influence of clanship and blood-compensation agreements that we are mainly concerned. In Somaliland the clash of interests is not so much between traditional chiefs and a new élite— although there is something of this especially among the Sab of Somalia. The real struggle is between the ideal of national unity as opposed to the reality of the values of clanship and sectional kinship interests in the lineage system.

As a whole, the Somalilands, because of their poverty in natural resources, have been little affected economically by European colonization. Pastoral nomadism remains the basic economy, carrying with it for the majority of the population the traditional political structure and kinship values described above. There has been no general local industrial revolution[23] and correspondingly little large-scale urbanization. The main towns in the Somali territories are tabulated here for comparison with estimates of their population.

| | |
|---|---|
| French Somaliland | Jibuti, new town, population[24] *c.* 30,000 (15,000 Somali). |
| British Protectorate | Hargeisa, new town, population[25] *c.* 30,000 Somali. |

[21] Sir H. Maine, *Ancient Law*, 1912 edition, p. 140.

[22] This hypothesis suggests that clanship and tribalism exert unequal restraining forces. Further research might well examine which of these two principles of social organization is the more antagonistic to the development of nationalism and which is more favourable to its growth.

[23] This factor is justly stressed for other parts of Africa in T. Hodgkin's essay, *Nationalism in Colonial Africa*, London, 1956.

[24] *Documents et Statistiques*, No. xv., Feb. 1957, p. 6.

[25] *Colonial Reports, Somaliland Protectorate, 1952/3*, 1954, p. 20, gives a figure of 32,000.

| Harar Province of Ethiopia | Harar, ancient city, population[26] *c.* 60,000 (2,000? Somali). |
| Somalia | Mogadishu, ancient city, population[27] *c.* 110,000. |

The presence of a class of traders is no new phenomenon, although the Somali element in it, as opposed to the Asian immigrant, has probably considerably increased over the last twenty years. Through foreign colonization markets have widened and trade extended. In the absence of any large European settler community in Somaliland the middle class of 'new men', which has arisen elsewhere in Africa in response to colonial rule, has been largely absorbed in posts in the administrative services. The influence of a European alien community is most marked in Somalia, the former Italian colony and the foothold for the Italian conquest of Ethiopia. But, compared with other African colonies, the numbers are small—at present including expatriate administrative staff amounting to little over 4,000—and economic developments and the attraction of foreign investments have been correspondingly slight. Certainly in Somalia the work of the agricultural associations (the largest being the *Società Agricola Italo Somala,* S.A.I.S.) constitutes an economic development of some importance.[28] But the number of labourers employed here and in light industries is small. The population of Somalia is estimated[29] to consist of 40 per cent. nomads, 30 per cent. pastoralists who practise some agriculture, 20 per cent. riverine cultivators, and 10 per cent. town dwellers. In the British Protectorate 5 per cent. of the population are thought to practise cultivation (the northwestern cultivators), 5 per cent. to live in towns, and the remainder (90 per cent.) to be fully nomadic.[30]

In the small territory of French Somaliland, on the other hand, almost half of the mixed Somali, Danakil, and Arab population is concentrated in the relatively heavily industrialized port of Jibuti, on which the country's economy mainly depends.

As a whole, the Somali have not been harshly administered or savagely oppressed under the colonial régimes. This common spur to nationalism—in the form of opposition to colonial rule—was probably, however, of some significance in Somalia during the period of Fascist administration and may yet be so in the Ethiopian Province of Harar. But what seems in all the Somali territories to be of greater importance in forwarding demands for self-determination is the objection of a Muslim people to infidel rule.

---

[26] This seems a reasonable estimate for 1957 from 31,000 recorded in 1938 by Francolini, 1938, p. 1115.

[27] *Rapport . . . Somalie, 1955,* p. 149.

[28] See *Rapport . . . Somalie, 1955,* pp. 64–77; Lewis, 1955, pp. 80–82.

[29] *Rapport . . . Somalie, 1955,* p. 89.

[30] Hunt, 1951, p. 121.

Nationalist ideals—as I shall show—always tend to be associated in Somaliland with Islamic unity opposed to Christian Government.[31]

Another factor of general significance in Somaliland is the disruption which accompanied the East African Campaign (1940–1) and the placing of British, Ethiopian, and ex-Italian territories under a common administration. Under British Military Administration (1941–9) the artificial and arbitrary international boundaries which divide Somaliland were opened and new ideas and aspirations were widely disseminated.

As in other territories, the extension of Western education helps to foster nationalist aspirations and to promote the desire for independence, for which, indeed, in countries such as Somalia and British Somaliland committed to self-determination, it is intended. Contact through travel for work or education (many Somalis have worked abroad as seamen) and through the media of the radio and press, with events in the world at large and nationalist movements elsewhere, certainly plays a significant part. Recently an independent Somali newspaper was founded.[32]

It is evident that the forces conducive to nationalist inspiration should be most developed in Somalia under United Nations Trusteeship and Italian Administration with a ten years' apprenticeship to independence (1950–60).[33] The present policies of encouragement and preparation for self-government in Somalia and British Somaliland seem to constitute a more important factor in the stimulation of nationalist aspirations than the more common indirect effects of colonial government. New developments in French colonial policy (through the *loi cadre*) are beginning to have a similar effect in French Somaliland.

Before proceeding to examine the modern political movements one further general remark must be made. In all the parties only a small minority of leaders occupied in the central party administration are full-time professional politicians. The initiative comes from these men and much support, especially in the nationalist organizations, derives from traders in the towns[34] and from those of the young educated élite who have not been

---

[31] For comparative material see: R. Rézette, *Les Partis politiques marocains*, Paris, 1955; G. E. von Grunebaum (ed.), *Unity and Variety in Muslim Civilization*, Chicago, 1955; Hazem Zaki Nuseibeh, *The Ideas of Arab Nationalism*, New York, 1956; P. Rondot, *Les Forces religieuses dans la vie politique de l'Islam*, Paris, 1957.

[32] This is the *Somali Chronicle* printed in English and founded in Mogadishu in 1957. That few independent newspapers have so far appeared is to be attributed not to any censorship or legal restrictions but rather to the lack of any strong need for one, such is the ease of communication in a nomadic country.

[33] It is now understood that independence may be granted in 1959, one year earlier than the date of expiry of the mandate.

[34] Although often permanently domiciled in towns, townsmen are not 'de-tribalized' (except in parts of southern Somalia) and are still subject to the all-pervasive rights and obligations of clanship and *heer* however much they may try to escape them. This is one reason why I have suggested that in discussing the growth of nationalism it is necessary to distinguish between tribalism and clanship as retarding forces of a different order.

precluded from political campaigning by appointment to government service. In Somalia government servants are allowed a wider latitude in political affairs than they are in the Protectorate, and since also the spread of education is wider it is not surprising that the most effective political organizations are found in Somalia.

## III

Political parties in Somaliland fall roughly into three categories (see chart). First there are those parties which are simply the modern political organ of a particular clan or group of clans and which, whatever lip-service they may pay to the ideal of Somali nationalism, are fundamentally committed to promote and safeguard the interests of the particular clan or group of clans which they represent. Secondly, there are those parties which are entirely opposed to the traditional values of agnation and to the distinction between Samaale and Sab. Their principle aim is to further a truly pan-Somali nationalism. The extent to which these ideals are promoted in practice is another matter. A third type of party, in a sense intermediate in composition between the clan party and the pan-Somali party, is that founded on common residence in a particular region. This type founded on regional or territorial (tribal) values occurs only in Somalia. Only in part of Somalia, as we have seen, have residential ties to some extent replaced agnation as a political principle in the traditional social organization.

### TYPES OF PARTY[35]

*A. Clan Parties*

| | |
|---|---|
| Mahlia Party | Formerly in the British Protectorate. |
| Isḥaaqiya | Kenya, British East Africa. |
| Marrehaan Union | Somalia. |
| Hawiye Party | Somalia. |

*B. National Parties*

| | |
|---|---|
| The Somaliland National League | British Protectorate mainly. |
| The National United Front | British Protectorate. |
| The Somali Youth League | French Somaliland, Ethiopia, British Protectorate, Somalia, Kenya, East Africa, &c. |

---

[35] Following Somali usage the word 'party' is used here in a broad sense to denote organizations not all of which are designed to contest elections and not all of which are at the same level of political development.

|                            |                           |
|----------------------------|---------------------------|
| The Somali Democratic Party | Somalia.                 |
| United Somali Association   | Kenya, British East Africa. |
| Union Républicaine          | French Somaliland.[36]    |

## C. Regional (and tribal) Parties

|                            |          |
|----------------------------|----------|
| The Afgoi-Audegle Party    | Somalia. |
| The Banadir Youth          | Somalia. |
| The Ḥizbia Digil-Mirifleh[37] | Somalia. |
| Shidleh Party              | Somalia. |
| Bajuni Fiqarini            | Somalia. |

## A. Clan Parties

We take first those organizations which are founded on ties of clanship and whose aim is to promote the interests of a particular agnatic group. Parties of this type are less developed in the British Protectorate than they are in Somalia. This is to be ascribed to a feebler degree of political consciousness in the modern sense in the Protectorate, and not to a weakening of the ties of clanship, for it is, as we have seen, in Somalia that the tendency to overcome the bonds of kinship is most developed and associated in the south with an agricultural economy. The Habar Awal, ʿIise Muuse of the British Protectorate, had, however, from 1952 to 1954 a short-lived political party, the Mahlia, whose aims were principally the promotion of ʿIise Muuse interests. And at the moment there is a strong movement towards the formation of similar purely clan parties, although in 1957 no well organized or clearly defined political party of this kind had made its appearance in the Protectorate. In British East Africa the interests of Somali immigrants (mainly Isḥaaq) are served by the Isḥaaqiya society, whose aims, despite some connexion with the Somaliland National League of the Protectorate, seem to be less political than simply those of an association or club. The Isḥaaqiya is, moreover, basically concerned with emphasizing Somali claims to Arabian descent in order that the Isḥaaq settlers may be classed with the Asian section of the East African populations and in return for paying a higher tax[38] enjoy the advantages of Arabian education and other privileges. Africans regard this as typical Somali snobbery, and there is no doubt that whatever tangible benefits

---

[36] The constitution of this party, which is an alliance of Somali, Danakil, and Arabs, is discussed in the second part of this study.

[37] This party changed its name in 1950 to *Ḥizbia Dastuur Muustaqiil,* the Independent Constitutional Party.

[38] Somali immigrants are not classed as 'natives' in Kenya and pay a 'non-native' tax graduated by income. The special tax paid by clansmen in the Northern (Frontier) Province is discussed in a succeeding article.

may result from their classification as 'non-Natives', Isḥaaq honour is at stake.[39]

The Marrehaan Union is the organ of the Marrehaan (Daarood) of the trans-Juban region of Somali. It is a splinter group of Daarood (Daarood in the main being S.Y.L.)[40] and has some slight influence with one seat in the Somalia Legislative Assembly. The Hawiye Party represents some of the Hawiye of Somalia (other Hawiye support the S.Y.L.) but is of little importance and has no representative in the Legislative Assembly. Hawiye supporters were in 1956 estimated to comprise some 30 per cent.[41] of the S.Y.L. following which indicates that, although there is a Hawiye Party frankly seeking support on clan lines, it has not yet achieved much success in its appeal to traditional kinship ties. To promote and encourage Hawiye support, however, the party was instrumental in organizing a memorial service (*siyaaro*) for the eponymous ancestor of the Hawiye clan-family at Mogadishu on 12 October 1956.[42] This was an attempt to marry the traditional expression of Hawiye clan solidarity with modern political aims.

## B. National Parties

Of the second class of political parties—those whose declared goal is the establishment of Somali nationalism and the destruction of the crippling ties of kinship and clan allegiance—the oldest is the Somaliland National League (S.N.L.) which has existed intermittently under various titles in the British Protectorate since 1935. This organization, with some connexion with the Isḥaaqiya of Kenya, is principally confined to the Protectorate where it assumed its present form and title in 1951. It draws most of its support from the Isḥaaq clans although it includes also some Dir and Daarood amongst its members. The League has a central committee, local (or district) committees, and a general assembly. The composition of the central and local committees includes a president, secretary, treasurer, and other members. The League's headquarters are at Burao and there are other branches at Hargeisa, Berbera, Borama, Erigavo, Sheikh, and Odweina. Admission to the League is by entrance fee (3s. E.A.) and a monthly subscription of 1s.6d. is payable. Members wear a badge bearing the

---

[39] The recently formed United Somali Association at Nairobi appears to have wider aims than the Isḥaaqiya and to be more nationalistic in outlook.

[40] The Somali Youth League nationalist party is discussed below.

[41] It will be appreciated that estimates of the clan membership of different political parties can only give approximate indications of party membership.

[42] For this information I am indebted to Dr. M. Pirone of the Education Department of the Government of Somalia, and to Mr. John Gethin, sometime H.M. Consul, Mogadishu.

legend in Arabic, 'Be united in the name of God' and 'S.N.L.'[43] members are required to swear to sacrifice their lives for their country if necessary. The League is predominantly Muslim in outlook and aims, is in contact with Egypt, and has ties with the local Islamic Somali Association in Aden. The original programme was:

(a) to work for the unification of the Somali race and Somali territories;
(b) to work for the advancement of the Somali race by abolishing clan fanaticism and encouraging brotherly relations among Somalis;
(c) to encourage the spread of education[44] and the economic and political development of the country;
(d) to co-operate with the British Government or any other local body whose aims are the welfare of the inhabitants of the country.

With the return to Ethiopia, by an Anglo-Ethiopian Agreement of 29 November 1954, of the Haud and former Reserved Areas,[45] in fulfilment of the Anglo-Ethiopian Treaty of 1897,[46] a treaty which Somalis have

---

[43] The badge also bears a replica of the Black Stone of Mecca, and costs 3s.

[44] Seventy-six Somali school boys who went for education to Egypt under the auspices of the S.N.L. and S.Y.L. have now applied for assistance from the British Government: *War Somali Sidihi,* No. 109, 9 March 1957, p. 9.

[45] This is the region of rich grazing, some 25,000 square miles in extent and occupied by a shifting nomadic population of some 200,000–300,000 persons which lies to the south of the British Protectorate. The region was incorporated in Somalia by the Italians during their expansionist movement in East Africa and Ethiopia, but, with the exception of a few police posts, was hardly administered and in 1941 was placed under the British Military Administration. Under a British Civil Affairs Administration portions of the Haud and Reserved Areas were returned to Ethiopia over the years until in 1954 there remained only two British Civil Affairs Officers. By the terms of the 1954 Anglo-Ethiopian Agreement these were withdrawn and replaced by a British Liaison staff with headquarters at Jigjiga. The duties of the British Liaison Officer and his assistants are to safeguard the grazing rights of British subjects from the Protectorate, whose rights to pasture in the former Reserved Areas were acknowledged by Ethiopia in the original Treaty of 1897 and reiterated in the Agreement of 1954. It is said to have been assumed by some of the British officials responsible for drawing up the terms of the Agreement that Ethiopia would not in fact actually go to the length of setting up a local administrative staff, and that, consequently, there would be little or no difficulty in the operation of the Agreement. As is well known, this prediction has proved to be very far from accurate and the difficulties which British Protected Somalis have experienced in their movements to and from the Reserved Areas (now known as 'the Territories') have given rise to repeated representations being made to the British Government to seek the return of the Territories, to Anglo-Ethiopian Conferences on the working of the Agreement in which both sides have alleged infringements, and to an abortive attempt on the part of the British Government in a mission in April 1956 led by Mr. Dodds-Parker (then Joint Parliamentary Under-Secretary of State for Foreign Affairs) to return the administration of the Territories to Great Britain.

[46] For the terms of the Treaty see under 'Abyssinia' in A. H. Oakes and F. H. T. Streatfield, *A Complete Collection of the Treaties and Conventions and Reciprocal Regulations Subsisting between Great Britain and Foreign Powers,* London, for H.M. Stationery Office, 1898, vol. xx.

never recognized,[47] and the independence which Somalia is destined to attain in 1960 (or 1959), the S.N.L. is now pressing for a grant of similar status to the Somaliland Protectorate. Recent (1956–7) events in the Middle East, the Egyptian seizure of the Suez Canal and Anglo-French intervention in Suez, have stimulated the pro-Egyptian and pro-Arab World tendencies of the League.

Another nationalist movement of importance in the British Protectorate is the National United Front (N.U.F.). This organization, which is entirely confined to the Protectorate, is a convention or congress rather than a party. It was founded in 1955 at a public conference with the aims of obtaining the return of the former Reserved Areas to the Protectorate,[48] and of working for the independence of the Protectorate within the British Commonwealth. A further aim now being given increasing prominence is that of federation to Somalia. Originally an alliance of the S.N.L. and S.Y.L. in the Protectorate and of other associations and private individuals and district representatives, it received wide support at the time of its inception.[49] Because of its character as a convention rather than a party and its failure hitherto in the first of its objectives—the return of the Haud and Reserved Areas—much S.Y.L. and S.N.L. support has been lost, and it now tends, although impressive in the calibre of its leaders, to lack any constant fol-

---

[47] Somalis consider that the terms of the previous treaties of the British Government with the Gadabuursi (1884) and with the Habar Awal (1884 and 1886) preclude Britain's right to cede territorial rights to Foreign Powers (Ethiopia) by any subsequent treaty (the Anglo-Ethiopian Treaty of 1897). Whatever the *prima facie* justness of the Somali view in alleging a transgression by Great Britain of prior treaties, it seems now to be generally accepted that in International Law the Treaty of 1897 with Ethiopia remains valid.

[48] A delegation consisting of Sultan ʿAbdillahi ('Iidagale), Sultan ʿAbdarahiim (Habar Awal), Dube ʿAli Maḥammad (Habar Tol Jaʿlo), and Michael Mariano (Habar Tol Jaʿlo) visited England in February 1955 to interview the Colonial Secretary and to arouse English public opinion and support against the transfer of the Reserved Areas to Ethiopia. This, of course, was a purely Isḥaaq delegation and received considerable publicity in the British Press. See *The Times*, 5, 8, 14, 15, and 23 Feb. 1955; *The Manchester Guardian*, 23 Feb. 1955. A second delegation consisting of Mr. Mariano and Sultan Biḥi (Ogaadeen), a refugee from Ethiopia, visited England in September of 1956 to discuss the Haud and Reserved Areas again with the British Colonial Secretary before proceeding to New York where it was intended to petition the United Nations Assembly and to seek their intervention or approval to put the Somali case to the International Court. The delegation's visit to the United Nations proved abortive and the dispute has still not been placed before the International Court.

[49] Conferences are periodically held at the N.U.F. Headquarters in Hargeisa attended by representatives of all districts and parties. At a Conference held on 15 May 1957, for instance, representatives of the following were present: Burao, Berbera, Borama, Las Anod, and Hargeisa Districts; S.N.L. and S.Y.L.; the Somali Officials Union (Hargeisa); the Somali Old Boys' Association (former pupils of Sheikh School); and the Somali Association, Aden. A report of the proceedings was circularized to all those mentioned and in addition to the Somali Brethren Society, England; the Somalis in Dahran (Saudi Arabia); the Somalis in Jiddah (Saudi Arabia); and the Somalis in Salalla (Aden). Financial contributions for the N.U.F. from Somalis in Saudia Arabia have been particularly generous.

lowing in the country. Its force lies in its flexibility of organization, which is open to all and not bound by a party system, and in its extremely able administrative core. Unlike the S.N.L. and S.Y.L., the N.U.F. does not have local branches throughout the country, but that does not mean that it cannot on occasion receive support from all quarters. The amounts of donations and financial aid received from all sections of the Protectorate community, and not only in British Somaliland, are impressive. And in keeping with its mediatory character as an all-party convention the N.U.F. have on occasion successfully intervened in clan and lineage-group disputes.[50]

The Somali Youth League (S.Y.L.) was founded in Somalia in 1943.[51] From its inception it has championed the cause of a greater Somalia—of a linking together under one Somali government of all the Somali territories from French Somaliland to the Northern Province of Kenya. When the British Military Administration of Somalia (then ex-Italian Somaliland) was disbanded in 1949, the party campaigned strongly for the unification of all the Somali territories and this proposal was supported by Britain's Foreign Minister at the time (Ernest Bevin). This solution was not acceptable to the Great Powers who returned Italy to Somalia as administering authority of a United Nations Trusteeship Territory which was to attain independence in 1960.[52] The S.Y.L. played a prominent part in the Mogadishu riots of 1949[53] which were held to demonstrate dissatisfaction at the return of Italian administration. Elections were held in Somalia during February 1956 for sixty seats in the newly created Legislative Assembly and voting took place both in the municipalities and the interior.[54] The S.Y.L. won a decisive majority of 43 seats. The organization of the Assembly and the scope and policy of Somalia's S.Y.L. government will be discussed in [parts IV–VI].

---

[50] The leaders of the National United Front have recently (1957) returned from a visit to Mogadishu where they discussed with the Government of Somalia the possible future of the Somali territories. This mission seems to have given a fillip to the Party's influence.

[51] As its name implies, more than any of the other present nationalist organizations it depends for support upon the new élite—the educated younger generation most numerous in Somalia.

[52] The status of the U.N. Trusteeship Territory of Somalia in International Law was approved by the General Assembly of the United Nations on 2 December 1950 and ratified by an Agreement with Italy (Law No. 1301 of 4 Nov. 1951).

[53] Cf. Trimingham, 1952, p. 280.

[54] Voting was confined to the masculine population, and candidates for the legislature were required to be over 30 years of age, literate in Italian and Arabic, and to have been resident at least one year in Somalia. In the municipalities voters were required to be registered on the municipal electoral lists. In the interior, where, in accordance with Somali custom, every sane male over 21 years of age could vote (as long as he had no grievous criminal record); voting took place through *ad hoc* councils or gatherings (*shirs*, see above) at which representatives were appointed to carry votes to the recorders. It is alleged and generally recognized that a considerable amount

The headquarters organization of the party at Mogadishu includes a president,[55] a deputy, a secretary, treasurer, comptrollers, and some twelve other members of council. District branches in Somalia and other Somali territories have a similar organization. Membership requires payment of an entrance fee and a small monthly subscription. A membership card is issued and a badge bearing the inscription 'S.Y.L.' As with the S.N.L. of the Protectorate, wherever there is a party branch weekly meetings are held in a building used as a meeting-place and club by the local party members. The proceedings at these meetings are generally formal. When the local party leaders enter the premises all present stand up as a sign of respect. Young members are appointed as ushers responsible for the discipline of the meeting. When the young members act as stewards at local meetings, and especially at public demonstrations, they wear a uniform consisting of white slacks and a white shirt crossed diagonally from shoulder to hip by a red and blue bandolier with the slogan 'S.Y.L.'[56] The introduction of a measure of formal discipline and of coloured uniforms and banners is a modern innovation foreign to traditional Somali clan life. Some precedent, however, exists in the organization (although less formal) of the Sufi Dervish Orders. The local weekly meetings are generally of much the same form. They are largely taken up with discussions and addresses on the aims of the party and with debates on matters of topical interest. A prominent feature common to all is the recitation and singing of patriotic verse (usually in the form of *gabay*)[57] and songs epitomizing the aims of the party. It is particularly interesting that the *gabay*, which in the traditional social context is often an effective vehicle for clan and lineage-group enmity, should here be used to promote the extension of nationalist sentiments and unity. In the partly Bantu culture of southern Somalia the meetings, in which women also participate,[58] include entertainments and dancing.

The pan-Somali and non-kinship character of the S.Y.L. is illustrated

---

of bribery and buying of votes took place. Out of a population represented at the time as twice as many, a total of 858,122 male adults are supposed to have voted. Either the election results had been very considerably exaggerated or the population of Somalia had been grossly underestimated. The most recent (1957) estimate of approximately 2 million for the population of Somalia is at least in better accord with the election figures.

[55] The present office-holder, Haaji Maḥammad Ḥusseen Ḥamud, who is also a former president, was elected in July 1957. Ḥaaji Maḥammad belongs to the Reer Ḥamar tribal section of Mogadishu. The Reer Ḥamar are a mixed urban population of part Somali origin. See Lewis, 1957 (1), p. 12.

[56] The S.N.L. wear a similar uniform but their sash is green and bears their own slogan. Proceedings at S.N.L. meetings are little different from those of the S.Y.L.

[57] *Gabay* is the traditional highly stylized Somali poem, the highest form of Somali verse. See Kirk, 1905, pp. 170 ff.; Maino, 1953, pp. 44 ff.; and Laurence, 1954, pp. 5 ff.

[58] Among the northern nomads women do not attend local political meetings. At a mixed meeting which I attended in southern Somalia the dancers sang the refrain: 'We are Somali, what can the person who resists the cry "Somali" do?'

in its membership in Somalia which was in 1956 estimated to comprise: Daarood, 50 per cent., Hawiye 30 per cent., Digil-Mirifleh 10 per cent., and others 10 per cent. Its strength in Somalia is indicated by the over-whelming majority which the party gained in the elections for the Legis-lative Assembly. There are branches throughout Somalia. In the British Protectorate there are branches at Burao, Hargeisa, Borama, Las Anod, Erigavo, and along the Makhir coast in the east of the Protectorate. The central council for the Protectorate is established at Berbera. Although in close contact with the Somalia headquarters organization, the S.Y.L. in the Protectorate lacks the vitality of the movement in Somalia. Its leaders are not of the same calibre as those in the south. With a following in the Protectorate smaller than that of its rival the S.N.L., the party derives much of its support from the eastern Dulbahante and Warsangeli (Daarood). The S.Y.L. exists also, necessarily under cover, in French Somaliland, Ethiopia, and the Northern Province of Kenya. In all these territories it is banned.[59] In every region of Somaliland its policy is nation-alistic and pan-Somali, but the extent to which these ideals are promoted in practice should not be judged too harshly, for it should be compared with other mainly clan organizations such as the Hawiye Party and Mar-rehaan Union, discussed above.

Finally, among the present parties striving to overcome the bonds of clanship must be mentioned the Somali Democratic Party of Somalia, which although a small party, nevertheless managed to gain three seats in the legislature. It exists only in Somalia and has an estimated following of: Daarood 50 per cent., Hawiye 40 per cent., others 10 per cent.

## C. Regional (and Tribal) Parties

The final group of parties are those which represent territorial rather than clan interests. These existed in 1957 only in Somalia, where, as we have seen in the south, the traditional lineage structure has been superseded to a considerable extent. There are four small parties, none of which returned a candidate to the Assembly in the 1956 elections. The Young Banadir, representing the interests of some of the peoples of the Banadir coast and based on Mogadishu, is currently estimated to be composed of: Reer Hamar[60] 80 per cent., Digil-Mirifleh 10 per cent., and others 10 per cent. The Afgoi-Audegle Party represents the cultivators (mainly Rahanweyn) based in the region between the villages of Afgoi and Audegle on the Shebelle River to the south-west of Mogadishu. This party is much smaller than the Young Banadir which in the 1956 elections ranked fourth amongst

---

[59] Under the new régime in French Somaliland, established by the *loi cadre*, greater freedom will presumably be allowed to the S.Y.L.

[60] For the Reer Hamar see Lewis, 1957 (1), p. 12.

the parties in the poll. It was primarily a combination of interests for the purpose of gaining seats in the elections and had almost completely collapsed in 1957. The remaining two small parties of this class and with little influence are the Bajuni-Fiqarini which caters for the interests of the coastal Bajuni of southern Somalia, and the Shidle Party which represents the Negroid Shidle cultivators of the Shebelle River.[62]

The most important party of this type is the Digil-Mirifleh Party (Digil and Mirifleh, including Raḥanweyn 90 per cent.; Reer Baraawa 5 per cent.;[63] others 5 per cent.), which represents the interests of the Digil and Raḥanweyn cultivators (or most of them) and associated tribes, and includes the support of the people of the town of Brava (Reer Baraawa). They gained 13 seats in the Assembly of Somalia in the 1956 elections, the largest number of seats held by any single party on the opposition benches, and with their good organization and vitality are the nucleus of an effective opposition. The existence of the Ḥizbia[64] Digil-Mirifleh was in 1957 the nearest approach in Somalia to a modern political cleavage between Samaale and Sab and following traditional lineage principles. In classing the Ḥizbia Digil-Mirifleh with the regional parties, I have been guided by the fact that, although their name refers to the eponymous ancestors of the Digil and Raḥanweyn clan-families, their organization as a political party is not based on lineage affiliation. As was shown above, it is in this region that tribalism founded on territorial ties is taking the place of clanship, and it is the common cultural, economic, and territorial interests of the Digil and Raḥanweyn inhabiting the most fertile region of Somalia that their party represents. At times, indeed, the Digil-Mirifleh Party has gone so far in expressing the sense of independence and identity of the Digil and Raḥanweyn tribes as to advocate the creation in southern Somalia of a separate and autonomous Digil-Mirifleh state. This aim had not been achieved in 1957, nor can it command much support, for the riverine area occupied by the Sab is the richest and most capable of economic development in Somalia.

In this article I have examined the organization of modern Somali political movements in relation to the traditional political organization. I have argued that there are three principal types of party; clan, national and regional or tribal. To some extent these three types reflect regional variations in the traditional social organization and traditional cleavages. Only in southern Somalia, where regional tribalism partly replaces agnation as a political principle, are regional and tribal political parties found. In the concluding part of this study, . . . I shall discuss the present consti-

---

[61] For the non-Somali Bajuni see Grottanelli, 1955.

[62] For the Shidle see Lewis, 1955, p. 41.

[63] For the Reer Baraawa see Lewis, 1955, p. 42; 1957 (1), p. 13.

[64] Cf. Arabic, ḥ-z-b, party.

tutional position and the activities of the parties in the different Somali territories.

· · ·

IV[65]

## Somali Nationalism and Constitutional Changes in the Somali Territories

### 1. French Somaliland

The *Côte des Somalis* has a currently estimated population of 63,000 of whom 3,000 are European, 26,000 Danakil ('Afar),[66] 17,000 'Iise Somali, and the remaining 17,000, which includes Arab (6,000) and other immigrants, mainly Somali (Habar Awal, Gadabuursi, &c.). It thus seems that the total Somali population is slightly in excess of the Danakil. Since the Danakil and 'Iise are traditional enemies their administration and the promotion of Somali nationalism aiming ultimately at the formation of a greater Somalia, set special problems.[67]

Prior to June 1957 there was a local Representative Council consisting of two sections. One contained representatives of the expatriate French community and the other Somali, Danakil, and Arab members. This assembly appointed a representative to the Council of the French Republic and to the Assembly of the French Union.[68] The total electorate of the territory appointed one Deputy to the metropolitan National Assembly.

The constitutional position was radically altered by the establishment,

---

[65] . . . In the preparation of [parts iv–vi] I am particularly indebted to the stimulating criticism of Professor J. C. Mitchell.

[66] For the Danakil ('Afar) a people closely related to the Somali and their neighbours to the north-west, see Lewis, 1955, pp. 155–73.

[67] The 'Afar (Danakil) are known to Somali, particularly to the 'Iise, not by their own name 'Afar', but as *Ood 'Ali* which some Somali consider a 'Somalization' of the Arabic 'he harmed' (a-dh-a) combined with the proper name 'Ali. There are different opinions as to whom the name 'Ali refers; some say it is 'Ali Abu Taalib, the uncle and son-in-law of the Prophet, and equate the Danakil with those who supported the Ummayad rebellion against 'Ali in the struggle for the Caliphate about A.D. 657. Others say it refers to 'Ali Samarroon, ancestor of the Gadabuursi clan, although the Danakil and Gadabuursi are separated by the 'Iise and rarely come into contact. There is little intermarriage between the 'Iise and 'Afar, and 'Iise informants in the Protectorate said that the Danakil were little better than bondsmen (*sab*). While among themselves the 'Iise nominally pay blood-wealth of a hundred camels or their equivalent for the death of a man, between 'Iise and 'Afar thirty camels or less are usually paid. Many 'Iise songs (*geeraar* and *gabay*) boast of the murder of Danakil and, although perhaps less common now than formerly, for an 'Iise youth to kill a Danakil brings prestige and honour. Camel-raiding between them is common. Even in the towns of French Somaliland fights between 'Iise and Danakil are quite frequent. While I was in Jibuti in January 1957 a small riot broke out between Danakıl and Somali in the town.

[68] The first was an 'Iise Somali, and the second a Danakil. For the constitution of the Representative Council see H. Deschamps *et al., Côte des Somalis; Réunion-Inde, Paris,* 1948, pp. 61–62.

in accordance with the *loi-cadre*,[69] of a Territorial Assembly for which elections were held in June 1957. As in Somalia[70] the right to vote was limited to the adult male population. Two parties contested thirty seats in the Assembly divided among three constituencies, Jibuti, Tajura, and Obock, of which the capital Jibuti was allocated the largest number of seats. The elections were won by the *Union Républicaine* led by Maḥamuud Harbi ('Iise Deputy in the metropolitan Chamber) who defeated his opponents in all three constituencies. The *Union* is a Somali-Danakil coalition with the financial backing of immigrant Arab merchants. These interests are reflected in the composition of the council of ministers of whom four are Somali, two Danakil, one Arab, and one European. External and military affairs remain in the control of the metropolitan government and the Council is presided over by the Governor of the *Côte* as President. The Vice-President is Maḥamuud Harbi, and the Arab member, 'Ali Kubeesh, a prominent merchant, is Minister of Finance. The European member is Minister of Education. The allocation of portfolios, where the Arab minister holds the responsibility for finance, represents the balance struck between Somali nationalistic aims in the person of Maḥamuud Harbi and economic considerations, since the Arab community has a greater interest in commerce than the Somali or Danakil. The economy of the *Côte* depends almost entirely upon the trade flowing through the port of Jibuti from Ethiopia. Since, in Eritrea, Ethiopia now has the alternative ports of Massawa and Assab, the Ethiopian Government is in a position to use economic sanctions to restrain Somali nationalism. There is also the question of resolving Somali and Danakil rivalry as well as providing for the security of Arab traders, to say nothing of French colonial policy.

In spite of the apparent resolution of these points of issue in the victory of the *Union Républicaine,* and its at least partial support of the pan-Somali movement, the bulk of the Somali population has so far shown little interest in Somali nationalism. The 'Iise are the only Somali clan who customarily graze in strength in French territory. They are less affected by external influences than most of the northern Somali and most strongly devoted to their traditional mode of life. Generally they think of themselves as 'Iise' rather than 'Somali' and show little evidence of that wider consciousness of nationhood which is manifest, at least to some extent, in Somalia.[71] But in French Somaliland there is a greater difference between

---

[69] The terms of the *loi-cadre*, No. 56.619 of 23 June 1956, are discussed in *Chroniques d'Outre-Mer*, No. 35, May 1957, pp. 3–19.

[70] See *Africa*, loc. cit. p. 257.

[71] United in long-standing hostility to the Danakil and also frequently at war with the Gadabuursi of the Protectorate, the 'Iise exhibit greater unity and internal solidarity than do most other Northern Somali clans. In this and other ways they are generally recognized as unusual. Other Somali often say 'the 'Iise are 'Iise' (*'Iise waa 'Iise*), with the implication that they are 'Iise and no one else.

town and interior than elsewhere in Northern Somaliland. The town of Jibuti, with a mixed urban population of about 30,000 (nearly half the total population) includes over 15,000 Somali of whom a significant proportion are Isḥaaq and Gadabuursi from the British Protectorate. With its Arab and other immigrants it has something of a cosmopolitan character and is much more industrialized than the capital of the British Protectorate. Trade unions are more developed and better organized than in British Somaliland. Here the influence of the Somali Youth League and Somaliland National League continues and through a party such as the *Union Républicaine* may eventually find fertile soil for a strong Somali nationalist movement. The victory of the *Union* is already an indication of such a movement.[72] The facility with which parties were organized to contest the elections compared with the failure of the parties in the Protectorate to put forward party rather than clan candidates for nomination to the Legislative Council, shows a wider political consciousness in French Somaliland.

The traditional division between the Somali and Danakil is clearly crucial. In recent years prior to the formation of the legislative assembly the French Government appears to have been attempting to minimize the demands of the Somali section of the population, arguing that its interests are no more important than those of the Danakil. An impressive degree of solidarity between the two rival communities was shown in the elections. A further indication of unity is given by an S.Y.L. slogan which asserts that not only are all the Somali one, but that they are at one with the Danakil ('Afar) and Galla of Ethiopia and Kenya.[73] Probably the more control Somali and Danakil gain in their government the more clearly their traditional differences will reappear. This at least is what is happening in Somalia, where, since the inauguration of the legislative assembly, there has been an upsurge of clanship.[74] Because of their close economic relationship with Ethiopia, Ethiopian imperialism may, more than in any other Somali territory, serve as a focus of unity sufficient even to overcome the traditional difference between the Somali and Danakil.

The new government may be expected to further education and the appointment of Danakil and Somali to officer grades in the administration in the direction already taken in British Somaliland and Somalia. But even

---

[72] The elections have shown that the enthusiasm for the maintenance of the *status quo* with the *Côte* as an integral part of the French Union and the hostility towards a greater Somali federation, expressed by Ḥassan Guuleed, Senator for the *Côte* (in *Union Française et Parlement*, July 1957, pp. 8–9) are not representative of popular feeling.

[73] This is expressed by S.Y.L. members in terms of the (Cushitic) cultural unity of the Somali, Danakil, and Galla. Mr. B. W. Andrzejewski tells me that there is some similar feeling of political solidarity between the Galla Booraan and Somali of the Northern Province of Kenya.

[74] See below pp. 340–342.

without this, the new constitutional changes in French Somaliland have given an impetus to demands for fuller Somali representation in the Protectorate legislative council.

## 2. British Somaliland

There is in the Protectorate no resident European community other than that of government servants who enjoy no local representation. Up to 1957 the only central organization for the expression of Somali opinion has been the Protectorate Advisory Council which has, in principle, met annually.[75] The Council's last meeting was held in October 1957, and delegates were sent to the Council from each District in the Protectorate. These were appointed largely in the first instance at clan and lineage-group meetings (*shirs*) in the Districts, with the aid of District Commissioners who tried to ensure that a reasonably representative party of delegates was sent from each District. A Legislative Council was inaugurated on 21 May 1957.[76]

At its inception the Legislative Council[77] included fifteen members: the Governor; and three *ex-officio* members; the Chief Secretary, the Attorney-General, and the Financial Secretary; five official members; and six unofficial members nominated by the Governor. The Advisory Council continues to meet and it is envisaged that the functions of the two councils should be complementary, providing for the representation of public opinion at different levels. The Advisory Council has, of course, no legislative powers. The six unofficial members were appointed by the Governor from a list of twenty-four candidates submitted on the last meeting of the 1956 Advisory Council. The government had, in fact, asked for sixteen nominations but great difficulty was experienced in selecting candidates and the smallest number which could be agreed upon was twenty-four. Starting in the Advisory Council, the process of selection overflowed into a series of hotly debated public meetings in Hargeisa. The N.U.F. leaders particularly, tried to maintain the principle that candidates should represent the three political parties (N.U.F., S.Y.L., and S.N.L.) and be selected irrespective of their clan and lineage-group affiliation. They maintained that the criteria for election should be capability and education irrespective of whether the final selection ensured an even representation of the major clan and lineage groups in the Protectorate. What actually happened, however, was that candidates were proposed to represent the major clans and lineage groups in each of the six Administrative Districts very much on the same lines as

---

[75] The Council's powers are not defined in the Protectorate Laws.

[76] See *War Somali Sidihi*, No. 115, 1 June 1957, pp. 2 ff.

[77] Powers defined by the Somaliland (Constitution) Ordinance in Council 1955.

the composition of the Advisory Council. That lineage group and not party political representatives were proposed is an index of the rudimentary character of party allegiance in British Somaliland.

In 1953 Local Government Councils[78] were established in two municipalities, Hargeisa and Berbera, and were also set up at Burao and Gebile towards the end of 1957.

With the developments in local and central government there is increasing scope for party political activity. Of the three main parties (the S.Y.L., S.N.L., and the National United Front) at present working in the Protectorate, the S.N.L. with its more extreme opposition to a continuation of British influence tends to command a wider appeal and a popular but fluctuating following. With its policy of independence within the Commonwealth, its failure so far to retrieve the Haud and Reserved Areas,[79] and its (in many people's eyes) excessive moderation, the National United Front has little permanent support. But because its organization is not exclusive and is open to members of all other parties and interest-groups it has potentially the widest following.[80]

As has been indicated important stimuli to anti-Ethiopian feeling and patriotism were provided by Britain's transfer of the Reserved Areas in 1954, the unsatisfactory working of the Agreement by which the transfer was effected, and the Ethiopian Emperor's imperialist speech on Somali-Ethiopian relations at Qabradare in the Haud in August 1956.[81] But although the enmity generated by these actions was considerable it has not yet led to any effective political unity. As in all the Somali territories attempts to promote effective national unity—in any cause, no matter how wide and compelling its appeal—are vitiated by clan and lineage rivalries. Such jealousies founded in daily nomadic life are more important than national unity. The slight degree of modern political consciousness which exists in the Protectorate at the moment explains why no purely clan political parties (such as the Hawiye Party of Somalia)[82] have yet been formed.

Those of the new élite, particularly, are acutely conscious of the crippling hold of clanship and blood-compensation agreements. For several years now, at District Council meetings, political meetings, and informal discussions, there has been talk of abolishing Somali *heer* (contract, agreement: in the widest sense, custom) which with clanship is regarded as the supreme impediment to the growth of political party and 'national soli-

---

[78] Local Government Council Ordinance, No. 1 of 1953.

[79] See pp. 324–325.

[80] For an occasion in which widespread popular support was achieved, see p. 325.

[81] The Emperor's address is recorded in a brochure published by the Ethiopian Press and Information Department. It is printed in Amharic, English and Arabic, and has been the subject of comment in the local Somali press of Somalia, see below, p. 344.

[82] See p. 323.

darity'.[83] Demands for the abolition of these inhibiting forces have come from most sections of the community, especially, of course, from religious leaders (particularly those with modernist tendencies) and nationalist politicians.[84] At a session of the Protectorate Legislative Council held in November 1957 a motion was tabled calling for consideration of how best to overcome 'Somali tribal *Heer*'. The government agreed that a public enquiry should be held. But in spite of vociferous pleas for their abolition on the part of a small section of the community the ties of clanship (*tol*) and treaty (*heer*) remain firmly rooted in Somali pastoral nomadism. Not withstanding the work of the S.Y.L., S.N.L. and N.U.F. patriotic nationalism is little more than an empty slogan and has little reality as a permanently effective political sentiment. Agnation is far more important than party solidarity. Thus although local government councils have been established there is no question yet of municipal elections being contested on a party basis. They are conducted on lineage-group principles, members of one lineage-group supporting their candidate in opposition to a candidate from a rival lineage-group. The business of the councils is ruled by agnation. Proposals made by a member of a certain clan or lineage-group are supported by those of the council who are his agnates and opposed by those who are not. I give one further indication of the primacy of agnatic support in the field of recent political developments. In 1957 a certain well-known sheikh of the Habar Yuunis clan who had been studying for several years in Egypt returned to the Protectorate and attempted to establish a strongly anti-government (i.e. anti-Christian imperialism) religious party. Among other things he attacked the disrupting forces of clan and lineage-group rivalry and the illegal (according to the Shariah) Somali system of paying blood-compensation. He encountered apathy and also hostility from the religious leaders of other clans. Even amongst the Habar Yuunis he was opposed by many and supported (in opposition to this hostility) by a party of his own close agnates. The nature of his support was in strict contradiction to the nationalist ideals which he sought to promote.

Outside the towns, as might be expected, there is little permanent interest in the political parties, whose functions have little appeal. Clan and lineage-group support is most effectively solicited through agnatic connexions. But at the moment the parties and the modern political ideals which they propagate have not made much impression in the interior. Occasionally I have met clansmen who in reply to my greeting and question 'of what clan are you' answered ostentatiously 'Somali' and refused to

---

[83] In spite of the urgency of the question of the Reserved Areas in the deliberations of the Advisory Council in 1956, the first item on the agenda was 'that the present Somali custom governing the payment of blood-money should be abolished'.

[84] Opposition to the collective payment of blood compensation by treaty (*heer*) is particularly strong among traders in the towns who seek to escape from paying compensation for actions in which they are not directly involved.

divulge their lineage. But this attempt to impress the stranger with a show of national unity—in opposition to the nationality of the questioner—is no indication of effective political unity. Members of the parties are often found in the interior with their party membership card carefully guarded among their valuables. But as far as their actions are concerned—as has been illustrated—party membership is not an effective principle of political grouping for the majority of the adherents of any party. But the local party meetings, if they do nothing else, at least maintain the existence of the party and occasionally increase its membership.

In 1957 there were about thirty Somali in the officer *cadre* out of a total of just over 200 officers in the Protectorate Administration. This degree of replacement of expatriate staff is in contrast to the rudimentary character of national feeling discussed above.

## 3. Ethiopia[85]

The Somali inhabitants of Ethiopia are a minority of less than three-quarters of a million, who probably do not comprise more than one-sixteenth of the total populations of Ethiopia and Eritrea,[86] and they are concentrated almost entirely in Harar Province. In considering the electoral rights of Somalis and their participation in government, therefore, it must be remembered that in contrast to their position in neighbouring territories (other than in Kenya) in Ethiopia they constitute only one fraction of a large and heterogeneous population.

The Ethiopian Parliament consists of an Upper House of Senators, and a Lower House of Deputies in which, in the spring of 1957, there was one Somali nominee from the Ogaden. Under Article 77 of the New Constitution of Ethiopia, promulgated by the Emperor on 4 November 1955, provision was made for the holding within two years of the first general election to the Lower House, the Chamber of Deputies. Elections[87] by direct suffrage and secret ballot were to be held throughout the Empire, including Eritrea, all men and women over twenty-one years of age having the right to vote. No property or literacy qualifications are required of the voters, but candidates for election must possess 1,000 dollars (Ethiopian) worth of immovable or $2,000 of movable property and deposit $250 with

---

[85] For the background to Ethiopian administration, see Perham, 1948, and Howard, 1956.

[86] The current official estimate of the population of Ethiopia and Eritrea is 16 million. According to Trimingham, 1952, p. 15, the total Christian population is greater than the combined population of Muslims and 'pagans'. It goes without saying that estimates of this kind are only approximate.

[87] The legislation governing the elections is the Chamber of Deputies Electoral Law, the terms of which are printed in the *Negarit Gazeta,* Addis Ababa, 27 August 1956.

the regional Electoral Boards set up under the Electoral Law. Voters must have lived for at least one year in their electoral district. Those serving criminal sentences, or who have lost their civil rights (the punishment for political offences) are excluded from voting. Voters are required to register their names and certain particulars in electoral registers in every electoral district and are provided with a voting card. The management of the elections as a whole is entrusted to a National Board of Registration and Elections established for the purpose in the Ministry of the Interior and consisting of three officials appointed by the Emperor. It has considerable powers and could, conceivably, influence the appointment of candidates.[88]

The elections originally scheduled to commence on the 9th of January 1957 (and every four years thereafter) were not actually held until September, owing to various delays in the preparation of the election organization. To what extent the new representation will enable Ethiopian Somali subjects to participate in their government remains to be seen. The banning of all opposition political parties in Ethiopia contrasts sharply with the apparently highly democratic character of the electoral charter as defined in the Electoral Law. Although the Somali Youth League continues to operate underground the atmosphere of intense rivalry and competition among a large number of political parties, which formed the background to the 1956 elections in Somalia, is completely absent.

Some concessions have been made to Somali by appointments to the junior ranks of the officer *cadre* of administrative officials in Harar Province. If their standard falls short of that of Somali in similar administrative positions in surrounding territories, in the present undeveloped state of the Ogaden this may be of little consequence to those whom they administer. Current events show the mainly nomadic Somali of Harar Province to be content for the present to accept gifts from the Ethiopian Government, the appointment of *'aaqils* (*balabats*), and payment of stipends to traditional titular authorities (Sultans, *Garaads*, &c.) as adequate recognition of their rights. If they were thus left undisturbed from further interference, taxation, and the injustices of an allegedly oppressive and corrupt administration, they would probably continue content with their lot for some time to come. Indeed, while as we have seen, some Ethiopian Somali subjects have sought political asylum in the British Protectorate and lent their active support to the representations made by the National United Front to the British Government to seek the return of the administration of the former Haud and Reserved Areas to Great Britain,[89] on the other hand some British subjects from the Protectorate have freely sought appointment as Ethiopian *'aaqils*. This applies only to members of clans such as the 'Iise, Gadabuursi, Habar, Awal, Arab, 'Iidagale, Habar Yuunis,

---

[88] See Chamber of Deputies Electoral Law, paras. 3–5.

[89] See p. 325.

in the west, and the Dulbahante in the east, who straddle the artificial and purely arbitrary boundary which separates British from Ethiopian territory. The current of defections is in both directions. It is thus difficult to infer the direction in which Somali loyalties really lie.[90] While at the moment Somali under Ethiopian rule may complain that they are oppressed, the new constitution of the Chamber of Deputies and an increased participation in government may satisfy their demands. The extensions in education and health services and the development of the Haud promised in the Emperor's speech at Qabradare in the Eastern Haud in August 1956 may, if not fulfilled, create dissatisfaction even among the nomadic inhabitants of the region.

It remains to be seen whether the concessions made and promised to Somali interests in the Ethiopian territories will be sufficiently strong to counteract the internal tendencies towards disaffection and the external forces of attraction of the progress towards self-determination of Somali in adjacent territories. At the moment, the greatest attractive force is vested in the pan-Somali nationalist government of Somalia. Here men of the same clans and lineage-groups as those living in Ethiopia are participating fully in the government of a country which aims at the formation of a greater and united Somaliland. The continued 'Somalization' of the administration of the British Protectorate, and the development of increasing Somali representation provided for in the Legislative Council, together

---

[90] It is perhaps misleading to suggest that those Somali clans and lineage-groups which straddle the Anglo-Ethiopian boundary are particularly attached to one side or the other. As long as the nomad can, preferably without interference, move with his kin and stock to the grazing areas and watering-places which are vital to his existence, the national character of those non-Somali governments under whose administration he comes is not very important. Naturally, of course, other things being equal, he prefers an unoppressive to an oppressive administration. But in the present situation it is essential for the nomad who customarily grazes both sides of the Anglo-Ethiopian boundary to be on good, or at least fair, terms with both the British and Ethiopian administrations. Some difference, however, is bound to occur in his allegiance, when he is administered on one side of a boundary by his own kinsmen in Somalia and on the other by Ethiopians. As regards British Somali subjects, in addition to the present necessity of being on good terms with both governments (the British and the Ethiopian), many Somalis are not convinced of British intentions for the future, and fear that they may in time find themselves entirely under Ethiopian control. In the course of my work in the interior, the return of the Haud and Reserved Areas to Ethiopia by what was regarded as an underhand and undeserved breach of faith, was a constant topic of conversation. It was generally impossible for me to question informants on anthropological topics until I had been subjected to a barrage of complaints and objections about the Haud. I was frequently told that if the British Government broke its treaties with the Somali no confidence could be placed in British assurances that the inhabitants of the Protectorate would be encouraged to achieve their own form of self-determination, if they wished, in federation to Somalia. There is therefore, I think, in the defections of Protectorate clansmen to Ethiopia, as well as the present necessity to have adequate grazing rights in Ethiopian territory, an element of safeguarding their future relations with Ethiopia. Many border clansmen in the interior have told me that they fear that the Protectorate will eventually be handed over to Ethiopia and that the return of the Haud is only the thin end of the wedge.

with the statement of policy made by Lord Lloyd on behalf of the British Government in May 1956, which expressed modified approval of the eventual unification of the Protectorate with Somalia, constitute in British Somaliland an attraction comparable to, if weaker than, that exercised by Somalia. As the time approaches for Somalia's independence in 1960, there is bound to be increasing Somali nationalist activity in Ethiopia even if it is still an underground movement. Whether or not it will be strong enough in Harar, the centre to which Somali in Ethiopia traditionally look[91] and where political activity would probably have the strongest foothold, to combat Ethiopian suppression and to arouse strong nationalist opposition to Ethiopian rule in the Province as a whole is impossible to predict. Quite apart from these movements in Ethiopia the future of Somalia itself, economically insecure and requiring considerable external aid, remains precarious in spite of the progress made towards self-government.

## 4. Somalia

The nascent state of Somalia is politically as well as economically (though still a poor country) the most developed of the Somali territories. In the elections held in February 1956 for the newly constituted Legislative Assembly the S.Y.L., as we have seen, were returned with forty-three seats and a clear majority.[92] Thirteen seats went to the Ḥizbia Digil-Mirifleh, three to the Somali Democratic Party, and one to the Marrehaan Union: the remaining ten seats in the legislature were filled by members chosen to represent the minorities; four Italians, four Arabians, one Indian, and one Pakistani. The President of the Assembly is Aaden 'Abdallah of the Hawiye clan-family. The S.Y.L. government is led by a council of five ministers, two of whom are Daarood, two Hawiye, and one Dir.[93] The Prime Minister, 'Abdallahi 'Iise is also Hawiye, so that in the Council of Ministers Hawiye members are in a majority. The extent to which, on the face of it, Daarood interests are subordinated to Hawiye is especially inter-

---

[91] For the role of Harar in Somali history see Trimingham, 1952, pp. 60 ff. Francolini, 1938, p. 1115, gives the population of Harar as 2,000 Amharas (Christians); 12,000 Hararis speaking the city language; 10–15,000 Galla; 1,000 Arabs; and about 1,000 Somali. See also Cerulli, 1936.

[92] Of the total votes cast the S.Y.L. gained 333,780, and 43 seats as against the Ḥizbia Digil-Mirifleh's 159,932 votes and 13 seats. In the Municipal elections held in March 1954, in which sixteen parties presented candidates, out of a total of 281 seats, the S.Y.L. won 142 and the H.D.M. 57. The 1956 elections for the legislature thus show a gain for S.Y.L. from the earlier municipal elections.

[93] The Ministers are: Minister of the Interior, Ḥaaji Muuse Boqor (Daarood, Majeerteen, of the 'Ismaan Maḥamuud lineage of Sultans); Minister of Economic Development, Haaji Faaraḥ 'Ali 'Umar (Hawiye); Minister of Social Affairs, Sheikh 'Ali Jumaaleh (Hawiye); Minister of Finance, Salaad 'Abdi Maḥamuud (Daarood); and Minister of General Affairs, Maḥamuud 'Abdi Nuur (Dir). External affairs remained under the control of the Italian Administering Authority.

esting since, as we have seen, membership of the League is at least half Daarood. And the S.Y.L. party as a whole is generally identified by members of other parties with the interests of the Daarood clan-family.

THE 1956 SOMALIA ASSEMBLY ELECTIONS[94]

(Only the main parties are shown)

| Party | Votes cast | Seats gained |
|---|---|---|
| S.Y.L. | 333,780 | 43 |
| H.D.M. | 159,932 | 13 |
| S.D.P | 81,454 | 3 |
| Young Banadir | 21,619 | |
| Marrehaan Union | 11,358 | 1 |
| Afgoi/Audegle | 3,441 | |
| Hawiye Party | 1,841 | |
| Shidle Party | 1,549 | |
| Bajuni Fiqarini | 426 | |
| *Minority communities* | | |
| Italian | | 4 |
| Arabian | | 4 |
| Indian | | 1 |
| Pakistani | | 1 |
| Total seats in Legislature | | 70 |

The programme of the newly elected S.Y.L. government as outlined by the Premier in 1956 had the following principal objectives.

1. Clarification and settlement of the Somalia-Ethiopian frontier.[95]
2. Stabilization of Somalia's precarious economy: to balance the budget by attracting foreign capital and external aid,[96] and by increasing taxation.

---

[94] These are the figures shown after the elections in *Il Corriere della Somalia,* their total is less than that reported in *Rapport . . . Somalie, 1955,* p. 25.

[95] The frontier with Ethiopia has never been defined. Following a convention of May 1908 an Italo-Ethiopian Commission was appointed in 1910 to determine the principles of allocation of Somali clans and lineage-groups to Ethiopian and Italian jurisdiction. But the commission was only able to establish a boundary over a stretch of 80 kilometres between the wells of Rabodi and Dolo on the Juba River. Since coming under United Nations Trusteeship the question has on several occasions been brought before the General Assembly of the United Nations. A Resolution of December 1955 urged that the Ethiopian and Italian Governments should continue negotiations, in the endeavour to reach agreement regarding their frontiers. But in 1957, despite repeated representations, the boundary still remained unsettled.

[96] The annual budgets over the last few years (1951–6) show a grant-in-aid contribution from the Italian State of about three million pounds sterling annually. This includes military expenses. A mission of World Bank financial experts visited Somalia in 1957 and estimated that external financial aid would be required for at least twenty years after 1960, the official date set for self-government. The vital question

3. The question of votes for women and the official language.[97]
4. Press and radio to be controlled by the Somalia government.[98] The Citizenship Law defining Somali citizenship and deciding the status of immigrants. State properties. The fuller Somali control of legal matters.[99]

With this policy the Ḥizbia Digil-Mirifleh opposition expressed their complete disapproval and stated that it contained nothing new.[100]

With a central legislature in which the majority of members are Somali, and with a considerable number of municipal councils (47 in 1956), there is greater scope in Somalia for political party activity than in any other Somali territory. The standard of education[101] of the Somali members of the legislative council is higher than in British Somaliland, and several members and some government ministers have had experience of political missions to foreign countries including America. In their attitudes towards clanship and *heer*, politicians in Somali show a striking difference to those in the British Protectorate. Whereas in the latter territory the stranglehold of these traditional political principles is a burning question widely discussed, in Somalia their continued influence is discounted and even denied. In Somalia a deliberate effort is made to give the impression that the force

---

for the Somali government is, of course, how to attract this assistance. It is understood that the United Nations have made pledges to the government of Somalia to continue grants-in-aid after self-determination is achieved.

[97] The question of the choice of official language between Arabic and Somali and the related problem of writing Somali in Arabic or Roman characters or in *'Ismaaniyya* has, for many years now, been of great interest in Somalia. See my article 'The Gadabuursi Somali Script', *B.S.O.A.S.*, February 1958. This controversy can be followed in articles and letters published in the *Corriere della Somalia*, Mogadishu, over the last few years and in the new bi-monthly magazine, *Somalia d'Oggi*, Mogadishu; see e.g. Yassiin 'Ismaan Kenadiid, *Somalia d'Oggi*, Anno 1, No. 1, 12 Oct. 1956, pp. 28 ff.; on the subject of teaching written Somali in schools, see *Somalia d'Oggi*, Anno 2, No. 1, January 1957, pp. 14 ff. Other references may be found in the Italian journal, *Affrica*. The recent appearance (9 March 1957) of a weekly supplement *Wargeyska Somaliyed* (The Somali Messenger) written entirely in Somali in a phonetically accurate, but simple, Roman script, has been precipitate, for popular S.Y.L. agitation has caused it to be withdrawn.

[98] These passed under Somali control by a law of 1 January 1957.

[99] For further details of the personalities and policies of Somalia's S.Y.L. government see *Affrica*, April–May 1956, p. 96; ibid., March 1956, p. 69. See also *Somalia d'Oggi*, 12 October 1956, pp. 4 ff. It is difficult outside Somalia to follow the course of Somalia political events, but some coverage is given in the *Corriere della Somalia*, and in *Somalia d'Oggi*, as well as in occasional articles in *Affrica*. There is also a daily newssheet published by the Agenzia Somala d'Informazioni, Rome, which sometimes contains items of interest. This was suspended as being too costly in 1957.

[100] The recent inauguration of the Order of Somali Solidarity, an order to be awarded to individuals for outstanding patriotic services to Somalia, was violently opposed by the Ḥizbia Digil Mirifleh, who urged that there were far more important issues for the Assembly to debate.

[101] All members of the legislature are literate either in Italian or Arabic and some in both. Some are also literate in English.

of agnation is a thing of the past. The end desired is westernization and the fiction is maintained that the goal has already been reached and that clanship is now so unimportant that it has no relevance in the new political field. Those of the educated élite particularly, and also many townspeople, resent being asked what clan they belong to. The reply 'Somali' to the question 'What is your agnatic group?'[102] is obtained in other Somali territories only from a few S.Y.L. adherents, but in Somalia it is commonly given in urban districts. When I tried to discover the clan and lineage identity of informants they told me their 'ex-clan' only with reluctance. Traditionally the polite form of address for a stranger is 'agnate' (inaadeer) but, especially in the southern towns, it has now changed to 'brother' (walaal). This change in greeting has clearly some significance, for it represents the ideal of a new unity in opposition to peoples of other nations.

But in spite of these manifestations of pan-Somali unity it is not to be supposed that clanship is dead in the traditional organization of the country as a whole, or even in the new central legislature and municipal councils. On the contrary the basic economy of the greater part of Somalia remains pastoral nomadism and carries with it traditional kinship and customary values. And it is not surprising, since there has been no major economic change, that this tradition should be carried over into the field of modern politics. In [parts I–II of this] article I showed how clan parties such as the Hawiye Party have been formed to promote traditional lineage values. Even those parties which on a basis of their ideals I classified as nationalist (e.g. the S.Y.L.) still utilize lineage values in the new political field. In the total membership of the Somali Youth League the Daarood are dominant and when the majority of the remainder, who are Hawiye, are included the party clearly represents 'Samaale' (or northern nomadic) interests as opposed to 'Sab' (or southern cultivating).[103] This is the basis of the intense rivalry between the S.Y.L. and the Hizbia Digil-Mirifleh. In canvassing for votes in the 1956 elections to the Assembly full use was made of agnatic support and the S.Y.L. were not behindhand in calling upon their agnates. The continued importance of agnatic solidarity is equally evident in debates in the Assembly and it would be strange if this were not so. What is significant, however, is that political leaders in Somalia should lay such stress on appearing 'westernized' and on claiming to have overcome their traditional lineage values.

In southern Somalia, however, as I have indicated,[104] a different pattern

---

[102] This is the question traditionally put to any stranger to find out what agnatic connexion, if any, subsists between him and the questioner. The degree of agnation revealed determines the social relation of the persons involved and decides whether, and with what degree of intimacy, a stranger will be received with friendship and hospitality.

[103] See p. 311.

[104] See p. 317.

prevails. Nomadism has largely given place to cultivation and urban settlement and the traditional clan structure is decaying. In the wedge of arable land between the Juba and Shebelle Rivers, the Sab (Rahanweyn and Digil) cultivators have evolved a political structure which depends on residential and tribal solidarity rather than on agnation. Here and in the ancient cosmopolitan coastal centres (Mogadishu, Merca, Brava, &c.) residential, and in the towns professional, ties formed the principle of association in tribal hunting societies, village self-help associations, and craft guilds, which existed before the formation of the new political parties.[105] With this tradition it is not surprising that the ethnic and cultural unity, and common economic interests, of the Digil and Rahanweyn tribes should find expression in a strong tribal party—the Hizbia Digil-Mirifleh. In addition to tribal solidarity pan-Somali sentiments among the Sab are such that in 1957 Digil and Rahanweyn support was thought to constitute some 10 per cent. of the strength of the Somali Youth League. But the majority of the Rahanweyn and Digil support their own party, and the traditional rivalry between the noble northern nomads (the 'Samaale') and the southern cultivators (the 'Sab') continues in the hostility of the Hizbia Digil-Mirifleh to the S.Y.L. Examples of this feud have already been given[106] but a few more may not be out of place. The H.D.M. has alleged discrimination on the part of S.Y.L. adherents against Rahanweyn and Digil members of the Government service.[107] More recently, in opposition to the strongly anti-Ethiopian policy of the S.Y.L., the Hizbia Digil-Mirifleh has displayed willingness to reach a friendly agreement with the Ethiopians. Petitions have even been sent to the British Administration of the Northern Province of Kenya seeking for the transfer of the Digil and Rahanweyn area to British administration. This gives some idea of the depth of animosity between the two parties consonant with the traditional

---

[105] See Lewis, 1955, pp. 74–78.

[106] See pp. 328–329.

[107] In 1956 the proportions by clan and ethnic group in the government service of Somalia were estimated at: Daarood, 35%; Hawiye 28%; Digil and Rahanweyn 15%; Reer Baraawa, 5%; Reer Hamar, 5%; and others including Arabs, 12%. The percentages in the total population of Daarood, Hawiye, and Digil-Mirifleh, are compared with these in the following table. The greater recruitment of Daarood and Hawiye is largely due to more people from these clan-families having sought employment. There are more unemployed nomads in search of work than unemployed cultivators.

|  | Government | Population |
|---|---|---|
| Daarood | 35% | 22% |
| Hawiye | 28% | 36% |
| Digil and Rahanweyn | 15% | 25% |

cleavage between the Sab and the Samaale. In the relations between Samaale and Sab members of the Assembly some strain is also evident. The Samaale politician still feels something of his people's traditional scorn for the sedentary and partly Negroid cultivator.[108] Another internal political factor of some importance, and not related to the dichotomy between the northern nomads and southern Digil and Raḥanweyn cultivators, is a territorial schism between the north and the south. In north-eastern Somalia there is some opposition to government from as distant a centre as Mogadishu in the south. Similar feelings are sometimes expressed in the Protectorate. As well as reflecting the differences created by different systems of colonial rule, this seems also to refer to the medieval pattern of government, when the two main centres were Zeila in the north and Mogadishu in the south.[109]

In external affairs recent Ethiopian moves have had much the same effect in Somalia as they have had in the Protectorate, although of course the return of the Reserved Areas excited less interest in Somalia. The Emperor's imperialist speech at Qabradare[110] in the Haud, in which he advocated the federation of Somalia with Ethiopia on the Eritrean pattern, attracted little enthusiasm in Somalia. Expressing the general sentiments of the Assembly, the Prime Minister stated that his country had no wish to be subject to Ethiopian rule. Other expressions of hostility have appeared elsewhere.[111] The government of Somalia continues to aim at the eventual fusion of the five Somali territories in an autonomous Somaliland.[112] But the economic difficulties are recognized. As well as seeking to obtain foreign aid and to attract foreign investments, the government attaches considerable hope to the search for oil. In the development plans for the country the approach is realistic, and it is accepted that, for the majority of the people, nomadism must remain the basic economy. No attempt is being made to develop an indirect system of administration in the interior (beyond the existing system of 'aaqils and stipended 'chiefs'). As a whole the government is becoming increasingly bureaucratic. Local government

---

[108] See p. 317.

[109] See Lewis, 1956, p. 589.

[110] See above, p. 330.

[111] See for example, Somalia d'Oggi, Anno 2, No. 1, January, pp. 4 ff. In this connexion it may be of interest to mention briefly the nature of popular reaction in Somalia where there are several Egyptian Consular officials and others, to the Suez Crisis. While some people in Mogadishu went so far as to volunter at the Egyptian consulate to fight with their Muslim brothers against the Anglo-French invasion of Egypt, there have been complaints from other Somalis of Egyptian interference and propaganda activity in Somalia. See, for example, letters in Corriere della Somalia, 4 January 1957.

[112] The five-pointed Somali star, which is the sole emblem on the flag of Somalia and is also a prominent feature of the national coat of arms, represents the unity of the five Somali territories.

already established in the towns and urban centres may develop, but the administration of the nomads seems destined to remain that of the District Commissioner following traditional methods of direct colonial rule.

Although, for the reasons given above, national unity is not as widespread as politicians in Somalia claim, it is more developed than in any other Somali territory. The replacement of expatriate Italian staff by Somali officials is well advanced and is more in keeping with this development than in other parts of Somaliland. In 1955 out of six provinces there was one Somali Provincial Commissioner, and out of thirty districts seventeen Somali District Commissioners.[113] By July 1956 all the Provincial and District Commissioners were Somali.

## 5. British East Africa: Kenya

Although there are small immigrant Somali communities in other British East African Territories, Kenya contains the largest Somali population, currently estimated, probably somewhat generously, at 100,000. The majority[114] live as nomadic pastoralists in the Northern Province, and the remainder as mainly commercial immigrant communities in other parts of Kenya. This latter group belongs principally to the Ishaaq clan-family. The total Somali population is thus only a small fraction of the population of Kenya (currently estimated at over 6 million) and cannot hope to play any very significant part in the government of the country. Even in the Northern Province, with its estimated total population of 230,000, the Somali element constitutes only about a third of the population of the Province. The Somali are here militant invaders who entered the Province less than sixty years ago and would, if given the chance, overrun the territory and impose their dominion upon the less resilient and less warlike Booraan, Rendille, and other pre-Somali conquest peoples who are in the majority.

As we have seen, in the Kenya legislation[115] Somalis with Arabs and Abyssinians are classified as 'non-Africans' and 'non-Natives', and I have referred above to the role of the Somali Ishaaqiya Society in stressing the peculiarly Arab or Asian, and non-African character of the Somali, in particular the Ishaaq immigrant communities. In the Northern Province, a special Poll Tax is levied.[116] An amount not in excess of 20s. (East

---

[113] *Rapport . . . Somalie, 1955,* 1956, p. 18.

[114] 80,000; approximately half Daarood, and half Hawiye, but including a considerable proportion of extraneous non-Somali or only part-Somali elements.

[115] Laws of Kenya, Cap. I, section 4.

[116] The Kenya Poll Tax (Northern Frontier Province) Ordinance, Cap. 253 of the Laws, amended by Ordinance No. 24 of 1954. In no other Somali territory is a poll tax levied.

African) is payable annually by every clansman over eighteen years of age and may be paid on a clan or lineage-group basis although it has never, in fact, been collected otherwise than individually. This tax provides exemption from taxation under the provisions of the African Poll Tax Ordinance (Cap. 252 of the Laws). In 1957 the Northern Province Poll Tax had not entitled any of the inhabitants of the Province to voting rights. The position is complicated by the fact that the Province is held to be too small to act as a separate constituency for the election of a representative to the Kenya legislature and in the 1956/7 elections would have to have been included with another African constituency. When this was put to the inhabitants of the province at the time, they unanimously decided to adhere to their present system of administration in which they have no elected representation. Opposition to voting for an African representative with an African constituency was particularly strong on the part of the Somali inhabitants of the Province. The constitutional changes introduced in 1958, provide for the nomination to the legislative council of a Somali representative for the Northern Province.

In 1957 there were no local government bodies in the Province. Attempts had been made to establish District Councils among the Rendille and Galla Booraan but these proved abortive and had not been extended to Somali. The Somali are a militant and troublesome minority and the government of Kenya has for long assumed the role of protecting the other inhabitants of the Province, and indeed of Kenya, by arresting Somali expansion from the north and west at the expense of the Booraan and other pre-Somali populations.[117] This policy dominates all administrative action in respect of Somali in Kenya.

There are no Somali administrative officers in the Northern Province, although there are a number of Somali Police Inspectors in Kenya. There is no 'Somalization' in the Northern Province—a lack which is thrown into relief in Somali eyes by progress towards autonomy in Somalia—because the Somali are in the minority and any policy encouraging their advancement at the expense of the non-Somali majority would, government maintains, be subject to opposition from the latter.

Immigrant[118] Somali communities elsewhere in Kenya had, in 1957, no electoral rights, but may gain the right to vote in the constitutional changes planned for 1960. In the 1957/60 Kenya Development Plans provision is made for a special school for the children of Somali immigrants.

Although they are a minority of little over fifty years standing in Kenya, Somali regard the Northern Province as their territory and feel the need

---

[117] For an outline of the history of the Somali conquest of pre-Somali peoples in Southern Somalia and Northern Kenya see Lewis, 1955, p. 45. The Somali advance into Kenya was halted at the Tana River in 1909 by the creation of fixed grazing areas.

[118] Immigration is strictly controlled.

for the enhancement of their rights in it.[119] While the majority of the nomadic Somali population of the Province are probably no more politically conscious in the modern sense than in the Ethiopian Ogaden, or in the British Protectorate, for that matter, the contrast between Somali conditions in the Province and across the border in Somalia is so great that developments in Somalia can hardly fail to produce some dissatisfaction in Kenya. 'Somalization' even in the Ethiopian Ogaden is, at least nominally, more advanced. All Somali political activity is prohibited but the Somali Youth League continues its nationalist campaign underground and everything points to its probable intensification as the date of Somalia's independence approaches. As mentioned earlier, the British Government has assured the inhabitants of the Protectorate (although they may feel doubts as to the assurances given) that they will be free to seek self-determination and, if they choose, federation with Somalia.[120] While these assurances have been given for the Protectorate, Somali nationalists cannot help regarding the destiny of the Northern Province as lying equally closely with Somalia. The progress towards independence of their fellow clansmen across the border is bound to stimulate demands which may not be satisfied sufficiently under British administration in Kenya. And it is certain that pan-Somali aspirations will be encouraged by the eventual establishment of a Somalia consulate in Kenya.[121]

## V

### Unity through Islam

I now discuss in wider perspective the unifying influence of Islam. Through religion, opposed both to the disruptive force of clanship and of European colonialism, some precedent for national patriotism exists. Despite the high degree of cultural homogeneity of the Somali as a whole[122] effective national unity is so slight that the appeal to unity is framed in terms of Muslim solidarity. The hostility between clans and clan-families is normally such that despite community of culture and language the only permanent bridge along which unity may be established is religion. The call to pan-Somali nationalism is to a large extent founded on the Islamic

---

[119] It is hardly necessary to point out that their position and claims are similar to those of other conquering minorities—such as European settler communities—in other parts of Africa.

[120] See above, p. 338.

[121] To represent the independent state of Somalia.

[122] With, of course, the exception of the Digil and Raḥanweyn-Sab.

ideal of the brotherhood of Muslims within the Somali community.[123] As we have seen, all the national parties stress the brotherhood of Somali as Muslims,[124] which is only to be expected, since the Somali are deeply attached to Islam which permeates all aspects of their life. We have noted that in the organization of the national parties and in that of the Somali Dervish Orders there are common features. Both possess uniforms or distinguishing features of dress, religious slogans, and a hierarchal administrative structure. As the national parties now advocate, the leaders of the religious orders have always preached the ideal of the equality of Somali irrespective of lineage affiliation. And the forces of agnation and custom which have opposed the realization of this ideal have weakened the strength of the Sufi *ṭariiqas* just as much as they now also undermine the strength of national party solidarity. Lineage-groups among the Samaale nomads are still stronger than Dervish Order or political party. A man may belong to a political party and to a *ṭariiqa*, but his primary allegiance is to his lineage of birth. Nor in the present economic conditions is this surprising. Nevertheless, the doctrine of Muslim unity propagated by the Sufi Orders has to some extent prepared the ground for the emergence of nationalism,[125] and this is true even when the Somali religious orders have themselves habitually been at loggerheads and constituted a dividing force in the country. Already, particularly in Somalia, the religious rebellion (*jihaad*) led against Christian Colonialism by Sayyid Maḥammad 'Abdille Ḥassan (the so-called 'Mad Mullah' of the Saaliḥiya Order) from 1899 to 1920, is beginning to be viewed as a turn of the century expression of Somali nationalism.[126] Somali who recall the struggles of their forefathers in the medieval wars between the Sultanates of Awdal and Christian Abyssinia regard these also as nationalistic in scope.[127] At the present time none of

---

[123] In the traditional lineage system (see p. 312) this is what is represented by the ascription of all Somali (both Samaale and Sab) descent groups to Quraysh, the lineage of the Prophet Maḥammad.

[124] One of the most active and capable leaders of the National United Front is, however, a Christian—and this does not escape notice and adverse comment at times.

[125] It is not implied that the national parties have evolved directly from the *ṭariiqa* organization. There is generally no particular or necessary connexion between *ṭariiqa* and political party affiliation. But a son of the famous Sheikh Uwais bin Maḥammad (founder of the Uwaisiiya branch of the Qaadiriya *ṭariiqa* in Somalia) played a prominent part in the formation of the Somali Youth League. For further information on the Somali *ṭariiqas*, see Lewis, 1956.

[126] For not very sympathetic, and not entirely accurate, accounts of the Sayyid's revolt, see Jardine, 1923; Caroselli, 1931; and for a brief biography, Cerulli, *Encyclopaedia of Islam*, vol. iii, pp. 667–8. While it is legitimate to compare this rising of *Daraawiish* to the Mahdiate in the Sudan, Sayyid Maḥammad, contrary to what has been written, never himself claimed to be the Mahdi, although he may sometimes have been so styled by some of his followers.

[127] In attempting to understand current politics it is important not to under-estimate the part played by the memory of the medieval religious wars in contributing to Somali attitudes towards Ethiopia. For an excellent account of this period see Trimingham, 1952.

the nationalistic parties has adopted the banner of the *jihaad* in summoning popular support, but a strong religious element persists in all their activities and could assume this character, particularly in Christian Ethiopia.[128] The degree to which Islam may play a significant part in reinforcing internal Somali nationalist aspirations seems to depend largely upon the role adopted by Ethiopia, and, to a lesser extent, on future French policy in the *Côte des Somalis* and on British policy in Kenya.

Religious leaders, especially those who have modernist leanings or who have been trained at El-Azhar in Egypt, now play a prominent part in politics. In spite of a certain and understandable hostility from the more humble *wadaads* of the interior, who are not generally politically conscious, such sheikhs can inspire a considerable following. The ordinary *wadaad* in the interior has usually no direct contact with the external Muslim World, but the prestige of El-Azhar and other foreign Islamic centres attracts support among the religious authorities. The influence of men of religion in the interior has already been discussed in the first part of this essay.[129] Broadly, as long as the religious interests which they champion do not run counter to dominant clan or lineage interests they usually acquire support, particularly when the question at issue can be converted into an attack upon the non-Muslim administering authority. Thus, through religion, political leaders who are at the same time prominent sheikhs may be instrumental in swaying public opinion in the interior.

On the other hand, while religion can act as a channel for the transmission of nationalist political aims, it can also constitute a formidable barrier to rapid development. With their authority in religion, sheikhs and *wadaads* tend to view as primarily religious, questions which politicians regard as primarily secular. The nominally pan-Muslim rather than Somali outlook of sheikhs sometimes exerts a retarding influence on progress towards nationalism. This conflict appears most clearly in Somalia where, although Italian influence continues, it is at a minimum. The S.Y.L. government has already experienced considerable embarrassment in the proposed introduction of legislation concerning among other things, the status of women, women's education, modern legal developments and the adoption of a national written language.[130]

Politicians and officials are not, as a whole, in sympathy with the *tariiqa*

---

[128] As was pointed out above, some of the S.Y.L. claim that they are united in religion and culture with Muṣlim Danakil and Galla (*Qoti*) in their nationalistic aspirations. But what depth of feeling, if any, this slogan really represents is difficult to assess.

[129] A sheikh cannot, and will not if he wishes to preserve his influence, ever advocate a course of action which is fundamentally contrary to clan interests. Thus, while there has long been religious opposition to the collective payment of blood-compensation, it has never been voiced very effectively amongst the nomads. To preserve their influence sheikhs must always proceed with caution.

[130] See above. Where non-Muslim influence is dominant—as in the other Somali territories—it is easy to arouse popular support against an infidel (*gaal*) government.

movements which they view with clanship as a dividing force in Somali society. They point to the frequent rivalry and strife between the Orders and to the abuses of which the descendants of saints have been guilty in collecting money and livestock in the name of the blessing (*baraka*) of their saintly founders. Few of them are active members of the Sufi Orders. Their general outlook tends in some respects towards Wahhabism, inasmuch as they are opposed to the cult of saints and its alleged abuses. But while many side with the reformist movement in Islam, they are generally modernist in outlook and do not wish to achieve a Muslim state founded on the rigid application of the Shariah. There seems little doubt that the influence of the established orders has waned over the past fifty years although it is still strong, particularly in the interior. Secular politicians look to the spread of education, to which they attach great importance, to weaken further the hold of the *tariiqas*.

I have already alluded to the fact that in their external relations the political parties nominally support the Arab World and have in many cases close ties with Egypt. This was evidenced in the 1956/7 Suez crisis. But there is little doubt that the parties as a whole are influenced by materialistic considerations rather than by strong sentiments of purely religious unity. In Somalia there is always the hope that Egypt may supply the economic aid so urgently required, or that in supporting the Arab block against the West help may come from some other quarter. There are, however, definite limits to Somali support of foreign co-religionists. There is no indication of any desire to be administered internally by a foreign Muslim power such as Egypt. In expressions of pro-Egyptian feeling and hostility to the non-Muslim administering powers, whether French, British, Italian, or Ethiopian, there is no suggestion of a longing for the days of the Egyptian rule of the Somali Coast (1870–85).[131]

Through the press and radio, and in Somalia by the action of propagandists, all the Somali countries are open to Egyptian propaganda.[132] Some Somali students have taken advantage of the Egyptian Government's offer of scholarships for study in Egypt. Egyptian influence cannot, therefore, be ignored. Mention has been made above[133] of protest in Somalia at Egyptian interference in the internal affairs of the country, but such evidence of anti-Egyptian feeling should not be allowed to obscure the nominal identification of external Somali policies with those of the Arab World.

---

[131] The Egyptians withdrew from Harar in 1885. Treaties of protection had been signed by Britain with the Habar Awal and Gadabuursi (1884), and from this time the British Protectorate was gradually established.

[132] An Egyptian mission led by two sheikhs from El-Azhar University spent three months in 1951 in Somaliland, Eritrea, and Aden. The Mission's Report (*Report on the Conditions of the Muslims living in Somaliland, Eritrea, Aden, and Ethiopia*) attacks Christian Colonialism and especially the Ethiopian Government.

[133] See above, p. 349.

It is significant that the new President of the S.Y.L. (the leader of the government party in Somalia) has recently been studying in Egypt. A wave of pro-Egyptian sympathy followed the assassination, in April 1957, of the Egyptian Member of the United Nations Advisory Council in Mogadishu. The murderer, a Somali who had returned from a visit to Egypt, was apparently not actuated by political motives. The crime has become something of a *cause célèbre,* and the government of Somalia has taken great pains to placate the Egyptian Government. A posthumous award of the Order of the Somali Star (First Class) was made to the dead Minister, and his widow has been provided with a pension. Beneath the surface of popular expressions of this kind, however, the truth probably remains, as we should expect, that Somali are Somali first and anything else second.

Another tendency among some Somali politicians, and recently publicly voiced by the Premier of Somalia, is to regard Somali as Africans[134] and the destiny of a Somali independent state, whether Somalia alone or a greater Somalia, as bound up with the future of African self-determination. This trend, running counter to external Muslim solidarity, recalls the impatience of some Somali politicians and officials at the disruptive and inhibiting influence of religion, particularly through the actvities of the Sufi Dervish Orders. Such conflicting tendencies have, of course, fullest scope in Somalia, shortly to attain self-government. Future political trends depend, as well as on the internal factors discussed, on the roles adopted by Ethiopia and France and on events in the Arab World, and at least to some extent also on political developments in other parts of Africa.

## VI

In the first part of this study a brief account of traditional Somali political organization was given. Against this background the organization, aims, and activities of the modern political movements have been examined. Clan parties such as the Hawiye Party and tribal parties such as the Ḥizbia Digil-Mirifleh represent a straightforward translation into modern political terms of traditional agnatic and territorial values. In the secular (as opposed to the religious) organization of society the nationalist parties are a new type of organization. The patriotic sentiments and pan-Somali values which they seek to establish find no general precedent in the traditional secular order. With their outspoken and constantly reiterated opposition to clan and tribal ties they do not base their nationalist aims upon the traditional lineage system or upon the total genealogy.[135] The total genealogy

---

[134] This is an untraditional attitude. As conquerors of the pre-Somali negroid and ('pagan') Galla populations of southern Somalia and with some participation in the slave trade, Somali traditionally despise negroes. Among other things this colour-bar reflects the nomad's scorn for the sedentary cultivator.

[135] See p. 311.

which unites all Samaale (with the exception of the Daarood) as the children of Samaale but leaves the division between his descendants and those of Sab (the Digil and Raḥanweyn) is gradually being forgotten. Pan-Somali clan ties are, in any case, too weak at this level to unite the Somali people as a nation in the face of the disruptive forces of agnation and contractual agreement at lower levels of the lineage system. A person more frequently acts as a member of a small corporate group[136] at the base of the lineage system than as a member of a larger unit at the top. At the highest level the organization is extremely unstable and soon disintegrates. The sustained opposition which could, in theory, knit together the whole Somali community at this level has not yet been experienced. This illustrates the difficulty of establishing a stable national policy in a lineage society without permanently stable political units and where the boundaries of political cleavage are constantly shifting. Where the élite is largely the product of superficial westernization, achieved through education and not the result of fundamental economic changes in the country as a whole, the traditional pattern of political cleavages is not changed but simply translated into a new idiom. This process operates at several levels. On the one hand, there are the new political organizations such as the Hawiye Party which express traditional clan political values. At a higher level the traditional lineage and cultural cleavage between the noble Samaale nomads and the Southern Sab cultivators recurs in modern politics in the schism between the Somali Youth League and the Ḥizbia Digil-Mirifleh.[137] Western procedure has been adopted but the traditional pattern persists.

### References

CAROSELLI, F. S. *Ferro e Fuoco in Somalia.* Rome, 1931.

CERULLI. E. *Studi Etiopici, I. La Lingua e la Storia di Harar.* Rome, 1936.

COLEMAN, J. S. 'Current Political Movements in Africa', *The Annals of the American Academy of Political and Social Science.* March, 1955, pp. 95–109.

COLUCCI, M. *Principi di Diritto Consuetudinario della Somalia Italiana Meridionale.* Florence, 1924.

CONSTANZO, G. A. 'The development of a middle class in British Somaliland, French Somaliland, and in Somalia under Italian Trusteeship', in *Dévelopment d'une classe moyenne dans les pays tropicaux,* Institut International des Civilisations Différentes, Bruxelles, 1956.

FRANCOLINI, B. 'I Somali del Harar,' *A.A.I.,* 3–4, 1938, pp. 1114–30.

GLUCKMAN, MAX. *Custom and Conflict in Africa.* Oxford, 1955.

---

[136] These are the "Dia-paying groups' described in [part I].

[137] To a significant extent the unity of the Hawiye and Daarood in the S.Y.L. is a function of the opposition of the Ḥ.D.M.

GROTTANELLI, V. L. *Pescatori del'Oceano Indiano*. Rome, 1955.

GRUNEBAUM, G. E. VON (Ed.) *Unity and Variety in Muslim Civilization*. Chicago, 1955.

HAZEM ZAKI NUSEIBEH. *The Ideas of Arab Nationalism*. New York, 1956.

HODGKIN, T. *Nationalism in Tropical Africa*. London, 1956.

HOWARD, W. E. H. *Public Administration in Ethiopia*. Groningen, 1956.

HUNT, J. A. *A General Survey of the Somaliland Protectorate, 1944–50*. London, 1951.

ITALIAN GOVERNMENT, MINISTRY OF FOREIGN AFFAIRS. *Rapport du Gouvernement Italien a l'Assemblée Générale des Nations Unies sur l'administration de tutelle de la Somalie*. Rome, 1956.

JARDINE, D. *The Mad Mullah of Somaliland*. London, 1923.

KIRK, J. W. C. *A Grammar of the Somali Language*. Cambridge, 1905.

LAURENCE, M. *A Tree for Poverty: Somali Poetry and Prose*. Nairobi, 1954.

LEWIS, I. M. *Peoples of the Horn of Africa: Somali, Afar and Saho*, Ethnographic Survey of Africa, North-Eastern Africa, Part I. London, 1955.

————. 'Sufism in Somaliland: A study in tribal Islam—I and II', London, reprinted from *B.S.O.A.S.* 1955, xvii/3; and 1956, xviii/I.

————. 'La communità ('Giamia') di Bardera sulle rive del Giuba', *Somalia d'Oggi*, Anno II, No. I, 1957 (3), pp. 36–37.

————. 'Population Movements in Somaliland: Current and projected research.' Communication to the Second Conference on African History and Archaeology, School of Oriental and African Studies, London, 1957 (2).

————. *The Somali Lineage System and the Total Genealogy: An introduction to the basic principles of Somali political institutions*, Hargeisa (British Somaliland), cyclostyled, 1957 (I).

————. 'The Gadabuursi Somali Script', *B.S.O.A.S.*, February, 1958.

————. 'Modern Political Movements in Somaliland (Parts I and II)', *Africa*, xxviii. 3, 1958, pp. 244–60, 4, 1958, pp. 344–362.

MAINO, M. *La Lingua Somala Strumento d'Insegnamente Professionale*. Alessandria, 1953.

MITCHELL, J. C. 'The Kalela Dance', *Rhodes-Livingstone Papers*, No. 27, 1956.

PERHAM, M. *The Government of Ethiopia*. Oxford, 1948.

REECE, SIR G. 'The Horn of Africa', *International Affairs*, vol. xxx, No. 4, Oct. 1954, pp. 440–50.

RÉZETTE, R. *Les Partis politiques marocains*. Paris, 1955.

RONDOT, F. *Les Forces religieuses dans la vie politique de l'Islam*. Paris, 1957.

SHARIIF' AYDARUUS, SHARIIF'ALI. *Bughyat al-Amaal fii Taariikh as-Soomaal*. Mogadishu, 1955.

TRIMINGHAM, J. S. *Islam in Ethiopia*. Oxford, 1952.

# 4

# Belief
# and Judgment

A. In Ghana, a boating expedition represents the importance of religion in the economy of Africa. African peoples see themselves as an integral part of the natural world. In their attitude toward nature, there is an absence of aggression, and, instead, a sense of cooperation and unity.

B. These miners in West Virginia are part of a culture in which advancing technology encourages an aggressive attitude toward the world and toward life itself. The desire to dominate and control what is around us may serve as a means of our own destruction.

C. Girls of the **elima** initiation in the Ituri Forest paint themselves white to mourn the death of their childhood and announce the recognition of their approaching responsibilities as adults.

D. This personal protest against war is remarkably reminiscent of African tradition, where white, painted on face and body, symbolizes mourning.

E. The old pass along their faith to the young, and this old woman with her grandchild is providing, with love, the sense of continuity that, with a community of belief, helps make the existence of physical coercion unnecessary.

F. Individual struggles for survival intensify as government responsibility increases and family influence lessens. Prostitution, while still legally and morally condemned, is necessary and inevitable and, for many deprived of other opportunities, it has become an acceptable way to earn a living and in many cases support a family.

At this point it is necessary to be as clear as possible about personal faith and belief: the one is unquestionable and the other is unquestioning. Because both are held with tenacity (if held at all), they are likely to present obstacles to the understanding of other faiths and beliefs and even greater obstacles to proper judgment. Yet both are indispensable to judgment if that judgment is to be moral.

A critical examination of various aspects of Western society has shown them to be wanting in terms of human relationships that are both affective and effective. The implicit question remains: Can they ultimately be effective without being affective? It is possible that continued separation of the two will result in either conflict of a catastrophic nature or the final dehumanization of our species. It would be intolerable to think that we had no control in the matter, although many do shrug the issue off as beyond control. But before thinking in terms of control, it is necessary to consider the direction in which we are heading and to make an initial judgment about that direction.

It would take an unusually ardent optimist to claim that the future, either immediate or distant, holds much promise of anything but technological advance, and that such advance is not as likely to add to our destructive potential as it has added to the burden of our present excess of necessary luxuries. The even less questionable dangers of our exploding population growth and increasing pollution are still, at this critical stage, ignored by many. Some escapists assume that "by that time," we will be colonizing the stars. According to reasonable estimates, there will be less than one square foot of dry land per person by the year 2070 if the present trend continues; the recent success in landing a few men on the moon for a few hours is a rather modest beginning toward any solution of this problem in terms of celestial emigration. Those who refer to "that" time are also ignoring the fact that time does not just stop and start; it is continuous. "That" time has already begun, and no time is too soon to begin to prepare for it. Continued lack of concern for the not-so-rosy future is exactly the attitude that the present Western social system encourages and against which the youth, with good reason, are rebelling. It is only to be expected of a legalistic, individual-oriented society that the older half of the population, which jealously monopolizes the power, is concerned with maintaining the status quo that assures its security and is opposed to changes that could benefit its children or grandchildren but threaten its own present comfortable position.

It is a difficult matter to assess just what the prospects are for the twenty-first century, but there are certainly no valid grounds for optimism in terms of socioeconomic or political progress. The best approach is to maintain an open mind and say that given a change in the present direction (and most would agree it would have to be a radical change), all may be well. But equally, there are no valid grounds for pessimism, unless it is claimed that change is impossible; and such defeatism is surely unacceptable to anyone with a shred of social conscience. However, a comparison of social organization in small-scale societies with that in large-scale societies reveals a trend that can be projected with reasonable certainty into the future in order to indicate the direction in which we are heading. Large-scale societies grow still larger; the population density increases still further; and life becomes even more. sedentary. These changes are already taking place, and there is no indication that any alteration in course is likely. The contemporary trend will merely be heightened. From moral coercion we have moved to physical coercion, and the next step, already being taken, is toward violent compulsion. We have moved from justice and democracy to law and order and are continuing onward toward order without law. We have shifted our attention and concern from the rights of the society to the rights of the individual and are heading toward the point where the demands of the system will be the central hub around which life revolves. Whereas the focus once was on the society and also on the human beings that constitute society, the shift now is from such a collectivity of social human beings through the present agglomeration of individuals to a mechanical structure of which human beings will be a mere incidental part. Wealth, once a concept applicable only to societies or social segments, is now primarily thought of in individual terms; the currency in which we measure wealth has shifted from human relationships through land and goods to cash. The resultant inequalities are so enormous that it is possible that in the future not only currency but also the concept of wealth will be eliminated; the necessities and comforts of life, as determined by the system, will then be distributed by the system. This seems the only efficient way in a non-moral society.

The following table attempts to give some idea of the process in which we are involved. It indicates a direction comprised of decreasing alternatives of action, decreasing diversity, decreasing sociality, decreasing humanity, and increasingly rigid control by a self-perpetuating system. It indicates that we are abandoning control over our lives to the system and moving toward servile automatism.

It seems inescapably true that we are moving along a steady path of depersonalization and dehumanization; some might say from God through Man to System, others, who prefer to eschew the notion of God, may substitute the notion of Society, which in no way alters the picture or lessens the chill of creeping paralysis. Reading across the columns, each

## INDICATED DIRECTION OF CHANGE

| | Small-scale society (Moralistic) | Large-scale society (Legalistic) | Future society (Deterministic) |
|---|---|---|---|
| *Economy* | | | |
| Characteristic | Social wealth | Individual wealth | Absence of wealth |
| Manifest in | Equal sharing | Unequal sharing | Distribution of necessities |
| *Family* | | | |
| Characteristic | | | |
| Functions in the | Social | Biological | Eugenic |
| interests of | Community | Individual | State |
| *Social Control* | | | |
| Characteristic | Justice | Law | Order |
| Achieved by | Moral coercion | Physical coercion | Violent compulsion |
| *Government* | | | |
| Characteristic | Affective democracy | Effective democracy | Autocracy |
| Based on | Community of belief | Community of behavior | Conformity |
| *Religion* | | | |
| Characteristic | Faith (unquestionable) | Belief (unquestioning) | Acceptance (unthinking) |
| Emphasis on | Spirit | Matter | System |
| Resulting in | Humanity | Individuality | Servility |

entry may evoke only disquiet; but reading down the columns, we can hardly avoid alarm since some modern societies, particularly the "great" nations are already partly into the third column. Beyond that it is impossible to predict, although it seems likely that the only possible form of progress left open would be the perfection of all technological development so that the machine becomes self-operating, with man swinging back and forth as an unthinking part of it, going through the necessary movements in unconscious and inconscient perpetual motion.

In trying to grapple with the problem of dehumanization, I have made use of the distinction between faith and belief, as is apparent in the table. I contrast the unquestionability of faith with the unquestioning nature of belief; the one seems to me to be suprarational and the other rational. This may not be in accord with definitions preferred by others, but the suggested usage is of critical importance in dealing with the role of religion in society, which in turn is crucial to the issues of the direction and directability of change. An act of faith, it seems to me, is an act whereby one accepts as truth a notion that cannot in any way be proven or substantiated. It may be the result of a hunch, an intuition, or at its most dramatic, a divine revelation. It is intensely personal and by its very suprarational nature, utterly unquestionable; yet it need not be individual. That is to say, a given social system may induce, at the individual level, a given act of faith that is thus held in common by all members of that society, providing a prime, unquestionable unity. This is the binding force of religion at its strongest; whether it is spiritual or social in nature, whether it is determined by God or by society, is irrelevant for present purposes.

An act of belief, on the other hand, is an acceptance of a notion that is only partly substantiated or that one does not bother to or wish to substantiate fully, accepting it because of its evident rationality. The power of belief is similar to the power of faith so long as it remains unquestioned, but its strength differs in that it *can* be questioned. Although its questionability is obviously also its weakness, it at least allows a rational way that is open to change; such a way is not open to faith. In considering any total change, a change of belief is only one step less vital than a change of faith, which at the moment seems like the kingpin of a true, human, moral society.

An example of both faith and belief at work as political forces is easily seen by consideration of the white South African attitude toward apartheid. To some extent, it rests on a belief that the black African is innately inferior. The desperate attempts of the whites (and some of their racist European and American counterparts) to prove this alleged inferiority is an indication of one weakness of belief: it puts a man within reach of his enemy, and there is always the possibility that his enemy may be better armed and better equipped intellectually. This particular belief is still under siege, and despite overwhelming rational evidence, the white South African remains unshaken because his belief, when most sorely tried, is superseded by a faith in his God-given white supremacy resulting from the descent of Africans from the children of Ham, conveniently cursed by God. Although it seems strange that a benevolent, omnipotent, and omniscient God should have cursed such a large portion of his creation for the benefit of a few white South Africans, the act of faith is unquestionable because it is beyond reason.

Fanaticism most frequently has its source in faith; but in small-scale societies so do democratic government, justice, equality, social responsibility, and morality. When a man cannot reason because of ignorance or lack of intelligence, belief may serve as a power comparable to faith despite the danger of contradiction. In modern society, it does not pay to question, and increasingly the tendency is not to do so, leading slowly to unthinking acceptance, the ultimate defeat of man himself.

South Africa is an important example because the credibility gap has reached the breaking point; rational justification of apartheid has been undermined, not by intelligence or morality, but by sheer expediency. South Africa is in the position where, if apartheid is to be maintained, it has to move even more firmly in the direction described in the third column of the table and be even more despotic, violently compulsive, and unhuman than it already is. In face of the growing powers of physical coercion of hostile nations, African and otherwise, some South Africans seem to be considering the only alternative: the abandonment of apartheid. But this abandonment would mean that both a belief and a faith that have been the central pillars of white South African society would have to be changed. The very antirational nature of the belief seems to have resulted in a warping of the white South African's intellectual ability, so that the problem of changing the belief is almost as great as that of changing the faith. As yet, the indications are unclear. Moves such as the creation of "independent" African states within South Africa, the holding of talks with black Africans on an "equal basis," and the many apparently trivial but significant gestures on the home front where prominent whites may increasingly be seen putting on a brave show of the "equal but separate" farce may all be moves in either direction—either toward ultimate reconciliation or as a temporary anesthesia leading to ultimate, total, violent suppression.

Anyone who thinks that the present degree of suppression in South Africa is total underestimates man's ability for violence. There is much the whites in South Africa can yet do, and will have to do, if they are unable or unwilling to change the belief and faith that dominate their present society. It will result in the physical destruction of the blacks and the destruction of the humanness of the whites. Yet perhaps in that explosive situation and out of the present dilemma there may come the solution to the problem that in general faces us all, South Africa is only one of the more obvious manifestations. That problem is: How do we induce change that is total before some terrible catastrophe does it for us?

In addition to contrasting faith and belief, I have contrasted spirit and matter; and although the contrast is easy enough to make without misunderstanding, there may be some dispute concerning its significance. I am impressed, for instance, by the African's willingness to consider what for us is the inconsiderable—the invisible, the unknown, the spiritual—and by his willingness to incorporate this spiritual world with his physical world in a single, total reality. Whereas for the African, the two worlds are part of one reality, for us they have little or nothing to do with each other, even if both are accepted as being of the same order of reality (which by no means all people do). Society for us is a material thing, devoid of spirit, to be considered in practical terms. It is the system that counts, and people are increasingly willing to fight for a particular system, regardless of the material loss and disaster it brings to themselves or to others, as though the system mattered more than lives and happiness.

After all, lives and happiness have to do with human beings; and in terms of the system, human beings do not count for much. The current emphasis on individualism is merely a prelude to the ultimate dehumanization of society. From the social point of view, an individual is only partly human; his essentially social personality (seen so clearly in the model provided by the small-scale society) does not fully emerge until he is seen as a part of a whole complex of interrelating human beings. Only then is it possible to talk of humanity. In the other direction lies the negation of humanity; human beings become automatons, and the life process becomes synchronized with that of the system, a monstrous master clock that has found the secret of perpetual motion and turns men on and off as programmed.

The increasingly humdrum, material nature of the lives of urban dwellers shows how far we are along that road. The monotonous daily routine is timed with precision around the major, if not the only, focus of interest: the repetitive wage-earning activity. There is little time for or interest in family life and virtually no opportunity for the family to thrive as a corporate unit. Thus, we are destroying our basic model, if not the basis itself, of sociality. The mechanical nature of much of the work that is done and the constant process of automation serve to reduce the human being to the role of yet another tool, and not a very efficient one. The human being reacts to this, rather desperately, by a growing delight in violent and blood sports, including such demonstrations of team spirit as football (where the success of the game can be measured in terms of the violent emotions it engenders and, in some cases, in terms of its actual physical violence) and such manly arts as boxing (where a match without blood and bestiality is a dismal failure). Alternative escapes from the monotony of life measure that monotony and the atrophy of our emotions equally well by their suicidal nature. Automobile racing, mountain climbing, free falling, sailing around the world in flimsy boats, and other such acts of near insanity often cause danger to others and cost innocent lives; yet they are acclaimed as acts of courage and manliness. In fact, they are all too often acts of cowardice and immaturity performed by people who are afraid to face up to the infinitely greater challenge of life, an adventure that calls for its own measure of skill, strength, and courage. It is to be noted that in small-scale societies and still in some rural areas, there is no such felt need for symbolic or real violence or suicide; life offers its own more worthwhile challenge and rewards, and the less involved in the by-products of industrialization, the more human life is at all stages and in all aspects.

Although all this is, in part, mere personal opinion and does not constitute adequate evidence, it is not without a reasonable level of probability. There is enough evidence at least to suggest that this may prove a fruitful line of investigation and that we are bound in a general direction that even by today's standards is not altogether desirable. If the possibility, let alone probability, of the direction is agreed upon as outlined, then it becomes necessary to make a judgment about whether that direction is acceptable. Those who are not prepared to accept it can reject it only on moral grounds; no other grounds are possible since none of us living at this moment are likely to be alive when it is no longer going to be worthwhile to be alive. Rejection of this direction implies concern for the future and for others. Once we admit in this way to being moral, which is to say to being human as well as humanitarian, we admit to an obligation to make further judgments, the most important of which concerns what can and should be done to alter the trend, to change the direction.

As I have said before, there can be no question of reversing the process; those who talk of its irreversibility are merely begging the question. Nonetheless, it is worth looking to the rapidly disappearing past, when societies were small in scale and the emphasis was on humanity, to see what the vital ingredients were and how far they necessarily relate to smallness of size. I am assuming that most of those who have read this far will find the characteristics listed in the table for small-scale societies more attractive than those listed for the larger societies. Although the last few entries in the table have not yet been discussed, it is clear that for small-scale societies, the emphasis all the way down is on the affective and social essence of human relationships, a combination that leads to effectivity. Most of the characteristics do seem to be related to the smallness of the society, which makes more intimate personal relationships possible. Yet in considering successively larger sizes of small-scale societies, from hunting bands through segmentary societies to centralized societies formed into nations, the descriptions have remained valid. This gives a glimmer of hope that even in the leviathan societies of the West there might be some room for humanity.

This hope becomes more substantial and the prerequisites emerge more clearly when the last three entries, under "Religion," are considered. Neither faith, spirit, nor humanity are much in fashion these days, having been dismissed as topics suitable for discussion in Sunday Schools, the church itself having become little more than an adult Sunday School. But in small-scale societies, they are not divorced from everyday life; they are an integral part of it. It is this integration that may be the very factor that enables the other qualities to persist even as society grows larger. This assumption is confirmed by the fact that the religious element is implicit in the smallest societies, becomes more and more explicit as the society grows in size, and is most formalized at the state or national level. But whereas African nations have formalized their religious life without losing its spiritual and human nature, the Western nations have formalized spirit out of existence, so that all that remains is a tired convention, a secular pattern of behavior divorced from social context, a rite without social significance. It is no longer even the opiate, to which level we reduced it when we separated church and state; and the lie is given to religious life and the promise of an afterlife by the manifest hypocrisy of so many of the church leaders, by their anxiety to compromise and surrender principle to expediency, insisting that religion should be divorced from politics and concern itself merely with man's relation to God, who apparently is not concerned enough with man to authorize his priests to suit their actions to their words. Religion, in this sense, can be forgotten when social purposes are concerned; it has become a flimsy world of fantasy and delusion for those who cannot or will not think. But although the church, as opposed to religion, is largely to blame for this degeneration (the triumph of system over spirit), as an institution, it is by no means to be ignored. The conflict within the various churches, Christian and otherwise, is itself indicative of at least a remnant of vitality. Some clerics, usually the younger ones, have shown themselves increasingly militant in the prosecution of their beliefs, feeling morally bound to judge political action and, in this way, to offer moral leadership to their congregations. Consequently, they have attracted more youth than before because youth belong to the future and they want their world to be livable. Sometimes consciously and sometimes unconsciously, they recognize that the prime cause of the degeneration of modern society, with all its narrowness of vision, bigotry, and violence, is the lack of faith and belief, resulting in the lack of all morality. The same self-seeking, self-centered quality that characterizes the individual we praise so highly—encouraging him in his eternal quest for wealth and power—also characterizes economic and political groups. The pursuit of national advancement is as ruthless as the pursuit of individual advancement and as lacking in consideration for others, except insofar as such consideration might further self-interests.

It is worth pointing to the difference between rural and urban churches and, in America, between black and white churches. Rural churches tend to be more involved than urban churches in the total community life, economic and political as well as familial and religious. In the rural southern states and even in some urban areas, the churches of Black Americans are even more a vital and functioning part of the community, even more politically conscious and active, even more a normal part of everyday life. Therefore, to a greater extent, they make of religion what by etymology it is meant to be: a unifying force binding people together, helping to provide a powerful sentiment and a truly distinct moral, social identity. If the church as a whole, of whatever religion or sect, were to involve itself actively and publicly in political life, it might just possibly rediscover its original religious nature. Religion is nothing if divorced from politics, and politics can be moral only if religious.

It is plainly time to attempt to define just what religion is, although I have begged the question already by referring to its definition by etymology as a binding together of people into a moral society. Since up to this point we have taken our cue from small-scale societies in examining our own, we will do so again. I have already suggested that by contrast with our own, African social life is religious or inextricably interwoven with religious life; it is concerned at all stages with human beings and relations between them, and this is its religious nature.

But in order to appreciate this fully, it is first necessary to clear away some of the many misconceptions about the nature of African religion, which is so often confused by the careless use of words like "mystical," "magic," and "witchcraft." Such terms are too frequently defined by reference to a specific society or situation; therefore, the disparity of usage is enormous. They are descriptive definitions, of little general use, and must be redefined on each new occasion. What I am seeking here is a definition that will explain a process rather than describe a phenomenon. Thus, as already defined, it is possible to see that the true opposition that highlights the difference between Western and African systems of thought is not so much between science and belief (for both are rational) as it is between science and faith. Magic, as practiced in Africa, clearly belongs to the camp of science and is in no way mystical (in the sense of "supra-rational"). This would be more easily seen if we used the local terminology instead of forcing our own categoric interpretation upon an act we have not bothered to understand. In many African languages, the word most frequently used for what we translate as "magic" really means "medicine." It covers any kind of curative, from a shot of penicillin through a local herbal remedy to a fetish or amulet, none of which is infallible, but all of which have some curative potential. Although many of us would dismiss the charm or amulet as demonstrably ineffective in medical terms, their psychological effectiveness may be considerable; and they are not without their own counterparts in Western medical science. But the point that I wish to make is not concerned with effectiveness; it is that however absurd magical remedies may seem to us, they are *conceived* of in the same terms as we conceive of penicillin, as something that works effectively and practically, without recourse to supernatural or spiritual agencies.

Furthermore, the African thinks not only of curing bodily ills by such means but also of curing social ills, and frequently both are the job of the same doctor. But whereas most of the cures for bodily illness are medicinal (although in some cases supernatural agencies may be invoked), most cures for social ills involve the concept of spiritual or supernatural force. Here again, we get confused because the terms "spiritual" and "supernatural," although less misleading than "magical," must not be understood to cover exactly the same categories in Africa that they cover elsewhere. For instance, in many African societies, death is regarded as unnatural; but since it seems to happen with remarkable inevitability, long life is therefore considered supernatural. Thus, old people are frequently regarded as witches or people possessed by supernatural powers. The same thing is true of spirits, which to us are supranatural, but which in Africa they (or certain classes of them) may well be classified as natural, that is, a part of nature or the natural world. Thus, the African is not being unduly mystical when he talks of having just met, heard, or seen a certain kind of spirit. He is communicating a reality that we too often dismiss as superstition because he is using a different idiom. (Robin Horton discusses this at length in his article, "African Traditional Thought and Western Science.")

In curing social ills, the appeal to spiritual or supernatural force indicates an increase in the gravity of the situation over physical illness, although there, too, spiritual or supernatural force may be invoked in some particularly serious or important cases. This also indicates that society, not the individual, is the concern of spiritual and supernatural beings. The lesser of these forces can to some extent be controlled; others can only be invoked and left to act as they see fit, in which case the outcome is accepted with as much equanimity as we piously express in "Thy will be done," but without adding the rider "but be sure to do it my way."

This area of spiritual and supernatural force crosses over from belief to faith, from science to religion. Thus as long as the doctor is using medicines or calling on "natural" spirits ("sprites" might be a better word) to help with the cure, he is being a scientist. But the moment the malady is beyond cure by natural powers, he invokes supernatural or spiritual force, a different thing from making use of mere spirits.* It is perhaps then that the term "priest" should be used, rather than the term "doctor," because he is fulfilling a very different role. In the more complex societies, the roles are divided and even subdivided into other categories of specialists such as diviners, fetish makers, and herbalists. But the fact that in the smaller societies it is one and the same person who attends to all bodily and social ills is significant of the basic unity of social life and of the pervasiveness of religious belief.

In African systems of belief, the terms "spiritual" and "spirit" must be taken as going beyond what we habitually refer to as "spirits." A totally different level of existence is involved, one that may well be related to the world but is not a part of it. The role of the priest is that of an intermediary. For this reason he is often a medial character himself[†] and (as mentioned before) may even accentuate his supernatural aspect by assumed oddity of dress and behavior. In Western eyes, this makes him a comic character, the superstitious "witch doctor" so beloved of cartoonists. If only we could see ourselves as we see others. What else does our Christian priest do when he dresses up in clothes that would make anyone else the laughing stock of society if he wore them in public and went walking down the main street swinging incense and ringing silver bells? When the priest changes vestments during the service, he signalizes a change of role; he is also symbolizing his separateness, his mediality.

One other figure who should be considered is the prophet, a figure that arises in times of exceptional crisis. It is useful to think of him as dealing with the supranatural rather than the supernatural. He is a much rarer category and is of major significance in this discussion, although, unfortunately, he is the figure about whom the least is known. However, it is plain that in his person, he unites the realms of religion and politics; and it is equally clear that he has the power to overthrow the established order temporarily or permanently and virtually create a new society. The kinds of crisis in which he appears are those in which the old social order is threatened or found inadequate and a new vehicle of authority

---

* See Robin Horton's article on Kalabari religion, "A Hundred Years of Kalabari Religion," in J. Middleton (ed.), *Black Africa* (New York: Macmillan, 1970), pp. 192–211.

† For much stimulating discussion of mediality, I am indebted to Joseph A. Towles and to the as-yet-unpublished results of his current researches into this aspect of a Congolese society.

is required. His position is quite different from that of the Divine King, for instance, who is usually removed from active participation in political life. He is also different from the priest, who although involved in politics does not take a leading political role. The prophet's religiosity or supranaturalness is well demonstrated in his person, usually more so than with other medial figures. His political potential is adequately testified to by the fact that he is the first person the colonial powers seek to remove from the political scene.* It has been suggested that there are close similarities between the behavior and role played by classical prophets such as Buddha, Jesus, and Mohammed and the traditional African prophets.† They are figures intimately involved with revolution in some form; they provide immensely powerful foci for the formation of unities that never existed before; out of revolution they bring a new order, a new faith, at least in the classical form, and a new set of beliefs to uphold and integrate the new order. It seems rather obvious then, that we stand in desperate need of a new prophet, bringing us a new faith and a new order out of the present social chaos.

Brief mention must also be made of the terms "witchcraft" and "sorcery." These English terms can seldom, if ever, be applied to an African counterpart. It is regrettable that they have been used as loosely and indiscriminately by anthropologists as by others and that there is still no consensus about how they should be used. They are second-best alternatives that most anthropologists make do with rather than load down their ethnographies and discussions with an impossible number of vernacular terms. It is therefore necessary for an author to define these terms each time he uses them because in each specific instance it is possible that the meaning will be slightly different. Personally, I find a measure of generality in African religious systems that makes one general definition of the terms possible and useful. It takes into account that factor so central to justice: intent. Both witchcraft and sorcery may be described as the manipulation by humans of supernatural forces for anti-social purposes. But whereas witchcraft is not intended to do harm, sorcery is. A witch is someone who has contracted the power of manipulation, perhaps through the inheritance of "witchcraft substance" (as with the Zande),‡ and may not even know that he has contracted this power

---

* See Banton in Middleton, 1970.

† Joseph A. Towles, "Prophets, Politics and People" (unpublished papers, Makerere University, Kampala, Uganda, 1970), and "Ritual and Structure: A Structural Approach" (unpublished papers, Makerere University, Kampala, Uganda, 1972).

‡ See E. E. Evans-Pritchard, *Witchcraft, Oracles and Magic Among the Azande* (Oxford, Eng.: Clarendon Press, 1937).

or may not be able to control it. Witchcraft is frequently thought of as a substance in the stomach or intestines that may compel the body to do things it would or could not normally do. Or it may leave the body at night, in itself do harm to others, and then return to the body. People who possess this substance are not blamed for their actions but are placed under control through periodic rituals of purification. But a person possessed of such powers who consciously uses them for personal gain or other antisocial ends is immediately condemned in all African societies. He is the essence of evil: the sorcerer.

A person who uses supernatural powers for social *good* should not be termed a witch nor referred to as using witchcraft; he is more appropriately placed in one of the other categories, probably a priest, doctor, or diviner. These definitions, as stated, are neither conclusive nor all-embracing; but at least they point to fundamentally different categories rather than to superficially different ones and are arrived at by consideration of the African system of thought rather than by the facile application of Western categories.

Apart from its excellence, Robin Horton's article, "African Traditional Thought and Western Science," is included partly because it does not agree with all that I have been saying in this, the most crucial of all areas. It will give the reader a different perspective. It is also recommended for its admirable lucidity and depth of perception. Horton and I may define or interpret terms such as "spirit" and "matter" somewhat differently, but there can be no disagreement over the point that Horton makes so clearly: that the seeming difference in focus of interest between the two systems of thought is more often apparent than real, at least in terms of thought process.

This kind of approach helps us to understand African religion in its own terms and to recognize more easily its prime and practical integrative role. If I were to attempt a generalization about African religion, I would include two qualities: its essential spirituality and its fundamental practicality. When I say that it is essentially spiritual, I mean that it derives its power from an initial act of faith in a divinity, a remote spiritual entity, providing a single authority that is utterly unquestionable. It is spiritual, also, because (although accounts seldom provide much supporting data) it seems that something of this spiritual essence is thought of as pervading the entire world as a kind of life force and is thus accessible to man, and even within man, in varying degrees and varying ways. A society that defines itself, as African societies do, by common adherence to such a faith is impregnable as long as the faith holds. The major manifestation and vehicle for the expression of this faith is what I have already referred to as a community of belief. Just as faith provides authority, belief provides power.

The spirituality and practicality of African religion can probably best be seen in the institution of Divine Kingship, which is to say, almost any traditional African kingship. There the locus of authority is divine and unquestionable and has the additional force of being symbolized in a living being. The task of preserving the aura of respectability and spirituality is not an easy one, and I have already mentioned something of the physical separation that such figures must undergo. The article by T. O. Beidelman, "Swazi Royal Ritual," discusses another, even more vital, aspect of separation and shows its operation in detail, first providing the reader with the necessary ethnographic background. He examines ritual practice, that necessary adjunct of religion. Although Beidelman discounts Gluckman's interpretation of the same ritual as ritualization of rebellion, he does not discount it completely; rather, he shifts the emphasis, suggesting that the notion of separation is more basic and better explains the facts. The one notion does not exclude the other, however, and Gluckman's accounts* should be read by anyone not familiar with them because they further demonstrate the fundamental practicality of a religion that, through ritualization, can literally ex-press conflict. The difference between the two accounts is a result of the different modes of interpretation, the one symbolic, the other functional. Both are valid, and, happily, both confirm much of what I have been saying about the conjunction of religion and politics and about the democratic nature of African politics as it is supported and symbolized in such rites.

Rodney Needham's article, "The Left Hand of the Mugwe: An Analytical Note on the Structure of Meru Symbolism," deals in a typically minute and painstaking manner with ritual separation in another context, again showing the extreme importance attached to the spiritual nature of certain figureheads as measured by the lengths to which society may go to maintain their aura of divinity. Beneath this divinity and apart from it, but drawing authority from it, lies the body of belief that forms the charter for society. This body of belief reflects the nature of society sometimes realistically, sometimes ideally, but always functionally. It manifests itself in family life, giving the family head something of the sacred nature ascribed to the Divine King (in segmentary societies, the family head, in some respects, is not unlike a Divine King shorn of all the trappings).

---

* See M. Gluckman, *Rituals of Rebellion in South-east Africa* (Manchester, Eng.: Manchester University Press, 1954); and *Order and Rebellion in Tribal Africa* (New York: Free Press, 1963).

Belief is called into play in economic life, as it is in family life, to account for fortunes and misfortunes, and through ritual it again becomes a normal, daily part of life. The political and jural realms offer perhaps the greatest avenues of expression for religious belief and ritual that ensure the high measure of justice and democracy to be found in traditional societies. The detail to which Needham points is indicative of the great importance of the concept of separation, not just as a primitive ritual but as a functional necessity for total social order.

"The *Mäsqal*-Pole: Religious Conflict and Social Change in Gurageland," by William A. Shack, explores the strength of religion in the face of change, its power to continue through faith to support the community of belief essential to social unity. This article looks at a traditional community adapting to the imposition of centralized state government and dealing with a conflict of loyalties. The account illustrates the total and integrated nature of society and the power of traditional belief in maintaining that integration even in the face of such enormously superior powers of physical coercion. When change of this magnitude comes, it can only come to such a society through a change of faith. Lesser change may be accommodated by change of belief.

The role of religion—of faith and belief and their manifestations in ritual—is difficult to define because in Africa it is so all-pervasive and diffuse. To describe it as a reflection of society is too passive, and in any case may be putting the cart before the horse. Society and belief reflect each other and tend to change in sympathy with each other. For those who are interested in the introduction of social change of major order, it is worthwhile to determine whether or not religion is a kind of central nervous system that can be stimulated to affect the body of society. Such a system would suggest a single line of attack, enabling them to induce change rather than impose it.

Too often, when change has been imposed, only the immediate effects have been considered; and however desirable those effects may have been, the consequences in other directions have sometimes more than negated their value to society as a whole.* The imposed introduction of Christianity in Africa is an example. Aside from the fundamentalists who came as though they were gods and tried to remake man in their own limited images, leaving a bitter emptiness in their wake, even those who came with the true desire to improve the lot of their fellow human beings often failed. They tried to impose a set of beliefs that to them were functional and supported by faith, but to the Africans were nonfunctional

---

* See Colin M. Turnbull, *The Lonely African* (New York: Simon and Schuster, 1962).

and unsupported by faith. The result was often that the new beliefs were manipulated to be of use to the new convert in his new context, and it was quickly found that the strange Christian belief in individual salvation suited the new cutthroat world admirably. The new religion then became a means of justifying the grossest immorality of all: unsociality. The converts were a part of society but no longer felt any obligations toward it; they were no longer integrated and interconnected by that all-important web of human interrelationships. And they were no longer even bound together by a common faith because that was the first thing the missionaries sought to destroy, replacing it with mere belief. The only faith possible in this modern civilized world is faith in oneself, and that does not have much integrative force.

Similarly imposed changes in other areas, familial, economic or political, were designed to achieve a specific goal; and by achieving that goal, these changes also brought a train of consequences that were by no means equally desirable and always further weakened the total social structure. The net result has been the real triumph of colonialism. Up to this point, modern African society has increasingly followed the pattern of amoral legalism with which we infected it. The new generation of leaders seems more alive to these dangers and to the positive power of certain traditions, but the process, once begun, is not easy to halt. Youth—in Africa, as elsewhere, the voice of the future—has been given the golden vision of progress and has not yet seen enough of it to know the disillusionment it brings. There may be more hope, oddly enough, in Western nations where there would seem to be an even more irrevocable commitment to progress.

The Ik are an example of the most extreme and adverse effects of social tinkering. As nomadic hunters and gatherers within their own ample territory, they lived an entirely adequate life. But the tinkering with national boundaries and the pursuit of national interests (such as the establishment of a game reserve in the middle of their former hunting territory) so effectively altered their physical world that they were unable to survive as hunters. They had to turn to other economic activities, and since agriculture in that area is totally inadequate, they have come to rely more and more upon their neighbors and the latent hostility between them. They prey upon their neighbors; they live on them like parasites; they encourage intertribal hostilities that they can manipulate to their own advantage. They are thorough and consistent, so they treat each other in the same way. It is the only way that they can possibly survive. They have become the most perfect individualists; they have become civilized. Their faith was destroyed because the adequacy of their world was destroyed and they had no time to adapt. In two generations they were reduced to the level that has taken us some 2,000 years to reach.

The Mbuti hunters of Zaïre are an example of an opposite extreme They, too, are faced with the dangers of unplanned social change in response to new national needs, but their world, the gigantic rain forest, is virtually unchangeable for the immediate future. Thus their faith, which springs from the source of their being, remains intact. The world changes around the hunters; roads and railways are built; villages become towns; there is a sudden influx of foreign people, foreign things, and foreign ideas; but the forest remains, and with it remains their faith. They have so far stayed intact as a people and, as such, stand a good chance of being able to adapt to the contemporary changes more successfully than the Ik. If, in the necessary task of introducing the Mbuti hunters to national life, to the responsibilities of citizenship, something of their world (and faith) can be preserved, they may make a unique contribution, being a moralistic society in the midst of a legalistic one.

"Primitive" life is not idyllic. It is often hard, sometimes short, and certainly not without its setbacks or without quarrel. But when they discuss the changes taking place around them and compare their own way of life with that which they are being encouraged to adopt, it becomes clear that what the Mbuti Pygmies themselves value in it is that almost everything they do, every minute of every day, involves them with each other. They act together at all times, in mutual though sometimes divided interests. Theirs is a world of human beings and human relationships, and the survival of the human being is seen in terms of the survival of the relationships. Their values are rooted, not in luxuries, but in necessities—family, friends, food, shelter, warmth, sex—all of which they enjoy in abundance.

What is important for us is not the actual physical way of life, which obviously we cannot emulate, but rather these human values and the exceptionally well-integrated nature of their social life. The goal of the rebellion of youth today and the revolution they wish to accomplish is precisely what the Mbuti already have and are fighting to retain in the face of the threat of civilization: a life that is human, that is rooted in humanity, that is concerned with humanity, that is organized as a system of essentially human relationships. The one thing that seems to make this possible is the integration of religious faith and belief into daily life; where this breaks down, the human focus also breaks down. Religion as a binding force is the essence of society, at least of a moralistic society. Technological advance has blinded us to that fact and has diverted our focus of attention from sociality, from humanity, to mere technicality, to system. Just as religious faith and belief are the essence of the moralistic society, so individualism, that jeweled diadem of civilization, is the essence of our modern legalistic society. The revolt of youth in the West is probably the most potentially significant event of the millennium because it is clearly a revolt against individualism and legalism, an attempt to reassert human values rather than technical ones.

The youth revolt is making use of all the prime social principles that are at work in small-scale societies. In itself it is the manifestation of the age principle at work. Its emphasis on community is a recognition of the importance of a sociological family as the source of a value system, as the home and cradle of faith. By its insistence on community of residence as well, it heightens still further its recognition of the necessity of community life, where community of behavior follows from community of belief, and where community of residence provides for the daily manifestation of social values in community of action and interrelationship. All these things are essential to a moralistic society. And youth is demonstrating that morality and humanity are not mere pipedreams to be relegated to moments of nostalgia; as principles of social behavior, they are as alive and as vital as ever. Humanity itself is the new faith, just as it was the old; and whatever today's youth may be losing in terms of material comfort, "social" respectability, formal education, and so forth, they are gaining in terms of human relationships. The basic way of life they are clamoring for is not by any means necessarily antagonistic to the material world in which we live, and which we cannot as realistically abandon as the leaders of the revolt can. All that we have to abandon, if we take our lesson from the small-scale societies, is our misplaced focus of interest. The technological world will then retreat into proper perspective and become our servant rather than our master.

How this may be accomplished is, of course, another matter. Youth in revolt may not accomplish it themselves; their revolt is perhaps more in the nature of a ritual rebellion. But in destroying, at least for themselves, the very validity of the old order, they have created a void that is the hope for the future. It is precisely the situation that in small-scale societies calls for the figurehead who precedes all true revolutions: the prophet. So, ironically, it may be an individual in every sense of the word who saves us from the blight of individualism and reasserts social values. The time is ripe, for not only youth feel in need of a new faith, of a new prophet. The surge of emotion felt toward figures like Pope John, Chairman Mao, John F. Kennedy, Martin Luther King, Billy Graham, and George Wallace indicates that in many diverse realms and communities people feel the need of a new savior. He may come in the form of a new kind of leader in an established church, or he may create a new church, a new community of believers. Only in this way can there come the faith that is essential to truly social life, be it a faith in God, a faith in Society, or a faith in Humanity; the difference between them may not be as great as we customarily think. Without such a faith, we are condemned to continued progress toward that technological nirvana where we will no longer need to be human because human beings will no longer be needed. The change in direction that needs to be effected calls for nothing short of a revolution; no amount of petty sociological tinkering can achieve it. The revolution that is called for is a revolution in faith, a moral revolution rather than a physical one. That, too, is a lesson to be learned from small-scale societies. Such a revolution is the prerequisite of the solution of the dangers posed by technology and our current notion of "progress" because what is needed, above all else, is a shift in values back to humanity, a shift from comfort and technological progress and the present concept of political stability back to the most essential of all: affective and effective human relationships. Whether such a revolution will cause or necessitate any material or technological sacrifice cannot be said, but even if it does, to those who value mankind above machinery, that would seem a small price to pay. For those of the new faith it will be no price at all because the only alternative seems to be the utter destruction of humanity.

# Swazi Royal Ritual[1]

# T. O. Beidelman

Upon the king! Let us our lives, our souls,
Our debts, our careful wives,
Our children, and our sins, lay on the king!
We must bear all. O hard conditions
Twin-born with greatness . . .
O Ceremony, show me but thy worth!
What is thy soul of adoration?
Art thou aught else but place, degree, and form,
Creating awe and fear in other men?
Wherein thou art less happy being fear'd
Than they in fearing.
What drink'st thou oft, instead of homage sweet,
But poison'd flattery? O, be sick, great greatness,
And bid thy Ceremony give thee cure!

*Henry V, iv. i*

---

[1] This paper was completed during the leisure afforded by a fellowship at the Center for Advanced Study in the Behavioral Sciences, Stanford. I wish to thank the Center, the National Institute of Mental Health, and Duke University for making this possible. An early version of this paper was presented in lectures at Harvard University where I benefited greatly by discussion with Dr. Terence Turner.

In writing this paper I have received valuable comments from Miss Jean Carter, Professor John Middleton, Dr. Rodney Needham, Professor M. N. Srinivas, and Professor Victor Turner. They are not, however, responsible for any errors which this paper may contain.

I have not been able to use all the Swazi literature although I have consulted more items than appear in my bibliography which contains only sources related to the problems at hand. I have utilized all the major sources cited by Gluckman, as well as many others. I have no knowledge of Afrikaans and cannot use those sources. I have not been to South Africa and I do not consider myself widely read in its ethnographic literature; doubtless, some useful sources have been neglected. Since no comparable Swazi dictionary is available, I have used Doke and Vilakazi's monumental *Zulu–English Dictionary* (1958) as the authority for many words whose meanings relate to my argument. In defence of using a Zulu dictionary in analysing Swazi, I cite Kuper (1952, pp. 13–14) 'Swati (siSwait, siNgwane) commonly known in its Zulu-ised form as Swazi, falls within the south-eastern zone of Bantu languages. It is further classified with Zulu and Xhosa. . . . It is clear that Swazi is sufficiently similar to Zulu for Zulu to serve efficiently as the only written and official vernacular. The main differences between them are phonetical and there are also slight variations in vocabulary.' It seems that Gluckman would allow a cautious use of a wide range of Zulu material to gain insight on the Swazi (1963, p. 19), but I have confined myself mainly to supplementary information on certain words and their meanings. Zulu terms and definitions from Doke and Vilikazi are preceded by the notation (Z). In most cases, the Zulu term is a perfect or near cognate of the Swazi. In transcribing Swazi and Zulu words I have avoided special linguistic signs and rendered these into what seem to be their nearest conventional equivalent.

Ideally, a detailed account of the Swazi royal rites of *Incwala* should accompany this paper, but space does not permit this. Both Kuper's account and Gluckman's analysis have been published twice and are readily available: Kuper, 1944; 1947,

## I. Introduction

In his Frazer Lecture of 1952, *Rituals of Rebellion in South-East Africa* (1954), Professor Max Gluckman considers certain types of ritual behaviour as institutionalized expressions of rebellion against authority. He maintains that this expression is an important function of such ritual. The following quotations present the gist of his interpretation:

I shall therefore consider the social components of ceremonies, analogous to those which concerned Frazer, among the South-Eastern Bantu. . . . Here there are . . . performed, as elsewhere in Africa, national and local ceremonies at the break of the rains, sowing, first fruits, and harvest. . . . But whatever the ostensible purpose of the ceremonies, a most striking feature of their organization is the way in which they openly express social tensions. Women have to assert license and dominance as against their formal subordination to men, princes have to behave to the kings as if they covet the throne, and subjects openly state their resentment of authority. Hence I call them rituals of rebellion. I shall argue that some ritual rebellions proceed within an established distribution of power, and not about the structure of the system itself. This allows for instituted protest, and in complex ways renews the unity of the system (1954, p. 3).

We are here confronted with a cultural mechanism which challenges study by sociologists, psychologists, and biologists, the analysis in detail of the process by which this acting of conflict achieves a blessing—social unity. Clearly we are dealing with the general problem of *catharsis* set by Aristotle . . . the purging of emotion through 'pity, fear and inspiration'. Here I attempt only to analyze the sociological setting of the process (1954, p. 20).

Although this approach provides some interesting insights into the societies discussed, it focuses upon a very narrow aspect of ritual and in so doing diverts attention from the main themes and purposes of such rites. Gluckman begins with a consideration of latent functions of such rites, that is, sociological and psychological results not consciously intended by the par-

---

chapter xiii; Gluckman, 1954; 1963, chapter iii. Important supplementary information is provided in Marwick (1940) and Ziervogel (1957).

This paper is only possible because of the superb ethnographic accounts of the Swazi provided by Kuper. It is reassuring that after completing all but the conclusion of this paper, I had the pleasure of meeting Professor Kuper and discovered that we had been pursuing somewhat similar lines of further analysis of her earlier material. Professor Kuper has kindly read over this paper; she is in disagreement with some of my conjectures on word relations and is not responsible for any errors which may appear in this paper. She has saved me from some blunders, but I have persisted in some points, even in the face of her disagreement. Some of my analysis is clearly speculative, but I believe that this does call attention to certain unclarified and important sectors in Swazi cosmology and symbolic thought. Examples of such speculation which Professor Kuper does not think warranted may be found in the following footnotes: page 403, footnote 16; page 404, footnote 17; page 405, footnote 19.

ticipants themselves. But before one may do this (if, indeed, it is a useful task), one must first determine what the members of the society concerned say (and thus probably think) that they are doing.

The problem of determining what the members of a preliterate society believe and think is difficult, since such peoples rarely if ever consider their ideas and symbols as forming an extensive analytical system such as the social anthropologist desires. However, it is often possible through considering the ethnographic facts available to obtain a fairly clear idea of the kind of system of ideas and symbols held by a people. This is certainly possible in the case of the two societies considered by Gluckman, where the data are among the richest in Africa.

Before one can write about the various themes in rites, such as aggression, humiliation, harmony, sexual differences, one must understand the symbolic vocabulary and grammar used by a particular society. In short, one must understand the cosmology of the people involved so that one has some idea of what they themselves believe that they are doing with such ritual. Otherwise one's interpretation of the significance of certain acts may be in terms of one's own perspective rather than that of the actors. In the case of ritual, which is, by definition, symbolic, such a cultural perspective is of the utmost importance. One may then proceed to search out sociological and psychological relationships of another order, if one wishes. Gluckman does not seem to have made such initial analysis with the symbolic acts he considers and I believe that this has led him to some misplaced emphases and misinterpretations, in that he has sometimes found conflict, aggression, and rebellion as dominant themes where this does not seem to be so.

To demonstrate my point, I must reanalyse the rites which Gluckman describes, and to do this in the manner I advocate, I must first provide analyses of the cosmologies for the societies concerned. Gluckman employs examples from two societies: fertility rites among the Zulu and the annual royal rites among the Swazi. I do not agree with his analyses of either, but I limit myself to consideration of only one of these, the main Swazi royal rites of *Incwala*. I hope this is sufficient to indicate the nature of my argument and the type of procedure which I advocate.[2]

The remainder of this paper is divided into three sections: (1) a presentation of what seem to be the basic concepts and values behind the main royal rites for the Swazi people, in short, a Swazi cosmology, or at least part of one; (2) a discussion of the most important of these rites in order to indicate how they conform to the preceding analysis and how they relate to Swazi kingship and society; in doing this I implicitly indicate many of the points I question in Gluckman's interpretation; (3) a short concluding

---

[2] I have already presented one such analysis dealing with a female initiation ceremony (Beidelman, 1964).

discussion of some of the possible implications which such analysis may
have for understanding ritual. Here, I touch upon the more basic problems
related to the study of ritual. I deal briefly with some issues related to
sociological and psychological aspects of ritual which have figured prominently in the earlier published criticisms of Gluckman's work. I do not
propose to solve such difficult issues, but only to indicate what I consider
the implications involved and to suggest what methods of further research
may be fruitful. This discussion of Swazi symbolism limits the space for
analysis of the rites themselves, yet no analysis would be possible without
first undertaking such a discussion. With regret, I therefore confine myself
in Section III to an analysis of the Great *Incwala,* the final and more important of the two national rites. The discussion of Swazi cosmology should
equip the reader himself to interpret the preliminary aspects of these rites
such as setting their date, fetching of waters, and other themes. Some minor
themes in all the rites, such as the significance of hornless cattle (representing some kind of inversion), of cattle skulls and horns mounted on roof-
tops, of certain plants and animals, cannot now be fully explained because
no data are available; others, such as token-fines and token-pillaging, and
the nature of the asylum huts (Kuper, 1944, pp. 233, 235–6), seem difficult
but perhaps soluble, and these I draw into the concluding analysis.


## II. Swazi Cosmology

The Swazi are a Bantu people inhabiting south-eastern Africa. Their kingdom is now a British protectorate, Swaziland, whose modern government
is founded upon the traditional kingship of the Swazi people. Swaziland
remains a kingdom and the rituals of its kingship epitomize all that Swazi
traditionally value in defining themselves as a nation. The literature on the
Swazi is large and I provide no background discussion of most aspects of
Swazi society; a bibliography of the main sources appears at the end of this
paper. Professor Kuper's fine ethnography, arranged mainly around the
problems of social rank and status, provides rich material from which a
picture of Swazi cosmology can be constructed; other sources supplement
her material. In this section I first present what seem to me to be the basic
ideas and symbols with which Swazi categorize their world; I then consider some of the processes by which Swazi see these categories interrelating with one another and some of the ways, through ritual acts, by which
Swazi believe that they themselves can manipulate symbols to achieve
certain states and effects in themselves and the world about them.

Swazi see an order both in the sphere of natural objects and events and
in human society. In most respects it would seem that a distinction between
nature and society is not made by them; rather, the two are manifestations
of the same principles of order in the universe, interdependent and validat-

ing one another. Order in one effects order in the other, and disorder in either jeopardizes the order of both.

The classical derivation of *cosmetics* from *cosmos*, from the idea of making something orderly and therefore attractive and right, seems especially appropriate in considering royal rituals which the Swazi call *Incwala*. Doke and Vilakazi note that the ideophone (Z) *cwa* conveys the idea of tidiness and order; the word (Z) *incwalacwala*, a tidy, neat, nice-looking person, thing, or act; and the verb (Z) *cwala*, to dress the hair, combing it out below the head-ring by using a pointed instrument, or to polish the head-ring. The head-ring, (Z) *isicoco*, is the most important of the traditional insignia worn by socially adult Zulu and Swazi men, that is, by married men. It is not worn by bereaved men for its removal is one of the main signs of male mourning, an expression of the chaotic disturbance of the individual and his relation to the deceased (Kuper, 1947, pp. 178–9).

## A. The Basic *Incwala* Pattern

The *Incwala* rites coincide, as much as possible, with the commencement of the sun's movement northward after the December solstice and with the waxing of the moon. The Small *Incwala* requires two days; after about a fortnight the Great *Incwala* is held, completing the annual celebrations. The Great *Incwala* requires four days followed by two days whereby, in van Gennep's terms, the king is reincorporated within the nation. The two *Incwala* rites resemble one another, except that the first is shorter, simpler, and not followed by any reincorporation. An extremely brief outline of the two *Incwala* provides orientation to the reader of my discussion of Swazi cosmology. I emphasize that this is no substitute for the reader's checking the original accounts, cf. the first footnote of this paper:

The Small *Incwala* [Kuper, 1944, pp. 232–9]: The king's ritual representatives undertake a quest outside the country to secure river and sea water to invigorate him. *En route* they collect fines from Swazi whom they encounter. Returning, they deposit the waters and other medicines in the *inhlambelo* (royal sacred enclosure). The warriors and public praise the king and a black ox is slain for medicines to doctor him. On a moonless night, as the warriors change their dance formation from a crescent to a full circle, the king enters the *inhlambelo* to be doctored for supernatural power. The sea and river waters, parts of the slain ox, and other items are used. The people sing the *simemo*, a song expressing rejection and hatred of the king, his isolation. Filled with medicines, the king spits east and west, through apertures in the enclosure, 'stabbing' the new year. The royal clan and aliens are excluded from his vicinity. Upon this, the public sing his praises for 'biting' into the year. The next dawn, the king again enters the *inhlambelo*, is doctored, and his kin and aliens excluded. He again spits east and west and 'bites' into the year, whereupon the public praise him. The rites end and later the warriors perform agricultural work for the royal family.

The Great *Incwala* [ibid., pp. 241–53]: The king's warriors undertake a ritual quest for sacred, invigorating vegetation growing far from the capital. They return by night and next dawn place this at the *inhlambelo*. The following dawn warriors place other vegetation at the *inhlambelo*. About noon they undress and then pummel to near-death a pitch black ox which is termed 'bull', after it has been driven wild by the king striking it with a doctored wand. The ox-bull is slain and its parts deposited in the *inhlambelo*. A black ox from the king's sacred herd is put in contact with the nude king in his cattle byre and both are washed in medicines. The king makes a gesture of eating part of an ox's liver. The warriors go from a crescent to a circular formation, singing the *simemo*. The carcass of the slain ox-bull is left overnight in the *inhlambelo* to be 'tasted' by the royal ghosts. On the morning of the fourth day, the king is doctored in the *inhlambelo*. He appears nude except for an ivory penis-cap, and walks through the crowd to the hut where he consummated the marriage to his first ritual queen. About him the crowd weeps and sings the *simemo*. Inside he is doctored and 'stabs' and 'bites' the new year. He spits medicine east and west. Later, undressed boys eat the 'stale' flesh of the ox-bull which has been in the *inhlambelo* overnight, and then they are cleansed in a river. Adults, following the king, 'bite' medicines for the new year. Later, people gather to dance about the king. His royal kinsmen encircle him singing that they plan to depart with him. The people lament. The royal clan dance, trying to encircle the king and force him back into the *inhlambelo*. The people dance and sing, trying to entice him out. He emerges in demonic costume, powerfully doctored and painted black, a wild beast dancing aggressively and showing reluctance to join the people. He disappears and reappears, back and forth. Finally, he disappears and royal kin and aliens leave the vicinity. Then he emerges, still doctored and painted but without demonic garb, holding a green calabash which he finally hurls at his warriors. One receives it on a sacred black shield. The celebrations end, dancers cleanse themselves, and the king, still doctored, spends the night 'darkened' with his first ritual queen. The people are supposed to observe restrictions that night and the next day. Those who do not, if caught, pay fines. On the sixth day the remaining meat of the ox-bull, the fines collected from the people, the remaining medicines and costumes, and all the 'dirt' of the rites and of the nation are heaped for a fire in the royal cattle byre. A black cow is slain. The king kindles a fire to burn all the 'dirt'. He washes off his medicines and walks nude about the byre aspersing himself and the royal herd with cleansing medicines. People gather and rain is supposed to fall, quenching the flames and blessing the rites. Praises are sung for the king and nation, and the rites end with feasts and dancing. On the following days the warriors perform agricultural work for the royal family.

The Great *Incwala* has a simple form: (*a*) The first half gradually increases all the powerful supernatural attributes of the king. When these have reached their maximum, he may partake of and act upon the supernatural forces which animate the world. These powerful forces are set loose and the climax of this supernatural 'charging' of the king is his appearance as a monster, cut off from men and society owing to the very strength and disorder of the varied opposing attributes condensed within him. (*b*) The second half is a gradual decreasing of this dangerous but potent concentration, sorting out these mixed attributes so that the more socially dangerous aspects may be discarded. The turning-point in the rites is the king's hurling of the sacred gourd on to the black shields, showing his decision to rejoin the nation and place his previously unrestricted powers within the confines of the social order. Through observance of various prohibitions, basic categories are again clearly defined and may then be readily separated into those aspects to be retained and those whose embodying objects are burned. I now consider these motifs in more detail.

## B. Space and the Heavens

Perhaps the most basic ordination of the Swazi cosmos relates to the regularity of the heavenly bodies and their correspondence to the seasons of the year. Swazi seem to place primary emphasis upon the east–west axis with reference to the passage of the sun across the sky: (Z) *impumalanga*, east (*ilanga*, sun + *phuma*, come forth); and (Z) *intshonalanga*, west (*shona*, go down, die). Movement from west to east seems to be inauspicious. Recent types of possession by spirits are thought to have come from the west (Kuper, 1952, p. 49; however, Engelbrecht seems to disagree, 1930*b*, p. 24). Ethnographic data are not clear concerning Swazi concepts relating to north and south; from Swazi ritual and organization of villages, it seems that primary orientation is facing from east, aligning north with the right (superior) and south with the left (inferior) (Marwick, pp. 12–13; Kuper, 1947, p. 235). Many rites progress from east to west; Swazi kings are buried oriented in an eastward direction (Marwick, p. 55), and Swazi brides walk from east to west, but face eastward in certain marriage rites (Kuper, 1945, pp. 150, 152).[3]

The key agents for Swazi in this orientation of space and time are the sun (*ilanga*) and moon (*inyanga*). The 'Great Sun' or 'Male of the Heavens' moves regularly back and forth across the skies, (Z) *izulu*, heavens (Kuper, 1947, p. 36). He makes two great treks across the skies, one going southward and ending with the summer solstice of the southern latitudes when he rests in his hut in the south, and one, beginning the year, going northward and ending in the other solstice. To Swazi, the sun's movement out of the south must coincide with the annual rites to rejuvenate the king

---

[3] I could not be sure that Zulu terms for south and north parallel Swazi; for Zulu, at least, south seems to have a negative connotation: (Z) *iningizimu*, south, so called because storms, winds, and fog are said to be associated with cannibals coming from the south (*amazimu*, cannibals). This term *amazimu* does not seem linked with ancestral ghosts, but seems related to the *simu, zimu* root often appearing in Bantu languages and referring to ancestral ghosts. The Swazi term ancestral ghosts, *emadloti*, relates probably to the Zulu terms (Z) *amadlozi*, ancestral spirits before they are put to rest; (Z) *dloza*, to seize violently, look after, keep an eye on.

The meaning of north remains unclear; this direction is associated with the royal clan among the Swazi (Kuper, 1964, p. 70), though what significance may be attached to this is hard to tell.

and nation. The sun does not die, but rather, each evening (Z) *ilanga selingene kunina,* the sun has already gone into its mother's (hut).[4] The moon is the female consort of the sun (Kuper, 1952, p. 42) and follows her mate. The moon grows until it becomes full: (Z) *inyanga inidindile,* the moon has now become full, (Z) *dinda,* to expose fully, or (Z) *inyanga ehlangene,* the moon has now become full, from (Z) *hlangana,* to come together, assemble, be dense, complete, have sexual connexion (euphemism). When the moon becomes dark, it is 'covered' by the sun, and 'dies' (Kuper, 1944, p. 234). (Z) *Inyanga isiyafa,* the moon is about to die, waning moon, dying moon, (Z) *inyanga isifile,* the moon has disappeared. The sexual connotations of 'covered' and 'die' should be clear in terms of solar and lunar symbolism in the royal rites and their association with lightness and darkness and with male and female sexuality.

The masculine sun is superior to the female moon. Its nature (size) is in flux, each phase being a product of its coupling with its heavenly mate. The Zulu dictionary is full of terms associating herbs and medicines with what appear to be lunar and female terms and the word *inyanga,* doctor, diviner, herbalist, is a homonym in both Zulu and Swazi for moon. This may have some association with the medial character which both diviners and the moon share. The Swazi royal clan, the sun's people, are strongly discouraged from becoming such doctors or diviners themselves; if one should be possessed, it is said to have come from the mother's family (Kuper, 1947, p. 165). (Similarly, witchcraft, though possessed by either men or women, is transmitted by women, Kuper, 1947, p. 173.)

Swazi find a relation between heavenly movement and certain processes of men, herds, and crops. This has a negative as well as a positive aspect: things are born and grow, but they also age and die. Swazi rites of growth and birth and also those of death are closely related to the waxing and waning moon. 'Ceremonies to introduce someone into the fullness of a new status take place when the moon is growing, or when it is full; those which temporarily isolate him from his fellows, when it is waning or disappearing' (Kuper, 1952, p. 44). The Swazi child is transformed from a 'thing' to a person by being presented to the waxing moon; some show a boy to the nearly full moon, a girl to the very new one: male/female: complete/incomplete (Kuper, 1947, pp. 75–76; Marwick, p. 87), but certain other rites, such as the annual *Incwala,* should commence in such darkness. At these ceremonies the queen mother is related to the waxing moon and the king to the full moon (Kuper, 1944, p. 252).

The moon may also be associated with the sea, although this is only conjecture. Royal rites involve the use of sea water and require close correlation with the darkness and subsequent waxing of the moon. I do not know

---

[4] I do not know how widespread this concept is; it is held by Kaguru in Tanzania. Kaguru also contrast the immortal sun with the succession of dying moons.

whether Swazi associate or compare the tides with the phases of the moon, but certain important medicines are reported to come from the bones of animals of the sea (Kuper, 1952, p. 49) and the term for becoming a diviner and herbalist is the same as the term (Z) *ethwasa*, to come out anew, emerge, show signs of change in oneself as by spirit possession, to wax (as the moon), (Kuper, 1947, p. 164).

## C. The Complementary Attributes of Sense, Sex, and Orientation

Darkness, as in the 'covered' moon, is an ambiguous quality. Black symbolizes 'impenetrability of the future' but also the 'sins and evils of the past year' (Marwick, p. 193). Marwick describes a human sacrifice being termed a black bushbuck (p. 202), fertility magic utilizing a pregnant black cow or sheep (p. 211), magic for preparing pegs for a new house utilizing the fat of a black sheep (p. 36), and a black beetle worn in the hair to brink luck with cattle (p. 174). With equal paradox, Twala describes black beads symbolizing marriage and wealth in cattle, but also symbolizing evil, disappointment, and misfortune (1951, pp. 115, 118). In Swazi ceremonies participants dress conspicuously in black finery (Twala, 1952, pp. 99–100). Most beasts slain in ritual must be black. The beasts slain or utilized in the annual *Incwala* are all pitch black. The Swazi king is buried with a live black goat (Kuper, 1947, p. 87), and over the royal corpse's head is stuck the [gall] bladder of a black goat (ibid., p. 86). Corpses of all men of authority, from the king and princes to headmen, are wrapped in the hides of black oxen, as is the corpse of the queen mother (ibid., pp. 178–9). At the king's puberty rites a black goat is slain and the young king's hair[5] deposited in its head-cavity and the young king given insignia including a spear washed in the gall of a black ox (Kuper, 1947, pp. 77).

This ambiguous quality of blackness is shared by whiteness. White beads are associated with the moon and the cleansing it can involve (Twala, 1951, pp. 115–16), and this whiteness is compared to the cleanness of sea-sand and to purity in both women and medicine (ibid., p. 121; cf. also Engelbrecht, 1930*b*, p. 16). The whiteness of the moon, like the whiteness of ashes, also implies transition. An infant decked out in white beads is shown to the white moon at rites to change its status from a thing to a person, being held at the time over an ash-heap (Marwick, p. 147), and

---

[5] The fascinating problem of the detachment of a part from the whole, as in castration, sexual ejaculation, birth, defecation, shaving, has been provocatively treated by Leach, cf. his essays on time (1961) and his Curl Bequest essay on magical hair. Such motifs appear throughout the Swazi material. Leach also observes how tears seem to be the only bodily emission which is invariably pure, cf. the liquor presented at the *Incwala* is referred to as the tears of the English king (Kuper, 1944, p. 244).

thus (Z) *ithambo*, bone, white bead, hatred. Perhaps because of this it is associated with diviners and mediums (Marwick, p. 231), who make contact with the dead for their prowess. The Swazi king is praised as the bright sun and royal children are washed in medicines to make their blood 'shine' (Kuper, 1947, p. 75), yet the king is also praised as one 'born amidst black shields' and as the 'black hero of the Swazi' (Kuper, 1947, pp. xi–xii). To a large extent, then, the two colours, although opposed in many senses, also contain similar qualities; when combined in a king, in a rainstorm, or a certain kind of magic, these produce the utmost power.

The word (Z) *mnyama* means black and dark, but also means deep, profound, unfathomable, and even confused, dizzy, angry. A black ox or bull is referred to as (Z) *inzima* and a black cow as (Z) *inzimakazi*, relating to (Z) *isinzima*, heaviness, weight, prestige, dignity. Doke and Vilakazi relate the ideophone (Z) *nzi* to heavy pressure, firmness, tightness; (Z) *inzima* may also mean black, dark-skinned, awe-inspiring, strong, forcible, heavy, weighty, difficult, important, grievous, onerous. The expression (Z) *Umabani usenzima*, she is heavy, is a euphemism for being pregnant. The idea of darkness and weight in (Z) *isithunzi*, shadow, allows that term's extension to moral weight, influence, prestige, soul, and personality. The king has great *isithunzi* (Kuper, 1947, p. 70); he is also the bull (*inkunzi*) of the nation. One can understand the frequent pouring of gall from black beasts over ritual objects and medicines when one knows that Swazi consider gall the epitome of this same heaviness and impenetrability. The term for gall bladder, (Z) *inyongo*, is used to refer to personality, dignity (as exemplified by being allowed to wear a gall bladder, thus (Z) *ukufaka inyongo*, to wear a gall bladder, an idiom for being an important person, such as a diviner or doctor). A person important enough to merit the slaughter of a bovine beast on his behalf should wear its gall bladder on his left wrist (Twala, 1952, p. 97). To Swazi, ritual knowledge is 'deep' and 'heavy' (Kuper, 1947, p. 161). That which is dark is unknown and ambiguous and dangerous, but it is also profound, latent with unknown meanings and possibilities.[6]

(Z) *Mhlophe* means white, pale, pure, innocent, perfect, but this may also mean destitute and empty. The whiteness of the full moon, (Z) *inyanga isidindile*, relates to fullness; but this term (Z) *dinda* can also mean to be useless, simply because it refers to that which is fully exposed and having no further unknown potentialities.

The combinations of black and white occur in key Swazi rituals. Some maintain that Swazi resemble Zulu closely in many respects. If so, then they

---

[6] In his article on Swazi marriage, Engelbrecht introduces Zulu data of some relevance to this idea of heaviness being related to fertility: women with watery, thin menstrual flow are thought to lack fertile strength and are induced to have thicker flow possessing *ithunzi*, shadow; he also notes that sterile women are thought to lack *ithunzi*, 1930*b*, p. 24.

too have both black and white medicines as Hoernlé describes (Schapera, p. 229): black medicines which are powerful, purgative, and activating; white which are soothing and purifying. The black and white aspects of rain (heavy clouds and lightning) require a discussion apart: so do the black and white associations of the king, his homestead, and his wives' sections in the harem. I provide one example here: while he is still a boy and 'in darkness', *emnyameni* (*mnyama*, black) (Ziervogel, 1957, p. 31), the king's embryonic capital's main compound (*lusasa*) is divided into two parts: the white is accessible to most persons, but the black, where the boy-king is doctored with vitalizing medicines, may be entered only by men (until later when the king is mature and takes sweethearts), and cannot be entered by women, not even his own mother (Kuper, 1947, p. 73). This same division into black and white is maintained in the harem of the adult king's capital and the attributes of both these black and white elements seem to be combined and utilized in royal ritual.

Right and left orientation figures prominently in Swazi symbolism; unfortunately, the ethnographic data appear somewhat inconsistent, perhaps because southern Swazi are more preoccupied with such distinctions than are those to the north. It has been suggested that these differences are due to variation in Zulu influence upon the Swazi; this may also account for some of the differences between the reports of Kuper and Marwick. There are a number of terms for right and left. The term (Z) *isandla*, forearm, hand, itself relates to the term (Z) *amandla*, strength, power, moral strength, authority, ability. Hence, (Z) *amandla enkosi*, power of the king, and (Z) *amandla obudoda*, power of the male, viz., semen. The right hand or arm has a number of names, each deriving from one of its attributes: (Z) *isandla sokudla* (*dla*, eat); (Z) *isandla sokunene* (*nene*, appropriately, correctly; *inene*, address term proper to a man; *ubunene*, kindness, courtesy, the right side of something; (Z) *isinene*, the front part of a man's loincloth); (Z) *isandla sokuphosa* (*phosa*, to hurl, as a spear). The association of the right with power and bravery lies behind war medicines being made from the right foreleg of a still-living bull noted for its ferocity (Kuper, 1947, p. 125); it also may account for the king's commander in war having his quarters to the right (north) of the king's compound (ibid., p. 235). The left hand is called (Z) *isandla sokunxele* or (Z) *isandla sekhohlo* (both derivations are unclear) and also (Z) *isandla semfene*, baboon's hand. (Z) *Ubunxele* means left-handedness or left-handed direction; (Z) *inxele*, a left-handed person or an ox with one horn receding downward; and (Z) *inxeleha*, a person who has killed another in battle and is thus polluted, or that person's weapon which is polluted as well. One addresses persons of authority as 'You of the right hand' (Marwick, p. 45). Swazi ritual and village arrangements bear out the association of the right side with superiority and masculinity, and the left with femininity and weakness. When Swazi build a house, work starts on the men's side, the right, and ends on the women's side or left; and the house of the first wife is placed on the right side of the entrance (north) and the second wife's house on the left (south) (Ziervogel, 1957, pp. 15, 23). Marwick states that Swazi villages are divided into a right side (*kunene*) and left (*kholwa*), and that ideally wives are ranked with the first to the right, second to the left, third to the right, etc. (p. 28). Kuper states that this is only true of southern Swazi where Zulu influence is strong (1947, p. 39). But Kuper herself devotes considerable space to indicating the importance of spatial orientation in the Swazi royal capital and notes that this is followed, more modestly, by the king's subjects. Her descriptions should be considered with her diagrams; she does not state whether right–left orientation is based on a person's entering or leaving a gateway. From the sum of her data and from other observers it is clear that Swazi figure right and left in terms of entering: thus, one comes from the east, facing west, so that right is brought into association with north and left with south (cf. Kuper's statements and diagrams, 1947, pp. 42–43, 235).

In sexual relations a Swazi youth should lie on his right side, a girl on her left (Marwick, p. 97); this would allow the boy to have his unclean hand free for sex play and cover his right, but would force the girl to use her right hand. Male corpses are placed on the man's side of the hut, facing toward the back (ibid., p. 222). Doke and Vilakazi seem to clarify this: (Z) *isilili somfazi* (*isilili*, sleeping place + *fazi*, female), the left-hand side where women sleep; (Z) *isilili sendoda* (*doda*, male), the right side where men sleep. Mourning women remove the right-hand post from their hut-entrances (Marwick, p. 224) and a bride is anointed with gall on her right side, first arm, then leg, because her left side is inauspicious (Marwick, p. 102; Kuper, 1945, p. 146; Engelbrecht, 1930b, p. 14). Kuper (Beemer, 1937, p. 186) notes that the left is an inappropriate side for a beast to be stabbed upon, except on certain 'bad' occasions which she does not specify; contrast with Ziervogel, 1957, pp. 124–5. She also notes that the right side of an entrance is the proper and auspicious side for entry at ceremonies (1945, p. 148).

The Swazi king undergoes many rituals in which right–left distinctions are crucial. When an infant, he is given medicines on the right side of the entrance to his mother's house, whereas his sister is treated on the left (Kuper, 1947, p. 75). When he reaches maturity and makes his first blood comrades or *tinsila*, he takes a right-hand *insila* first, then a left (ibid., p. 77). The blood of the right side of the first *insila* and the blood of the king's right are mingled; the blood of the left side of the second *insila* is mingled with the blood of the king's left. The king may take additional *tinsila*, but does not exchange blood with these; but each *insila* is associated ritually to one side or the other of the king and is available to apply medicines and tend the king's bodily needs, each of the particular side he is bound to (ibid., pp. 80–82). The king also exchanges blood with his first queen, the one to whom he has special ritual connexions; in this case blood from both sides, first his right side's blood with hers, then their left (ibid.).

Although right and left and east and west seem the most prominent aspects of ritual orientation, there are others: the front, in both space and time. The ritually first queen's section in the 'white' part of the harem is located at the gate before the 'black' section for the other queens (Kuper, 1947, p. 43). Swazi men eat the forelegs, women the hindlegs, of sacrificial animals (Ziervogel, 1957, p. 127).

Men are considered 'hard' and 'firm', whereas women are considered 'weak' and 'soft' (Kuper, 1947, p. 139; 1950, p. 95). The sexual act itself, however desirable and productive, is considered dangerous and defiling to both participants, but women are seen as especially defiling because of menstruation and the pollution of childbirth. Kuper states (1947, p. 107):

The blood of a menstruating woman, however, is considered capable of destroying the fertility of cattle and the production of crops, and it may bring illness on men. During menstruation, a woman may not walk through a herd, for it is said, the cattle would grow thin, nor may she eat curdled milk, lest the future milk yield be tinged with red; should she walk through a garden, the 'fruits of the earth'—monkey nuts, sweet potatoes, ground beans—and 'those fruits with seeds embedded in pulp'—pumpkins and gourds—will wither, and this disaster can only be avoided by special ritual precautions. The illness her blood causes men is named *lugolo,* and is described as a wasting illness that leads to coughing of blood. Menstrual blood is also considered part of the foetus that grows within the womb—its discharge is analogous to a miscarriage, though less terrifying and polluting. . . . [At both menstruation and miscarriage women] must avoid all physical contact with the opposite sex, they may neither cook for men, nor touch their clothes, and the women themselves are in a state of danger as well as being a source of danger to others . . . in certain situations, however, menstrual blood is not destructive, but is considered a life symbol or rather a life force; thus the recurrence of menstruation after a woman gives birth 'washes her' and enables her to cohabit again with her husband, and after a death in the family circle, a man should not cohabit with his wife until she has menstruated.

Menstruating women should also avoid a smith when he is at work (ibid., p. 143).

Red is the colour of fertility, (Z) *ibomvu*, red, ripe, red referring to ripeness even in crops which do not actually become red when ripe. Red is also, obviously, the colour of blood and thus of some kinds of danger. This may explain the danger that menstrual discharge may turn cattle's milk red. Cows of the royal herd (*mfukwane*), which embody the nation and whose fat is so potent that only the king, queen mother, and ritually first queen may come into contact with it without going mad, are thought to have feelings like humans and to give red milk (Kuper, 1947, p. 218). Although ordinary Swazi brides are smeared with the red clay (*libovu*) of wifehood (ibid., p. 97), perhaps to express fertility, the main queen, the one who will bear his heir, is not so smeared but instead is smeared with dung from the royal herd (ibid., p. 85), the same herd from which payment has been made by the nation for her marriage. This smearing takes place within the new husband's cattle byre and seems to incorporate the new wife into the group represented by the byre (Ziervogel, 1957, pp. 48–49; 179).

Blood is too polluting for contact with the royal clan under most circumstances, perhaps products of the royal herd take its place not only in bridal symbolism but also in conveying potency in the smearing of caul on the king in certain rites which create potency. Blood cannot be shed in the royal capital and members of the royal clan were never slain by stabbing but were strangled or clubbed (ibid., p. 108). These restrictions may account for the king not taking part in battle. They prevent a queen from bearing her baby within her own hut as any other Swazi woman would, and require her to move out of the royal enclosure and remain in seclusion for many months. Nor are the queen mother or ritually first queen who come into frequent contact with the king permitted to visit the new mother during her period of pollution (Kuper, 1947, pp. 74–75). At construction of a new national shrine-hut, only old women past menopause may take part (ibid., pp. 240–2). The chaotic and defiling aspect of women also seems expressed in the idea of the moistness of the vagina, a moistness different in some respects from the purifying aspects of rapidly moving water.

Doke and Vilakazi state that among Zulu the labia majora are termed (Z) *ilebe* and the perpetually moist lower lips of cattle and horses are termed (Z) *isilebe*.[7] These two terms seem to be associated with various medicinal plants, perhaps because these all mediate between various states of being and non-being, such as health and sickness or death.

This Zulu information may perhaps help us to understand why Swazi diviners are thought to gain power through moistness of the noses of hyenas[8] and dogs (Kuper, 1947, p. 167) and why the lower lip of a slain ox is used to doctor the king, cf. later. A similar idea of fluidity of the female seems the basis of the custom in the past that warriors preparing for battle ate an unborn calf to 'make them slippery' (Marwick, p. 279).

Young queens may not help build the royal shrine-hut because they are 'too hot', too 'sexually impure' to touch the hut of the powerful affines whose ghosts dwell there (Kuper, 1947, p. 241). Although sexual relations are associated with danger, disorder, and uncleanness, this 'hotness' appears especially associated with female sexuality manifested in menstruation, since women beyond menopause are not ritually 'hot'. Hotness is also asso-

---

[7] I found such association of feminine moistness with the muzzles of animals among the Kaguru and Ngulu of Tanzania.

[8] The hyena has an added medial quality through being considered hermaphroditic, if we may assume Doke and Vilakazi's findings also fit the Swazi. This seems likely, since belief in the bisexuality of the hyena seems to be one of the most widely spread notions in Africa.

ciated with the emotional involvement of kinship, for Swazi distinguish between 'our folk' and kin and 'cold people' (Kuper, 1950, pp. 91, 102).

Sexuality, the sign of vigour and power, has its sinister side as well: (Z) *thomba*, to reach puberty, menstruate or ejaculate for the first time, may also refer to the corroding away of iron or the deposit of an unclean film on stagnant water, cf. also Engelbrecht, 1930*a*, p. 13; and (Z) *amalotha*, semen, may perhaps derive from the verb (Z) *lotha*, to subside, die down. Perhaps for these reasons 'hot' queens are kept separated from their affinal ghosts of the national shrine-hut (*kabayethe*). Kuper observes (1947, p. 42):

Here the king and queen mother speak to the ancestral spirits on behalf of their subjects, and perform rites to bring rain; here princes and princesses gather for important family occasions; and here matters of national concern may be discussed. No one impure, no one who has recently had sexual relations, no menstruating women, no one with the ropes of mourning may enter. Swazi say that such a person would bring madness on himself or herself, and disaster on the land. Swazi in European dress take off their shoes and hats before going inside, and accept the rules of behaviour dictated by tradition. The King's wives may not enter, nor even pass in front of the low doorway: it is the hut of the powerful males of their husband's clan, and queens must avoid them more rigorously than ordinary wives avoid their husband's in-laws. Royal children, on the other hand, perpetuators of the paternal lineage, sleep in the *kabayethe*, except when it is required for special ceremonies. Behind it lies a sacred store hut, containing in pots and 'shop-bought' boxes ancient ceremonial objects.

Yet sexual relations lead also to social definition, order, and continuity through the establishment of households and production of children. A man's first wife takes him out of 'darkness' (*emnyameni*) and puts him in a proper house, and she may be referred to as *isisulamsiti*, the wiper-away of darkness (Ziervogel, 1957, p. 31; Kuper, 1950, p. 93).

The king, the bull of his nation, serves as the link between the super-natural world and the world of the living. In a lesser way this is true also of each male householder, as assisted by his widowed mother. Every Swazi home consecrates an ox to its ancestral ghosts and this beast may not be slain or beaten. The king has his special sacred herd, *mfukwane,* which establishes a similar connexion, though these may be slaughtered at certain rites (Kuper, 1952, p. 43). The term (Z) *inkabi* means ox or any castrated animal, but it also refers to any close friend. In the most important Swazi rites the sacrifice is usually a pitch-black ox. Sometimes the beast is referred to as 'bull' even though it is an ox (Kuper, 1944, p. 233).[9] The term *sifutsa*

---

[9] Leach discusses the problems of animal terms provocatively but not always convincingly (1964). None of the superb ethnographies of the Nilotes and Nilo-Hamites have posed this problem even though it is usually oxen rather than bulls which must be sacrified among many of these peoples. In a later paper I hope to consider this question, using the Nuer data. Leach discusses the symbolism of castration with characteristic brilliance (1961, pp. 129–31); I make use of his theories toward the end of this paper.

indicates the place where testicles have been removed from a castrated ox; this place is also called *uncubula* (scrotum), and when the udder of a cow has no milk, the cow is slain and its removed udders called *sifutsa* (Ziervogel, 1957, p. 125).

With castration the beast becomes a kind of transcendent bull, that is, it continues to be termed bull in the sense that it epitomizes certain masculine and powerful attributes. It is called *inkunzi*, a term for large male animals such as the bull, horse, lion, and for certain species of plants known as strong emetics. Although it comes from the Ur-Bantu *kunda*, to copulate, *inkunzi* seems to carry the connotation of weight and force rather than sexuality. It is a praise term given to Swazi kings and probably relates to ideas of dignity and personality associated with them, as in *isithunzi*, shadow, prestige. If this is right, then this 'bull' has shed other limiting aspects related to its sex even as it keeps more positive ones. To use Turner's phrase, it is 'betwixt-and-between'. This should make more sense after I indicate what ambigious attributes are shared by bulls-oxen and by the Swazi man-king and to a lesser extent by the queen mother and the ritual queens, who become kinds of women/non-women, mothers/non-mothers.

## D. The Nature of Rain and Water

Swazi depend almost entirely on rain for good harvests; there is considerable danger of drought in eastern Swaziland and some such problem exists in more or less all areas (Kuper, 1947, p. 34). Rainmaking is one of the most important ritual tasks of Swazi royalty (Beemer, 1935; Schoeman, 1935; Kuper, 1952, p. 44);[10] and rain is one of the crucial signs that the annual royal rites have been a success (Kuper, 1944, p. 253).

Rain, (Z) *imvula*, is only one aspect of water. Water (Z) *amanzi*, appears to be a term of considerable ambiguity. In Doke and Vilakazi, the adjective (Z) *manzi* means wet, but also weak, feeble, morally weak, deceptive, plausible. Persons should not be buried in wet soil (Engelbrecht, 1930*b*, p. 24). The dead Swazi king lies in state drying until the spring, viz., the dry season, before being interred (Kuper, 1947, p. 178). Rain also has a purifying and cooling aspect: (Z) *izulu lihlanza inyanga,* the sky is washing the moon, said of rain at the time of new moon. After royal burial there are said to be four days of rain (Bryant, p. 334; are we to assume that this is unusual for that time of year, considering the preceding information by Kuper? If the king has to be buried in the dry season and there has to be four days of rain after his burial, it may be a tribute to his rain-

---

[10] Kuper's (*née* Beemer) criticisms of Schoeman lead one to cite his work with hesitation, Beemer, 1935.

making powers). A widow in mourning discards her restricted status during the rainy season (Kuper, 1947, p. 35). And the ritual hotness of the *Incwala* ceremonies is terminated by rain.[11]

Rain clouds are associated with the female because they are wet, like the uterus (Schoeman, p. 172); also, like the feminine, rain is associated with looseness and softness, for certain cattle must be got 'soft' to encourage rain (ibid., pp. 170–1). If the heavens remain 'firm', those in charge of rain wash themselves in foamy medicines (Kuper, 1947, p. 171). Schoeman's remarks on the parallel with the uterus may be supported by Kuper's remarks that rain medicines involve the treatment of a pregnant ewe or pregnant black cow (ibid.). Like water, rain is ambiguous; Marwick notes (p. 172):

Thunder is of two kinds. There is that which accompanies the storms which are sent by the king, and there is that which is sent by wizards who are able to control thunder and lightning. The former is innocuous and does not harm, and indeed, is regarded as having the property of making crops grow (cf. also, Kuper, 1947, p. 174).

Kings are associated with the fertility and power related to a storm; a kingship legend tells of a youth destined to be a king who was dramatically associated with thunder and lightning (Kuper, 1947, p. 273) and the king is praised: 'You play with the waters and they speak' (ibid., p. xii). 'Thus throughout his life he [king] may not drink water, lest, by connexion with his personality, this bring lightning and destruction' (ibid., p. 86). Rain speaks in thunder, (Z) *duma,* to thunder, also, to be famous, notorious, well known. To be struck by lightning, (Z) *ukushawa lizulu* (*shaya,* to strike + *izulu,* sky, lightning), involves the same polluting death as that in warfare (ibid., p. 125). *Izulu,* sky, is a praise-name for the king.

Swazi seek separation from the negative aspects of storms: rites to strengthen a house against lightning seem to take two forms: emphasis upon the beneficial aspects of rain, as manifested in portentous but innocuous storm clouds (e.g. a black sheep is slain, Ziervogel, 1957, p. 113); negation of the dangerous aspects of lightning:

I remember a sultry night in the bush veld when lightning flashed and crackled and the inmates of the homestead covered everything that was white and shiny with dark cloth . . . (Kuper, 1947, p. 163).

But rites to separate lightning from houses are prohibited during the time when rain is needed for crops, and then the population must bear the

---

[11] At his puberty ceremonies the Swazi boy-king (or crown-prince) is placed in contact with a riverstone. This may have the purpose of cooling (Kuper, 1947, p. 77); similar practice is reported as a cooling process for the Lovedu (Krige, p. 8), so it may be so among the Swazi as well.

dangers of rain's mixed blessings (ibid., p. 51). Those in charge of rain send clouds of smoke skyward and flash metal imitating lightning. A black cow is slain, cooked by men or by women past menopause. A sheep (black?) is slain and eaten by the king's messengers (rain priests?), and an unborn calf eaten by a woman beyond menopause; no one involved in these rites may have sexual relations (Schoeman, pp. 173–4), perhaps because of the unclean wetness involved in sexuality.

Lightning is believed to be caused by a sky-bird which dwells in certain pools (Kuper, 1952, p. 44), and the dead are also associated with deep pools (ibid., p. 48). The idea of a reflecting pool as the entry to another, supernatural world or even as a reflection of the sky-world or the land of ghosts is common throughout Bantu Africa.

## E. The Nature of Ritual Action[12]

Ritual is often discussed in terms of the gift of sacrifice, using the ideas of Hubert and Mauss. Recently Evans-Pritchard (1956) and Leach (1961) have expanded some of these ideas involving the separation of a sacrificial object into various components, some relating more closely to the sphere of the person making the sacrifice and some to the sphere of the supernatural recipient. In sacrifice this breakdown of the sacrificial object transforms it into a thing 'betwixt-and-between', thus allowing it to bridge the natural and supernatural spheres or, as Mauss and Hubert term these, the profane and sacred. This idea of transition involves two related but different notions of separation: (1) There is the broad separation of two states which form the universe: that of living men and that of supernatural beings. Behind any sacrifice there is the assumption that in some sense this separation must, at least temporarily, be bridged, even if, as in many cases, this is in order that a separation may be made all the firmer afterwards. (2) The other notion is that to bridge these two spheres, some kind of separation must be effected within the object which serves to join these divided categories. The object is seen as a combination of several attributes which, when separated out, as through mutilation, death, or both, each take on greater efficacy for being in an uncombined, ideal state. At that point the sacrificial object exists as a kind of sacred monster, as something partaking of both worlds and thus of neither. Its component attributes exist in a released state. The object exists within the natural world as defined by men through its resemblance to its previous state, its outward appearance, before it became a sacrifice. It exists in the other world through some disturbance in that

---

[12] After completing this paper I came across Krige's perceptive article (1944) which concerns itself with somewhat similar problems of attributes and symbolic action, cf. especially pp. 6–10.

ordinary state, through immolation, castration, aberration, costume, mask, etc., so as to accentuate and throw off-balance these same natural attributes and cut it off from normal and ordered life. The beast sacrificed by Swazi must be castrated yet is termed a 'bull' because of these contradictory features combined within it.

Cosmology is a system of categories, and ritual involves manipulation of symbolic objects from these various categories. This takes two basic, antithetical forms: (1) a mixing or confounding of categories which is both dangerous and potent. This is often achieved through ritual patterned on bodily ingestion and conception; or (2) a separation out, a reordering or check upon the existing ordering of categories, which should be kept apart. This is achieved through acts of avoidance and separation or through acts of purgation, often patterned on bodily emissions, evacuation, birth. All these ritual acts may be expressed through certain modes of violent, forceful action. I consider each of these aspects of ritual process in turn using Swazi examples.

## F. The Sacrifice as Separation and Transformation

Among Swazi, sacrifice is made only to ghosts of the dead; Swazi do not sacrifice to God or other high spirits. Each householder sacrifices to the ghosts of his father, mother, and other deceased kin; the Swazi king and queen mother sacrifice to royal ghosts whose powers protect the entire nation. Though ancestral ghosts are thought to live below ground, it seems that at least royal ghosts have some supernatural connexion with the sky and rain (Kuper, 1947, pp. 165–96). Disturbance in the sphere of the living or dead brings these two spheres into contact with one another, resulting in troubles in the previously undisturbed sphere as well. Much Swazi ritual attempts to end such disturbance by reseparating these two spheres. Death constitutes a disturbance in both worlds, an entrance into one and an exit from the other; it marks the most extreme rites of separation by Swazi; for example (Kidd, p. 249):

The people in the kraal are all unclean. They may not drink milk, nor may they transact business with other kraals, until the doctor has cleansed them. Those who touched the dead body are especially unclean, and so is every implement which was used to make the grave with, or which the dead body touched. Those who touched the dead body, or the dead man's things, have to wash in running water.

Dissension among the living, through incest, ill will, disputes, fratricide, or ignoring customs, may lead to illness and other difficulties caused by ancestral ghosts. Unaccountable disturbances of ancestral ghosts lead them to possess their living kin, manifesting themselves through sickness, bad dreams, and aberrant behaviour of the possessed. These should be driven off, but if this is not possible, their disturbance must at least be confined into socially approved ways. Possessed persons become diviners and doctors, spanning the worlds of the living and the ghosts (Kuper, 1952, pp. 42–49; 1947, pp. 163–6; Engelbrecht, 1930b, p. 20). They bridge two sets of categories normally kept apart. The ghost of a royal child which died as the result of its mother breaking certain important prohibitions is thought sometimes to hold back the rain until propitiated (Schoeman, p. 174). Sacrifice is an ambiguous act: it gives to the dead to make contact with them and to receive benefits of their power, but it also respects or bribes them to keep them separate from the living.

## G. The Condensation of Symbols and the Confounding of Categories

Swazi ritual knowledge is 'deep' and 'heavy', as indicated through the analysis of the attributes of darkness, weight, shadow. Much ritual is aimed at creating a kind of thick, complex condition in which various attributes form an impenetrable and pregnant state, potent and dangerous. Thus, too, entangling of the spheres of the ghosts and the living may cause sickness or madness, yet, if controlled, may bestow valuable supernatural powers such as the ability to divine and cure. The Swazi king himself possesses such gifts inherently (Kuper, 1947, p. 165). One says of the royal rites (Z) *kanye ngonyaka inkosi ibiqungwa ngamakhubalo*, once annually the king would be strengthened (darkened) with strong medicines; instead of (Z) *quanga*, perf. *qungile,* Kuper transcribes *cungiwe* to refer to this 'darkening' of the king (1944, p. 251); (Z) *qunga*, to discolour, darken, make cloudy, invigorate, strengthen, fortify with medicines, make callous, fearless; and perhaps, thus, *luqunga*, 'the passion that is roused in men, particularly those in authority, when their position is threatened. They tremble like the *luqunga* (reed). "They are like hollow things moved by the angry wind" ' (Kuper, 1947, p. 159). Swazi manhood at its finest in battle may be filled with 'the same uncontrollable lust to kill that enters a man when once he has slain and against which he must be purified; it is a power that pervades the very weapons that he has used so that they too need to be tempered and cooled' (ibid.). This is *silwane*, being like a wild beast, which maddens the warriors who pummel the sacrificial ox-bull in the royal rites (Ziervogel, 1957, p. 17). This accounts for demonic aspects of the king himself, for (Z) *isilwane* may also refer to a person of outstanding qualities and the king himself has the title of *silo,* wild beast or monster, cf. ibid., pp. 56–57, and appears as such in the royal rites. (A somewhat similar disorder, the rankling of ill will among kin, provokes the wrath of ghosts.)

The royal rites involve a dangerous but potent process of increasing animation, a combination of various symbolic attributes (in terms of the king) not normally together. One says: (Z) *ukuguba umkhosi*, to hold the royal rites; (Z) *guba*, to tremble, toss about wildly, be in a wild commotion, shiver, draw up into dance positions, flutter about, dance with violent body movements, observe, and solemnize.

Mixing attributes is vital, but dangerous and unbearable over a long period. Swazi rites provide ways by which such disorderly combinations are restored to safer, separate elements.

## H. Purgations and the Separation of Categories

In discussions of Swazi social relations where we have Swazi terms given for acts in such situations, one often finds words relating to the expression of respect between Swazi of various ranks and particularly between men and women who stand as affines to one another. Kuper, Doke and Vilakazi, and others translate *hlonipha* as respect or shame (1950, p. 93; cf. also Engelbrecht, 1930a, pp. 11–13; Ziervogel, 1957, pp. 82–91). The meaning seems to be far wider than this, nearer the idea of separation. In Swazi rites which protect a house against lightning the term is *livahlonishwa*, a passive form of *hlonipha*, which Ziervogel translates as 'be respected' (1957, p. 13).[13] In discussing blood and feminine sexuality, I indicated other separations normally made by Swazi. I here provide three further examples: (1) the king's corpse, his umbilical cord, the corpses of his rain-messengers, his rain medicines, must all be kept dry if rain is to fall (Schoeman, p. 172); (2) while the main house of a homestead is under construction (in disorder), no one in the household may make fire or have sexual relations (Kuper, 1947, p. 38);[14] (3) during royal rites when the king is in 'darkness', persons should abstain (*kutilwa*) from sexual relations, washing, scratching themselves, sleeping late (Kuper, 1944, pp. 251–2; Engelbrecht, 1930a, p. 11).

Swazi seem to see such separation of attributes as purgation, washing away of certain undesirable attributes while retaining others in a purer form. This is a form of sacrifice whereby objects take on certain undesirable attributes and then shed them to be apotheosized, stronger and more impressive than before. Related to this is the notion of dirt, something out of place and therefore undesirable.[15] The *Incwala* rites provide dramatic

---

[13] Similarly, Nuer *thek* their totems, lightning, affines, etc., a term which Professor Evans-Pritchard translates as 'respect' rather than 'separate' (1956, pp. 64–65, 79, 103, 129, 177–83, 241, 291).

[14] Many Bantu peoples speak of kindling fire by fire-sticks as a euphemism and ritual expression of sexual relations. It is very likely so amongst the Swazi.

[15] For many insights into the notion of dirt, I am indebted to Douglas's study of Leviticus xi.

examples of this which I discuss later. I confine myself here to two motifs:
(1) A child loses its non-human attributes while held over an ash-heap, a
place for depositing refuse. When an infant can finally crawl it is allowed
into the great house of its paternal grandmother, who puts ash from her
hearth on its forehead so that 'it will be one with its forefathers' (Kuper,
1950, p. 105). This woman is an intermediary between the living and the
ghosts of her husband and his kin. Ashes are dirt; they are out of place
between the state of things and the state of non-things; between that of
the living and that of the ghosts. The word (Z) *izala*, rubbish-heap, ash-
heap, occurs in another form: (Z) *umzala*, which also means ashes and
dumping ground, but may also mean cross-cousin (cf. *mzala*, Kuper, 1950,
pp. 101, 104). This may be a 'false-cognate'; it is true that cross-cousins,
too, are out of place; they are neither entirely kin, for one may marry them;
but many say such marriage often is not good, because one should marry
people who are truly 'cool', that is, non-kin (ibid., p. 104).[16] Nor do their
offspring seem like those from other marriages (cf. Ziervogel, 1957, pp.
72–75).

(2) Upon coming of age and starting to undertake his full burden of
office as king, the Swazi ruler exchanges blood with two men called *tinsila*
and also, later, with his first ritual wife. Today no other Swazi exchange
blood in such fashion. The word *insila* (pl. *tinsila*) means the king's
attendant, body servant, close resemblance, but also dirt or body filth. The
*tinsila* or doubles of the king are thought to absorb many supernatural
dangers otherwise injurious to him; they should not be healthy. As extensions of the king, they perform ritual to cleanse him and assist him, the
right-hand *insila* being a leader in war ritual, the left being a leader of
national rites both for fertility and royal deaths. Like ashes, dirt, and cross-
cousins, and like the king, the *tinsila* are, in a sense, anomalous. Like the
king, they have no real family but are considered the fathers of the entire
nation; should one die, he cannot be mourned or recognized as dead until
the king dies (ibid., pp. 80–82). The senior *tinsila* are apart from any
single group and, like the king, mediate in disputes between various sec-

---

[16] Carrying such conjecture dangerously far, I note that Doke and Vilakazi give:
(Z) *zala*, to bear, give birth, generate, be full, all of which have possible ambiguous
suggestions of mediation. They also give another word for ash-heap: (Z) *ilotha*; for
what it is worth, I note that they give (Z) *lotha*, to die down (as a fire), and (Z)
*amalotha*, semen, which, in turn, is also dirt. It would seem that some further research
on this might be worth while.

Ant-hills also seem important intermediary zones, but data are lacking (Engelbrecht,
1930*a*, p. 13; 1930*b*, p. 20). Kuper makes no mention of these, but she does report
King Sobhuza referring to his young warriors (nearly nude and childless), back from
their ritual quest for sacred leaves for the annual rites, as being shiny like 'wings
of flying ants', 1944, p. 243. Taken together, Engelbrecht's and Kuper's comments
suggest some value in pursuing this topic. Doke and Vilakazi give the following Zulu
terms: (Z) *umuhlwa*, a white-ant heap; (Z) *inhlwa*, a flying termite, someone who is
destitute, naked, an unmarried or childless person.

tions of the country (ibid., p. 58). A ritual queen is also an anomaly, cohabiting with the king when others dare not because of his ritual 'darkening'; she is a queen who is, with her ritual co-queens, expressly denied the right to bear the heir to the kingship. What could better express her anomalous position than her sometimes being spoken of as 'a man' (Kuper, 1947, p. 50)?

There are two interrelated themes in Swazi purificatory rites: one is the idea of removal through washing away, scraping away, evaporating away, cooling; the other is the idea of loosening or separating through making something assume a more liquid state. The two concepts are expressed by washing, bowel movements, purgatives, vomiting, etc. (cf. Kidd, pp. 125–6). The *inhlambelo* is the most sacred enclosure where the most vital and secret rites of 'darkening' and later of cleansing the king take place. *Inhlambelo*, besides referring to this enclosure, also means wash-basin.[17] In the account of the *Incwala* one finds frequent examples of cleansing or normalizing through bathing, aspersing with water, drenching with rain, etc.

The verb (Z) *geza,* to wash, purify after death, is a euphemism for menstruation. The flow of blood pollutes women yet also cleanses after death or bearing a child (Kuper, 1947, p. 107). The king is excluded from death and blood, yet Kuper remarks that the king assists in purification after death by biting ritually (*kuluna*) [*kuluma*?] into a red root (*mdzambane*) (from *kudzamba,* to disappoint or weaken) (ibid., pp. 185–6); for *geza,* cf. also Ziervogel (1957, pp. 170–1).

Purgation also involves softening and cooling; (Z) *thomba,* to become soft, impressionable, supple, tame, domesticated, cool down, become gentle, become limp, lack energy, but also to have one's first sexual emission (cf. Engelbrecht, 1930a, p. 13). (All aspects of *thomba* would seem to occur to the 'darkened' and ritually charged king when he sleeps with his ritual queen at the close of the *Incwala.*)[18]

---

[17] I am struck by the apparent similarities between certain Zulu terms conveying the ideas of washing, cleansing, vomiting, obscenity, abuse, diarrhoea, purgation, etc. I do not know whether these indicate any valid linguistic relationships.

Detailed linguistic analysis of such terms and phrases seems likely to provide deep insight into some features of Swazi ritual processes. The possible relationship between notions of purgation and obscenity seems particular interesting. The dissolving of distinctions seems to have two possible aspects in many societies: purification or pollution. If this is so, it provides insight into some of the features of institutionalized joking in many parts of Africa.

[18] From Swazi material it is not possible to be sure what other verbs for cooling also have ritual connotations. The following two Zulu terms from Doke and Vilakazi probably occur in such contexts: (Z) *phola,* to cool, calm, be mild, heal up, recover, be unblemished, be of good repute, be well behaved; (Z) *thambisa,* to soften, tame, domesticate, cool. This latter term may well relate to the East African terms such as *tambika,* to propitiate ancestral ghosts, to worship, to normalize a disturbed supernatural relation; while the former term may perhaps relate to such East African terms as *hosa,* to cool, normalize, expiate. I am not competent to judge such problems.

Finally, there is the idea of drying up through heat and burning. Swazi term old women and grandmothers *gogo* and the term *imgogodla*, backbone, cf. later, refers to the last burning rite of *Incwala*. Doke and Vilakazi give (Z) *gogo* as an ideophone for emaciation, drying up, stooping, crouching, huddling: (Z) *ugogo,* emaciated person; (Z) *ugogo,* grandmother; (Z) *umgogodla*, backbone, dry hide-bag. This notion may also relate to the practice of allowing the royal corpse to dry until it no longer smells, before it is interred (Schapera, p. 266; Bryant, p. 334).

## I. The Expression of Force

Three types of violent bodily acts figure in royal rites: biting, stabbing (also with the idea of piercing with the penis), and beating. All three have the apparent connotations of consuming, subordinating, absorbing, or dispersing, and are themes in rites among people throughout the world, expressing sexual and political conquest and success. (Z) *Luma*, to bite, suffer sharp pain, itch, figures in ritual acts of the king. Those in authority 'bite' to partake of medicines (Kuper, 1944, pp. 238, 247), 'bite' the first crops of the new year (ibid., p. 247); and ghosts 'bite' the living when they disturb them on account of their wrong-doing (Kuper, 1952, p. 42). 'Bite' also connotes a separation; the king 'bites' separating the old and new years and royal kin 'bite' separating lightning from homesteads (Marwick, p. 188).

The notion of stabbing or piercing is involved in the king's success in war and in the consummation of his first marriage which is compared to war, and to strengthening the new year by spitting medicines (Kuper, 1944, pp. 238, 247; 1952, p. 21). The notion of striking against something sometimes conveys the separation, as in the previously noted rites and as Swazi strike (*bethelela*) stakes which ward off lightning from a house (cf. Ziervogel, 1957, pp. 12, 178).

Beating involves a dispersion through force: (Z) *dubula*, to give a resounding, thudding blow, exert great physical force, sweep off, resound, shoot, put forth shoots from a stem; (Z) *bula,* to beat.[19] The idea of loosening or softening through pounding or pummelling (*dubula*) figures in the *Incwala*. Swazi beat a youth being cleansed after his first seminal emission (Engelbrecht, 1930*a*, p. 13).

---

[19] Doke and Vilakazi state that *bula*, to beat, may also mean to consult a diviner or to divine, explaining that Zulu divine by tapping with sticks. However, this does not seem a Swazi practice since Kuper provides rich information on Swazi divination and makes no reference to such beating.

### III. The Royal Rites of the *Incwala:* Swazi Ritual Symbolism and Swazi Society

#### A. The Kingship and Swazi Society

What probably led Kuper to characterize Swazi as an 'aristocracy' is that they see their society as a pyramid of ascending social layers, each a more intense and effective version of the one beneath. At the base is the Swazi household, each hamlet headed by a mature man and his widowed mother, who hold authority over the group and who propitiate the ancestral ghosts which affect the group supernaturally. At the apex, based on the same principles expanded and made awesome in their political and religious importance, are the royal capitals of the king and queen mother. In between is a gradation from local headmen and elders through chiefs and princes. The social world of each is linked to the layers above and below, not only through ties of social rights and obligations, but through the basic ideas and values which provide the model on which each develops and maintains his own particular segment of this world. The same pattern is thought to exist in the ghostly world as well.

The king and queen mother and their capitals are the visible realization of the basic values and ideas of Swazi society. Swazi speak of the land being like a cow to be divided amongst men; if so, the king provides direction how this is done. Swazi sometimes compare a hamlet to a cow's head with the arcs of houses swinging out from the centre as horns. This places the core of animation in the compound of the headman's widowed mother, who links her son to his father's ghost and whose particular marriage as the paramount wife to his father accounts for his inheritance as heir over his brothers. It is over her hut's doorway that the horns and skulls of sacrificed animals are mounted.

Swazi describe the king and his mother as 'twins', as inseparable complements governing the nation. He is *ingwenyama* (lion) and she is *indlovukati* (cow elephant). In both political affairs and national ritual a balance is maintained between them, each with his and her own capitals, regiments, courts, duties (Kuper, 1947, pp. 54–55; 1952, p. 34). Swazi legend describes how an early Swazi king persecuted his people, 'Who is it that soils the spear of the Lion? Let him be killed', but his mother restrained him and won a permanent place in the rulership of the nation (Kuper, 1947, pp. 12–13).

Traditionally, the king did not pay bridewealth for most wives, but for the prospective mother of his heir, the future queen mother, cattle from the royal herd, from the whole nation, were given and she was smeared not with red earth but with their dung (ibid., pp. 54, 85). She is wife and mother for the nation and her son, the heir, is *umutfwana,* child of the nation (ibid., p. 72; Beemer, 1937, p. 64). The king himself 'has no children; the people are his children', and his children are taught to reply, when asked who their father is, with the name of one of the king's brothers (Kuper, 1947, p. 62). After her son is born the queen mother should bear no more children and this deviation from the usual ideals of feminine fertility is unique in Swaziland. When her son is king she may be addressed, like a man in authority, as *inkosi* (Kuper, 1952, p. 35); the ritual queens are also so addressed, and they too are severely restricted through their duties. Such a queen 'is a man, an *inkosi* . . .' (Kuper, 1947, p. 80). These women are sometimes called 'mothers' of the entire nation (ibid., p. 85). The burden of authority cuts royal leaders off from normal familial ties treasured by ordinary Swazi, for these are transformed into grander relations involving the entire nation.

The king rules because of his membership in the Dlamini royal clan, the people of the sun; he rules through the support of such kinsmen, but he also may be said to rule in spite of them:

Because of the positive and constructive aspects of the bond of blood, princes are sent to act as *titfundzi telive* (literally, shadows, i.e. personalities, of the realm), to report important events, investigate rumours of treason, and see that subjects respond to the summons for national service. They are expected to keep alive the prestige of royalty by generosity to commoners and tribute to the central rulers. But the bond of blood also makes the princes rivals of the king. . . . Important princes should never be settled too near the king lest they usurp his powers and interfere with his 'personality' by ritual. No close brother may live permanently at the capital, eat from the king's dish, be at all familiar with his queens, or treat the queen mother's enclosure at though it were his own mother's (Kuper, 1947, p. 57; cf. also, 1952, p. 36).

The king counteracts this through his use of commoners:

The king is careful not to give too much power to male kinsmen, and certain highly-coveted administrative posts are monopolized by commoners. In this fashion a balance is maintained between the rights of the Dlamini aristocracy and members of other clans (Kuper, 1947, p. 60).

More closely identified with the king than with the princes are the two senior *tinsila* and it is part of their duty to watch and guide the princes and report any hint of treason. They have administrative authority equal to that of the most important princes (Kuper, 1952, p. 36).

National ritual is usually monopolized by special clans which co-operate with, and support, the Dlamini. Medicines required for national ritual are transmitted from father to son, subject always to the ultimate approval of the Dlamini king (Kuper, 1947, p. 114).

The royal clan is isolated from the common people through its political and ritual privileges and the economic and social advantages related to these (Kuper, 1947, p. 17) and through special prohibitions and dialect which distinguishes them. Royal Swazi are also isolated from their kinsman, the king himself, who is their leader but also leader of the nation.

Because of these various important ties, the king must transcend loyalties towards any particular group if he is to unify all his people. He holds power in his authority only to the degree that he meets some but never all of the cross-cutting obligations towards his supporters. A king has no friends, and divide-and-rule has been a tactic for governing in parts of Africa long before colonial days. These conflicting demands upon a king, the burden of his office, subject him to the dangers of sorcery and witchcraft from his enemies within and outside the country. The *tinsila* absorb some of this 'dirt'. Through the annual rites he is revivified. In this some of Gluckman's interpretation makes sense, but in different terms from those presented by him as the 'function' of such ritual. These dangers and sufferings of the Swazi king are part of his admirable strength and compelling attractiveness, his pathos.

The king is 'father' (*babe*) to the nation, as are his *tinsila* (Kuper, 1947, pp. 77, 82). He is uniquely beyond all other men: 'Men with little sense of inferiority or humility complained that when they were long with the king they trembled and shook "Because the medicines he uses together with his royal blood are too strong"' (ibid., p. 71). His life and that of the nation are literally one. His death is not announced or even mentioned by anyone until his successor is appointed, for were the land to lack a king, it would be dangerously 'light' (lacking in *isithunzi*) and thus vulnerable to its enemies (ibid., p. 86). When the new child-king and queen mother mourn the old king, the land is in 'darkness' with them (Kuper, 1944, p. 253). The annual royal rites grow in scope and intensity with the youthful king himself; his personality (*isithunzi*, weight, shadow) lacks strength and substance during his immaturity so that it cannot at first bear the full burden of the rites: the medicines of the sacrificial ox-bull, the sacred and invigorating vegetation, and the hurling of the gourd. This is possible only when he has reached manhood and his ritual wife has 'wiped away the darkness' of his immaturity (Kuper, 1947, p. 80; 1944, pp. 253–4).

### B. The Great *Incwala*

The Great *Incwala* is a ritual separation of the king so that he may take on certain supernatural attributes which provide him with power. To recall some of these attributes to the reader before proceeding, I quote extracts from the royal praise-song to King Sobhuza which forms a prelude to Kuper's book and which displays the kingship's full grandeur as the Swazi symbolize it (Kuper, 1947, pp. xi–xii):

Dawn, you of the Inner House! Dawn, Strong Lion with mighty claws that grabbed protection overseas! Thou art cold. Cold as the waters of Mangwaneni [a waterfall]. Thou art the ice of Mangwaneni. I called Sobhuza, Sobhuza of the High Mountains. Cast your shadow on the hills. Cast your shadow on the huts. You play with the waters and they speak. Sobhuza, Somkiti, born amidst black shields. He himself is fearful. He has outwitted me. Miraculous body that grows feathers in winter while others are without plumage. Master in weapons. Your voice brings you to people. . . . I appeal to you, You enter into all matters. . . . You from the fountains of a Zulu clan [Sobhuza's mother is a Zulu]. The Zulu shall drink of your waters. They drink of the waters of friendship. Waters cleanse Sobhuza, lave his feet, cleanse him of pollution. He is polluted. He trod the grave of wizards. Sobhuza is a mightly force concentrated in mystical waters. He destroys people when he handles them, he tracked Shaka like an antelope. He danced in two worlds. . . . You point a spear at the Sotho, black hero of the Swazi. They hate Sobhuza and are right to hate. Jaw that cracks all bones. Spotted beast! Great Conqueror! Hail! You of the inner House![20]

## 1. *The Process of Condensation and Separation*

When these rites begin, the king may already be in a state of some 'darkening' since he does not appear to have undergone any extensive purgative rites following the Small *Incwala* a fortnight earlier. The first two days of the Great *Incwala* are devoted to providing ritual plant substance (*lusekwana*)[21] to increase the king's vitality. This plant is separated from the divisive aspects of sexuality: only warriors who have never fathered children or committed adultery with married women (i.e., possibly fathered children) are considered strong enough to fetch this plant and not cause it to wither. Warriors fight amongst themselves and their plants wither if one steps over another's plant when they camp overnight prior to bestowing the plants to the king (Ziervogel, 1957, p. 167).[22] The warriors sleep outside the village because 'the *lusekwane* must not be contaminated by the sex life of the village' (Kuper, 1944, p. 243). The vitality of the king and his warriors remains strong because it is not divided by domestic interests and obligations. The king and warriors serve the entire nation and neither has children in the full social sense. The warriors have children only when they cease to be warriors, and the king's own son is formally referred to as his heir only when he has succeeded to his father's kingship. The king ritually exerts his sexuality for the nation only with the queen who is 'a man' and may never bear his heir. The presentation of *lusekwane* is synchronized with the dawn and is bestowed as the regi-

---

[20] 'Inner House' apparently refers to one of the inner enclosures where the king is doctored or communes with royal ghosts. The 'Two Worlds' is unclear; it may refer to the worlds of men and supernatural, or the worlds of Swazi and outsiders, or both. The Sotho are the traditional tribal enemies of Swazi and they fear and hate the Swazi king. Cf. also, Cook (1931).

[21] Full significance of ritual plants is unclear; Kuper indicates that they involve strength, endurance, and vitality; but why, for example, are they gathered in a particular sequence or placed in a particular order?

[22] Stepping over a person symbolized sexual connexion in many Bantu societies. A warrior is angered if another steps over his plant and withers it, since plants are here associated with sexual purity and warriorhood.

mental crescent enters the royal byre chanting a lullaby (ibid., pp. 241–3). The *lusekwane* and the *emacembe* plants collected the following day cover the *inhlambelo* where the king is doctored to gain vitality.

Through both *Incwala,* songs are correlated to the supernatural development. Lullabies are sung at the onset of rites which strengthen the king; the *simemo* or song of rejection is sung when he enters his most potent state, when he has undertaken his heaviest ritual burden for the nation. It is sung as he strikes, separating the new and old years; as he consummates his first marriage, striking to separate his immaturity from his new life of full kingly power; when he is interred with his royal ancestors, and when he confronts the royal herd which has been put into contact with the royal ghosts. It is not sung by his royal competitors for office or by the nation's potential enemies, for these have been excluded from most scenes of such singing. It is sung by warriors and ordinary people expressing the burden assumed by the king (cf. ibid., pp. 239–40). Following the *simemo,* and the successful reincorporation of the king, Swazi sing national hymns praising him and his triumphant, powerful aspects.

On the third day a large black ox seized from a commoner's herd is pummelled by undressed warriors and then slain by the rain-priests in the *inhlambelo.* In the Small *Incwala* a black ox to provide leather for the ritual water-calabashes was also seized from a commoner's herd. The significance of such seizures is unclear. Both beasts establish contact between the king and royal ghosts; both slaughterings are preceded by collection of fines representing 'dirt' from the people. Perhaps this ox establishes the bond between the king and the people, whose common devitalizing dirt is transformed, through the king, into power enabling the ruler to undertake a new ordering of the world.

The black ox is referred to as 'bull' (*inkunzi*) (ibid., p. 244). This usage expresses the ambiguity of the sacrificial beast.[23] The ox possesses the heavy, dark, potent (*nzi*) aspects of the male beast, but, as with the warriors and the king, its divisive sexuality is removed. It exists for the king and nation and for consumption by the royal ghosts; it does not exist, as do most beasts, for its progeny and herd. It is betwixt-and-between and in this confused and dark state links the king and royal ghosts so that the king gains supernatural powers. The beast's dark, confused state is intensified by the king striking it with a stick doctored with aphrodisiacal medicines which drive it wild (*msululeke*, ibid., p. 245). Even looking at it drives the warriors into acting like wild beasts who pummel the ox (Ziervogel, 1957, pp. 170–1). This pummelling (*kudubula*) subdues the beast and seems to loosen the potent attributes confined within it. The beast is called *umdutshulwa* (passive of *kudubula*) and is slain and placed

---

[23] The distinction between oxen and bulls may have confused Frankfort, cf. 1948, chapter xiv, footnotes 50 and 51, p. 385.

within the *inhlambelo*. Some of its organs, including its lower lip (cf. *isilebe*) and gall bladder, which 'have power', are removed for doctoring the king. The king himself assumes the filth of the nation, and though endangered by this, gains power. Royal ghosts are thought to partake in the carcass, which explains why Swazi describe its meat as tasting stale and without essence when fed to undressed prepubescent boys. These eat until 'overcome' (*ibehlule*) and are then cleansed in a river (Ziervogel, 1957, p. 167). Like the ritualized king and ghosts, the children lack full incorporation into the social structure, and are, along with the grandparental group which opens the *Incwala* rites, a link between the world of the living and the ghosts and the past (ibid.; Kuper, 1944, p. 247; Schoeman, p. 171).

The condensation of the king's supernatural attributes is increased by his being put into contact with a black ox from the royal herd. This ox, called *incwambo* (a muscle near the testicles), is forced to the ground and the king sits nude on it and his *tinsila* wash him with *umtuso*, aphrodisiacal medicines (*kutusa*, to stir, awaken); he tastes another medicine related to part of the liver which causes disorderly, confused behaviour (Kuper, 1944, p. 246). The name of the ox, by its reference to sexuality, seems to connote its ambiguous ox-bull category. By nightfall the king is highly doctored; the regiments sing the *simemo* and then wash in a river, but the king himself remains doctored.

At dawn of the fourth day the lullaby is sung by the regiments as the *incwambo* is again driven into the royal byre, 'songs of hate' are sung. The king is washed in the *inhlambelo* and emerges nude[24] except for an ivory penis-cap (*lupondvo lwendlovu*). The women weep. Kuper quotes the queen mother, 'It is pain to see him a king; my child goes alone through the people'. The queens said, 'We pity him. There is no other man who could walk naked in front of everybody', and another said, 'The work of a king is indeed heavy' (ibid., p. 247). It is not nakedness denoting humiliation but a unique, lonely, denuded status outside any single social category. In the *Incwala* only the king appears so nude, but others also undress. Warriors doff their finery and wear only loincloths when they pummel the ox-bull (ibid., p. 252); the queen mother's bodyguard undresses to escort the king to the *inhlambelo* (ibid., p. 248); the boys who eat the *umdutshulwa's* carcass wear only loincloths (Ziervogel, 1957, pp. 168–71); the king lies nude all day on a lionskin during the period of his 'darkness' before his final reincorporation (Kuper, 1944, p. 251) and he is nude at his ritual contacts with the royal herd during these rites (ibid., pp. 246, 252). The other holders of such terrible asocial powers, involving lightning itself, are Swazi witches who appear naked (Marwick, p. 243).

The term *lupondvo lwendlovu* does not seem to be the usual term for

---

[24] I distinguish between the positive (nude) and negative (naked) aspects of undress, taking this distinction from Sir Kenneth Clark's *The Nude* (1956).

ivory substance; whatever its wider connotations, it is clear that like the lion and bull, the elephant is an awesome beast associated with kingship; the queen mother is the cow elephant. (Z) *Lwendlovu* means, of an elephant, and is associated, perhaps with the striking violence essential to rites of 'biting': (Z) *dlova*, to treat roughly, override violently; (Z) *isidlova*, a person who acts roughly, a wild beast; (Z) *dlovo*, of trampling underfoot, stabbing; (Z) *umdlovu*, horn of an ox when growing with the point downward like the tusk of an elephant. The term (Z) *uphondo*, horn, may perhaps also suggest the notion of a pointed, striking object.

The whiteness covers the moist and ambiguous glans penis.[25] Here, the king seems to appear in terms of his attributes of striking force, like white lightning, which breaks through the confusion and separates the old and new years and impels time back on to its course. Whiteness and nudity may also both possibly signify the utmost in potentiality which may sometimes be suggested by an empty or clear state. The recurrent themes of castration and genital-emphasis found here and elsewhere seem to be two aspects of the same symbolic notion of implementing time. As Leach observes:

. . . it is the sexual act itself which provides the primary image of time . . . the 'beginning of time' occurred at that instant when, out of an initial unity, was created not only polar opposition but also the sexual vitality that oscillates between one and the other . . . not only must male be distinguished from female but one must postulate a third element, mobile and vital, which oscillates between the two (Leach, 1961, pp. 127, 129).

The nude king enters the 'white' harem area where he consummated his first marriage and came out of darkness, and warriors sing the lullaby outside as he spits medicine east then west through the hut's apertures and as the elders cry out, 'He stabs it'. 'As the king spits his strength goes "right through" and awakens his people' (Kuper, 1944, p. 247). Later, lesser persons in authority also 'bite' medicines to open the new year.

The king undergoes further doctoring inside the *inhlambelo* and then emerges to be surrounded by his royal kinsmen who sing songs about forsaking the nation and taking him off with them. These songs are interpreted by some as expressing aggression and hatred towards him. The royal kin force the king within the *inhlambelo* but then sing trying to coax him to come out again.

He emerges as *silo*, a monster (cf. *silwane*; cf. also Ziervogel, 1957, pp. 56–57), covered in bright green grass and black medicines and wearing a headband of lion-skin. He is said to present an extremely fierce and terrifying sight. He wears fat from the royal herd, thought to produce

---

[25] The Swazi no longer circumcise, but did so traditionally. The king went through initiation rites based on the traditional pattern. The penis-cap covers the glans, even in the case of an uncircumcised person, since it keeps the prepuce drawn forward.

madness in others, a gall bladder, and a silver monkey skin embodying enduring life (Kuper, 1944, pp. 249–50). The king dances demonically in a way Swazi insist cannot be taught but is instinctive to kings. He dances expressing reluctance to rejoin the people; warriors surround him with their black ceremonial shields. In his left hand he carries a shield smeared in madness-producing fat, but his right hand, the hand of order, is empty.

Dangerous but awesome wild beasts such as lions might be referred to as *silo*; the king is termed 'lion' and is compared to the terrible mamba, a back, aggressive, deadly serpent (Kuper, 1952, p. 42). Such terrible aspects of kingliness, emphasized here, occur outside the annual rites and contribute to the awful grandeur associated with the traditional kings of the south-eastern Bantu. The cruelties of the Zulu king Shaka are legendary, but retold with pride as well as fear; some of the cruelties of the Swazi king Bunu, father of the present ruler, match Shaka's. Despite the white ethnocentrism and obtuse brutality of these European authors, the accounts of Kidd (p. 291) and the horrifying eyewitness accounts of O'Neil (1921, pp. 68–72, 75–77, 113–16) display the royal court as a scene of terrible cruelty by a true royal monster.[26] A revealing aspect of these revolting accounts is the implication of individual and national pride in the bravery and devotion of the warriors and the terrible and absolute power of the king. These accounts suggest a kind of ambiguous love–hate relation between the king and his primary victims, the warriors of his own regiments, in terms of their mutual view of one another as embodiments of ideals of national devotion and kingship. The king and his warriors are alike in representing the nation rather than any particular section of the country.

Later, the king comes out dancing with a black wand similar to those held by doctors, diviners, and witches.

## 2. *The Process of Purgation and Return*

When the king next retreats within the *inhlambelo,* his royal kin and aliens are excluded from the byre and only loyal Swazi commoners remain. The king emerges still doctored but without demonic costume, bearing a vivid

---

[26] This is no place for long discussion of the problems of evaluating early historical reports of the cruelties of African divine kings. However, the horror of some of these, for example, the conduct of the early kabakas of Uganda and some of the rulers of southern Nigeria, Dahomey, and Ghana, may have been accentuated by European observers simply because they did not share the cultural ethos of divine rule held in the societies concerned. In many societies the divinity of rulers has been demonstrated or affirmed by awful acts, beyond the conventions of these societies. The terrible aspects of certain Roman emperors seem related to their claims to divinity and their attempts to confirm this to their people. For an amusing application of a similar line of analysis towards de Gaulle and Churchill, cf. J. Weightman, *The Observer,* 28 Feb. 1965.

green gourd. The gourd was collected during the preceding year and is called *luselwa lwembo*, the wild gourd from Embo, the northern district from which the royal clan migrated into Swaziland (Kuper, 1944, p. 250). Marwick claims that this gourd is found near the sea (p. 190), which fits with certain symbolism in the Small *Incwala*. The wild gourd is called *luselwa* and the rites *kulahlwa luselwa*; the wild gourd is thrown away (Kuper, 1952, p. 46). Royalty may be praised as (Z) *amakhosi oselwa*, rulers of the wild gourd. The king has discarded his demonic green costume and his royal kinsmen and aliens have been excluded from his midst. He hurls the last greenery from himself, indicating his decision to rejoin his people. This must be caught on the back of one of the black shields (*tihlangu*). 'If anyone by accident during the year touches the black shields he immediately goes to wash . . .' (Kuper, 1944, p. 250).[27] It was believed in the past that the warrior whose shield caught the gourd would be the first slain in future battle (ibid., p. 251); the gourd bears the demonic, 'dirty' attributes which previously animated the monster-king. The dance ends, the regiments wash themselves, and the king retires to the *inhlambelo* where the rest of his costume is removed. He is purged of the strongest medicines, but spends the night *cungiwe* (painted in blackness) and *emnyameni* (in darkness),[28] dangerous to himself and others. He sleeps with his first ritual queen, she who is 'a man'.

### 3. The Final Achievement of Normality

Like his *tinsila* or ritual doubles, the ritual queen takes on some of the 'dirt' of the king, the energy generated by doctoring is expended through his loss of strength, his emission of semen (dirt) into her body.

On the fifth day the court and people of the capital should observe restrictions. These involve prohibitions related to bodily comfort. Those who break these, if detected, pay fines. Collection of fines is in the hands of the rain-priests (Kuper, 1944, pp. 233, 235, 251, 252). Fines are pillaged (*kuhlamahlama*,[29] ibid., p. 233; the term may perhaps suggest the

---

[27] It is reported that long ago some Swazi cremated their dead; the wood required was of the *ishlangu* tree, Dumbrell, p. 190. The black shields may be associated with certain nihilistic aspects of warrior regiments. Like the king, they too are outside the ordinary groups of Swazi society and yet are the instruments by which that society works. Their instrumentality is in large part a product of their separation from ordinary domestic obligations. Certain aspects of this, associated with warfare, are highly negative and self-destructive. Supernatural dirt here passes from one out-of-place group to another; but this exchange makes sense only because of the similarities between the two.

[28] I use Kuper's translation, but the reverse translations seem more appropriate: *cungiwe* (darkened, obscured); *emnyameni* (in blackness).

[29] The same term is used when the herd-boy messenger conveying bridewealth cattle to a bride's father spears one of these beasts to provide a feast. This may only be done if the groom's kin have been lucky enough to provide the entire payment

notion of purgation). Their possible relation to 'dirt' is suggested by the mode of their disposal. On the sixth day the regiments, wearing loincloths, deposit articles which must be burned to end the disturbed state of the king and nation achieved by rites. The king is still not completely separated from the disorderly forces which enabled him to 'bite' the year. So long as the various objects connected with this condition exist in the capital, full order may not be reached. The warriors fetch the costumes worn by the king on the fourth day, the remains of the *umdutshulwa* ox-bull (except the hide), the hide of the preceding year's *umdutshulwa* and that year's wild gourd,[30] worn-out utensils and garments of the king, and the fines pillaged by the rain-priests from the people. Swazi say 'the filth of the king and all the people lies here on the fire' (ibid., p. 252). The rain-priests deal with dirt. They obtain objects with attributes which darken the king, making him a dangerous but potent amalgam of conflicting attributes. Within the context of *Incwala*, dirt and disorder become desirable. If we see rain-priests as bearers of dirt, we can understand why they are forbidden entry to sacred storehuts and shrines and clubhouses of the regiments (ibid., pp. 235–6). Kuper states that she could not discover why this should be, and yet she rightly sees a connexion between the prohibition and the fact that men sentenced to death find sanctuary in these same places. Spilling of blood, menstruation, death itself, sexual relations, the pillaging rain-priests with the filth of the nation, are all polluting. The regimental clubhouses and royal shrines involve attributes associated with men belonging to the nation who should not lose their strength in the dirt[31] of parochial loyalties and domestic quarrels.

The royal herd is driven into the byre and a black cow slaughtered and its gall bladder used for medicines. (There are no data on why a cow is used.) The king kindles a fire with friction sticks (probably with sexual connotations) and the filth is ablaze. He wanders nude around the byre aspersing himself and the herd with medicines, the herd representing both the nation which he tends and also his contact with the royal ghosts. The rain-priests strew rain-producing leaves on the ground. According to Kuper

---

(Engelbrecht, 1930b, pp. 17–18). This marks the end of payments, whereas in most Swazi marriages payments are made by instalment over several years, with all the ambiguous social difficulties this implies between the two groups involved. The payment ends the 'dirty' difficulties over such exchanges between affines.

[30] Continuity in these rites may be expressed by use of certain objects over two successive years, e.g. the wild gourd, the *umdutshwa* hide. There are no data on this.

[31] Swazi themselves see petty quarrels as 'dirt': *tibi tendlu,* dirt of the huts, Kuper, 1947, p. 65. A man sentenced to death may himself bear pollution, but apparently this is minor compared to the pollution of shedding blood or seizing him (for death) within such sanctuaries. Although data are inadequate, there seem to be different types and degrees of pollution. Thus, for example, the pollution of homicide appears far more terrible than that of sexual relations, since murderers are forbidden sexual connexion.

this is 'to turn around, to normalize' (*kupotula*) the king (ibid., p. 252). This verb has other important connotations: (Z) *phothula,* to scrape, shave, rub, massage, grind, crush, purify ceremonially after death or childbirth. This day is called *kushisa kukhuni* (consuming the firewood) (Kuper, 1952, p. 46): (Z) *shisa,* to consume, set alight, be burning hot, dry up, be unhealthy in the sense of wasting away; but the materials burned away are also called *ungogodla,* backbone (Ziervogel, 1957, p. 175). We should recall the ideophone (Z) *gogo,* connoting a searing away of filth, transforming it into ashes which may pass from one world to another, from that of men to that of ghosts. As the smoke, the essence of this dirt, ascends, the fire is put out by rain.[32] The transformed dirt of the world is exchanged for rain, a substance separated off from the sphere of the supernatural. This final exchange is both a bridge and a separation, for as the mediating dirt is consumed in flames, this link is washed away until the annual rites of the following year.

## IV. Conclusion

The preceding analysis suggests that the main theme of the *Incwala* is not rebellion or the expression of aggression and conflict, as Gluckman maintains, but the separation of the king from the various groups within his nation so that he is free and fit to assume the heavy supernatural powers of his office as king-priest of the nation. Much of both Gluckman's and Kuper's accounts of the themes of hatred and aggression towards the king depend upon their interpretation of the *simemo* songs at these rites. These are sung when the king, or objects associated with him, are being isolated so that they may take on increased supernatural powers. Far from being periods when the king is symbolically weak, they mark his assumption of great power. If there is an aspect of strain, it involves the 'heaviness' and isolation of the king's task. On Gluckman's thesis, one would expect those who sing the *simemo* and similar songs of 'hatred' to be those Swazi contending against the king for power. But royal kinsmen are excluded at most such scenes in the rites. This is consistent with my interpretation: the king's ties to his royal kin are being minimized; it is not their hostility towards him that is expressed nor is it that of the people. Perhaps deeper examination of the *simemo* might bear this out. In a similar sense, the king's nudity expresses the king's isolation and this is consistent with the ceremonial undress of warriors and certain others in these ceremonies.

The interpretation of these acts which I present here seems more in keeping with the sum total of Swazi beliefs and symbolism than is the con-

---

[32] Long ago, the ashes of cremated dead are said to have been washed away by water diverted through dams built for such purposes, Dumbrell, p. 190.

flict theme suggested by Gluckman. At the least, I hope that I have shown these rites to be more complex than his interpretation suggests. But it is difficult to verify any analysis of such a system of ideas. One can only maintain that an interpretation which seems consistent with all the reported ethnographic facts, and which is the most parsimonious available, is acceptable until facts may be shown inconsistent with it or until a better model is provided. My disagreement with Gluckman is also concerned with his method of considering latent functions or results of a rite prior to considering their culturally manifest purpose. This second area of difference relates to my own view of the more important problems to be tackled in the study of ritual. This leads to the very difficult problem of the relation of sociological and psychological factors in the explanation of ritual acts.

Definitions of ritual explicitly or implicitly admit the manipulation of symbols as an essential aspect of such acts. Rituals may exist in a very wide range of societies and as parts of ideological systems of all degrees of complexity and sophistication. Why is it that most men do not consider it sufficient to contemplate their social values and ideas but must also go through certain ritual acts as well? Why is a Christian, for example, not content with reading and contemplating Christian theology and philosophy, but also goes through the rites of a theophagic feast in order to make communion with the supernatural? What are the attributes or qualities of such symbols that give them a force or efficacy apparently not provided by other abstract ideas? This is a question with which Durkheim grappled in his *Elementary Forms of the Religious Life*. In his analysis of the problem of totemism, Lévi-Strauss attacks Durkheim's solution: 'His theory of totemism starts with an urge, and ends with a recourse to sentiment' (1963, pp. 70–71). Lévi-Strauss himself insists that such phenomena may be explained either in terms of biology or the intellect, but he seems reluctant to deal with any interrelationship between these two spheres (p. 104). Yet ultimately such a relationship must be dealt with in order to gain insight into the bases of ritual acts. Lévi-Strauss's work pursues the line of 'intellect', but it is difficult to see how in the long run this can avoid psychological and physiological issues.

Most competent sociologists and social anthropologists studying symbolism and ritual stress that such data should initially be examined as social and not psychological phenomena, that the significance of symbols depends upon the meanings and values assigned within a particular culture. Such a cultural analysis indicates the particular themes to which a symbol may relate, e.g. the attributes of hotness, moistness, elusiveness, redness, uncleanness, leftness, downwardness, may relate to the choice of certain objects to express feminine sexuality, as among many African Bantu peoples. But such an analysis does not explain why modes of sensation (heat, wetness, texture) or orientation (up-down, right-left) or bodily acts (ingestion, evacuation, birth) should be associated with certain social values of goodness and badness, cleanness and pollution, order and chaos. I have touched upon this problem elsewhere (1964) and it has been brilliantly discussed by Turner (1962a, 1962b, 1964, 1966). His argument runs something like this: basic cultural values or ideologies are existential, and yet ritual behavior seems to suggest that individuals do not maintain such beliefs simply because these are part of a cognitive system shared by the members of a society. Some features of such ideologies, especially those involving moral notions, tend to be expressed emotionally through certain psycho-physiological terms, e.g. body states and sensations. These bodily experiences have had important bearing on each individual's interpretation of his surroundings, even before speech, and they appear to have provided important metaphorical means by which many word concepts developed. According to this neo-Freudian approach, for example, feelings of oral gratification, satiety, body states related to bodily emissions, temperature, body surface contacts, lightness and darkness, bodily spatial orientation, etc., begin to be associated with various human interrelations. These individual relations, in turn, form the core from which certain social relations are built up and made meaningful in each child's thought. The ideology of any particular social group may represent, in large part, an abstract elaboration based upon these more primitive sets of psycho-physiological associations. Because these most basic psycho-physiological associations are often preverbal, they possess an immediacy inviolate to the onslaughts of verbal, rational argument and it is this intractable aspect of such sense-oriented attributes that provides some of the impetus of symbols and the resilience of many religious and political ideologies which make prominent use of such symbols. In short, the particular configuration of any symbolic value system is a social or cultural problem; but the efficacy of such symbols must be studied by psycholinguists, social psychologists, and similar specialists. It presents an important though uncharted field for interdisciplinary research, provided that each expert remains acutely aware of the limits of his own field and his own capabilities.[33]

Gluckman's reliance on the concept of catharsis depends upon psychological principles, though ones not directly related to the peculiar nature of ritual, viz., its symbolic character. His theory relates to a hydraulic model of personality projected on to entire social groups. Gluckman himself maintains that his interpretation is strictly sociological.[34] But I find his argument unclear and suggest that he may not have seen where his

---

[33] For a discussion of some of these problems, cf. Devons and Gluckman's remarks on Turner's work, Gluckman (1964), pp. 213–18.

[34] Gluckman, 1963, pp. 27, 32; 1965, pp. 259–60. Norbeck recently criticizes Gluckman's theory; he draws attention to the problem of defining conflict and recognizes some of the psychological implications of the argument, but he ignores the issues regarding the nature and need for ritual acts, Norbeck, 1963, 1965; cf. van den Berghe, 1965; Cohen, 1965.

theory ultimately leads. He sidesteps the crucial issue of how such rites produce catharsis when he provides the following type of explanations: (*a*) 'This allows for institutionalized protest, and in complex ways renews the unity of the system' (1954, p. 3); and (*b*) 'A dropping of normal restraints, and inverted and transvestite behaviour, in which women were dominant and men suppressed *somehow* were believed to achieve good for the community—an abundant harvest' (ibid., p. 10). He does not pursue this further but merely states: 'I have not time to enter into these mechanisms, of which indeed as yet we understand little' (ibid.). These are extremely difficult issues not worked out by sociologists or psychologists; but they require a clearer distinction between psychological and sociological explanations than he provides. In any case, Gluckman's analysis veers close to teleological functionalism, a danger inherent in any explanation using 'latent' functions.

My interpretation is not a wide departure from earlier attempts to explain the efficacy of symbols, except that it stresses that in a final sense the efficacy of symbols is essentially a psychological problem. The existential, non-rational nature of such value systems was emphasized by Lévy-Bruhl and, in a more explicit and sophisticated form, this idea is a cornerstone to Evans-Pritchard's masterpiece on Zande witchcraft. It is the basis, too, for one of the earlier insights on the analysis of African political systems:

Bonds of utilitarian interest between individuals and between groups are not as strong as the bonds implied in common attachment to mystical symbols. It is precisely the greater solidarity, based on these bonds, which generally gives political groups their dominance over social groups of other kinds (Fortes and Evans-Pritchard, p. 23).

Such a passage is very Durkheimian both in its laudable emphasis upon the importance of analysing ideology in order to understand behaviour and in its vague recognition that in explaining the power of symbolic moral systems, we may be getting at the very core of ideas which determine the workings of a society; but such a passage is also Durkheimian in its blindness to the psychological issues involved which are implicitly raised but hardly clarified by the perplexing adjective 'mystical'. Furthermore, it is not made clear why political groups possess an ideological, symbolic reference different from that for the other units of a particular society, especially in the case of simpler, preliterate groups. The Anglo-French sociological tradition has fathered some profound analyses of primitive philosophies, but it has also perpetuated Durkheim's dilemma in trying to account for the individual effect of symbols and ritual without recourse to psychological as well as sociological concepts.

## Bibliography

ANONYMOUS, 1950. 'Witchcraft in Swaziland', *Nature,* cxlv. 664.

BEEMER, H. 1935. 'The Swazi Rain Ceremony', *Bantu Studies,* ix. 273–80.

———— 1937. 'The Development of the Military Organisation in Swaziland', *Africa,* x. 55–75, 176–205.

BEIDELMAN, T. O. 1964. 'Pig *(Guluwe)*: an Essay on Ngulu Sexual Symbolism and Ceremony', *Southwestern Journal of Anthropology,* xx. 359–92.

BRYANT, A. T. 1929. *Olden Times in Zululand and Natal,* Longmans, Green & Co., London.

COHEN, R. 1965. 'Review Article', *American Anthropologist,* lxvii. 950–7.

COOK, P. A. W. 1930. 'The Inqwala Ceremony of the Swazi', *Bantu Studies,* iv. 205–10.

———— 1931. 'History and Isibongo of the Swazi Chiefs', Ibid., v. 181–201.

DOKE, C. M., and VILAKAZI, B. W. 1958. *Zulu-English Dictionary,* Witwatersrand University Press, Johannesburg.

DOUGLAS, MARY, 1966. *Purity and Danger,* Routledge & Kegan Paul, London.

DUMBRELL, H. J. P. 1952. 'Pyre Burning in Swaziland', *African Studies,* xi. 190–1.

ENGELBRECHT, J. A. 1930*a.* 'Swazi Texts with Notes', *Annals of the University of Stellenbosch,* 8B, no. 2.

———— 1930*b.* 'Swazi Customs relating to Marriage', Ibid., no. 3.

EVANS-PRITCHARD, E. E. 1956. *Nuer Religion,* Clarendon Press, Oxford.

FORTES, M., and EVANS-PRITCHARD, E. E. 1940. 'Introduction' to *African Political Systems,* Oxford University Press( for International African Institute), London.

FRANKFORT, H. 1948. *Kingship and the Gods,* University of Chicago Press.

GLUCKMAN, M. 1938. 'Social Aspects of the First Fruits Ceremonies among the South-Eastern Bantu', *Africa,* xi. 25–41.

———— 1954. *Rituals of Rebellion in South-East Africa,* Manchester University Press.

———— 1963. *Order and Rebellion in Africa,* Cohen & West, London.

———— 1964. (ed.) *Closed Systems and Open Minds,* Oliver & Boyd, Edinburgh.

———— 1965. *Politics, Law and Ritual in Tribal Society,* Blackwell, Oxford.

KIDD, D. 1925. *The Essential Kaffir,* Black, London.

KRIGE, J. D. 1944. 'The Magical Thought-Pattern of the Bantu in Relation to Health Services', *African Studies,* xi. 1–13.

KUPER, H. *(née* BEEMER), 1944. 'A Ritual of Kingship among the Swazi', *Africa,* xiv. 230–56.

———— 1945. 'The Marriage of a Swazi Princess', Ibid., xv. 145–55.

———— 1947. *An African Aristocracy: Rank among the Swazi,* Oxford University Press (for International African Institute), London.

———— 1950. 'Kinship among the Swazi', pp. 86–110, in *African Systems of Kinship and Marriage,* eds. A. Radcliffe-Brown and D. Forde, Oxford University Press (for International African Institute), London.

———— 1952. *The Swazi,* Oxford University Press (for International African Institute), London.

———— 1964. *The Swazi: a South African Kingdom,* Holt, Rinehart and Winston, New York.

LEACH, E. 1961. *Rethinking Anthropology,* Athlone, London.

———— 1964. 'Some Anthropological Aspects of Language', pp. 23–63, in *New Directions in the Study of Language,* ed. E. Lenneberg, Massachusetts Institute of Technology, Cambridge, Mass.

LÉVI-STRAUSS, C. 1963. *Totemism,* Beacon, Boston.

MARWICK, B. A. 1940. *The Swazi,* Cambridge University Press.

NORBECK, E. 1963. 'African Rituals of Conflict', *American Anthropologist,* lxv. 1254–79.

———— 1965. 'Reply to van den Berghe', Ibid., lxvii. 487–9.

O'NEILL, O. R. 1921. *Adventures in Swaziland,* Century, New York.

SCHAPERA, I. (ed.). *The Bantu-Speaking Tribes of South Africa,* Routledge, London.

SCHOEMAN, P. J. 1935. 'The Swazi Rain Ceremony', *Bantu Studies,* ix. 168–75.

SUNDKLER, B. 1965. 'Chiefs and Prophets in Zululand and Swaziland', pp. 276–90, in *African Systems of Thought,* eds. M. Fortes and G. Dieterlen, Oxford University Press (for International African Institute), London.

TURNER, V. 1962a. *Chihamba the White Spirit,* Rhodes-Livingstone Paper No. 33, Manchester University Press.

———— 1962b. 'Three Symbols of *Passage* in Ndembu Circumcision Ritual', pp. 124–73, in *Essays in the Ritual of Social Relations,* ed. M. Gluckman, Manchester University Press.

———— 1964. *Betwixt and Between: the Liminal Period in Rites de Passage,* mimeograph.

———— 1966. 'Colour Classification in Ndembu Ritual', pp. 47–85, in *3 Anthropological Approaches to the Study of Religion,* Tavistock (A.S.A. Monograph), London.

TWALA, R. 1951. 'Beads as Regulating the Social Life of the Zulu and Swazi', *African Studies,* x. 113–25.

———— 1952. 'Umhlanga (Reed) Ceremony of Swazi Maidens', Ibid., xi. 93–104.

VAN DEN BERGHE, P. 1965. 'Some Comments on Norbeck's "African Rituals of Conflict"', *American Anthropologist,* lxvii. 485–7.

WEIGHTMAN, J. 1965. 'The Sacred Monster', *The Observer,* 28 February 1965, London.

ZIERVOGEL, D. 1952. *A Grammar of Swazi,* Witwatersrand University Press, Johannesburg.

———— 1957. *Swazi Texts,* van Schaik, Pretoria.

# The Left Hand of the Mugwe: An Analytical Note on the Structure of Meru Symbolism*

## Rodney Needham

**I**

In his admirable study of the Mugwe, a religious dignitary among the Meru of Kenya, Bernardi reports a singular fact which raises a problem of comparative and theoretical interest: viz. that the left hand of the Mugwe possesses and symbolizes his ritual power. The issue is best seen, to begin with, in the following passage:

> Among the Imenti [a sub-tribe] an unusual aspect of the people's conception of the Mugwe concerns his left hand. It is this hand . . . that should always hold the *kiragu* [insignia] and be used only to bless. It is a most sacred member of the Mugwe's body and no one is allowed to see it. During the day, the Mugwe spends his time playing *kiothi*, the Meru draughts, but even while he plays, he must always keep his left hand covered and no one must see it. Sudden death would overtake anyone who dared to look at the left hand of the Mugwe.[1]

Neither in this place, nor in any other of the references to this hand, does Bernardi offer an explanation. The object of this note is to suggest a possible answer.

That the position of the left hand of the Mugwe does raise a problem hardly needs demonstration. Hertz showed fifty years ago the universality of a symbolic differentiation of right and left, and examined in his classic paper[2] the grounds for the preeminence of the right; and Wile has brought

---

* This paper, in a slightly altered form, is included in Rodney Needham (ed.), *Right and Left: Essays on Dual Symbolic Classification* (London: Routledge and Kegan Paul). [Ed.]

[1] B. Bernardi, *The Mugwe, a Failing Prophet*, London 1959, p. 74.

[2] Robert Hertz, 'La Prééminence de la main droite: étude sur la polarité religieuse', *Revue Philosophique*, vol. lxviii, 1909, pp. 553–80. Also in English translation by R. and C. Needham, in *Death and The Right Hand*, London (1960).

together in his work on handedness[3] an overwhelming amount of evidence on the distinction of the sides and the practically universal privilege of the right. These two works alone show that in every quarter of the world it is the right hand, and not the left, which is predominant; and this is so whether in the great civilizations of China and India, or among the most primitive and isolated peoples known. The issue can be studied in such varied fields as the Homeric poems, alchemy, and thirteenth-century French religious art, in Hindu iconography, classical Chinese state ceremonies, emblem books and bestiaries, as well as in Maori ritual, Bornean divination, and the myths of the most disparate cultures. This differentiation and opposition of right and left is the very type of symbolic classification, and its logical simplicity and universal distribution make it a fundamental concern in the social anthropologist's study of symbolism. If, then, we are clearly told by a reliable authority that the *left* hand of a certain personage is sacred and used exclusively for his religious functions, we have every reason to be surprised and to look for an explanation.

Let me begin by compounding the remaining evidences in Bernardi's monograph relating specifically to the left hand of the Mugwe. Enemies try to strike the left hand of the Mugwe of the Imenti 'because it was said to hold the power of the Mugwe'; the *kiragu,* insignia of power, the things by which the Mugwe is made to be the Mugwe, are held in his left hand, and for this reason the Mugwe of the Imenti keeps his left hand always under cover of his mantle; a very special power in connexion with his blessings is popularly attributed to his left hand, and anyone going to him is advised above all never to look at this hand; in it the Mugwe holds the power of his blessing; it is enough for him to lift his left hand in order to stop any enemy attacking his people; it is a source of great awe; respect and fear are felt for this hand, and no one may look on it without dying.[4]

The facts are thus quite clear. The most valuable relate to the Imenti sub-tribe, but I draw whatever usable evidence I can from other sub-tribes also, and my interpretation should essentially apply to the Meru in general. It would be inappropriate for me, as an orientalist, to introduce ethnographic or cultural considerations by pursuing a comparative study of the matter in other Bantu societies, and I base my analysis entirely on the evidence presented by Bernardi in his monograph. The theoretical problem is one which may properly be tackled by any social anthropologist, whatever the area of his special competence, but I should nevertheless feel

---

[3] Ira S. Wile, *Handedness: Right and Left,* Boston, Mass., 1934. (I am indebted to Professor E. Adamson Hoebel for my acquaintance with this useful compilation.)

[4] Bernardi, pp. 61, 103, 110, 120. At the ritual of accession among the Imenti the new Mugwe runs with an old woman, keeping hold of her hand: if she dies, he is a fit successor (p. 93). It is not stated by which hand the Mugwe holds hers; and it is unclear if it is because of the touch of his left hand that she dies, though one might infer so, since she is supposed to be overwhelmed by his supernatural power.

hesitant about advancing my interpretation if it were not for the fact that any proposed answer is readily testable by Africanists and by persons in Africa in close touch with the Meru. What I present, therefore, is not merely a speculative exercise of some technical interest, but a testable hypothesis. If correct, it may add to our understanding of the Meru; and in any case it will permit a test, in a new field, of a method of inquiry which has already proved illuminating in others.

There are now two elucidatory matters, one cultural and the other structural, to be examined before dealing with the evidence. The first is that the Meru have been influenced by Christianity. A number of Meru informants in Bernardi's work bear Christian first names, and Christian elements have clearly been introduced into Meru mythology. This, so far as one can see in the monograph, is the most considerable extraneous cultural influence powerful enough to affect their symbolic notions. However, it is certain that the attributes of the left hand of the Mugwe have nothing to do with Christian belief or teaching; for in all the references to the right and left hands in the Bible which Wile has listed, 'in no single instance is the left hand given a position of honor, superiority or righteousness'.[5] Also it is common knowledge that in western cultural notions in general (such as might have influenced the Meru) it is the right, where any differentiation is made, which is pre-eminent and not the left. The position of the left hand of the Mugwe is not, therefore, due to influence by western culture in general or by Christianity in particular.

The second, structural, matter is that in societies based on descent such symbolic representations may be expected to correlate with the type of descent system. Roughly, in cognatic societies the relation of symbolic to social order may be indefinite or minimal; in lineal systems the relationship may be discernible in a limited range of particulars but not commonly in a comprehensive manner; and in lineal systems with prescriptive affinal alliance there is usually a correspondence of structure between the two orders such that one may speak of a single scheme of classification under which both are subsumed.[6] Meru society is at present based on exogamous patrilineal descent groups, so that we may therefore expect some elucidation of their symbolic notions by examining their social structure, though not so certainly or profitably as if we were dealing with a system of prescriptive alliance. There is, furthermore, certain evidence on the social system (which I shall examine below) which brings Meru society closer to one form of prescriptive system and makes such an approach even more promising.

---

[5] Wile, pp. 339–40.

[6] R. Needham, 'A Structural Analysis of Purum Society', *American Anthropologist*, vol. 60, 1958, pp. 75–101; 'An Analytical Note on the Kom of Manipur', *Ethnos*, vol. 24, 1959.

What I shall do now is to abstract from Bernardi's account isolated evidences of a scheme of symbolic classification by which the Meru may be taken to order their universe, and within which the peculiar character of the Mugwe's left hand may make sense. This involves the establishing of analogical connexions between very different institutions and situations; and this type of analysis brings with it, I fear, the likelihood of a rather disjointed exposition. However, as the evidence accumulates and the conceptual connexions are elicited a certain coherence should emerge, the key to which I shall try to set out clearly and briefly towards the end.

## II

According to Bernardi, all Meru believe they came from the land of Mbwa, to the north. The word by which they designate the north is *urio,* which 'literally' means the right hand.[7]

There are distinct traces in Meru society, connected with their myth of origin, of a dual division. This has now lost its significance, but appears to have been typical of all the nine sub-tribes. Clans in the Imenti sub-tribe have names which refer to the intensity of the light while they were crossing the great water in the tribe's exodus from Mbwa: some are called 'black', some 'red', and some 'white'. Those who crossed during the night are black; those who crossed at dawn, red; and those who crossed when the sun was up, white. The elders say, however, that there was 'really no distinction' between red and white, and that these formed a single group. The clans may thus be distinguished simply as 'black clans' and 'white clans'. It seems certain, says Bernardi, that this distinction had in the past some effective territorial, social, and probably political significance.[8]

This division of the clans is concordant wtih a division of the Imenti into two groupings, the Nkuene and the Igoki. These were territorial, Nkuene being on the south and Igoki on the north. Igoki seems to have included all the white clans, and the two designations appear to have become synonymous. The divisions were also referred to geographically, as those of *urio,* north, and those of *umotho,* south. The Igoki are said by

---

[7] Bernardi, pp. 2–3. It is not clear why Bernardi isolates a literal meaning, implying that only by a kind of extension does the word mean 'north'. (Cf. Sanskrit *dakshina,* Hebrew *jamīn,* Irish *dess,* 'right, south'.)

[8] Bernardi, pp. 9, 58. Though the clear statement about the equation of red and white clans is highly satisfactory for my present purpose, the triadic division presumably 'means' something, and is possibly connected with the number of other contexts in which three seems to have a special significance: see Bernardi, pp. 21, 25–26, 58, 68, 90. Also, W. H. Laughton, *The Meru,* Nairobi, 1944, pp. 11, 14, 15; H. E. Lambert, *Kikuyu Social and Political Institutions,* London, 1956, p. 27. Laughton, p. 2, says that it is the red and the black clans which have 'merged into one group'.

the elders to have been 'always very proud; they wanted always to be first in grazing and watering their cattle'.[9]

In the Tharaka sub-tribe there was a similar division, and the Mugwe came from the *umotho* (southern) group. Only the people of Umotho were privileged to take part in full array at his ceremonial blessings. Those of Urio are described as 'alien to the Mugwe', and were not expected to visit him at his residence. 'It seems there was, or could be, some kind of friction between the two divisions.' The divisions were not exogamous.[10]

In the Tigania sub-tribe the divisions were named Athwana and Igoki: the former was also referred to as *umotho* and the latter as *urio*. The Mugwe of the Tigania resides among the Igoki, i.e. in the northern grouping, a fact which will acquire some significance later. Bernardi reports that the Athwana are described (like the Urio of Tharaka) as alien to the Mugwe, and regards his presence in a specified division as indicative of a former social and political significance to the dual division in this sub-tribe also.[11]

In the Igembe sub-tribe the only mention of *urio* and *umotho* refers not to moieties but to the location of the huts of wives in a polygynous household: 'the first wife is always *Urio*, the right'.[12]

Another institutionalized duality is seen in the age-set system: all the age-sets were related in a dual division, sets of alternate division being successively in power.[13]

Men and women are differentially evaluated. An Imenti elder, to affirm that 'to be circumcised is nothing', says that 'even women are operated upon', clearly implying a depreciation of women. More explicitly, elders use the term 'woman' to describe their present subordinate political condition: 'We are all *women*: the real *man* is the government', expressing also the superiority of man over woman. Further, at the official ceremonies of the Mugwe, on which the stability and continuity of Meru society are said to rest, women and children are not allowed.[14]

'The sun rises at the place of Mukuna-Ruku and sets at the place of the Mugwe.' Mukuna-Ruku is a name applied by Meru to a legendary ivory-trader, probably an Arab. His residence is said to have been Mombasa, 'i.e. the east, where the sun rises'. Mukuna-Ruku is also a mythical figure

---

[9] Bernardi, p. 9. I understand from Dr. J. H. M. Beattie that *umotho* or one or other cognate word means 'left' in at least some neighbouring Bantu languages. See, e.g., M. B. Davis, *Lunyoro-Lunyankole-English . . . Dictionary*, Kampala–London, 1938, p. 95, s.v. *moso*.

[10] Bernardi, pp. 10, 42.

[11] Bernardi, pp. 11, 76.

[12] Bernardi, p. 10.

[13] Bernardi, pp. 21–23. See also, Laughton, p. 4: 'There is a traditional and ceremonial antipathy between successive age-sets.'

[14] Bernardi, pp. 17, 39, 90.

with a body that is all eyes and gives light to the sun. The obvious inference is that the Mugwe is symbolically associated with the west, but Bernardi says that this 'cannot so easily be implied'. The elucidation he presents is that the house of the Mugwe cannot come to an end, the Mugwe cannot die; and it is therefore at his dwelling that the sun sets. 'The sun, as the Mugwe, cannot fail to give its light and warmth, it cannot die, and therefore it sets at the dwelling of the Mugwe in order to renew its power for the next day. There is a parallel between the two figures of Mukuna-Ruku and the Mugwe, both possessing a very special character and a very special power: light and immortality.'[15] Bernardi does not cite here, as he usually does elsewhere, Meru statements to show that this interpretation is that of the people themselves, and it has the air of being his own. I think, in any case, that it is inconsistent with what else can be discerned of Meru symbolism, and shall try to show why later. For the moment, I suggest that Mukuna-Ruku is associated with east and light, and the Mugwe with west and darkness. This is supported, to give a brief indication, by the colour of the sacrificial bull, which must be black, 'a colour sacred to God', and by that of the Mugwe's staff, which is 'the ritual black',[16] permitting the inference that darkness is not symbolically incompatible with the Mugwe's ritual position.

We have already seen that the Mugwe keeps his left hand concealed while he plays 'draughts', and although there is no other information on his right hand the tenor of the evidence is that this is his profane hand. His left hand is reserved for his sacred function, viz. to bless, which is described as his 'essential work'. His authority, in fact, is 'basically religious'; while it is the elders who control all forms of social and political activity and are 'the real masters of the country'. 'The eternal machinery of tribal government and of social life would appear to work satisfactorily even without the Mugwe', and this is underlined by Bernardi's discovery that, apparently until very recently, the very existence of the Mugwe had entirely escaped the Administration. The Meru are admittedly described as looking up to the Mugwe as their father, and the elders say that before the European administration there was no other 'chief' but the Mugwe; but these statements do not really conflict with the clear distinction of function between the Mugwe and the elders, especially when we further learn from the elders themselves that they protect the Mugwe as though he were a queen bee. The Mugwe was in a literally singular position, the one person on whom the society could be said to focus, and whose presence and (ritual) services could be regarded as essential; and in view of his functions it is easily comprehensible that he should be referred to in such terms. The fact is clear, I think, that there was a distinct partition of

---

[15] Bernardi, pp. 73, 74.
[16] Bernardi, pp. 92, 99.

sovereignty into the religious authority of the Mugwe, seen in his indispensable blessing in the major social institutions, and the political power of the elders, seen in their effective jural and administrative control.[17] The apparently conflicting evaluations of the respective status of Mugwe and elders are made within different contexts and characterized by different criteria.

Finally, the possible significance of temporal succession deserves some attention. In the myth of the exodus of the Meru from Mbwa the people come to the water and their leader (= Mugwe) divides it with his staff to make a passage for them. He first sends across a small girl and a small boy, and then a young woman and a young man; and only when they have crossed does he take the main body over. This suggests the possibility that those who are first, the forerunners, are of inferior status, and that those whom they precede, the main body, are of superior status. It would probably be going too far to infer that the order in which the sexes are mentioned—first female, then male—makes the same point; but if this is a culturally conventional order it is at least consistent with the fact that first the younger cross and then the older, and with the relative status of women and men.[18] The second illustration also comes from myth. All peoples are said to come from the same place, but the first to be born was a black man, and after him a white[19] man. In this case the predecessors are (whatever their other qualities and however they regard themselves in other respects) political inferiors, and their successors are superiors, an opposition explicitly made by the elders quoted above. Related to this theme, also, is the myth of the origin of the exploitation of natural resources: first came the age-set with the Mugwe, and this is the one which started honey-collecting; next came the set which was the first to cultivate. We cannot be sure of the relative evaluation of these two subsistence activities, but one would think that basic sustenance would depend more on the latter than on honey, which is described merely as one of the staple elements of diet among the Tharaka. Moreover, we can see here another instance of the theme of complementary functions; for sacred honey-beer is one of the insignia of the Mugwe, and the rite of blessing itself consists in the Mugwe sipping some honey-beer and gently spitting it on to the people;

---

[17] Bernardi, pp. 160, 161, 150, 155, 136, 174, 142, 151, 161. This is not to say that the Mugwe is quite without political influence, and we are indeed told that his religious authority is capable of 'political extension' (p. 139) and a source of political power which a strong and ambitious man could exploit (p. 161); but this is a contingent matter of fact, whereas I am concerned with a conceptual system.

[18] In one myth, God is described as creating man and then woman; but this is said by Bernardi (pp. 52, 55) to be Christian. However, there is still one clear contrary indication: in an invocation by the Mugwe, he refers to his people as 'male, female . . . boys and girls', which tends to dispose of the idea. Bernardi, pp. 192, 121.

[19] Bernardi, pp. 193–4. 'White': lit. umutune, red; cf. the equation of red and white clans.

whereas according to Laughton (to cite another authority for once) all rights in land lie with the elders, and it is they who control its preservation and exploitation.[20]

## III

Having completed a survey of the evidence, we are now in a position to make a systematic interpretation by which the position of the left hand of the Mugwe may be comprehensible. The first step is to construct a table such as that which follows: this represents a symbolic classification in which pairs of opposite terms are analogically related by the principle of complementary dualism.[21] It relates specifically to the Imenti, though the principle exhibited appears valid for at least some of the other sub-tribes. The oppositions are listed seriatim as they have been elicited in the exposition of the relevant facts.

| left | right |
|---|---|
| south | north |
| Umotho | Urio |
| Nkuene | Igoki |
| black clans | white clans |
| night | day |
| co-wife | first wife |
| junior | senior |
| subordinate age-division | dominant age-division |
| woman/child | man |
| inferior | superior |
| west | east |
| sunset | sunrise |
| ——— (moon?) | sun |
| darkness | light |
| (blindness) | sight (eyes) |
| black | ——— |
| Mugwe | elders |
| religious authority | political power |
| predecessors | successors |
| younger | older |
| black man | white man |
| honey-collecting | cultivation |

---

[20] Bernardi, pp. 100–1, 110; Laughton, pp. 3, 5.
[21] Cf. Needham, 1958, pp. 97, 99.

It will readily be seen that the scheme is coherent, and that it displays a systematic order which can immediately be apprehended. A few clarificatory notes may, however, be helpful, and there are also certain difficulties which have to be discussed.

A matter which may occasion some reserve is that the Mugwe should be associated, however indirectly, with feminine. This may be thought in conflict with his paternal authority and with the statements that the Mugwe is 'higher' than the elders and 'above' them.[22] But we have to remember, firstly, the matter of context: ritually, as a symbol of the unity of Meru society, the Mugwe is superior to the elders, but politically he is definitely not. Even this is misleading, though. It is the *complementarity,* I think, which should be emphasized, rather than differential status in opposed contexts.

Secondly, it has to be kept in mind that the ascription of terms to one series in the scheme does not entail that they all share the particular attributes of any one term. The association of these terms rests on analogy, and is derived from a mode of categorization which orders the scheme, not from the possession of a specific property by means of which the character or presence of other terms may be deduced. One does not, therefore, say that the Mugwe *is* feminine, any more than one would say that night or south or the subordinate age-division is feminine.

Nevertheless, the association in any way of religious authority with feminine may still seem to call for an explanation. This question, it seems to me, can be resolved by comparison with other societies. I select two particularly clear parallels from widely separated and disparate cultures, in which a symbolic association of religion with feminine is quite explicitly and directly made. Among the Ngaju of south Borneo, most religious functionaries are priestesses, and religious matters are so intimately associated with the feminine that men who professionally assume such functions also assume feminine social status. They wear women's clothes and dress their hair like women; they are commonly homosexual or impotent, and they even marry men. A man who has thus assumed femininity is thought to be more efficacious in the supernatural sphere than a woman.[23] Among the Chukchi of Siberia, there are four stages in becoming a particularly prominent kind of shaman, each marked by an increased assumption of feminine attributes. In the first, the man adopts woman's hair-style; in the second he wears woman's dress; in the third he throws away all his masculine appurtenances and undertakes woman's tasks, his voice changes and his body acquires the helplessness of a woman; and in the final stage he 'changes sex', taking a lover and after a time a husband, and may even claim

---

[22] Bernardi, pp. 139, 152–3.

[23] A. Hardeland, *Dajacksch–Deutsches Wörterbuch,* Amsterdam, 1859, pp. 53–54, s.v. *basir;* M. T. H. Perelaer, *Ethnographische Beschrijving der Dajaks,* Zalt-Bommel, 1870, p. 35; H. Schärer, *Die Gottesidee der Ngadju–Dajak in Süd-Borneo,* Leiden, 1946, pp. 64–67.

to give birth to children. Such a shaman has a special relation with the supernatural, marked by the protection and guidance of a guardian spirit, and he is dreaded, even by untransformed shamans.[24] On the most general grounds, therefore, and taking the most extreme cases, the inclusion of the Mugwe in a category which includes feminine may be considered not at all unusual. I may now adduce a superficially isolated and otherwise incomprehensible fact, reported in connexion with sexual intercourse, which also associates the Mugwe (of the Imenti) with feminine. An elder says: 'Another wonder for the common people: the Mugwe never asks for his wife; it is his wife who asks for him.'[25] This very unusual practice can now be seen as an elaboration on a symbolic classification which gives it meaning.[26]

These points made, we may now understand from the scheme why the Igoki were so proud, and why they demanded always to be first in grazing and watering their cattle; for by analogical inference they were the senior of the moieties (Igoki: Nkuene:: north: south:: senior: junior), and these may well have been their traditional and distinctive rights. To take another case, it is even possible that the scheme may give a lead as to whether the Meru came from the north, as Bernardi reports, or from the east, as is said by Lambert, Holding, and, by implication, Laughton.[27] In addition to the equation north = right, which is consistent with an eastern origin, there are the elements of white, day, sun, and light in the right-hand (dominant, privileged) series—all commonly assigned, not to the north, but generally and naturally to the east. One might therefore tend to think (assuming some connexion between traditions of origin and Meru symbolic classification) that they came from the east rather than the north. Finally, historical questions aside, it may be seen on what grounds I suggested above that predecessors may be classed as junior. Whether moving from the north or from the east, the children and young people are the first to the south or west; and they are therefore associated with the juniority of the co-wife and the inferiority (asserted, it appears, by the Igoki) of the Nkuene.

However, this last matter brings us now to some difficulties. The predecessor in the advancement of the age-sets is not junior but senior; the

---

[24] W. Bogoras, *The Chukchee*, Leiden–New York, 1909, pp. 449 ff.

[25] Bernardi, p. 107.

[26] Bernardi at one place even suggests that a reference to a certain woman could have been 'an indirect way of referring to the Mugwe' (p. 39). Note that these cases relate to the Imenti. I do not overlook the possible relevance of the theme of reversal which so often characterizes ritual; but this is an enormous topic which I cannot broach here.

[27] H. E. Lambert, *The Systems of Land Tenure in the Kikuyu Land Unit* (Communications, School of African Studies, 22), Cape Town, 1950, p. 7; E. M. Holding, 'Some Preliminary Notes on Meru Age-grades', *Man*, vol. xlii, 1942, p. 58; Laughton, p. 2.

predecessor in marriage to a man is not a junior co-wife but the senior; and the elders, similarly, are predecessors to all their younger juniors. Meru ethnography is not extensive or detailed enough to permit useful speculation on my part about these points. It may be that my formulation of the defining relation is mistaken, or that the formal resemblance between the situations from which I elicited it is misleading, e.g. that it is not simply predecession that is decisive, but that some other kind of distinction is symbolically significant. This one couple of terms (predecessors: successors) aside, though, the subsequent and derivative couples remain consistent with the scheme.

Though it is only the Mugwe who is clearly associated with black in a ritual context, it is not only he who wears a black mantle, but the elders as well.[28] If black were a sign of superior social status there would be no difficulty in seeing that the Mugwe and the elders might together be distinguished in this way as social leaders; but in the face of the ritual associations of black, the ritual office of the Mugwe, and the secular status of the elders as a body, this fact creates a contradiction to the scheme which does not seem resoluble by resort to the published ethnography.

There are other points, too, which cause difficulty, such as the relationships focusing on the concept of *ntindiri*.[29] I have not felt sure enough to include them in the scheme: the ethnography on these points is too slender for any compelling logic to emerge as directive, and a speculative review of the formal possibilities would not be decisive.

## IV

The only assumption I have made in constructing the scheme of classification is that Meru symbolism is consistent; and so far as I know I have not omitted from the account any relevant facts which are contradictory to the scheme, or which would lend another interpretation to the significance of the facts to which it relates. I now proceed to the problem.

The resolution which I propose is that it is in accordance with this symbolic order, and consistent with the total scheme of relations between the particular terms, that the left hand of the Mugwe should be regarded as sacred. By a conceptual dichotomy operative in a number of contexts he is symbolically assigned to the category of the left, and it is consistent with this that in some cases his own left should symbolize his status.

There is one point, however, to be made directly. Given that the Mugwe himself belongs symbolically to the category which includes left, it does not necessarily follow that his sacred hand shall also be his left. It is per-

---

[28] Bernardi, p. 95.
[29] Bernardi, pp. 13, 39, 60, 91, 94, 138, 139, 159.

fectly conceivable that his right hand should be endowed with this value, without contradiction to the classification; and Bernardi's account gives reason to suppose that in most of the nine sub-tribes this is indeed the case. Of the five references which he makes to the left hand, three (comprising the greater and most explicit part of the evidence) relate specifically to the Imenti, and one appears to relate to earlier statements about them; while only the remaining one refers to other sub-tribes as well. This is that in which is described the Mugwe's power to halt enemy attacks by raising his left hand: 'This belief was common with the Tharaka, the Chuka, the Igembe and the Imenti; but it is especially with the Imenti that the left hand of the Mugwe has become a source of great awe.'[30] We are told, furthermore, in the quotation first cited, that among the Imenti the people's conception of the Mugwe's left hand is 'unusual'. In most of the sub-tribes, then, the Mugwe's sacred hand may well be his right; while in some, and typically the Imenti, it is his left. This situation has to be taken into account when we try to relate the sacred left hand to the scheme of classification.

It is thus evident that in this context the fundamental distinction to be registered in the scheme must be that between the profane hand of the Mugwe and the sacred hand. By analogical inference we have no choice about the series to which they must respectively be assigned: the sacred, efficacious hand must enter the series on the right of the scheme, in company with what is socially and mythically dominant and superior; while the profane hand must be assigned to the complex of opposite and complementary terms. Note that this is a purely symbolic ascription: which of the hands, organically speaking, shall be reckoned sacred, and which profane, is indeterminate. In fact, among most of the sub-tribes the sacred hand will apparently be the right (as on the most universal grounds we should anticipate), and it is the right hand which will be assigned to the right-hand series in the scheme, where it will be explicitly associated with 'right'. But among the Imenti (to take them as typical of the other sub-tribes in this respect, and among whom this symbolic elaboration is most marked) it is the left hand of the Mugwe which, exceptionally, is sacred; and in accordance with its determining character it must be assigned to the right-hand series in the scheme, in company with the generally dominant hand among the other Mugwe. This may seem puzzling at first, but it is obvious that to assign the left hand of the Imenti Mugwe to the left-hand series simply because of the common feature of leftness, which is a *factual* but not necessarily symbolic attribute, would reverse the ascription of *symbolic* value and constitute a direct contradiction to the symbolic order. The association of the Imenti Mugwe's left hand with the terms of the right-hand series is therefore analogically valid. For Meru in general, I take it, the formula is:—profane hand: sacred hand:: common left: com-

---

[30] Bernardi, p. 110.

mon right. But in the case of the Mugwe of the Imenti the profane hand is his physical right, so that as far as symbolic attributes are concerned his right hand is his left.

The point is made, I hope, that the selection of one hand or the other as sacred (efficacious, pre-eminent) is not necessarily determined, and certainly not by matters of physical fact; and, in general, that the categorization of a term is not in principle deducible from any one of its properties. Symbolic attributes are not necessary, and one's task in elucidating them is not to claim that they have been determined but to show their coherence. I have tried to explain the symbolic attributes of the Mugwe by relating them to the system of ideas of which they are part, and to the mode of classification by which the ideas are ordered. It still remains to say something about why, in the exceptional case of the Mugwe of the Imenti, the left hand should be pre-eminent.

It may be claimed that the position of his left hand is consistent with the classification in a peculiarly satisfactory way. Even in the scheme I have constructed, which must be a very attenuated version of what might be detected in field investigations directed specifically to the issue, the symbolic reinforcement of the Mugwe's position is striking. He belongs to the left, the south (=left), and he is connected with the black clans (he is theirs), the night (in which he and they crossed the water), the west, sunset, darkness, and the colour black. It may be thought appropriate and intellectually satisfying, then, that the ascription of the Mugwe to the left-hand series should be symbolically intensified, among the Imenti, by the value attached to his left hand.

This contention is not a sophistical expedient adopted to give plausibility to an argument, for such re-emphasis of symbolic value has been recorded from other cultures. I shall mention two cases, one from another part of Africa and the other from the Indo-Burma border.

In a recent account of the pastoral Fulani, the following oppositions are recognizable: [31]

| left | right |
| --- | --- |
| east | west |
| back | front |
| north | south |
| feminine | masculine |
| junior homestead | senior homestead |
| genealogical junior | genealogical senior |

---

[31] D. J. Stenning, *Savannah Nomads*, London, 1959, pp. 39–40, 104–5, 106–8. Stenning himself appears not to have paid particular attention to Fulani ideology, and I should like to suggest that a structural analysis to elicit its ruling ideas may prove sociologically illuminating in a most general and profound fashion.

There is no need to expatiate on this scheme, which is easily confirmed by reference to the source. One recognizes in it a differentiation between the two series of terms similar to that of the Meru classification, and even without recounting the ethnographic evidence a consistency of character can be seen between a number of the terms in each series. The point I wish to make concerns the relations north: south:: junior: senior. Within the homestead the bed-shelters of the wives are ranged north to south according to rank. At first sight one would expect the senior wife to be associated with south; but instead, within the feminine part of the homestead, her shelter is placed to the *north,* and the shelters of her junior co-wives in descending order of seniority to the south. Moreover, the senior wife is explicitly called 'north-one', and any junior wife 'south-one'. Here we have, then, an intensification of symbolic character precisely similar to that of the Mugwe's left hand among the Imenti.[32]

The second example relates to the Purum of Manipur. They seek augury by sacrificing a fowl and observing the relative positions of its legs: if the right rests on the left the augury is good, and if the left rests on the right it is bad. (Right is generally regarded as superior to left among all the Kuki tribes of this area, and this kind of symbolic distinction is radical to their culture.) At the name-giving ceremony for a boy a cock is sacrificed and the above rules of interpretation are followed, but at the ceremony for a girl there is a reversal of the symbolism: a hen is sacrificed this time, and it is the left leg resting on the right that is accounted good augury for her.[33]

These examples from very distant and different cultures demonstrate that the symbolic process which I have posited to explain the case of the left hand of the Imenti Mugwe is not a forced interpretation or a cultural singularity. On the contrary, it is an understandable manipulation of symbolic concepts which has its own validity, and which depends for its effect on the categorization with which it at first appears to be in conflict.

It might be emphasized, finally, that in proposing my explanation I do not intend to claim that for Meru in general the left hand has anything of the value which is attached to that of the Imenti Mugwe. Indeed, though Bernardi's ethnography says nothing on this point, I feel sure that for them it is the right hand (as one would expect) that is pre-eminent. I should think, also, that it is the exceptional status of the Imenti Mugwe's left hand, in contrast to the general evaluation of the right, which in his case

---

[32] Unfortunately, we are not told whether the traditional Meru homestead is oriented or whether the relative positions of its members within it are of any significance. Laughton (p. 9) reports merely that the hut of the owner of the homestead is on the right as one enters, and that the huts of his wives are disposed anti-clockwise from this; but this, though it suggests a conventional arrangement, is not symbolically informative.

[33] T. C. Das, *The Purums: an Old Kuki Tribe of Manipur,* Calcutta, 1945, pp. 195, 234; cf. Needham, 1958, pp. 90–91, 97.

marks particularly his exceptional personal status and the nature of his authority.[34]

## V

There is one possible objection to the type of analysis that I have made which I should like to comment on briefly. Hertz has written that dualism is of the essence of primitive thought;[35] and I should go further to say that the symbolic opposition of right and left, and a dualistic categorization of phenomena of which this opposition is paradigmatic, are so common as to seem natural proclivities of the human mind.[36] Does this sort of analysis then have any explanatory merit? That is, if we are dealing with a fundamental mode of thought, the demonstration of the existence of a dualistic classification among the Meru might be thought nugatory or tautological. But this is not the case. Firstly, even a fundamental feature of thought is not necessarily formally manifested in a scheme which is based upon it. Secondly, whatever their logical grounds, symbolic classifications are not everywhere of this dualistic kind: some are triadic, and others feature four, five, or more major categories. They may be reducible, but they are formally distinct from the Meru scheme. Thirdly, although it is possible to maintain that in certain contexts there is a 'natural' symbolism which is immediately apprehensible, irrespective of culture, the particulars of a classification are not necessary; so that to elicit from an ethnographic description the symbolic classification and mode of conceptual relation characteristic of a culture is in fact informative. Finally, the construction of this sort of scheme does not depend simply on ingenuity in relating concepts and values which one has some reason to expect in any case. To the extent that the ethnography is comprehensive and reliable, the form of the classification by which a people order their world imposes itself on the analytical construction: 'Le système est vraiment dans les faits' (Dumézil).

If, in spite of these considerations (which are advanced, after all, in an excessively summary manner for such a large topic), it is still thought that the approach is faulty, there will yet remain a considerable problem: viz. to explain how it is, in that case, that the ethnography permits the coherent interpretation which I have put upon it, and which I would decline to think fortuitous. And a sociological enterprise would still remain to be

---

[34] There is a weaker, because less singular, parallel to this among the Ibo. The right hand is clearly superior and the use of the left is prohibited; but a warrior who has killed a man with his own hands is permitted, as a privilege, to drink with his left. A. G. Leonard, *The Lower Niger and its Tribes*, London, 1906, p. 310.

[35] Hertz, 1909, p. 559.

[36] Needham, 1958, p. 97.

carried out, viz. to determine the range of symbolic significance in social systems of different type, and to explain the correlations of social and symbolic structure.

## VI

I conclude with an indication of the wider theoretical significance of this inquiry. It derives from the work of Durkheim and Mauss[37] and of Hertz, and nearer to our time takes as models the publications of the Leiden school[38] and Hocart,[39] and latterly the stimulating analyses of Lévi-Strauss.[40] A particular issue connected with the continuing theme of these studies, and to which I wish to draw attention in connexion with the Mugwe, is that of the dual nature of sovereignty: the complementary functions of priest and king, the ordering of social life by dualistic notions of religious authority and secular power of which these figures are exemplars. Dumézil has with fascinating effect exploited this type of opposition, compendiously represented by the couple Mitra–Varuṇa, in his analysis of sovereignty in Indo-European society;[41] and Coomaraswamy has similarly, and more minutely, examined the ancient Indian theory of government in terms of the complementary opposites of spiritual authority and temporal power.[42] In contrast to the superficially rather trivial interest of the left hand, it is to these studies that I should wish to relate this modest and tentative note on the Mugwe.

---

[37] E. Durkheim and M. Mauss, 'De quelques formes primitives de classification: contribution à l'étude des représentations collectives', *Année Sociologique*, vol. vi, 1903, pp. 1–72.

[38] e.g. W. H. Rassers, *De Pandji-Roman*, Antwerp, 1922. (It is not generally realized that the Leiden school of anthropology inherited and effectively exploited French sociological ideas at a time when they were all but ignored in Britain and the United States.)

[39] Especially *Kings and Councillors*, Cairo, 1936.

[40] C. Lévi-Strauss, 'The Structural Study of Myth', in T. A. Sebeok (ed.), *Myth: A Symposium*, Philadelphia, 1955, pp. 50–66; 'La Geste d'Asdiwal', *Annuaire 1958–9, École Pratique des Hautes Études* (Section des Sciences Religieuses), Paris, 1958.

[41] G. Dumézil, *Mitra-Varuna: Essai sur deux représentations indo-européennes de la souveraineté*, Paris, 1948 (1st edn. 1940). At the end of his examination of Indo-European notions of sovereignty, Dumézil makes a brief comparison with the Chinese philosophy of *yin-yang* and concludes with the observation: 'Il sera intéressant de confronter le mécanisme indo-européen ici dégagé avec d'autres mécanismes que le *yang* et le *yin*' (p. 211). It is satisfying and intriguing, then, to note how clearly we find in the present African context a Mitra–Varuṇa type of representation of sovereignty: elders = Mitra, the jurist, associated with this world, the day, masculine, senior, and the right; Mugwe = Varuṇa, the magician, associated with the other world, night, feminine, junior, and the left. Cf. also Dumézil, *Les Dieux des Indo-Européens*, Paris, 1952, ch. ii.

[42] A. K. Coomaraswamy, *Spiritual Authority and Temporal Power in the Indian Theory of Government*, New Haven, 1942.

If we are to understand his position in Meru society, it may be more illuminating, it seems to me, and less potentially misleading, to make a structural analysis of the sort I have proposed rather than to try to decide whether he is best described, in our language and symbolic ambience, as leader, public figure, judge, diviner, priest, bishop, prophet, God, chief, or king. All these various appellations, severally applied in order to define one or other aspect of his status, are, as Bernardi himself points out, inexact and misleading. The Mugwe is the Mugwe. What this means may best be understood, I suggest, by concentrating on the functions, attributes, and conceptual associations of the Mugwe in terms of the structure, symbolic as well as social, which gives his office its proper significance. The most general notion by which this structure may be defined is that of complementary dualism, which appears to be a pervasive feature of traditional Meru culture. In the context of the present problem this is expressed in the opposition of secular and religious status: political power is complemented by religious authority.[43]

The distinction of the hands is the commonest manifestation of the mode of classification isolated by this inquiry, and it is the pursuit of an explanation for the singular attributes of the left hand of the Mugwe of the Imenti which has permitted this glimpse of the conceptual order of Meru society.

---

[43] To pursue an indication of the former constitution of Meru society which I have already touched upon, I should guess that Igoki was the politically dominant moiety, while Nkuene possessed the complementary religious authority of which the presence of the Mugwe was the sign. Cf. also the balance between the social superiority of the wife-givers and the ritual indispensability of the wife-takers in certain systems of asymmetric alliance (Needham, 1958).

# The *Mäsqal*-Pole: Religious Conflict and Social Change in Gurageland

# William A. Shack

In *An Analysis of a Social Situation in Modern Zululand,* Professor Gluck-man argued that in situations of conflict, pre-existing groups do not divide neatly into opposing halves, but that groups realign themselves according to the values, motives, and interests governing them at a given time; and that groups who are opposed when facing one situation may find them-selves aligned when the nature of the situation differs.[1] Similar studies of social change in Africa and elsewhere have further advanced Gluckman's contention.[2] In all these studies the analytical procedure adopted was to interpret the situational behaviour of the actors in terms of the influence of the wider social system of which they were a part.[3] However, a great deal of the ethnographic data anthropologists gather in the course of field research are derived from chance observations of social phenomena occurring in relatively unstructured situations within which the individuals involved have a wide range of choice in determining the way they interact with others. This paper is based upon just these sorts of 'imponderable' facts of Gurage life which, when first recorded in the field,[4] appeared less clearly a part of what Malinowski once called 'the real substance of the social fabric'[5] of a changing tribal society than they do now in retrospect. I attempt here to interpret the spontaneous and contradictory behaviour of individual Gurage and groups in the setting of an Ethiopian Christian religious ceremony known as *Mäsqal*. This analysis of situational behaviour is` made in terms of selected aspects of historical or 'processive' social change in Gurageland, a tribal district in south-west Ethiopia.

[1] Gluckman, 1958, p. 26.

[2] See for example, Mitchell, 1956; Turner, 1957; Epstein, 1958; cf. also Geertz, 1957.

[3] Mitchell, 1966, p. 58.

[4] Field research among the western Gurage tribes was carried out in 1957–9, and in 1962–5 under National Institutes of Health Research Grants Nos. MH–07141–03.

[5] Malinowski, 1922, p. 19.

Ethiopian Copts interpret *Mäsqal* as meaning literally 'commemoration of finding the true holy cross'. Thus even nominal participation by only a small number of Gurage tribesmen, people who by tradition are non-Christian believers, is, in itself, a fact of social change. In historical terms, the imposition in the nineteenth century of Christian Ethiopian rule over the western Gurage tribal grouping who call their political federation the 'Seven Gurage Houses', brought substantial changes to Gurage polity. But as I have explained elsewhere,[6] there was no wholesale conversion by Gurage to accept Christian beliefs immediately following *pax Aethiopica* and perhaps fewer than one-tenth of the 350,000 Gurage ardently profess Christianity today. In a later section of this paper I show that the Gurage had practised their own religious tradition of *Mäsqal* long before military conquest of the tribal district was finally achieved by Emperor Menilek II in 1889. But first I describe the politico-religious features of the Ethiopian *Mäsqal* ceremony, for it is against the background of this traditional Christian ritual that later discussion proceeds.

### *Mäsqal* in Christian Ethiopia

Among the Amhara and Tigrinya peoples who inhabit the central highlands of Ethiopia, *Mäsqal* is considered the largest and most important of religious festivals. To these 'Abyssinians', whose introduction to the monophysite doctrine of Christianity took place more than 1,000 years ago, *Mäsqal* replicates the European Christian legend of St. Helena who, upon discovering the 'true cross', is said to have caused bonfires to be lighted on the hills of Palestine and that these were seen by the people of Constantinople.[7] The Ethiopic version of this legend attributes to King Dawit I (1382–1411), a great heroic defender of Christian Ethiopia against Islamic incursions, the introduction of the *Mäsqal* tradition among Ethiopian Copts. Historical records of Ethiopia in the Middle Ages are scanty but some writers have credited the innovation of *Mäsqal* to the reign of Emperor Zara Yacob (1434–68).

Historical traditions apart, *Mäsqal* is, at least today, associated with the agricultural cycle of the highland Christians. In their calendrical reckoning of seasonal changes, the small yellow, so-called '*Mäsqal*-daisy' (*Coreopsis negriana*) coming into full bloom across the highland plateaux in mid

---

[6] Throughout this paper I refer specifically to the western tribal grouping of Gurage, the social structure and religious organization of which I have described fully in *The Gurage* (1966). Although this analysis of the *Mäsqal* ritual is based upon observations carried out among the mainly pagan Chaha tribe of Gurage, the traditional form and meaning of *Mäsqal* obtains as well among other tribes of the 'seven houses' where, as with the Chaha, there also are to be found Christian and Islamic converts.

[7] Hyatt, 1928, p. 165.

September, the Amhara month of *mäsqram*, symbolically announces the ending of the 'big rains', ushering in a new cycle of economic and religious events. *Mäsqal* also has political significance. The annual celebration provides religious ground for repetitive symbolization of the political values of Christian Ethiopians. Customarily the reigning King of Ethiopia (or Emperor since the late nineteenth century) re-enacts the politico-religious role first performed by King Dawit I. In this portrayal the Emperor sets a torch to the ceremonial '*Mäsqal*-pyre'. Nowadays it is fashioned of a pyramid-shaped heap of young eucalyptus trees stripped bare of their bark and branches, and erected near the principal church in the public centre of the political capital and seat of the empire.[8] Since 1911 the royal capital has been located permanently in Addis Ababa. After the ritual torch lighting, Christians who have gathered to join in the *Mäsqal* celebration circle the burning pyre, all the while jubilantly dancing and chanting praise songs to the Emperor. In outlying provinces where Christian churches have now been built in traditionally non-Christian areas, such as Gurageland and other tribal districts in south-west Ethiopia, the ceremonial role of the Emperor is assumed by his principal administrative representative, the District Governor. Here, as in Addis Ababa, the *Mäsqal*-pyre is erected in the public area of the provincial capital, next to the local church, the most conspicuous symbol of the government's presence in a tribal district. Taking the Emperor's role on *Mäsqal*-eve, the District Governor kindles the ceremonial pyre and then leads the laity of Christian converts drawn from among local tribesmen in the ritual of circling the fire, as the entire assembly follow in procession behind the clergy.

## *Mäsqal* in Gurageland

The *Mäsqal* incident next described and from which the analysis of conflict and change in Gurageland proceeds, is set against the background of political and religious relationships between the Gurage and the 'Amhara-Ethiopian' Government.[9]

After more than a decade (1878–89) of devastating warfare, the armies of Emperor Menilek II brought to an end over 400 years of Gurage political independence. Military colonies posted in Gurageland, whose personnel were chiefly Amhara soldiery, frequently quelled Gurage uprisings aimed against Ethiopian rule and assisted the military government in administer-

---

[8] The use of *Podocarpus eucalyptus* in the *Mäsqal* ceremony is obviously of recent origin, certainly not earlier than the reign of Emperor Menilek II (1889–1911) who introduced the arboriculture of this species into Ethiopia.

[9] Although the conquest and subsequent occupation of Gurageland was not exclusively an act of Amhara military aggression, the Gurage refer to this as if it were so. Significantly, they use the terms 'Amhara' and 'government' synonymously.

ing the conquered territory. Coptic priests soon followed the soldiery. Gurage clan chiefs, the highest traditional political authorities, were obliged to accept baptism and to adopt Ethiopic Christian names (Muslim clan chiefs being exempted) in order to retain their chieftainships; but relatively few subjects of chiefs became converts, and then only nominally. In addition to assisting the District Governor in his administration of the tribal lands by keeping peace, collecting tithes (later monetary taxes), and mustering corvée labour for public works, chiefs were also obliged to participate in all religious festivals the government deemed to be of 'national' importance, for instance, *Mäsqal, Timqat* (Epiphany), and *Gəna* (Christmas). If chiefs failed in this, penalties could be exacted from them.

Generally honorific titles such as 'Balabbat'[10] were conferred upon chiefs of traditionally dominant clans who had held political pre-eminence over constituent clans of the same tribe at the time of the conquest. Because of flagrant abuses of the former system of local administration permitted under military rule, a few 'major' clan chiefs gradually usurped the authority of 'minor' clan chiefs and came to be recognized for certain purposes by administrative officials as 'tribal chiefs'.[11] In some clan districts the government installed magistrate courts and police detachments, and built churches near the principal market site where tribal dignitaries had customarily held public meetings. In other clan districts, administrative officials, acting on government orders, destroyed ritual shrines the Gurage had dedicated to their deities, and inside the sacred groves (*gärärä*) which had sheltered them erected Christian churches.

The largest congregation of *Mäsqal* celebrants gathers at the church located in the provincial 'capital' of Gurageland and, appearing alongside the District Governor and other appointed officials, are the most prominent of Gurage clan chiefs and elder dignitaries. When the Christian rituals end, chiefs return to their respective villages joining with the elders there in celebrating *Mäsqal* according to the Gurage way. As with Christian Amhara and Tigrinya, *Mäsqal* is for Gurage also the most important event in their religious calendar, and each of the eight days over which the feasting extends signals a special ritual activity, performance of which symbolically reaffirms ties of kinship and clanship. It is beyond the scope of this discussion to describe in detail the nature of these yearly communal rituals and the ceremonial gift-exchanges through which Gurage kinship sentiments are expressed. But the context and meaning of *Mäsqal* in the Gurage tradition needs to be understood, if only in general terms.

Before the coming of 'Amhara-Ethiopian' rule the Gurage celebrated *Mäsqal* according to their own calendar, that is, in their month called

---

[10] Literally 'owner of the father' and one of the few Amhara-Ethiopian non-military honorific titles which confer status.

[11] See Shack, 1966, pp. 18 ff.; also Perham, 1948, pp. 293 ff.

*Yədar* (June–July), as the rains begin.[12] Traditionally the season of marriage in Gurageland coincided with the celebration of *Mäsqal*. And despite the calendrical changes, neither the form nor meaning of the communal rituals which Gurage perform annually to renew fertility for women and for the earth have declined in their importance. Symbolically, the dual nature of this spiritual function is expressed at the highpoint of the village-organized ritual. Each adult male whose powers of procreation have not yet waned (or at least who still lays claim to fecundity, for 'old' men show a reluctance to admit otherwise) presents a '*Mäsqal*-pole', a long eucalyptus sapling, at the village *mʷəqʸər*, the Gurage version of the Christian *Mäsqal*-pyre. Afterwards, virgin girls from each homestead pay homage at the *mʷəqʸər*-shrine by spreading about freshly collected *Mäsqal*-flowers, all the while chanting praises to Gurage deities. As already mentioned, Christian influences have now encouraged the Gurage to celebrate *Mäsqal* in the Amhara month of *Mäsgram* (September), as do other Ethiopian Copts. So also, in one sense, Christian churches erected in Gurageland under government sponsorship provided for the Gurage permanent shrines for their otiose 'high god' (Yəgzär) who throughout the year is ceremonially honoured only at *Mäsqal*.[13] According to the conceptual hierarchy by which Gurage have ordered their major deities and lesser spirits, Yəgzär appears to have withdrawn some time in the dim past in favour of more active tribal deities and clan spirits around whom important ritual cults now centre. Ritual cults of this nature express a wide variety of Gurage notions pertaining to war and hero worship, illness and good health, ritual transgression and atonement.

On *Mäsqal*-eve each village (*ğäfʷarä*) performs publicly the communal ritual in front of the local earth-shrine, a large *zəgba*-tree (*yäğäfʷarä zəgba*).[14] At other times throughout the year men and women of the village perform sacrifices at this earth-shrine to Božä, the Gurage 'thunder god', and customarily village courts conducted by the headman and elders, especially informal moots called for settling minor disputes, convene under the cooling shade the earth-shrine provides. In Gurage villages where no sacred *zəgba* stands there is usually to be found a prominent 'stele', well-

---

[12] On early Christian influences in southern Ethiopia see Haberland, 1964. However, I would contend that the form and meaning of *Mäsqal* as celebrated by the Gurage, Wallamo, Janjero, and other culturally related tribes in south-west Ethiopia suggests that the rite predates sixteenth-century Christian influences.

[13] The *Mäsqal* rite at which Yəgzär is honoured is performed at earth-shrines, the sacred *zəgba-trees*, dedicated to Božä, the 'thunder god'; it is the latter, an intermediary deity, to whom the high god handed down the responsibility for regulating the social and moral conduct of Gurage in everyday affairs. On the role of Božä in social control among the Gurage see Shack, 1966, p. 159, *passim*.

[14] *Podocarpus gracilior*.

rubbed and bloodstained from repeated sacrificial acts.[15] Whatever its symbolic form, next to the earth-shrine are stood long, freshly cut eucalyptus saplings fashioning a shape which resembles an overcrowded wooden frame of a Plains Indian tepee; and, as already mentioned, the Gurage call their *Mäsqal*-pyre 'yäg̈af<sup>ʷ</sup>arä m<sup>ʷ</sup>əq<sup>y</sup>ər', literally 'the m<sup>ʷ</sup>əq<sup>y</sup>ər of the village'. At the twelfth hour, which in Gurage time-reckoning marks the onset of night (about 6 p.m.), the village headman inaugurates the week-long ceremony by setting a torch (*čənarä*) to the communal *m<sup>ʷ</sup>əq<sup>y</sup>ər,* and each adult village male follows suit. Women and youths of the village then kindle the small *m<sup>ʷ</sup>əq<sup>y</sup>ər* (*yäwäraža*) erected at the entrance to each of their homesteads. The Gurage have no songs or chants praising Yəgzär, at least so far as I am aware, thus customarily this phase of their *Mäsqal* ritual closes with praise songs to Božä, and to Waq, the 'sky god' of Gurage men.[16]

On the following morning about mid-day each homestead head sacrifices a bull on behalf of his family and himself. His wife and unmarried sons and daughters, and married sons with their spouses and children, form a circle encompassing the sacrificial animal as the elder recites a highly stylized prayer to Yəgzär. This rhythmical invocation entreats the high god to bestow on his family blessings of good health and prosperity. All the while calling upon Yəgzär, the elder repeatedly strokes the bull's back from shoulder-hump to hindquarter; and the married sons, standing beside their father, each with his right hand placed on the animal's back, help to strengthen his petition by reciting repetitiously and in unison with other family members—'*amən-amən*'.

The family head severs the bull's jugular vein, after which his wife collects the sacrificial blood in a clay dish (*sera*) whereupon each family member dips in a finger and anoints his or her forehead; the wife later smears with blood the door frames and centre posts of all the sleeping-houses in the compound. The fatty lining (*səwä*) of the bull's stomach is divided among the married sons, the father taking for himself the largest portion which he places around the upper section of the centre post of the main house, at the point where the ceiling rafters join; there it remains

---

[15] These sacrificial stelae are not to be confused with the so-called 'Gran stones' found throughout Gurageland said to mark the invasion route travelled by Mohammad Gran in the sixteenth century during the Islamic conflict with Christian Ethiopia.

[16] Traditionally, each Gurage clan had its own personal Waq who ranked below Yəgzär and Božä, the 'national' deities for the 'Seven Gurage Houses.' When internecine warfare between clans and tribes was rife in the past, Gurage warriors petitioned their clan Waq to bestow upon them ritual blessings to insure against defeat before embarking on military campaigns. The elevation of the Chaha-Mogämänä clan Waq to the status of a tribal or national deity, and hence frequently extolled in praise songs at tribal celebrations like *Mäsqal,* coincided with the formation in the mid nineteenth century of a 'segmentary state', and in this political development the Chaha gained supremacy over other tribes in the federation. For a discussion of these political changes see my paper 'On Gurage Judicial Structure and African Political Theory' (1967).

until the next *Mäsqal*. Afterwards, the dried *səwä* can be taken to a 'wizard' (*šägʷära*) who fashions from it an amulet to be worn about the neck for warding off illness, or evil spirits, or simply as a sign of 'good luck'. Soon after each married son has performed a similar rite on behalf of his own household, the feasting on raw meat begins. Each day of the week-long festival is distinguished by eating a special portion of the sacrificial meat. By the final day, called *adabʷənna*, or 'week from sacrifice day', all of the meat is expected to have been consumed, signifying the close of *Mäsqal*.

## The *Mäsqal* Incident

I identify the principal actors in the 'social drama' now to be described solely by their political titles: District Governor, Chief, Balabbats, Police Chief, Policemen, and 'friends of the Chief'. My role in the drama was chiefly that of an observer, having accepted an invitation from the Chief to witness the *Mäsqal* ceremony in which he was to participate.

On the afternoon of *Mäsqal*-eve I arrived at the home of the Chief to accompany him to the ceremony being held at the local church near the market site in his clan district. As a chief his presence was expected not only for the sake of 'political appearances' but also so that he could participate alongside other tribal dignitaries in the ritual lighting of the Christian *mʷəqʸər*, even though the most prominent ceremonial role, as already explained, would be assumed by the District Governor. *En route* to the church the Chief reminisced freely about what, as he would have it, were the 'good old days' in Gurageland, this bygone era being before the coming of 'Amhara' administration and especially Christianity. Much of the Chief's recall of the pre-conquest era had been experienced personally, but mostly these memories had been relived countless times in the oral traditions handed down from his father, the former Chief, and his contemporaries alive even today. In recounting past events, the Chief underscored the point that when the Gurage practised only their traditional religion there was 'peace' throughout the tribal lands.[17] Coptic Christianity, the Chief held, more than Islamic and Catholic influences, had stripped from *Mäsqal* its traditional meaning for the Gurage, and as an example he cited the ceremony I was about to witness.

The ceremony had already begun when we arrived. Priests were loudly reading selected passages from the Coptic bible in *Ge'ez*, the liturgical language of the Ethiopian church. Several deacons assisted the clergy, chanting psalms in a partly audible off-key monochromatic scale. Young acolytes waving in front of the priests pewter censers burning fragrant

---

[17] On the contrary, internecine tribal warfare in Gurageland was commonplace before the imposition of Ethiopian government rule.

incense sent forth smoke puffs which floated above the sparse assembly of laity. There were in all fewer than thirty men present. The District Governor, Police Chief, and Balabbats all stood on one side of the large ceremonial $m^w \partial q^y \partial r$; and the policemen, when not engaged in ushering into position the late-arriving celebrants, were kept busy chasing away young children from the ceremonial grounds who were jokingly misbehaving. Other men in the assembly assumed the usual solemn religious posture observable at Coptic church services; leaning against long staffs which serve as supports during the several hours of church services for which most people stand. Two old nuns were the only women present, widows who had taken religious vows never to remarry, as only women of this spiritual state are allowed to participate in the ritual. Moreover, they had long ago passed the child-bearing stage of life and their presence could in no way pollute this sacred occasion for men. As more lay worshippers arrived the ceremonial $m^w \partial q^y \partial r$ became almost fully circled. Meanwhile, solemnly engrossed in praying, the priests remained apparently undisturbed by the prankish behaviour of a group of young virgins away in the distant fields who were raucously singing and dancing in preparation for taking part later in the ceremony.

Upon joining the assembly we took places among the Chief's friends who had stationed themselves on the opposite side of the $m^w \partial q^y \partial r$, facing the District Governor. Soon after, the Chief's servant arrived shouldering an immense eucalyptus-pole and showing obvious signs of straining under its weight. Custom prescribed that the pole presented by the Chief to the ceremonial $m^w \partial q^y \partial r$ should be more impressive in length and girth than those of his subjects. It was also customary for each participant on arrival to stand his pole on the $m^w \partial q^y \partial r$ before joining the assembly. But most of the late-arriving celebrants, including the Chief, were unaware of changes in the ceremonial procedure ordered by the District Governor. The Police Chief had been instructed by him to prohibit late arrivals from presenting their poles on the $m^w \partial q^y \partial r$ until the prayer phase of the ceremony ended. Thus when the Chief's servant attempted to approach the $m^w \partial q^y \partial r$ and stand his pole, the policemen, carrying out their instructions, blocked the way, and when an argument ensued they backed up their authority by repeating the orders of the Governor. The Chief's vexation at this action was manifest; and his friends openly expressed their support of him by grumbling disapproval of the Governor's arbitrary orders, which they interpreted as not only unnecessary interference in customary ritual procedure, but still more as a personal slight against their Chief. But the Governor stood firm. Policemen ordered about in the same way other late-comers who attempted to stand their *Mäsqal*-poles while the ceremony was in progress. On each occasion a mild disturbance spread among the Chief and his friends, for most, if not all, of the late-arriving participants were clans-men of the Chief. And before the priests ended their prayers, the assembly had awkwardly divided itself into opposing halves: on one side stood a displeased group consisting of the Chief and his friends; on the other side stood the District Governor, the Police Chief, and the Balabbats.

Near the close of the long prayer-reading service, the monotony of which perhaps had partly dulled the assembly, the Chief seized an opportunity to make a second bid at erecting his *Mäsqal*-pole, ignoring the Governor's orders. By a discreet nod of the head, he signalled his servant to bring forth his ceremonial pole, this time with another of the Chief's servants assisting. Before the policemen became fully aware of what the servants were about, the two men raced forward, attempting to erect the pole by driving its butt-end into the ground, in the manner of pole-vaulting. While the force of the drive enabled the large pole to raise itself, once it reached an upright position it was beyond the control of the servants to steady it. In a matter of seconds the Chief's pole crashed on to the ceremonial $m^w \partial q^y \partial r$, razing it to the ground. The stunned assembly stood motionless. But the priests and deacons, absorbed in their religious duties and giving outwardly the impression of being unmindful of the confusion, continued praying and chanting without interrupting even a stanza of the psalms.

The imprudent actions of the Chief had not only disturbed the sacredness of the ceremony, but with the collapse of the $m^w \partial q^y \partial r$, the highpoint of the ritual, the torch lighting, could not be performed. Friends of the Chief were visibly disappointed by his actions, and the Governor more so: the incident denied him the temporary role of imitating the Emperor, one of the few important events which makes tolerable an otherwise unrewarding political appointment in provincial administration. To reerect the $m^w \partial q^y \partial r$ would delay the ceremony and create even more disorder; yet not having the $m^w \partial q^y \partial r$ would deprive the entire assembly of the full spiritual benefits of the *Mäsqal* ritual. The dilemma worsened for the Chief as the Balabbats openly muttered disapproval of his actions, thus verbally articulating their allegiance to the Governor; the friends of the Chief cautiously avoided indicating their position on the issue. Finally the Chief broke the impasse. Stepping forward into the tumbled mass of poles he began clearing the site to erect a new $m^w \partial q^y \partial r$, his servants promptly following his lead. Still the friends of the Chief showed reluctance to joining with him, though one or two of his most loyal supporters awkwardly pretended to assist him after first seeking a sign of approval from the District Governor. He gave none.

While the Chief and his servants hastily attempted to set up the $m^w \partial q^y \partial r$, the priests began chanting the closing psalms of the religious service. Friends of the Chief joined in with him, this time without seeking the Governor's approval, and together they hastily erected a crude replica of the original $m^w \partial q^y \partial r$. But again the task of setting the Chief's pole upright proved difficult even though several men assisted, and by the time it had been erected and made steady, the ceremony closed. Now the priests made no attempt at disguising their annoyance at the Chief's actions, and without lighting the $m^w\partial q^y\partial r$ abruptly led from the ceremonial grounds a procession consisting of the District Governor, Police Chief, policemen, and Balabbats. However, sensing that even the newly erected $m^w\partial q^y\partial r$ was straining under the weight of his pole and was on the verge of collapsing, the Chief quickly called for a torch and assuming the role of the Emperor's representative, he kindled the pyre. Before the fire could spread, the $m^w\partial q^y\partial r$ fell again, quenching the small blaze. By then the District Governor and his party were well out of sight; the Chief and his friends remained the only witnesses from the original assembly.

The second collapse of the $m^w\partial q^y\partial r$ spontaneously agitated the Chief and his friends into rebellious behaviour. No longer constrained by the District Governor's presence, they gathered dry brush to kindle a new fire, and broke into smaller pieces the long *Mäsqal*-poles. But the Chief's pole remained protruding conspicuously from the pyre and after his friends failed in several attempts to break the pole by hand, an axe was finally employed. This done, young girls from the village approached the pyre carrying bouquets of '*Mäsqal*-daisies' which they tossed on to the fire, as they circled round it, dancing and singing traditional Gurage songs. Then the Chief joined in the ritual dance, leading in procession his friends around the *Mäsqal* pyre. This occasioned the singing of heroic songs honouring the Chief, his late father, and famous old warriors; these chants inevitably include praises to Waq and Božä. Leaving the church-yard, the procession headed towards the village of the Chief, collecting in its wake those men who had absented themselves from the Christian ceremony. As the procession passed groups of women stationed along the way, they greeted the Chief with ululations of joy, the shrilling form of praise reserved for important tribal dignitaries. To signal the arrival of the Chief at his compound the small *yäwäražä* was kindled, as his wife, children, and retainers greeted him with song and dance. After an hour or so of ceremonial singing and dancing, largely encouraged by the Chief passing around *tallä*-beer and the more potent distilled *areq*, his friends and other subjects finally dispersed into the night, ringing the stillness with traditional Gurage songs.

## Social Conflict and Social Change in Gurageland

The *Mäsqal* incident described above is, I suggest, symptomatic of a wide range of everyday social situations which reflect the relationships of co-operation and conflict between Amhara and Gurage. Following Gluckman's usage, I have termed the incident which arose out of the contradictory behaviour of the principal actors in the *Mäsqal* ceremony a 'social situation': that is 'the behaviour on some occasion of members of a community as such, analysed and compared with their behaviour on other occasions, so that the analysis reveals the underlying system of relationships between the social structure of the community'.[18] Gurage and Amhara are involved in a network of relationships, the integrating factors of which promote separation of the two groups in particular situations and co-operation between them in other situations. The *Mäsqal* incident has analytical value in demonstrating the process of social conflict and change taking place in Gurageland when set in the wider context of relationships between Gurage and Amhara which I now summarily describe.

For over three-quarters of a century Amhara-Ethiopian rule in Gurage-land has chiefly been extended through the Gurage tribal authority system. Like the Native Authority System formerly administered under British Indirect Rule in colonial Africa, Gurage clan chiefs, by and large, retained their traditional positions of authority and where necessary received government backing in enforcing tax collections and keeping peace. No 'Paramount Chieftainship' was established in Gurageland, however. One effect of government intervention in the tribal district was to stabilize the office of clan chieftainship by eliminating rivalry over political succession between powerful clan segments which, in the past, often erupted in open hostility. In turn this provided fertile ground for the expression of old political grievances in new modes; for the authority of chiefs of some dominant clans was extended beyond their traditional territorial-political boundaries while the authority of other clan chiefs was limited to that of government-sponsored 'go-betweens' bearing, as has been shown above, the honorary title of Balabbat.

It appears that the association of the Balabbats with the District Governor and his party, in opposition to that of the chief, in the *Mäsqal* ceremony reflects the longstanding conflict between chiefs and Balabbats and the exclusion of the latter from positions of authority under 'Amhara' rule. With the gradual change towards bureaucracy in tribal administration, Balabbats who align themselves in opposition to the Chief, whenever situations are created which allow for such alignments, stand to gain political patronage in the form of lower-grade civil service appointments which, as with traditional tribute, is reapportioned among kinsmen and faithful subjects. But an ostentatious display of aggressiveness or antagonism towards the Chief on the part of Balabbats would obviously alienate them from most Gurage who whole-heartedly support the Chief in his political opposition to the Amhara. Friends of the Chief manifest their loyalty to him whenever and wherever the circumstances permit, the *Mäsqal* incident being one such event. In short, Balabbats must select particular situations within which shifting attachment from one group to that of another is made less conspicuous by the nature of the occasion; the *Mäsqal* incident allowed for such an expression of structural differences in a changing tribal authority system on at least two scores. One was the way Balabbats seized

[18] Gluckman, 1958, p. 9. Cf. also Gluckman, 1949, p. 6.

upon the opportunity created by the Chief's late arrival at the ceremony to align themselves with the District Governor, whereas customarily they constitute the Chief's personal retinue at all his public appearances. For another, the series of events which led up to the unfortunate *Mäsqal* incident provided for the Balabbats a ready-made situation for faintly concealing their political opposition to the Chief behind a veil of sacro-religious values which masked the credibility of their loyalty to him.

The Chief, the guardian of Gurage tradition, law, custom, and values, symbolizes the 'Gurage nation'. In public relations with the District Governor, the Chief reflects Gurage-Amhara political opposition at the highest level. He pleads on behalf of Gurage tribesmen generally, let alone his own clansmen, brought to trial in government courts,[19] and he loans money and cattle to meet judicial assessments levied against them; he exercises leniency in collecting taxes from Gurage who have experienced some personal hardship, even at the risk of placing in jeopardy his own political future.

A similar expression of group opposition was evident in the behaviour of Christian Gurage who abstained from participating in the church-held *Mäsqal* ceremony but welcomed the Chief on his return in the traditional style, thereby announcing the values they associate with the Gurage form of *Mäsqal*. Even so this separation of Gurage and Amhara into opposing political groups is not to be interpreted as a static equilibrium of the social structure whereby a fictional balance of some sort is maintained, as the following facts show. For when political conflict between Gurage tribes was suppressed under Amhara rule the Gurage tribes jointly opposed the government; but Gurage and Amhara soldiery fought side-by-side in helping to liberate Ethiopia from Italian occupation (1936–41),[20] thus showing that in certain contexts of political relationships they form a single Ethiopian community. After the restoration of the central government and of Amhara rule, Gurage–Amhara political relationships assumed their pre-war form.

Gurage integration into the wider Ethiopian community, in the field of economic relationships, takes place principally through wage-labour migration and cash-crop farming. The economic return from these activities provide Gurage with cash to pay government tax, part of which is utilized to provide the administration of their country. Chiefs, Balabbats, and village headmen are obliged to co-operate with the District Governor in tax collections and in so doing often bring themselves into open conflict with their subjects who, in the main, view land tax as an unnecessary burden imposed upon them by the government. Unlike traditional tribute

---

[19] However, the Gurage traditional court system is still retained and continues to operate alongside government-appointed courts in Gurageland. For a description of the former see Shack, 1966, p. 157 ff., and 1967.

[20] So also, the Gurage took up arms in support of Menilek II against Italian armies at the Battle of Aduwa (1895–6).

which the Gurage paid to chiefs and ritual dignitaries who used to redis-
tribute part of their wealth to their subjects, the Gurage do not see any
tangible benefit in such government-financed development schemes as all-
weather roads, public-health clinics, and improved schools. In fact, major
improvements in tribal welfare have been brought about principally
through self-help schemes instigated by migrant Gurage in the towns
together wtih the assistance of rural kinsmen, and in these voluntary
sponsored programmes the government takes no part.[21]

Thus tribal authority figures who are often in conflict with one another,
in such political situations as rivalry over appointments in the local
bureaucratic administration, here form a group in co-operation, supporting tribal welfare schemes, even at the risk of fines and imprisonment for
failing to carry out government orders. Labour migration for wage employment and cash-crop farming bring Gurage workers, traders, and entre-
preneurs into the wider economic sector of the Amhara community. Gurage
exchange cheap wage labour, coffee, and ensete-fibres, the by-products of
their staple crop, in return for low-quality manufactured trade goods,
livestock, grains, and a few luxury items.

*Mäsqal* is only one of several religious ceremonies which link together
Gurage and Amhara. Annual celebrations to such popular saints of
Ethiopian Christendom as Mariam, Michael, Gabriel, as with the observ-
ances of *Fasiqa* (Esaster) and *Gəna* (Christmas), all similarly concern
Gurage–Amhara relationships in the religious sphere of Ethiopian community life. As do other Ethiopian Copts, Christian Gurage abstain from
meat for more than 100 days of the year; they present gifts to priests on
special religious occasions for past services performed; they distribute
alms to the destitute in the name of a patron saint as an act of Christian
charity; they are baptized and buried according to Coptic prescriptions.
But Christian Gurage are also polygynous; they invoke traditional deities
whenever an extra spiritual uplift is needed; they resort to special paraphernalia to ward off misfortune; they consult traditional diviners to
diagnose illnesses and to render explanations for unusual phenomena; and
they are often possessed by evil spirits, the exorcism of which can be
effected only by performing sacrificial placation rites and periodically
presenting tribute to the ritual dignitary who controls malevolent forces.[22]

---

[21] I discuss the role of Gurage urban voluntary associations in maintaining the rural–
urban network of relationships in a forthcoming article, 'Urban Tribalism and the
Cultural Process of Urbanization in Ethiopia'.

[22] Although Amhara and Gurage Christians both share among some of these features,
there are to be noted obvious differences between them, especially in the resort to
magical cures. While the *däbtära* (scribe or canon) practising exorcising magic is
tacitly tolerated by the Ethiopian Church, the *tänqway*, or sorcerer, whose activities
are performed secretly, is not. Christian Gurage remain clients of the *šägwära* and
other traditional ritual agents of magic and sorcery, rather than consulting the *däbtära*,
as do most Christian Amhara.

During the Menilek period of rule over Gurageland, Amhara efforts to destroy the sacred forests in Gurageland, which symbolize to Gurage the shrines of their deities, to be replaced by Christian churches, had the unforseen negative consequence of increasing traditional cult activities and giving renewed impetus to Islam to which many Gurage became converts; the emergence of the Islamic prophetic cult of Shaikh Sayyid Budella is a striking example.[23] In describing the background to the *Mäsqal* incident, I have already pointed out how chiefs nominally support the religious aspects of government administration in Gurageland by participating in Christian festivities which reflect 'national' policy. Yet at the same time, chiefs symbolically uphold the traditional religious values of the Gurage by participating in annual cult ceremonials held in honour of Waq, the 'sky god', and Božä, the 'god of thunder'. And in these rituals, chiefs provide continuity for traditional politico-religious customs, thereby minimizing the radical effects of socio-cultural change.

To sum up, I have attempted to show that the spontaneous behaviour of Gurage actors in a particular *Mäsqal* ceremony, in reacting to the series of events centring round the erection of the $m^w \partial q^y \partial r$, expressed the various contradictory motives, values, and interests which they share as individuals and groups in a changing Gurage society. In social interaction these contradictions most likely become recognizable conflicts whenever the traditional beliefs and values which are expressive of the group's socio-cultural system are inconsistent with the particular situation that change has forced upon them. Because of the 'optative' element in social life, individuals and groups can, in the daily round of life, select from these contradictions those beliefs and interests which allow shifts in allegiance and position according to the factors influencing their decisions at a given time.[24] Thus whether they are Gurage celebrants at a *Mäsqal* rite, Zulu onlookers at the dedication ceremony of a bridge, or Javanese mourners at a funeral, there is an element of choice open which enables individuals to define the social situation and to behave according to its dictates. The analysis of situational behaviour is a useful operational device, a point of departure for defining the field of social interaction within which the actions of opposing individuals and groups minimize conflict.

**Bibliography**

EPSTEIN, A. L. 1958. *Politics in an Urban African Community*. Manchester University press.

GEERTZ, C. 1957. 'Ritual and Social Change: A Javanese Example', *American Anthropologist*, lix. 32–54.

---

[23] Shack, 1966, pp. 190–4.

[24] Mitchell, 1966, pp. 59–60.

GLUCKMAN, M. 1949. *An Analysis of the Sociological Theories of Bronislaw Malinowski*. Rhodes-Livingstone Paper, no. 16. Oxford University press.

———— 1958. *An Analysis of a Social Situation in Modern Zululand*. Rhodes-Livingstone Paper, no. 28. Manchester University press.

HABERLAND, E. 1964. 'The Influence of the Christian Ethiopian Empire on Southern Ethiopia', *Journal of Semitic Studies*, ix. 235–8.

HYATT, H. 1928. *The Church of Abyssinia*. Luzac, London.

MALINOWSKI, B. 1922. *Argonauts of the Western Pacific*. Routledge & Kegan Paul, London.

MITCHELL, C. 1956. *The Kalela Dance*. Rhodes-Livingstone Paper, no. 27. Manchester University press.

———— 1966. 'Theoretical Orientations in African Urban Studies', in *The Social Anthropology of Complex Societies*, ed. M. Banton. Tavistock, London.

PERHAM, M. 1948. *The Government of Ethiopia*. Oxford University press.

SHACK, W. A. 1966. *The Gurage: A People of the Ensete Culture*. Oxford University press for the International African Institute.

———— 1966. 'Urban Tribalism and the Cultural Process of Urbanization in Ethiopia', in *Urban Anthropology*, eds. A. W. Southall and E. Bruner. Aldine press, Chicago.

———— 1967. 'On Gurage Judicial Structure and African Political Theory', *Journal of Ethiopian Studies*, v. 89–101.

TURNER, V. W. 1957. *Schism and Continuity in an African Society*. Manchester University press.

# African Traditional Thought and Western Science[1]

# Robin Horton

## Part I. From Tradition to Science

The first part of this paper seeks to develop an approach to traditional African thought already sketched in several previous contributions to this journal.[2] My approach to this topic is strongly influenced by the feeling that social anthropologists have often failed to understand traditional religious thought for two main reasons. First, many of them have been unfamiliar with the theoretical thinking of their own culture. This has deprived them of a vital key to understanding. For certain aspects of such thinking are the counterparts of those very features of traditional thought which they have tended to find most puzzling. Secondly, even those familiar with theoretical thinking in their own culture have failed to recognise its African equivalents, simply because they have been blinded by a difference of idiom. Like Consul Hutchinson wandering among the Bubis of Fernando Po, they have taken a language very remote from their own to be no language at all.

My approach is also guided by the conviction that an exhaustive exploration of features common to modern Western and traditional African thought should come before the enumeration of differences. By taking things in this order, we shall be less likely to mistake differences of idiom for differences of substance, and more likely to end up identifying those features which really do distinguish one kind of thought from the other.

Not surprisingly, perhaps, this approach has frequently been misunderstood. Several critics have objected that it tends to blur the undeniable

---

[1] I am grateful to the Institute of African Studies, University of Ibadan, for a grant towards the publication of this paper. The Institute is, however, in no way responsible for the opinions expressed.

[2] 'Destiny and the Unconscious in West Africa', *Africa*, April 1961; 'The Kalabari World-View: an Outline and Interpretation', *Africa,* July 1962; 'Ritual Man in Africa', *Africa*, April 1964.

distinction between traditional and scientific thinking; that indeed it presents traditional thinking as a species of science.[3] In order to clear up such misunderstandings, I propose to devote the second part of this paper to enumerating what I take to be the salient differences between traditional and scientific thinking and to suggesting a tentative explanation of these differences. I shall also explore how far this explanation can help us to understand the emergence of science in Western culture.

In consonance with this programme, I shall start by setting out a number of general propositions on the nature and functions of theoretical thinking. These propositions are derived, in the first instance, from my own training in Biology, Chemistry, and Philosophy of Science. But, as I shall show, they are highly relevant to traditional African religious thinking. Indeed, they make sense of just those features of such thinking that anthropologists have often found most incomprehensible.

### 1. *The Quest for Explanatory Theory Is Basically the Quest for Unity Underlying Apparent Diversity; for Simplicity Underlying Apparent Complexity; for Order Underlying Apparent Disorder; for Regularity Underlying Apparent Anomaly*

Typically, this quest involves the elaboration of a scheme of entities or forces operating 'behind' or 'within' the world of common-sense observations. These entities must be of a limited number of kinds and their behaviour must be governed by a limited number of general principles. Such a theoretical scheme is linked to the world of everyday experience by statements identifying happenings within it with happenings in the everyday world. In the language of Philosophy of Science, such identification statements are known as Correspondence Rules. Explanations of observed happenings are generated from statements about the behaviour of entities in the theoretical scheme, plus Correspondence-Rule statements. In the sciences, well-known explanatory theories of this kind include the kinetic theory of gases, the planetary-atom theory of matter, the wave theory of light, and the cell theory of living organisms.

One of the perennial philosophical puzzles posed by explanations in terms of such theories derives from the Correspondence-Rule statements. In what sense can we really say that an increase of pressure in a gas 'is' an increase in the velocity of a myriad tiny particles moving in an otherwise empty space? How can we say that a thing is at once itself and something quite different? A great variety of solutions has been proposed to this puzzle. The modern positivists have taken the view that it is the things of common sense that are real, while the 'things' of theory are mere fictions

---

[3] See, for instance, Beattie, 1966.

useful in ordering the world of common sense. Locke, Planck, and others have taken the line that it is the 'things' of theory that are real, while the things of the everyday world are mere appearances. Perhaps the most up-to-date line is that there are good reasons for conceding the reality both of common-sense things and of theoretical entities. Taking this line implies an admission that the 'is' of Correspondence-Rule statements is neither the 'is' of identity nor the 'is' of class-membership. Rather, it stands for a unity-in-duality uniquely characteristic of the relation between the world of common sense and the world of theory.

What has all this got to do with the gods and spirits of traditional African religious thinking? Not very much, it may appear at first glance. Indeed, some modern writers deny that traditional religious thinking is in any serious sense theoretical thinking. In support of their denial they con-trast the simplicity, regularity, and elegance of the theoretical schemas of the sciences with the unruly complexity and caprice of the world of gods and spirits.[4]

But this antithesis does not really accord with modern field-work data. It is true that, in a very superficial sense, African cosmologies tend towards proliferation. From the point of view of sheer number, the spirits of some cosmologies are virtually countless. But in this superficial sense we can point to the same tendency in Western cosmology, which for every common-sense unitary object gives us a myriad molecules. If, however, we recog-nize that the aim of theory is the demonstration of a limited number of *kinds* of entity or process underlying the diversity of experience, then the picture becomes very different. Indeed, one of the lessons of such recent studies of African cosmologies as Middleton's *Lugbara Religion,* Lien-hardt's *Divinity and Experience,* Fortes's *Oedipus and Job,* and my own articles on Kalabari, is precisely that the gods of a given culture do form a scheme which interprets the vast diversity of everyday experience in terms of the action of a relatively few *kinds* of forces. Thus in Middleton's book, we see how all the various oppositions and conflicts in Lugbara experience are interpreted as so many manifestations of the single underlying opposi-tion between ancestors and *adro* spirits. Again, in my own work, I have shown how nearly everything that happens in Kalabari life can be inter-preted in terms of a scheme which postulates three basic *kinds* of forces: ancestors, heroes, and waterspirits.

The same body of modern work gives the lie to the old stereotype of the gods as capricious and irregular in their behaviour. For it shows that each category of beings has its appointed functions in relation to the world of observable happenings. The gods may sometimes appear capricious to the unreflective ordinary man. But for the religious expert charged with the diagnosis of spiritual agencies at work behind observed events, a basic

[4] See Beattie, op. cit.

modicum of regularity in their behaviour is the major premiss on which his work depends. Like atoms, molecules, and waves, then, the gods serve to introduce unity into diversity, simplicity into complexity, order into disorder, regularity into anomaly.

Once we have grasped that this is their intellectual function, many of the puzzles formerly posed by 'mystical thinking' disappear. Take the exasperated, wondering puzzlements of Levy-Bruhl over his 'primitive mentality'. How could primitives believe that a visible, tangible object was at once its solid self and the manifestation of an immaterial being? How could a man literally see a spirit in a stone? These puzzles, raised so vividly by Levy-Bruhl, have never been satisfactorily solved by anthropologists. 'Mystical thinking' has remained uncomfortably, indigestibly *sui generis*. And yet these questions of Levy-Bruhl's have a very familiar ring in the context of European philosophy. Indeed, if we substitute atoms and molecules for gods and spirits, these turn out to be the very questions cited a few paragraphs back—questions posed by modern scientific theory in the minds of Berkeley, Locke, Quine, and a whole host of European philosophers from Newton's time onwards.

Why is it that anthropologists have been unable to see this? One reason, as I suggested before, is that many of them move only in the common-sense world of Western culture, and are unfamiliar with its various theoretical worlds. But perhaps familiarity with Western theoretical thinking is not by itself enough. For a thoroughly unfamiliar idiom can still blind a man to a familiar form of thought. Because it prevents one from taking anything for granted, an unfamiliar idiom can help to show up all sorts of puzzles and problems inherent in an intellectual process which normally seems puzzle-free. But this very unfamiliarity can equally prevent us from seeing that the puzzles and problems are ones which crop up on our own doorstep. Thus it took a 'mystical' theorist like Bishop Berkeley to see the problems posed by the materialistic theories of Newton and his successors; but he was never able to see that the same problems were raised by his own theoretical framework. Again, it takes materialistically inclined modern social anthropologists to see the problems posed by the 'mystical' theories of traditional Africa; but, for the same reasons, such people can hardly be brought to see these very problems arising within their own theoretical framework.

## 2. *Theory Places Things in a Causal Context Wider than that Provided by Common Sense*

When we say that theory displays the order and regularity underlying apparent disorder and irregularity, one of the things we mean is that it provides a causal context for apparently 'wild' events. Putting things in a causal context is, of course, one of the jobs of common sense. But although it does this job well at a certain level, it seems to have limitations. Thus the principal tool of common sense is induction or 'putting two and two together', the process of inference so beloved of the positivist philosophers. But a man can only 'put two and two together' if he is looking in the right direction. And common sense furnishes him with a pair of horse-blinkers which severely limits the directions in which he can look. Thus common-sense thought looks for the antecedents of any happening amongst events adjacent in space and time: it abhors action at a distance. Again, common sense looks for the antecedents of a happening amongst events that are in some way commensurable with it. Common sense is at the root of the hard-dying dictum 'like cause, like effect'. Gross incommensurability defeats it.

Now one of the essential functions of theory is to help the mind transcend these limitations. And one of the most obvious achievements of modern scientific theory is its revelation of a whole array of causal connexions which are quite staggering to the eye of common sense. Think for instance of the connexion between two lumps of a rather ordinary looking metal, rushing towards each other with a certain acceleration, and a vast explosion capable of destroying thousands of people. Or think again of the connexion between small, innocuous water-snails and the disease of bilharziasis which can render whole populations lazy and inept.

Once again, we may ask what relevance all this has to traditional African religious thinking. And once again the stock answer may be 'precious little'. For a widely current view of such thinking still asserts that it is more interested in the supernatural causes of things than it is in their natural causes. This is a misinterpretation closely connected with the one we discussed in the previous section. Perhaps the best way to get rid of it is to consider the commonest case of the search for causes in traditional Africa —the diagnosis of disease. Through the length and breadth of the African continent, sick or afflicted people go to consult diviners as to the causes of their troubles. Usually, the answer they receive involves a god or other spiritual agency, and the remedy prescribed involves the propitiation or calling-off of this being. But this is very seldom the whole story. For the diviner who diagnoses the intervention of a spiritual agency is also expected to give some acceptable account of what moved the agency in question to intervene. And this account very commonly involves reference to some event in the world of visible, tangible happenings. Thus if a diviner diagnoses the action of witchcraft influence or lethal medicine spirits, it is usual for him to add something about the human hatreds, jealousies, and misdeeds, that have brought such agencies into play. Or, if he diagnoses the wrath of an ancestor, it is usual for him to point to the human breach of kinship morality which has called down this wrath.

Although I do not think he has realized its full significance for the study of traditional religious thought, Victor Turner has brought out this point beautifully in his analyses of divination and the diagnosis of disease amongst the Ndembu people of Central Africa.[5] Turner shows how, in diagnosing the causes of some bodily affliction, the Ndembu diviner not only refers to unseen spiritual forces, but also relates the patient's condition to a whole series of disturbances in his social field. Turner refers to divination as 'social analysis', and says that Ndembu believe a patient 'will not get better until all the tensions and aggressions in the group's interrelations have been brought to light and exposed to ritual treatment'. Although Turner himself does not refer to comparable material from other African societies, Max Gluckman, drawing on data from Tiv, Lugbara, Nyakyusa, Yao, and several other traditional societies, has recently shown that the kind of analysis he has made of divination among the Ndembu is very widely applicable.[6] The point in all this is that the traditional diviner faced with a disease does not just refer to a spiritual agency. He uses ideas about this agency to link disease to causes in the world of visible, tangible events.

The situation here is not very different from that in which a puzzled American layman, seeing a large mushroom cloud on the horizon, consults a friend who happens to be a physicist. On the one hand, the physicist may refer him to theoretical entities. 'Why this cloud?' 'Well, a massive fusion of hydrogen nuclei has just taken place.' Pushed further, however, the physicist is likely to refer to the assemblage and dropping of a bomb containing certain special substances. Substitute 'disease' for 'mushroom cloud', 'spirit anger' for 'massive fusion of hydrogen nuclei', and 'breach of kinship morality' for 'assemblage and dropping of a bomb', and we are back again with the diviner. In both cases reference to theoretical entities is used to link events in the visible, tangible world (natural effects) to their antecedents in the same world (natural causes).

To say of the traditional African thinker that he is interested in supernatural rather than natural causes makes little more sense, therefore, than to say of the physicist that he is interested in nuclear rather than natural causes. In fact, both are making the same use of theory to transcend the limited vision of natural causes provided by common sense.

Granted this common preoccupation with natural causes, the fact remains that the causal link between disturbed social relations and disease or misfortune, so frequently postulated by traditional religious thought, is one which seems somewhat strange and alien to many Western medical scientists. Following the normal practice of historians of Western ideas, we can approach the problem of trying to understand this strange causal notion from two angles. First of all, we can inquire what influence a particular theoretical idiom has in moulding this and similar traditional notions. Secondly, we can inquire whether the range of experience avail-

---

[5] Turner, 1961 and 1964.

[6] Gluckman, 1965. See especially chapter vi: 'Mystical Disturbance and Ritual Adjustment'.

able to members of traditional societies has influenced causal notions by throwing particular conjunctions of events into special prominence.

Theory, as I have said, places events in a wider causal context than that provided by common sense. But once a particular theoretical idiom has been adopted, it tends to direct people's attention toward certain kinds of causal linkage and away from others. Now most traditional African cultures have adopted a personal idiom as the basis of their attempt to understand the world. And once one has adopted such an idiom, it is a natural step to suppose that personal beings underpin, amongst other things, the life and strength of social groups. Now it is in the nature of a personal being who has his designs thwarted to visit retribution on those who thwart him. Where the designs involve maintaining the strength and unity of a social group, members of the group who disturb this unity are thwarters, and hence are ripe for punishment. Disease and misfortune are the punishment. Once a personal idiom has been adopted, then, those who use it become heavily predisposed towards seeing a nexus between social disturbance and individual affliction.

Are these traditional notions of cause merely artefacts of the prevailing theoretical idiom, fantasies with no basis in reality? Or are they responses to features of people's experience which in some sense are 'really there'? My own feeling is that, although these notions are ones to which people are pre-disposed by the prevailing theoretical idiom, they also register certain important features of the objective situation.

Let us remind ourselves at this point that modern medical men, though long blinded to such things by the fantastic success of the germ theory of disease, are once more beginning to toy with the idea that disturbances in a person's social life can in fact contribute to a whole series of sicknesses, ranging from those commonly thought of as mental to many more commonly thought of as bodily. In making this rediscovery, however, the medical men have tended to associate it with the so-called 'pressures of modern living'. They have tended to imagine traditional societies as psychological paradises in which disease-producing mental stresses are at a minimum. And although this view has never been put to adequate test, it is one held by many doctors practising in Africa.

In criticism of this view, I would suggest that the social life of the small, relatively self-contained and undifferentiated communities typical of much of traditional Africa contains its own peculiar and powerful sources of mental stress. Let me recall a few:

(a) When tension arises between people engaged in a particular activity, it tends to colour a large sector of their total social life. For in societies of this kind a person performs a whole series of activities with the same set of partners.

(b) Being caught up in hostilities or caught out in a serious breach of social norms is particularly crushing, since in societies of this kind it is often extremely hard to move out of the field in which the trouble arose.

(c) There are a limited number of roles to be filled, and little scope for personal choice in the filling of them. Hence there is always a relatively large number of social misfits.

Apart from these sources of stress peculiar to such communities, there are others commonly thought to be absent from them, but which they in fact share with modern industrial societies. I am thinking here of fundamental inconsistencies in the values taught to members of traditional communities. Thus aggressive, thrusting ambition may be inculcated on one hand, and a cautious reluctance to rise above one's neighbour on the other. Ruthless individualism may be inculcated on one hand, and acceptance of one's ascribed place in a lineage-system on the other. Such inconsistencies are often as sharp as those so well known in modern industrial societies. As an anthropological field-worker, one has come close enough to these sources of stress to suspect that the much-advertised 'pressures of modern living' may at times be the milder affliction. One may even suspect that some of the young Africans currently rushing from the country to the towns are in fact escaping from a more oppressive to a less oppressive psychological environment.

The point I am trying to make here is that if life in modern industrial society contains sources of mental stress adequate to causing or exacerbating a wide range of sicknesses, so too does life in traditional village communities. Hence the need to approach traditional religious theories of the social causation of sickness with respect. Such respect and readiness to learn is, I suggest, particularly appropriate with regard to what is commonly known as mental disease. I say this because the grand theories of Western psychiatry have a notoriously insecure empirical base and are probably culture-bound to a high degree.

Then again, there are the traditional social-cause explanations of all those mysterious bodily ailments doctors try in vain to cure in their hospitals, and which finally get cleared up by traditional religious healers. Though we have no statistics on such cases, there is little doubt that they are always cropping up. Judging from a recent symposium on traditional medicine,[7] even unromantic, hard-headed social anthropologists are now generally convinced of their reality. Accounts of cases of this kind suggest that they very often fall into the category which Western medical practitioners themselves have increasingly come to label psychosomatic—i.e. marked by definite bodily changes but touched off or exacerbated by mental stress. This category includes gastric and duodenal ulcer, migraine,

---

[7] Kiev (ed.) 1964, *passim*.

chronic limb pains, and certain kinds of paralysis, hypertension, diabetes, and dermatitis. It includes many agonizing and several potentially lethal complaints. Forward-looking Western medical men now agree that effective treatment of this kind of illness will eventually have to include some sort of diagnosis of and attempt to combat stress-producing disturbances in the individual's social life. As for trying to find out what the main kinds of stress-producing disturbances are in a particular traditional society, the modern doctor can probably do no better than start by taking note of the diagnoses produced by a traditional religious healer working in such a society.

Finally, there are those diseases in which the key factor is definitely an infecting micro-organism. Even here, I suggest, traditional religious theory has something to say which is worth listening to.

Over much of traditional Africa, let me repeat, we are dealing with small-scale, relatively self-contained communities. These are the sort of social units that, as my friend Dr. Oruwariye puts it, 'have achieved equilibrium with their diseases'. A given population and a given set of diseases have been co-existing over many generations. Natural selection has played a considerable part in developing human resistance to diseases such as malaria, typhoid, small-pox, dysentery, etc. In addition, those who survive the very high peri-natal mortality have probably acquired an extra resistance by the very fact of having lived through one of these diseases just after birth. In such circumstances, an adult who catches one of these (for Europeans) killer diseases has good chances both of life and of death. In the absence of antimalarials or antibiotics, what happens to him will depend very largely on other factors that add to or subtract from his con-siderable natural resistance. In these circumstances the traditional healer's efforts to cope with the situation by ferreting out and attempting to remedy stress-producing disturbances in the patient's social field is probably very relevant. Such efforts may seem to have a ludicrously marginal importance to a hospital doctor wielding a nivaquine bottle and treating a non-resistant European malaria patient. But they may be crucial where there is no niva-quine bottle and a considerable natural resistance to malaria.

After reflecting on these things the modern doctor may well take some of these traditional causal notions seriously enough to put them to the test. If the difficulties of testing can be overcome, and if the notions pass the test, he will end up by taking them over into his own body of beliefs. At the same time, however, he will be likely to reject the theoretical frame-work that enabled the traditional mind to form these notions in the first place.

This is fair enough; for although, as I have shown, the gods and spirits do perform an important theoretical job in pointing to certain interesting forms of causal connexion, they are probably not very useful as the basis of a wider view of the world. Nevertheless, there do seem to be a few cases in which the theoretical framework of which they are the basis may have something to contribute to the theoretical framework of modern medicine. To take an example, there are several points at which Western psycho-analytic theory, with its apparatus of personalized mental entities, resembles traditional West African religious theory. More specifically, as I have suggested elsewhere,[8] there are striking resemblances between psycho-analytic ideas about the individual mind as a congeries of warring entities, and West African ideas about the body as a meeting place of multiple souls. In both systems of belief, one personal entity is identified with the stream of consciousness, whilst the others operate as an 'unconscious', sometimes co-operating with consciousness and sometimes at war with it. Now the more flexible psycho-analysts have long suspected that Freud's allocation of particular desires and fears to particular agencies of the mind may well be appropriate to certain cultures only. Thus his allocation of a great load of sexual desires and fears to the unconscious may well have been appropriate to the Viennese sub-culture he so largely dealt with; but it may not be appropriate to many other cultures. A study of West African soul theories, and of their allocation of particular desires and emotions to particular agencies of the mind, may well help the psycho-analyst to reformulate his theories in terms more appropriate to the local scene.

Earlier, I said that modern Western medical scientists had long been distracted from noting the causal connexion between social disturbance and disease by the success of the germ theory. It would seem, indeed, that a conjunction of the germ theory, of the discovery of potent antibiotics and immunization techniques, and of conditions militating against the build-up of natural resistance to many killer infections, for long made it very difficult for scientists to see the importance of this connexion. Conversely, perhaps, a conjunction of no germ theory, no potent antibiotics, no immunization techniques, with conditions favouring the build-up of considerable natural resistance to killer infections, served to throw this same causal connexion into relief in the mind of the traditional healer. If one were asked to choose between germ theory innocent of psychosomatic insight and traditional psychosomatic theory innocent of ideas about infection, one would almost certainly choose the germ theory. For in terms of quantitative results it is clearly the more vital to human well-being. But it is salutary to remember that not all the profits are on one side.

From what has been said in this section, it should be clear that one commonly accepted way of contrasting traditional religious thought with scientific thought is misleading. I am thinking here of the contrast between traditional religious thought as 'non-empirical' with scientific thought as 'empirical'. In the first place, the contrast is misleading because traditional

---

[8] Horton, 1961.

religious thought is no more nor less interested in the natural causes of things than is the theoretical thought of the sciences. Indeed, the intellectual function of its supernatural beings (as, too, that of atoms, waves, etc.) *is* the extension of people's vision of natural causes. In the second place, the contrast is misleading because traditional religious theory clearly does more than postulate causal connexions that bear no relation to experience. Some of the connexions it postulates are, by the standards of modern medical science, almost certainly real ones. To some extent, then, it successfully grasps reality.

At this point, I must hasten to reassure the type of critic I referred to earlier that I am not claiming traditional thought as a variety of scientific thought. I grant that, in certain crucial respects, the two kinds of thought are related to experience in quite different ways, and I shall consider these differences in Part II of this paper. Meanwhile, I want to point out that it is not only where scientific method is in use that we find theories which both aim at grasping causal connexions and to some extent succeed in this aim. Scientific method is undoubtedly the surest and most efficient tool for arriving at beliefs that are successful in this respect; but it is not the only way of arriving at such beliefs. Given the basic process of theory-making, and an environmental stability which gives theory plenty of time to adjust to experience, a people's belief system may come, even in the absence of scientific method, to grasp at least some significant causal connexions which lie beyond the range of common sense. It is because traditional African religious beliefs demonstrate the truth of this that it seems apt to extend to them the label 'empirical'.

All this does not mean that we can dispense with the term 'non-empirical'. The latter remains a very useful label for certain other kinds of religious thinking which contrast sharply with that of traditional Africa in their lack of interest in explaining the features of the space-time world. Here I am thinking in particular of the kind of modern Western Christianity which co-exists, albeit a little uneasily, with scientific thought. I shall be saying more about this kind of religious thinking in Part II.


3. *Common Sense and Theory Have Complementary Roles in Everyday Life*

In the history of European thought there has often been opposition to a new theory on the ground that it threatens to break up and destroy the old, familiar world of common sense. Such was the eighteenth-century opposition to Newtonian corpuscular theory, which, so many people thought, was all set to 'reduce' the warm, colourful beautiful world to a lifeless, colourless, wilderness of rapidly moving little balls. Not surprisingly, this eighteenth-century attack was led by people like Goethe and Blake—poets whose job was precisely to celebrate the glories of the world of common sense. Such, again, is the twentieth-century opposition to Behaviour Theory, which many people see as a threat to 'reduce' human beings to animals or even to machines. Much of the most recent Western Philosophy is a monotonous and poorly reasoned attempt to bludgeon us into believing that Behaviour Theory cannot possibly work. But just as the common-sense world of things and people remained remarkably unscathed by the Newtonian revolution, so there is reason to think it will not be too seriously touched by the Behaviour-Theory revolution. Indeed, a lesson of the history of European thought is that, while theories come and theories go, the world of common sense remains very little changed.

One reason for this is perhaps that all theories take their departure from the world of things and people, and ultimately return us to it. In this context, to say that a good theory 'reduces' something to something else is misleading. Ideally, a process of deduction from the premises of a theory should lead us back to statements which portray the common-sense world in its full richness. In so far as this richness is not restored, by so much does theory fail. Another reason for the persistence of the world of common sense is probably that, within the limits discussed in the last section, common-sense thinking is handier and more economical than theoretical thinking. It is only when one needs to transcend the limited causal vision of common sense that one resorts to theory.

Take the example of an industrial chemist and his relationships with common salt. When he uses it in the house, his relationships with it are governed entirely by common sense. Invoking chemical theory to guide him in its domestic use would be like bringing up a pile-driver to hammer in a nail. Such theory may well lend no more colour to the chemist's domestic view of salt than it lends to the chemically uneducated rustic's view of the substance. When he uses it in his chemical factory, however, common sense no longer suffices. The things he wants to do with it force him to place it in a wider causal context than common sense provides; and he can only do this by viewing it in the light of atomic theory. At this point, someone may ask: 'And which does he think is the real salt; the salt of commonsense or the salt of theory?' The answer, perhaps, is that both are equally real to him. For whatever the philosophers say, people develop a sense of reality about something to the extent that they use and act on language which implies that this something exists.

This discussion of common sense and theory in Western thought is very relevant to the understanding of traditional African religions. Early accounts of such religions stressed the ever-presence of the spirit world in the minds of men. As Evans-Pritchard has noted, this stress was inevitable where the authors in question were concerned to titillate the imagination of the European reader with the bizarre.[9] Unfortunately, however, such accounts were seized upon by serious sociologists and philosophers like

---

[9] Evans-Pritchard, 1965, p. 8.

Levy-Bruhl, who used them to build up a picture of Primitive Man continuously obsessed by things religious. Later on, field-work experience in African societies convinced most reporters that members of such societies attended to the spirit world rather intermittently.[10] And many modern criticisms of Levy-Bruhl and other early theorists hinge on this observation. For the modern generation of social anthropologists, the big question has now become: 'On what kinds of occasion do people ignore the spirit world, and on what kinds of occasion do they attend to it?'

A variety of answers has been given to this question. One is that people think in terms of the spirit-world when they are confronted with the unusual or uncanny. Another is that they think this way in the face of anxiety-provoking situations. Another is that they think this way in the face of *any* emotionally charged situation. Yet another is that they think this way in certain types of crisis which threaten the fabric of society. Of all of these answers, the most one can say is: 'sometimes yes, sometimes no.' All of them, furthermore, leave the 'jump' from common sense to religious thinking fundamentally mysterious. One wants to ask: 'Even if this jump does occur in a certain type of situation, why should the latter require specifically *religious* thinking?' A better answer, I think, is one that relates this jump to the essentially theoretical character of traditional religious thinking. And here is where our discussion of common sense and theory in European thought becomes relevant.

I suggest that in traditional Africa relations between common sense and theory are essentially the same as they are in Europe. That is, common sense is the handier and more economical tool for coping with a wide range of circumstances in everyday life. Nevertheless, there are certain circumstances that can only be coped with in terms of a wider causal vision than common sense provides. And in these circumstances there is a jump to theoretical thinking.

Let me give an example drawn from my own field-work among the Kalabari people of the Niger Delta. Kalabari recognize many different kinds of diseases, and have an array of herbal specifics with which to treat them. Sometimes a sick person will be treated by ordinary members of his family who recognize the disease and know the specifics. Sometimes the treatment will be carried out on the instructions of a native doctor. When sickness and treatment follow these lines the atmosphere is basically commonsensical. Often, there is little or no reference to spiritual agencies.

Sometimes, however, the sickness does not respond to treatment, and it becomes evident that the herbal specific used does not provide the whole answer. The native doctor may rediagnose and try another specific. But if this produces no result the suspicion will arise that 'there is something else in this sickness'. In other words, the perspective provided by common sense is too limited. It is at this stage that a diviner is likely to be called

---

[10] See for instance Evans-Pritchard, op. cit., p. 88.

in (it may be the native doctor who started the treatment). Using ideas about various spiritual agencies, he will relate the sickness to a wider range of circumstances—often to disturbances in the sick man's general social life.

Again, a person may have a sickness which, though mild, occurs together with an obvious crisis in his field of social relations. This conjunction suggests at the outset that it may not be appropriate to look at the illness from the limited perspective of common sense. And in such circumstances, the expert called in is likely to refer at once to certain spiritual agencies in terms of which he links the sickness to a wider context of events.

What we are describing here is generally referred to as a jump from common sense to mystical thinking. But, as we have seen, it is also, more significantly, a jump from common sense to theory. And here, as in Europe, the jump occurs at the point where the limited causal vision of common sense curtails its usefulness in dealing with the situation on hand.

## 4. Level of Theory Varies with Context

A person seeking to place some event in a wider causal context often has a choice of theories. Like the initial choice between common sense and theory, this choice too will depend on just how wide a context he wishes to bring into consideration. Where he is content to place the event in a relatively modest context, he will be content to use what is generally called a low-level theory—i.e. one that covers a relatively limited area of experience. Where he is more ambitious about context, he will make use of a higher-level theory—i.e. one that covers a larger area of experience. As the area covered by the lower-level theory is part of the area covered by the higher-level scheme, so too the entities postulated by the lower-level theory are seen as special manifestations of those postulated at the higher level. Hence they pose all the old problems of things which are at once themselves and at the same time manifestations of other quite different things.

For an example of how this matter of levels works out in modern Western thought, let us go back to our manufacturing chemist and his salt. Suppose the chemist to be in the employ of a very under-developed country which has extensive deposits of salt and can supply a limited range of other simple chemicals, but which has no electricity. The government asks him to estimate what range of chemical products he can 'get out of' the salt, given the limited resources they can make available to him. Here the limited range of means implies a limited causal context and the appropriateness of a correspondingly low level of theory. In working out what he can do with his salt deposits under these straitened circumstances, the chemist may well be content to use the low-level, 'ball-and-bond' version of atomic theory, whose basic entities are homogeneous spheres linked by girder-like bonds. This level of theory will enable him to say that, with the aid of a few simple auxiliaries like chalk and ammonia, he can derive from his salt such important substances as washing soda and caustic soda.

Now suppose that after some time the chemist is told to assume that an electric power supply will be at his disposal. This additional element in the situation promises a wider range of possibilities. It also implies that salt is to be placed in a wider causal context. Hence a theory of wider coverage and higher level must be brought into play. Our chemist will now almost certainly make his calculations in terms of a more-embracing version of the atomic theory—one which covers electrical as well as strictly chemical phenomena. In this theory the homogeneous atoms of the lower-level schema are replaced by planetary configurations of charged fundamental particles. The atoms of the lower-level theory now become mere manifestations of systems of particles postulated by the higher-level theory. For philosophical puzzle-makers, the old teaser of things that are at once themselves and manifestations of something else is with us again. But the puzzle becomes less acute when we see it as an inevitable by-product of the way theories are used in the process of explanation.

Once again, we find parallels to all this in many traditional African religious systems. It is typical of such systems that they include, on the one hand, ideas about a multiplicity of spirits, and on the other hand, ideas about a single supreme being. Though the spirits are thought of as independent beings, they are also considered as so many manifestations or dependants of the supreme being. This conjunction of the many and the one has given rise to much discussion among students of comparative religion, and has evoked many ingenious theories. Most of these have boggled at the idea that polytheism and monotheism could coexist stably in a single system of thought. They have therefore tried to resolve the problem by supposing that the belief-systems in question are in transition from one type to the other. It is only recently, with the Nilotic studies of Evans-Pritchard and Lienhardt,[11] that the discussion has got anywhere near the point—which is that the many spirits and the one God play complementary roles in people's thinking. As Evans-Pritchard says: 'A theistic religion need be neither monotheistic nor polytheistic. It may be both. It is the question of the level, or situation, of thought, rather than of exclusive types of thought.'[12]

On the basis of material from the Nilotic peoples, and on that of material from such West African societies as Kalabari, Ibo, and Tallensi,[13] one can make a tentative suggestion about the respective roles of the many and the one in traditional African thought generally. In such thought, I suggest, the spirits provide the means of setting an event within a relatively limited causal context. They are the basis of a theoretical scheme which

---

[11] Evans-Pritchard, 1956; Lienhardt, 1961.

[12] Evans-Pritchard, op. cit., p. 316.

[13] Horton, 1962, 1964*b*, 1954; Fortes, 1949, especially pp. 21–22 and p. 219.

typically covers the thinker's own community and immediate environment. The supreme being, on the other hand, provides the means of setting an event within the widest possible context. For it is the basis of a theory of the origin and life course of the world seen as a whole.

In many (though by no means all) traditional African belief-systems, ideas about the spirits and actions based on such ideas are far more richly developed than ideas about the supreme being and actions based on them. In these cases, the idea of God seems more the pointer to a potential theory than the core of a seriously operative one. This perhaps is because social life in the communities involved is so parochial that their members seldom have to place events in the wider context that the idea of the supreme being purports to deal with. Nevertheless, the different levels of thinking are there in all these systems. And from what we have said, it seems clear that they are related to one another in much the same way as are the different levels of theoretical thinking in the sciences. At this point the relation between the many spirits and the one God loses much of its aura of mystery. Indeed there turns out to be nothing peculiarly religious or 'mystical' about it. For it is essentially the same as the relation between homogeneous atoms and planetary systems of fundamental particles in the thinking of our chemist. Like the latter, it is a by-product of certain very general features of the way theories are used in explanation.

## 5. All Theory Breaks Up the Unitary Objects of Common Sense into Aspects, then Places the Resulting Elements in a Wider Causal Context. That Is, It First Abstracts and Analyses, then Re-integrates

Numerous commentators on scientific method have familiarized us with the way in which the theoretical schemas of the sciences break up the world of common-sense things in order to achieve a causal understanding which surpasses that of common sense. But it is only from the more recent studies of African cosmologies, where religious beliefs are shown in the context of the various everyday contingencies they are invoked to explain, that we have begun to see how traditional religious thought also operates by a similar process of abstraction, analysis, and reintegration. A good example is provided by Fortes's recent work on West African theories of the individual and his relation to society. Old-fashioned West African ethnographers like Talbot long ago showed the wide distribution of beliefs in what they called 'multiple souls'. They found that many West African belief-systems invested the individual with a multiplicity of spiritual agencies, and they baptized these agencies with fanciful names such as 'spirit double', 'bush soul', 'shadow soul', and 'over soul'. The general impression they gave was one of an unruly fantasy at work. In his recent book,[14] how-

---

[14] Fortes, 1959.

ever, Fortes takes the 'multiple soul' beliefs of a single West African people (the Tallensi) and places them in the context of everyday thought and behaviour. His exposition dispels much of the aura of fantasy.

Fortes describes three categories of spiritual agency especially concerned with the Tale individual. First comes the *segr*, which presides over the individual as a biological entity—over his sickness and health, his life and death. Then comes the *nuor yin*, a personification of the wishes expressed by the individual before his arrival on earth. The *nuor yin* appears specifically concerned with whether or not the individual has the personality traits necessary if he is to become an adequate member of Tale society. As Fortes puts it, evil *nuor yin* 'serves to identify the fact of irremediable failure in the development of the individual to full social capacity'. Good *nuor yin*, on the other hand, 'identifies the fact of successful individual development along the road to full incorporation in society'. Finally, in this trio of spiritual agencies, we have what Fortes calls the *'yin* ancestors'. These are two or three out of the individual's total heritage of ancestors, who have been delegated to preside over his personal fortunes. *Yin* ancestors only attach themselves to an individual who has a good *nuor yin*. They are concerned with the fortunes of the person who has already proved himself to have the basic equipment for fitting into Tale society. Here we have a theoretical scheme which, in order to produce a deeper understanding of the varying fortunes of individuals in their society, breaks them down into three aspects by a simple but typical operation of abstraction and analysis.

Perhaps the most significant comment on Fortes's work in this field was pronounced, albeit involuntarily, by a reviewer of 'Oedipus and Job'.[15] 'If any criticism of the presentation is to be made it is that Professor Fortes sometimes seems to achieve an almost mystical identification with the Tallensi world-view and leaves the unassimilated reader in some doubt about where to draw the line between Tallensi notions and Cambridge concepts!' Now the anthropologist has to find *some* concepts in his own language roughly appropriate to translating the 'notions' of the people he studies. And in the case in question, perhaps only the lofty analytic 'Cambridge' concepts did come anywhere near to congruence with Tallensi notions. This parallel between traditional African religious 'notions' and Western sociological 'abstractions' is by no means an isolated phenomenon. Think for instance of individual guardian spirits and group spirits—two very general categories of traditional African religious thought. Then think of those hardy Parsonian abstractions—psychological imperatives and sociological imperatives. It takes no great brilliance to see the resemblance.[16]

---

[15] R. E. Bradbury in *Man*. September 1959.

[16] Such parallels arouse the more uncomfortable thought that in all the theorizing we sociologists have done about the working of traditional African societies, we may often have done little more than translate indigenous African theories about such workings.

One can of course argue that in comparing traditional African thought with modern Western sociological thought, one is comparing it with a branch of Western thought that has attained only a low degree of abstraction. One can go on to argue that traditional African thought does not approach the degree of abstraction shown, say, by modern nuclear physics. Such comparisons of degrees of abstraction are, I think, trickier than they seem at first glance. In any case, they cannot affect the validity of the point already made, which is that abstraction is as essential to the operation of traditional African religious theory as it is to that of modern Western theory, whether sociological or physical.

6. *In Evolving a Theoretical Scheme, the Human Mind Seems Constrained to Draw Inspiration from Analogy between the Puzzling Observations to Be Explained and Certain Already Familiar Phenomena*

In the genesis of a typical theory, the drawing of an analogy between the unfamiliar and the familiar is followed by the making of a model in which something akin to the familiar is postulated as the reality underlying the unfamiliar. Both modern Western and traditional African thought-products amply demonstrate the truth of this. Whether we look amongst atoms, electrons, and waves, or amongst gods, spirits, and entelechies, we find that theoretical notions nearly always have their roots in relatively homely everyday experiences, in analogies with the familiar.

What do we mean here by 'familiar phenomena'? Above all, I suggest, we mean phenomena strongly associated in the mind of the observer with order and regularity. That theory should depend on analogy with things familiar in this sense follows from the very nature of explanation. Since the overriding aim of explanation is to disclose order and regularity underlying apparent chaos, the search for explanatory analogies must tend towards those areas of experience most closely associated with such qualities. Here, I think, we have a basis for indicating why explanations in modern Western culture tend to be couched in an impersonal idiom, while explanations in traditional African society tend to be couched in a personal idiom. The reader may see the point most readily if I introduce a little personal reminiscence. The idea that people can be much more difficult to cope with than things is one that has never been far from my own mind. I can recall long periods of my own boyhood when I felt at home and at ease, not with friends, relatives, and parents round the fire, but shut up alone for hours with bunsen burners and racks of reagents in a chemistry laboratory. Potassium hydroxide and nitric acid were my friends; sodium phosphate and calcium chloride my brothers and sisters. In later life I have been fortunate enough to break through many times into a feeling of at-homeness with people. But such break-throughs have always been things to wonder at; never things to be taken for granted. My joy in people is all the more intense for being a joy in something precarious. And in the background there is always the world of things beckoning seductively towards the path of escape from people. English colleagues may shrug their shoulders and say I am a freak in this. But if they are honest with themselves, they will admit I am saying things which strike echoes in all their hearts. Nor do I have to depend on their honesty in this; for the image of the man happier with things than with people is common enough in modern Western literature to show that what I am talking about here is the sickness of the times.

Not long ago I was having a discussion with a class of Nigerian students, all of whom, I suppose, still had strong roots in traditional community life. We were discussing some of the characteristic ways in which life in Western industrial cities differed from life in traditional village communities. When I came to touch on some of the things I have just been saying, I felt that I had really 'gone away from them'. What I was saying about a life in which things might seem a welcome haven from people was just so totally foreign to their experience that they could not begin to take it in. They just stared. Rarely have I felt more of an alien than in that discussion.

Now the point I wish to make is this. In complex, rapidly changing industrial societies the human scene is in flux. Order, regularity, predictability, simplicity, all these seem lamentably absent. It is in the world of inanimate things that such qualities are most readily seen. This is why many people can find themselves less at home with their fellow men than with things. And this too, I suggest, is why the mind in quest of explanatory analogies turns most readily to the inanimate. In the traditional societies of Africa, we find the situation reversed. The human scene is the locus *par excellence* of order, predictability, regularity. In the world of the inanimate, these qualities are far less evident. Here, being less at home with people than with things is unimaginable. And here, the mind in quest of explanatory analogies turns naturally to people and their relations.

### 7. *Where Theory Is Founded on Analogy between Puzzling Observations and Familiar Phenomena, It is Generally Only a Limited Aspect of Such Phenomena that Is Incorporated into the Resulting Model*

When a thinker draws an analogy between certain puzzling observations and other more familiar phenomena, the analogy seldom involves more than a limited aspect of such phenomena. And it is only this limited aspect which is taken over and used to build up the theoretical schema. Other aspects are ignored; for, from the point of view of explanatory function, they are irrelevant.

Philosophers of science have often used the molecular (kinetic) theory of gases as an illustration of this feature of model-building. The molecular theory, of course, is based on an analogy with the behaviour of fast-moving, spherical balls in various kinds of space. And the philosophers have pointed out that although many important properties of such balls have been incorporated into the definition of a molecule, other important properties such as colour and temperature have been omitted. They have been omitted because they have no explanatory function in relation to the observations that originally evoked the theory. Here, of course, we have another sense in which physical theory is based upon abstraction and abstract ideas. For concepts such as 'molecule', 'atom', 'electron', 'wave' are the result of a process in which the relevant features of certain prototype phenomena have been abstracted from the irrelevant features.

Many writers have considered this sort of abstraction to be one of the distinctive features of scientific thinking. But this, like so many other such distinctions, is a false one; for just the same process is at work in traditional African thought. Thus when traditional thought draws upon people and their social relations as the raw material of its theoretical models, it makes use of some dimensions of human life and neglects others. The definition of a god may omit any reference to his physical appearance, his diet, his mode of lodging, his children, his relations with his wives, and so on. Asking questions about such attributes is as inappropriate as asking questions about the colour of a molecule or the temperature of an electron. It is this omission of many dimensions of human life from the definition of the gods which gives them that rarefied, attenuated aura which we call 'spiritual'. But there is nothing peculiarly religious, mystical, or traditional about this 'spirituality'. It is the result of the same process of abstraction as the one we see at work in Western theoretical models: the process whereby features of the prototype phenomena which have explanatory relevance are incorporated into a theoretical schema, while features which lack such relevance are omitted.

## 8. A Theoretical Model, Once Built, Is Developed in Ways which Sometimes Obscure the Analogy on which It Was Founded

In its raw, initial state, a model may come up quite quickly against data for which it cannot provide any explanatory coverage. Rather than scrap it out of hand, however, its users will tend to give it successive modifications in order to enlarge its coverage. Sometimes, such modifications will involve the drawing of further analogies with phenomena rather different from those which provided the initial inspiration for the model. Sometimes, they will merely involve 'tinkering' with the model until it comes to fit the new observations. By comparison with the phenomena which provided its original inspiration, such a developed model not unnaturally seems to have a bizarre, hybrid air about it.

Examples of the development of theoretical models abound in the history of science. One of the best documented of these is provided by the modern atomic theory of matter. The foundations of this theory were laid by Rutherford, who based his original model upon an analogy between the passage of ray-beams through metal foil and the passage of comets through our planetary system. Rutherford's planetary model of the basic constituents of matter proved extremely useful in explanation. When it came up against recalcitrant data, therefore, the consensus of scientists was in favour of developing it rather than scrapping it. First of the consequent modifications was the introduction of the possibility that the 'planets' might make sudden changes of orbit, and in so doing emit or absorb energy. Then came the substitution, at the centre of the planetary system, of a heterogeneous cluster of bodies for a single 'sun'. Later still came the idea that, at a particular moment, a given 'planet' had a somewhat ambiguous position. Finally, along with this last idea, came a modification inspired by the drawing of a fresh analogy. This was the introduction of the idea that, in some contexts, the 'planets' were to be considered as bundles of waves. Each of these modifications was a response to the demand for increased explanatory coverage. Each, however, removed the theoretical model one step further away from the familiar phenomena which had furnished its original inspiration.

In studying traditional African thought, alas, we scarcely ever have the historical depth available to the student of European thought. So we can make few direct observations on the development of its theoretical models. Nevertheless, these models often show just the same kinds of bizarre, hybrid features as the models of the scientists. Since they resemble the latter in so many other ways, it seems reasonable to suppose that these features are the result of a similar process of development in response to demands for further explanatory coverage. The validity of such a supposition is strengthened when we consider detailed instances: for these show how the bizarre features of particular models are indeed closely related to the nature of the observations that demand explanation.

Let me draw one example from my own field-work on Kalabari religious thought which I have outlined in earlier publications. Basic Kalabari religious beliefs involve three main categories of spirits: ancestors, heroes, and water-people. On the one hand, all three categories of spirits show many familiar features: emotions of pleasure and anger, friendships, enmities, marriages. Such features betray the fact that, up to a point, the spirits are fashioned in the image of ordinary Kalabari people. Beyond this point, however, they are bizarre in many ways. The ancestors, perhaps, remain closest to the image of ordinary people. But the heroes are decidedly odd. They are defined as having left no descendants, as having disappeared rather than died, and as having come in the first instance from outside the community. The water-spirits are still odder. They are said to be 'like men, and also like pythons'. To make sense of these oddities, let us start by sketching the relations of the various kinds of spirits to the world of everyday experience.

First, the ancestors. These are postulated as the forces underpinning the life and strength of the lineages, bringing misfortune to those who betray lineage values and fortune to those who promote them. Second, the heroes. These are the forces underpinning the life and strength of the community and its various institutions. They are also the forces underpinning human skill and maintaining its efficacy in the struggle against nature. Third, the water-spirits. On the one hand, these are the 'owners' of the creeks and swamps, the guardians of the fish harvest, the forces of nature. On the other hand, they are the patrons of human individualism—in both its creative and its destructive forms. In short, they are the forces underpinning all that lies beyond the confines of the established social order.

We can look on ancestors, heroes, and water-spirits as the members of a triangle of forces. In this triangle, the relation of each member to the other two contains elements of separation and opposition as well as of co-operation. Thus by supporting lineages in rivalry against one another, the ancestors can work against the heroes in sapping the strength of the community; but in other contexts, by strengthening their several lineages, they can work with the heroes in contributing to village strength. Again, when they bring up storms, rough water, and sharks, the water-spirits work against the heroes by hampering the exercise of the village's productive skills; but when they produce calm water and an abundance of fish, they work just as powerfully with the heroes. Yet again, by fostering anti-social activity, the water spirits can work against both heroes and ancestors; or, by supporting creativity and invention, they can enrich village life and so work with them.

In this triangle, then, we have a theoretical scheme in terms of which Kalabari can grasp and comprehend most of the many vicissitudes of their daily lives. Now it is at this point that the bizarre, paradoxical attributes of heroes and water-spirits begin to make sense: for a little inspection shows that such attributes serve to define each category of spirits in a way appropriate to its place in the total scheme. This is true, for example, of such attributes of the heroes as having left no human descendants, having disappeared instead of undergoing death and burial, and having come from outside the community. All these serve effectively to define the heroes as forces quite separate from the ancestors with their kinship involvements. Lack of descendants does this in an obvious way. Disappearance rather than death and burial performs the same function, especially when, as in Kalabari, lack of burial is almost synonymous with lack of kin. And arrival from outside the community again makes it clear that they cannot be placed in any lineage or kinship context. These attributes, in short, are integral to the definition of the heroes as forces contrasted with and potentially opposed to the ancestors. Again, the water-spirits are said to be 'like men, and also like pythons'; and here too the paradoxical characterization is essential to defining their place in the triangle. The python is regarded as the most powerful of all the animals in the creeks, and is often said to be their father. But its power is seen as something very different from that of human beings—something 'fearful' and 'astonishing'. The combination of human and python elements in the characterization of the water-people fits the latter perfectly for their own place in the triangle—as forces of the extra-social contrasted with and potentially opposed to both heroes and ancestors.

Another illuminating example of the theoretical significance of oddity is provided by Middleton's account of traditional Lugbara religious concepts.[17] According to Middleton, Lugbara belief features two main categories of spiritual agency—the ancestors and the *adro* spirits. Like the Kalabari ancestors, those of the Lugbara remain close to the image of ordinary people. The *adro*, however, are very odd indeed. They are cannibalistic and incestuous, and almost everything else that Lugbara ordinarily consider repulsive. They are commonly said to walk upside down—a graphic expression of their general perversity. Once again, these oddities fall into place when we look at the relations of the two categories of spirits to the world of experience. The ancestors, on the one hand, account for the settled world of human habitation and with the established social order organized on the basis of small lineages. The *adro*, on the other hand, are concerned with the uncultivated bush, and with all human activities which run counter to the established order of things. Like the Kalabari water-spirits, they are forces of the extra-social, whether in its natural or its human form. The contrast and opposition between ancestors and *adro* thus provides Lugbara with a theoretical schema in terms of which they can comprehend a whole series of oppositions and conflicts manifest in the world of their everyday experiences. Like the oddities of the Kalabari gods, those of the *adro* begin to make sense at this point. For it is the bizarre, perverse features of these spirits that serve to define their position in the theory—as forces contrasted with and opposed to the ancestors.

In both of these cases the demands of explanation result in a model whose structure is hybrid between that of the human social phenomena which provided its original inspiration, and that of the field of experience to which it is applied. In both cases, oddity is essential to explanatory function. Even in the absence of more direct historical evidence, these examples suggest that the theoretical models of traditional African thought are the products of developmental processes comparable to those affecting the models of the sciences.

Some philosophers have objected to the statement that explanatory

---

[17] Middleton, 1960.

models are founded on analogy between the puzzling and the familiar, saying that the features of typical models in the sciences rather suggest that in them the relatively familiar is explained in terms of the relatively unfamiliar. They point to the abstract character of theoretical entities, contrasting this with the familiar concreteness of the world of everyday things. They point to the bizarre features of such entities, so far removed from anything found in the everyday world. These very objections, however, merely confirm the validity of the .view they aim to criticize. For what makes theoretical entities seem abstract to us is precisely that they have taken over some key features from particular areas of everyday experience, while rejecting other features as irrelevant to their purposes. Again, what makes theoretical entities seem bizarre to us is precisely these features drawn from areas of familiar experience. The presence of some such features leads us to expect others. But the processes of abstraction and development produce results that cheat these expectations: hence our sense of the odd.

In treating traditional African religious systems as theoretical models akin to those of the sciences, I have really done little more than take them at their face value. Although this approach may seem naïve and platitudinous compared to the sophisticated 'things-are-never-what-they-seem' attitude more characteristic of the social anthropologist, it has certainly produced some surprising results. Above all, it has cast doubt on most of the well-worn dichotomies used to conceptualize the difference between scientific and traditional religious thought. Intellectual versus emotional; rational versus mystical; reality-oriented versus fantasy-oriented; causally oriented versus supernaturally oriented; empirical versus non-empirical; abstract versus concrete; analytical versus non-analytical: all of these are shown to be more or less inappropriate. If the reader is disturbed by this casting away of established distinctions, he will, I hope, accept it when he sees how far it can pave the way towards making sense of so much that previously appeared senseless.

One thing that may well continue to bother the reader is my playing down of the difference between non-personal and personal theory. For while I have provided what seems to me an adequate explanation of this difference, I have treated it as a surface difference concealing an underlying similarity of intellectual process. I must confess that I have used brevity of treatment here as a device to play down the gulf between the two kinds of theory. But I think this is amply justifiable in reaction to the more usual state of affairs, in which the difference is allowed to dominate all other features of the situation. Even familiarity with theoretical thinking in their own culture cannot help anthropologists who are dominated by this difference. For once so blinded, they can only see traditional religious thought as wholly other. With the bridge from their own thought-patterns to those of traditional Africa blocked, it is little wonder they can make no further headway.[18]

The aim of my exposition has been to reopen this bridge. The point I have sought to make is that the difference between non-personal and personalized theories is more than anything else a difference in the idiom of the explanatory quest. Grasping this point is an essential preliminary to realizing how far the various established dichotomies used in this field are simply obstacles to understanding. Once it is grasped, a whole series of seemingly bizarre and senseless features of traditional thinking becomes immediately comprehensible. Until it is grasped, they remain essentially mysterious. Making the business of personal versus impersonal entities the crux of the difference between tradition and science not only blocks the understanding of tradition. It also draws a red herring across the path to an understanding of science. This becomes obvious from a look at history. So far as we know, an extensive depersonalization of theory has happened spontaneously only twice in the history of human thought. Once in Europe and once in China. In Europe this depersonalization was accompanied by a growth of science; in China it was not.[19] Again, where depersonalization *has* been accompanied by the growth of science, the two have often parted company very readily. Thus in Western lay culture we have a largely depersonalized view of the world which is at the same time totally unscientific.[20] And in many of the developing countries, for which science appears as a panacea, it seems likely that the depersonalized world of the West may get through without the scientific spirit.[21] Yet again, in the recent history

---

[18] Just how little headway British social anthropologists appear to be making with traditional religious thought is betrayed by their tendency to confine themselves to the study of its political manipulation, and to leave to psychologists the job of accounting for its substantive features. In this context, I should like to draw attention to the curiously menial role in which the modern British anthropologist has cast the psychologist—the role of the well disciplined scavenger. On the one hand, the psychologist is expected to keep well away from any intellectual morsel currently considered digestible by the anthropologist. On the other hand, he is tossed all indigestible morsels, and is expected to relieve the anthropologist of the embarrassing smell they would create if left in his house uneaten.

[19] See, for instance, *Scientific Change* (Symposium on the History of Science, University of Oxford 9–15 July 1961), ed. A. C. Crombie, London, 1963; especially the chapter on 'Chinese Science' and the subsequent interventions by Willy Hartner and Stephen Toulmin.

[20] 'Western society today may be said to harbour science like a foreign god, powerful and mysterious. Our lives are changed by its handiwork but the population of the West is as far from understanding the nature of this strange power as a remote peasant of the Middle Ages may have been from understanding the theology of Thomas Aquinas.' Barzun, 1961.

[21] Coming from Africa, this is something of a *cri de cœur*. In the authoritarian political climate of emergent African nations, there are particular dangers that this may be the outcome of 'westernization'. For since the spirit of science, as I shall emphasize in Part II, is essentially anti-authoritarian, there is a great temptation to take the preoccupation with impersonal models as the essence of science, and to reject the real essence as inconvenient. Hence the need to insist so strongly on disentangling the two.

of Western psychology, we find both personalized (psycho-analytic) and non-personalized (behaviouristic) theories. And for each category there are those who handle the theories scientifically and those who do not.

All this is not to deny that science has progressed greatly through working in a non-personal theoretical idiom. Indeed, as one who has hankerings after behaviourism, I am inclined to believe that it is this idiom, and this idiom only, which will eventually lead to the triumph of science in the sphere of human affairs. What I am saying, however, is that this is more a reflection of the nature of reality than a clue to the essence of scientific method. For the progressive acquisition of knowledge, man needs both the right kind of theories *and* the right attitude to them. But it is only the latter which we call science. Indeed, as we shall see, any attempt to define science in terms of a particular kind of theory runs contrary to its very essence. Now, at last, I hope it will be evident why, in comparing African traditional thought with Western scientific thought, I have chosen to start with a review of continuities rather than with a statement of crucial differences. For although this order of procedure carries the risk of one's being understood to mean that traditional thought is a kind of science, it also carries the advantage of having the path clear of red herrings when one comes to tackle the question of differences.

## Part II. The 'Closed' and 'Open' Predicaments

In Part I of this paper, I pushed as far as it would go the thesis that important continuities link the religious thinking of traditional Africa and the theoretical thinking of the modern West. I showed how this view helps us to make sense of many otherwise puzzling features of traditional religious thinking. I also showed how it helps us to avoid certain rather troublesome red herrings which lie across the path towards understanding the crucial differences between the traditional and the scientific outlook.

In Part II, I shall concentrate on these differences. I shall start by isolating one which strikes me as the key to all the others, and will then go on to suggest how the latter flow from it.

What I take to be the key difference is a very simple one. It is that in traditional cultures there is no developed awareness of alternatives to the established body of theoretical tenets; whereas in scientifically oriented cultures, such an awareness is highly developed. It is this difference we refer to when we say that traditional cultures are 'closed' and scientifically oriented cultures 'open'.[22]

---

[22] Philosophically minded readers will notice here some affinities with Karl Popper, who also makes the transition from a 'closed' to an 'open' predicament crucial for the take-off from tradition to science. For me, however, Popper obscures the issue by packing too many contrasts into his definitions of 'closed' and 'open'. Thus, for him,

One important consequence of the lack of awareness of alternatives is very clearly spelled out by Evans-Pritchard in his pioneering work on Azande witchcraft beliefs. Thus he says:

I have attempted to show how rhythm, mode of utterance, content of prophecies, and so forth, assist in creating faith in witch-doctors, but these are only some of the ways in which faith is supported, and do not entirely explain belief. Weight of tradition alone can do that. . . . There is no incentive to agnosticism. All their beliefs hang together, and were a Zande to give up faith in witch-doctorhood, he would have to surrender equally his faith in witchcraft and oracles. . . . In this web of belief every strand depends upon every other strand, *and a Zande cannot get out of its meshes because it is the only world he knows. The web is not an external structure in which he is enclosed. It is the texture of his thought and he cannot think that his thought is wrong.*[23]

And again:

And yet Azande do not see that their oracles tell them nothing! Their blindness is not due to stupidity, for they display great ingenuity in explaining away the failures and inequalities of the poison oracle and experimental keenness in testing it. It is due rather to the fact that their intellectual ingenuity and experimental keenness are conditioned by patterns of ritual behaviour and mystical belief. Within the limits set by these patterns, they show great intelligence, but it cannot operate beyond these limits. Or, to put it in another way; *they reason excellently in the idiom of their beliefs, but they cannot reason outside, or against their beliefs because they have no other idiom in which to express their thoughts.*[24]

Yet again, writing more generally of 'closed' societies in a recent book, he says:

Everyone has the same sort of religious beliefs and practices, and their generality, or collectivity, gives them an objectivity which places them over and above the psychological experience of any individual, or indeed of all individuals. . . . *Apart from positive and negative sanctions, the mere fact that religion is general means, again in a closed society, that it is obligatory, for even if there is no coercion, a man has no option but to accept what everybody gives assent to, because he has no choice, any more than of what language he*

---

the transition from one predicament to the other implies not just a growth in the awareness of alternatives, but also a transition from communalism to individualism, and from ascribed status to achieved status. But as I hope to show in this essay, it is the awareness of alternatives which is crucial for the take-off into science. Not individualism or achieved status: for there are lots of societies where both of the latter are well developed, but which show no signs whatever of take-off. In the present context, therefore, my own narrower definition of 'closed' and 'open' seems more appropriate.

[23] Evans-Pritchard, 1936, p. 194.

[24] Ibid., p. 338.

*speaks. Even were he to be a sceptic, he could express his doubts only in terms of the beliefs held by all around him.*[25]

In other words, absence of any awareness of alternatives makes for an absolute acceptance of the established theoretical tenets, and removes any possibility of questioning them. In these circumstances, the established tenets invest the believer with a compelling force. It is this force which we refer to when when we talk of such tenets as sacred.

A second important consequence of lack of awareness of alternatives is vividly illustrated by the reaction of an Ijo man to a missionary who told him to throw away his old gods. He said: 'Does your God really want us to climb to the top of a tall palm tree, than take off our hands and let ourselves fall?' Where the established tenets have an absolute and exclusive validity for those who hold them, any challenge to them is a threat of chaos, of the cosmic abyss, and therefore evokes intense anxiety.

With developing awareness of alternatives, the established theoretical tenets come to seem less absolute in their validity, and lose something of their sacredness. At the same time, a challenge to these tenets is no longer a horrific threat of chaos. For just as the tenets themselves have lost some of their absolute validity, a challenge to them is no longer a threat of absolute calamity. It can now be seen as nothing more threatening than an intimation that new tenets might profitably be tried. Where these conditions begin to prevail, the stage is set for change from a traditional to a scientific outlook.

Here, then, we have two basic predicaments: the 'closed'—characterized by lack of awareness of alternatives, sacredness of beliefs, and anxiety about threats to them; and the 'open'—characterized by awareness of alternatives, diminished sacredness of beliefs, and diminished anxiety about threats to them.

Now, as I have said, I believe all the major differences beween traditional and scientific outlooks can be understood in terms of these two predicaments. In substantiating this, I should like to divide the differences into two groups: A, those directly connected with the presence or absence of a vision of alternatives; and B, those directly connected with the presence or absence of anxiety about threats to the established beliefs.

## A. Differences Connected with the Presence or Absence of a Vision of Alternatives

### 1. *Magical Versus Non-Magical Attitude to Words*

A central characteristic of nearly all the traditional African world-views we know of is an assumption about the power of words, uttered under appro-

---

[25] Evans-Pritchard, 1965, p. 55.

priate circumstances, to bring into being the events or states they stand for.

The most striking examples of this assumption are to be found in creation mythologies where the supreme being is said to have formed the world out of chaos by uttering the names of all things in it. Such mythologies occur most notably in Ancient Egypt and among the peoples of the Western Sudan.

In the acts of creation which the supreme being has left to man, the mere uttering of words is seldom thought to have the same unconditional efficacy. Thus, so far as we know, there are no traditional cultures which credit man with the ability to create new things just by uttering new words. In most such cultures, nevertheless, the words of men are granted a certain measure of control over the situations they refer to. Often there is a technical process which has to be carried out in order to achieve a certain result; but for success, this has to be completed by a properly framed spell or incantation foreshadowing the result. Such a situation is vividly described by the Guinean novelist Camara Laye. His father was a goldsmith, and in describing the old man at work, he says:

Although my father spoke no word aloud, I know very well that he was thinking them from within. I read it from his lips, which were moving while he bent over the vessel. He kept mixing gold and coal with a wooden stick which would blaze up every now and then and constantly had to be replaced. What sort of words were those that my father was silently forming? I don't know—at least I don't know exactly. Nothing was ever confided to me about that. But what could these words be but incantations?

Beside the old man worked a sorcerer:

Throughout the whole process his speech became more and more rapid, his rhythms more urgent, and as the ornament took shape, his panegyrics and flatteries increased in vehemence and raised my father's skill to the heavens. In a peculiar, I would almost say immediate and effective, way the sorcerer did in truth take part in the work. He too was drunk with the joy of creation, and loudly proclaimed his joy: enthusiastically he snatched the strings, became inflamed, as if he himself were the craftsman, as if he himself were my father, as if the ornament were coming from his own hands.[26]

In traditional African cultures, to know the name of a being or thing is to have some degree of control over it. In the invocation of spirits, it is essential to call their names correctly; and the control which such correct calling gives is one reason why the true or 'deep' names of gods are often withheld from strangers, and their utterance forbidden to all but a few whose business it is to use them in ritual. Similar ideas lie behind the very

---

[26] Laye, 1965. Quoted in Jahn, 1961 (p. 125). As an attempt to make an inventory of distinctive and universal features of African culture, Jahn's book seems to me highly tendentious. But its imaginative sketch of the assumptions underlying magical beliefs and practices is one of the most suggestive treatments of the subject I have seen.

widespread traditional practice of using euphemisms to refer to such things as dangerous diseases and wild animals: for it is thought that use of the real names might secure their presence. Yet again, it is widely believed that harm can be done to a man by various operations performed on his name—for instance, by writing his name on a piece of paper and burning it.

This last example carries me on to an observation that at first sight contradicts what we have said so far: the observation that in a great deal of African magic, it is non-verbal symbols rather than words that are thought to have a direct influence over the situations they represent. Bodily movements, bits of plants, organs of animals, stones, earth, water, spittle, domestic utensils, statuettes—a whole host of actions, objects, and artefacts play a vital part in the performances of traditional magic. But as we look deeper the contradiction seems more apparent than real. For several studies of African magic suggest that its instruments become symbols through being verbally designated as such. In his study of Zande magic, for instance, Evans-Pritchard describes how magical medicines made from plants and other natural objects are given direction by the use of verbal spells Thus:

The tall grass *bingba*, which grows profusely on cultivated ground and has feather-like, branching stems, is known to all as medicine for the oil-bearing plant *kpagu*. A man throws the grass like a dart and transfixes the broad leaves of the plant. Before throwing it, he says something of this sort: 'You are melons, you be very fruitful like *bingba* with much fruit.' Or 'You are *bingba*; may the melons flourish like *bingba*. My melons, you be very fruitful. May you not refuse.'[27]

My own field-work in Kalabari constantly unearthed similar examples of non-verbal symbols being given direction and significance by verbal spells. My favourite example is taken from the preparation of a medicine designed to bring clients to an unsuccessful spirit medium. One of the important ingredients of this medicine was the beak of the voracious, mud-dredging muscovy duck—an item which the doctor put into the medicine with the succinct comment: 'Muscovy Duck; you who are always eating.'

Amongst the most important non-verbal magical symbols in Kalabari culture are the statuettes designed to 'fix' the various spirits at times of ritual. Of these, several Kalabari said: 'They are, as it were, the names of the spirits.' Explaining their use, one old man said: 'It is in their names that the spirits stay and come.' It is by being named that the sculpture comes to represent the spirit and to exert influence over it.[28]

In a recent essay on Malagasy magic,[29] Henri Lavondes discusses similar

[27] Evans-Pritchard, 1936, p. 449.

[28] Horton, 1965.

[29] Lavondes, 1963.

examples of the direction of magical objects by verbal spells. He shows
how the various ingredients of a compound medicine are severally related
by these spells to the various aspects of the end desired. And, following
Mauss, he goes on to suggest that the function of the spell is to convert
material objects into *mots realisés* or concrete words. In being given verbal
labels, the objects themselves become a form of language.

This interpretation, which reduces all forms of African magic to a verbal
base, fits the facts rather well. One may still ask, however, why magicians
spend so much time choosing objects and actions as surrogate words, when
spoken words themselves are believed to have a magical potential. The
answer, I would suggest, is that speech is an ephemeral form of words,
and one which does not lend itself to a great variety of manipulations.
Verbal designation of material objects converts them into a more permanent
and more readily manipulable form of words. As Lavondes puts it:

Le message verbal est susceptible de davantage de précision que le message
figuré. Mais le second a sur le premier l'avantage de sa permanence et de sa
matérialité, qui font qu'il reste toujours disponible et qu'il est possible de s'en
pénétrer et de le répandre par d'autres voies que celle du langage articulé (par
absorption, par onction, par aspersion).[30]

Considered in this light, magical objects are the preliterate equivalents
of the written incantations which are so commonly found as charms and
talismans in literate but prescientific cultural milieux.

Through a very wide range of traditional African belief and activity,
then, it is possible to see an implicit assumption as to the magical power
of words.

Now if we take into account what I have called the basic predicament
of the traditional thinker, we can begin to see why this assumption should
be so deeply entrenched in his daily life and thought. Briefly, no man can
make contact with reality save through a screen of words. Hence no man
can escape the tendency to see a unique and intimate link between words
and things. For the traditional thinker this tendency has an overwhelming
power. Since he can imagine no alternatives to his established system of
·concepts and words, the latter appear bound to reality in an absolute
fashion. There is no way at all in which they can be seen as varying independently of the segments of reality they stand for. Hence they appear so
integrally involved with their referents that any manipulaton of the one
self-evidently affects the other.

The scientist's attitude to words is, of course, quite opposite. He dis-
misses contemptuously any suggestion that words could have an immediate,
magical power over the things they stand for. Indeed, he finds magical
notions amongst the most absurd and alien trappings of traditional thought.
Though he grants an enormous power to words, it is the indirect one of

---

[30] Ibid., p. 115.

bringing control over things through the functions of explanation and prediction. Words are tools in the service of these functions—tools which like all others are to be cared for as long as they are useful, but which are to be ruthlessly scrapped as soon as they outlive their usefulness.

Why does the scientist reject the magician's view of words? One easy answer is that he has come to know better: magical behaviour has been found not to produce the results it claims to. Perhaps. But what scientist has ever bothered to put magic to the test? The answer is, none; because there are deeper grounds for rejection—grounds which make the idea of testing beside the point.

To see what these grounds are, let us return to the scientist's basic predicament—to his awareness of alternative idea-systems whose ways of classifying and interpreting the world are very different from his own. Now this changed awareness gives him two intellectual possibilities. Both are eminently thinkable; but one is intolerable, the other hopeful.

The first possibility is simply a continuance of the magical world-view. If ideas and words are inextricably bound up with reality, and if indeed they shape it and control it, then, a multiplicity of idea-systems means a multiplicity of realities, and a change of ideas means a change of things. But whereas there is nothing particularly absurd or inconsistent about this view, it is clearly intolerable in the extreme. For it means that the world is in the last analysis dependent on human whim, that the search for order is a folly, and that human beings can expect to find no sort of anchor in reality.

The second possibility takes hold as an escape from this horrific prospect. It is based on the faith that while ideas and words change, there must be some anchor, some constant reality. This faith leads to the modern view of words and reality as independent variables. With its advent, words come 'unstuck from' reality and are no longer seen as acting magically upon it. Intellectually, this second possibility is neither more nor less respectable than the first. But it has the great advantage of being tolerable whilst the first is horrific.

That the outlook behind magic still remains an intellectual possibility in the scientifically oriented cultures of the modern West can be seen from its survival as a nagging undercurrent in the last 300 years of Western philosophy. This undercurrent generally goes under the labels of 'Idealism' and 'Solipsism'; and under these labels it is not immediately recognizable. But a deeper scrutiny reveals that the old outlook is there all right—albeit in a strange guise. True, Idealism does not say that words create, sustain, and have power over that which they represent. Rather, it says that material things are 'in the mind'. That is, the mind creates, sustains, and has power over matter. But the second view is little more than a post-Cartesian transposition of the first. Let me elaborate. Both in traditional African cosmologies and in European cosmologies before Descartes, the modern distinction between 'mind' and 'matter' does not appear. Although everything in the universe is underpinned by spiritual forces, what moderns would call 'mental activities' and 'material things' are both part of a single reality, neither material nor immaterial. Thinking, conceiving, saying, etc. are described in terms of organs like heart and brain and actions like the uttering of words. Now when Descartes wrote his philosophical works, he crystallized a half-way phase in the transition from a personal to an impersonal cosmological idiom. Whilst 'higher' human activities still remained under the aegis of a personalized theory, physical and biological events were brought under the aegis of impersonal theory. Hence thinking, conceiving, saying, etc. became manifestations of 'mind', whilst all other happenings became manifestations of 'matter'. Hence, whereas before Descartes we have 'words over things', after him we have 'mind over matter'— just a new disguise for the old view.

What I have said about this view being intellectually respectable but emotionally intolerable is borne out by the attitude to it of modern Western philosophers. Since they are duty bound to explore all the alternative possibilities of thought that lie within the grasp of their imaginations, these philosophers mention, nay even expound, the doctrines of Idealism and Solipsism. Invariably, too, they follow up their expositions with attempts at refutation. But such attempts are, just as invariably, at farce. Their character is summed up in G. E. Moore's desperate gesture, when challenged to prove the existence of a world outside his mind, of banging his hand with his fist and exclaiming: 'It is there!' A gesture of faith rather than of reason, if ever there was one!

With the change from the 'closed' to the 'open' predicament, then, the outlook behind magic becomes intolerable; and to escape from it people espouse the view that words vary independently of reality. Smug rationalists who congratulate themselves on their freedom from magical thinking would do well to reflect on the nature of this freedom!

## 2. *Ideas-Bound-to-Occasions Versus Ideas-Bound-to-Ideas*

Many commentators on the idea-systems of traditional African cultures have stressed that, for members of these cultures, their thought does not appear as something distinct from and opposable to the realities that call it into action. Rather, particular passages of thought are bound to the particular occasions that evoke them.

Let us take an example. Someone becomes sick. The sickness proves intractable and the relatives call a diviner. The latter says the sickness is due to an ancestor who has been angered by the patient's bad behaviour toward his kinsmen. The diviner prescribes placatory offerings to the spirit and reconciliation with the kinsmen, and the patient is eventually cured. Now while this emergency is on, both the diviner and the patient's relatives may justify what they are doing by reference to some general statements

about the kinds of circumstance which arouse ancestors to cause sickness.
And it is when he is lucky to be around on such occasions that the
anthropologist picks up most of his hard-earned information about traditional theories of the world and its working. But theoretical statements of
this kind are very much matters of occasion, not likely to be heard out of
context or as part of a general discussion of 'what we believe'. Indeed, the
anthropologist has learned by bitter experience that, in traditional Africa,
the generalized, 'what do you chaps believe?' approach gets one exactly
nowhere.[31]

If ideas in traditional culture are seen as bound to occasions rather than
to other ideas, the reason is one that we have already given in our discussion of magic. Since the member of such a culture can imagine no alternatives to his established system of ideas, the latter appear inexorably bound
to the portions of reality they stand for. They cannot be seen as in any
way opposable to reality.

In a scientifically oriented culture such as that of the Western anthropologist, things are very different. The very word 'idea' has the connotation of
something opposed to reality. Nor is it entirely coincidental that in such a
culture the historian of ideas is considered to be the most unrealistic kind
of historian. Not only are ideas dissociated in people's minds from the
reality that occasions them: they are bound to other ideas, to form wholes
and systems perceived as such. Belief-systems take shape not only as
abstractions in the minds of anthropologists, but also as totalities in the
minds of believers.

Here again, this change can be readily understood in terms of a change
from the 'closed' to the 'open' predicament. A vision of alternative possibilities forces men to the faith that ideas somehow vary whilst reality remains
constant. Ideas thus become detached from reality—nay, even in a sense
opposed to it. Furthermore, such a vision, by giving the thinker an opportunity to 'get outside' his own system, offers him a possibility of his coming
to see it *as a system*.

### 3. *Unreflective Versus Reflective Thinking*

At this stage of the analysis there is no need for me to insist further on the
essential rationality of traditional thought. In Part I, indeed, I have already

---

[31] From the piecemeal, situation-bound character of traditional idea-systems, some
have been led to infer that the anthropologist must analyse them in an equally piecemeal, situational manner, and not as systems. Thus in her recent *Purity and Danger*
(1966), Mary Douglas talks about the error of pinning out entire traditional idea-
systems like Lepidoptera, in abstraction from the real-life situations in which their
various fragments actually occur. But abstraction is as abstraction does. Provided that
comparison of total idea-systems leads to interesting results, it is surely as justifiable
as any other kind of comparison. After all, what about the abstraction and comparison
of social structures?

made it out far too rational for the taste of most social anthropologists. And yet, there is a sense in which this thought includes among its accomplishments neither Logic nor Philosophy.

Let me explain this, at first sight, rather shocking statement. It is true that most African traditional world-views are logically elaborated to a high degree. It is also true that, because of their eminently rational character, they are appropriately called 'philosophies'. But here I am using 'Logic' and 'Philosophy' in a more exact sense. By Logic, I mean thinking directed to answering the question: 'What are the general rules by which we can distinguish good arguments from bad ones?' And by Philosophy, I mean thinking directed to answering the question: 'On what grounds can we ever claim to know anything about the world?' Now Logic and Philosophy, in these restricted senses, are poorly developed in traditional Africa. Despite its elaborate and often penetrating cosmological, sociological, and psychological speculations, traditional thought has tended to get on with the work of explanation, without pausing for reflection upon the nature or rules of this work. Thinking once more of the 'closed' predicament, we can readily see why these second-order intellectual activities should be virtually absent from traditional cultures. Briefly, the traditional thinker, because he is unable to imagine possible alternatives to his established theories and classifications, can never start to formulate generalized norms of reasoning and knowing. For only where there are alternatives can there be choice, and only where there is choice can there be norms governing it. As they are characteristically absent in traditional cultures, so Logic and Philosophy are characteristically present in all scientifically oriented cultures. Just as the 'closed' predicament makes it impossible for them to appear, so the 'open' predicament makes it inevitable that they must appear. For where the thinker can see the possibility of alternatives to his established idea-system, the question of choice at once arises, and the development of norms governing such choice cannot be far behind.[32]

### 4. Mixed Versus Segregated Motives

This contrast is very closely related to the preceding one. As I stressed in Part I of this essay, the goals of explanation and prediction are as powerfully present in traditional African cultures as they are in cultures where science has become institutionalized. In the absence of explicit norms of thought, however, we find them vigorously pursued but not explicitly reflected upon and defined. In these circumstances, there is little thought about their consistency or inconsistency with other goals and motives. Hence wherever we find a theoretical system with explanatory and predic-

---

[32] See Gellner, 1964, for a similar point exemplified in the Philosophy of Descartes (p. 105).

tive functions, we find other motives entering in and contributing to its development.

Despite their cognitive preoccupations, most African religious systems are powerfully influenced by what are commonly called 'emotional needs' —i.e. needs for certain kinds of personal relationship. In Africa, as elsewhere, all social systems stimulate in their members a considerable diversity of such needs; but, having stimulated them, they often prove unwilling or unable to allow them full opportunities for satisfaction. In such situations the spirits function not only as theoretical entities but as surrogate people providing opportunities for the formation of ties forbidden in the purely human social field. The latter function they discharge in two ways. First, by providing non-human partners with whom people can take up relationships forbidden with other human beings. Second, through the mechanism of possession, by allowing people to 'become' spirits and so to play roles *vis-à-vis* their fellow men which they are debarred from playing as ordinary human beings.

Examples of the first kind occur very commonly in association with the need for dependence created in children by the circumstances of their family upbringing. In some African societies male children are required to make an abrupt switch from dependence to independence as soon as they reach puberty. A prominent feature of the rites aimed at achieving this switch is the dramatic induction of the candidates into a relation of dependence with a powerful spiritual agency. The latter can be seen as a surrogate for the parents with whom the candidates are no longer allowed to continues their dependent relationships, and hence as a means of freeing the candidates for the exercise of adult independence and responsibility. This appears to be the basic significance of secret society initiations among the peoples of the Congo and the Western Guinea Coast. In other traditional societies, the early relation of dependence on parents is allowed to continue so long as the parents are still alive; and an abrupt switch to independence and responsibility has to be made on their death. Here, it is the dead parent, translated into ancestorhood, who provides for the continuance of a relationship which has had to be abruptly and traumatically discontinued in the purely human social field. This sequence, with its culmination in a highly devout worship of patrilineal ancestors, has been vividly described by Fortes in some of his writings on the Tallensi of Northern Ghana.[33]

Examples of the second kind occur more commonly in association with the need for dominance. Most societies stimulate this need more widely than they grant it satisfaction. In traditional African societies, women are the most common sufferers from this; and it is no accident that in the numerous spirit-possession cults that flourish up and down the continent

---

[33] See, for instance, Fortes, 1961.

women are generally rather more prominent than men. For in the male-authority roles which they tend to assume in possession, they gain access to a whole area of role-playing normally forbidden them.

Aesthetic motives, too, play an important part in moulding and sustaining traditional religious systems. This is especially true of West Africa, where narrative, poetry, song, dance, music, sculpture, and even architecture use the spirits and their characters as a framework upon which to develop their various forms. These arts in turn influence the direction in which ideas about the spirits develop. In my own field-work on Kalabari religion, I have found a gradual shading of the cognitive into the aesthetic which can at times be most confusing. In oral tradition, for example, serious myths intended to throw light on the part played by the gods in founding social institutions shade into tales which, although their characters are also gods, are told for sheer entertainment. And although Kalabari do make a distinction between serious myth and light tale, there are many pieces which they themselves hesitate to place on one side or the other. Belief shades through half-belief into suspended belief. In ritual, again, dramatic representations of the gods carried out in order to dispose them favourably and secure the benefits which, as cosmic forces, they control, are usually found highly enjoyable in themselves. And they shade off into representations carried out almost solely for their aesthetic appeal. In the Kalabari water-spirit masquerades, for instance, religion seems to have become the servant of art.[34]

There is little doubt that because the theoretical entities of traditional thought happen to be people, they give particular scope for the working of emotional and aesthetic motives. Here, perhaps, we do have something about the personal idiom in theory that does militate indirectly against the taking up of a scientific attitude; for where there are powerful emotional and aesthetic loadings on a particular theoretical scheme, these must add to the difficulties of abandoning this scheme when cognitive goals press toward doing so. Once again, I should like to stress that the mere fact of switching from a personal to an impersonal idiom does not make anyone a scientist, and that one can be unscientific or scientific in either idiom. In this respect, nevertheless, the personal idiom does seem to present certain difficulties for the scientific attitude which the impersonal idiom does not.

Where the possibility of choice has stimulated the development of Logic, Philosophy, and norms of thought generally, the situation undergoes radical change. One theory is judged better than another with explicit reference to its efficacy in explanation and prediction. And as these ends become more clearly defined, it gets increasingly evident that no other ends are compatible with them. People come to see that if ideas are to be used as efficient tools of explanation and prediction, they must not be allowed to

---

[34] See Horton, 1963.

become tools of anything else. (This, of course, is the essence of the ideal of 'objectivity'.) Hence there grows up a great watchfulness against seduction by the emotional or aesthetic appeal of a theory—a watchfulness which in twentieth-century Europe sometimes takes extreme forms such as the suspicion of any research publication not written out in a positively indigestible style. Also there appears an insistence on the importance of 'pure' as opposed to 'applied' science. This does not mean that scientists are against practical application of their findings. What it does mean is that they feel there should always be some disjunction between themselves and the people who apply their discoveries. The reasons for this are basically the same as those which lead the scientist to be on his guard against emotional or aesthetic appeals. For one thing, if a scientist is too closely identified with a given set of practical problems, he may become so committed to solving these as to take up any theory that offers solution without giving it adequate testing. Again, those lines of inquiry most closely related to the practical problems of the day are not necessarily those which lead to the most rapid advances in explanation and prediction. Finally, in so far as practical interests involve inter-business and inter-national competition, over-identification with them can lead to a fundamental denial of the scientific ideal by encouraging the observance of rules of secrecy. Since it is a primary canon of the scientific ideal that every new theory be subjected to the widest possible testing and criticism, free circulation of new findings is basic to the code of the scientific community. (See below.) Hence, in so far as commercial and international competition leads to the curtailment of such circulation, it is inimical to science. This is why brilliant and dedicated scientists tend to be among the most double-edged weapons in wars either hot or cold.

The traditional theoretical scheme, as we have noted, brings forth and nourishes a rich encrustation of cultural growths whose underlying motives have little to do with explanation and prediction. Notable among these are elaborate systems of personal relationships with beings beyond the purely human social order, and all manner of artistic embellishments.

As the insistence on segregation of theoretical activity from the influence of all motives but those defined as essential to it gains strength, these various growths are forcibly sloughed off and have to embark on an independent existence. To survive without getting involved in a losing battle with the now-prestigious 'science', they have to eschew loudly all explanatory pretensions, and devote great energy to defining their 'true' ends. In doing this, they have often been accused of making a virtue out of sad necessity—of putting a brazen face on what is simply a headlong retreat before science. But their activities in this direction can, I think, also be seen in a more positive way. That is, they too can be seen as a direct outcome of the 'open' predicament, and thence of the general tendency to reflect on the nature of thought, to define its aims, and to formulate its norms. Now the conclusion such reflective activity arrives at for Theory-Making also holds for Spiritual Communion and for Art: that is, there are several distinct modes of thought; and a particular mode, if it is to fulfil itself completely, must be protected from the influence of all motives except those defined as essential to it. Hence when we hear a Western theologian proclaim loudly the 'modern discovery' that the essence of religion has nothing to do with explanation and prediction of worldly events, but is simply communion with God for its own sake, we are only partly right when we sneer at him for trying to disguise retreat as advance. For in fact he can claim to be undertaking much the same kind of purifying and refining operation as the scientist. The force of this contention emerges when we come to consider the case of the artist. For when the latter proclaims that his activity is no longer the handmaid of religion, of science, or even of representation, we do in fact grant that this drastic circumscription of aims represents a form of progress akin to that of the scientist purging his subject in the pursuit of objectivity. The rationalist who says that the modern theologian is retreating whilst the modern artist is advancing is thus merely expressing an agnostic prejudice. Both, in fact, are in an important sense caught up in the same currents of thought as those that move the scientist.

It will now be clear that the scientist's quest for 'objectivity' is, among other things, a purifying movement. As has happened in many such movements, however, the purifying zeal tends to wander beyond its self-appointed bounds, and even to run to excess within these bounds. Such tendencies are well exemplified in the impact of the quest for objectivity on metaphor.

In traditional Africa, speech abounds with metaphor to a degree no longer familiar in the scientifically oriented cultures of the modern West. The function of such metaphor is partly, as anthropologists never tire of saying,[35] to allude obliquely to things which cannot be said directly. Much more importantly, perhaps, its function is to underline, emphasize, and give greater impact to things which *can* be said literally. 'Proverbs are the palm oil with which words are eaten', say the Ibo.[36] In this capacity, it is clearly a vital adjunct to rational thought. Often, however, metaphor subtly misleads. The analogy between the things which constitute its literal reference and the things which constitute its oblique reference usually involves only limited aspects of both. But there is always a temptation to extend the analogy unduly, and it can then run its users right off the rails. In sociology, for instance, this has happened with the use of organismic metaphors for thinking about societies and social relations. Organisms and societies do perhaps resemble each other in certain limited ways; but sociologists who

---

[35] See Beattie, 1966.
[36] Achebe, 1957.

have become addicted to organismic metaphor often go beyond these limited resemblances and end up by attributing to societies all sorts of properties possessed only by organisms.

These occasional dangers have led the purists to regard metaphor and analogy as one great snare and delusion. No palm-oil with our words, they have decreed with grim satisfaction. The resulting cult of plain, literal speaking, alas, has spread beyond the bounds of strictly scientific activity right through everyday life, taking much of the poetic quality out of ordinary, hum-drum social relations. Not only this. The distrust of metaphor and analogy has in some places gone so far as to threaten intellectual processes which are crucial to the advance of science itself. Thus the positivist philosophers of science have often denigrated the activity of theoretical model-building. At best, some of them have contended, such model-building is a dubious help to serious scientific thought; and at worst, its reliance on the process of analogy may be extremely misleading. According to this purist school, induction and deduction are the only processes of thought permissible to the scientist. His job is not to elaborate models of a supposed reality lying 'behind' the data of experience. It is simply to observe; to make inductive generalizations summarizing the regularities found in observation; to deduce from these generalizations the probable course of further observation; and finally to test this deduction against experience. A then B, A then B, A then B; hence all A's are followed by B's; hence if there is an A in the future, it will be followed by a B; check. The trouble about this purist paradigm, of course, is that it condemns the scientist to an eternity of triteness and circularity. It can never account for any of the great leaps in explanatory power which we associate with the advance of science. Only in relation to some model of underlying reality, for instance, can we come to see that A and X, B and Y, so different in the eye of the casual observer, are actually outward manifestations of the same kinds of events. Only in relation to such a model are we suddenly moved to look for a conjunction between X and Y which we would never have noticed otherwise. And only thus can we come to see AB, XY as two instances of a single underlying process or regularity. Finally, so it seems, the only way yet discovered in which scientists can turn out the new models of underlying reality necessary to set such explanatory advance in motion is through the drawing of bold analogies.

To sum up on this point: one of the essential features of science is that it is a purifying movement. But like other purifying movements, alas, it provides fertile soil for obsessional personalities. If we can compare the traditional thinker to an easy-going housewife who feels she can get along quite nicely despite a considerable accumulation of dirt and dust on the furniture, we can compare the positivist who is so often a fellow traveller of science to an obsessional housewife who scrubs off the dirt, the paintwork, and finally the handles that make the furniture of use!

## B. Differences Connected with the Presence or Absence of Anxiety about Threats to the Established Body of Theory

### 5. *Protective Versus Destructive Attitude towards Established Theory*

Both in traditional Africa and in the science-oriented West, theoretical thought is vitally concerned with the prediction of events. But there are marked differences in reaction to predictive failure.

In the theoretical thought of the traditional cultures, there is a notable reluctance to register repeated failures of prediction and to act by attacking the beliefs involved. Instead, other current beliefs are utilized in such a way as to 'excuse' each failure as it occurs, and hence to protect the major theoretical assumptions on which prediction is based. This use of *ad hoc* excuses is a phenomenon which social anthropologists have christened 'secondary elaboration'.[37]

The process of secondary elaboration is most readily seen in association with the work of diviners and oracle-operators, who are concerned with discovering the identity of the spiritual forces responsible for particular happenings in the visible, tangible world, and the reasons for their activation. Typically, a sick man goes to a diviner, and is told that a certain spiritual agency is 'worrying' him. The diviner points to certain of his past actions as having excited the spirit's anger, and indicates certain remedial actions which will appease this anger and restore health. Should the client take the recommended remedial action and yet see no improvement, he will be likely to conclude that the diviner was either fraudulent or just incompetent, and to seek out another expert. The new diviner will generally point to another spiritual agency and another set of arousing circumstances as responsible for the man's condition, and will recommend fresh remedial action. In addition, he will probably provide some explanation of why the previous diviner failed to get at the truth. He may corroborate the client's suspicions of fraud, or he may say that the spirit involved maliciously 'hid itself behind' another in such a way that only the most skilled of diviners would have been able to detect it. If after this the client should still see no improvement in his condition, he will move on to yet another diviner— and so on, perhaps, until his troubles culminate in death.

What is notable in all this is that the client never takes his repeated failures as evidence against the existence of the various spiritual beings named as responsible for his plight, or as evidence against the possibility

---

[37] The idea of secondary elaboration as a key feature of prescientific thought-systems was put forward with great brilliance and insight by Evans-Pritchard in his *Witchcraft, Oracles and Magic*. All subsequent discussions, including the present one, are heavily indebted to his lead.

of making contact with such beings as diviners claim to do. Nor do members of the wider community in which he lives ever try to keep track of the proportion of successes to failures in the remedial actions based on their beliefs, with the aim of questioning these beliefs. At most, they grumble about the dishonesty and wiles of many diviners, whilst maintaining their faith in the existence of some honest, competent practitioners.

In these traditional cultures, questioning of the beliefs on which divining is based and weighing up of successes against failures are just not among the paths that thought can take. They are blocked paths because the thinkers involved are victims of the closed predicament. For them, established beliefs have an absolute validity, and any threat to such beliefs is a horrific threat of chaos. Who is going to jump from the cosmic palm-tree when there is no hope of another perch to swing to?

Where the scientific outlook has become firmly entrenched, attitudes to established beliefs are very different. Much has been made of the scientist's essential scepticism toward established beliefs; and one must, I think, agree that this above all is what distinguishes him from the traditional thinker. But one must be careful here. The picture of the scientist in continuous readiness to scrap or demote established theory contains a dangerous exaggeration as well as an important truth. As an outstanding modern historian of the sciences has recently observed,[38] the typical scientist spends most of his time optimistically seeing how far he can push a new theory to cover an ever-widening horizon of experience. When he has difficulty in making the theory 'fit', he is more likely to develop it in the ways described in Part I of this essay than to scrap it out of hand. And if it does palpably fail the occasional test, he may even put the failure down to dirty apparatus or mistaken meter-reading—rather like the oracle operator! And yet, the spirit behind the scientist's actions *is* very different. His pushing of a theory and his reluctance to scrap it are not due to any chilling intuition that if his theory fails him, chaos is at hand. Rather, they are due to the very knowledge that the theory is not something timeless and absolute. Precisely because he knows that the present theory came in at a certain epoch to replace a predecessor, and that its explanatory coverage is far better than that of the predecessor, he is reluctant to throw it away before giving it the benefit of every doubt. But this same knowledge makes for an acceptance of the theory which is far more qualified and far more watchful than that of the traditional thinker. The scientist is, as it were, always keeping account, balancing the successes of a theory against its failures. And when the failures start to come thick and fast, defence of the theory switches inexorably to attack on it.

If the record of a theory that has fallen under a cloud is poor in all circumstances, it is ruthlessly scrapped. The collective memory of the Euro-

---

[38] Kuhn, 1962.

pean scientific community is littered with the wreckage of the various unsatisfactory theories discarded over the last 500 years—the earth-centered theory of the universe, the circular theory of planetary motion, the phlogiston theory of chemical combination, the aether theory of wave propagation, and perhaps a hundred others. Often, however, it is found that a theoretical model once assumed to have universal validity in fact has a good predictive performance over a limited range of circumstances, but a poor performance outside this range. In such a case, the beliefs in question are still ruthlessly demoted; but instead of being thrown out altogether they are given a lesser status as limiting cases of more embracing generalities—still useful as lower-level models or as guides to experience within restricted areas. This sort of demotion has been the fate of theoretical schemes like Newton's Laws of Motion (still used as a guide in many mundane affairs, including much of the business of modern rocketry) and the 'Ball-and-Bond' theory of chemical combination.

This underlying readiness to scrap or demote established theories on the ground of poor predictive performance is perhaps the most important single feature of the scientific attitude. It is, I suggest, a direct outcome of the 'open' predicament. For only when the thinker is able to see his established idea-system as one among many alternatives can he see his established ideas as things of less than absolute value. And only when he sees them thus can he see the scrapping of them as anything other than a horrific, irretrievable jump into chaos.

## 6. *Divination Versus Diagnosis*

Earlier in this essay I drew certain parallels between the work of the traditional African diviner and the work of the Western diagnostician. In particular, I showed how both of them make much the same use of theoretical ideas: i.e. as means of linking observed effects to causes that lie beyond the powers of common sense to grasp. I now propose to discuss certain crucial differences between these two kinds of agent.

As I noted in the last section, in traditional cultures anxieties about threats to the established theories effectively block many of the paths thought might otherwise take. One path so blocked is the working out of any body of theory which assigns too distinctive an effect to any particular pattern of antecedents. Why this path should be blocked is not hard to see. Suppose that there is a theory X, which makes the following causal connexions:

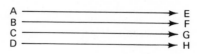

Now if situation E is disagreeable, and is unambiguously ascribable to cause A, action will be taken to get rid of E by manipulating A. If it fails, then the most obvious verdict is that A→E is invalid. A similar argument applies, of course, to B→F, C→G, D→H.

Suppose, on the other hand, that theory X makes the following connexions:

Now things are very different. If E is ascribed to A, action will still be taken to get rid of E by manipulating A. But if it fails, we are no longer compelled to admit that A→E is invalid. We can now say that perhaps B was present as a complicating factor, and that failure to take account of it was responsible for our disappointment. Or we can say that A was not present at all, but only D. So the theory remains protected.

Coming back to concrete terms, we find that traditional African theories of, say, disease approximate to the second of these patterns rather than to the first, and that this is their ultimate protection. In most traditional cultures, diseases are thought to be caused by the anger of several categories of spirits. Each of these categories is aroused by a different kind of situation. Thus in Kalabari thought heroes, ancestors, water-spirits, and medicine spirits are the main unseen bringers of disease. Heroes tend to be activated by offences against 'town laws', ancestors by offences against kinsmen, water-spirits by failure to heed certain tangible signs that they wish to form personal attachments with human partners, medicine-spirits by the machinations of enemies with whom one 'has case'. Hence there is a fairly clear correlation between the kind of activating situation and the kind of spirit brought into play. But although there are the beginnings of a second correlation, between the kind of spirit brought into play and the kind of misfortune inflicted, this has not gone very far. By and large, if a diviner attributes a disease to a certain spirit aroused by certain antecedent circumstances, and if the remedy based on this attribution fails, another diviner can always say that the first attribution was a mistake, and that it was really another spirit, aroused by another set of circumstances, who caused the trouble. Studies like those of Evans-Pritchard on the Zande,[39] Nadel on the Nupe,[40] and Forde on the Yakö[41] suggest that this particular defensive pattern, based on converging causal sequences, is very widespread.

But a theory which postulates converging causal sequences, though self-

[39] 1936, *passim.*

[40] Nadel, 1956, esp. chap. vi.

[41] Forde, 1958.

protective to a high degree, faces serious problems in its application to everyday life. For the man who visits a diviner with misfortune E does not want to be told that it could be due to any one of four different kinds of spirits, activated by circumstances A, B, C, or D. He wants a definite verdict and a definite remedial prescription.

Now given the nature of the theoretical model the diviner operates with, any amount of minute inspection and definition of E will not allow him to give a definite verdict as between A, B, C, or D. Sometimes, he can and does find out from the client whether A, B, C, or D have occurred in his life-history. But the client may well have forgotten the crucial activating circumstance. Indeed, as it is often a guilt-provoking circumstance, he is likely to have forgotten it. Or, the client may remember that happenings answering to both A, B, and C have occurred at various times in his life; and the diviner is still left with the problem of which of these happenings and which category of spirit is actually responsible for the present occurrence of E.

We have, then, an apparently insoluble conflict. For the diviner to give a causal verdict which transcends the limited vision of common sense, he must operate with a theory. But for the theory to survive, it must be of the converging-sequence type which makes the giving of a definite causal verdict very difficult.

As I see it, the essence of divination is that it is a mechanism for resolving this conflict. Faced with a theory postulating several possible causes for a given event, and no means of inferring the actual cause from observable evidence, divination goes, as it were, 'over the head of' such evidence. It elicits a direct sign from the realm of those unobservable entities that govern the causal linkages it deals with—a sign that enables it to say which of the several sequences indicated by the theory is the one actually involved.

Just how it elicits this sign seems immaterial. Indeed, there is a fantastic variety of divination procedures on the African continent. The diviner may enter into a privileged contact with the realm of unobservable entities postulated by his theory, 'seeing' and 'hearing' them in a manner beyond the powers of his client. The diviner may force his client to choose from a collection of twigs, each representing one of the various spirits and causal linkages potentially involved in the situation. He may set spiders to chew leaves, and give his verdict on the basis of a series of correlations between patterns of chewing and kinds of causal sequence. He may cause a dead body to be carried by several men, suggest to the body the various possible causes of its death, and obtain from its consequent movements a reply as to which is the cause actually involved. He may administer poison to a series of fowls, put one of the several potential sequences as a question to each fowl, and infer from the life or death of the animal whether this particular sequence is the one actually involved. One might cite up to a hundred more ingenious procedures.

All of these divination techniques share two basic features. First, as I have said, they are means of selecting one actual causal sequence from several potential sequences. Secondly, they all carry a subtle aura of fallibility which makes it possible to 'explain everything away' when remedial prescriptions based on them turn out not to work. Thus many divination procedures require an esoteric knowledge or faculty which the client does not share with the operator. Hence the client has no direct check on the operator; and in retrospect there is always the possibility of the latter's dishonesty or sheer incompetence. Again, nearly all of these procedures are thought to be very delicate and easily thrown out of kilter. Among other things, they may be affected by pollution, or by the machinations of those who have a grudge against the client.

So, whereas the positive features of the divining process make it possible to arrive at a definite causal verdict despite a converging-sequence theory, the aura of fallibility provides for the self-protecting action of such a theory by making it possible, in the event of a failure, to switch from one potential sequence to another in such a way as to leave the theory as a whole unimpugned. In the last section, we noted that the context of divination provided some of the clearest illustrations of the defence-mechanism known as 'secondary elaboration'. Now, I think, we can go further: that is, we can say that divination owes its very existence to the exigencies of this mechanism.

Where the 'open' predicament prevails, anxieties about threats to the established theories decline, and previously blocked thought-paths become clear. We now witness the development of theories that assign distinctive effects to differing causes; and in the face of this development the type of theory that assumes converging sequences tends to disappear. Nowadays, of course, it is more fashionable to talk of covariation than to talk of cause and effect. But the continuous-covariation formula of the type $ds = f. \, dt$, so prominent in modern scientific theory, is in fact an instance of the tendency I am referring to. For, spelled out, the implication of such a formula is that, to an infinite number of values of a cause-variable, there correspond an infinite number of values of an effect-variable.

Where this type of theory comes into the ascendant, the diviner gives place to the diagnostician. The latter, whether he is concerned with bodily upsets or with aeroplane disasters, goes to work in a way which differs in important respects from that of his traditional counterpart. Dealing as he does with theories that postulate non-converging causal sequences, he has a task altogether more prosaic than that of the diviner. For, given non-convergence, a complete and accurate observation of effect, plus knowledge of the relevant theory, makes it possible for him to give an unambiguous causal verdict. Once these conditions have been fulfilled, there is no need for the additional operations of the diviner. No need for special mechanisms to elicit signs from the realm of unobservable entities. No need for a way of going 'over the head of' observable evidence in order to find out which of several potential causes is the actual one.

Modern Western diagnosis, it is true, has not lost all of the aura of fallibility that surrounds traditional divining. Incomplete and inaccurate observation of effect may sometimes provide a plausible defence for failures of diagnosis based on outmoded theory. But such a defence is a poor thing compared with that provided by converging-sequence theory and a divining mechanism characterized as inherently delicate and subject to breakdown. In the modern West, of course, the diagnosticians and remedialists are usually not the same as the people who are actively concerned with the developing and testing of theory. (Hence the division between 'pure' and 'applied' scientists.) Nevertheless, it is often through reports of failure from these men that the developers and testers get their stimulus for the replacement of an old theory with a new one. Thus in medicine, reports from general practitioners about widespread breakdown of well-tried diagnostic and healing procedures have often provided the stimulus for medical researchers to make drastic revisions in the theory of disease.

Far from being an integral part of any mechanism for defending theory, then, the diagnostician often contributes his share to the circumstances that lead to the abandonment of old ideas and the adoption of new ones.


## 7. Absence Versus Presence of Experimental Method

Anyone who has read Part I of this paper should be in little doubt as to how closely adjusted traditional African theoretical systems often are to the prevailing facts of personality, social organization, and ecology. Indeed, although many of the causal connexions they posit turn out to be red herrings when subjected to scientific scrutiny, others turn out to be very real and vital. Thus an important part of traditional religious theory posits and attempts to explain the connexion between disturbed social relationships and disease—a connexion whose reality and importance Western medical scientists are only just beginning to see. Nevertheless, the adjustments of these systems to changing experience are essentially slow, piecemeal, and reluctant. Nothing must happen to arouse public suspicion that basic theoretical models are being challenged. If changes are to take place, they must take place like movements in the game of Grandmother's Footsteps: i.e. when Grandma is not looking, and in such a way that whenever she turns round, she sees somebody standing stock-still and in a position not too obviously different from the one he was in when last she looked. The consequence of all this, if the reader will excuse me for mixing my metaphors, is that traditional idea-systems are usually catching up on experience from a position of 'one jump behind'.

Scientific thought, by contrast, is characteristically 'one jump ahead' of experience. It is able to be so because of that distinctive feature of the scientist's calling: the Experimental Method. This method is nothing more nor less than the positive extension of the 'open' attitude to established beliefs and categories which we referred to in Section 5. For the essence of experiment is that the holder of a pet theory does not just wait for events to come along and show whether or not it has a good predictive performance. He bombards it with artificially produced events in such a way that its merits or defects will show up as immediately and as clearly as possible.

Often, the artificially produced events involved in an experiment are ones that would take a long time to observe if left to occur of their own accord. Thus a medical research worker who has a theory about the destructive effect of a certain chemical upon pneumonia germs does not wait for the next severe English winter to bring its heavy toll of pneumonia victims. He gets a large batch of monkeys (or, in America sometimes, condemned human volunteers), deliberately infects them with pneumonia, gives some the chemical and others an inert substance, and observes the results. In many cases, the artificially produced events are of a kind which would almost certainly never occur were nature left to take her own course; but the experimentalist sets great store by them because they are expressly designed to provide a more unequivocal test of theory than any naturally occurring conditions. Most laboratory experiments in biology, chemistry, and especially physics are of this kind.

We can say, then, that whereas in traditional thought there is continual if reluctant adjustment of theories to new experience, in science men spend much of their time deliberately creating new experience in order to evaluate their theories. Whilst in traditional thought it is mostly experience that determines theory, in the world of the experimental scientist there is a sense in which theory usually determines experience.

## 8. *The Confession of Ignorance*

The European anthropologist working in a traditional African community often has the experience of soliciting people's theories on a number of (to him) interesting topics, and of getting the reply 'we don't know anything about that' with the implication 'we don't really care'. Thus the anthropologist usually comes to Africa with ideas about the wonderful 'creation myths' to be found there. Very often, however, he finds that the people he has come to live with are not at all curious about the creation of the world; and apart from acknowledging that it was the work of a supreme being, they are apt to say with a shrug of their shoulders 'the old people did not tell us anything about it'. (Often, of course, an equal lack of curiosity on the anthropologist's part leads him to miss an elaborate body of indigenous explanatory theory covering some area of experience his own lack of interest prevented him from enquiring about.)

What the anthropologist almost never finds is a confession of ignorance about the answer to some question which the people themselves consider important. Scarcely ever, for instance, does he come across a common disease or crop failure whose cause and cure people say they just do not know.

Given the basic predicament of the traditional thinker, such an admission would indeed be intolerable. For where there are no conceivable alternatives to the established theoretical system, any hint that this system is failing to cope must be a hint of irreparable chaos, and so must rouse extreme anxiety.

In the case of the scientist, his readiness to test every theory to destruction makes it inevitable that he will have to confess ignorance whenever a theory crumbles under testing and he has no better one immediately available. Indeed, it is only in a culture where the scientific attitude is firmly institutionalized that one can hope to hear the answer 'we don't know' given by an expert questioned on the causes of such a terrible human scourge as cancer. Such willingness to confess ignorance means that the world-view provided by scientists for wider consumption is apt to seem far less comprehensive and embracing than many of the world-views of pre-scientific cultures. In fact, it tends to give the impression of a great expanse of darkness illuminated only at irregular intervals. This impression, of course, is tolerable to scientists precisely because the beliefs they hold at a given time are not things of absolute value to which they can imagine no possible alternatives. If current beliefs let in the dark, this does not rule out the possibility of other beliefs which may eventually shut it out.


## 9. Coincidence, Chance, Probability

Closely related to the development of a capacity to tolerate ignorance is the development of concepts which formally recognize the existence of various kinds of limitation upon the possible completeness of explanation and prediction. Important among such concepts are those of coincidence, chance, and probability.

Let us start with the idea of coincidence. In the traditional cultures of Africa, such a concept is poorly developed. The tendency is to give any untoward happening a definite cause. When a rotten branch falls off a tree and kills a man walking underneath it, there has to be a definite explanation of the calamity. Perhaps the man quarrelled with a half-brother over some matter of inheritance, and the latter worked the fall of the branch through a sorcerer. Or perhaps he misappropriated lineage property, and the lineage ancestors brought the branch down on his head. The idea that the whole thing could have come about through the accidental convergence of two independent chains of events is inconceivable because it is psychologically intolerable. To entertain it would be to admit that the episode was inexplicable and unpredictable: a glaring confession of ignorance.

It is characteristic of the scientist that he is willing to face up to the inexplicability and unpredictability of this type of situation, and that he does not shrink from diagnosing an accidental convergence of different chains of events. This is a consequence of his ability to tolerate ignorance.

As with the idea of coincidence, so with that of probability. Where traditional thought is apt to demand definite forecasts of whether something will or will not happen, the scientist is often content to know the probability of its happening—that is, the number of times it will happen in a hypothetical series of, say, a hundred trials.

When it was first developed, the probability forecast was seen as a makeshift tool for use in situations where one's knowledge of the factors operating was incomplete, and where it was assumed that possession of all the relevant data would have made a definite forecast possible. This is still an important context of probability forecasting, and will continue to be so. An example of its use is in prediction of incidence of the mental disease schizophrenia. Psychiatrists have now come to believe that heredity plays a large part in causing the disease; and given a knowledge of the distribution of previous cases in a person's family history, they are able to calculate the probability of his contracting it. Their forecasts only run to probabilities, because they are not yet sure that they know all the other factors which reinforce or inhibit the effect of heredity, and also because they are seldom in a position to observe all those factors they do know to be relevant. Nevertheless, the assumption remains that if all the relevant factors could be known and observed, the probability forecasts could be replaced by unequivocal predictions.

In the twentieth century, a yet more drastic step has been taken in acknowledging the limits of explanation and prediction. For physicists now admit that the entities they postulate as the ultimate constituents of all matter—the so-called Elementary Particles—have properties such that, even given all obtainable data about their condition at any instant, it is still impossible to give more than a probability forecast of their condition at any instant in the future. Here, the probability forecast is no longer a makeshift for an unequivocal prediction: it is ultimate and irreducible.

From one angle, then, the development of the scientific outlook appears more than anything else as a growth of intellectual humility. Where the prescientific thinker is unable to confess ignorance on any question of vital practical import, the good scientist is always ready to do so. Again, where the prescientific thinker is reluctant to acknowledge any limitation on his power to explain and predict, the scientist not only faces such limitations with equanimity, but devotes a good deal of energy to exploring and charting their extent.

This humility, I suggest, is the product of an underlying confidence—

the confidence which comes from seeing that one's currently held beliefs are not the be-all and end-all of the human search for order. Once one has seen this, the difficulty of facing up to their limitations largely dissolves.[42]

## 10. *Protective Versus Destructive Attitude to the Category-System*

If someone is asked to list typical features of traditional thinking, he is almost certain to mention the phenomenon known as 'taboo'. 'Taboo' is the anthropological jargon for a reaction of horror and aversion to certain actions or happenings which are seen as monstrous and polluting. It is characteristic of the taboo reaction that people are unable to justify it in terms of ulterior reasons: tabooed events are simply bad in themselves. People take every possible step to prevent tabooed events from happening, and to isolate or expel them when they do occur.

Taboo has long been a mystery to anthropologists. Of the many explanations proposed, few have fitted more than a small selection of the instances observed. It is only recently that an anthropologist has placed the phenomenon in a more satisfactory perspective by the observation that in nearly every case of taboo reaction, the events and actions involved are ones which seriously defy the established lines of classification in the culture where they occur.[43]

Perhaps the most important occasion of taboo reaction in traditional African cultures is the commission of incest. Incest is one of the most flagrant defiances of the established category-system: for he who commits it treats a mother, daughter, or sister like a wife. Another common occasion for taboo reaction is the birth of twins. Here, the category distinction involved is that of human beings versus animals—multiple births being taken as characteristic of animals as opposed to men. Yet another very generally tabooed object is the human corpse, which occupies, as it were, a classificatory no-man's-land between the living and the inanimate. Equally widely tabooed are such human bodily excreta as faeces and menstrual blood, which occupy the same no-man's-land between the living and the inanimate.

Taboo reactions are often given to occurrences that are radically strange or new; for these too (almost by definition) fail to fit in to the established category system. A good example is furnished by a Kalabari story of the

---

[42] Some similar comments on the themes of ignorance and uncertainty in relation to the scientific outlook are made by R. G. Armstrong in a brief but trenchant critique of 'The Notion of Magic' by M. and R. Wax (1963).

[43] This observation may well prove to be a milestone in our understanding of traditional thought. It was first made some years ago by Mary Douglas, who has developed many of its implications in her recent book *Purity and Danger*. Though we clearly disagree on certain wider implications, the present discussion is deeply indebted to her insights.

coming of the Europeans. The first white man, it is said, was seen by a fisherman who had gone down to the mouth of the estuary in his canoe. Panic-stricken, he raced home and told his people what he had seen; whereupon he and the rest of the town set out to purify themselves—that is, to rid themselves of the influence of the strange and monstrous thing that had intruded into their world.

A sort of global taboo reaction is often evoked by foreign lands. As the domains of so much that is strange and unassimilable to one's own categories, such lands are the abode *par excellence* of the monstrous and the abominable. The most vivid description we have of this attitude is that given for the Lugbara by John Middleton.[44] For this East African people, the foreigner is the inverted perpetrator of all imaginable abominations from incest downwards. The more alien he is, the more abominable. Though the Lugbara attitude is extreme, many traditional African cultures would seem to echo it in some degree.[45]

Just as the central tenets of the traditional theoretical system are defended against adverse experience by an elaborate array of excuses for predictive failure, so too the main classificatory distinctions of the system are defended by taboo avoidance reactions against any event that defies them. Since every system of belief implies a system of categories, and vice versa, secondary elaboration and taboo reaction are really opposite sides of the same coin.

From all this it follows that, like secondary elaboration, taboo reaction has no place among the reflexes of the scientist. For him, whatever defies or fails to fit in to the established category-system is not something horrifying, to be isolated or expelled. On the contrary, it is an intriguing 'phenomenon' —a starting point and a challenge for the invention of new classifications and new theories. It is something every young research worker would like to have crop up in his field of observation—perhaps the first rung on the ladder of fame. If a biologist ever came across a child born with the head of a goat, he would be hard put to it to make his compassion cover his elation. And as for social anthropologists, one may guess that their secret dreams are of finding a whole community of men who sleep for preference with their mothers!

## 11. *The Passage of Time: Bad or Good?*

In traditional Africa, methods of time-reckoning vary greatly from culture to culture. Within each culture, again, we find a plurality of time-scales used in different contexts. Thus there may be a major scale which locates

---

[44] Middleton, 1960.

[45] This association of foreign lands with chaos and pollution seems to be a universal of prescientific thought-systems. For this, see Eliade, 1961, esp. chap. 1.

events either before, during, or after the time of founding of the major institutions of the community: another scale which locates events by correlating them with the life-times of deceased ancestors: yet another which locates events by correlating them with the phases of the seasonal cycle: and yet another which uses phases of the daily cycle.

Although these scales are seldom interrelated in any systematic way, they all serve to order events in before-after series. Further, they have the very general characteristic that *vis-à-vis* 'after', 'before' is usually valued positively, sometimes neutrally, and never negatively. Whatever the particular scale involved, then, the passage of time is seen as something deleterious or at best neutral.

Perhaps the most widespread, everyday instance of this attitude is the standard justification of so much thought and action: 'That is what the old-time people told us.' (It is usually this standard justification which is in the forefront of the anthropologist's mind when he applies the label 'traditional culture'.)

On the major time-scale of the typical traditional culture, things are thought of as having been better in the golden age of the founding heroes than they are today. On an important minor time-scale, the annual one, the end of the year is a time when everything in the cosmos is run-down and sluggish, overcome by an accumulation of defilement and pollution.

A corollary of this attitude to time is a rich development of activities designed to negate its passage by a 'return to the beginning'. Such activities characteristically depend on the magical premiss that a symbolic statement of some archetypal event can in a sense recreate that event and temporarily obliterate the passage of time which has elapsed since its original occurrence.[46]

These rites of recreation are to be seen at their most luxuriant in the ancient cultures of the Western Sudan—notably in those of the Bambara and Dogon. In such cultures, indeed, a great part of everyday activity is said to have the ulterior significance of recreating archetypal events and acts. Thus the Dogon labouring in the fields recreates in his pattern of cultivation the emergence of the world from the cosmic egg. The builder of a homestead lays it out in a pattern that symbolically recreates the body of the culture-hero Nommo. Even relations between kin symbolize and recreate relations between the primal beings.[47]

One might well describe the Western Sudanic cultures as obsessed with the annulment of time to a degree unparalleled in Africa as a whole. Yet

---

[46] In these rites of recreation, traditional African thought shows its striking affinities with prescientific thought in many other parts of the world. The world-wide occurrence and meaning of such rites was first dealt with by Mircea Eliade in his *Myth of the Eternal Return*. A more recent treatment, from which the present analysis has profited greatly, is to be found in the chapter entitled 'Le Temps Retrouvé', Lévi-Strauss, 1962.

[47] See Griaule and Dieterlen, 1954, and Griaule, 1965.

other, less spectacular, manifestations of the attempt to 'get back to the beginning' are widely distributed over the continent. In the West African forest belt, for instance, the richly developed ritual dramas enacted in honour of departed heroes and ancestors have a strong recreative aspect. For by inducing these beings to possess specially selected media and thus, during festivals, to return temporarily to the company of men, such rituals are restoring things as they were in olden times.[48]

On the minor time-scale provided by the seasonal cycle, we find a similar widespread concern for recreation and renewal. Hence the important rites which mark the end of an old year and the beginning of a new one—rites which attempt to make the year new by a thoroughgoing process of purification of accumulated pollutions and defilements.

This widespread attempt to annul the passage of time seems closely linked to features of traditional thought which I have already reviewed. As I pointed out earlier, the new and the strange, in so far as they fail to fit into the established system of classification and theory, are intimations of chaos to be avoided as far as possible. Advancing time, with its inevitable element of non-repetitive change, is the vehicle *par excellence* of the new and the strange. Hence its effects must be annulled at all costs. Rites of renewal and recreation, then, have much in common with the processes of secondary elaboration and taboo behaviour. Indeed, their kinship with the latter can be seen in the idea that the passage of the year is essentially an accumulation of pollutions, which it is the function of the renewal rites to remove. In short, these rites are the third great defensive reflex of traditional thought.[49]

When we turn from the traditional thinker to the scientist, we find this whole valuation of temporal process turned upside down. Not for the scientist the idea of a golden age at the beginning of time—an age from which things have been steadily falling away. For him, the past is a bad old past, and the best things lie ahead. The passage of time brings inexorable progress. As C. P. Snow has put it aptly, all scientists have 'the future in their bones'.[50] Where the traditional thinker is busily trying to annul the passage of time, the scientist may almost be said to be trying frantically to hurry time up. For in his impassioned pursuit of the experimental method, he is striving after the creation of new situations which nature, if left to herself, would bring about slowly if ever at all.

Once again, the scientist's attitude can be understood in terms of the 'open' predicament. For him, currently held ideas on a given subject are

---

[48] For some interesting remarks on this aspect of West African ritual dramas, see Tardits, 1962.

[49] Lévi-Straus, I think, is making much the same point about rites of renewal when he talks of the continuous battle between prescientific classificatory systems and the non-repetitive changes involved in the passage of time. See Lévi-Strauss, 1962.

[50] Snow, 1959, p. 10.

one possibility amongst many. Hence occurrences which threaten them are not the total, horrific threat that they would be for the traditional thinker. Hence time's burden of things new and strange does not hold the terrors that it holds for the traditionalist. Furthermore, the scientist's experience of the way in which successive theories, overthrown after exposure to adverse data, are replaced by ideas of ever greater predictive and explanatory power, leads almost inevitably to a very positive evaluation of time. Finally, we must remember that the 'open' predicament, though it has made people able to tolerate threats to their beliefs, has not been able to supply them with anything comparable to the cosiness of the traditional thinker ensconced amidst his established theories. As an English medical student, newly exposed to the scientific attitude, put it:

You seem to be as if when learning to skate, trying to find a nice hard piece of ice which you can stand upright on instead of learning how to move on it. You continue trying to find something, some foundation piece which will not move, whereas everything will move and you've got to learn to skate on it.[51]

The person who enjoys the moving world of the sciences, then, enjoys the exhilaration of the skater. But for many, this is a nervous, insecure sensation, which they would fain exchange for the womb-like warmth of the traditional theories and their defences. This lingering sense of insecurity gives a powerful attraction to the idea of progress. For by enabling people to cling to some hoped-for future state of perfect knowledge, it helps them live with a realization of the imperfection and transcience of present theories.

Once formed, indeed, the idea of Progress becomes in itself one of the most powerful supports of the scientific attitude generally. For the faith that, come what may, new experience must lead to better theories, and that better theories must eventually give place to still better ones, provides the strongest possible incentive for a constant readiness to expose oneself to the strange and the disturbing, to scrap current frameworks of ideas, and to cast about for replacements.

Like the quest for purity of motive, however, the faith in progress is a double-edged weapon. For the lingering insecurity which is one of the roots of this faith leads all too often to an excessive fixation of hopes and desires on an imagined Utopian future. People cling to such a future in the same way that men in prescientific cultures cling to the past. And in doing so, they inevitably lose much of the traditionalist's ability to enjoy and glorify the moment he lives in. Even within the sciences, an excessive faith in progress can be dangerous. In sociology, for instance, it has led to a number of unfruitful theories of social evolution.

---

[51] Johnson Abercrombie, 1960; quoted on p. 131.

At this point, I should like to draw attention to a paradox inherent in the presentation of my subject. As a scientist, it is perhaps inevitable that I should at certain points give the impression that traditional African thought is a poor, shackled thing when compared with the thought of the sciences. Yet as a man, here I am living by choice in a still-heavily-traditional Africa rather than in the scientifically oriented Western subculture I was brought up in. Why? Well, there may be lots of queer, sinister, unacknowledged reasons. But one certain reason is the discovery of things lost at home. An intensely poetic quality in everyday life and thought, and a vivid enjoyment of the passing moment—both driven out of sophisticated Western life by the quest for purity of motive and the faith in progress. How necessary these are for the advance of science; but what a disaster they are when they run wild beyond their appropriate bounds! Though I largely disagree with the way in which the 'Négritude' theorists have characterized the differences between traditional African and modern Western thought, when it gets to this point I see very clearly what they are after.

So much, then, for the salient differences between traditional and scientific thought. There is nothing particularly original about the terms in which I have described the contrast between the two. Indeed, all of my eleven points of difference are to be found mentioned somewhere or other in previous anthropological literature. This literature, however, leaves much to be desired when it comes to interpretation. Thus one author deals with secondary elaboration, another with magic, another with taboo, and so on. A particular explanation covers a particular trait of traditional thought, but seems to have very little relevance to the others. Most social anthropologists would acknowledge that the eleven characteristic traits of traditional thought listed in this essay tend to occur together and vanish together; but so far they have offered no over-all interpretation that does justice to this concomitance.

In so far as my paper makes a fresh contribution, I think this lies precisely in its provision of just such an over-all interpretation. For the concept of the 'closed' predicament not only provides a key to the understanding of each one of the eleven salient traits of traditional thought, it also helps us to see why these eleven traits flourish and perish as a set. Where formerly we saw them as an assemblage of miscellaneous exotica, we can now see them as the components of a well-defined and comprehensible syndrome.

So far, however, the interpretation, though it breaks new ground, remains largely intellectualist. At this stage, it does not allow us to relate ideational differences to broader sociocultural differences. It does not as yet allow us to suggest answers to such questions as 'Why did the scientific attitude emerge spontaneously in Europe but not in Africa?' or, 'Why, in Europe, did it emerge at particular times and places?' None the less, I think it does give a valuable clue as to the sort of circumstances we should be looking for: i.e. circumstances tending to promote awareness of alternatives to established theoretical models. Three relevant factors of this kind suggest themselves at once :

(I) DEVELOPMENT OF WRITTEN TRANSMISSION OF BELIEFS.[52] Earlier on in this essay, I talked of the paradox of idea-systems whose users see them as static, but which are in fact constantly, albeit slowly, changing. This paradox, as I said, seems to imply something like a game of Grandmother's Footsteps, with Grandson moving a little at a time when Grandma's back is turned, but always taking care to be still when Grandma rounds on him.

Now it is, above all, the oral transmission of beliefs which makes this intellectual Grandmother's Footsteps possible. For in each generation, small innovations, together with the processes of selective recall, make for considerable adjustments of belief to current situation. But where they cannot refer back to the ideas of a former generation 'frozen' in writing, both those responsible for the adjustments and those who accept them remain virtually unaware that innovation has taken place. In a similar manner, a small and seemingly marginal innovation in belief can occur without anyone realizing that it is part of a cumulative trend which, over several generations, will amount to a very striking change.

In these circumstances, everything tends to give the main tenets of theory an absolute and timeless validity. In so doing, it prevents the development of any awareness of alternatives. Oral transmission, then, is clearly one of the basic supports of the 'closed' predicament.

Where literacy begins to spread widely through a community, the situation changes radically. The beliefs of a particular period become 'frozen' in writing. Meanwhile, oral transmission of beliefs goes on, and with it the continuous small adjustments to changing circumstances typical of pre-literate society. As time passes these adjustments produce an idea-system markedly different from that originally set down in writing. Now in an entirely oral culture, as we have seen, no one has the means of becoming aware of this change. But in a literate culture, the possibility of checking current beliefs against the 'frozen' ideas of an earlier era throws the fact of change into sharp relief.

In these circumstances, the main tenets of theory can no longer be seen as having an absolute and timeless validity. In the consciousness that one's own people believed other things at other times, we have the germ of a

---

[52] The discussion that follows leans heavily upon Goody and Watt, 1963. Goody and Watt are, I believe, among the first to have spelled out the probable importance of the transition from oral to written transmission of beliefs for the take-off from tradition into science. I have drawn heavily here upon their characterization of the contrasting predicaments of thinkers in oral and literate cultures; though my argument diverges somewhat from theirs in its later stages.

sense of alternatives. The stage is set for the emergence of the 'open' predicament.

Not only does attention to the question of literacy help us to understand why the 'open' predicament developed in Europe but not in Africa. It also helps us to understand why, in Europe, this predicament developed just when and where it did. Thus in their sketch of the history of writing,[53] Goody and Watt point out that pictographic writing developed in the Middle and Far East from the end of the fourth millennium B.C. But the various pictographic systems were so unwieldy and their assimilation so time-consuming that they tended to be the exclusive possessions of specially trained, conservative ruling *élites*. The interests of such *élites* in preserving the *status quo* would naturally counteract the 'opening' tendencies of written transmission. It was in sixth-century-B.C. Greece that a convenient, easily learnable phonetic alphabet became in some communities a majority possession; and it was in this same sixth-century Greece that the 'open' predicament made its first notable appearance. The subsequent fortunes of literacy in the Mediterranean world seem to correspond rather well with the subsequent fortunes of the 'open' predicament. Thus what we term the 'Dark Ages' was at once a period which saw the restriction of literacy to small, conservative ruling *élites*, and at the same time a period in which the 'closed' predicament reasserted itself in full force. And in the reawakening of the twelfth–seventeenth centuries, a great expansion and democratization of literacy was the precursor of the final, enduring reappearance of the open predicament and the scientific outlook. Notable during the early part of this period was the rediscovery, via Arab sources, of the 'lost' writings of the great Greek philosopher-scientists. Since in early Medieval times current theoretical tenets were taught very much in the 'this is what the ancients handed down to us' spirit of the closed society, the sudden forced confrontation with the very different reality of what these ancestral heroes actually did believe must have had an effect which powerfully supplemented that due to the growth of literacy generally.

(ii) DEVELOPMENT OF CULTURALLY HETEROGENEOUS COMMUNITIES. There is one obvious, almost platitudinous answer to the question: what gives members of a community an awareness of alternative possibilities of interpreting their world? The answer, of course, is: meeting other people who do in fact interpret the world differently. But there are meetings and meetings; and it is clear that whilst some make very little difference to the outlooks of those involved, others are crucial for the rise of the 'open' predicament.

Now neither traditional Africa nor early Europe lacked encounters between bearers of radically different cultures. So our aim must be to

---

[53] Ibid., pp. 311–19.

show why, in Africa, such encounters did little to promote the 'open' predicament, when in Europe they did so much.

My own very tentative answer goes something like this. Traditional African communities were as a rule fairly homogeneous as regards their internal culture, and their relations with culturally alien neighbours tended to be restricted to the context of trade. Now such restricted relations did not make for mutual encounter of a very searching kind. In extreme cases, indeed, they were carried on without actual face-to-face contact: take for instance, the notorious 'silent trade' between North African merchants and certain peoples of the Western Sudan—an exercise in which the partners neither met nor spoke. Much trade between bearers of radically different cultures was, of course, carried out under conditions far less extreme than these; and it was even common for members of a given community to speak the languages of the culturally alien peoples they traded with. Yet culturally contrasted trading partners remained basically rooted in different communities, from which they set out before trade, and to which they returned after it. Under these limitations, confrontation with alien world-views remained very partial. The trader encountered the thought of his alien partners at the level of common sense but not usually at the level of theory. Since common-sense worlds, in general, differ very little in comparison with theoretical worlds, such encounters did not suffice to stimulate a strong sense of alternatives.[54]

Even where the member of a traditional community did make contact with his alien neighbours at the level of theory, the content of theory was such that it still presented an obstacle to the development of a real sense of alternatives. As I pointed out in Part I of this paper, the bulk of traditional theory was concerned with its users' own particular community. There was an implicit premiss that the world worked one way within one's own community, and another way outside it. Hence if one's neighbours believed some very strange and different things, this was in no way surprising or disturbing in terms of one's own beliefs. In such circumstances, radically contrasting belief-systems could seldom be seen as genuine alternatives.

---

[54] This point, I think, is relevant to an argument advanced against my analysis of magic. (John Beattie, personal communication.) The argument is that once a person learns another language, he becomes aware of alternative possibilities of dividing up the world by words and, on my premisses, must inevitably adopt a non-magical outlook.

In rebuttal, I would say that where a person learns another people's language and thought only at the common-sense level, he is not exposed to a radically different way of dividing up the world by words. Indeed, he is liable to see most of the common-sense words and concepts of the alien language as having equivalents in his own. They are 'the same words' and 'the same thoughts'. It is only when he learns the alien language and thought at the theoretical level that he becomes aware of a radically different way of dividing the world.

When we turn from Africa to Europe, it is important to note just when and where the 'open' predicament came to prevail. Its first home, historians seem to agree, was in certain parts of sixth-century-B.C. Greece. Not in such centrally placed, culturally homogeneous states as Sparta, whose self-contained agricultural society remained rigidly 'closed'; but in the small, cosmopolitan trading communities on the frontiers of the Greek world— old established Ionian cities like Miletus and Ephesus, and more recently established colonies like Abdera and Syracuse.[55]

After declining in this area the fortunes of the 'open' predicament flourished for several centuries in Alexandria. Later, they waxed briefly in the cities of the Arab world. Thence, in late Medieval times, the current passed to the cities of the Iberian Peninsula and coastal Italy. Finally, it passed to the cities of north-western Europe.

What was it about the communities that lay along this devious path that made them such excellent centres for the development of the 'open' predicament? First and foremost, perhaps, it was the conditions of contact between the bearers of different cultures. Whereas in Africa intercultural boundaries tended to coincide with intercommunity boundaries, in these Mediterranean and European cities they cut right through the middle of the community. In these centres, people of diverse origins and cultures were packed together within single urban communities. And although the 'sons of the soil' were frequently the only people who had full citizenship rights, most of the inhabitants had feelings of common community membership and common interests vis-à-vis such outsiders as territorial rulers, the lords of the local countryside, other cities, and so on.

Under these conditions, relations between bearers of different cultures were much broader in scope than the purely commercial relations which typically linked such people over much of traditional Africa. And a broader context of social relationship made for a deeper and more searching intellectual encounter. Here, the encounter was not merely at the level of common sense where differences were negligible. It was also at the level of basic theory where differences were striking. Much of the 'open' temper of late and Medieval and Renaissance times, for instance, can probably be traced to the confrontation of the basic tenets of the Christian, Islamic, and Jewish thought-traditions in the twelfth-century cities of Spain and coastal Italy.[56]

Another factor making for more searching encounter was the actual content of the theories involved. The various traditions of thought making

---

[55] For a brilliant sketch of the beginnings of the 'open' predicament in the Greek city-states, see Popper, 1945. Although, as I said earlier, Popper's definition of 'closed' and 'open' differs somewhat from my own, much of what he says is relevant to my argument and has indeed provided inspiration for it.

[56] For the importance of the confrontation between these three thought-traditions, see Heer, 1962.

up the intellectual inheritance of these Mediterranean and European cities were the products of peoples who had long been living in communities far more integrally linked to the wider world than was usual in traditional Africa. As such, they were more universalistic in their content. So here, when a confrontation took place, it was no longer possible to rest content with saying: 'My theory works for my little world, and his works for his.' My theory and his theory were now patently about the same world, and awareness of them as alternatives became inescapable.

(III) DEVELOPMENT OF THE TRADE-TRAVEL-EXPLORATION COMPLEX. So much for encounter between bearers of different cultures within a single community. A second important kind of encounter arises from voyages of travel and exploration in which members of one community go to live temporarily amongst members of a culturally alien community, with the express aim of intellectual and emotional contact at all levels from the most superficial to the deepest.

Now although individual members of many traditional African cultures must have made such voyages from time to time, these, so far as we know, have never become a dominant theme of life in any of the traditional cultures. But in sixth–third-century-B.C. Greece, in the medieval Arab world, and finally in fifteenth–seventeenth-century western Europe—all crucial centres for the development of the 'open' predicament—these voyages were such important features of social life that they coloured everyone's outlook on the world.

The evidence we have from ancient Greece indicates that many of the great independent thinkers such as Thales, Anaximander, Democritus, Herodotus, and Xenophanes probably made extensive exploratory voyages themselves. And in some of their writings, the connexion between first-hand experience of a variety of alien ways of looking at the world and an 'open' sceptical tenor of thought becomes explicit.[57] Again in fifteenth–eighteenth-century western Europe, exotic world-views personified in figures like the Noble Savage, the Wise Egyptian, and the Chinese Sage haunt the pages of many of the sceptical writings of the times; and here too the link between confrontation with alien world-views and 'open' thinking is often explicit.[58]

---

[57] Take, for instance, the following passage from Xenophanes, quoted in Toulmin, 1961:

'Mortals consider that the gods are begotten as they are, and have clothes and voices and figures like theirs. The Ethiopians make their gods black and snub-nosed; the Thracians say theirs have blue eyes and red hair. Yes, and if oxen and horses or lions had hands, and could paint with their hands, and produce works of art as men do, horses would paint the gods with shapes like horses, and oxen like oxen, and make their bodies in the image of their several kinds.'

[58] For this see Hazard, 1964. (Especially chap. 4.)

It is, of course, possible to argue that these voyages and these confrontations were a consequence and not a cause of the 'open' predicament; that 'open-minded' people embarked on them with the idea of putting parochial views to the deliberate test of wider horizons of experience. This may have been true once the voyages had become a dominant feature of the life of the times. But I believe the beginnings of the eras of exploration can still be best understood in terms of the aims and interests of essentially 'closed-minded' societies.

One's suspicions on this score are aroused in the first instance by the fact that in both of the great eras of exploration, many of the voyages were encouraged if not directed by the pillars of tradition: in early Greece by the Delphic Oracle, and in western Europe by the Popes.

Again, it is clear that the motive forces behind the voyages included the aim of reducing population pressure by overseas settlement and that of extending commerce to include new items to be found only in faraway lands. The detailed probings of alien world-views can thus be understood as intelligence operations directed toward solving the problems of human coexistence involved in overseas settlement and commerce. There was probably little 'open-mindedness' in the intentions which originally lay behind them.

Perhaps the most interesting example of the essentially 'closed' motivations behind activities which were to make a great contribution to the development of the 'open' predicament is provided by the operations of Christian missionaries in the fifteenth–eighteenth centuries. The fanaticism with which the missionaries worked to convert distant peoples of alien faith can, I think, be understood as a product of the 'closed' society's determination to protect itself from the possibility of being disturbed by confrontation with alien world-views—a possibility which loomed large in this era of exploration. But the more intelligent missionaries saw that effective evangelization required a prior understanding of the faiths of those to be converted; and they set themselves, however reluctantly, to acquire such an understanding. The result was a body of records of alien world-views that came to colour much of the thought of the times, and that was undoubtedly one of the important contributions to the genesis of the open thinking of the seventeenth century.

The eras of exploration encouraged the growth of the 'open' predicament in a second way. This was through the rich material fruits of the voyages. In traditional cultures, as we have seen, distant lands tend to epitomize all that is new and strange, all that fails to fit into the established system of categories, all that is tabooed, fearful, and abominable. Hence, whether among the Lugbara of East Africa or among Dark Age Europeans, we find them peopled with abominations and monsters. In the eras of exploration, however, reports came back not of monsters but of delights and riches. Slowly, these pleasant associations of the Great Beyond extended themselves to new and strange experience generally. The quest for such experience came to be seen not as something dangerous and fool-hardy, but as something richly rewarding and pleasantly exciting. This relation between the fruits of exploration and the new attitudes to the strange and category defying is portrayed very clearly in some of the metaphors of these eras. Take, for instance, Joseph Glanvill's notion of 'An America of Secrets and an Unknown Peru of Nature', waiting to overthrow old scholastic ideas and force men to replace them with something better.[59]

Not only, then, did the events of these eras undermine the feeling that one's established beliefs were the only defence against chaos and the void. They gave a less horrifying, nay benign, face to chaos itself.

In naming these three factors as crucial for the development of the 'open' predicament, I am not implying that wherever they occur, there is a sort of painless, automatic, and complete transition from 'closed' to 'open' thinking. On the contrary, the transition seems inevitably to be painful, violent, and partial.

Even in ancient Greece, the independent thinking of the great pre-socratic philosophers evoked strong and anxious reactions.[60] In late Medieval times, a few decades of confrontation with alien world-views and 'open' sceptical thinking tended to be succeeded by decades of persecution of those responsible for disturbing established orthodoxy and by a general 'closing-up' of thought.[61] In present-day Nigeria, we seem to be seeing yet another example of the atrocious birth-pangs of the 'open' society.

Why should the transition be so painful? Well, a theme of this paper has been the way in which a developing awareness of alternative world-views erodes attitudes which attach an absolute validity to the established outlook. But this is a process that works over time—indeed over generations. Throughout the process there are bound to be many people on whom the confrontation has not yet worked its magic. These people still retain the old sense of the absolute validity of their belief-systems, with all the attendant anxieties about threats to them. For these people, the confrontation is still a threat of chaos of the most horrific kind—a threat which demands the most drastic measures. They respond in one of two ways: either by trying to blot out those responsible for the confrontation, often down to the last unborn child; or by trying to convert them to their own beliefs through fanatical missionary activity.

Again, as I said earlier, the moving, shifting thought-world produced by the 'open' predicament creates its own sense of insecurity. Many people

[59] Quoted from *The Vanity of Dogmatizing*, in Willey, 1962, p. 168.

[60] See Popper, 1945, for some of these reactions to pre-socratic 'open' thinking.

[61] See Heer, 1962, for a vivid picture of the way in which the Medieval world oscillated crazily between 'open' and 'closed' attitudes.

find this shifting world intolerable. Some adjust to their fears by developing an inordinate faith in progress toward a future in which 'the Truth' will be finally known. But others long nostalgically for the fixed, unques-. tionable beliefs of the 'closed' culture. They call for authoritarian establishment and control of dogma, and for persecution of those who have managed to be at ease in a world of ever-shifting ideas. Clearly, the 'open' predicament is a precarious, fragile thing.

In modern western Europe and America, it is true, the 'open' predicament seems to have escaped from this precariousness through public acknowledgement of the practical utility of the sciences. It has achieved a secure foothold in the culture because its results maximize values shared by 'closed-' and 'open-' minded alike. Even here, however, the 'open' predicament has nothing like a universal sway. On the contrary, it is almost a minority phenomenon. Outside the various academic disciplines in which it has been institutionalized, its hold is pitifully less than those who describe Western culture as 'science-oriented' often like to think.

It is true that in modern Western culture, the theoretical models propounded by the professional scientists do, to some extent, become the intellectual furnishings of a very large sector of the population. The moderately educated layman typically shares with the scientist a general predilection for impersonal 'it-' theory and a proper contempt for 'thou-' theory. Garbled and watered-down though it may be, the atomic theory of matter is one of his standard possessions. But the laymen's ground for accepting the models propounded by the scientist is often no different from the young African villager's ground for accepting the models propounded by one of his elders. In both cases the propounders are deferred to as the accredited agents of tradition. As for the rules which guide scientists themselves in the acceptance or rejection of models, these seldom become part of the intellectual equipment of members of the wider population. For all the apparent up-to-dateness of the content of his worldview, the modern Western layman is rarely more 'open' or scientific in his outlook than is the traditional African villager.

This takes me back to a general point about the layout of this paper. If I spent the whole of Part I labouring the thesis that differences in the content of theories do more to hide continuities than reveal genuine contrasts, this was not, as some readers may have imagined, through a determination to ignore the contrasts. Rather, it was precisely to warn them away from the trap which the Western layman characteristically falls into—the trap which makes him feel he is keeping up with the scientists when in fact he is no nearer to them than the African peasant.

## References

ACHEBE, CHINUA. 1957. *Things Fall Apart*, London.

BARZUN, JACQUES. 1961. Introduction to Stephen Toulmin, *Foresight and Understanding*, London.

BEATTIE, J. H. M. 1966. 'Ritual and Social Change' (The Malinowski Lecture), *Man. Journal of the Royal Anthropological Institute*, vol. i, no. 1.

CROMBIE, A. C. (ed.). 1963. *Scientific Change* (Symposium on the History of Science, University of Oxford, 9–15 July 1961), London.

DOUGLAS, MARY. 1966. *Purity and Danger*, London.

ELIADE, MIRCEA. 1954. *Myth of the Eternal Return*, New York.

————. 1961. *The Sacred and the Profane*, New York.

EVANS-PRITCHARD, E. E. 1936. *Witchcraft, Oracles and Magic among the Azande*, Oxford.

————. 1956. *Nuer Religion*, Oxford.

————. 1965. *Theories of Primitive Religion*, Oxford.

FORDE, DARYLL. 1958. 'Spirits, Witches and Sorcerers in the Supernatural Economy of the Yakö', *Journal of the Royal Anthropological Institute*, vol. lxxxviii, no. 2.

FORTES, M. 1949. *The Web of Kinship among the Tallensi*, London.

————. 1959. *Oedipus and Job in West African Religion*, Cambridge.

————. 1961. 'Pietas in Ancestor Worship', *Journal of the Royal Anthropological Institute*, vol. xci, pt. 2.

GELLNER, ERNEST. 1964. *Thought and Change*, London.

GLUCKMAN, MAX. 1965. *Politics, Law, and Ritual in Tribal Society*, Oxford.

GOODY, J., and WATT, I, 1963. 'The Consequences of Literacy', *Comparative Studies in Society and History*, vol. v, no. 3.

GRIAULE, M. 1965. *Conversations with Ogotemmêli*, London. (Translation of *Dieu d'Eau*.)

———— and DIETERLEN, G. 1954. 'The Dogon', in *African Worlds*, ed. D. Forde, London.

HAZARD, P. 1964. *The European Mind 1680–1715*, London.

HEER, FRIEDRICH. 1962. *The Mediaeval World*, London.

HORTON, ROBIN. 1956. 'God, Man, and the Land in a Northern Ibo Village Group', *Africa*, xxvi, 1, pp. 17–28.

————. 1961. 'Destiny and the Unconscious in West Africa', ibid., xxxxii, 2, pp. 110–116.

————. 1962. 'The Kalabari World-View: an Outline and Interpretation', ibid., xxxii, 3, pp. 197–220.

————. 1963. 'The Kalabari *Ekine* Society: a Borderland of Religion and Art', ibid., xxxiii, no. 2.

————. 1964a. 'Ritual Man in Africa', ibid., xxxiv, 2, pp. 85–104.

————. 1964b. 'A Hundred Years of Change in Kalabari Religion'. (Unpublished paper for the University of Ife Conference on 'The High God in Africa', December 1964.)

————. 1965. *Kalabari Sculpture*, Lagos.

JAHN, JAHNHEINZ. 1961. *Muntu: an Outline of Neo-African Culture*, London.

JOHNSON, ABERCROMBIE, M. L. 1960. *The Anatomy of Judgement*, London.

KIEV, ARI (ed.). 1964. *Magic, Faith, and Healing*, London.

KUHN, T. 1962. *The Structure of Scientific Revolutions*, Chicago.

LAVONDES, H. 1963. 'Magie et langage', *L'Homme*, tome iii, num. 3.

LAYE, CAMARA. 1965. *The Dark Child*, London.

LÉVI-STRAUSS, CLAUDE. 1962. *La Pensée sauvage*, Paris.

LIENHARDT, GODFREY. 1961. *Divinity and Experience: the Religion of the Dinka*, London.

MIDDLETON, JOHN. 1960. *Lugbara Religion: Ritual and Authority among an East African People*, London.

NADEL, S. F. 1956. *Nupe Religion*, London.

POPPER, KARL, 1945. *The Open Society and Its Enemies*, London.

SNOW, C. P. 1959. *The Two Cultures and the Scientific Revolution*, Cambridge.

TARDITS, C. 1962. 'Religion, Epic, History: Notes on the Underlying Functions of Cults in Benin Civilisations', *Diogenes*, no. 37.

TOULMIN, S. 1961. *The Fabric of the Heavens*, London.

TURNER, VICTOR W. 1961. *Ndembu Divination*. Rhodes-Livingstone Paper, No. 31. Manchester.

_____. 1964. 'An Ndembu Doctor in Practice', in Ari Kiev (ed.), *Magic, Faith, and Healing*, London.

WAX, M. and R. 1963. 'The Notion of Magic', *Current Anthropology*, December.

WILLEY, BASIL. 1962. *The Seventeenth Century Background*, London.

# Selected Bibliography

APTER, D. E. 1963. *Ghana in Transition.* New York: Atheneum.

——. 1965. *The Politics of Modernization.* Chicago: University of Chicago Press.

APTHORPE, R. J. 1958. *Present Inter-relations in Central African Rural and Urban Life.* Lusaka, Northern Rhodesia: Rhodes-Livingstone Institute.

BALANDIER, G. 1954. *Conséquences Sociales de l'Industrialisation et Problèmes Urbaines en Afrique.* Paris: Bureau International de Recherche.

——. 1957. *Afrique Ambiguë.* Paris: Plon.

BANTON, M. 1957. *West African City.* London: Oxford University Press.

BARNES, J. A. 1954. *Politics in a Changing Society.* Cape Town: Oxford University Press.

BASCOM, W. R., and M. J. HERSKOVITS (eds.). 1959. *Continuity and Change in African Cultures.* Chicago: University of Chicago Press.

BEATTIE, J. 1960. *Bunyoro.* New York: Holt, Rinehart and Winston.

BEIDELMAN, T. O. 1960. "The Baraguyu," *Tanganyika Notes and Records* 55:245–278.

——. 1961. "Beer Drinking and Cattle Theft in Ukaguru," *American Anthropologist* 63(3): 534–548.

BERNARDI, B. 1959. *The Mugwe, a Failing Prophet.* London: Oxford University Press.

BOHANNAN, P. J. 1957. *Justice and Judgement among the Tiv.* London: Oxford University Press.

BOHANNAN, P. J., and G. DALTON (eds.). 1958. *Markets in Africa.* Garden City, N.Y.: Natural History Press.

COLSON, E. 1953. "Social Control and Vengeance in Plateau Tonga Society," *Africa* 23(3):199–212.

——. 1958. *Marriage and the Family among the Plateau Tonga.* Manchester, Eng.: Manchester University Press.

——. 1962. *The Plateau Tonga of Northern Rhodesia.* Manchester, Eng.: Manchester University Press.

COLSON, E., and M. GLUCKMAN (eds.). 1951. *Seven Tribes of British Central Africa.* London: Oxford University Press.

CRAWFORD, J. R. 1968. *Witchcraft and Sorcery in Rhodesia.* London: Oxford University Press.

CUNNISON, I. 1959. *The Luapula Peoples of Northern Rhodesia.* Manchester, Eng.: Manchester University Press.

DAVIDSON, B. 1959. *The Lost Cities of Africa.* Boston: Little, Brown.

————. 1964. *The African Past.* Boston: Little, Brown.

DOUGLAS, M. M. 1963. *The Lele of the Kasai.* London: Oxford University Press.

ELIAS, T. O. 1956. *The Nature of African Customary Law.* Manchester, Eng.: Manchester University Press.

EMERSON, R. 1963. "The Erosion of Democracy in the New States," in D. Apter and H. Eckstein (eds.), *Comparative Politics.* New York: Free Press, 625–644.

EPSTEIN, A. L. 1967. "Urbanization and Social Change in Africa," *Current Anthropology* 8(4):275–295.

EVANS-PRITCHARD, E. E. 1937. *Witchcraft, Oracles and Magic among the Azande.* Oxford, Eng.: Clarendon Press.

————. 1940. *The Nuer.* Oxford, Eng.: Clarendon Press.

————. 1951. *Kinship and Marriage among the Nuer.* Oxford, Eng.: Clarendon Press.

————. 1956. *Nuer Religion.* Oxford, Eng.: Clarendon Press.

FAGE, J. D. 1955. *Introduction to the History of West Africa.* Cambridge, Eng.: Cambridge University Press.

FALLERS, L. A. 1955. "The Predicament of the Modern African Chief: An Instance from Uganda," *American Anthropologist* 57(2): 290–305.

————. 1956. *Bantu Bureaucracy.* Cambridge, Eng.: Heffer.

FANON, F. 1965. *The Wretched of the Earth.* C. Farrington (tr.). New York: Grove.

————. 1967a. *Toward the African Revolution: Political Essays.* H. Chevalier (tr.). New York: Monthly Review Press.

————. 1967b. *Black Masks, White Faces.* C. Markmann (tr.). New York: Grove.

FIRTH, R. 1954. "Social Organization and Social Change," *Journal of the Royal Anthropological Institute* 84:1–20.

FORDE, D. 1941. *Marriage and the Family among the Yako in Southeastern Nigeria.* London: International African Institute.

————. (ed.). 1954. *African Worlds.* London: Oxford University Press.

————. (ed.). 1956. *Social Implications of Industrialization and Urbanization in Africa South of the Sahara.* Paris: UNESCO.

FORDE, D., and P. M. KABERRY (eds.). 1967. *West African Kingdoms in the Nineteenth Century.* London: International African Institute.

FORTES, M. 1945. *The Dynamics of Clanship among the Tallensi.* London: Oxford University Press.

————. 1949. *The Web of Kinship among the Tallensi.* London: Oxford University Press.

FORTES, M., and G. DIETERLEN (eds.). 1965. *African Systems of Thought.* London: Oxford University Press.

FORTES, M., and E. E. EVANS-PRITCHARD (eds.). 1940. *African Political Systems.* London: Oxford University Press.

Gibbs, J. R. (ed.). 1965. *The Peoples of Africa.* New York: Holt, Rinehart and Winston.

Gluckman, M. 1954. *Rituals of Rebellion in South-east Africa.* Manchester, Eng.: Manchester University Press.

————. 1955a. *The Judicial Process among the Barotse of Northern Rhodesia.* Manchester, Eng.: Manchester University Press.

————. 1955b. *Custom and Conflict in Africa.* Oxford, Eng.: Blackwell.

————. 1963. *Order and Rebellion in Tribal Africa.* New York: Free Press.

————. 1965a. *The Ideas in Barotse Jurisprudence.* New Haven, Conn.: Yale University Press.

————. 1965b. *Politics, Law and Ritual in Tribal Society.* Oxford, Eng.: Blackwell.

Goody, J. 1962. *Death, Property and the Ancestors.* Stanford, Calif.: Stanford University Press.

Gulliver, P. H. 1957. "Nyakyusa Labour Migration," *Rhodes-Livingstone Journal* 21:32–63.

————. 1958. "Land Tenure and Social Change among the Nyakyusa: An Essay in Applied Anthropology," *East African Studies* 11 (Kampala, Uganda).

————. 1961. "Land Shortage, Social Change and Social Conflict in East Africa," *Journal of Conflict Resolution* 5(1):16–26.

————. 1963. *Social Control in an African Society.* London: Routledge and Kegan Paul.

Gutkind, P. C. W. 1961. "Urban Conditions in Africa," *Town Planning Review* 32(1):20–32.

————. 1962a. "The African Urban Milieu: A Force in Rapid Change," *Civilisations* 12(2):156–195.

————. 1962b. "African Urban Family Life," *Cahiers d'Etudes Africaines* 10:149–217.

————. 1963. "African Urban Marriage and Family Life," *Bulletin de l'Institut Fondamental d'Afrique Noire,* ser. B 25(3–4):266–287.

Herskovits, M. J. 1962. *The Human Factor in Changing Africa.* New York: Knopf.

Krige, E. J., and J. D. Krige. 1943. *The Realm of a Rain Queen.* London: Oxford University Press.

Kuper, H. 1947. *An African Aristocracy.* London: Oxford University Press.

————. 1952. *The Swazi.* London: International African Institute.

Legum, C. 1962. *Pan Africanism.* New York: Praeger.

Lewis, I. 1961. *A Pastoral Democracy.* London: Oxford University Press.

Lienhardt, R. G. 1961. *Divinity and Experience: Religion among the Dinka.* Oxford, Eng.: Clarendon Press.

Little, K. L. 1951. *The Mende of Sierra Leone.* London: Routledge and Kegan Paul.

Llewellyn, R. 1961. *A Man in a Mirror.* Garden City, N.Y.: Doubleday.

Lloyd, P. C. (ed.). 1966. *The New Elites of Tropical Africa.* London: Oxford University Press.

Mair, L. P. 1953. "African Marriage and Social Change," in A. Phillips (ed.),

*Survey of African Marriage and Family Life.* London: Oxford University Press.

MAQUET, J. J. 1961. *The Premise of Inequality in Rwanda.* London: Oxford University Press.

MARRIS, P. 1951. *Family and Social Change in an African City.* London: Routledge and Kegan Paul.

MAUSS, M. 1967. *The Gift.* New York: Norton.

MIDDLETON, J. 1961. *Land Tenure in Zanzibar.* London: Her Majesty's Stationery Office.

————. 1966. *The Effects of Economic Development on Traditional Political Systems in Africa South of the Sahara.* The Hague: Mouton.

————. 1969. *Lugbara Religion.* London: Oxford University Press.

MIDDLETON, J., and D. TAIT (eds.). 1958. *Tribes Without Rulers.* London: Routledge and Kegan Paul.

MIDDLETON, J., and E. WINTER (eds.). 1963. *Witchcraft and Sorcery in East Africa.* London: Routledge and Kegan Paul.

MITCHELL, J. C. 1956. *The Kalela Dance: Aspects of Social Relationships among Urban Africans in Northern Rhodesia.* Manchester, Eng.: Manchester University Press.

————. 1960. "The Anthropological Study of Urban Communities," *African Studies* 19(3):169–172.

MURDOCK, G. P. 1959. *Africa: Its People and Their Culture History.* New York: McGraw-Hill.

NADEL, S. F. 1942. *A Black Byzantium.* London: Oxford University Press.

————. 1952. "Witchcraft in Four African Societies: a Comparison," *American Anthropologist* 54:18–29.

————. 1954 *Nupe Religion.* London: Routledge and Kegan Paul.

NEEDHAM, R. 1967. "Right and Left in Nyoro Symbolic Classification," *Africa* 37(4): 425–452.

NIEHOFF, A. H. 1966. *A Casebook of Social Change.* Chicago: Aldine.

NORBECK, E. 1963. "African Rituals of Conflict," *American Anthropologist* 65(6):1254–1279.

OLIVER, R. (ed.). 1961. *The Dawn of African History.* London: Oxford University Press.

OLIVER, R., and J. D. FAGE. 1961. *A Short History of Africa.* Harmondsworth, Eng.: Penguin Books.

OTTENBERG, S., and P. OTTENBERG (eds.). 1960. *Cultures and Societies of Africa.* New York: Random House.

PAULME, D. (ed.). 1963. *Women of Tropical Africa.* London: Routledge and Kegan Paul.

PLOTNICOV, L. 1967. *Strangers to the City.* Pittsburgh: University of Pittsburgh Press.

POWDERMAKER, H. 1963. *Copper Town.* New York: Harper & Row.

RADCLIFFE-BROWN, A. R., and D. FORDE (eds.). 1950. *African Systems of Kinship and Marriage.* London: Oxford University Press for the International African Institute.

RATTRAY, R. S. 1923. *The Ashanti.* Oxford, Eng.: Clarendon Press.

————. 1927. *Religion and Art in Ashanti*. Oxford, Eng.: Clarendon Press.

————. 1929. *Ashanti Law and Constitution*. Oxford, Eng.: Clarendon Press.

RICHARDS, A. I. 1956. *Chisungu: A Girl's Initiation Ceremony among the Bemba*. London: Faber.

RIGBY, P. 1970. *The Gogo*. Ithaca, N.Y.: Cornell University Press.

ROSCOE, J. 1911. *The Baganda*. London: Macmillan.

RUEL, M. J. (ed.). 1963. *Urbanization in African Social Change*. Edinburgh: Edinburgh University, Centre of African Studies.

SCHNEIDER, H. K. 1970. *The Wahi Wanyaturu: Economics in an African Society*. Viking Fund Publications in Anthropology, No. 48. Chicago: Aldine.

SMITH, M. G. 1960. *Government in Zazau*. London: Oxford University Press.

————. 1964. "Historical and Cultural Conditions of Political Corruption among the Hausa," *Comparative Studies in Society and History* 6 (2) : 164–194.

SOUTHALL, A. (ed.). 1961. *Social Change in Modern Africa*. London: Oxford University Press.

STENNING, D. J. 1959. *Savannah Nomads*. London: Oxford University Press.

SUNDKLER. B. 1948. *Bantu Prophets in South Africa*. London: Butterworth.

TAIT, D. 1961. *The Konkomba of Northern Ghana*. London: Oxford University Press.

TEMPELS, P. 1949. *La Philosophie Bantoue*. A. Rubbens, Paris: Editions Africaines.

THOMAS, E. M. 1959. *The Harmless People*. New York: Knopf.

TOWLES, J. A. (with C. M. TURNBULL). 1968. "The White Problem in America," *Natural History Magazine* 77 (6) : 6–18.

TOWLES, J. A. 1970. "Prophets, Politics and People." Kampala, Uganda: Makerere University, unpublished paper.

————. 1972. "Ritual and Structure: A Structural Approach." Kampala, Uganda: Makerere University, unpublished paper.

TURNBULL, C. M. 1961. *The Forest People*. New York: Simon and Schuster.

————. 1962. *The Lonely African*. New York: Simon and Schuster.

————. 1965a. *Wayward Servants*. Garden City, N.Y.: Natural History Press.

————. 1965b. *The Mbuti Pygmies: An Ethnographic Survey*. New York: The American Museum of Natural History, Anthropological Papers, Vol. 50, part 3.

————. 1966. "A People Apart," *Natural History Magazine* 75 (8) : 8–14.

————. 1967. "The Ik: Alias the Teuso," *Uganda Journal* 31 (1) : 63–71 (Kampala, Uganda).

————. 1972. *The Mountain People*. New York: Simon and Schuster.

TURNER, V. W. 1961. *Ndembu Divination*. Manchester, Eng.: Manchester University Press.

————. 1962. *Chihamba, the White Spirit*. Manchester, Eng.: Manchester University Press.

————. 1967. *The Forest of Symbols*. Ithaca, N.Y.: Cornell University Press.

UCHENDU, V. 1965. *The Igbo of Southeastern Nigeria*. New York: Holt, Rinehart and Winston.

VANSINA, J. 1966. *Kingdoms of the Savannah*. Madison: University of Wisconsin Press.

VAN VELSEN, J. 1964. *The Politics of Kinship*. Manchester, Eng.: Manchester University Press.

WATSON, W. 1958. *Tribal Cohesion in a Money Economy*. Manchester, Eng.: Manchester University Press.

WILSON, G. 1941–1942. *An Essay on the Economics of Detribalization in Northern Rhodesia*. Rhodes-Livingstone Papers 5 and 6. Livingstone, Northern Rhodesia: Rhodes-Livingstone Institute.

WILSON, G., and M. WILSON. 1945. *The Analysis of Social Change*. Cambridge, Eng.: Cambridge University Press.

WILSON, M. 1957. *Rituals of Kinship among the Nyakyusa*. London: Oxford University Press.

————. 1959. *Communal Rituals of the Nyakyusa*. London: Oxford University Press.

WINTER, E. H. 1955. *Bwamba Economy*. Kampala, Uganda: East African Institute of Social Research.

————. 1959. *Beyond the Mountains of the Moon: The Lives of Four Africans*. Urbana: University of Illinois Press.

WRAITH, R., and E. SIMPKINS. 1963. *Corruption in Developing Countries*. London: Allen and Unwin.

Colin M. Turnbull is Professor of Anthropology at Hofstra University, where he has taught since 1968. Born in England, he received both the master's and doctor's degrees from Oxford University. Dr. Turnbull has traveled extensively in Africa, conducting research on half a dozen field trips. Between the years 1951 and 1971, he covered the Congo, Uganda, and North and West Africa. He served as Associate Curator of African Ethnology at the American Museum of Natural History in New York City from 1959 to 1968, and is the author of many distinguished books on anthropology, among which are *The Forest People* (1961), *The Lonely African* (1962), *Tradition and Change in Tribal Africa* (1966), and *The Mountain People* (1972).

## A Note on the Type

The text of this book was set on the Linotype in a face called TIMES ROMAN, designed by Stanley Morison for the Times (London), and first introduced by that newspaper in 1932.

Among typographers and designers of the twentieth century, Stanley Morison has been a strong forming influence, as typographical advisor to the English Monotype Corporation, as a director of two distinguished English publishing houses, and as a writer of sensibility, erudition, and keen practical sense.

Composed by Cherry Hill
Composition, Pennsauken, N.J.
Printed and bound by
The Kingsport Press, Kingsport, Tenn.